SEVENTH EDITION

Literacy
for the 21st Century

A Balanced Approach

GAIL E. TOMPKINS

California State University, Fresno, Emerita

PEARSON

Boston • Columbus • Indianapolis • New York • San Francisco
Amsterdam • Cape Town • Dubai • London • Madrid • Milan • Munich • Paris • Montréal • Toronto
Delhi • Mexico City • São Paulo • Sydney • Hong Kong • Seoul • Singapore • Taipei • Tokyo

Vice President/Editorial Director: Jeffrey Johnston
Executive Editor: Meredith D. Fossel
Editorial Assistant: Maria Feliberty
Executive Marketing Managers: Christopher Barry/Krista Clark
Executive Development Editor: Linda Ashe Bishop
Program Manager: Miryam Chandler
Project Manager: Karen Mason
Manufacturing Buyer: Deidra Skahill
Text Designer: Cenveo® Publisher Services
Manager, Rights and Permissions: Johanna Burke
Rights and Permissions Project Manager: Terenia McHenry
Full-Service Project Management: Cenveo® Publisher Services
Cover Design: Studio Montage
Media Production: Allison Longley
Cover Art: NB Illustration/Galia Bernstein; stripes: Kalenik Hanna/Shutterstock;
   circles: gudinny/Shutterstock
About the Author Photo: by Ann K. Brandon

Acknowledgments of third party content appear on the page with the feature, which constitutes an extension of this copyright page.

Library of Congress Cataloging-in-Publication Data Is Available on Request

13 2022

www.pearsonhighered.com

ISBN 10: 0-13-481310-3
ISBN 13: 978-0-13-481310-3

Dedication

In memory of my parents,
Ruth and Charles Tompkins,
who took me around the world and
celebrated my accomplishments.

About the Author

I'm a teacher, first and foremost. I began my career as a first grade teacher in Virginia in the 1970s. I remember one student who cried as the first day of school was ending. When I tried to comfort him, he sobbed accusingly, "I came to school to learn to read and write, and you forgot to teach me." The next day, I taught that child and his classmates. We made a small patterned book about "Tom," a stuffed animal in the classroom. I wrote some of the words and the students supplied the others, and I duplicated and bound copies of the book for each child. We practiced reading it until everyone memorized our little book. The children proudly took their books home to read to their parents. I've never forgotten that child's comment and what it taught me: Teachers must understand their students and meet their expectations.

My first few years of teaching left me with more questions than answers, and I wanted to become a more effective teacher, so I started taking graduate courses. In time I earned a master's degree and then a doctorate in Reading/Language Arts, both from Virginia Tech. Through my graduate studies, I learned a lot of answers, but more importantly, I learned to keep on asking questions.

Then I began teaching at the university level. I taught at Miami University in Ohio, then at the University of Oklahoma, and finally at California State University, Fresno. I've taught preservice teachers and practicing teachers working on master's degrees, and I've directed doctoral dissertations. I've received awards for my teaching, including the Provost's Award for Excellence in Teaching at California State University, Fresno, and I was inducted into the California Reading Association's Reading Hall of Fame. Through the years, my students have taught me as much as I've taught them, and I'm grateful to all of them for what I've learned.

I've been writing college textbooks for more than 30 years, and I think of the books I write as teaching, too: I'll be teaching you as you read this text. When I write a book, I try to anticipate the questions you might ask and provide that information so that you'll become an effective teacher. I've written other books published by Pearson Education, including *Language Arts: Patterns of Practice*, 9th ed. (2016); *Teaching Writing: Balancing Process and Product*, 6th ed. (2012); *50 Literacy Strategies*, 4th ed. (2014); and two grade-level-specific versions of this text: *Literacy in the Early Grades*, 3rd ed. (2015); and *Literacy in the Middle Grades*, 2nd ed. (2010).

Preface

Teaching reading and writing effectively is a great responsibility. I think it's one of the most critical responsibilities teachers have because literacy makes a huge difference in students' lives—good readers and writers have many more opportunities throughout their school years and beyond. Meeting challenges for developing readers and writers has never been more important, because new technologies have changed what it means to be literate. And, learning to read and write well closes the achievement gap among students, affecting not only their academic success but also their future.

This text, *Literacy for the 21st Century: A Balanced Approach*, shares my vision for reading and writing instruction. It covers the fundamental components of literacy, illustrates how to teach strategies, identifies how to differentiate instruction to meet the diverse needs of students today, and supports digital teaching and learning. In a nutshell, I've written *Literacy for the 21st Century* to help you create a classroom climate where literacy flourishes, technology is a tool to meet the needs of contemporary teaching and learning, and differentiated instruction scaffolds instruction so all students can be successful.

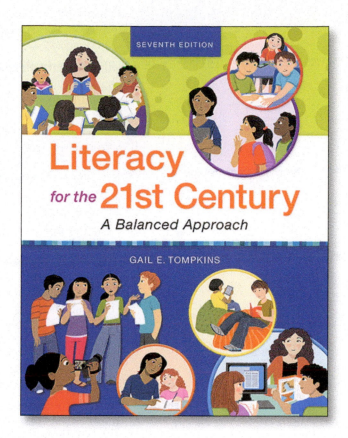

NEW TO THIS EDITION

This seventh edition of *Literacy for the 21st Century* is exciting because it incorporates a variety of new features and digital applications. I share detailed information in this Preface of what is new to this edition, but here's a brief list:

- **First Time as REVEL** This seventh edition is offered in a new immersive online format called REVEL that's been designed to accommodate 21st-century learning on laptops and tablets. REVEL offers a variety of interactive experiences:
  - **Learning Outcomes** The REVEL format guides the chapter structure. Specifically, I list the learning outcomes at the beginning of each chapter, organize the chapter's content into sections addressing each learning outcome, and include self-assessments at the end of the section. The Evaluate & Reflect projects at the end of the chapter invite you to apply the learning outcomes authentically—with teachers and students in real K–8 classrooms.
  - **Classroom Videos*** Important concepts in each chapter are illustrated in videos, showing you how teachers apply them in authentic classroom settings.
  - **Self-Assessments*** Short-answer and multiple-choice self-assessments at the end of each chapter section check your understanding and identify gaps in your learning, and project-based assessments at the end of each chapter invite you to

*These features are available only in REVEL, exclusively from http://www.pearsonhighered.com/revel/ or by ordering the Tompkins REVEL plus Loose-Leaf Version (ISBN 0134090195) or the Tompkins REVEL Access Code Card (ISBN 0134303202).

delve more deeply into the chapter content and apply what you're learning through classroom observations, interviews with students and teachers, and real teaching experiences.

ॐ **Organizational Change** In Chapter 10, *Organizing for Instruction*, I've added guided reading as an effective approach for teaching reading. Responding to reviewer requests, I've described and discussed the purpose, components, theory base, applications, strengths, and limitations of this instructional approach.

ॐ **Teach Kids to Be Strategic** Reviewers also requested a change to the feature Teach Kids to Be Strategic, so it has been thoroughly revised to specify what you need to do to ensure that your students have ample practice with the strategic behaviors they need to use to be successful readers and writers.

ॐ **New Topics** In every edition I explain new literacy concepts. These are some of the critical new discussions in this edition:

  ॐ **Oral Language** In Chapter 1, *Becoming an Effective Literacy Teacher*, and Chapter 4, *The Youngest Readers and Writers*, I discuss the critical role of oral language in literacy development for both native English speakers and English learners. In addition, I explain how to nurture and monitor children's oral language proficiency through grand conversations, choral reading, hot seat interviews, oral reports, retelling stories, and other literacy activities.

  ॐ **Close Reading** In Chapter 2, *The Reading and Writing Processes*, and Chapter 8, *Promoting Comprehension: Reader Factors*, I discuss close reading—helping students understand the deeper meaning of complex text—and I describe how to implement it in grades K–8.

  ॐ **Standards** New features in this text address the Common Core State Standards for English Language Arts, demonstrate how to use them in your classroom, and point to the value of addressing Standards in lesson planning. The Standards hold you accountable for teaching grade-level-specific content, and the vignettes at the beginning of each chapter and in the Compendium of Instructional Procedures show you how effective teachers integrate the Standards into their teaching.

  ॐ **The Instruction–Assessment Cycle** Assessment is a crucial part of effective literacy instruction. You'll be held accountable for determining students' literacy levels, monitoring their progress, diagnosing strengths and weaknesses, and documenting student learning. In Chapter 1, *Becoming an Effective Literacy Teacher*, and Chapter 3, *Assessing Literacy Development*, I teach you how to follow an instruction–assessment cycle; in other chapters, the information about how to assess phonics, fluency, comprehension, and other topics also follows this four-step cycle. In addition, this text is organized using the instruction–assessment cycle; you'll notice that the terms *planning*, *monitoring*, *evaluating*, and *reflecting* are used throughout to call your attention to the learning outcomes, quizzes, and end-of-chapter projects.

MY GOALS

First and foremost, I have written this text for you. I know you want to become a successful teacher of reading and writing, capable of using the instructional approaches that unlock reading and writing for all the students you have the privilege to teach. It's why I've loaded *Literacy for the 21st Century: A Balanced Approach* with the most effective instructional methods for kindergarten through eighth grade, methods that are based on scientific research

and classroom-tested practice. I've also written it to help you meet the needs of every student in your classroom—children who come to school well prepared for literacy learning and those who struggle with learning to read and write, including children whose first language isn't English.

To make this text and its valuable resources accessible, I have organized it into four distinct parts, and I present pedagogy and classroom applications through five text themes—*teacher accountability, instructional support, diverse learners, assessment resources,* and *technology tools.* These themes illustrate the significant roles and responsibilities teachers must learn to teach reading and writing effectively.

TEACHER ACCOUNTABILITY

As a teacher, you'll be responsible for your students' literacy achievement, and your accountability will depend on how well you address reading and writing standards in your literacy lessons and how successfully you use instructional methods. This text will advance your understanding of what you're expected to teach and the instructional approaches you're expected to use. These text features point to ways you can be an accountable teacher:

Teacher Checklists

Teaching reading and writing requires understanding a number of important components—the processes of reading and writing; literacy assessment; and the procedures for teaching phonemic awareness and phonics, fluency, vocabulary, comprehension, and writing. You can answer the questions in Teacher Checklists to ensure you address key elements for each literacy component.

Common Core State Standards

You'll be responsible for ensuring that the literacy lessons, strategies, and skills you teach align with standards. Your state may use its own standards or use some adaptation of the Common Core State Standards for English Language Arts. Three features in this text illustrate how to integrate the Common Core State Standards into your instruction.

- **NEW Standards Check!** At the end of each chapter-opening vignette are directives for identifying the Standards the vignette teachers address while teaching their lessons.
- **Common Core State Standards Boxes** Look for Common Core State Standards boxes that point out how to plan purposeful literacy lessons that align with state and national literacy standards.
- **NEW Standards in the Classroom** In a number of instructional procedures in the Compendium, Pearson REVEL users can hyperlink to Standards in the Classroom vignettes that illustrate how classroom teachers use specific procedures to address Common Core State Standards.

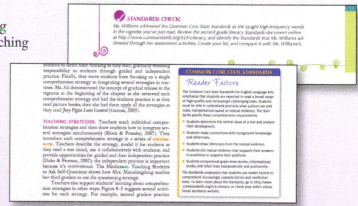

Teachers use these features to ensure that students meet grade-level standards.

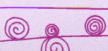

INSTRUCTIONAL SUPPORT

Balance is key to teaching reading and writing effectively: balancing reading instruction with writing, balancing explicit instruction with practice, and balancing instruction with assessment so that teachers use the results of assessment to inform their instruction. Knowing how to balance the teaching of reading and writing strategies—when, why, and how—is also vital. These features, many of which are supported by authentic classroom scenarios, illustrate the balanced approach to literacy instruction:

Chapter-Opening Vignettes

As a signature feature of this text, chapter-opening classroom stories describe how effective teachers integrate reading and writing instruction to maximize students' learning.

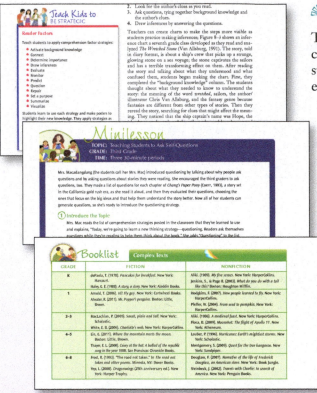

Teach Kids to Be Strategic

This revised feature will be invaluable in the classroom. Specific guidelines list the cognitive and metacognitive strategies students need to learn and then explain what to check for to ensure students are applying them effectively.

Minilessons

These popular step-by-step features model a clear and concise instructional procedure for teaching literacy strategies and skills, and they're intended to serve as ready-to-use tools for your classroom teaching.

Booklists

Well-written children's books can serve as mentor texts to support the development of literacy and advance children's fluency, vocabulary, comprehension, and writing. Throughout the text, Booklists identify grade-appropriate literature for your classroom use or for students' independent reading. These lists are vetted in every edition to ensure currency.

Student Artifacts

Nothing illustrates connected teaching and learning better than models of children's work. To that end, this text is peppered with examples of students' writing projects and other work products to help you learn to recognize grade-appropriate literacy development.

Chapter 10, Organizing for Instruction

Five instructional approaches—*guided reading*, *basal reading programs*, *literature focus units*, *literature circles*, and *reading and writing workshop*—provide concrete methods for teaching reading and writing. Chapter 10 digs into these approaches, illustrating how

to plan for and manage each of them and determine which approaches are most appropriate for your students.

Compendium of Instructional Procedures

Part Four of this text is a bank of step-by-step, evidence-based teaching procedures, popular because of their value as a classroom resource.

Literacy Portraits

Literacy Portraits features in the text draw your attention to five children—Rhiannon, Rakie, Michael, Curt'Lynn, and Jimmy—who are students in Ms. Janusz's second grade class. They're introduced in the openers to Parts One and Two, and the Literacy Portraits features provide direct links to video case studies so you can track these children's reading and writing development through their second grade year.

Embedded Classroom Videos

Look for play button icons located in navigation bars below interior chapter photos; clicking on these play buttons in REVEL will enable you to review videos that exemplify concepts covered in each chapter. Captions below the photos draw your attention to the focus of each video.

DIVERSE LEARNERS

No two students are alike. Children come to school with different background knowledge, language experiences, and literacy opportunities; they also differ in the way they learn and in the languages they speak. Throughout this text, and in these features in particular, I address the vast diversity of students and what it means to differentiate instruction to meet individual students' literacy needs:

Classroom Interventions

These features present information on topics such as dysfluency, phonics mismatches, vocabulary in content area texts, revising writing, and comprehension strategies. These suggestions for classroom intervention detail specific ways to assist struggling readers and writers.

Nurturing English Learners

Throughout the text, expanded chapter sections focus on ways to scaffold students who are learning to read and write at the same time they're learning to speak English. These sections provide in-depth guidance for planning instruction that addresses the needs of culturally and linguistically diverse students.

remember what they've just read and what they do when they run into difficulty. Students also write about their thinking on small self-stick notes and place them in their books, next to text that stimulated their thinking. Later, students share their notes during a discussion about how they monitor their reading.

Predicting

Readers make thoughtful "guesses" or predictions about what will happen or what they'll learn in the book they're reading. These guesses are based on what students already know about the topic and genre or on what they've read thus far. Students often make a prediction before beginning to read and several others at pivotal points in a text—no matter whether they're reading stories, nonfiction books, or poems—and then as they read, they either confirm or revise their predictions. Predictions about nonfiction are different than for stories and poems here students are generating questions about the topic that they would like to find answers to as they read.

When teachers share a big book with young children using shared reading, they prompt children to make predictions at the beginning of the book and again at key points during the reading. They model how to make reasonable predictions and use think-alouds to talk about their predictions.

Questioning

Readers ask themselves questions about the text as they read (Duke & Pearson, 2002). They ask self-questions out of curiosity, and as they use this strategy, they become more engaged with the text and want to keep reading to find answers (Harvey & Goudvis, 2007). These questions often lead to making predictions and drawing inferences. Students also ask themselves questions to clarify misunderstandings as they read. They use this strategy throughout the reading process—to activate background knowledge and make predictions before reading, to engage with the text and clarify confusions during reading, and to evaluate and reflect on the text after reading.

Traditionally, teachers have been the question-askers and students have been the question-answerers, but when students learn to generate questions about the text, their comprehension improves. In fact, students comprehend better when they gener-

Classroom INTERVENTIONS

Strategic Readers

Struggling students often complain that they don't understand what they're reading. Comprehension difficulties are due to a variety of problems, but one of the most common is that students don't read strategically (Cooper, Chard, & Kiger, 2006). They read passively, without using comprehension strategies to think about what they're reading. Unless they learn to thoughtfully engage in the reading process, it's unlikely that students who struggle with comprehension will improve very much.

The good news is that teachers can help struggling students become more thoughtful and strategic readers by teaching them to use comprehension strategies (Allington, 2012). The most important strategies for struggling readers are activating background knowledge, determining importance, summarizing, questioning, visualizing, and monitoring.

As teachers teach comprehension strategies, they explain each strategy, including how, when, and why to use it, and they make the strategy visible by demonstrating how to use it during minilessons, interactive read-alouds, and guided reading lessons. They use think-alouds to show that capable readers are active thinkers while they're reading. Students participate in small-group and partner activities as they practice using the strategy and verbalize their thinking. At first, teachers provide lots of support, and they withdraw it slowly as students become responsible for using the strategy independently. Once students have learned to apply two or three strategies, they begin to use them together. Integrating strategy use is important because capable readers don't depend on a single comprehension strategy; instead, they have a repertoire of strategies available that they use as needed while they're reading (Allington, 2012).

Differentiated Instruction

Because teachers need to recognize individual students' progress and personalize learning, this edition includes three features that zero in on nine students whose cultural backgrounds and literacy progress differ. *Differentiated Instruction* features appear in Chapters 4, 8, and 11 to showcase the developmental differences you might see in beginning readers and writers, readers and writers who are learning comprehension strategies, and older readers and writers who differ greatly in their achievement levels. In addition, many of the featured students are learning English at the same time they're becoming literate.

ASSESSMENT RESOURCES

Although summative assessment is often a part of a formal whole-school program, teachers often use formative assessment measures to monitor and evaluate students' achievement. I offer a variety of authentic assessment examples in this text so you'll learn how to plan for assessment that really measures what's intended, glean useful information about student progress, and personalize instruction to meet students' needs. Assessment requires teachers to engage in all four steps of the instruction–assessment cycle—plan for, monitor, evaluate, and reflect on students' literacy progress plus their own effectiveness; this link with instruction is crucial to ensure that all students are successful.

Chapter 3, Assessing Literacy Development

This chapter is placed early in the text to lay the groundwork for assessing students in line with backward design, ensuring that you know how you're going to measure literacy progress as you set literacy goals. Information in this chapter also addresses how to use student performance to inform instructional planning and how to prepare students for high-stakes achievement tests.

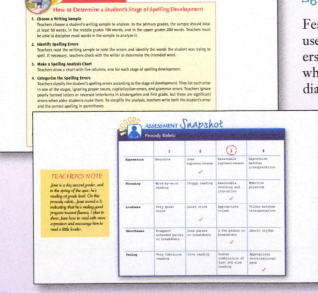

Assessment Tools

Features throughout the text identify well-respected and widely used assessment tools that measure literacy development. Teachers are responsible for knowing about these assessment choices, when it's appropriate to use them, and the kinds of screening or diagnostic information they impart.

Assessment Snapshots

A variety of authentic assessment examples that portray the literacy performance of individual students are presented in most chapters. Teacher's Notes accompany each assessment example to illustrate how teachers gather information from each assessment and use the results to guide further instruction.

TECHNOLOGY TOOLS

Technology is changing the way we live and communicate; this change affects not only our use of technology but also students' ability to access and learn from it. In these two features, I introduce digital programs, products, or processes that support students in learning to read and write:

Go Digital!

Many schools across the country are expecting teachers to engage students in digital learning. The Go Digital! features provide practical ideas and guidance for using specific programs and products that benefit students in using technology and in developing new media skills.

New Literacies

These features describe the research behind and the use of new technologies and how they support the development of 21st-century literacy strategies. Carefully researched, each featured technology identifies specific ways to prepare students for the reading and writing demands of 21st-century learning, including information and communication technologies.

REVEL. . . . learning reimagined. Reading has been the cornerstone of education since the invention of the printing press. Yet even as technology has connected us and guaranteed us a way to interact differently with the world, the means through which learners and educators have had to interact with written text has remained largely static. REVEL, a new learning experience offered by Pearson, engages you in a new way to read, think, and learn. REVEL allows you to interact with course material on devices you use—laptops, tablets, and smartphones—anytime and anywhere, and apply new learning and assessment strategies that weren't possible in the past with a printed textbook. Immersive learning experiences enliven familiar and respected course content with media interactives and assessments.

REVEL also is designed to make a measurable impact on defined learner outcomes related to access, completion, competence, and progression. It's the first product at Pearson to have an efficacy framework built in from the very beginning. REVEL was developed over several years and with more than 23,000 educators and students, and its key aspects—from features to content to performance dashboard reporting—were guided by interactions with customers like you. The result is a new approach to digital learning that gives educators and students precisely what they need—and nothing more. You can download a full efficacy report at http://www.pearsonhighered.com/revel/educators/index.html.

REVEL reflects several learning design principles:

- *Effective learning experiences clearly communicate goals to learners.* They feature content that directly aligns with the stated objectives.
- *Embedding formative assessment has a positive impact on both learning and instruction.* Assessments allow instructors to gauge student comprehension frequently, provide timely feedback, and address learning gaps along the way. When assessments are implemented appropriately and with specific, timely feedback, they engage students in the retrieval process, and this act of retrieving solidifies the original learning (Schecter, Durik, Miyamoto, & Harackiewicz, 2011*).

At Pearson, we believe that learning is a life-changing opportunity and that education should have a measurable impact on learners' lives. It's why we have spent so much time creating an immersive new learning environment that will empower you to take an active role in your own learning: engaging in familiar learning and eStudy tools (highlighting, note-taking, and accessing a glossary when needed), utilizing interactives that make the content dynamic, and participating in assessments that allow you to check your understanding at regular intervals.

By listening to instructors and students, by leveraging the best thinking and instructional research and design, and by applying new learning and assessment strategies, Pearson created REVEL. It's meant to make learning a valued and personalized experience for you. It is meant to prepare you for your future career.

*Schecter, O. G., Durik, A. M., Miyamoto, Y., & Harackiewicz, J. M. (2011). The role of utility value in achievement behavior: The importance of culture. *Personality and Social Psychology Bulletin, 37*(3): 303–317. doi: 10.1177/0146167210396380

Support Materials for Instructors

Instructors can download the following resources at **www.pearsonhigher.com/educators**. They enter the author or title of this book, select this particular edition of the book, and then click on the "Resources" tab to log in and download these textbook supplements:

Instructor's Resource Manual and Test Bank

The Instructor's Manual and Test Bank includes chapter-by-chapter materials with learning outcomes, suggested readings, discussion questions, in-class activities, and guidance on how to use the vignettes meaningfully in your instruction. You'll also find a bank of multiple-choice and essay questions.

PowerPoint Slides

The PowerPoint slides specifically designed for this text expand concepts and clarify chapter ideas to help instructors create a lecture or classroom activity that will engage students and share important chapter concepts.

TestGen

TestGen is a powerful test generator that instructors install on a computer and use in conjunction with the TestGen test bank file for this text. Assessments can be created for both print and online testing.

TestGen is available exclusively from Pearson Education publishers. Instructors install TestGen on a personal computer (Windows or Macintosh) and create tests for classroom assessments and for other specialized delivery options, such as over a local area network or on the Web. A test bank, which is also called a Test Item File (TIF), typically contains a large set of test items, organized by chapter and ready for use in creating an assessment, based on the related textbook material.

The tests can be downloaded in the following formats:

TestGen Testbank file—PC
TestGen Testbank file—MAC
TestGen Testbank—Blackboard 9 TIF
TestGen Testbank—Blackboard CE/Vista (WebCT) TIF
Angel Test Bank (zip)
D2L Test Bank (zip)
Moodle Test Bank
Sakai Test Bank (zip)

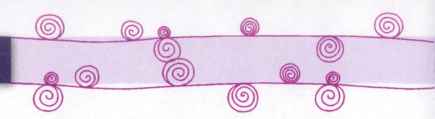

Many people helped and encouraged me as I developed and revised this text; my heartfelt thanks go to each of them. First, I want to thank my students over the years at California State University, Fresno, the University of Oklahoma, and Miami University, who taught me while I taught them, and the Teacher Consultants in the San Joaquin Valley Writing Project and the Oklahoma Writing Project, who shared their expertise with me. Their insightful questions challenged and broadened my thinking. I will always be grateful to the teachers who welcomed me into their classrooms, showed me how they created a balanced literacy program, and allowed me to learn from them and their students. In particular, I want to express my appreciation to Kimberly Clark, Whitney Donnelly, Stacy Firpo, Laurie Goodman, Lisa Janusz, Susan McCloskey, Kristi McNeal, Carol Ochs, Gay Ockey, Pam Papaleo, Holly Reid, Jenny Reno, Kacey Sanom, Troy Wagner, Darcy Williams, and Susan Zumwalt. I also want to recognize Van Vang for the excellent artwork he rendered for this text.

To my editors and the production team at Pearson Education, I offer my heartfelt thanks. A special thank you to Linda Bishop; I value your insightful approach to my books and your nurturing manner. I also want to express my appreciation to Meredith Fossel, my acquisitions editor, for her support, and I extend my unflagging gratitude to Susan McNally and Karen Mason, who have moved this text through the maze of production details. And to Melissa Gruzs, who has again cleaned up my manuscript and proofread the typeset text: I'm grateful for your careful attention to detail.

Finally, I want to thank the professors and teaching professionals who reviewed my text for their insightful comments that informed my development of this revision: Stan Barrera, IV, Louisiana State University; Frannie Franc, The College of New Jersey; Kristi Kallio, Mooresville (NC) Graded School District; Sharla Snider, Texas Woman's University; Christine Tate, Granite State College; and Amy W. Thornburg, Queens University of Charlotte. I sincerely appreciate your guidance.

Gail E. Tompkins

Brief Contents

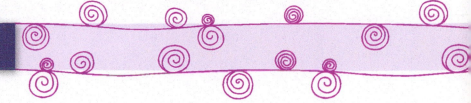

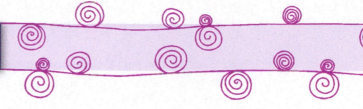

Table of Contents

PART one
Literacy in the 21st Century 1

chapter 1
Becoming an Effective Literacy Teacher 4

chapter 2

The Reading and Writing Processes   36

PART two
Components of Literacy Development   103

chapter 5
Cracking the Alphabetic Code   142

chapter 6

Developing Fluent Readers and Writers 182

chapter 7

Expanding Academic Vocabulary 216

PART *three*
Organizing for Instruction   325

chapter 10

Organizing for Instruction   328

chapter 11

Differentiating for Success   366

chapter 12

Reading and Writing Across the Curriculum 398

PART *four*

Compendium of Instructional Procedures 435

Special Features

Booklist

Literacy Portraits

DIVERSE LEARNERS

Classroom Interventions

Nurturing English Learners

Differentiated Instruction

ASSESSMENT RESOURCES

Assessment Tools

Assessment Snapshot

TECHNOLOGY TOOLS

Go Digital!

New Literacies

PART one

Literacy in the 21st Century

Classrooms are different today: They've become communities of learners where students assume more responsibility for learning. There's a hum as students talk about books they're reading, share their writing, and work in small groups. The students are more culturally and linguistically diverse, and many are English learners. Teachers guide and nurture students' learning through their instructional programs. Here's what they do:

- Balance explicit instruction with authentic application
- Address state standards
- Integrate reading and writing
- Teach with trade books as well as textbooks
- Incorporate digital technologies into literacy instruction
- Differentiate instruction so every student can succeed
- Link assessment and instruction

In this part opener, you meet Ms. Janusz and her second grade class, who exemplify this 21st-century view of literacy instruction. **Click here** to meet Ms. Janusz and students from her class. You'll also find several of her students featured in Literacy Portraits throughout this text.

Ms. Janusz works to develop her students' abilities to read and write fluently. She's teaching them to decode and spell words, use literacy strategies, and focus on meaning when they're reading and writing.

Students read leveled books with Ms. Janusz in guided reading groups, and she assesses their progress by listening to them read aloud.

Because the students' reading levels range from first to fourth grade, and some are English learners, Ms. Janusz differentiates instruction by varying grouping **patterns** and instructional materials.

The second graders practice the phonics skills that Ms. Janusz is teaching as they do a making words activity.

After she shares a trade book, Ms. Janusz often uses it to teach a minilesson on a reading or writing strategy or skill.

Visualizing

I make pictures in my mind when I read.

During reading workshop, students read "just right" books independently and with buddies.

Ms. Janusz balances explicit instruction with authentic reading and writing in her literacy program. Guided reading is the teaching component, and reading and **writing workshop are the authentic application activities.**

During writing workshop, the second graders draft, conference with Ms. Janusz, and revise and edit their writing with classmates. Later, they publish their books, sometimes using word processing so their writing will look professional.

Chapter 1

Becoming an Effective Literacy Teacher

PLAN: Preview the Learning Outcomes

After studying this chapter, you'll be prepared to respond to these points:

1.1 Compare teacher-centered and student-centered theories about learning.

1.2 Examine the role of each of the four cueing systems.

1.3 Describe the characteristics of a community of learners.

1.4 Explain the balanced approach to instruction.

1.5 Discuss the Common Core State Standards.

1.6 Describe how to scaffold students' reading and writing.

1.7 Summarize the programs that teachers use to organize instruction.

1.8 Explain how and why teachers differentiate instruction.

1.9 Describe how teachers link instruction and assessment.

*E*ffective teachers are the key to ensuring that students learn to read and write successfully. Most researchers agree that teacher quality is the most important factor in determining how well students learn (Vandevoort, Amrein-Beardsley, & Berliner, 2004). Teachers need to be knowledgeable about how students learn to read and write, how to teach literacy, and how to respond to the needs of struggling students and those learning English as a new language.

Today, teachers are held accountable for their effectiveness. In 2002, the federal No Child Left Behind (NCLB) Act ushered in a new era by holding schools responsible for educating all students to meet mandated standards. Teachers have always been responsible for advancing their students' achievement, but NCLB has led to annual standardized tests to measure student achievement and then using the scores to determine whether teachers and schools are effective. The assumption is that if students don't do well, teachers aren't effective, even though this logic is faulty. Standardized tests don't take into account students' growth over time. For example, some struggling readers make less than one year's growth each year, so by fourth grade, they're reading at the second grade level. Then they have an especially effective teacher, and these students make a whole year's growth—now they're reading at the third grade level; but because they're still below grade level, their teacher's effectiveness isn't recognized. In addition, learning to read and write is a complex endeavor, so a single test can never be a complete measure of student learning and teacher effectiveness.

President Obama called for "a new culture of accountability" in schools that builds on NCLB (Dinan, 2009). He described these components of accountability: better tracking of teachers' performance, higher standards for teachers, and assistance for teachers who aren't effective. He also recommended that exemplary teachers be recognized for their effectiveness and asked to serve as grade-level mentors or leaders in their schools. Obama's notion of teacher accountability still translates to how well students perform on standardized tests, but new ways of determining teacher effectiveness are being implemented.

The National Board of Professional Teaching Standards (2002) developed a system of standards that represent a national consensus of the characteristics of effective teachers. These 15 standards describe what teachers need to know and how they support student learning:

Knowledge of Learners. Teachers use their knowledge of learning theories to inform their teaching.

Knowledge About Literacy. Teachers understand current research and theories about literacy instruction and apply their knowledge to their teaching.

Equity, Fairness, and Diversity. Teachers provide equal access to learning, capitalize on diversity, and encourage all students to respect themselves and their classmates.

Learning Environment. Teachers establish a community of learners in their classroom that's safe, supportive, inclusive, and democratic.

Instructional Resources. Teachers collect, create, and adapt instructional resources, involve students in creating resources, and invite community members to enrich the instructional program.

Instructional Decision Making. Teachers set informed goals for their students, provide meaningful learning experiences, and interact effectively with students.

Assessment. Teachers use a range of assessment tools to monitor instructional progress, evaluate students' learning, and make instructional decisions.

Integration. Teachers understand the reciprocal nature of reading and writing and integrate written language with oral and visual language.

Reading. Teachers use their knowledge of the reading process, types of texts, and instructional procedures to develop strategic, lifelong readers.

Writing. Teachers apply their knowledge of the writing process, writer's craft, and instructional procedures to develop writers who can write for a variety of purposes and audiences.

Listening and Speaking. Teachers teach listening and speaking as essential components of literacy and provide opportunities for students to use oral language for a variety of purposes and audiences.

Viewing. Teachers value viewing as an essential component of literacy and use a variety of print and multimedia resources to develop students' visual literacy capabilities.

Collaboration With Families and Communities. Teachers develop positive and purposeful relationships with families and community members.

Teachers as Learners. Teachers improve their knowledge about literacy learning and teaching through professional reading and inquiry.

Professional Responsibility. Teachers actively contribute to the improvement of teaching and learning and to the advancement of knowledge and professional practice.

To read more about these characteristics of teacher effectiveness, go to the National Board of Professional Teaching Standards website.

The goal of literacy instruction is to ensure that all students achieve their full literacy potential, and in that light, this chapter introduces nine principles of balanced literacy instruction. These principles are stated in terms of what effective teachers do, and they provide the foundation for the chapters that follow.

Principle 1: Effective Teachers Understand How Students Learn

Understanding how students learn influences how teachers teach. Until the 1960s, behaviorism, a teacher-centered theory, was the dominant view of learning; since then, student-centered theories that advocate children's active engagement in authentic literacy activities have become more influential. The three most important theories are constructivism, sociolinguistics, and information processing. During the last two decades, however, behaviorism has begun a resurgence as evidenced by NCLB, renewed popularity of basal reading programs, current emphasis on curriculum standards, and mandated high-stakes testing. Tracey and Morrow (2006) argue that multiple theoretical perspectives improve the quality of literacy instruction, and the stance presented in this text is that instruction should represent a realistic balance between teacher-centered and student-centered theories. Figure 1–1 summarizes these learning theories.

Behaviorism

Behaviorists focus on the observable and measurable aspects of students' behavior. They believe that behavior can be learned or unlearned, and that learning is the result of stimulus-and-response actions (O'Donohue & Kitchener, 1998). Reading is viewed as a conditioned response. This theory is described as teacher centered because it focuses on the teacher's active role as a dispenser of knowledge. Skinner (1974) explained that students learn to read by learning a series of discrete skills and subskills.

Teachers use **explicit instruction** to teach skills in a planned, sequential order. Information is presented in small steps and reinforced through practice activities until students master it because each step is built on the previous one. Students practice skills they're learning by completing fill-in-the-blank worksheets. They usually work individually, not in small groups or with partners. Behavior modification is another key feature: Behaviorists believe that teachers control and motivate students through a combination of rewards and punishments.

Constructivism

Constructivist theorists describe students as active and engaged learners who construct their own knowledge. According to this student-centered theory, learning

FIGURE 1–1 Learning Theories

ORIENTATION	THEORY	CHARACTERISTICS	APPLICATIONS
Teacher-Centered	Behaviorism	• Focuses on observable changes in behavior • Views the teacher's role as providing information and supervising practice • Describes learning as the result of stimulus-response actions • Uses incentives and rewards for motivation	• Basal readers • Minilessons • Repeated readings • Worksheets
Student-Centered	Constructivism	• Describes learning as the active construction of knowledge • Recognizes the importance of background knowledge • Views learners as innately curious • Advocates collaboration, not competition • Suggests ways to engage students so they can be successful	• Literature focus units • KWL charts • Learning logs • Thematic units • Word sorts
	Sociolinguistics	• Emphasizes the importance of language and social interaction on learning • Views reading and writing as social and cultural activities • Explains that students learn best through authentic activities • Describes the teacher's role as scaffolding students' learning • Advocates culturally responsive teaching • Challenges students to confront injustices and inequities in society	• Literature circles • Shared reading • Reading and writing workshop • Author's chair
	Information Processing	• Compares the mind to a computer • Recommends integrating reading and writing • Views reading and writing as meaning-making processes • Explains that readers' interpretations are individualized • Describes students as strategic readers and writers	• Guided reading • Graphic organizers • Grand conversations • Interactive writing • Reading logs

occurs when students integrate new information with their existing knowledge. Teachers engage students with experiences so that they construct their own knowledge.

SCHEMA THEORY. Knowledge is organized into cognitive structures called **schemas**, and schema theory describes how students learn. Jean Piaget (1969) explained that learning is the modification of schemas as students actively interact with their environment. Imagine that the brain is a mental filing cabinet, and that new information is organized with existing knowledge in the filing system. When students are already familiar with a topic, the new information is added to that mental file, or schema, in a revision process Piaget called **assimilation**. But when students begin studying a new topic, they create a mental file and place the new information in it; this more difficult construction process is **accommodation**. Everyone's cognitive structure is different, reflecting their knowledge and past experiences.

INQUIRY LEARNING. John Dewey advocated an inquiry approach to develop citizens who could participate fully in our democracy (Tracey & Morrow, 2006). He theorized that learners are innately curious and actively create their own knowledge and concluded that collaboration is more conducive to learning than competition. Students collaborate to conduct investigations in which they ask questions, seek information, and create new knowledge to solve problems.

ENGAGEMENT THEORY. Theorists examined students' interest in reading and writing and found that engaged learners are intrinsically motivated; they do more reading and writing, enjoy these activities, and reach higher levels of achievement (Guthrie & Wigfield, 2000). Engaged students have **self-efficacy**, the confidence that they'll succeed and reach their goals (Bandura, 1997). Students with high self-efficacy are resilient and persistent, despite obstacles and challenges that get in the way of success. These theorists believe that students are more engaged when they participate in authentic literacy activities and when they collaborate with classmates in a nurturing classroom community.

Sociolinguistics

Sociolinguists theorized that learners use language to organize their thoughts. Lev Vygotsky (1978, 1986) recommended that teachers incorporate opportunities into their instruction for students to talk about what they're learning; students can work in small groups, for example, and talk about books they're reading or share their writing with classmates. Vygotsky realized that students can accomplish more challenging tasks in collaboration with adults than on their own, but they learn very little when they perform tasks that they can already do independently. He recommended that teachers focus instruction on children's **zone of proximal development**, the level between their actual development and their potential development. Teachers gradually withdraw their support or scaffolding as students learn so that they eventually perform the task independently. Then the cycle begins again.

SOCIOCULTURAL THEORY. Reading and writing are viewed as social activities that reflect the culture and community in which students live, and students from different cultures have different expectations about literacy learning and preferred ways of learning (Heath, 1983; Moll & Gonzales, 2004). Teachers apply this theory as they create culturally responsive classrooms that empower everyone, including those from marginalized groups, to become more successful readers and writers (Gay, 2010).

Teachers often use powerful multicultural literature to develop students' global awareness, including *Goin' Somewhere Special* (McKissack, 2001), a story about the mistreatment of black children in the segregated South; *Esperanza Rising* (Ryan, 2002), a story about a Mexican American girl who creates a new future for herself in a migrant camp; and *Project Mulberry* (Park, 2007), a story about a Korean American girl who creates a silkworm project for the state fair while dealing with issues of prejudice, patriotism, and conservation. Additional books are included in the Booklist: Multicultural Books.

Culturally responsive teaching acknowledges the legitimacy of all children's cultures and social customs and teaches children to appreciate their classmates' diverse heritages. This theory emphasizes that teachers are responsive to their students' instructional needs. When children aren't successful, teachers examine their instructional practices and make changes so that all children become capable readers and writers.

SITUATED LEARNING THEORY. Learning is a function of the activity, context, and culture in which it occurs (Lave & Wenger, 1991). Situated learning theory rejects the notion of separating learning to do something from actually doing it and emphasizes the idea of apprenticeship, where beginners move from the edge of a learning community to its center as they develop expertise (Brown, Collins, & Duguid, 1989). For example, if you want to become a chef, you could either go to a cooking school or learn as you work in a restaurant; situated learning theory suggests that working in a restaurant is more effective. In the same way, children learn best through

Booklist — Multicultural Books

CULTURE	BOOKS
African American	Bridges, R. (1999). *Through my eyes*. New York: Scholastic. M
	Bryan, A. (2009). *Ashley Bryan: Words to my life's song*. New York: Atheneum. M
	Curtis, C. P. (2000). *The Watsons go to Birmingham—1963*. New York: Laurel Leaf. MU
	Rappaport, D. (2007). *Martin's big words: The life of Dr. Martin Luther King, Jr.* New York: Hyperion Books. PM
	Ringgold, F. (1996). *Tar beach*. New York: Dragonfly Books. PM
	Taylor, M. D. (2004). *Roll of thunder, hear my cry*. New York: Puffin Books. MU
	Williams-Garcia, R. (2011). *One crazy summer*. New York: Amistad. MU
	Woodson, J. (2005). *Show way*. New York: Putnam. M
Arab American	Bunting, E. (2006). *One green apple*. New York: Clarion Books. P
	Ellis, D. (2001). *The breadwinner*. Toronto, ON: Groundwood Books. MU
	Nye, N. S. (1997). *Sitti's secrets*. New York: Aladdin Books. P
	Nye, N. S. (1999). *Habibi*. New York: Simon & Schuster. U
	Nye, N. S. (2005). *19 varieties of gazelle: Poems of the Middle East*. New York: Greenwillow. U
	Wolf, B. (2003). *Coming to America: A Muslim family's story*. New York: Lee & Low. PM
Asian American	Lai, T. (2013). *Inside out and back again*. New York: HarperCollins. M
	Look, L. (2006). *Ruby Lu, brave and true*. New York: Atheneum. PM
	Look, L. (2009). *Alvin Ho: Allergic to girls, school, and other scary things*. New York: Yearling. P
	Park, L. S. (2008). *Bee-bim bop!* New York: Sandpiper. P
	Park, L. S. (2011). *A single shard*. New York: Sandpiper. MU
	Perkins, M. (2008). *Rickshaw girl*. Watertown, MA: Charlesbridge. PM
	Say, A. (2008). *Grandfather's journey*. New York: Sandpiper. PM
	Yang, G. L. (2008). *American born Chinese*. New York: Square Fish Books. U
Hispanic American	Ada, A. F. (1999). *The lizard and the sun / La lagartija y el sol*. New York: Dragonfly Books. P
	Bunting, E. (1998). *Going home*. New York: HarperCollins. P
	Cisneros, S. (1991). *The house on Mango Street*. New York: Vintage. MU
	Dorros, A. (1997). *Abuela*. New York: Puffin Books. P
	Jiménez, F. (2002). *The circuit: Stories from the life of a migrant child*. Boston: Houghton Mifflin. U
	Krull, K. (2004). *Harvesting hope: The story of Cesar Chavez*. New York: Scholastic. M
	Ryan, P. M. (2010). *The dreamer*. New York: Scholastic. MU
	Soto, G. (1996). *Too many tamales*. New York: Puffin Books. P
Native American	Alexie, S. (2009). *The absolutely true diary of a part-time Indian*. Boston: Little, Brown. U
	Bruchac, J. (1997). *13 moons on turtle's back*. New York: Puffin Books. PM
	Bruchac, J. (2001). *The heart of a chief*. New York: Puffin Books. MU
	Bruchac, J. (2006). *Code talker: A novel about the Navajo marines of World War II*. New York: Speak. U
	Erdrich, L. (2002). *The birchbark house*. New York: Hyperion Books. MU
	Goble, P. (2010). *The boy and his mud horses*. Bloomington, IN: World Wisdom. M
	McDermott, G. (2001). *Raven: A trickster tale from the Pacific northwest*. New York: Sandpiper. P
	O'Dell, S. (2010). *Sing down the moon*. New York: Sandpiper. U

P = primary grades (K–2); M = middle grades (3–5); U = upper grades (6–8)

authentic and meaningful activities. They join a community of learners in the classroom and become more expert readers and writers through interaction with classmates. The teacher serves as an expert model, much like a chef does in a restaurant.

CRITICAL LITERACY. Paulo Freire (2000) called for sweeping educational change so that students examine fundamental questions about justice and equity. **Critical literacy** theorists view language as a means for social action and advocate that students become agents of social change (Johnson & Freedman, 2005). This theory has a political agenda, and the increasing social and cultural diversity in American society adds urgency to resolving inequities and injustices.

Reading and responding to books that deal with social issues are ways that teachers address social literacy (Lewison, Leland, & Harste, 2008). For example, *The Breadwinner* (Ellis, 2001) is the story of a girl in Taliban-controlled Afghanistan who pretends to be a boy to support her family; *Smoky Night* (Bunting, 1999) is a Caldecott Medal–winning story about overcoming racism set during the Los Angeles riots; and *Homeless Bird* (Whelan, 2000) is the story of an Indian girl who has no future when she is widowed. The books in the Booklist: Books That Foster Critical Literacy describe injustices that students can understand and work to change.

Information Processing

Information processing theory compares the mind to a computer and describes how information moves through a series of processing units—sensory register, short-term memory, and long-term memory—as it's stored (Tracey & Morrow, 2006). There's a

Booklist   Books That Foster Critical Literacy

LEVEL	BOOKS
Primary Grades (K–2)	Baker, J. (2010). *Mirror*. Somerville, MA: Candlewick Press. Bunting, E. (1997). *A day's work*. New York: Clarion Books. Bunting, E. (1999). *Smoky night*. San Diego: Voyager. Chinn, K. (1997). *Sam and the lucky money*. New York: Lee & Low. Uchida, Y. (1996). *The bracelet*. New York: Putnam. Winter, J. (2008). *Wangari's trees of peace: A true story from Africa*. San Diego: Harcourt. Woodson, J. (2001). *The other side*. New York: Putnam.
Middle Grades (3–5)	Curtis, C. P. (2000). *The Watsons go to Birmingham—1963*. New York: Laurel Leaf. Deedy, C. A. (2009). *14 cows for America*. Atlanta, GA: Peachtree. Fleischman, P. (2004). *Seedfolks*. New York: Harper Trophy. Golenbock, P. (1992). *Teammates*. San Diego: Voyager. King, M. L., Jr. (1997). *I have a dream*. New York: Scholastic. Milway, K. S. (2008). *One hen: How one small loan made a big difference*. Toronto, ON: Kids Can Press. Ringgold, F. (2003). *If a bus could talk: The story of Rosa Parks*. New York: Aladdin Books. Ryan, P. M. (2002). *Esperanza rising*. New York: Scholastic/Blue Sky Press.
Upper Grades (6–8)	Avi. (2011). *Nothing but the truth*. New York: Scholastic. Hesse, K. (2005). *Witness*. New York: Scholastic. Hiaasen, C. (2006). *Hoot*. New York: Yearling. Hiaasen, C. (2007). *Flush*. New York: Knopf. Lowry, L. (2006). *The giver*. New York: Delacorte. Rhuday-Perkovich, O. (2011). *8th grade superzero*. New York: Levine Books. Staples, S. F. (2006). *Dangerous skies*. New York: Farrar, Straus & Giroux.

control mechanism, too, that oversees learning. Theorists create models of the reading and writing processes to describe the complicated, interactive workings of the mind (Hayes, 2004; Kintsch, 2004; Rumelhart, 2004); they believe that reading and writing are related, and their models describe a two-way flow of information between what readers and writers know and the words written on the page.

INTERACTIVE MODELS. Reading and writing are interactive processes of meaning-making. The interactive model of reading emphasizes that readers focus on comprehension and construct meaning using a combination of reader-based and text-based information. This model also includes an executive monitor that oversees children's attention, determines whether what they're reading makes sense, and takes action when problems arise (Ruddell & Unrau, 2004).

Hayes's (2004) model of writing describes what writers do as they write; it emphasizes that writing is also an interactive meaning-making process. Students move through a series of stages as they plan, draft, revise, and edit their writing to ensure that readers will understand what they've written. Writers use the same control mechanism that readers do to make plans, select strategies, and solve problems.

TRANSACTIONAL THEORY. Louise Rosenblatt's transactional theory (2004) explains how students create meaning as they read. She describes comprehension, which she calls *interpretation*, as the result of a two-way transaction between readers and the text. Instead of trying to figure out the author's meaning, readers negotiate an interpretation based on the text and their knowledge about literature and the world. Interpretations are individualized because each student brings different knowledge and experiences to the reading event. Even though interpretations vary, they can always be substantiated by the text.

STRATEGIC BEHAVIORS. Children employ strategic or goal-oriented behaviors to direct their thinking. Cognitive strategies such as visualizing, organizing, and revising are used to achieve a goal, and metacognitive strategies, such as monitoring and repairing, determine whether that goal has been reached (Dean, 2006; Pressley, 2002). The word **metacognition** is often defined as "thinking about your own thinking," but more accurately, it refers to a sophisticated level of thinking that students use to actively control their thinking (Baker, 2002). Metacognition is a control mechanism that involves both students' awareness about their thinking and their active control of thinking.

MONITOR: Check Your Understanding 1.1

Principle 2: Effective Teachers Support Students' Use of the Cueing Systems

Language is a complex system for creating meaning through socially shared conventions (Halliday, 1978). English, like other languages, involves four **cueing systems**:

- The phonological, or sound, system
- The syntactic, or structural, system
- The semantic, or meaning, system
- The pragmatic, or social and cultural use, system

Together, these systems make communication possible; children and adults use all four systems simultaneously as they read, write, listen, and talk. The priority people place on cueing systems varies; however, the phonological system is especially important for

FIGURE 1–2 The Four Cueing Systems

SYSTEM	TERMS	APPLICATIONS
Phonological System The sound system of English with approximately 44 sounds and more than 500 ways to spell them	• *Phoneme* (the smallest unit of sound) • *Grapheme* (the written representation of a phoneme using one or more letters) • *Phonological awareness* (knowledge about the sound structure of words, at the phoneme, onset-rime, and syllable levels) • *Phonemic awareness* (the ability to orally manipulate phonemes in words) • *Phonics* (instruction about phoneme–grapheme correspondences and spelling rules)	• Pronouncing words • Detecting regional and other dialects • Decoding words when reading • Using invented spelling • Reading and writing alliterations and onomatopoeia • Noticing rhyming words • Dividing words into syllables
Syntactic System The structural system of English that governs how words are combined into sentences	• *Syntax* (the structure or grammar of a sentence) • *Morpheme* (the smallest meaningful unit of language) • *Free morpheme* (a morpheme that can stand alone as a word) • *Bound morpheme* (a morpheme that must be attached to a free morpheme)	• Adding inflectional endings to words • Combining words to form compound words • Adding prefixes and suffixes to root words • Using capitalization and punctuation to indicate beginnings and ends of sentences • Writing simple, compound, and complex sentences • Combining sentences
Semantic System The meaning system of English that focuses on vocabulary	• *Semantics* (meaning) • *Synonyms* (words that mean the same or nearly the same thing) • *Antonyms* (opposites) • *Homonyms* (words that sound alike but are spelled differently)	• Learning the meanings of words • Discovering that many words have multiple meanings • Using context clues to figure out an unfamiliar word • Studying synonyms, antonyms, and homonyms • Using a dictionary and a thesaurus
Pragmatic System The system of English that offers language choices according to social and cultural uses	• *Function* (the purpose for which a person uses language) • *Standard English* (the form of English used in textbooks and by television newscasters) • *Nonstandard English* (other forms of English)	• Varying language to fit specific purposes • Reading and writing dialogue in dialects • Comparing standard and nonstandard forms of English

beginning readers and writers as they apply phonics skills to decode and spell words. Information about the four cueing systems is summarized in Figure 1–2.

The Phonological System

There are approximately 44 speech sounds in English. Children learn to pronounce these sounds as they learn to talk, and they associate the sounds with letters as they learn to read and write. Sounds are called **phonemes**, and they're represented in print with diagonal lines to differentiate them from **graphemes**, letters or letter combinations. Thus, the first grapheme in *mother* is m, and the phoneme is /m/. The phoneme in *soap* that is represented by the grapheme *oa* is called "long o" and is written /ō/.

The phonological system is important for both oral and written language. Regional differences exist in the way people pronounce phonemes; for example, New Yorkers pronounce sounds differently from Georgians. Students learning English as a second language learn to pronounce the sounds in English, and not surprisingly, they have more difficulty with sounds that differ from those in their native language. For example, because Spanish doesn't have /th/, native Spanish speakers have difficulty pronouncing it, often substituting /d/ for /th/ because the sounds are articulated in similar ways. Younger children usually learn to pronounce the difficult sounds more easily than older children and adults do.

This system plays a crucial role in reading instruction during the primary grades. In a purely phonetic language, there's a one-to-one correspondence between letters and sounds, which means teaching students to decode words is easy. But English is not a purely phonetic language: There are 26 letters and 44 sounds and many ways to combine the letters to spell some sounds, especially vowels. Consider these ways to spell long *e*: *sea*, *green*, *Pete*, *me*, and *people*. And the patterns used to spell long *e* don't always work—*head* and *great* are exceptions. **Phonics**, which describes the phoneme–grapheme correspondences and related spelling rules, is an important component of reading instruction. Students use phonics to decode many words, but it isn't a complete reading program because many common words can't be decoded easily and because reading involves more than just decoding. Comprehension is the goal of reading instruction.

The Syntactic System

The syntactic system is the structural organization of English. It's the grammar that regulates how words are combined into sentences; here the word **grammar** means the rules governing how words are combined in sentences, not parts of speech. Students use the syntactic system as they combine words to form sentences. Word order is important in English, and English speakers must arrange words into a sequence that makes sense. Spanish speakers who are learning English, for example, learn to say "This is my red sweater," not "This is my sweater red," the literal translation from Spanish.

Students use their syntactic knowledge as they read: They expect that the words have been strung together into sentences, and when they come to an unfamiliar word, they recognize its role in the sentence even if they don't know the labels for parts of speech. In the sentence "The horses galloped through the gate and out into the field," students may not know the word *through*, but they can substitute a reasonable word or phrase, such as *out of* or *past*.

Another component of **syntax** is word forms. Words such as *dog* and *play* are **morphemes**, the smallest meaningful units in language. Word parts that change the meaning of a word are also morphemes; when the plural marker *-s* is added to *dog* to make *dogs*, for instance, or the past-tense marker *-ed* is added to *play* to make *played*, these words now have two morphemes because the inflectional endings change the meaning of the words. The words *dog* and *play* are **free morphemes** because they convey meaning while standing alone; the endings *-s* and *-ed* are **bound morphemes** because they must be attached to free morphemes to convey meaning. **Compound words** are two or more morphemes combined to create a new word: *Birthday*, for example, is a compound word made up of two free morphemes.

The Semantic System

The semantic system focuses on meaning. Vocabulary is the key component of this system: Researchers estimate that children have a vocabulary of 5,000 words by the time they enter school, and they continue to acquire 3,000 to 4,000 words each year so that by the time they graduate from high school, their vocabularies reach 50,000 words (Stahl & Nagy, 2005). Students learn some words through instruction, but they learn many more words informally through reading and through social studies and science units. Students' depth of knowledge about words increases, too, from knowing one meaning for a word to knowing how to use it in many different ways. The word *fire*, for instance, has more than a dozen meanings; many are related to combustion, but others deal with an intense feeling, discharging a gun, or dismissing someone. *To light a fire under* someone and *being under fire* are idiomatic expressions, and compound words using *fire* include *firearm, fire extinguisher, firefly, fireproof,* and *fireworks.*

The Pragmatic System

Pragmatics deals with the social aspects of language use. People use language for many purposes; how they talk and write varies according to their purpose and audience. Language use also varies among social classes, ethnic groups, and geographic regions; these varieties are **dialects**. School is one cultural community, and the language of school is **Standard English**. This dialect is formal—the one used in textbooks, newspapers, and magazines, and by television newscasters. Other forms, including those spoken in urban ghettos or in Appalachia, are generally classified as **nonstandard English**; these nonstandard forms are alternatives in which the phonology, syntax, and semantics differ from those of Standard English. They're neither inferior nor substandard; instead, they reflect the communities of the speakers, and the speakers communicate as effectively as those who use Standard English. The goal is for students to add Standard English to their repertoire of language registers, not to replace their home dialect with Standard English.

Students use all four cueing systems as they read and write. For example, when students correctly read the sentence "Jimmy is playing ball with his father," they're probably using information from all four systems. On the other hand, when they misread certain words, they may be focusing on one cueing system more than the others. For example, a child who substitutes *dad* for *father* and reads "Jimmy is playing ball with his dad" is probably focusing on the semantic or pragmatic system rather than on the phonological system. When a child substitutes *basketball* for *ball* and reads "Jimmy is playing basketball with his father," he might be relying on an illustration or his own experience playing basketball. Or, because both *basketball* and *ball* begin with *b*, he might have noticed the beginning sound but not have considered the length of the word *basketball* compared with the word *ball*. A child who changes the syntax, as in "Jimmy, he play ball with his father," probably speaks a nonstandard dialect. And sometimes a child reads the sentence so that it doesn't make sense, such as "Jump is play boat with his father": The child chooses words with the correct beginning sounds and uses appropriate parts of speech for at least some of the words, but there's no comprehension. This is a serious problem because the child doesn't seem to understand that what he reads must make sense.

 MONITOR: Check Your Understanding 1.2

Principle 3: Effective Teachers Create a Community of Learners

Classrooms are social settings. Together, students and their teacher create their classroom community, and the type of community they create strongly influences the learning that takes place (Angelillo, 2008). The classroom community should feel safe and respectful so students are motivated to learn and actively involved in reading and writing activities. Perhaps the most striking quality is the partnership between the teacher and students: They become a "family" in which all members respect one another and support each other's learning. Students value culturally and linguistically diverse classmates and recognize that everyone makes important contributions.

Think about the differences between renting and owning a home. In a classroom community, students and the teacher are joint "owners" where they assume responsibility for their behavior and learning, work collaboratively with classmates, complete assignments, and care for the classroom. In contrast, the classroom belongs to the teacher in traditional classrooms, and students are "renters" for the school year. Joint ownership doesn't mean that teachers abdicate their responsibility; on the contrary, they're the guides, instructors, coaches, and evaluators. Sometimes these roles are shared with students, but the ultimate responsibility remains with the teacher.

Characteristics of a Classroom Community

A successful classroom community has specific, identifiable characteristics that are conducive to learning:

Safety. The classroom is a safe place that promotes in-depth learning and nurtures students' physical and emotional well-being.

Respect. Students and the teacher interact respectfully with each other. Harassment, bullying, and verbal abuse aren't tolerated. Students' cultural, linguistic, and learning differences are honored so that everyone feels comfortable and valued.

High Expectations. Teachers set high expectations and emphasize that all students can be successful. Their expectations promote a positive classroom environment where students behave appropriately and develop self-confidence.

Risk Taking. Teachers challenge students to explore new topics and try unfamiliar activities, and they encourage students to take intellectual risks and to develop higher level thinking skills.

Collaboration. Students work with classmates on reading and writing activities and other projects. Because students value opportunities for social interaction and belong to a group, working together often increases students' motivation and enhances their achievement.

Choice. Students make choices about the books they read, the topics they write about, and the projects they pursue within the parameters set by the teacher. When students have opportunities to make choices, they're more motivated to succeed, and they place more value on the activity.

Responsibility. Students are valued members of the classroom community who are responsible for their learning, their behavior, and the contributions they make. Teachers and students share learning and teaching responsibilities, and students assume leadership roles in small-group activities.

Family and Community Involvement. Teachers involve parents and community members in classroom activities and develop home–school bonds through regular communication and special programs. Researchers report that when parents and other adults are involved in classroom activities, student achievement soars (Edwards, McMillon, & Turner, 2010).

Literacy Portraits

Ms. Janusz spent the first month of the school year creating a community of learners in her classroom. She taught the second graders how to participate in reading and writing workshop, including procedures for choosing books, reading with a buddy, and keeping a writer's notebook. They learned to work cooperatively, take responsibility for their work and behavior, and show respect to their classmates.

Listen to Ms. Janusz as she talks about Curt'Lynn, and listen to a story Curt'Lynn shares about her family. Which of the characteristics of a community of learners described in the third principle do you observe in this video clip? Why do you think Ms. Janusz tries to build a community of learners in her classroom?

Curt'Lynn

These characteristics emphasize the teacher's role in creating an inviting, supportive, and safe classroom climate.

How to Create the Classroom Culture

Teachers are more successful when they take the first several weeks of the school year to establish the classroom environment; it's unrealistic to assume that students will instinctively be cooperative, responsible, and respectful of classmates. Teachers explicitly explain classroom routines, such as how to get supplies out and put them away and how to work with classmates in a small group, and they expect that everyone will adhere to the routines. They demonstrate literacy procedures, including how to choose a book, how to provide feedback about a classmate's writing, and how to participate in a **grand conversation**. Teachers also model ways of interacting with classmates and assisting them with reading and writing projects.

Check the Compendium of Instructional Procedures, which follows Chapter 12.

Teachers are the classroom managers: They set expectations and clearly explain to students what's expected of them and what's valued in the classroom. The classroom rules are specific and consistent, and teachers also set limits: For example, students are permitted to talk quietly with classmates when they're working, but they're not allowed to shout across the classroom or talk when the teacher's talking or when classmates are presenting to the class. Teachers also model classroom rules themselves as they interact with students. This process of socialization at the beginning of the school year is crucial to the success of the literacy program.

Not everything can be accomplished quickly, however; teachers continue to reinforce classroom routines and literacy procedures. One way is to have student leaders model the desired routines and behaviors; this way, classmates are likely to follow the lead. Teachers also continue to teach additional literacy procedures as students become involved in new types of activities. The classroom community evolves, but the foundation is laid at the beginning of the year.

When the classroom environment is predictable, with familiar routines and literacy procedures, students feel comfortable, safe, and more willing to take risks. This is especially true for students from varied cultures, English learners, and students who struggle (Fay & Whaley, 2004).

 MONITOR: Check Your Understanding 1.3

Principle 4: Effective Teachers Adopt a Balanced Approach to Instruction

Literacy is the ability to use reading and writing for a variety of tasks at school and outside of school. **Reading** is a complex process of understanding written text: Readers interpret meaning in a way that's appropriate to the type of text they're reading and their purpose. Similarly, *writing* is a complex process of producing text: Writers create meaning in a way that's appropriate to the type of text and their purpose. Peter Afflerbach (2012) describes reading as a dynamic, strategic, and goal-oriented process; the same is true of writing:

> *Dynamic* means that readers and writers are actively involved in reading and writing.
> *Strategic* means that readers and writers consciously monitor their learning and take action when problems arise.

New LITERACIES

Digital Technology

Teachers are blending digital technology with traditional literacy practices: Their students read books on eReaders, use search engines to do online research, blog about books they're reading, and use word processing software to draft and refine their writing. K–8 students are using digital technology in a myriad of ways, including these:

Collaboration. Students work with classmates and students in the next state or around the world using wikis, Internet-based face-to-face calls with Skype, photo-sharing tools such as Flickr, and ePals software (safe email and blogs).

Communication. Students use blogs to share ideas with classmates, post responses on the Wallwisher website, and send and receive messages on cell phones.

Creation. Students use tools, including Scratch, Twine, Hopscotch, and Kodu, to construct games, and programs and apps, including Do Ink, Cartoonster, and Go Animate, to make animations for digital devices.

Reading. Students read books and magazines on Kindle or other eReaders, and younger children read books interactively using Fisher Price's iXL digital learning system or LeapFrog's digital books.

Games. Students play video games with appropriate content and useful learning tools, including those on consoles such as the Wii U, Xbox One, and PlayStation 4 and on computers; and simulation games, such as The Oregon Trail.

Interactive Whiteboards. Teachers and students write, display Internet images, and use a variety of interactive programs on SMART boards, Promethean boards, and other interactive whiteboards. Students use clickers to input answers to questions.

Multimedia Tools. Students combine text, images, video, talk, and sound into projects to document their learning using software programs including iMovie, Flickr, Audacity, Glogster, and Photoshop.

Presentation Tools. Students use podcasts, PowerPoint presentations, and publication websites to document their learning.

Research. Students use a search engine such as Google to find answers to questions and search for information.

Writing. Students use word processors to write stories, essays, and other compositions. They use brainstorming tools to generate, sort, and organize ideas; spelling and grammar checks; online dictionaries; and publication websites.

Goal-oriented means that reading and writing are purposeful; readers and writers have a plan in mind.

Traditional definitions of literacy focused on students' ability to read words, but now literacy is viewed as a tool for participating more fully in our technological society. In addition, Kress (2003) and Kist (2005) talk about *new literacies*—sophisticated digital ways to read and write multimedia texts incorporating words, images, and sounds—which provide opportunities for students to create innovative spaces for making meaning, exploring the world, and voicing their lives. These texts often combine varied forms of representation, including computer graphics, video clips, and digital photos, and students read and write them differently than traditional books (Karchmer, Mallette, Kara-Soteriou, & Leu, 2005).

The **balanced approach** to instruction is based on a comprehensive view of literacy that combines explicit instruction, guided practice, collaborative learning, and independent reading and writing (Madda, Griffo, Pearson, & Raphael, 2011). It's grown out of the so-called "reading wars" of the late 20th century in which researchers argued for either teacher-centered or student-centered instruction. Even though balanced programs vary, they usually embody these characteristics:

Teaching from a balanced approach to literacy means using a variety of developmentally appropriate strategies. What are the five critical elements of reading instruction that Tim Shanahan identifies?

ℓ Literacy involves both reading and writing.
ℓ Oral language is integrated with reading and writing.

FIGURE 1–3 Components of the Balanced Literacy Approach

COMPONENT	DESCRIPTION
Comprehension	Students apply reader factors, including comprehension strategies, and text factors, including text structures, to understand what they're reading.
Content Area Study	Students use reading and writing as tools to learn about social studies and science topics in thematic units.
Literacy Strategies and Skills	Students use problem-solving and monitoring behaviors called *strategies* and automatic actions called *skills* as they read and write.
Literature	Students read and respond to fiction and poetry and learn about genres, text structures, and literary features.
Oral Language	Students talk with classmates, participate in grand conversations, give oral presentations, and listen to the teacher read aloud.
Phonemic Awareness and Phonics	Students manipulate sounds in words and apply the alphabetic principle and phonics rules to decode words.
Reading	Students participate in modeled, shared, interactive, guided, and independent reading experiences using picture-book stories and novels, nonfiction books, poetry, basal readers, content area textbooks, and Internet materials.
Spelling	Students apply what they're learning about English orthography to spell words, and their spellings gradually become conventional.
Vocabulary	Students learn the meaning of academic vocabulary through wide reading, listening to books read aloud, and content area study; and they apply word-learning strategies to figure out the meaning of unfamiliar words.
Writing	Students employ the writing process and their knowledge about the six traits to draft and refine stories, poems, reports, essays, and other compositions.

- Reading instruction includes phonemic awareness, phonics, fluency, vocabulary, and comprehension.
- Writing instruction includes the writing process, the writer's craft, and the conventions of writing that make ideas more legible.
- Reading and writing are used as tools for content-area learning.
- Strategies and skills are taught explicitly, with a gradual release of responsibility to students.
- Students often work collaboratively and talk with classmates.
- Students are more motivated and engaged when they participate in authentic literacy activities.

Cunningham and Allington (2016) compare the balanced approach to a multivitamin, suggesting that it brings together the best of teacher- and student-centered learning theories.

Madda, Griffo, Pearson, and Raphael (2011) explain that "achieving balance is a complex process that requires flexibility and artful orchestration of literacy's various contextual and conceptual aspects" (p. 40). The characteristics of the balanced approach are embodied in an instructional program that includes these components, which are described in Figure 1–3:

- Comprehension
- Content Area Study
- Literacy Strategies and Skills
- Literature
- Oral Language
- Phonemic Awareness and Phonics
- Reading
- Spelling
- Vocabulary
- Writing

A balanced literacy program integrating these components is recommended for all students, including those in high-poverty urban schools, struggling readers, and students learning a new language (Braunger & Lewis, 2006). Creating a balance is essential, according to Peterson (2013), because when one component is over- or underemphasized, the development of the others suffers. To examine the effectiveness of your instruction, use the Teacher Checklist: Am I an effective teacher?

 MONITOR: Check Your Understanding 1.4

TEACHER *Checklist*

Am I an effective teacher?

- Do I apply theories about how children learn to my teaching?
- Do I support students' use of the cueing systems as they read and write?
- Have I created a community of learners in my classroom?
- Have I adopted a balanced approach to instruction?
- Have I integrated Standards into my instruction?
- Do I scaffold students as they read and write?
- Have I organized my literacy program with instruction, practice opportunities, and independent reading and writing?
- Do I differentiate instruction to meet students' needs?
- Do I link instruction and assessment?

Principle 5: Effective Teachers Address Standards

The **Common Core State Standards** (CCSS) Initiative has identified the knowledge students are expected to learn at each grade level, K–12. Collier (2011) explains that "the standards are not a rigid, one-size-fits-all checklist of materials and lessons teachers must march in lock-step to employ in their classrooms. Rather, the Common Core Standards show teachers what should be taught—but leave up to them how this can be accomplished" (p. 8). The Standards are organized into five strands: Reading, Writing, Speaking and Listening, Language, and Media and Technology. The Initiative was spearheaded by the National Governors Association and the Council of Chief State School Officers with the goal of ensuring that all students graduate from high school able to succeed in college or in the workforce. More than 40 states and the District of Columbia have adopted the CCSS.

The Common Core State Standards

The Common Core State Standards for English Language Arts are a framework for improving teaching and learning, with clear and consistent academic benchmarks (Kendall, 2011). Click to review the Standards document online (http://www.corestandards .org/ELA-Literacy). The Standards are research based and include rigorous content that requires students to use higher level thinking skills as they apply their knowledge, and they're designed to be relevant to the real world because they reflect what students need for success in college and careers. The curriculum spirals, from kindergarten through 12th grade, and at each grade level students are required to read and write more complex texts. Reading and writing are integrated across the curriculum, and students are required to conduct research to answer questions and solve problems.

READING STRAND. The Reading strand consists of three sections: Foundational Skills, Literature, and Informational Texts. As young children learn to read, they develop foundational skills—print concepts, **phonological awareness**, phonics, word recognition, and **fluency**. The emphasis in the Literature and Informational Texts sections is on students' comprehension of complex texts: Students read increasingly sophisticated grade-level texts and grow in their ability to make inferences and connections among ideas and between texts. The Standards in these three sections are grouped into these topics:

🎴 Key Ideas and Details
🎴 Craft and Structure
🎴 Integration of Knowledge and Ideas
🎴 Range of Reading and Level of Text Complexity

WRITING STRAND. Students learn to use the **writing process** to compose texts representing a variety of genres—in particular arguments, informative texts, and **narratives**. They also write to respond to literature and conduct research projects related to content area study. The Standards in the Writing strand are organized under these topics:

🎴 Text Types and Purposes
🎴 Production and Distribution of Writing
🎴 Research to Build and Present Knowledge
🎴 Range of Writing

SPEAKING AND LISTENING STRAND. Students gain mastery of oral language skills, using speaking and listening informally in discussions and more formally in oral presentations. Standards in this strand are arranged under two topics:

🎴 Comprehension and Collaboration
🎴 Presentation of Knowledge and Ideas

LANGUAGE STRAND. Students apply vocabulary, grammar, and Standard English conventions to increasingly sophisticated oral and written presentations. These Standards are grouped into these topics:

🎴 Conventions of Standard English
🎴 Knowledge of Language
🎴 Vocabulary Acquisition and Use

MEDIA AND TECHNOLOGY STRAND. The CCSS integrate the critical analysis of media and the creation of multimedia projects within the other strands.

For each topic, the Standards clearly specify what students should know at each grade level. Figure 1–4 shows how the Common Core State Standards are addressed in each chapter of this text.

Now that most states have adopted the CCSS, teachers are developing curriculum that incorporates the Standards. Groups of teachers in schools and school districts have developed more challenging curriculum, and Common Core teams of teachers from across the United States have developed six multidisciplinary units. Versions are available online and in print: *Common Core Curriculum Maps in English Language Arts, Grades K–5* (2012a) and *Common Core Curriculum Maps in English Language Arts, Grades 6–8* (2012b). Review the Standards at http://www.corestandards .org/ELA-Literacy.

MONITOR: Check Your Understanding 1.5

FIGURE 1–4 The Common Core State Standards

CHAPTER	READING STRAND: LITERATURE	READING STRAND: INFORMATIONAL TEXT	READING STRAND: FOUNDATIONAL SKILLS	WRITING STRAND	SPEAKING AND LISTENING STRAND	LANGUAGE STRAND
2 The Reading and Writing Processes	•	•		•		
3 Assessing Literacy Development	•	•	•	•	•	•
4 The Youngest Readers and Writers			•	•		•
5 Cracking the Alphabetic Code			•			•
6 Developing Fluent Readers and Writers			•	•		
7 Expanding Academic Vocabulary	•	•				•
8 Promoting Comprehension: Reader Factors	•	•			•	
9 Promoting Comprehension: Text Factors	•	•		•		
10 Organizing for Instruction	•		•	•		•
11 Differentiating for Success	•	•	•	•	•	•
12 Reading and Writing Across the Curriculum	•	•		•	•	•

Principle 6: Effective Teachers Scaffold Students' Reading and Writing

Teachers **scaffold** students' reading and writing as they demonstrate, guide, and teach, and they vary the amount of support they provide according to the instructional purpose and students' needs. Sometimes teachers model how experienced readers read or record children's dictation when the writing's too difficult for them

Teachers scaffold reading and writing instruction to meet the needs of their students. How does this teacher meet her students' literacy needs?

to do on their own; at other times, they guide students to read a leveled book or proofread their writing. Teachers use five levels of support, moving from more to less as students assume responsibility (Fountas & Pinnell, 1996). Figure 1–5 summarizes these five levels of support—*modeled, shared, interactive, guided,* and *independent*—for reading and writing activities.

Modeled Reading and Writing

Teachers provide the greatest amount of support when they model how expert readers read and expert writers write. When teachers read aloud, they're modeling: They read fluently and with expression, and they talk about their thoughts and the strategies they're using. When they model writing, teachers write a composition on chart paper or an interactive whiteboard so everyone can see what the teacher does and how the text is being written. This support level is useful for demonstrating procedures, such as choosing a book to read or doing a **word sort**, and for introducing new writing genres, such as writing an "I Am . . ." poem. Teachers often do a **think-aloud** to share what they're thinking as they read or write, the decisions they make, and the strategies they use. They use modeling for these purposes:

- ⟡ Demonstrate fluent reading and writing
- ⟡ Explain how to use reading and writing strategies
- ⟡ Teach the procedure for a literacy activity
- ⟡ Show how reading and writing conventions and other skills work

FIGURE 1–5 Levels of Scaffolding

LEVEL	READING	WRITING
Modeled	Teachers read aloud, modeling how good readers read fluently using books that are too difficult for students to read themselves.	Teachers demonstrate how to write a composition for students, creating the text, doing the writing, and thinking aloud about their use of strategies and skills.
Shared	Teachers and students read books together, with students following as the teacher reads and then repeating familiar refrains.	Teachers and students create the text together; then the teacher does the actual writing. Students may assist by spelling familiar or high-frequency words.
Interactive	Teachers and students read instructional-level texts together and take turns doing the reading. Teachers help students read fluently and with expression.	Teachers and students create the text and share the pen to do the writing. They spell words correctly and add capitalization, punctuation, and other conventions.
Guided	Teachers plan and teach reading lessons to small, homogeneous groups using instructional-level books. The focus is on supporting and observing students' use of strategies.	Teachers plan and teach lessons on a writing strategy, skill, or procedure, and students participate in supervised practice activities.
Independent	Students read self-selected books independently. Teachers conference with students to monitor their progress.	Students use the writing process to develop reports, essays, poems, and other compositions. Teachers monitor students' progress.

Shared Reading and Writing

Teachers "share" reading and writing tasks with students at this level. Probably the best known shared activity is **shared reading**, which teachers use to read big books with young children. The teacher does most of the reading, but children join in to read familiar and predictable words and phrases. Teachers who work with older students can also use shared reading (Allen, 2002): When a novel is too difficult for students to read independently, for example, teachers often read it aloud while students follow along, reading silently when they can.

Teachers use shared writing in a variety of ways. Primary grade teachers often use the **Language Experience Approach** to write children's dictation on paintings and brainstorm lists of words on the whiteboard, for example, and teachers of older students use shared writing when they make **KWL charts**.

Sharing differs from modeling in that students actually participate in the activity rather than simply observing the teacher. In shared reading, students follow along as the teacher reads, and in shared writing, they suggest the words and sentences that the teacher writes. Teachers use shared reading and writing for these purposes:

- ℮ Involve students in literacy activities they can't do independently
- ℮ Create opportunities for students to experience success in reading and writing
- ℮ Provide practice before students read and write independently

Interactive Reading and Writing

Students assume an increasingly important role in interactive reading and writing. They no longer observe the teacher reading or writing, repeat familiar words, or suggest words that the teacher writes; instead, they're more actively involved. They support their classmates by sharing the reading and writing responsibilities, and their teacher provides assistance when needed. **Choral reading** and **readers theatre** are two examples of interactive reading. In choral reading, students take turns reading lines of a poem, and in readers theatre, they assume the roles of characters and read lines in a script. In these activities, the students support each other by actively participating and sharing the work. In **interactive writing**, students and the teacher create a text and write a message (Button, Johnson, & Furgerson, 1996; Tompkins & Collom, 2004). The text is composed by the group, and the teacher assists as students write the text on chart paper. Teachers use interactive reading and writing for these purposes:

- ℮ Practice reading and writing high-frequency words
- ℮ Apply phonics and spelling skills
- ℮ Read and write texts that students can't do independently
- ℮ Have students share their literacy expertise with classmates

Guided Reading and Writing

Even though teachers continue to provide support, in guided reading, students do the reading and writing themselves. Small, homogeneous groups of students meet with the teacher to read a book at their instructional level; the teacher introduces the book and guides students as they read it. **Minilessons** are another example: As teachers teach lessons about strategies and skills, they provide practice activities and supervise as students apply what they're learning. In guided writing, teachers supervise students as they complete writing activities. For example, when students make pages for a **collaborative book**, it's guided writing because the teacher structures the activity and supervises students as they work. Teachers also provide guidance as they conference with students about their writing.

Classroom INTERVENTIONS

More Reading and Writing

Struggling students need to increase their volume of reading and writing. Allington (2012) recommends that teachers dramatically increase the amount of time struggling readers spend reading each day so that they can become more capable and confident readers and develop greater interest in reading. Reading volume matters: Better readers typically read three times as much as struggling readers do. This recommendation for increased volume applies to writing, too: Struggling writers need to spend more time writing.

In addition to explicit instruction and guided practice, students need large blocks of uninterrupted time for authentic reading and writing, and reading and writing workshop are two of the best ways to provide this opportunity. During reading workshop, students read self-selected books at their own reading level, and during writing workshop, they draft and refine compositions on self-selected topics. Practice is just as important for reading and writing as it is when you're learning to ride a bike or play the piano.

How much classroom time should students spend reading and writing? Although there's no hard-and-fast rule, Allington (2012) recommends that each day students spend at least 90 minutes reading and 45 minutes writing. Researchers have found that the most effective teachers provide more time for reading and writing than less effective teachers do (Allington & Johnston, 2002). It's often difficult for struggling students to sustain reading and writing activities for as long as their classmates do, but with teacher support, they can increase the time they spend reading and writing.

Teachers choose this level of scaffolding to provide instruction and assistance as students are actually reading and writing. Teachers use guided reading and writing for these purposes:

- Support students' reading in appropriate instructional-level materials
- Teach literacy strategies and skills
- Involve students in collaborative writing projects
- Teach students to use the writing process—in particular, how to revise and edit

Independent Reading and Writing

Students do the reading and writing themselves at the independent level, applying the strategies and skills as they work on authentic literacy activities, such as reading and writing workshop. Students choose their own books and work at their own pace as they read and respond to books. Similarly, during independent writing, students choose their own topics and move at their own pace as they develop and refine their writing. It would be wrong to suggest, however, that teachers play no role in independent-level activities; they continue to monitor students, but they provide much less guidance at this level.

Through independent reading, students learn how pleasurable reading is and, teachers hope, become lifelong readers. In addition, as they write, students come to view themselves as authors. Teachers use independent reading and writing for these purposes:

- Create opportunities for students to practice literacy strategies and skills
- Provide authentic literacy experiences
- Develop lifelong readers and writers

These five levels of support illustrate Pearson and Gallagher's (1983) gradual release of responsibility model. As students move from modeled to independent reading and writing, they increasingly do more of the reading and writing as teachers gradually transfer responsibility to them.

 MONITOR: Check Your Understanding 1.6

Principle 7: Effective Teachers Organize for Instruction

No single instructional program best represents the balanced approach to literacy; instead, teachers organize for instruction by creating their own program that fits their students' needs and their school's standards and curricular guidelines. Instructional programs should reflect these principles:

- Teachers create a community of learners in their classroom.
- Teachers incorporate the components of the balanced approach.
- Teachers scaffold students' reading and writing experiences.

Five of the most popular programs are *guided reading, basal reading programs, literature focus units, literature circles,* and *reading and writing workshop*.

Guided Reading

Teachers use guided reading to personalize instruction and meet students' individual needs. They meet with small groups of children who read at approximately the same proficiency level for teacher-directed lessons (Fountas & Pinnell, 1996). In these 20-minute lessons, teachers teach word-identification and comprehension strategies and have students apply what they're learning as they read books at their instructional level. Teachers emphasize that the goal of reading is comprehension—understanding what you're reading, not just saying all the words correctly. At the same time teachers are working with one guided reading group, classmates work at literacy centers or pursue other activities that they can complete independently. This instructional approach is often used in kindergarten through third grade, but it can also be adapted to use with older, struggling readers.

Basal Reading Programs

Commercially produced reading programs are known as **basal readers**. These programs feature a textbook of reading selections with accompanying workbooks, supplemental books, and related instructional materials at each grade level. Phonics, vocabulary, comprehension, grammar, and spelling instruction is coordinated with the reading selections and aligned with grade-level standards. The teacher's guide provides detailed procedures for teaching the selections and related skills and strategies. Instruction is typically presented to the whole class, with reteaching to small groups of struggling students. Testing materials are also included so that teachers can monitor students' progress. Publishers tout basal readers as a complete literacy program, but effective teachers realize that they aren't.

Literature Focus Units

Teachers create literature focus units featuring high-quality picture-book stories and novels. The books are usually included in a district- or state-approved list of award-winning books that all students are expected to read at a particular grade level. These books include classics such as *The Very Hungry Caterpillar* (Carle, 2002) and *Charlotte's Web* (White, 2006) and award winners such as *Officer Buckle and Gloria* (Rathmann, 1995), *Holes* (Sachar, 2008), and *Flora & Ulysses* (DiCamillo, 2013). Everyone in the class reads and responds to the same book, and the teacher supports students' learning through a combination of explicit instruction and reading and writing activities. Through these units, teachers teach students about literary genres and authors, and they develop students' interest in literature.

Literature Circles

Small groups of students get together in literature circles or book clubs to read a story or other book. To begin, teachers select five or six books at varying reading levels to meet the needs of all students in the class. Often, the books are related in some way—for instance, representing the same genre or written by the same author. They collect multiple copies of each book and give a **book talk** to introduce them. Then students choose a book to read and form a group to read and respond to the book. They set a reading and discussion schedule and work independently, although teachers sometimes sit in on the discussions. Through the experience of reading and discussing a book together, students develop responsibility for completing assignments.

Reading and Writing Workshop

Students do authentic reading and writing in workshop programs. They select books, read independently, and conference with the teacher about their reading; and they

Listen to Ms. Janusz talk about writing workshop and how it helps meet her school's "targets" or standards. How does she modify writing workshop during the school year?

write books on topics that they choose and conference with the teacher about their writing. Teachers set aside a time for reading and writing workshop, and all students read and write while the teacher conferences with small groups. Teachers also teach mini-lessons on reading and writing strategies and skills and read books aloud to the whole class. In a workshop program, students read and write more like adults do, making choices, working independently, and developing responsibility.

These programs can be divided into authentic and textbook approaches. Literature focus units, literature circles, and reading and writing workshop are classified as authentic because they use trade books and involve students in meaningful activities. Basal readers, not surprisingly, are textbook programs that reflect the behaviorist theory. Teachers generally combine authentic approaches and textbook programs because students learn best through a variety of reading and writing experiences. Sometimes the books that students read are challenging, or teachers are introducing a new writing genre; these situations require more teacher support and guidance. Some teachers alternate literature focus units or literature circles with reading and writing workshop and basal readers, and others use some components from each approach throughout the school year.

GO DIGITAL!   **Incorporating Technology Into Instruction.** Teachers integrate 21st-century technology into all the instructional approaches, as Figure 1–6 shows. They use digital software, the Internet, and computer technology for many purposes, including these:

- Present information to students
- Scaffold students' reading and writing
- Involve students in activities and projects
- Respond to students' work
- Assess students' achievement

Teachers often display information on interactive whiteboards as part of whole-class presentations and minilessons, and they teach students to use a variety of digital tools such as eReaders, digital cameras, and software programs. For instance, students write blogs, use apps, create wikis, complete WebQuests, and produce podcasts and vodcasts as they read books and write compositions.

Some reading programs have completely online versions that are very engaging for students. One example is Scholastic's Read 180 Next Generation, an intervention program for struggling readers in grades 4–8.

Nurturing English Learners

What is effective classroom instruction? English learners (ELs) benefit from participating in the same instructional programs that mainstream students do, and teachers create classroom learning contexts that respect minority students and meet their needs (Brock & Raphael, 2005; Peregoy & Boyle, 2013; Shanahan & Beck, 2006). Learning to read and write is more challenging for students learning English as a new language because they're learning to speak English at the same time they're developing literacy. Teachers scaffold students' oral language acquisition and literacy development in these ways:

FIGURE 1–6 Technology in the Classroom

APPROACH	TEACHERS	STUDENTS
Guided Reading	• Use online materials for planning lessons and collecting assessment data. • Choose leveled books using online resources.	• Read leveled books on eReaders and iPads for independent practice. • Listen to books read aloud on eReaders and iPads. • Use familiar eBooks as models for writing.
Basal Reading Programs	• Display text excerpts and activities on an interactive whiteboard. • Assign online textbook support activities. • Monitor students' achievement using the program's online assessment system.	• Play online phonics and grammar games. • Read books independently online or using eReaders. • Listen to audio books. • Take online quizzes.
Literature Focus Units	• Display text excerpts on an interactive whiteboard. • Read and respond to entries in students' blogs. • View author websites. • Work with students to create a wiki about the book.	• Complete a WebQuest related to the book. • Read the book using eReaders or listen to the audio version of the book. • Respond to the book in a blog. • Listen to author podcasts or create a podcast from one character's perspective. • Create multimedia projects.
Literature Circles	• Monitor students' reading and discussion schedules. • Read and respond to entries in students' blogs.	• Read the book using eReaders or listen to the audio version. • Complete role assignments online. • Research the author or other topics online. • Create a wiki about the book to share with the class.
Reading Workshop	• Conference with students about their reading using online entries. • Monitor students' progress by checking their weekly or monthly schedules online.	• Read books on eReaders. • Conference with the teacher or student partners about the book using online entries. • Post weekly or monthly reading schedules online. • Keep lists of books they've read online.
Writing Workshop	• Monitor students' progress using an online "Status of the Class." • Read and respond to students' rough drafts online. • Create a classroom website or wiki where students post their published writing. • Collect students' writing in ePortfolios.	• Use AlphaSmarts or other portable keyboards for drafting. • Print out rough draft copies for revising groups and final copies to share with classmates. • Create slide show stories. • Use digital storytelling software. • Post writing on classroom websites or wikis.

Explicit Instruction. Teachers present additional instruction on literacy strategies and skills because ELs are more at risk than other students (Genesee & Riches, 2006). They also spend more time teaching unfamiliar academic vocabulary related to reading and writing (e.g., *vowel, homonym, paragraph, index, quotation marks, predict, revise, summarize*).

Oral Language. Teachers provide many opportunities each day for students to practice speaking English comfortably and informally with partners and in small groups. Through these conversations, ELs develop both conversational and academic language, which supports their reading and writing development (Rothenberg & Fisher, 2007).

Small-Group Work. Teachers provide opportunities for students to work in small groups because classmates' social interaction supports their learning (Genesee & Riches, 2006). English learners talk with classmates as they read and write, and at the same time, they're learning the culture of literacy.

Reading Aloud to Students. Teachers read aloud a variety of stories, nonfiction books, and books of poetry, including some that represent students' home cultures (Rothenberg & Fisher, 2007). As they read, teachers model fluent reading, and students become more familiar with English sounds, vocabulary, and written language structures.

Background Knowledge. Teachers organize instruction into themes to build students' world knowledge about grade-appropriate concepts, and they develop ELs' literary knowledge through minilessons and a variety of reading and writing activities (Braunger & Lewis, 2006).

Authentic Literacy Activities. Teachers provide daily opportunities for students to apply the strategies and skills they're learning as they read and write for authentic, real-life purposes (Akhavan, 2006). ELs participate in meaningful literacy activities through literature circles and reading and writing workshop.

These recommendations promote English learners' academic success.

Teachers' attitudes about minority students and knowledge about how they learn a new language play a critical role in the effectiveness of instruction (Gay, 2010). It's important that teachers understand that English learners have different cultural and linguistic backgrounds and plan instructional programs accordingly. Most classrooms reflect the European American middle-class culture, which differs significantly from minority students' backgrounds. Brock and Raphael (2005) point out that "mismatches between teachers' and students' cultural and linguistic backgrounds matter because such mismatches can impact negatively on students' opportunities for academic success" (p. 5). Teachers and students use language in different ways. For example, some students are reluctant to volunteer answers to teachers' questions, and others may not answer if the questions are different than those their parents ask (Peregoy & Boyle, 2013). Teachers who learn about their students' home language and culture and embed them into their instruction are likely to be more successful. 🐌

 MONITOR: Check Your Understanding 1.7

Principle 8: Effective Teachers Differentiate Instruction

Effective teachers adjust their instruction because students vary in their levels of development, academic achievement, and ability. Tomlinson (2004, 2014) explains that the one-size-fits-all instructional model is obsolete, and teachers respect students by honoring both their similarities and their differences. Differentiation is based on Vygotsky's idea of a zone of proximal development. If instruction is either too difficult or too easy, it isn't effective; instead teachers must provide instruction that meets students' instructional needs.

As they differentiate instruction, teachers vary instructional arrangements, choose instructional materials at students' reading levels, and modify assignments (Opitz & Ford, 2008). They monitor students' learning and make adjustments, when necessary, and they assess learning in multiple ways, not just using paper-and-pencil tests. Differentiation involves adjusting the content, the process, and the product:

Differentiating the Content. Teachers identify the information that students need to learn to meet grade-level standards so that every child will be successful. They differentiate the content in these ways:

- Choose instructional materials at students' reading levels
- Consider students' developmental levels as well as their current grade placement in deciding what to teach
- Use assessment tools to determine students' instructional needs

Differentiating the Process. Teachers vary instruction and application activities to meet students' needs. They differentiate the process in these ways:

- Provide instruction to individuals, small groups, and the whole class
- Scaffold struggling readers and writers with more explicit instruction
- Challenge advanced readers and writers with activities requiring higher level thinking
- Monitor students' learning and adjust instruction when they aren't successful

Differentiating the Product. Teachers vary how students demonstrate what they've learned. Products include both the projects that students create and the tests used to measure their academic achievement. Teachers differentiate the products in these ways:

- Have students create projects individually, with partners, or in small groups
- Design projects that engage students with literacy in meaningful ways
- Assess students using a combination of visual, oral, and written formats

As teachers differentiate instruction, they consider the **background knowledge** and literacy demands of the reading selection, create a text set of related books, design activities with varied grouping patterns, consider students' preferred language modalities and thinking styles, and determine how much support students are likely to need. Figure 1–7 lists some of the ways teachers differentiate instruction.

 **MONITOR: Check Your Understanding 1.8**

Principle 9: Effective Teachers Link Instruction and Assessment

Assessment is an integral and ongoing part of both learning and teaching (Mariotti & Homan, 2005). Sometimes teachers equate standardized high-stakes achievement tests with assessment, but classroom assessment is much more than a once-a-year test. It's a daily part of classroom life. Teachers collect and analyze data from observations, conferences, and classroom tests, and then use the results to make decisions about students' academic achievement and plan interventions. They assess students' learning for these purposes:

Determining Instructional Levels. Teachers determine students' achievement levels so that they can plan appropriate instruction.

Monitoring Progress. Teachers regularly assess students to ensure that they're understanding instruction and making expected progress, and when they're not, teachers take action to get them back on track.

FIGURE 1–7   Ways to Differentiate Instruction

TECHNIQUE	DESCRIPTION
Books	Teachers create text sets with a variety of fiction and nonfiction books and magazines about a topic. The collection includes interesting resources that are appropriate for grade-level readers as well as for those who read above and below grade level.
Grouping Patterns	Teachers consider grouping patterns—whole class, small groups, partners, and individual students—as they plan instruction. Grouping patterns are important because students are often more motivated when they work with classmates, and struggling students are more likely to be successful when classmates provide support.
Instruction	Teachers provide explicit instruction to build students' background knowledge, introduce vocabulary, and present information. Then they supervise students as they complete practice activities and, finally, provide opportunities for independent application.
Language Modes	Teachers encourage students to use a combination of oral, written, and visual language modes to learn and demonstrate new knowledge. Some students learn best by listening to oral presentations or reading a book, but others are more successful when they view video presentations. Similarly, some students can more effectively show what they've learned by making graphic representations or performing dramatizations, but others prefer to create artistic posters or written reports.
Modalities	Teachers recognize that students learn through different modalities, so they allow students to choose activities that incorporate auditory, visual, or tactile modalities.
Scaffolding	Teachers provide varying levels of support so that all students can be successful. They use a combination of modeled, shared, interactive, guided, and independent reading and writing activities.
Technology	Teachers provide opportunities for students to use digital tools, including word processing, online games, digital cameras, and WebQuests, to increase engagement and support their learning.
Thinking Styles	Teachers design projects that provide opportunities for students to apply newly learned knowledge in analytical, relational, and creative ways that reflect their thinking styles.
Tiered Activities	Teachers create a range of related projects that take into account students' reading and writing achievement levels, their preferred language modes, and their thinking styles. They also consider students' motivation, their interest in technology, and whether they prefer to work independently, with a partner, or in a group.

Diagnosing Strengths and Weaknesses. Teachers examine work samples to identify students' strengths and weaknesses. Diagnosis is especially important when students are struggling or aren't meeting grade-level expectations.

Documenting Learning. Teachers use a combination of collections of students' work and test results to provide evidence of students' academic achievement and document that they've met grade-level standards.

These purposes highlight the wide range of ongoing assessment activities that effective teachers use.

The Instruction–Assessment Cycle

Assessment is linked to instruction (Snow, Griffin, & Burns, 2005). Teachers do some assessments before they begin to teach, some while they're teaching, and others afterward. They link instruction and assessment in this four-step cycle:

Step 1: Planning. Teachers use their knowledge about students' reading levels, their background knowledge, and their strategy and skill competencies to plan appropriate instruction that's neither too easy nor too difficult.

Step 2: Monitoring. Teachers monitor instruction that's in progress as they observe students, conference with them, and check their work to ensure that their instruction is effective, and they make modifications, including reteaching when necessary, to improve the quality of their instruction and meet students' needs.

Step 3: Evaluating. Teachers evaluate students' learning using rubrics and checklists to assess students' reading and writing projects and administering teacher-made tests. They also collect samples to document students' achievements.

Step 4: Reflecting. Teachers judge the effectiveness of their instruction by analyzing students' reading and writing projects and test results and consider how they might adapt instruction to improve student learning.

It's easy to blame students when learning isn't occurring, but teachers need to consider how they can improve their teaching through planning, monitoring, evaluating, and reflecting so their students will be more successful.

Classroom Assessment Tools

Teachers use both a variety of informal assessment tools that they create themselves and tests that are commercially available (McKenna & Dougherty Stahl, 2015). Informal assessment tools include the following:

- 🌀 Observation of students as they participate in instructional activities
- 🌀 **Running records** of students' oral reading to analyze their ability to solve reading problems
- 🌀 Examination of students' work
- 🌀 Conferences to talk with students about their reading and writing
- 🌀 Checklists to monitor students' progress
- 🌀 **Rubrics** to assess students' performances, written products, and multimedia projects

These assessment tools support instruction, and teachers choose which ones to use according to the kind of information they need. They administer commercial tests to individual students or the entire class to determine their overall reading achievement or their proficiency in a particular component, such as phonics, spelling, fluency, or comprehension.

High-Stakes Tests

Beginning in second grade, the results of yearly, **high-stakes tests** also provide evidence of students' literacy achievement against grade-specific Common Core State Standards. The usefulness of these data is limited, however, because the tests are usually administered in the spring and the results aren't released until after the school year ends. At the beginning of the next school year, teachers do examine the data and use what they learn in planning for their new class, but the impact isn't as great as it would be for the teachers who worked with those students during the previous year. Another way the results are used is in measuring the effectiveness of teachers' instruction by examining how much students grew since the previous year's test and determining whether students met grade-level standards.

 MONITOR: Check Your Understanding 1.9

Review

TEACHING READING AND WRITING

Effective teachers demonstrate their responsibility and commitment to ensuring that their students are successful when they adopt these nine principles presented in this chapter:

1.1 Teachers apply learning theories as they teach reading and writing.

1.2 Teachers teach students to use the four cueing systems.

1.3 Teachers create a community of learners in their classrooms.

1.4 Teachers adopt the balanced approach to literacy instruction.

1.5 Teachers address Standards in their instruction.

1.6 Teachers support students' reading and writing development.

1.7 Teachers organize their instruction using more than one program.

1.8 Teachers differentiate instruction so all students can be successful.

1.9 Teachers link instruction and assessment.

EVALUATE & REFLECT

Apply your understanding of the principles underlying effective literacy instruction. The questions ask you to collect and analyze data, and report the results. Your response should meet academic standards and adhere to Standard English conventions.

1. Examine your beliefs about how students learn and how teachers teach reading and writing. Then consider how your beliefs will influence your instruction. Your response should include answers to these questions:

    ℮ Is your orientation teacher centered or student centered?
    ℮ Which theories reflect your beliefs?
    ℮ What are the classroom implications of your beliefs?

2. Observe in a K–8 literacy classroom, and use the Teacher Checklist presented in this chapter to examine what it means to be an effective teacher. In your response, describe the classroom, and address these points:

    ℮ Which items on the Teacher Checklist did you observe?
    ℮ Do you think the teacher is effective?
    ℮ How could the teacher become more effective?

3. Interview a K–8 teacher to learn how he or she teaches reading and writing. Ask questions to examine these points:

    ℮ how the teacher creates a community of learners
    ℮ how the teacher organizes for instruction
    ℮ which instructional programs the teacher uses
    ℮ how the teacher nurtures English learners
    ℮ how the teacher links instruction and assessment

In your response, describe the teacher and his/her teaching assignment and explain what you've learned about the teacher.

4. Observe in two K–8 classrooms to see how the teachers differentiate instruction to meet students' needs. In your response, describe the classrooms, explain how teachers differentiate instruction, and evaluate the effectiveness of the teachers' approaches.

5. Interview a K–8 teacher about his or her assessment program. In your response, describe the teacher, organize the teacher's assessment procedures into the four steps of the instruction–assessment cycle, and suggest ways the teacher could expand his/her assessment program.

REFERENCES

Afflerbach, P. (2012). *Understanding and using reading assessment, K–12* (2nd ed.). Newark, DE: International Reading Association.

Akhavan, N. (2006). *Help! My kids don't all speak English: How to set up a language workshop in your linguistically diverse classroom.* Portsmouth, NH: Heinemann.

Allen, J. (2002). *On the same page: Shared reading beyond the primary grades.* Portland, ME: Stenhouse.

Allington, R. L. (2012). *What really matters for struggling readers: Designing research-based programs* (3rd ed.). Pearson.

Allington, R. L., & Johnston, P. H. (Eds.). (2002). *Reading to learn: Lessons from exemplary fourth-grade classrooms.* New York: Guilford Press.

Angelillo, J. (2008). *Whole-class teaching.* Portsmouth, NH: Heinemann.

Baker, L. (2002). Metacognition in comprehension instruction. In C. C. Block & M. Pressley (Eds.), *Comprehension instruction: Research-based best practices* (pp. 77–95). New York: Guilford Press.

Bandura, A. (1997). *Self-efficacy: The exercise of control.* New York: W. H. Freeman.

Braunger, J., & Lewis, J. P. (2006). *Building a knowledge base in reading* (2nd ed.). Newark, DE: International Reading Association/National Council of Teachers of English.

Brock, C. H., & Raphael, T. E. (2005). *Windows to language, literacy, and culture: Insights from an English-language learner.* Newark, DE: International Reading Association.

Brown, J. S., Collins, A., & Duguid, S. (1989). Situated cognition and the culture of learning. *Educational Researcher, 18*(1), 32–42.

Bunting, E. (1999). *Smoky night.* San Diego: Voyager.

Button, K., Johnson, M. J., & Furgerson, P. (1996). Interactive writing in a primary classroom. *The Reading Teacher, 49,* 446–454.

Carle, E. (2002). *The very hungry caterpillar.* New York: Puffin Books.

Collier, L. (2011). Keeping students at the center of the Common Core classroom: Recommendations for using the CCSS productively. *The Council Chronicle, 21*(1), 6–9, 26.

Common Core curriculum maps in English language arts, grades K–5. (2012a). San Francisco: Jossey-Bass.

Common Core curriculum maps in English language arts, grades 6–8. (2012b). San Francisco: Jossey-Bass.

Cunningham, P. M., & Allington, R. L. (2016). *Classrooms that work: They can all read and write* (6th ed.). Boston: Pearson.

Dean, D. (2006). *Strategic writing: The writing process and beyond in the secondary English classroom.* Urbana, IL: National Council of Teachers of English.

DiCamillo, K. (2013). *Flora & Ulysses.* Somerville, MA: Candlewick Press.

Dinan, S. (2009, March 10). Obama wants teacher "accountability." Retrieved from http://www.washingtontimes.com/news/2009/mar/10/obama-calls-accountability-education

Edwards, P. A., McMillon, G. T., & Turner, J. D. (2010). *Change is gonna come: Transforming literacy education for African American students.* New York: Teachers College Press.

Ellis, D. (2001). *The breadwinner.* Toronto, ON: Groundwood Books.

Fay, K., & Whaley, S. (2004). *Becoming one community: Reading and writing with English language learners.* Portland, ME: Stenhouse.

Fountas, I. C., & Pinnell, G. S. (1996). *Guided reading: Good first teaching for all children.* Portsmouth, NH: Heinemann.

Freire, P. (2000). *Pedagogy of the oppressed* (30th anniversary ed.). New York: Continuum.

Gay, G. (2010). *Culturally responsive teaching: Theory, research, and practice* (2nd ed.). New York: Teachers College Press.

Genesee, F., & Riches, C. (2006). Literacy: Instructional issues. In F. Genesee, K. Lindholm-Leary, W. M. Saunders, & D. Christian (Eds.), *Educating English language learners: A synthesis of research evidence* (pp. 109–175). New York: Cambridge University Press.

Guthrie, J. T., & Wigfield, A. (2000). Engagement and motivation in reading. In M. L. Kamil, P. B. Mosenthal, P. D. Pearson, & R. Barr (Eds.), *Handbook of reading research* (Vol. 3, pp. 403–422). Mahwah, NJ: Erlbaum.

Halliday, M. A. K. (1978). *Language as social semiotic: The social interpretation of language and meaning.* Baltimore: University Park Press.

Hayes, J. R. (2004). A new framework for understanding cognition and affect in writing. In R. B. Ruddell & N. J. Unrau (Eds.), *Theoretical models and processes of reading* (5th ed., pp. 1399–1430). Newark, DE: International Reading Association.

Heath, S. B. (1983). Research currents: A lot of talk about nothing. *Language Arts, 60,* 999–1007.

Johnson, H., & Freedman, L. (2005). *Developing critical awareness at the middle level.* Newark, DE: International Reading Association.

Karchmer, R. A., Mallette, M. H., Kara-Soteriou, J., & Leu, D. J., Jr. (Eds.). (2005). *Innovative approaches to literacy education: Using the Internet to support new literacies.* Newark, DE: International Reading Association.

Kendall, J. (2011). *Understanding Common Core State Standards.* Alexandria, VA: Association for Supervision and Curriculum Development.

Kintsch, W. (2004). The construction-integration model and its implications for instruction. In R. B. Ruddell & N. J. Unrau (Eds.), *Theoretical models and processes of reading* (5th ed., pp. 1270–1328). Newark, DE: International Reading Association.

Kist, W. (2005). *New literacies in action: Teaching and learning in multiple media.* New York: Teachers College Press.

Kress, G. (2003). *Literacy in the new media age.* London: Routledge.

Lave, J., & Wenger, E. (1991). *Situated learning: Legitimate peripheral participation.* Cambridge, UK: Cambridge University Press.

Lewison, M., Leland, C., & Harste, J. C. (2008). *Creating critical classrooms: K–8 reading and writing with an edge.* New York: Erlbaum.

Madda, C. L., Griffo, V. B., Pearson, P. D., & Raphael, T. E. (2011). Balance in comprehensive literacy instruction: Evolving conceptions. In L. M. Morrow & L. B. Gambrell (Eds.), *Best practices in literacy instruction* (4th ed., pp. 37–63). New York: Guilford Press.

Mariotti, A. S., & Homan, S. P. (2005). *Linking reading assessment to instruction*. London: Routledge.

McKenna, M. C., & Dougherty Stahl, K. A. (2015). *Assessment for reading instruction* (3rd ed.). New York: Guilford Press.

McKissack, P. (2001). *Goin' somewhere special*. New York: Atheneum.

Moll, L. C., & Gonzales, N. (2004). Engaging life: A funds of knowledge approach to multicultural education. In J. A. Banks & C. A. M. Banks (Eds.), *Handbook of research on multicultural education* (2nd ed., pp. 699–715). San Francisco: Jossey-Bass.

National Board of Professional Teaching Standards. (2002). *Early and middle childhood literacy: Reading-language arts standards*. Arlington, VA: Author.

O'Donohue, W., & Kitchener, R. F. (Eds.). (1998). *Handbook of behaviorism*. New York: Academic Press.

Opitz, M. F., & Ford, M. P. (2008). *Do-able differentiation: Varying groups, texts, and supports to reach readers*. Portsmouth, NH: Heinemann.

Park, L. S. (2007). *Project mulberry*. New York: Yearling.

Pearson, P. D., & Gallagher, M. C. (1983). The instruction of reading comprehension. *Contemporary Educational Psychology 8*(3), 317–344.

Peregoy, S. F., & Boyle, O. F. (2013). *Reading, writing, and learning in ESL: A resource book for teaching K–12 English learners* (6th ed.). Boston: Pearson.

Peterson, D. S. (2013). Balanced, differentiated teaching. In B. M. Taylor & N. K. Duke (Eds.), *Handbook of effective literacy instruction: Research-based practice K–8* (pp. 88–105). New York: Guilford Press.

Piaget, J. (1969). *The psychology of intelligence*. Paterson, NJ: Littlefield, Adams.

Pressley, M. (2002). Comprehension strategies instruction. In C. C. Block & M. Pressley (Eds.), *Comprehension instruction: Research-based best practices* (pp. 11–27). New York: Guilford Press.

Rathmann, P. (1995). *Officer Buckle and Gloria*. New York: Putnam.

Rosenblatt, L. M. (2004). The transactional theory of reading and writing. In R. B. Ruddell & N. J. Unrau (Eds.), *Theoretical models and processes of reading* (5th ed., pp. 1363–1398). Newark, DE: International Reading Association.

Rothenberg, C., & Fisher, D. (2007). *Teaching English language learners: A differentiated approach*. Upper Saddle River, NJ: Merrill/Prentice Hall.

Ruddell, R. B., & Unrau, N. J. (2004). Reading as a meaning-construction process: The reader, the text, and the teacher. In R. B. Ruddell & N. J. Unrau (Eds.), *Theoretical models and processes of reading* (5th ed., pp. 1462–1521). Newark, DE: International Reading Association.

Rumelhart, D. E. (2004). Toward an interactive model of reading. In R. B. Ruddell & N. J. Unrau (Eds.), *Theoretical models and processes of reading* (5th ed., pp. 1149–1179). Newark, DE: International Reading Association.

Ryan, P. M. (2002). *Esperanza rising*. New York: Scholastic/Blue Sky Press.

Sachar, L. (2008). *Holes*. New York: Farrar, Straus & Giroux.

Shanahan, T., & Beck, I. (2006). Effective literacy teaching for English-language learners. In D. August & T. Shanahan (Eds.), *Developing literacy in second-language learners: Report of the National Literacy Panel on Language-Minority Children and Youth* (pp. 415–488). Mahwah, NJ: Erlbaum.

Skinner, B. F. (1974). *About behaviorism*. New York: Random House.

Snow, C. E., Griffin, P., & Burns, M. S. (Eds.) 2005. *Knowledge to support the teaching of reading: Preparing teachers for a changing world*. San Francisco: Jossey-Bass.

Stahl, S. A., & Nagy, W. E. (2005). *Teaching word meanings*. Mahwah, NJ: Erlbaum.

Tomlinson, C. A. (2004). *How to differentiate instruction in mixed-ability classrooms* (2nd ed.). Alexandria, VA: Association for Supervision and Curriculum Development.

Tomlinson, C. A. (2014). *The differentiated classroom: Responding to the needs of all learners* (2nd ed.). Alexandria, VA: Association for Supervision and Curriculum Development.

Tompkins, G. E., & Collom, S. (Eds.). (2004). *Sharing the pen: Interactive writing with young children*. Upper Saddle River, NJ: Merrill/Prentice Hall.

Tracey, D. H., & Morrow, L. M. (2006). *Lenses on reading: An introduction to theories and models*. New York: Guilford Press.

Vandevoort, L. G., Amrein-Beardsley, A., & Berliner, D. C. (2004, September 8). National board certified teachers and their students' achievement. *Education Policy Analysis Archives, 12*(46). Retrieved from http://epaa.asu.edu/epaa/v12n46

Vygotsky, L. S. (1978). *Mind in society*. Cambridge, MA: Harvard University Press.

Vygotsky, L. S. (1986). *Thought and language*. Cambridge, MA: MIT Press.

Whelan, G. (2000). *Homeless bird*. New York: HarperCollins.

White, E. B. (2006). *Charlotte's web*. New York: HarperCollins.

Chapter 2

The Reading and Writing Processes

PLAN: Preview the Learning Outcomes

After studying this chapter, you'll be prepared to respond to these points:

2.1 Describe the five stages of the reading process.

2.2 Discuss the five stages of the writing process.

2.3 Describe the writer's craft.

2.4 Compare the reading and writing processes.

2.5 Explain the purpose of strategies in reading and writing.

The Reading Process in Action.   The seventh graders in Mrs. Goodman's class use the reading process to read the Newbery Medal–winning novel *The Giver* (Lowry, 2006). In this futuristic story, 12-year-old Jonas is selected to become the next Keeper of the Memories, and he discovers the terrible truth about his "perfect" community. To introduce the book, Mrs. Goodman asks her students to get into small groups to brainstorm lists of what they'd like to change about their community; their lists include no homework, school days starting at 10 AM, no gangs, no taking out the garbage, no soldiers dying in war, and being allowed to drive at age 10. The groups project their lists on the whiteboard and share them. Next, Mrs. Goodman explains that the class is going to read a story about life in the future. She explains that *The Giver* takes place in a planned utopian, or "perfect," society with some of the qualities students mentioned.

She passes out copies of the book and uses **shared reading** to read the first chapter aloud as students follow along in their books. Then the class talks about the first chapter in a **grand conversation**, asking many questions: Why are there so many rules? Doesn't anyone drive a car? What does "released" mean? Why are children called a "Seven" or a "Four"? What does it mean that people are "given" spouses—don't they fall in love and get married? Why does Jonas have to tell his feelings? Classmates share their ideas and are eager to continue reading. Mrs. Goodman's reading aloud of the first chapter and the questions that the students raised generate excitement. The power of this story grabs them all.

They set a schedule for reading and discussion. Every three days, they'll come together to talk about the chapters they've read, and over two weeks, the class will complete the book. They'll also write in **reading logs** after reading the first chapter and then five more times as they're reading; in these logs, students write reactions to the story. Maria wrote this journal entry after finishing the book:

In this chapter, you'll read about the reading and writing processes. These two essential processes both have five stages, with similar activities at each stage. As you read this vignette, notice how Mrs. Goodman uses the five stages of the reading process as her students participate in a literature focus unit on *The Giver*. Try to pick out the stages: *prereading, reading, responding, exploring,* and *applying*.

Jonas had to do it. He had to save Gabriel's life because the next day Jonas's father was going to release him and release means K-I-L-L. He had it all planned out. That was important. He was very brave to leave his parents and his home, but they weren't his parents really. I don't know if I could be that brave, but he did the right thing. He saved himself and he saved little Gabe. I'm glad he took Gabriel. That community was supposed to be safe, but it was dangerous. I guess that sometimes things that at first seem to be good could be really, really bad.

Ron explored some of the themes of the story:

Starving. Jonas has memories of food. But he's still hungry. At least he's free. Food is safe. Freedom is surprises. Before Jonas was starved for colors, memories and choice. Choice. To do what you want. To be all you can be. He won't starve.

Alicia thought about a lesson her mother taught her as she wrote:

As Jonas fled from the community he lost his memories so that they would go back to the people there. Would they learn from them? Or would life go on just the same? That's the question. I think you have to do it yourself if you are going to learn. That's what my mom says. Somebody else can't do it for you.

Tomas wrote about the Christmas connection at the end of the story:

It was Christmas. Jonas and Gabe came to the town at Christmas. Why did Lois Lowry do that? I think Gabe is like the baby Jesus. It's like a rebirth—they're being born again. His old community didn't go to church. Maybe they didn't believe in God. Now Jonas will be a Christian and the people in the church will welcome them. Gabe is sort of like Jesus because people tried to release Jesus.

During their grand conversations, students talk about many of the same points they raise in their journal entries. The story fascinates them—at first they think about how simple and safe life would be, but then they think about all the things they take for granted that they'd have to give up to live in Jonas's ordered society. They talk about bravery and making choices, and they applaud Jonas's decision to flee with Gabriel. They also wonder if Jonas and Gabe survive.

The students collect "important" words from the story for the **word wall**. After reading the fourth, fifth, and sixth chapters, they add these words to the word wall displayed in the classroom:

relinquish	*bikeports*	*regulated*	*infraction*
invariably	*gravitating*	*rehabilitation*	*stirrings*
serene	*chastisement*	*assignment*	*reprieve*

Sometimes students choose unfamiliar or long words, but they also choose words such as *assignment* that are important to the story. Students refer to the word wall when they're writing. Later during the unit, Mrs. Goodman teaches a minilesson about root words using some of these words.

As students read the book, Mrs. Goodman teaches a series of **minilessons** about reading strategies; after they read about colors in the story, for example, she teaches a minilesson on visualizing. The teacher rereads excerpts about Jonas being selected to be the next Receiver and asks students to create a picture of the scene in their minds. She asks them to focus on the sights, sounds, smells, and feelings, and she talks about how important it is for readers to bring a story to life in their minds. Then students draw pictures of their visualizations and share them in small groups.

Another minilesson focuses on literary opposites. Mrs. Goodman explains that authors often introduce conflict and develop themes by using contrasts or opposites. She asks students to think of opposites in *The Giver*; she suggests *safe—danger* and *freedom—imprisoned*. The students offer these opposites:

alive—released	*families—family units*
choice—no choice	*memories—no memories*
color—black and white	*rules—anarchy*
conform—do your own thing	*stirrings—the pill*

Mrs. Goodman asks the class to think about how the opposites relate to the story and how Lois Lowry made them explicit in *The Giver*. Students talk about how the community seemed safe at the beginning of the story, but chapter by chapter, Lowry uncovered the community's shortcomings. They also talk about themes of the story reflected in these opposites.

After they finish reading *The Giver*, the students have a read-around in which they select and read aloud favorite passages. Then the class makes a quilt to probe the story's themes: Each student prepares a paper quilt square with an illustration and several sentences of text; check the figure A Quilt Square. The students decide to use white, gray, and black to represent the sameness of Jonas's community, red because it was the first color Jonas saw, and a colorful center to represent Elsewhere.

For the final activity in the unit, the seventh graders write argumentative essays, defending either Jonas's perfect society or their own societies. She asks half of the students to brainstorm a list of the characteristics of the "perfect" society while the others prepare a list of the characteristics of their own society. When they've completed their lists, the two groups share them, and quickly the students join in to refine some of the characteristics and suggest additional ones. Before they started reading *The Giver*, most of the students thought a perfect society sounded good, but now they appreciate the benefits of their own society, especially the freedoms they take for granted. Most students decide to write in defense of their own society, but Isaac, Petra, and Zoe take on the challenge of arguing in favor of Jonas's society.

Before they begin writing, Mrs. Goodman briefly reviews what she's taught them about the argumentative writing genre using a chart they developed during a series of minilessons two months ago. The chart presents this information about argumentative essays:

1. *Provide background about the issue.*
2. *State your position strongly.*

A QUILT SQUARE

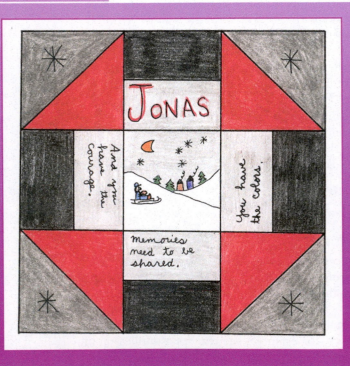

3. *Present a convincing argument with at least 3 pieces of supporting evidence.*

4. *Argue against the opposing viewpoint.*

5. *Answer the question "So what?" in the conclusion.*

The students read the information on the chart and talk through how they might address each point in their essays.

Then the students get down to work on their essays. They use the writing process as they prepare their first drafts, share them with classmates, get feedback that they use to revise their drafts, work with partners to correct mechanical errors during editing, and finally publish their final drafts. They share their essays in small groups and then self-assess their writing using a rubric that Mrs. Goodman developed that incorporates the five points listed on the chart about argumentative essays.

 STANDARDS CHECK!

Mrs. Goodman addressed the Common Core State Standards as she used the reading and writing processes in the vignette you've just read. Review the seventh grade literacy Standards document online at http://www.corestandards.org/ELA-Literacy, and identify the Standards that Mrs. Goodman and her students addressed. Create your list, and compare it with Mrs. Goodman's.

The reading process that Mrs. Goodman used represents a significant shift in thinking about what students do as they read. She understood that readers construct meaning as they negotiate the texts they're reading, and that they use their background experiences and knowledge of written language as they read. She also knew that it's quite common for two students to read the same book and come away with different interpretations because meaning doesn't exist on the pages of a book; instead, comprehension is created through the interaction between readers and the texts they're reading. This individualized view of readers' interpretations reflects Rosenblatt's transactional theory (2004).

The **reading process** involves a series of stages during which readers comprehend the text. The term *text* refers to all reading materials—stories, maps, newspapers, cereal boxes, textbooks, email, and so on; it's not limited to basal reading textbooks. The writing process is a similar recursive process involving a variety of activities as students gather and organize ideas, write rough drafts, revise and edit the drafts, and, finally, publish their writings. Students learn to use the writing process to craft and refine their compositions—autobiographies, stories, reports, poems, and essays.

The Reading Process

Reading is a constructive process of creating meaning that involves the reader, the text, and the purpose within social and cultural contexts. The goal is comprehension, understanding the text and being able to use it for the intended purpose. Readers don't simply look at the words on a page and grasp the meaning; rather, it's a complex process involving these essential components:

Phonemic Awareness and Phonics. Students use their knowledge about the phonological system, including how to manipulate sounds in spoken words and apply

As you listen to educators talk about the reading process and watch teachers teach reading, consider how these teachers use the reading process. Why is the reading process the foundation for literacy instruction?

phoneme–grapheme correspondences and phonics rules, as they read. They develop these abilities through phonemic awareness and phonics instruction in the primary grades.

Word Identification. Students recognize common or high-frequency words automatically and use their knowledge of phonics and word parts to decode unfamiliar words. Until students can recognize most of the words they're reading, they're slow, word-by-word readers.

Fluency. Students become fluent readers once they recognize most words automatically and read quickly and with expression. This is a milestone because students have limited cognitive resources to devote to reading. Beginning readers use most of this energy to decode words; fluent readers, in contrast, devote most of their cognitive resources to comprehension.

Vocabulary. Students think about the meaning of words they're reading, choosing appropriate meanings, recognizing figurative uses, and relating them to their background knowledge. Knowing the meaning of words influences comprehension because it's difficult to understand when the words being read don't make sense.

Comprehension. Students use a combination of reader and text factors to understand what they're reading. To create meaning, they predict, connect, monitor, repair, and use other comprehension strategies as well as their knowledge of genres, organizational patterns, and literary devices.

These components are supported by scientifically based reading research (National Reading Panel, 2000).

Teachers use the reading process to involve students in activities to teach, practice, and apply these components. The reading process is organized into five stages: *prereading, reading, responding, exploring,* and *applying.* This process is used, no matter which instructional program teachers choose, even though some activities at each stage differ. Figure 2–1 summarizes the reading process.

FIGURE 2–1 **The Reading Process**

Stage 1: Prereading
- Activate or build background knowledge and related vocabulary.
- Think about the genre.
- Set purposes.
- Introduce key academic vocabulary words.
- Make predictions.
- Preview the text.

Stage 2: Reading
- Read independently or with a partner.
- Read with classmates using shared or guided reading.
- Listen to the teacher read aloud.
- Read the entire text or specific sections, depending on purpose.
- Apply reading strategies and skills.
- Examine illustrations, charts, and diagrams.

Stage 3: Responding
- Write in reading logs.
- Participate in grand conversations or other discussions.

Stage 4: Exploring
- Reread all or part of the text.
- Learn new vocabulary words.
- Participate in minilessons.
- Examine genre, other text features, or the writer's craft.
- Learn about the author.
- Collect memorable quotes.

Stage 5: Applying
- Construct projects.
- Read related books.
- Use information in thematic units.
- Reflect on the reading experience.

Stage 1: Prereading

The reading process begins before readers open a book. The first stage, **prereading**, occurs as readers prepare to read. In the vignette, Mrs. Goodman built her students' background knowledge and stimulated their interest in *The Giver* as they talked about how wonderful life would be in a "perfect" world. As readers get ready to read, they activate background knowledge, set purposes, and make plans for reading.

ACTIVATING BACKGROUND KNOWLEDGE. Students have both general and specific **background knowledge** (Braunger & Lewis, 2006). General knowledge is world knowledge, what students have acquired through life experiences and learning in their home communities and at school, and specific knowledge is literary knowledge, what students need to read and comprehend a text. Literary knowledge includes information about reading, genres, and text structures. In this stage, students activate their world and literary background knowledge: To trigger this activation, they think about the title of a book, examine the book cover and inside illustrations, and read the first paragraph.

When students don't have enough background knowledge to read a text, teachers build their knowledge base. They build knowledge about reading by teaching reading strategies and skills; knowledge about genres by examining the structure of the genre and explaining how reading varies according to genre; and knowledge about a topic by providing a text set of books for students to read, engaging students in discussions, sharing artifacts, and introducing key vocabulary words. It's not enough just to build students' knowledge about the topic; literary knowledge is also essential!

SETTING PURPOSES. The purpose guides students' reading. It provides motivation and direction for reading, as well as a mechanism for students to monitor their reading to see if they're fulfilling their purpose. Sustaining a single purpose while students read the text is more effective than presenting students with a series of purposes (Blanton, Wood, & Moorman, 1990). Sometimes teachers set purposes for reading, and sometimes students set their own purposes. In literature focus units and basal reading textbooks, teachers usually explain how students are expected to read and what they'll do after reading. In contrast, students set their own purposes for reading during literature circles and reading workshop; they choose texts that are intrinsically interesting or that explain something they want to learn more about. As students develop as readers, they become more effective at choosing books and setting their own purposes.

PLANNING FOR READING. Once students activate their background knowledge and identify their purpose for reading, they take their first look at the text and plan for reading. Students vary how they make plans according to the type of selection they're preparing to read. For stories, they make predictions about the characters and events in the story, often basing their predictions on the book's title or the cover illustration. If they've read other stories by the same author or in the same genre, students also use this information in making their predictions. Sometimes students share their predictions orally, and at other times, they write predictions in their reading logs.

When students are preparing to read nonfiction books and content area textbook chapters, they preview the selection by flipping through the pages and noting section headings, illustrations, and diagrams. Sometimes they examine the table of contents to see how the book is organized, or they consult the index to locate specific information they want to read. They also notice highlighted terminology that's

Check the Compendium of Instructional Procedures, which follows Chapter 12.

unfamiliar to them. To help students plan, teachers often use **anticipation guides** and **prereading plans**.

Stage 2: Reading

Students read the book or other selection in the reading stage. Outside of school, most people usually read silently and independently, but in the classroom, teachers and students use five types of reading:

- Reading aloud to students
- Shared reading
- Guided reading
- Partner reading
- Independent reading

The types vary in the amount of teacher scaffolding: Teachers provide very little support during independent reading, and the most support when they read aloud to students. As they decide which type of reading to use, teachers consider the purpose for reading, students' reading levels, and the number of available copies of the text.

READING ALOUD TO STUDENTS. Teachers use the **interactive read-aloud** procedure to read aloud books that are developmentally appropriate but written above students' reading levels (Fisher, Flood, Lapp, & Frey, 2004). As they read, teachers engage students in activities rather than postponing student involvement until after reading; students become active participants, for example, as they make predictions, repeat refrains, ask questions, identify big ideas, and make connections. In addition, when teachers read aloud, they model what good readers do and how good readers use reading strategies (Cappellini, 2005). Reading aloud also provides an opportunity for teachers to think aloud about their use of reading strategies.

Read-alouds are an important component of literacy instruction at all grade levels, not just for young children who can't read many books on their own (Allen, 2000). Teachers read books aloud during literature focus units, reading and writing workshop, and thematic units. Reading aloud has many benefits, such as introducing vocabulary, modeling comprehension strategies, and increasing students' motivation (Rasinski, 2003).

SHARED READING. Teachers use **shared reading** to read aloud books and other texts that students can't read independently (Holdaway, 1979), modeling what fluent readers do as they involve students in enjoyable reading activities (Fountas & Pinnell, 1996). Often primary grade teachers use big books so that both small groups and whole-class groups can see the text and read along. After reading the text several times, teachers use it to teach phonics concepts and high-frequency words. Students can also read small versions of the book independently or with buddies and use the text's pattern or structure for writing activities. Shared reading differs from reading aloud because children see the text as the teacher reads. Children often join in the reading of predictable refrains and rhyming words, and after listening to the text read several times, they often remember enough of it to read along with the teacher.

Shared reading is also used with older students to read novels when the books are too difficult to read independently (Allen, 2002). Teachers distribute copies to everyone, and students follow along as the teacher reads aloud. Sometimes students take turns reading sections aloud, but the goal is not for everyone to have a turn reading; students who take turns reading must be fluent enough to keep the reading meaningful. Often the teacher begins reading, and when a student wants to take over the reading, he or she begins reading aloud with the teacher; then the teacher drops off and the student continues reading. After a paragraph or a page, another student joins in and the first student drops off. Many teachers call this technique "popcorn reading."

GUIDED READING. Teachers use guided reading to work with groups of four or five students who read at the same level. They use books that students can read at their instructional level, with approximately 90–94% accuracy, and they support students' reading and their use of reading strategies (Fountas & Pinnell, 1996; Richardson, 2009). Students do the reading themselves, although the teacher may read aloud to get them started on the first page or two. Young children often murmur the words softly as they read, which helps the teacher keep track of students' reading and the strategies they're using. Older, more fluent readers usually read silently during guided reading.

Guided reading lessons usually last 25 to 30 minutes. When the students arrive for the small-group lesson, they often reread, either individually or with a buddy, familiar books used in previous lessons. For the new guided reading lesson, students read books that they haven't read before. Beginning readers usually read small picture books in one sitting, but older students who are reading longer chapter books take several days to a week or two to read their books (Allen, 2000).

Teachers observe students as they read during guided reading lessons. They spend a few minutes observing each reader, sitting either in front of or beside the student. They watch for evidence of strategy use and confirm the student's attempts to identify words and solve reading problems. Teachers take notes about their observations and use the information to choose minilessons to teach and books for students to read.

PARTNER READING. Students read or reread a selection with a classmate or sometimes with an older student (Friedland & Truesdell, 2004). Partner reading is a good alternative to independent reading. It's an enjoyable social activity, and students can often read selections together that neither one could read individually; by working together, students are often able to figure out unfamiliar words and talk out comprehension problems.

As teachers introduce partner reading, they demonstrate how to read with a partner and how to support each other as they read. Students take turns reading aloud to each other or read in unison. They often stop and help each other identify an unfamiliar word or take a minute or two at the end of each page to talk about what they've read. Partner reading provides the practice that beginning readers need to become fluent; it's also an effective way to work with students with special learning needs and English learners. However, unless the teacher has explained the technique and taught students how to work collaboratively, partner reading often deteriorates into the stronger of the two partners reading aloud to the other student, but that isn't the intention of the technique.

INDEPENDENT READING. When students read independently, they read silently by themselves, for their own purposes, and at their own pace. It's essential that the books students select are at an appropriate reading level. Primary grade students often read the featured selection independently during literature focus units, but this is often after they've already read it once or twice with the teacher's assistance. Once students become fluent readers in second or third grade, students do more independent reading. They read chapter books independently for literature focus units and literature

FIGURE 2–2 Types of Reading

TYPE	STRENGTHS	LIMITATIONS
Reading Aloud to Students Teacher reads aloud and provides opportunities for students to be actively involved in the experience.	• Students have access to books they can't read themselves. • Teacher models fluent reading and reading strategies. • Students build background knowledge and vocabulary.	• Students have no opportunity to read. • Students may not be interested in the text.
Shared Reading Teacher reads aloud while students follow along using a big book or individual copies.	• Teacher teaches concepts about print. • Teacher models fluent reading and reading strategies. • Students become a community of readers.	• Big books or a class set of books are needed. • Text may not be appropriate for all students.
Guided Reading Teacher supports students as they apply reading strategies and skills to read a text.	• Teacher teaches reading strategies and skills. • Teacher provides scaffolding. • Teacher monitors students' reading.	• Multiple copies of texts at the appropriate reading level are needed. • Teacher controls the reading experience.
Partner Reading Two students take turns as they read a text together.	• Students collaborate and assist each other. • Students become more fluent readers. • Students talk to develop comprehension.	• One student may simply read to the other. • Teacher has little involvement or control.
Independent Reading Students read a text on their own without teacher scaffolding.	• Students develop responsibility. • Students learn to select texts. • The experience is authentic.	• Students may not choose texts that they can read independently. • Teacher has little involvement or control.

circles, and students at all grade levels independently read books written by favorite authors or books about interesting nonfiction topics during reading workshop.

Independent reading is an important part of a balanced reading program because it's the most authentic type of reading. It's the way students develop a love of reading and come to think of themselves as readers. The reading selection, however, must be at an appropriate level of difficulty so that students can read it independently; otherwise, teachers use another type of reading to scaffold students and make it possible for them to be successful.

The types of reading are compared in Figure 2–2. In the vignette at the beginning of this chapter, Mrs. Goodman used a combination of these approaches. She used shared reading as she read aloud the first chapter of *The Giver*, with students following along in their own copies. Later, students read together in small groups, with a partner, or independently. As teachers plan their instructional programs, they include reading aloud to students, teacher-led student reading, and independent reading each day.

Stage 3: Responding

Students respond to what they've read and continue to negotiate the meaning after reading. This stage reflects Rosenblatt's (2005) transactional theory. Two ways that students make tentative and exploratory comments immediately after reading are by writing in reading logs and participating in grand conversations or other discussions.

WRITING IN READING LOGS. Students write and draw their thoughts and feelings about the books they're reading in **reading logs**. As they write about what they've read, they unravel their thinking and, at the same time, elaborate on and clarify their responses. Students usually write in reading logs when they're reading stories and poems; sometimes they also write in reading logs when they're reading nonfiction books, but during thematic units, they make notes of important information or draw charts and diagrams in **learning logs**.

Students usually make reading logs by stapling together 10 to 12 sheets of paper. They decorate the covers, keeping with the theme of the book, and write entries after reading. Sometimes students choose topics for their entries, and sometimes teachers pose questions to guide students' thinking about their reading. Teachers monitor students' entries, reading and often responding to them. These journals are learning tools, so teachers rarely correct students' spellings; instead, they focus their responses on the ideas, but they expect students to spell the characters' names and high-frequency words accurately. At the end of the unit, teachers review students' work and often grade the reading logs based on whether students completed all the entries and on the quality of the ideas expressed in them.

PARTICIPATING IN DISCUSSIONS. Students also talk about the text with classmates in **grand conversations** about stories and poems and in discussions about nonfiction books and chapters in content area textbooks. Peterson and Eeds (2007) explain that in grand conversations, students share their personal responses and tell what they liked about the text. After sharing personal reactions, they shift the focus to "puzzle over what the author has written and . . . share what it is they find revealed" (p. 61). Often students make connections between the text and their own lives or between the text and other literature they've read. If they're reading a chapter book, they also make predictions about what might happen in the next chapter.

Teachers often share their ideas in grand conversations, but they act as interested participants, not leaders. The talk is primarily among the students, but teachers ask questions regarding things they're genuinely interested in learning more about and share information in response to questions that students ask. In the past, many discussions have been "gentle inquisitions" during which students recited answers to factual questions that teachers asked to determine whether students read an assignment. Although teachers can still judge whether students have read the assignment, the focus in grand conversations is on clarifying and deepening students' understanding of the story they've read.

Teachers and students also have discussions after reading nonfiction books and chapters in content area textbooks. Students talk about what interested them and what they learned about the topic, but teachers also focus students' attention on the big ideas, ask clarifying questions, share information, and reread brief excerpts to explore an idea.

These discussions can be held with the whole class or with small groups. Young children usually meet as a class, but older students often prefer to talk in small groups. When students meet as a class, there's a feeling of community, and the teacher can be part of the group. Small groups offer more opportunities for students to share their interpretations, but fewer viewpoints are expressed in each group, and teachers must move around, spending only a few minutes with each group. Teachers often compromise by having students begin their discussions in

As you watch this video, consider ways students respond to a text. Why is responding to text a critical stage in the reading process?

small groups and then come together as a class so that the groups can share what they discussed.

Stage 4: Exploring

Students go back into the text to examine it more analytically. This stage is more teacher directed than the others; it reflects the teacher-centered theory. Students re-read the selection or excerpts from it, examine the writer's craft, and focus on words and sentences from the selection. Teachers also teach minilessons on strategies.

REREADING THE SELECTION. As students reread the text, they think again about what they've read. Each time they reread a selection, students benefit in specific ways (Yaden, 1988): They deepen their comprehension as they move beyond their initial focus on the events of a story or the big ideas in a nonfiction book to under-standing the theme of the story or the relationships among the big ideas in a nonfic-tion text.

CLOSE READING. Teachers use **close reading** to guide students in rereading passages from a text to uncover deeper layers of meaning (Boyles, 2012/2013; Dalton, 2013). It's the purposeful rereading of a complex or challenging text to understand the big ideas, determine the author's purpose, and reflect on the meaning of individual words and sentences. The teacher's role is to scaffold stu-dents' thinking.

Teachers ask text-based questions to direct students back into the text. To ana-lyze a brief passage, they ask questions on one or more of these topics:

- the author's purpose
- ideas
- structural elements
- word choice
- sentence structure
- viewpoints

Text-dependent questions require students to pay attention as they reread the passage and locate evidence from the text to support their answers. For example, in *Skellig* (Almond, 1998), the story of Michael and his family who move into a new home, death seems to surround them. A seventh grade teacher is reading *Skellig* with his students, and after they read the first chapter, his close-reading questions focus on word choice:

> Go back into the text to see what word the author repeats.
>
> Are there other words that suggest death?
>
> What tone does the author evoke?
>
> Does the author offer any hope?

As the seventh graders reread the brief chapter and locate the death-related words, their comprehension grows. The most illuminating question is the last one. The stu-dents search for evidence that Michael will overcome his despair, and they find it: The story is set at the end of winter, and spring—a symbol for hope—will arrive soon. In addition, the thing in the garage is still alive. A student sums up what they've learned: "This story will get better. Life, not death, is going to win!"

Teachers choose grade-appropriate texts that are challenging enough to warrant repeated readings. Students need practice analyzing varied types of complex texts, including stories, newspaper articles, biographies, and other nonfiction books, songs, poems, and speeches. Younger students often listen to the teacher read the text aloud, but older students read it themselves. Students, even first graders, need individual copies of the passages used for close reading so they can add annotations. Teachers teach them how to annotate texts by highlighting words and sentences and writing notes in the margin. When students can't mark directly on the text, they write notes on small self-stick notes and attach them to the page.

EXAMINING THE WRITER'S CRAFT. Teachers plan exploring activities to focus students' attention on the genres, text structures, and literary devices that authors use. Students use **story boards** made from illustrations cut from picture books to sequence the events in the story, and make graphic organizers to highlight the plot, characters, and other elements of story structure. Another way students learn about the structure of stories is by writing books based on the selection they've read. In sequels, students tell what happens to the characters after the story ends.

Teachers share information about the author and introduce other books by the same author. Sometimes students read several books by an author and make comparisons among them. To focus on literary devices, students often reread excerpts to locate examples of onomatopoeia, similes and metaphors, and other types of figurative language.

FOCUSING ON WORDS AND SENTENCES. Teachers and students add "important" words to the **word wall** posted in the classroom. Students refer to it when they write and use the words for word-study activities, including drawing word clusters and posters to highlight particular words, doing **word sorts** to categorize words, and completing **semantic feature analysis** charts to examine relationships between words.

Students also locate "important" sentences in books they read; these sentences are worthy of examination because they contain figurative language, employ an interesting sentence structure, express a theme, or illustrate a character trait. Students often copy the sentences onto sentence strips to display in the classroom. Sometimes students copy the sentences in their reading logs and use them to begin their entries.

TEACHING MINILESSONS. Teachers present **minilessons** on procedures, concepts, strategies, and skills (Angelillo, 2008). They introduce the topic and make connections between the topic and examples in the featured selection students have read. In the vignette, Mrs. Goodman presented minilessons on visualizing and literary opposites using examples from *The Giver*.

Stage 5: Applying

Readers extend their comprehension, reflect on their understanding, and value the reading experience in this final stage. Often they create projects to apply what they've learned, and these projects take many forms, including stories, slide shows, posters, **readers theatre** performances, essays, and podcast presentations. Project ideas are listed in Figure 2–3. Usually students choose which project they want to do and work independently, with a classmate, or in a small group, but sometimes the class decides to work together on a project.

 **MONITOR: Check Your Understanding 2.1**

FIGURE 2–3   **Application Projects**

Digital Projects
- Write a blog about a book.
- Investigate an author's website and share information from it with classmates.
- Create a multimodal project about the book using text, images, and sounds.
- Search the Web for information on a topic related to the book and share the results with classmates.
- Create a podcast presentation about the book.
- Create or complete a WebQuest about the book.

Oral Language Projects
- Perform a readers theatre presentation of an excerpt from a book.
- Create a choral reading using an excerpt from a book and have classmates read it.
- Write a script and present a play based on a book.
- Dress as a book character and sit on the "hot seat" to answer classmates' questions.
- Present a rap, song, or poem about a book.

Social Action Projects
- Write a letter to the editor of the local newspaper on a topic related to a book.
- Get involved in a community project related to a book.

Visual Projects
- Design a graphic organizer or model about a book.
- Create a collage to represent the theme of a book.
- Prepare illustrations of a story's events for clothesline props to use in retelling the story.
- Make a book box and fill it with objects and pictures representing a book.
- Construct a paper quilt about a book.
- Create an open-mind portrait to probe one character's thoughts.

Writing Projects
- Rewrite a story from a different point of view.
- Write another episode or a sequel for a book.
- Write simulated letters from one character to another.
- Create a found poem using words and phrases from a book.
- Write a poem on a topic related to a book.
- Keep a simulated journal from one character's viewpoint.
- Write an essay to examine the book's theme or a controversial issue.
- Create a multigenre project about a book.

The Writing Process

The writing process is a series of five stages that describe what students think about and do as they write; the stages are *prewriting*, *drafting*, *revising*, *editing*, and *publishing*. Numbering the stages doesn't mean that the writing process is a linear series of neatly packaged categories; rather, research has shown that the process involves recurring cycles, and numbering is simply an aid to identifying writing activities. In the classroom, the stages merge and recur as students write. The key features of each stage are listed in Figure 2–4.

Stage 1: Prewriting

Prewriting is the "getting ready to write" stage. The traditional notion that writers have a topic completely thought out and ready to flow onto the page is ridiculous: If writers wait for ideas to fully develop, they may wait forever. Instead, writers begin tentatively—talking, reading, brainstorming—to see what they know and in what direction they want to go. Prewriting has probably been the most neglected stage in the writing process; however, it's as crucial to writers as a warm-up is to athletes. Murray (1982) stated that at least 70% of writing time should be spent in prewriting. During prewriting, students choose a topic, consider purpose and genre, and gather and organize ideas.

CHOOSING A TOPIC. Students should choose their own topics for writing—topics that they're interested in and know about—so that they'll be more engaged, but that isn't always possible. Sometimes teachers provide the topics, especially in connection with literature focus units and content area units. It's best when teacher-selected topics are broad enough so that students can narrow them in a way that suits them.

CONSIDERING PURPOSE AND GENRE. As students prepare to write, they think about their purpose for writing: Are they writing to entertain? to inform? to persuade? Setting a purpose for writing is just as important as setting the purpose for reading, because purpose influences decisions students make about genre. If students are writing to inform, for instance, they write reports, essays, letters, or podcast presentations. Or, they can use several genres and create a multigenre project. Students learn about a variety of writing genres; six are described in Figure 2–5. Through reading and writing, students become knowledgeable about these genres and how they're structured (Donovan & Smolkin, 2002). Langer (1985) found that by third grade, students respond in distinctly different ways to story- and report-writing assignments; they organize the writing differently and include varied kinds of information and elaboration. Because students are learning the distinctions between various genres, it's essential that teachers use the correct terminology and not call all writing "stories."

GATHERING AND ORGANIZING IDEAS. Students engage in activities to gather and organize ideas for writing during the prewriting stage. Graves (1983) calls what writers do to prepare for writing "rehearsal" activities. To gather ideas, they draw pictures, brainstorm lists of words, read books, do Internet research, and talk about ideas with classmates. Students make graphic organizers to visually display their ideas. Their

---

FIGURE 2–4 **The Writing Process**

Stage 1: Prewriting
- Choose a topic.
- Consider the purpose.
- Identify the genre.
- Engage in rehearsal activities to gather ideas.
- Use a graphic organizer to organize ideas.

Stage 2: Drafting
- Write a rough draft.
- Use wide spacing to leave room for revising and editing.
- Emphasize ideas rather than mechanical correctness.
- Mark the writing as a "rough draft."

Stage 3: Revising
- Reread the rough draft.
- Participate in revising groups.
- Work at one or more revising centers.
- Make substantive changes that reflect classmates' feedback.
- Conference with the teacher.

Stage 4: Editing
- Proofread the revised rough draft with a partner.
- Work at one or more editing centers.
- Correct spelling, capitalization, punctuation, and grammar errors.
- Conference with the teacher.

Stage 5: Publishing
- Format the composition.
- Make the final copy.
- Share the writing with an appropriate audience.

FIGURE 2–5 Writing Genres

GENRE	PURPOSE	ACTIVITIES
Argumentative Writing	Students present a clearly articulated position on a debatable issue, such as whether kids should be allowed to play football or how schools should address bullying. They cite evidence to support their claims and consider the other side's viewpoint.	Advertisements Book and film reviews Essays Letters to the editor Posters
Descriptive Writing	Students observe carefully and choose precise language as they write descriptions. They take notice of sensory details and create comparisons (metaphors and similes) to make their writing more powerful.	Character sketches Comparisons Descriptive essays Descriptive sentences Found poems
Expository Writing	Students collect and synthesize information. This writing is objective; reports are the most common type. Students use expository writing to give directions, sequence steps, compare one thing to another, explain causes and effects, or describe problems and solutions.	Alphabet books Autobiographies Directions Essays Posters Reports Summaries
Journals and Letters	Students write to themselves and to specific, known audiences. Their writing is personal and often less formal than other genres. They share news, explore new ideas, and record notes. Students learn the special formatting that letters, envelopes, and online messages require.	Business letters Courtesy letters Double-entry journals Email messages Friendly letters Learning logs Personal journals
Narrative Writing	Students retell familiar stories, develop sequels for stories they've read, write stories about events in their own lives, and create original stories. They include a beginning, middle, and end in the narratives to develop the plot and characters.	Original short stories Personal narratives Retellings of stories Sequels to stories Story scripts
Poetry Writing	Students create word pictures and play with rhyme and other stylistic devices as they create poems. Through their wordplay, students learn that poetic language is vivid and powerful but concise and that poems can be arranged in different ways on a page.	Acrostic poems Color poems Free verse Haiku "I Am . . ." poems Poems for two voices

choice of graphic organizer varies with the writing genre: For stories, they often use a three-part diagram to emphasize the beginning-middle-end structure of stories, and to write persuasive essays, they use a cluster with one ray to develop each argument.

Stage 2: Drafting

Students get their ideas down on paper and write a first draft of their compositions in this stage. Because they don't start writing with their pieces already composed in their minds, students begin tentatively with the ideas they've developed through prewriting activities. Their drafts are usually messy, reflecting the outpouring of ideas with cross-outs, lines, and arrows as they think of better ways to express ideas. Students write quickly, with little concern about legible handwriting, correct spelling, and careful use of capitalization and punctuation.

When they write rough drafts, students skip every other line to leave space for revisions. They use arrows to move sections of text, cross-outs to delete sections, and scissors and tape to cut apart and rearrange text, just as adult writers do. They write on only one side of a sheet of paper so it can be cut apart or rearranged. Wide spacing between lines is crucial. At first, teachers make small *x*s on every other line of students' papers as a reminder to skip lines during drafting, but once they understand the importance of leaving space, students skip lines automatically.

Students label their drafts by writing *rough draft* in ink at the top or by using a ROUGH DRAFT stamp. This label indicates to the writer, other students, parents, and administrators that the composition is a draft in which the emphasis is on content, not mechanics; it also explains why the teacher hasn't graded the paper.

Instead of writing drafts by hand, many students, even those in kindergarten through third grade, use computers to compose rough drafts, polish their writing, and print out final copies. There are many benefits of using computers for word processing. Students are often more motivated to write, and they tend to write longer pieces. Their writing looks neater, and they use spell-check programs to identify and correct misspelled words.

Stage 3: Revising

During the revising stage, writers refine ideas in their compositions. Students often break the writing process cycle as soon as they complete a rough draft, believing that once they've jotted down their ideas, the writing task is done. Experienced writers, however, know they must turn to others for reactions and revise on the basis of these comments. Revision isn't polishing; it's meeting the needs of readers by adding, substituting, deleting, and rearranging material. Revision means "seeing again," and in this stage, writers see their compositions again with the help of classmates and the teacher. Revising consists of three activities: rereading the rough draft, sharing the rough draft in a revising group, and revising on the basis of feedback.

REREADING THE ROUGH DRAFT. After finishing the rough draft, writers distance themselves from it for a day or two, then reread it from a fresh perspective, as a reader might. As they reread, students make changes—adding, substituting, deleting, and moving text—and place question marks by sections that need work; students ask for help with these trouble spots in their revising groups.

SHARING IN REVISING GROUPS. Students meet in **revising groups** to share their compositions with classmates. Group members respond to the writer's rough draft and suggest possible revisions. Revising groups provide a scaffold in which teachers and classmates talk about plans and strategies for writing and revising (Applebee & Langer, 1983; Calkins, 1983).

Revising groups can form spontaneously when several students have completed drafts and are ready to share their compositions, or they can be formal groupings with identified leaders. In some classrooms, revising groups form when four or five students

Classroom INTERVENTIONS

The Writing Process

Many struggling writers don't like to write, and they avoid writing whenever possible because they don't know what to do (Christenson, 2002). These students need to learn to use the writing process. One of the best ways to teach the writing process to struggling writers is to use interactive writing, a procedure normally used with young children, to demonstrate both the process and the strategies writers use, including organizing and revising. Because it's a group activity, students are more willing to participate.

Once they're familiar with the stages in the writing process, students apply what they've learned to write collaborative compositions. Each student drafts a paragraph or short section and then moves through the writing process; this way, the workload is manageable for both students and their teachers. Once students have learned to use the writing process and have developed a repertoire of writing strategies, they're better prepared to write independently.

Struggling writers who don't understand the writing process don't realize that they need to revise and edit their writing to communicate more effectively. The key to enticing struggling writers to revise and edit is to help them develop a sense of audience. Many novice writers write primarily for themselves, but when they want their classmates or another audience to understand their message, they begin to recognize the importance of refining their writing. Teachers emphasize audience by encouraging students to share their writing from the author's chair. Lots of writing and sharing are necessary before students learn to appreciate the writing process.

Revising improves students' writing. How do teachers motivate students to revise their work?

finish writing their rough drafts; students gather around a conference table or in a corner of the classroom and take turns reading their rough drafts aloud. Classmates in the group listen and respond, offering compliments and suggestions for revision. Sometimes the teacher joins the revising group, but if the teacher is involved in something else, students work independently.

In other classrooms, the revising groups are assigned; students get together when all students in the group have completed their rough drafts and are ready to share their writing. Sometimes the teacher participates in these groups, providing feedback along with the students. Or, the revising groups can function independently: Each is made up of four or five students, and a list of groups and their members is posted in the classroom. The teacher puts a star by one student's name, and that student serves as a group leader. The leader changes every quarter.

MAKING REVISIONS. Students make four types of changes to their rough drafts: additions, substitutions, deletions, and moves (Faigley & Witte, 1981). As they revise, students add words, substitute sentences, delete paragraphs, and move phrases. They often use a blue or red pen to cross out, draw arrows, and write in the space left between the double-spaced lines of their rough drafts so that revisions will show clearly; that way, teachers can see the types of revisions students make by examining their revised rough drafts. Revisions are another gauge of students' growth as writers.

REVISING CENTERS. Many teachers set up centers to give students revision options: They can talk with a classmate about the ideas in their rough draft, examine the organization of their writing, consider their word choice, or check that they've included all required components in the composition. Figure 2–6 presents a list of revising centers. Teachers introduce these centers as they teach their students about the writing process and the writer's craft, and then students work at these centers before or after participating in a revising group. Teachers usually provide a checklist of center options that students put in their writing folders, and then they check off the centers that they complete. Through these center activities, students develop a repertoire of revising strategies and personalize their writing process.

Stage 4: Editing

Editing is putting the piece of writing into its final form. Until this stage, the focus has been primarily on the content of students' writing. Once the focus changes to mechanics, students polish their writing by correcting spelling mistakes and other mechanical errors. Mechanics are the commonly accepted conventions of written Standard English; they consist of capitalization, punctuation, spelling, sentence structure, usage, and formatting considerations specific to poems, scripts, letters, and other writing genres. The use of these commonly accepted conventions is a courtesy to those who will read the composition.

Students are more efficient editors if they set the composition aside for a few days before beginning to edit. After working so closely with a piece of writing during drafting and revising, they're too familiar with it to notice many mechanical errors; with the distance gained by waiting a few days, students are better able to approach editing with a fresh perspective and gather the enthusiasm

Literacy Portraits

The students in Ms. Janusz's class are confident writers who willingly share their rough drafts and revise their writing. Watch Michael share his rough draft with Ben, and then listen as Ms. Janusz teaches a minilesson on writing effective endings and conferences with Michael about how he plans to end a story he's writing. Also click on Rhiannon's revising conference with Ms. Janusz. Because Rhiannon's writing is a challenge to read—ideas are born so quickly in her imagination that she forgets about inserting punctuation when she writes, and her abbreviated phonetic spellings are difficult to decipher—Ms. Janusz usually combines revising and editing when she works with her.

Getting students to revise isn't easy. What do you notice in these video clips to suggest why these second graders are successful?

Michael

Ms. Janusz

Rhiannon

FIGURE 2–6 Revising and Editing Centers

TYPE	CENTERS	ACTIVITIES
Revising	Rereading	Students reread their rough drafts with a partner, and the partner offers compliments and asks questions.
	Word Choice	Students choose 5–10 words in their rough drafts and look for more specific or more powerful synonyms using a thesaurus, word walls in the classroom, or suggestions from classmates.
	Graphic Organizers	Students draw a chart or diagram to illustrate the organization of their compositions, and they make revisions if the organization isn't effective or the writing isn't complete.
	Highlighting	Students use highlighter pens to mark their rough drafts according to the teacher's direction. Depending on the skills being taught, students may mark topic sentences, descriptive language, or sensory details.
	Sentence Combining	Students choose a section of their rough drafts with too many short sentences or sentence fragments and combine sentences to improve the flow of their writing.
Editing	Spelling	Students work with a partner to proofread their writing. They locate misspelled words and consult a dictionary to correct errors.
	Homophones	Students check their rough drafts for homophone errors (e.g., *there–their–they're*), and consulting a chart posted in the center, they correct the errors.
	Punctuation	Students proofread their writing, checking for punctuation errors. After correcting the errors, students highlight all punctuation marks in their compositions.
	Capitalization	Students check that each sentence begins with a capital letter, the word *I* is capitalized, and proper nouns and adjectives are capitalized. After correcting the errors, students highlight all capital letters in the compositions.
	Sentences	Students analyze the sentences in their rough drafts and categorize them as simple, compound, complex, or fragment on a chart. Then they make any necessary changes.

necessary to finish the writing process. Then students move through two activities in the editing stage: proofreading to locate errors and correcting the ones they find.

PROOFREADING. Students **proofread** their compositions to locate and mark possible errors. Proofreading is a unique type of reading in which students read word by word, hunting for errors rather than reading for meaning. Concentrating on mechanics is difficult because of our inclination to read for meaning; even experienced proofreaders often find themselves focusing on comprehension and thus overlooking errors that don't inhibit meaning. It's important, therefore, to take time to explain proofreading to students and to demonstrate how it differs from regular reading.

To demonstrate proofreading, teachers display a piece of writing on the whiteboard and read it aloud several times, each time hunting for a particular type of error. During each reading, they read the composition slowly, softly pronouncing each word and touching it with a pencil or pen to focus attention on it. Teachers mark possible errors as they're located.

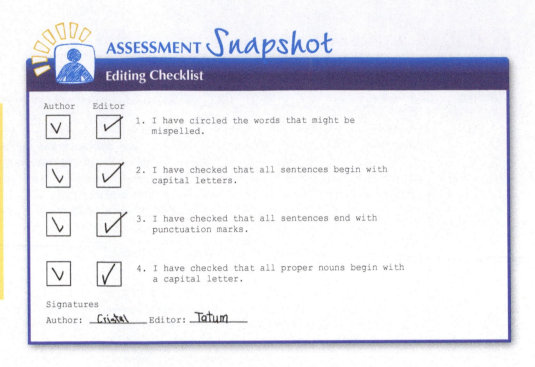

ASSESSMENT *Snapshot*

Editing Checklist

Author	Editor	
✓	✓	1. I have circled the words that might be mispelled.
✓	✓	2. I have checked that all sentences begin with capital letters.
✓	✓	3. I have checked that all sentences end with punctuation marks.
✓	✓	4. I have checked that all proper nouns begin with a capital letter.

Signatures

Author: _Cristal_   Editor: _Tatum_

TEACHER'S NOTE

Cristal responsibly corrects errors in her rough drafts. She works well with Tatum, welcoming her assistance. In this piece, Cristal corrected 11 errors; I caught only 2 misspelled words and one unnecessary capital letter.

Editing checklists help students focus on particular types of errors. Teachers develop checklists with two to six items appropriate for the grade level. A first grade checklist, for example, might have only two items—perhaps one about capital letters at the beginning of sentences and another about periods at the end. In contrast, a middle grade checklist might contain items such as using commas in a series, indenting paragraphs, capitalizing proper nouns and adjectives, and spelling homonyms correctly. Teachers revise the checklist during the school year to focus attention on skills they've recently taught.

A third grader's editing checklist is presented in Assessment Snapshot: Editing Checklist. The writer and a classmate work as partners to edit their compositions. First, they proofread their own drafts, searching for errors in each category on the checklist, and after proofreading, they check off each item. After completing the editing checklist, students sign their names and trade checklists and drafts: Now they become editors and complete each other's checklist. Having both writer and editor sign the checklist helps them to take the activity seriously.

CORRECTING ERRORS. After students proofread their rough drafts and locate as many errors as they can, they use red pens to correct the errors independently or with an editor's assistance. Some errors are easy to correct, some require use of a dictionary, and others involve instruction from the teacher. It's unrealistic to expect students to locate and correct every mechanical error in their pieces; not even published books are always error-free! Once in a while, students may change a correct spelling or punctuation mark and make it incorrect, but they correct far more errors than they create.

Students also work at editing centers to identify and correct specific types of errors; a list of editing centers is also included in Figure 2–6. Teachers often vary the center activities to reflect the types of errors students are making. Students who continue to misspell common words can check for these words on a chart posted in the center. Or, after a series of lessons on contractions or punctuation marks, for example, one or more centers will focus on applying the newly taught skill.

Editing can end after students and their editors correct as many mechanical errors as possible, or after students meet with the teacher for a final editing conference. When mechanical correctness is crucial, this conference is important. Teachers proofread the composition with individual students, and they identify and make the remaining corrections together, or the teacher makes checkmarks in the margin to note errors for the student to correct independently.

Stage 5: Publishing

Students bring their compositions to life by writing final copies and by sharing them orally with an appropriate audience. When they share their writing with real audiences of classmates, other students, parents, and the community, students come to think of themselves as authors. Publication is powerful: Students are motivated not only to continue writing but also to improve the quality of their writing through revising and editing (Weber, 2002).

MAKING BOOKS. A popular way for students to publish their writing is by making books. Simple booklets can be made by folding a sheet of paper into quarters, like a greeting card. Students write the title on the front and use the three remaining sides for their composition. They can also construct booklets by stapling sheets of writing paper together and adding covers made out of construction paper. Sheets of wallpaper cut from old sample books also make sturdy covers. These stapled booklets can be cut into various shapes, too. Students can make more sophisticated books by covering cardboard covers with contact paper, wallpaper samples, or cloth. Pages are sewn or stapled together, and the first and last pages (endpapers) are glued to the cardboard covers to hold the book together.

SHARING WRITING. One of the best ways for students to share their writing is to sit in a special chair in the classroom called the *author's chair* and read their writing aloud to classmates. Afterward, classmates ask questions, offer compliments, and celebrate the completion of the writing project. Sharing writing is a social activity that helps writers develop sensitivity to audiences and confidence in themselves as authors. Beyond just providing the opportunity for students to share writing, teachers need to teach students how to make appropriate comments as they respond to their classmates' writing. Teachers also serve as a model for responding to students' writing without dominating the sharing.

Here are other ways for students to share their writing:

ℂ Read it to parents and siblings
ℂ Share it at a back-to-school event
ℂ Place it in the class or school library
ℂ Read it to students in other classes
ℂ Display it as a mobile or on a poster
ℂ Contribute it to a class anthology
ℂ Post it on the class website or wiki
ℂ Submit it to the school's literary magazine
ℂ Display it at a school or community event
ℂ Send it to a children's literary magazine
ℂ Submit it to an online literary magazine

The best literary magazines for students are *Stone Soup* and *Skipping Stones*. *Stone Soup* is a magazine of writing and artwork for children ages 8–13; this prestigious magazine seeks children's stories and poems. At its website, students can download a sample issue and listen to authors reading their own writing. Subscription information

𝒩𝑒𝓌 LITERACIES

Laptops for Writing

Technology has the potential to support writing instruction through word processing, spell-check apps, multimedia software, and the Internet (Karchmer-Klein, 2007). One exciting program is Maine's middle school laptop program. All seventh and eighth graders were given laptops as part of a 5-year program to get them ready for 21st-century literacy demands, and teachers learned to use laptops to teach writing. Students used Apple iBook computers with AirPort wireless networking, Internet access, and Web browsers. Software included AppleWorks, email, iMovie, iPhoto, and NoteShare. Students could take their laptops home in the evenings, on weekends, and on school vacations.

Teachers participated in professional development programs to learn more about the writing process and teaching writing with digital tools. The Maine Writing Project's Literacy Through Technology Team trained Teacher Leaders at each school site so they could both help colleagues integrate the laptops into their instructional programs and provide technical assistance.

Researchers reported a positive link between laptop use and the quality of students' writing (Silvernail & Gritter, 2007). Eighth graders' writing, as measured by the Maine Educational Assessment (MEA), the state's standardized assessment, improved significantly after the laptop program was implemented. MEA writing scores from 2000 show that 29% of eighth graders met the state's writing proficiency standard, but in 2005, 41% did! The researchers found that the way laptops were used influenced writing achievement. Students who reported using their laptops at each stage in the writing process received the highest test scores, and those who said they hadn't used the laptops earned the lowest scores. Silvernail and Gritter interviewed students and teachers about the program; they found that more than 70% of students believed that laptops improved their writing. The students reported doing more writing, working more quickly, and self-correcting a higher number of errors, and teachers' perceptions were similar. Now, more than 10 years later, students continue to successfully use laptops for writing, math, and other curricular areas.

---

is available there as well as directions for submitting students' writing. *Skipping Stones* is an international magazine for children ages 8–16 that accepts stories, articles, photos, cartoons, letters, and drawings. This award-winning publication focuses on global interdependence, celebrates cultural and environmental richness, and provides a forum for children from around the world to share ideas and experiences. To read excerpts from the current issue and to get information about subscribing and submitting writing to *Skipping Stones*, go to the magazine's website. Many teachers subscribe to these magazines and use the writings as models when they're teaching writing. Other literary magazines worth considering are *Magic Dragon* and *New Moon: The Magazine for Girls and Their Dreams*. Too often, literary magazines are labors of love rather than viable financial ventures, so even highly esteemed and popular magazines go out of business. Students should always check that a literary magazine is still accepting submissions before sending their writing.

GO DIGITAL! **Online Publishing.** The Internet offers unlimited opportunities for students to display their writing online, share it with a global audience, and receive authentic feedback from readers (McNabb, 2006). When students create multimodal projects that incorporate audio, video, animation, and graphics, electronic publication is essential so that readers can fully experience them. Students are using new literacies when they implement multimodal technologies to express their ideas and engage in online communication (Labbo, 2005).

These online publication sites are some of the best for students:

Amazing Kids! Magazine. This website posts K–8 students' stories and poems, but it's geared primarily toward grades 4–8. In addition, the site has Writer's Tips with useful information for student writers.

Cyberkids. This site publishes original writing by 7- to 12-year-olds, including multimodal stories.

KidsWWwrite. Students' stories and poems are published in this eZine that's divided into areas for 5- to 8-year-olds, 9- to 12-year-olds, and 13- to 16-year-olds.

Poetry Zone. This British website posts students' poetry, hosts competitions, and provides a variety of poetry resources for teachers.

Stories From the Web. This website, divided into ages 0–7, 7–11, and 11–16 areas, accepts submissions of students' stories, play scripts, poems, raps, and songs.

Students can also use Internet search engines to locate new eZines. It's inevitable that some online publication websites will shut down, but others will spring up to take their place.

Each electronic magazine posts its own submission information that students should read and follow. Most eZines specify that students' submissions must be original, and that writing dealing with violent or offensive topics or employing inappropriate language won't be published. Students usually aren't paid for their writing. Submissions must be ready for posting; it's naïve to assume that an editor will format students' writing or correct mechanical errors. Students usually complete an online information sheet and email their writing to the eZine's website, and parents must submit a statement giving permission.

Students can also display their writing on the class website or wiki for others to read and respond to in guest books, blogs, and email messages (Weber, 2002). Even first graders can access, read, and respond to writing posted on their class website (McGowan, 2005)!

Nurturing English Learners

How do teachers teach writing? Writing can be a daunting task for English learners. Students need to know English vocabulary, sentence structure, and spelling to communicate effectively in writing, but ELs can become good writers when their teachers set high expectations, teach them how to write, and involve them in daily writing activities. Teachers must be mindful of the increased linguistic demands placed on English learners and take into account these considerations when they teach writing:

Topics. At first, students write about personal topics—their families, after-school activities, friends, and family trips, for example—but with experience, they move on to writing about books they're reading and topics they're learning in thematic units. To nudge ELs toward new writing topics, teachers offer suggestions about content-related topics, demonstrate how to write a book on a topic related to a book or unit, and create a collaborative book where each student contributes a page. Making this switch is especially important because English learners need to take advantage of writing as a tool for learning academic vocabulary and understanding the big ideas they're studying.

Talk. All students need to talk before they begin writing to activate background knowledge and develop ideas, but conversation is even more important for English learners because they're also learning English vocabulary and sentence structures. Teachers often make a list of academic words that they call a *word bank* as they talk with ELs during prewriting so the students will have the words available when they're writing. They also refer ELs to the word wall hanging in the classroom and encourage them to incorporate these words in the sentences they're writing.

Models. English learners often use a pattern book as a model for writing. Pattern books help students move beyond personal writing, and they're useful in teaching new sentence structures. For example, young children learn to write questions and answers as they make their own versions or innovations of Bill Martin Jr.'s *Brown Bear, Brown Bear, What Do You See?* (2010) and other books in the series, and older students use alphabet books, such as *The Extinct Alphabet Book* (Pallotta, 1993), as a pattern for writing about science and social studies topics.

Focus on Ideas. Many students value correctly spelled words and neat handwriting over the clear communication of ideas; but as they learn to use the writing process, most students gradually understand that the focus is on developing ideas before they reach the editing stage, and that messy rough drafts are a good thing because they reflect thoughtful drafting and revising. English learners, however, often struggle to accept the notion that developing ideas precedes mechanical correctness. Teachers demonstrate the writing process using interactive writing to nurture ELs' appreciation of the concept that writers often make their papers messy as they improve them.

If teachers address these considerations, ELs are better able to grow as writers along with their native English-speaking classmates.

 MONITOR: Check Your Understanding 2.2

The Writer's Craft

Specific techniques that writers use to capture readers' attention and convey meaning are referred to as the **writer's craft**. Establishing a clear voice, incorporating a useful organization, choosing precise words, and fashioning effective sentences are often mentioned as essential components of the writer's craft. Nearly 20 years ago, researchers at Education Northwest identified six writer's craft techniques, which they called *traits*: *ideas, organization, voice, word choice, sentence fluency,* and *conventions*. Later *presentation* was added as the seventh trait, but these qualities are still referred to as "the six traits" or "the six traits plus one." Two of the researchers who developed the six traits—Ruth Culham (2003, 2005, 2010) and Vicki Spandel (2008, 2009)—continue to design instruction and assessment procedures and share them with teachers. Students learn to incorporate the six traits into their writing.

Ideas

The ideas are the heart of a composition—the message and its meaning. Students pick an interesting idea and then narrow and develop it using main ideas and details. They choose an idea during prewriting and develop it as they draft and revise their writing. This trait includes these components:

- Choosing a topic
- Focusing the topic
- Identifying the genre
- Developing the topic

Students know that they've developed their ideas effectively when readers keep reading because the ideas are compelling.

Organization

The organization is the skeleton of the composition. Students hook the reader in the beginning, identify the purpose, present ideas logically, provide transitions between ideas, and end with a satisfying conclusion so that the important questions are answered. Organization includes these components:

- Crafting the lead
- Structuring the composition
- Providing transitions between ideas
- Ending with a satisfying conclusion

Students need to know how to organize their writing and learn ways to make their structure clear and logical for readers. It's during prewriting that they organize their ideas, and they follow their plans as they draft.

Voice

The writer's distinctive style is known as *voice*; it's what breathes life into a piece of writing. Culham (2003) calls voice "the writer's music coming out through the words" (p. 102). This trait includes these components:

- Choosing personally meaningful topics
- Writing with knowledge and passion
- Adopting a tone

Writers' personalities emerge through these components. During the drafting and revising stages, students create voice in their writing through the words they use, the sentences they craft, and the tone they adopt.

Word Choice

Careful word choice makes the meaning clear and the composition more interesting to read. As they craft their pieces, students learn to choose lively verbs and specific nouns, adjectives, and adverbs; create word pictures; and use idiomatic expressions. The goal is to find a fresh, original way to express the message while being concise. This trait links ideas with voice (Spandel, 2009), and includes these components:

- Painting a picture with words
- Choosing precise words
- Energizing writing with strong verbs
- Playing with words

Students focus on word choice as they draft and revise their writing.

Sentence Fluency

Sentence fluency is the rhythm and flow of language. Students vary the length and structure of their writing so that it has a natural cadence and is easy to read aloud. This trait includes these components:

- Achieving a rhythmic flow
- Constructing effective sentences
- Varying sentence patterns
- Breaking the rules

Students develop sentence fluency as they draft, revise, and edit their writing.

Conventions

The **conventions** are *spelling, capitalization, punctuation,* and *grammar*. In the editing stage, students proofread their compositions and correct spelling and grammar errors to make the writing easier to read. This trait includes these components:

- Spelling words conventionally
- Paragraphing accurately
- Punctuating effectively
- Capitalizing correctly
- Applying Standard English grammar and usage rules

Students who have a good grasp of these conventions correct most errors during editing to make their compositions "reader ready" (Culham, 2010, p. 261).

Presentation

Presentation focuses on making the final copy look good. Students use titles, headings, and white space to emphasize their purpose, and they integrate the words and illustrations and make clear the connections between them. This trait includes these components:

- Adding text features
- Arranging words and illustrations on the page
- Using legible handwriting
- Using word processing effectively

This trait is important during the publishing stage because the way the text is formatted enhances readers' ability to understand the message.

Booklist   The Six Traits

TRAIT	BOOKS
Ideas	Baylor, B. (1995). *I'm in charge of celebrations.* New York: Aladdin Books. PMU
	Moss, T. (1998). *I want to be.* New York: Puffin Books. PM
	Van Allsburg, C. (1996). *The mysteries of Harris Burdick.* Boston: Houghton Mifflin. MU
	Wyeth, S. D. (2002). *Something beautiful.* New York: Dragonfly Books. PMU
Organization	Brown, M. W. (2006). *Another important book.* New York: Harper Trophy. PM
	Fanelli, S. (2007). *My map book.* New York: Walker. PM
	Fleischman, P. (2004). *Seedfolks.* New York: Harper Trophy. MU
	Ryan, P. M. (2001). *Mice and beans.* New York: Scholastic. PM
Voice	Browne, A. (2001). *Voices in the park.* New York: Dorling Kindersley. PM
	Hesse, K. (2005). *Witness.* New York: Scholastic. U
	Ives, D. (2005). *Scrib.* New York: HarperCollins. MU
	Raschka, C. (2007). *Yo! Yes?* New York: Scholastic. P
Word Choice	Barrett, J. (2001). *Things that are the most in the world.* New York: Aladdin Books. PM
	Leedy, L., & Street, P. (2003). *There's a frog in my throat! 440 animal sayings a little bird told me.* New York: Holiday House. PMU
	Scieszka, J. (2001). *Baloney (Henry P.).* New York: Viking. M
	Shannon, G. (1999). *Tomorrow's alphabet.* New York: Harper Trophy. PM
Sentence Fluency	Aylesworth, J. (1995). *Old black fly.* New York: Henry Holt. P
	Grimes, N. (2002). *My man blue.* New York: Puffin Books. M
	Grossman, B. (1998). *My little sister ate one hare.* New York: Dragonfly Books. PM
	Locker, T. (2003). *Cloud dance.* San Diego: Voyager. M
Mechanics	Holm, J. L. (2007). *Middle school is worse than meatloaf: A year told through stuff.* New York: Atheneum. U
	Pattison, D. (2003). *The journey of Oliver K. Woodman.* San Diego: Harcourt Brace. M
	Pulver, R. (2003). *Punctuation takes a vacation.* New York: Holiday House. PMU
	Truss, L. (2006). *Eats, shoots & leaves: Why commas really do make a difference!* New York: Putnam. M

P = primary grades (K–2); M = middle grades (3–5); U = upper grades (6–8)

As students learn about the six traits, they internalize what good writers do. They learn to recognize good writing, develop a vocabulary for talking about writing, become better able to evaluate their own writing, and acquire strategies for improving the quality of their writing.

Teachers use minilessons, mentor texts, and guided practice activities to teach the components of each trait, and then students apply what they've learned in their own writing. Fletcher (2010) recommends teaching students about the writer's craft because it energizes their writing. Booklist: The Six Traits is a compilation of mentor texts that teachers use in teaching the traits.

MONITOR: Check Your Understanding 2.3

Reading and Writing Are Reciprocal Processes

Reading and writing are reciprocal; they're both constructive, meaning-making processes. Researchers have found that reading leads to better writing, and writing has the same effect on reading (Spivey, 1997). Not surprisingly, they've also learned that integrating instruction improves both reading and writing (Tierney & Shanahan, 1996). It's possible that students use the same type of thinking for both reading and writing (Braunger & Lewis, 2006).

Comparing the Two Processes

The reading and writing processes have comparable activities at each stage (Butler & Turbill, 1984). A comparison of the two processes is shown in Figure 2–7. Notice, for example, the similarities between the activities in the third stage of reading and writing—responding and revising, respectively. Fitzgerald (1989) analyzed these two activities and concluded that they draw on the same reader-writer-text interactions. Similar analyses can also be made for the other stages.

Tierney (1983) explains that reading and writing involve concurrent, complex transactions between writers as readers and readers as writers. It seems natural that writers read other authors' books for ideas and to learn about organizing their writing, and they also read and reread their own writing as they revise to communicate more effectively. The quality of these reading experiences seems closely tied to success in writing. Thinking of readers as writers may be more difficult, but readers participate in many of the same activities that writers use—activating background knowledge, setting purposes, determining importance, monitoring, repairing, and evaluating.

Classroom Connections

Many classroom activities integrate reading and writing. Making connections between reading and writing is a natural part of classroom life. Students read and then write or write and then read: They write reading log entries after reading to deepen their understanding, for example, or they make graphic organizers to organize the information they're reading in a content area textbook or nonfiction book. Similarly, they read rough drafts aloud to make sure they flow and then read them to classmates to get feedback on how well they're communicating, or they use a structural pattern from a poem they've read in one they're writing. Shanahan (1988) outlined these

FIGURE 2–7   A Comparison of the Reading and Writing Processes

	WHAT READERS DO	**WHAT WRITERS DO**
Stage 1	**Prereading** Readers use knowledge about • the topic • reading • genres • cueing systems	**Prewriting** Writers use knowledge about • the topic • writing • genres • cueing systems
Stage 2	**Reading** Readers • use word-identification strategies • use comprehension strategies • monitor reading • create meaning	**Drafting** Writers • use writing strategies • use meaning-making strategies • monitor writing • create meaning
Stage 3	**Responding** Readers • respond to the text • deepen meaning • clarify misunderstandings • expand ideas	**Revising** Writers • respond to the text • deepen meaning • clarify misunderstandings • expand ideas
Stage 4	**Exploring** Readers • examine words and literary language • explore structural elements • compare the text to others	**Editing** Writers • identify and correct mechanical errors • review paragraph and sentence structure
Stage 5	**Applying** Readers • create projects • share projects with classmates • reflect on the reading process • feel success • want to read again	**Publishing** Writers • make the final copy of their compositions • share their compositions with genuine audiences • reflect on the writing process • feel success • want to write again

guidelines for connecting reading and writing so that students develop a clearer understanding of literacy:

- Involve students in daily reading and writing experiences.
- Introduce the reading and writing processes in kindergarten.
- Plan instruction that reflects the developmental nature of reading and writing.
- Make the reading–writing connection explicit to students.
- Emphasize both the processes and the products of reading and writing.
- Set clear purposes for reading and writing.
- Teach reading and writing through authentic literacy experiences.

It's not enough, however, for students to see themselves as both readers and writers; they need to grasp the relationships between the two roles and move flexibly between them. Readers think like writers to understand the author's purpose and viewpoint, for instance, and writers assume alternative viewpoints as potential readers.

 MONITOR: Check Your Understanding 2.4

Literacy Strategies

Reading and writing are complex, thoughtful processes involving both strategies and skills. Strategies represent the thinking that students do as they read and write; in contrast, skills are quick, automatic behaviors that don't require any thought. For example, readers use the connecting strategy to compare a story to their own lives, the world around them, and other books they've read. They're actively thinking as they make connections; however, noticing quotation marks that signal a character's dialogue is a skill because students don't have to think about what these punctuation marks are signaling—they recognize their meaning automatically. The terms *strategy* and *skill* can be confusing; sometimes they're considered synonyms, but they're not. It's important to clarify the distinctions between the two.

Strategies are deliberate, goal-directed actions (Afflerbach, Pearson, & Paris, 2008). Readers and writers exercise control in choosing appropriate strategies, using them flexibly, and monitoring their effectiveness. Strategies are linked with motivation. Afflerbach and his colleagues explain that "strategic readers feel confident that they can monitor and improve their own reading so they have both knowledge and motivation to succeed" (p. 370). Strategies reflect the information processing theory. In contrast, **skills** are automatic actions that occur without deliberate control or conscious awareness; the emphasis is on their effortless and accurate use. Skills reflect the behavioral theory, and they're used in the same way, no matter the reading or writing situation.

Reading Strategies

Comprehension strategies are probably the best known type, but readers use strategies throughout the reading process:

Decoding Strategies. Students use strategies, such as using phonic and morphemic analysis, to identify unfamiliar words.

Word-Learning Strategies. Students apply strategies, such as analyzing word parts, to figure out the meaning of unfamiliar words.

Comprehension Strategies. Students use strategies, such as predicting, drawing inferences, and visualizing, to understand what they're reading.

Study Strategies. Students apply strategies, such as taking notes and questioning, to learn information when they're reading content area textbooks.

These strategies highlight the kinds of thinking that students engage in while they're reading.

Digital Reading Strategies

Digital texts are different than books (Castek, Bevans-Mangelson, & Goldstone, 2006). Print materials are linear and sequential, but online texts are a unique genre with these characteristics:

Nonlinearity. Because digital text lacks the familiar linear organization of books, readers impose a structure that fits their needs and reconfigure the organization, when necessary.

Multiple Modalities. Online texts are multimodal, integrating words, images, and sound to create meaning, so readers interpret each mode and understand how it contributes to the overall meaning.

Intertextuality. Because many related texts are available on the Internet, they influence and shape each other. As students read these texts, they prioritize, evaluate, and synthesize the information being presented.

Interactivity. Webpages often include interactive features that engage readers and allow them to customize their searches, link to other websites, play games, and view video clips.

Because of these features, reading online requires students to become proficient in new ways of accessing and comprehending information.

Students learn to use these four digital reading strategies:

Navigating. Students navigate the Internet to search for and locate information.

Coauthoring. Students coauthor online texts as they impose an organization on the information they're reading.

Evaluating. Students evaluate the accuracy, relevance, and quality of information on webpages.

Synthesizing. Students synthesize information from multiple texts.

Literacy in the 21st century involves more than teaching students to read books and write using paper and pencil; it's essential that teachers prepare their students to use digital technologies successfully (Karchmer, Mallette, Kara-Soteriou, & Leu, 2005).

Writing Strategies

Writing strategies are like reading strategies: They're tools students use deliberately to craft effective compositions. Students apply many of the same strategies for both reading and writing, such as activating background knowledge, questioning, repairing, and evaluating, and they also use other strategies that are specific to writing. Dean (2006) explains that using the writing process makes writers more strategic, and writers use a variety of strategies at each stage:

Prewriting Strategies. Students use prewriting strategies, including organizing, to develop ideas before beginning to write.

Drafting Strategies. Students apply drafting strategies, including narrowing the topic and providing examples, to focus on ideas while writing the first draft.

Revising Strategies. Students use revising strategies, including detecting problems, elaborating ideas, and combining sentences, to communicate their ideas more effectively.

Editing Strategies. Students apply strategies, including proofreading, to identify and correct spelling and other mechanical errors.

Publishing Strategies. Students use strategies, including designing the layout, to prepare their final copies and share them with classmates and other authentic audiences.

Students use these writing strategies purposefully as they draft and refine their writing.

Strategy Instruction

Students need explicit instruction on strategies because they don't acquire the knowledge through reading and writing (Dowhower, 1999; Pressley, 2000). Teachers usually provide strategy instruction during minilessons where they explain the topic, provide examples, have students participate in guided practice activities, and then apply what they're learning in authentic reading and writing activities.

During minilessons, teachers provide three types of information about a strategy:

🌀 Declarative knowledge—what the strategy does
🌀 Procedural knowledge—how to use the strategy
🌀 Conditional knowledge—when to apply the strategy (Baker & Brown, 1984)

The questioning strategy, for instance, is a comprehension strategy that students use to ask themselves questions while they're reading. They use it to direct their reading, monitor whether they're understanding, and construct meaning (declarative knowledge). They ask themselves questions such as "What's going to happen next?" "How does this relate to what I know about?" and "Does this make sense?" (procedural knowledge). Students use this strategy again and again while they're reading (conditional knowledge).

Teachers use minilessons to teach students about strategies. They explain the strategy and model its use, and then students practice using it with teacher guidance and supervision before using it independently. Through this instruction, students develop metacognitive awareness, their ability to think about their strategy use (Paris, Wasik, & Turner, 1996).

Teachers demonstrate the thought processes readers and writers use as they read and write by using **think-alouds** (Wilhelm, 2001). Teachers think aloud or explain what they're thinking so that students become more aware of how capable readers and writers think; in the process, students also learn to think aloud about their use of strategies. When they're reading, students set a purpose for reading, predict what will happen next, make connections, ask questions, summarize what's happened so far, draw inferences, evaluate the text, and make other comments that reflect their thinking. Think-alouds are valuable both when teachers model them for students and when students engage in them themselves. When students use think-alouds, they become more thoughtful, strategic readers and writers and improve their ability to monitor their reading and writing.

Students record their strategy use during reading on small self-stick notes, which teachers distribute and explain how to use. Students can focus on their use of a single strategy or a group of strategies. They write comments about the strategies on the self-stick notes while they're reading and place them in the margins of the pages so they can locate them when the book is closed. Afterward, students share their notes and talk about the strategies they used in a discussion with classmates or in a conference with the teacher.

To assess your knowledge about strategy instruction, use the Teacher Checklist: How do I teach strategies?

 **MONITOR: Check Your Understanding 2.5**

In this minilesson, Mrs. Ockey thinks aloud about how she developed her story. How did she help her second graders learn to expand a single, undeveloped paragraph into multiple paragraphs?

TEACHER *Checklist*

How do I teach strategies?

○ Do I teach that strategies are problem-solving tactics?
○ Do I address Standards in my instruction?
○ Do I teach strategies in minilessons using explanations, demonstrations, think-alouds, and practice activities?
○ Do I provide step-by-step explanations and modeling so that students understand what the strategy does, and how and when to use it?
○ Do I hang student-made charts of strategies in the classroom, and encourage students to refer to them when they're reading and writing?
○ Do I provide both guided and independent practice opportunities so that students apply the strategy in new situations?
○ Do I have students apply the strategy in activities across the curriculum as well as in literacy activities?
○ Do I ask students to reflect on their use of strategies?

Review

TEACHING THE READING AND WRITING PROCESSES

Effective teachers demonstrate their responsibility and commitment to ensuring that their students are successful when they organize instruction using the reading and writing processes presented in this chapter, these points in particular:

2.1 Teachers use the reading process—*prereading, reading, responding, exploring,* and *applying*—to ensure that students comprehend texts they read.

2.2 Teachers teach students how to use the writing process—*prewriting, drafting, revising, editing,* and *publishing*—to write and refine their compositions.

2.3 Teachers teach students about the writer's craft, including the six traits.

2.4 Teachers integrate reading and writing because they're reciprocal meaning-making processes.

2.5 Teachers teach students to use strategies to organize, direct, and problem-solve as they read and write.

✓ EVALUATE & REFLECT

Apply what you've learned about teaching reading and writing. The questions ask you to collect and analyze data, and report the results. Your response should meet academic standards and adhere to Standard English conventions.

1. Observe in a K–8 literacy classroom to see how a teacher applies the reading process. In your response, explain what you've learned about teaching reading, and address these points:

    🐚 the classroom community
    🐚 the teacher's instruction
    🐚 the activities students participate in
    🐚 the teacher's plan for any stages not observed

2. Prepare to teach a series of minilessons on the writer's craft. Choose one of six traits, collect at least three mentor texts to use in teaching that trait, and create lesson plans for a series of three 15-to 20-minute lessons using the minilesson procedure presented in the Compendium of Instructional Procedures. Your lesson plans should include these points:

    🐚 develop students' knowledge about the trait
    🐚 incorporate three mentor texts
    🐚 identify the Standards addressed in the minilessons
    🐚 follow the minilesson procedure

    In your response, name the trait you chose, list the mentor texts, and summarize the minilessons, explaining how they address the points listed above.

3. Interview three students of varying grade levels to discover what they know about reading strategies. Ask questions to examine these points:

    🐚 students' understanding of the word *strategy*
    🐚 which reading strategies students can name
    🐚 how students use strategies when they're reading
    🐚 how students learned about reading strategies

In your response, describe the students you interviewed, and explain what they've learned about reading strategies. Address each of the four points.

4. Observe K–8 students who are involved in each of the five types of reading described in Figure 2–2. In your response, list your observations under the heads found in Figure 2–2, and draw conclusions about the usefulness of the reading types.

5. Compare a stage in the reading process to the similar stage in the writing process; Responding/Revising were compared in the chapter, so choose one of the other four stages to compare. In your response, describe the reading process stage and the writing process stage, make comparisons, and draw conclusions about their similarities and differences.

REFERENCES

Afflerbach, P., Pearson, P. D., & Paris, S. G. (2008). Clarifying differences between reading skills and reading strategies. *The Reading Teacher, 61*, 364–373.

Allen, J. (2000). *Yellow brick road: Shared and guided paths to independent reading, 4–12*. Portland, ME: Stenhouse.

Allen, J. (2002). *On the same page: Shared reading beyond the primary grades*. Portland, ME: Stenhouse.

Almond, D. (1998). *Skellig*. New York: Laurel Leaf.

Angelillo, J. (2008). *Whole-class teaching: Minilessons and more*. Portsmouth, NH: Heinemann.

Applebee, A. N., & Langer, J. A. (1983). Instructional scaffolding: Reading and writing and natural language activities. *Language Arts, 60*, 168–175.

Baker, L., & Brown, A. (1984). Metacognitive skills of reading. In P. D. Pearson, M. Kamil, P. Mosenthal, & R. Barr (Eds.), *Handbook of reading research* (pp. 353–394). New York: Longman.

Blanton, W. E., Wood, K. D., & Moorman, G. B. (1990). The role of purpose in reading instruction. *The Reading Teacher, 43*, 486–493.

Boyles, N. (December 2012/January 2013). Common Core: Now what? *Educational Leadership, 70*(4), 36–41.

Braunger, J., & Lewis, J. P. (2006). *Building a knowledge base in reading* (2nd ed.). Newark, DE: International Reading Association/National Council of Teachers of English.

Butler, A., & Turbill, J. (1984). *Towards a reading-writing classroom*. Portsmouth, NH: Heinemann.

Calkins, L. M. (1983). *Lessons from a child: On the teaching and learning of writing*. Portsmouth, NH: Heinemann.

Cappellini, M. (2005). *Balancing reading and language learning: A resource for teaching English language learners, K–5*. York, ME: Stenhouse.

Castek, J., Bevans-Mangelson, J., & Goldstone, B. (2006). Reading adventures online: Five ways to introduce the new literacies of the Internet through children's literature. *The Reading Teacher, 59*, 714–728.

Christenson, T. A. (2002). *Supporting struggling writers in the elementary classroom*. Newark, DE: International Reading Association.

Culham, R. (2003). *6 + 1 traits of writing, grades 3 and up*. New York: Scholastic.

Culham, R. (2005). *6 + 1 traits of writing: The complete guide for the primary grades*. New York: Scholastic.

Culham, R. (2010). *Traits of writing: The complete guide for middle school*. New York: Scholastic.

Dalton, B. (2013). Engaging children in close reading. *The Reading Teacher, 66*, 642–649.

Dean, D. (2006). *Strategic writing*. Urbana, IL: National Council of Teachers of English.

Donovan, C. A., & Smolkin, L. B. (2002). Children's genre knowledge: An examination of K–5 students' performance on multiple tasks providing differing levels of scaffolding. *Reading Research Quarterly, 37*, 428–465.

Dowhower, S. L. (1999). Supporting a strategic stance in the classroom: A comprehension framework for helping teachers help students to be strategic. *The Reading Teacher, 52*, 672–688.

Faigley, L., & Witte, S. (1981). Analyzing revision. *College Composition and Communication, 32*, 400–410.

Fisher, D., Flood, J., Lapp, D., & Frey, N. (2004). Interactive read-alouds: Is there a common set of implementation practices? *The Reading Teacher, 58*, 8–17.

Fitzgerald, J. (1989). Enhancing two related thought processes: Revision in writing and critical thinking. *The Reading Teacher, 43*, 42–48.

Fletcher, R. (2010). *Pyrotechnics on the page: Playful craft that sparks writing*. York, ME: Stenhouse.

Fountas, I. C., & Pinnell, G. S. (1996). *Guided reading: Good first teaching for all children*. Portsmouth, NH: Heinemann.

Friedland, E. S., & Truesdell, K. S. (2004). Kids reading together. *The Reading Teacher, 58*, 76–83.

Graves, D. H. (1983). *Writing: Teachers and children at work*. Exeter, NH: Heinemann.

Holdaway, D. (1979). *The foundations of literacy*. Portsmouth, NH: Heinemann.

Karchmer, R. A., Mallette, M. H., Kara-Soteriou, J., & Leu, D. J., Jr. (Eds.). (2005). *Innovative approaches to literacy education: Using the Internet to support new literacies*. Newark, DE: International Reading Association.

Karchmer-Klein, R. (2007). Best practices in using the Internet to support writing. In S. Graham, C. A. McArthur, & J. Fitzgerald (Eds.), *Best practices in writing instruction* (pp. 222–241). New York: Guilford Press.

Labbo, L. D. (2005). Fundamental qualities of effective Internet literacy instruction: An exploration of worthwhile classroom practices. In R. A. Karchmer, M. H. Mallette, J. Kara-Soteriou, & D. J. Leu, Jr. (Eds.), *Innovative approaches to literacy education: Using the Internet to support new literacies* (pp. 165–179). Newark, DE: International Reading Association.

Langer, J. A. (1985). Children's sense of genre. *Written Communication, 2*, 157–187.

Lowry, L. (2006). *The giver*. New York: Delacorte.

Martin, Bill, Jr. (2010). *Brown bear, brown bear, what do you see?* New York: Holt.

McGowan, M. (2005). My Internet projects and other online resources for the literacy classroom. In R. A. Karchmer, M. H. Mallette, J. Kara-Soteriou, & D. J. Leu, Jr. (Eds.), *Innovative approaches to literacy education: Using the Internet to support new literacies* (pp. 85–102). Newark, DE: International Reading Association.

McNabb, M. L. (2006). *Literacy learning in networked classrooms: Using the Internet with middle-level students.* Newark, DE: International Reading Association.

Murray, D. H. (1982). *Learning by teaching.* Montclair, NJ: Boynton/Cook.

National Reading Panel. (2000). *Teaching children to read: An evidence-based assessment of the scientific research literature on reading and its implications for reading instruction.* Washington, DC: National Institute of Child Health and Human Development.

Pallotta, J. (1993). *The extinct alphabet book.* Watertown, MA: Charlesbridge.

Paris, S. G., Wasik, D. A., & Turner, J. C. (1996). The development of strategic readers. In R. Barr, M. L. Kamil, P. B. Mosenthal, & P. D. Pearson (Eds.), *Handbook of reading research* (Vol. 2, pp. 609–640). Mahwah, NJ: Erlbaum.

Peterson. R., & Eeds, M. (2007). *Grand conversations: Literature groups in action* (Updated ed.). New York: Scholastic.

Pressley, M. (2000). What should comprehension instruction be instruction of? In M. L. Kamil, P. B. Mosenthal, P. D. Pearson, & R. Barr (Eds.), *Handbook of reading research* (Vol. 3, pp. 545–561). Mahwah, NJ: Erlbaum.

Rasinski, T. V. (2003). *The fluent reader.* New York: Scholastic.

Richardson, J. (2009). *The next step in guided reading: Focused assessments and targeted lessons for helping every student become a better reader.* New York: Scholastic.

Rosenblatt, L. (2005). *Making meaning with texts: Selected essays.* Portsmouth, NH: Heinemann.

Rosenblatt, L. M. (2004). The transactional theory of reading and writing. In R. B. Ruddell & N. J. Unrau (Eds.), *Theoretical models and processes of reading* (5th ed., pp. 1363–1398). Newark, DE: International Reading Association.

Shanahan, T. (1988). The reading-writing relationship: Seven instructional principles. *The Reading Teacher, 41,* 636–647.

Silvernail, D. L., & Gritter, A. K. (2007). *Maine's middle school laptop program: Creating better writers.* Gorham, ME: University of Southern Maine, Maine Education Policy Research Institute.

Spandel, V. (2008). *Creating young writers: Using the 6 traits to enrich the writing process in primary classrooms* (2nd ed.). Boston: Allyn & Bacon/Pearson.

Spandel, V. (2009). *Creating writers through 6-trait writing assessment and instruction* (5th ed.). Boston: Allyn & Bacon/Pearson.

Spivey, N. (1997). *The constructivist metaphor: Reading, writing, and the making of meaning.* New York: Academic Press.

Tierney, R. J. (1983). Writer-reader transactions: Defining the dimensions of negotiation. In P. L. Stock (Ed.), *Forum: Essays on theory and practice in the teaching of writing* (pp. 147–151). Upper Montclair, NJ: Boynton/Cook.

Tierney, R. J., & Shanahan, T. (1996). Research on the reading-writing relationship: Interactions, transactions, and outcomes. In R. Barr, M. L. Kamil, P. B. Mosenthal, & P. D. Pearson (Eds.), *Handbook of reading research* (Vol. 2, pp. 246–280). Mahwah, NJ: Erlbaum.

Weber, C. (2002). *Publishing with students: A comprehensive guide.* Portsmouth, NH: Heinemann.

Wilhelm, J. D. (2001). *Improving comprehension with think-aloud strategies.* New York: Scholastic.

Yaden, D. B., Jr. (1988). Understanding stories through repeated read-alouds: How many does it take? *The Reading Teacher, 41,* 556–560.

Chapter 3

Assessing Literacy Development

PLAN: Preview the Learning Outcomes

After studying this chapter, you'll be prepared to respond to these topics:

3.1 Explain how teachers link instruction and assessment.

3.2 Discuss how teachers use diagnostic tests to determine students' reading levels and diagnose their strengths and weaknesses.

3.3 Explain the role of high-stakes testing in literacy instruction and assessment.

3.4 Describe how teachers use portfolios to assess students' progress toward meeting grade-level standards.

Mrs. McNeal Does Second-Quarter Assessments. The end of the quarter is approaching, and Mrs. McNeal is assessing her first graders. She collects a variety of assessment data about her students' reading, writing, and spelling development, which she uses to document children's achievement, verify that they're meeting state standards, determine report card grades, and make instructional plans for the third quarter.

Today, Mrs. McNeal assesses Ethan, who's 6½ years old. He's a quiet, well-behaved child who regularly completes his work. The teacher has a collection of Ethan's writing, but she wants to assess his reading level. At the beginning of the school year, Mrs. McNeal considered him an average student, but in the past month, his reading has accelerated.

DETERMINING ETHAN'S INSTRUCTIONAL READING LEVEL. Mrs. McNeal regularly takes **running records** as she listens to children reread familiar books to monitor their ability to recognize high-frequency words, decode unfamiliar words, and use reading strategies. In addition, Mrs. McNeal assesses each child's instructional reading level using the Developmental Reading Assessment 2e PLUS (DRA2+), an assessment kit available from Pearson Instructional Resources that includes 45 leveled books and 95 leveled passages arranged from kindergarten to fourth grade reading levels, with an accompanying iPad and app that teachers use to make management easier.

At the beginning of the school year, most of Mrs. McNeal's first graders were reading at Level 4; by midyear, they should be reading at Level 8; and by the end of the school year, they're expected to reach Level 18. Like many of his classmates, Ethan was reading at Level 4 in August, and at the end of the first quarter, he was reading at Level 8. Now Mrs. McNeal decides to test him at Level 16 because he's reading a book at that level in his guided reading group.

Ethan reads *The Pot of Gold* (2001), a Level 16 book in the DRA2+ assessment kit. The book recounts an Irish folktale about a man named Grumble who makes an elf show him where his pot of gold is hidden. Grumble marks the spot by tying a scarf around a nearby tree branch and goes to get a shovel with which to dig up the gold. He admonishes the elf not to move the scarf, and he doesn't; instead he ties other scarves on nearby trees so that Grumble can't find the elf's gold. Mrs. McNeal takes a running record while Ethan reads; check the figure A Running Record Scoring Sheet that the teacher completed.

As indicated on the running record sheet, Ethan makes 14 errors but self-corrects 2 of them; his accuracy rate is 95%. Mrs. McNeal analyzes Ethan's errors and concludes that he overdepends on visual (or phonological) cues while ignoring semantic ones. Of the 12 errors, only one—*Grumply* for *Grumble*—makes sense in the sentence. When Ethan retells the story, he shows that he comprehends the big idea, but his retelling isn't especially strong: He tells the beginning and the end of the story but leaves out important details in the middle; however, he does make interesting connections between the story and his own life. Mrs. McNeal concludes that Level 16 is his instructional level and that his ability to read words is stronger than his comprehension.

Mrs. McNeal makes notes about Ethan's instructional priorities for the next quarter. She'll focus on comprehension and teach him more about story structure, and help him use semantic cues to support visual ones. She'll encourage him to structure his oral and written retellings in three parts—beginning, middle, and end—and to include more details. She also decides to introduce Ethan to easy chapter books, such as Tedd Arnold's Fly Guy series about the friendship between the fly and his friend Guy and Cynthia Rylant's Henry and Mudge series about the adventures of a boy named Henry and his dog, Mudge.

TESTING ETHAN'S KNOWLEDGE OF HIGH-FREQUENCY WORDS. Mrs. McNeal's goal for her first graders is to recognize at least 75 of the 100 high-frequency words by the end of the school year. In August, most children could read at least 12 words; Ethan read 16 correctly. Today, Mrs. McNeal asks Ethan again to read the list of 100 high-frequency words, which is arranged in order of difficulty. She expects that he'll be able to read 50 to 60 of the words and when he misses 5 in a row, she'll stop, but Ethan surprises her and reads the entire list! He misses only these 6 words: *don't, how, there, very, were,* and *would.* Ethan's high score reflects his results on the running record: He's a very good word reader.

CHECKING ETHAN'S ABILITY TO WRITE WORDS. Several days ago, Mrs. McNeal administered the "Words I Know" Test to the class, asking the children to write as many words as they could in 10 minutes without copying from classroom charts. In August, most children could spell 15 to 20 words correctly; Mrs. McNeal's goal is that they be able to write 50 words by the end of the school year. Ethan wrote 22 words in August, and on the recent test, he wrote 50 words, spelling them correctly, including *the, hat, bat, come, go, going, dog, dogs, God, cat, cowboys, from, fight, night, sun, run, fish, starfish, fin, trees, what,* and *you.* Mrs. McNeal reviews the list of words and notices that most are one-syllable words with short vowels, such as *cat* and *fin,* but he's beginning to write words with more complex spellings, such as *what, come,* and *night,* words with

A RUNNING RECORD SCORING SHEET

Name __Ethan_____ Date ___Jan. 17_____

Level __16__ Title ___The Pot of Gold_____ Easy (Instructional) Hard

Running Record	E	SC	E	SC
✓ ✓ ✓ ✓ ✓ ✓ ✓ ✓ grumply ✓ ✓ ✓ ✓ ✓ ✓ ✓ **2** Grumble|T ___ |A ✓ ✓ ✓ ✓ ✓ ✓ ✓ always|T ✓ ✓ ✓ ✓ ✓ ✓ ✓ ✓ ✓ ✓ ✓ ✓	1 1		m s Ⓥ	
✓ ✓ ✓ ✓ ✓ ✓ ✓ ✓ ✓ ✓ ✓ ✓ ✓ ✓ ✓ did not| **3** ✓ ✓ didn't| ✓ ✓ ✓ ✓ ✓ ✓ ✓ ✓ ✓ ✓ ✓ ✓ ✓ ✓ ✓ ✓ ✓ ✓ ✓	1		Ⓜ Ⓢ v	
✓ ✓ ✓ ✓ ✓ ✓ ✓ **4** ✓ ✓ ✓ ✓ ✓ ✓ ✓ ✓ ✓ ✓				
✓ ✓ ✓ ✓ ✓ ✓ ✓ ✓ ✓ ✓ ✓ ✓ ✓ I | make| ✓ ✓ ✓ **5** I'll| move| safr| ✓ ✓ ✓ ✓ ✓ or| ✓ ✓ ✓ scarf| of|	1 1 1 1		Ⓜ Ⓢ Ⓥ Ⓜ Ⓢ Ⓥ m s Ⓥ m s Ⓥ	
✓ ✓ ✓ ✓ ✓ ✓ me|sc self| ✓ ✓ ✓ my| scarf| **6** ✓ ✓ ✓ ✓ ✓ ✓ ✓ ✓	1	1	m s Ⓥ m s Ⓥ	Ⓜ Ⓢ Ⓥ
✓ ✓ ✓ ✓ ✓ ✓ ✓ **7** ✓ ✓ ✓ ✓ ✓ ✓ ✓ ✓ ✓ ✓ ✓ ✓ ✓ ✓				
✓ ✓ ✓ ✓ ✓ ✓ ✓ **8** ✓ ✓ ✓ ✓ ✓ ✓ ✓ ✓ ✓ ✓				
✓ ✓ ✓ take| ✓ scafer| ✓ ✓ ✓ **9** taken| scarf| ✓ ✓ ✓ ✓ ✓ ✓ ✓ ✓	1 1		Ⓜ s Ⓥ m s Ⓥ	
✓ ✓ ✓ ✓ ✓ ✓ ✓ ✓ ✓ they |sc ___ |R ✓ ✓ ✓ ✓ ✓ **10** that| ✓| maybe| sit| ✓ ✓ ✓ ✓ ✓ may| still|	1 1	1	m s Ⓥ m s Ⓥ m s Ⓥ	Ⓜ Ⓢ Ⓥ

Scoring	Picture Walk
12/266 95% accuracy	Gets gist of story
Types of Errors: M S Ⓥ Overdependent on V cues	Oral Reading Reads fluently
Self-correction Rate 1:5	Retelling/Questions Tells BME but middle is brief

ETHAN'S JOURNAL ENTRY

I ate piza for dinr My dad tok me
to Ron Tab. It was haf huyan and
haf peprone. We bot the lf ors home.

inflectional endings, such as *going*, and two-syllable words, such as *cowboys*. She concludes that Ethan is making very good progress, in both the number of words he can write and the complexity of the spelling patterns he's using.

SCORING ETHAN'S COMPOSITIONS. Mrs. McNeal looks through Ethan's journal and chooses several samples written in the past 3 weeks to score; check the figure Ethan's Journal Entry. Here's the text with conventional spelling and punctuation:

> *I ate pizza for dinner. My dad took me to Round Table. It was half Hawaiian and half pepperoni. We brought the leftovers home.*

Using the school district's 6-point rubric, Mrs. McNeal scores the composition as a 4. A score of 5 is considered grade-level at the end of the school year, and Mrs. McNeal believes that Ethan will reach that level before then. She notices that he's writing several sentences, even though he sometimes omits a word or two and often omits punctuation at the ends of sentences. Mrs. McNeal plans to talk to him about rereading his writing to catch any omissions, adding punctuation marks, and correcting misspelled words.

MEASURING ETHAN'S WORD KNOWLEDGE. The first graders take a dictation test each week. On Monday, they craft two sentences and write them on a chart displayed in the classroom. They practice writing the sentences on small whiteboards each day, and during **minilessons**, Mrs. McNeal draws their attention to high-frequency words, the phonetic features of various words, and capitalization and punctuation rules applied in the sentences. Last week's sentences focused on *The Magic School Bus Lost in the Solar System* (Cole, 1993), a book Mrs. McNeal read aloud:

> *Their bus turned into a rocket ship. They wanted to visit all of the planets.*

After practicing the sentences all week, Mrs. McNeal dictates them for children to write on Friday. She tells them to try to spell words correctly and to write all the sounds they hear in the words they don't know how to spell. Ethan wrote:

> *The bus turd into a rocket ship they wande to vist all of the planis.*

Ethan spelled 10 of the 15 words correctly and included 46 of 51 sounds in his writing. He also omitted the period at the end of the first sentence and failed to capitalize the first word in the second sentence.

Mrs. McNeal uses this test to check children's ability to apply phonics knowledge and spell high-frequency words. Ethan spelled most of the high-frequency words correctly, except that he wrote *the* for *their*; his other errors involved the second syllable of the word or inflectional endings. Mrs. McNeal concludes that Ethan is making good progress in learning to spell high-frequency words and that he's ready to learn more about two-syllable words and inflectional endings.

GRADING ETHAN'S LITERACY ACHIEVEMENT. Having collected and analyzed these data, Mrs. McNeal completes Ethan's report card. Her students receive separate number grades in reading, writing, and spelling: The grades range from 1, not meeting grade-level standards, to 4, exceeding standards. Ethan receives a 3 in reading, writing, and spelling; a score of 3 means that he's meeting grade-level standards. Even though his reading level is higher, his dependence on visual cues and his weak comprehension keep him at the third level in reading.

 STANDARDS CHECK!

Mrs. McNeal addressed the Common Core State Standards as she assessed Ethan's reading and writing achievement in the vignette you've just read. Review the first grade literacy Standards document online at http://www.corestandards.org/ELA-Literacy, and identify the Standards that Mrs. McNeal addressed through her assessment activities. Create your list, and compare it with Mrs. McNeal's.

Assessment has become a priority in 21st-century schools. School district, state, and federal education agencies have increased their demands for accountability, and today, most students take annual high-stakes tests to measure their achievement (International Reading Association & National Council of Teachers of English, 2009). Teachers collect more assessment data now, and do it more frequently, and they use the information to make instructional decisions, as Mrs. McNeal demonstrated in the vignette. Researchers explain that "a system of frequent assessment, coupled with strong content standards and effective reading instruction, helps ensure that teachers' . . . approaches are appropriate to each student's needs" (Kame'enui, 2000, p. 1). By linking assessment and instruction, teachers improve students' learning and their teaching.

The terms **assessment** and **evaluation** are often considered interchangeable, but they're not. *Assessment* is formative; it's ongoing and provides immediate feedback to improve teaching and learning. It's usually authentic, based on the literacy activities students are engaged in. In contrast, *evaluation* is summative; it's final, generally administered at the end of a unit or a school year to judge quality. Tests are the most common type of evaluation, and they're used to compare one student's achievement against that of other students or against grade-level standards.

Classroom Assessment

Classroom assessment drives instruction, ensures that students are making adequate progress, determines the effectiveness of instruction, and documents students' achievement. Every day, teachers use a combination of assessment tools to collect meaningful information about what students know and do (Afflerbach, 2007; Kuhs, Johnson, Agruso, & Monrad, 2001). Assessment involves four steps—planning, monitoring, evaluating, and reflecting. Each step serves a different purpose, so teachers need to integrate all of the steps into their literacy programs.

Step 1: Planning for Assessment

Teachers plan for assessment at the same time they're planning for instruction. They think about these questions and choose the assessment tools they'll use to get answers:

- Do students have adequate background knowledge and vocabulary about the topic to be taught?
- Are any students struggling to understand?
- Are students completing assignments?
- Are students exhibiting good work habits?
- Are students working responsibly with classmates?
- Have students learned the concepts that have been taught?
- Can students apply what they've learned in authentic literacy projects?

By planning for assessment before they begin teaching, teachers are prepared to use assessment tools wisely; otherwise, classroom assessment often turns out to be haphazard and impromptu.

Step 2: Monitoring Students' Progress

Monitoring is vital to student success (Braunger & Lewis, 2006). Teachers monitor students' learning every day and use the results to make instructional decisions. As they monitor students' progress through observations, conferences, and other informal, formative procedures, teachers learn about students and their individual strengths and weaknesses and about the impact of their instruction.

OBSERVATIONS. Effective teachers are "kid watchers," a term Yetta Goodman (1978) coined to describe the "direct and informal observation of students" (p. 37). To be effective kid watchers, teachers must focus on what students do as they read or write, not on whether they're behaving properly or working quietly. Of course, little learning can occur in disruptive situations, but during these observations, the focus is on literacy, not behavior. Observations should be planned: Teachers usually observe a specific group of students each day so that over the course of a week, they watch everyone in the class.

ANECDOTAL NOTES. Teachers write brief notes in notebooks or on self-stick notes as they observe students (Boyd-Batstone, 2004). The most useful notes describe specific events, report rather than evaluate, and relate the events to other information about the student. Teachers make notes about students' reading and writing activities, the questions students ask, and the strategies and skills they use fluently and those they don't understand; these records monitor and document students' growth and pinpoint problem areas to address in future minilessons. A teacher's notes about sixth grade students participating in a literature circle on *Bunnicula: A Rabbit-Tale of Mystery* (Howe & Howe, 2006) appear in the Assessment Snapshot: Anecdotal Notes About a Literature Circle.

ASSESSMENT *Snapshot*

Anecdotal Notes About a Literature Circle

March 6

Met with the <u>Bunnicula: A Rabbit-Tale of Mystery</u> literature circle as they started reading the book. They have their reading, writing, and discussion schedule set. Sari questioned how a dog could write the book. We reread the Editor's Note. She asked if Harold really wrote the book. She's the only one confused in the group. Is she always so literal? Mario pointed out that you have to know that Harold supposedly wrote the book to understand the first-person viewpoint of the book. Talked to Sari about fantasy. Told her she'll be laughing out loud as she reads this book. She doubts it.

March 7

Returned to <u>Bunnicula</u> literature circle for first grand conversation, especially to check on Sari. Annie, Mario, Ted, Rod, Laurie, and Belinda talked about their pets and imagined them taking over their homes. Sari is not getting into the book. She doesn't have any pets and can't imagine the pets doing these things. I asked if she wanted to change groups. Perhaps a realistic book would be better. She says no.

March 10

The group is reading chapters 4 and 5 today. Laurie asks questions about white vegetables and vampires. Rod goes to get an encyclopedia to find out about vampires. Mario asks about DDT. Everyone—even Sari—involved in reading.

March 13

During a grand conversation, students compare the characters Harold and Chester. The group plans to make a Venn diagram comparing the characters for the sharing on Friday. Students decide that character is the most important element, but Ted argues that humor is the most important element in the story. Other students say humor isn't an element. I asked what humor is a reaction to—characters or plot? I checked journals and all are up to date.

March 17

The group has finished reading the book. I share sequels from the class library. Sari grabs one to read. She's glad she stayed with the book. Ted wants to write his own sequel in writing workshop. Mario plans to write a letter to James Howe.

March 20

Ted and Sari talk about <u>Bunnicula</u> and share related books. Rod and Mario share the Venn diagram of characters. Annie reads her favorite part, and Laurie shows her collection of rabbits. Belinda hangs back. I wonder if she's been involved. Need to talk to her.

TEACHER'S NOTE

A successful literature circle! Students worked well together and studied story structure. Sari took a while to get involved, probably because of the genre. I will conference with Belinda about her engagement.

CONFERENCES. Teachers talk with students to monitor their progress as well as to set goals and help them solve problems. They often conduct these types of conferences with students:

On-the-Spot Conferences. The teacher visits with students at their desks to monitor some aspect of the students' work or to check on progress. These conferences are brief, with the teacher often spending less than a minute with each student.

Planning Conferences. The teacher and the student make plans for reading or writing: At a prereading conference, they talk about concepts or vocabulary related to the book or the reading schedule, and at a prewriting conference, they discuss possible writing topics or how to narrow a broad topic.

Revising Conferences. A small group of students meets with the teacher to share their rough drafts and get specific suggestions about how to revise them.

Book Discussion Conferences. Students meet with the teacher to discuss the book they've read. They may share reading log entries, discuss plot or characters, or compare the story to others they've read.

Editing Conferences. The teacher reviews students' proofread compositions and helps them correct spelling, punctuation, capitalization, and other mechanical errors.

Evaluation Conferences. The teacher meets with students after they've completed an assignment or project to talk about their growth as readers and writers. Students reflect on their accomplishments and set goals.

Often these brief conferences are informal, held at students' desks as the teacher moves around the classroom; at other times, however, the conferences are planned, and students meet with the teacher at a designated conference table.

CHECKLISTS. Checklists simplify assessment and enhance students' learning (Kuhs, Johnson, Agruso, & Monrad, 2001). To create them, teachers identify the evaluation criteria in advance so students understand what's expected of them before they begin working. Grading is easier because teachers have already set the evaluation criteria, and it's fairer, too, because they use the same criteria to grade all students' work. The Assessment Snapshot: Book Talk Checklist shows a teacher's evaluation of a fourth grader's **book talk**; the student's grade was B. At the beginning of the school year, the teacher introduced book talks, modeled how to do one, and developed the checklist with the students. Students use the checklist whenever they're preparing to give a book talk, and the teacher uses it as a rating scale to evaluate the effectiveness of their book talks.

Watch as a teacher discusses how she uses checklists to explain assignments and help students monitor their progress. What steps does the teacher take to develop effective checklists?

Check the Compendium of Instructional Procedures, which follows Chapter 12.

ASSESSMENT *Snapshot*

Book Talk Checklist

Name Jaime   Date November 13

Title Cockroach Cooties

Author Laurence Yep

✔ Hold up the book to show to classmates.

✔ State the title and author's name.

✔ Interest classmates in the book by asking a question, reading an excerpt, or sharing some information.

___ Summarize the book, without giving away the ending.

✔ Talk loud enough for everyone to hear you.

✔ Look at the audience.

___ Limit the book talk to 3 minutes.

TEACHER'S NOTE

Jaime's book talk was effective. She generated lots of excitement about the book even though she talked for 5+ minutes and didn't summarize the story. Her classmates really responded! Grade B

Step 3: Evaluating Students' Learning

Teachers document students' learning to make judgments about their achievement. At this stage, the assessment is summative. Tests are a traditional way to evaluate students' learning, but most teachers prefer to evaluate students' actual reading and writing to make judgments about their achievement.

STUDENTS' WORK SAMPLES. Teachers collect students' work samples, including audio files of them reading aloud, lists of books they've read, reading logs, writing samples, photos of projects, and flash drives with digital projects, and they use these data to document students' progress toward meeting grade-level standards and to assign grades. Students also choose some of their best work to place in their portfolios to document their own learning and accomplishments.

RUBRICS. Teachers use **rubrics**, or scoring guides, to evaluate student performance according to specific criteria and levels of achievement (Afflerbach, 2012; Stevens, Levi, & Walvoord, 2012). They're similar to checklists because they specify what students are expected to do, but they go beyond checklists because they describe specific criteria and levels of achievement. Writing rubrics are the most common type, but teachers use rubrics to assess students' reading and their achievement in other curricular areas.

Students also use the rubrics to self-assess their writing, and sometimes they use them to assess a classmate's achievement. To be successful, students first need to analyze anonymous work samples and identify the traits that demonstrate strong, average, and weak achievement; it's also helpful for teachers to model traits at each level in the rubric. Skillings and Ferrell (2000) taught second and third graders to develop the criteria for evaluating their writing, and the students moved from using the rubrics their teachers prepared to creating their own 3-point rubrics, which they labeled as the "very best" level, the "okay" level, and the "not so good" level. Perhaps the most important outcome of teaching students to create rubrics, according to Skillings and Ferrell, is that they develop metacognitive strategies and the ability to think about themselves as writers.

A 4-level rubric for assessing sixth graders' independent reading during reading workshop is shown in Assessment Snapshot: Independent Reading Rubric. Simone and her classmates use the rubric to assess their achievement at the end of each quarter. The quality levels, ranging from Outstanding (highest) to Beginning (lowest), are shown in the column on the far left, and the achievement categories are listed across the top row: number of books read during the quarter, reading level of the books, genres represented by the books, and students' interpretations. The Interpretation category assesses students' comprehension. Simone also reflects on her achievement in the accompanying Student's Note.

GO DIGITAL! **Creating Rubrics.** Teachers can find tools for generating rubrics and blank rubric templates online as well as a collection of rubrics that other teachers have developed at these websites:

- ⟳ Rubrics 4 Teachers
- ⟳ Rubistar
- ⟳ Teach-nology
- ⟳ Common Core State Standards
- ⟳ 6 + 1 Traits

There are rubrics for assessing K–8 students' reading, writing, oral performance, and multimedia projects at these websites, too. ⟳

ASSESSMENT *Snapshot*

Independent Reading Rubric

Name **Simone**   Quarter **3**

Level	Books Read	Difficulty	Genres	Interpretation
Outstanding	Finishes 5 or more books	Reads "just right" books and tries "too hard" books sometimes	Reads books from three or more genres	Makes insightful interpretation with evidence from the book, author's style, and genre
(Proficient)	Finishes 3 or 4 books ✓	Reads mostly "just right" books ✓	Reads books from two genres ✓	Shares accurate interpretation using a summary, inferences, and story structure
Developing	Finishes 2 books	Reads mostly "too easy" books	Tries a different genre once in a while	Provides literal interpretation by summarizing events and making personal connections ✓
Beginning	Finishes 1 book	Always reads "too easy" books	Sticks with one genre	Offers incomplete or inaccurate response

STUDENT'S NOTE

I did it! I read 3 books this quarter—James and the Giant Peach, Shiloh, and Volcanoes and Earthquakes. They are RL 6, and one is nonfiction! Yes, I kept my book log up-to-date.

MULTIMODAL ASSESSMENTS. Risko and Walker-Dalhouse (2010) urge teachers to broaden evaluation to examine more the multimodal ways students participate in reading and writing, both in and out of school. It's not enough to simply evaluate the projects that students create; instead, teachers should consider these points when assessing students' learning:

- The literacy strategies that students employ
- The variety of print and digital texts students read
- The digital resources students use
- Students' ability to collaborate with classmates
- The multiple ways—oral, written, and visual—that students demonstrate learning

Peverini (2009) urges teachers to design authentic assessments that address these points as well as meet their instructional goals and grade-level standards.

Teachers use these data to document students' progress toward meeting grade-level standards as well as to evaluate their own teaching effectiveness. Students also collect their best work in portfolios to document their own learning and accomplishments.

Step 4: Reflecting on Students' Learning

Teachers reflect on their instruction to improve their teaching effectiveness. They ask themselves questions about lessons that were successful and those that weren't and how they might adapt instruction to meet their students' needs. They also analyze students' achievement, because teachers aren't effective if students aren't learning.

FIGURE 3–1   Ways to Assess Students' Learning

Planning	Monitoring
• Determine students' reading levels using running records and informal reading inventories. • Choose appropriate books for students. • Match students' reading levels to instructional procedures and approaches.	• Observe students as they read and write. • Conduct conferences with students. • Make anecdotal notes. • Have students mark checklists and rubrics to track their progress.
Evaluating	**Reflecting**
• Use checklists and rubrics to evaluate and grade student work. • Examine collections of student work to determine grades. • Create tests, when necessary, to evaluate students' learning.	• Have students write self-reflections about their work habits and achievement. • Have students place work that highlights their accomplishments in portfolios. • Reflect on your teaching effectiveness by examining the results of students' evaluation.

Danielson (2009) recommends that teachers work with colleagues who can help to solve problems and improve instruction.

Students also reflect on their achievement to develop self-awareness and to learn to take more responsibility for their learning. Self-assessment is metacognitive: Students evaluate their achievement, ways of learning, and work habits. Teachers often provide questions such as these to prompt students' reflections:

What did you learn during this unit?
How could your teacher have improved your learning?
How did you feel at the beginning, middle, and end of the unit?
How did you contribute to our classroom community of learners?
What are your three greatest strengths as a reader or writer?
What would you like to get better at?

Students write journal entries, letters to the teacher, or essays to respond to these questions. Teachers read and respond to students' reflections, but they don't grade them. They often use students' reflections to generate conversation during conferences and to help students set goals for the next unit.

Each assessment step serves a different purpose, so it's important that teachers choose assessment tools carefully. Researchers recommend that teachers use a combination of assessment tools to improve the fairness and effectiveness of classroom literacy assessment (Kuhs, Johnson, Agruso, & Monrad, 2001). Figure 3–1 highlights the assessments teachers use during each step of assessment.

 MONITOR: Check Your Understanding 3.1

Diagnostic Tests

Teachers use commercial diagnostic tests to inform their instruction. In particular, these tests are used to determine students' reading levels and identify struggling readers' strengths and weaknesses. Then teachers use the results to differentiate instruction, make accurate placement decisions, and create meaningful classroom interventions.

Determining Students' Reading Levels

Teachers match students with books at appropriate levels of difficulty because students are more successful when they're reading books that are neither too easy nor too difficult; too-easy books don't provide enough challenge, and too-difficult books frustrate students. Researchers have identified three reading levels that take into account students' ability to recognize words automatically, read fluently, and comprehend the message:

Independent Reading Level. Students read books at their **independent reading level** comfortably, on their own. They recognize almost all words; their accuracy rate is 95–100%. The reading is fluent, and they comprehend what they're reading. Books at this level are only slightly easier than those at their instructional level, and they still engage students' interest.

Instructional Reading Level. Students read books at their **instructional reading level** with support, but not on their own. They recognize most words; their accuracy rate is 90–94%. Their reading may be fluent, but sometimes it isn't. With support from the teacher or classmates, students comprehend what they're reading, but if they're reading independently, their understanding is limited.

Frustration Reading Level. Books at the **frustration reading level** are too difficult for students to read successfully, even with assistance. Students don't recognize enough words automatically; their accuracy is less than 90%. Their reading is choppy and word by word, and it often doesn't make sense. In addition, students show little understanding of what's been read.

Students should be assessed regularly to determine their reading levels and monitor their progress.

These reading levels have important implications for instruction: Teachers need to know students' reading levels when they're planning for instruction. Students read independent-level books when they're reading for pleasure and instructional-level books when they're participating in guided reading and other instructional lessons. They shouldn't be expected to read books at their frustration level; when it's essential that struggling readers experience grade-appropriate literature or learn content area information, teachers should read the text aloud to students, have students read with partners, or for content area textbooks, have students work in small groups to read and report on short sections.

The Common Core State Standards for English Language Arts require teachers to plan instruction using grade-level requirements, not students' developmental reading levels (McLaughlin & Overturf, 2012; McLaughlin & Overturf, 2013). The 10th Standard at grades 2–8 clearly states that students should read and comprehend grade-level stories, poems, and nonfiction books independently and proficiently by the end of the school year, needing support only to succeed with the most challenging texts. Students who read at or above grade level typically meet this Standard, but struggling students who read more than two grades below their grade placement don't. This Standard emphasizes the importance of using grade-level texts with all students, but teachers must also consider students' current levels and provide developmentally appropriate instruction, too, to scaffold struggling students as they become more

Literacy Portraits

Ms. Janusz regularly monitors the second graders' reading achievement. Working one-on-one, she introduces a leveled book and asks the child to read the first part aloud while she takes a running record on a separate sheet of paper. Then the child reads the rest of the book silently. The teacher also asks questions after the child finishes reading orally and again after he or she reaches the end of the book.

Watch Ms. Janusz assess Jimmy's reading in October and again in March. As you watch the videos, think about how Jimmy grew as a reader during the school year. Does he decode unfamiliar words, read fluently, and comprehend what he's read orally and silently? Next, reflect on how Ms. Janusz linked instruction and assessment when she took advantage of teachable moments while assessing his reading.

Jimmy in October

COMMON CORE STATE STANDARDS

Assessment

Common Core State Standards don't identify how to assess learning or which evaluation instruments to use; instead, they specify what students should be able to demonstrate at each grade level, and Standard 10 emphasizes that students in grades 2–8 should be able to read and comprehend challenging grade-appropriate texts. Sample fiction and nonfiction texts are listed for each grade level in the Standards document. To learn more about the literacy Standards, go to http://www.corestandards.org/ELA-Literacy, or check your state's educational standards website.

proficient readers. That's why teachers teach guided reading groups while conducting literature focus units: Everyone is exposed to grade-level texts, and at the same time, they're reading at their instructional level. For more information, check the feature Common Core State Standards: Assessment.

READABILITY FORMULAS. For nearly a century, readability formulas have been used to estimate the ease with which students can read trade books and textbooks. The scores that the formulas provide serve as rough gauges of text difficulty and are traditionally reported as grade-level equivalents. If a book has a score of fifth grade, for example, teachers assume that average fifth graders can read it. Sometimes the scores are marked as RL, for *reading level*, and a grade, such as RL 5 (fifth grade) or 5.2 (fifth grade, second month).

Readability scores are determined by correlating semantic and syntactic features in a text. Several passages from a text are identified for analysis, and then vocabulary sophistication is measured by counting the number of syllables in each word or determining each word's familiarity, and sentence complexity by the number of words in each sentence. Syllable and word counts from each passage are averaged, and the readability score is calculated by plotting the averages on a graph. It seems reasonable to expect that texts with familiar words and shorter sentences would be easier to read than others with longer words and sentences. But readability formulas take into account only two text factors; they can't account for reader factors, including the experience and knowledge that readers bring to reading, their cognitive and linguistic backgrounds, or their motivation for reading.

One fairly quick and easy readability formula is the Fry Readability Graph, developed by Edward Fry (1968); it's available in *The Reading Teacher's Book of Lists* (Kress & Fry, 2015), and at numerous websites. This graph predicts the grade-level score for first grade through college-level texts. Teachers use a readability formula as an aid in evaluating textbook and trade-book selections for classroom use; however, they can't assume that materials rated as appropriate for a particular grade level will be appropriate for everyone because students' reading achievement within a typical class varies by three grade levels or more.

LEVELED BOOKS. Basal readers have traditionally been leveled according to grade level, but these designations, especially for kindergarten and first grade, are too broad. To match students to books in grades K–8, Fountas and Pinnell (2006) developed a text gradient, or classification system that arranges books along a 26-level continuum from easiest to hardest. Their system is based on these variables that influence reading difficulty:

- Genre and format of the book
- Organization and use of text structures
- Familiarity and interest level of the content
- Complexity of ideas and themes
- Language and literary features
- Sentence length and complexity
- Sophistication of the vocabulary
- Word length and ease of decoding
- Relationship of illustrations to the text
- Length of the book, its layout, and other print features

Booklist

Fountas and Pinnell's Levels

LEVEL	GRADE	BOOK
A	K	Burningham, J. (1985). *Colors*. New York: Crown.
B	K–1	Carle, E. (1997). *Have you seen my cat?* New York: Aladdin Books.
C	K–1	Martin, B., Jr. (2010). *Brown bear, brown bear, what do you see?* New York: Holt.
D	1	Peek, M. (2006). *Mary wore her red dress*. New York: Clarion Books.
E	1	Hill, E. (2005). *Where's Spot?* New York: Putnam.
F	1	Hutchins, P. (2005). *Rosie's walk*. New York: Aladdin Books.
G	1	Shaw, N. (2006). *Sheep in a jeep*. Boston: Houghton Mifflin.
H	1–2	Kraus, R. (2005). *Whose mouse are you?* New York: Aladdin Books.
I	1–2	Wood, A. (2005). *The napping house*. San Diego: Harcourt.
J	2	Rylant, C. (1996). *Henry and Mudge and the bedtime thumps*. New York: Simon & Schuster.
K	2	Heller, R. (1999). *Chickens aren't the only ones*. New York: Putnam.
L	2–3	Marshall, J. (2000). *The three little pigs*. New York: Grosset & Dunlap.
M	2–3	Park, B. (2007). *Junie B. Jones and the stupid smelly bus*. New York: Random House.
N	3	Danziger, P. (2006). *Amber Brown is not a crayon*. New York: Puffin Books.
O	3–4	Cleary, B. (1992). *Ramona Quimby, age 8*. New York: Harper Trophy.
P	3–4	Mathis, S. B. (2006). *The hundred penny box*. New York: Puffin Books.
Q	4	Howe, D., & Howe, J. (2006). *Bunnicula: A rabbit-tale of mystery*. New York: Aladdin Books.
R	4	Paulsen, G. (2007). *Hatchet*. New York: Simon & Schuster.
S	4–5	Norton, M. (2003). *The borrowers*. San Diego: Odyssey Classics.
T	4–5	Curtis, C. P. (2004). *Bud, not Buddy*. New York: Laurel Leaf.
U	5	Lowry, L. (2011). *Number the stars*. New York: Sandpiper.
V	5–6	Sachar, L. (2008). *Holes*. New York: Farrar, Straus & Giroux.
W	5–6	Choi, S. N. (1993). *Year of impossible goodbyes*. New York: Yearling.
X	6–8	Hesse, K. (1999). *Out of the dust*. New York: Scholastic.
Y	6–8	Lowry, L. (2006). *The giver*. New York: Delacorte.
Z	7–8	Hinton, S. E. (2006). *The outsiders*. New York: Puffin Books.

Based on Fountas, I. C., & Pinnell, G. S. (2009). *The Fountas and Pinnell leveled book list, K–8* (2010–2012 ed.). Portsmouth, NH: Heinemann.

Fountas and Pinnell used these criteria to identify levels, labeled A through Z, for their text gradient, which teachers also can use to level books in their classrooms. More than 35,000 books have been leveled using this text gradient. A sample trade book for each level is shown in Booklist: Fountas and Pinnell's Levels; other leveled books can be found in *The Fountas & Pinnell Leveled Book List, K–8+* (Fountas & Pinnell, 2013) and online at the Fountas and Pinnell Leveled Books Website.

THE LEXILE FRAMEWORK. Another approach to matching books to readers is the Lexile Framework, developed by MetaMetrics. This approach is different because it's used to measure both students' reading levels and the difficulty level of books. Word familiarity and sentence complexity are the two factors used to determine the difficulty level of books. Lexile scores range from 100 to 1300, representing kindergarten through 12th grade reading levels. The numerical scores have been organized into grade-level bands to coordinate with the Common Core State Standard 10 expectation

Classroom
INTERVENTIONS

"Just Right" Books

Struggling readers need books they can read. Too often, they pick up books that are too difficult, and when they attempt to read them, they give up in frustration. What students need are "just right" books that they can read fluently and can comprehend (Allington, 2012); when students read interesting books at their independent reading level, they're more successful. The "three-finger rule" is a quick way to determine whether a book is a good match for a student: Have the student turn to any page in the book, read it aloud, and raise a finger whenever there's an unknown word. If the student knows every word, it's too easy, but if one or two words on a page are difficult, the book is probably an appropriate choice. If there are three or more difficult words on a page, the book's too difficult for independent reading.

and then recently recalibrated to increase the challenge presented to students so that they'll be better prepared for college and careers after graduating from high school. For example, the grades 4–5 band increased from 645–845 to 770–980 in the recalibration. Booklist: The Recalibrated Lexile Grade Bands presents the grade bands with sample books.

Students' results on high-stakes tests are often linked to the Lexile Framework. Standardized achievement tests, including the Iowa Test of Basic Skills and the Stanford Achievement Test, report test results as Lexile scores, and a number of standards-based state reading tests do the same. With this information, students, parents, and teachers can match students to books by searching the online Lexile database to locate books at the student's reading level.

The wide range of scores in the Lexile Framework allows teachers to more closely match students and books. Plus, the availability of the online database with more than 200,000 leveled books, 80 million articles, and 60,000 websites that students, parents, and teachers can access makes it a very useful assessment tool; however, matching students to books is more complicated than determining a numerical score!

Booklist   The Recalibrated Lexile Grade Bands

GRADE BAND	LEVEL	BOOKS
K–1*	0–449	Allard, H. (1985). *Miss Nelson is missing!* Boston: Houghton Mifflin. (340)**
		Bridwell, N. (2002). *Clifford the big red dog.* New York: Scholastic. (220)
		Henkes, K. (2007). *Chrysanthemum.* New York: Greenwillow. (410)
		Lobel, A. (1979). *Frog and Toad are friends.* New York: HarperCollins. (400)
		Willems, M. (2003). *Don't let the pigeon drive the bus!* New York: Hyperion Books. (120)
2–3	450–790	Blume, J. (2007). *Tales of a fourth grade nothing.* New York: Puffin Books. (470)
		Brown, J. M. (2009). *Flat Stanley.* New York: Scholastic. (640)
		Howe, D., & Howe, J. (2006). *Bunnicula: A rabbit-tale of mystery.* New York: Aladdin Books. (710)
		Rathmann, P. (1995). *Officer Buckle and Gloria.* New York: Putnam. (510)
		Steig, W. (2009). *Amos & Boris.* New York: Square Fish Books. (690)
4–5	770–980	Dahl, R. (2007). *Charlie and the chocolate factory.* New York: Puffin Books. (810)
		Gantos, J. (2011). *Joey Pigza swallowed the key.* New York: Square Fish Books. (970)
		Lewis, C. S. (2005). *The lion, the witch and the wardrobe.* New York: HarperCollins. (940)
		Naylor, P. (2000). *Shiloh.* New York: Aladdin Books. (890)
		Rowling, J. K. (1999). *Harry Potter and the sorcerer's stone.* New York: Scholastic. (880)
6–8	955–1155	Curtis, C. P. (2000). *The Watsons go to Birmingham—1963.* New York: Laurel Leaf. (1000)
		King-Smith, D. (2005). *Babe: The gallant pig.* New York: Knopf. (1040)
		Lester, J. (2005). *To be a slave.* New York: Puffin Books. (1080)
		O'Dell, S. (2006). *Island of the blue dolphins.* Boston: Houghton Mifflin. (1000)
		Stevenson, R. L. (2009). *Treasure island.* Somerville, MA: Candlewick Press. (1100)

*This band isn't included on most Lexile documents because Common Core State Standard 10 for first grade specifies that students work toward reading grade-level books with prompting and support; mastery isn't required. The band is included here to highlight books at the K–1 level.

**Lexile score

ASSESSMENT TOOLS

Determining Students' Reading Levels

Teachers use screening assessments to determine students' instructional reading levels, monitor their progress, and document student achievement through a school year and across grade levels. They often use these three screening assessments:

- **Developmental Reading Assessment, 2nd Edition PLUS (DRA2+)**
  The DRA2+ is available as two kits, one for grades K–3 and the other for grades 4–8, to assess students' reading performance using leveled fiction and nonfiction books. The K–3 kit also includes an individualized diagnostic instrument to assess students' phonemic awareness and phonics knowledge. Teachers use an online system to manage students' scores and group students for instruction. Management apps are also available for iPads.

- **Fountas & Pinnell Benchmark Assessment System**
  The Fountas & Pinnell Benchmark Assessment System is sold as two kits, one for grades K–2 and the other for grades 3–8. Each kit contains 30 leveled fiction and nonfiction books written specifically for the kit and CDs with assessment forms to manage students' scores. Teachers use the books in the kit to match students' reading levels to the Fountas and Pinnell 26-level text gradient.

For both of these assessments, teachers test students individually. The teacher selects an appropriate book for the student to read, and then introduces it; the student reads the book, and the teacher takes a running record of the student's reading. Then the student retells the text and answers comprehension questions. The teacher scores and analyzes the results, and testing continues until the teacher determines the student's instructional level.

- **Scholastic Reading Inventory (SRI)**
  The SRI is a unique computer-adaptive assessment program for kindergarten through college readiness that reports students' reading levels using Lexile scores. There are separate reading foundation and comprehension subtests. Students take a 20-minute computerized test individually—they read a narrative or informational passage on the computer screen and answer multiple-choice comprehension questions. This test is computer-adaptive because if the student answers a question correctly, the next one will be more difficult, and if the answer is wrong, the next question will be easier. Students read passages and answer questions until their reading level is determined. They receive a customized take-home letter with their Lexile score and a personalized list of recommended books.

These assessments are usually administered at the beginning of the school year and periodically during the year to monitor students' progress. The results are also used to group students for guided reading and to identify students who need diagnostic testing.

Assessment Tools: Determining Students' Reading Levels describes three screening tools for measuring students' reading levels.

GO DIGITAL! **Online Book-Search Systems.** Teachers also consult online databases to locate books at students' reading levels so that they can match readers with appropriate books. One of the most popular search systems is the Book Wizard, a free book-search system at Scholastic's website. Teachers search the 50,000 books in its database to locate books at a specific reading level or check the level of a particular book. Teachers also download the Book Wizard app for easy access to the Scholastic database.

The search results present useful information about each book, including the title and author, a photo of the book cover, the book's interest and reading levels, the genre, a summary, and a list of topics related to the book. The reading level is expressed as a grade-level equivalent (e.g., RL 2.3 or second grade, third month) and according to both guided reading levels and Lexile Framework scores. Links are also provided to author information and teaching resources. 📖

USING READABILITY SCORES IN THE CLASSROOM. It's easy to locate different grade-level recommendations for a particular book because readability formulas result in varied reading-level equivalents. Patricia MacLachlan's *Sarah, Plain and Tall* (2005), for instance, is the award-winning story of a mail-order bride that teachers have traditionally shared with their students in third or fourth grade, depending on students' reading levels. Scholastic's Book Wizard lists the book's interest level as grades 3–5 and its grade-level equivalency as 4.2 (fourth grade, second month), and Fountas and Pinnell score it at level R (grade 4). This information is consistent with teachers' choices; however, its Lexile score is 560, which now places it one grade earlier, in the grades 2–3 band. This earlier placement highlights the Common Core State Standards' emphasis on increasing students' reading achievement.

Teachers have to take into account more than just reading levels when matching books to students: They also need to consider what they know about their students and about the texts they're reading. Students' background knowledge and related vocabulary, the structure of the text, and the complexity of the book's theme are also important considerations. *Number the Stars* (Lowry, 2011) and *Holes* (Sachar, 2008) are two award-winning novels that score in the grades 2–3 band, but they're intended for middle grade students; in *Number the Stars*, Lois Lowry addresses the Holocaust—a complex theme—and in *Holes*, Louis Sachar uses a sophisticated narrative structure.

Sometimes two very different books score at the same level. For example, Steven Kellogg's *Johnny Appleseed* (2008) and Mildred Taylor's *Roll of Thunder, Hear My Cry* (2004) both received Lexile scores of 920 (grades 4–5), but the books are very different and appropriate for older or younger students. *Johnny Appleseed* is a picture book about the larger-than-life folk hero that's 48 pages long and packed with colorful illustrations that fill two thirds of the page together with a brief text; most teachers read it aloud to students in grades 2–4. In contrast, *Roll of Thunder, Hear My Cry* is a novel, nearly 300 pages in length; it's the profoundly moving story of the social injustice faced by an African American family in the South during the 1930s. Most teachers consider it appropriate for students in grades 6–8 because of its powerful themes. These examples emphasize that teachers must be familiar with the books they're having students read to ensure that the texts are appropriate; they can't depend on readability scores alone.

Diagnosing Students' Strengths and Weaknesses

Teachers use diagnostic assessments to identify students' strengths and weaknesses, examine areas of difficulty in detail, and decide how to modify instruction to meet students' needs. They use diagnostic tests to examine students' achievement in phonemic awareness, phonics, fluency, vocabulary, comprehension, and other components of literacy development. Assessment Tools: Diagnostic Assessments lists recommended diagnostic tests and directs you to the chapter where you'll learn more about them.

RUNNING RECORDS. Running records are authentic assessment tools because students demonstrate how they read using their regular reading materials as teachers make a detailed account of their ability to read a book (Clay, 2015). Teachers take running records of students' oral reading to assess their word identification and reading fluency. They make notes on a copy of the book the student is reading and place

ASSESSMENT TOOLS

Diagnostic Assessments

Component	Tests	Where to Learn More
Comprehension	Comprehension Thinking Strategies Assessment (1–8)* Developmental Reading Assessment (K–8) Informal reading inventories (2–8)	Chapter 8, Promoting Comprehension: Reader Factors
Concepts About Print	Observation Survey of Early Literacy Achievement (K–2)	Chapter 4, The Youngest Readers and Writers
Fluency	**aims**web (K–8) Dynamic Indicators of Basic Early Literacy Skills (K–3) Fluency checks (1–8) Informal reading inventories (2–8) Running records (K–8)	Chapter 6, Developing Fluent Readers and Writers
Phonemic Awareness	Dynamic Indicators of Basic Early Literacy Skills (K–3) Phonological Awareness Literacy Screening (K–3) Yopp-Singer Test of Phonemic Segmentation (K)	Chapter 5, Cracking the Alphabetic Code
Phonics	Dynamic Indicators of Basic Early Literacy Skills (K–3) The Names Test (3–8) Observation Survey (K–2) The Tile Test (K–2)	Chapter 5, Cracking the Alphabetic Code
Spelling	Developmental Spelling Analysis (K–8) Phonological Awareness Literacy Screening (K–3) Qualitative Spelling Inventory (K–8)	Chapter 5, Cracking the Alphabetic Code
Vocabulary	Expressive Vocabulary Test (K–8) Informal reading inventories (2–8) Peabody Picture Vocabulary Test (K–8)	Chapter 7, Expanding Academic Vocabulary
Word Identification	Developmental Reading Assessment (K–8) The Names Test (3–8) Phonological Awareness Literacy Screening (K–3) Running records (K–8)	Chapter 6, Developing Fluent Readers and Writers
Word Recognition	High-frequency word lists (K–3) Observation Survey (K–2)	Chapter 6, Developing Fluent Readers and Writers
Writing	Rubrics (K–8)	Chapter 2, The Reading and Writing Processes

*Recommended grade levels

checkmarks above the words that the student reads correctly and use other marks to indicate words that the student substitutes, repeats, mispronounces, or doesn't know, as Mrs. McNeal did in the vignette. Then the student's miscues are classified and charted. The Assessment Snapshot: Miscue Analysis shows how Ethan's miscues were

ASSESSMENT *Snapshot*

Miscue Analysis

Child   Ethan   Date   Jan. 17

Text   The Pot of Gold (Level 16)

Words			Meaning	Visual	Syntax
Text	Child	Self-corrected?	Similar meaning?	Graphophonic similarity?	Grammatically acceptable?
Grumble	Grumply			✓	
always	——				
didn't	did not		✓	✓	✓
I'll	I		✓	✓	✓
move	make			✓	✓
scarf	safr			✓	
of	or			✓	
my	me	✓		✓	
scarf	self			✓	
taken	take		✓	✓	
scarf	scafer			✓	
that	they	✓		✓	
may	maybe			✓	
still	sit			✓	

TEACHER'S NOTE

Ethan fluently read <u>The Pot of Gold</u> with 95% accuracy. Level 16 is his current instructional level. The miscue analysis indicates that Ethan overrelies on visual cues and rarely self-corrects.

Look carefully at the score sheet Ms. Janusz is using while Jimmy reads in this video clip. How does Ms. Janusz act as she takes a running record?

categorized. Only words that students mispronounce or substitute can be analyzed; repetitions and omissions aren't calculated.

INFORMAL READING INVENTORIES. Teachers use commercial tests called **informal reading inventories** (IRIs) to evaluate students' reading performance. They can be used at first through eighth grade levels, but first grade teachers often find that IRIs don't provide as much useful information about beginning readers as running records do. These popular reading tests are often used as a screening instrument to determine whether students are reading at grade level, but they're also a valuable diagnostic tool (Nilsson, 2008). Teachers can use IRIs to identify struggling students' instructional needs, particularly in the areas of word identification, oral reading fluency, and comprehension.

These individualized tests consist of two parts: graded word lists and passages ranging from first to eighth grade levels. The word lists contain 10 to 20 words at each level, which students read until the words become too difficult; this indicates an approximate level for students to begin reading the passages. Because students who can't read the words on their grade-level list may have a word-identification problem, teachers analyze the words they read incorrectly, looking for error patterns and deciding whether students rely on only one cueing system.

The graded reading passages include both narrative and expository texts, presented in order of difficulty. Students read these passages orally or silently and then answer three types of comprehension questions; teachers ask students to recall specific information, draw inferences, and explain the meaning of vocabulary words. When students read the passages orally, teachers assess their fluency: Students beyond third grade should be able to read the passages at their grade level fluently, but if they can't, they may have a fluency problem. Teachers also examine students' comprehension; they check to see if there's a pattern to the types of questions that students miss. Do students answer the recall questions correctly, but they can't answer the other two types? Do students miss the vocabulary questions because they lack academic vocabulary knowledge? Or, do the inferential questions stymie students because they don't know how to think figuratively?

View this brief video clip that shows a teacher conducting an informal reading inventory. How does the student behave as she reads?

Teachers use scoring sheets to record students' performance data and calculate their independent, instructional, and frustration reading levels. When students' reading level is below their grade-level placement, teachers also check their listening capacity; that is, their ability to understand passages that are read aloud to them. Knowing whether students can understand and learn from grade-level texts that are read aloud is crucial because that's a common way that teachers differentiate instruction to support struggling readers.

🌀 Nurturing English Learners

How do teachers assess literacy development? Teachers assess English learners' developing language proficiency as well as their progress in learning to read and write. It's more challenging to assess ELs than native English speakers, because when students aren't proficient in English, their scores don't accurately reflect what they know (Peregoy & Boyle, 2013). Their cultural and experiential backgrounds also contribute to making it more difficult to assure that assessment tools being used aren't biased.

ORAL LANGUAGE ASSESSMENT. Teachers assess students who speak a language other than English at home to determine their English language proficiency. They typically use commercial oral language tests to determine if students are proficient in English; if they're not, teachers place them in appropriate English language development programs and monitor their progress toward English language proficiency. Two widely used tests are the Language Assessment Scales, published by CTB/McGraw-Hill, and the IDEA Language Proficiency Test, published by Ballard and Tighe; both tests assess K–12 students' oral, written, and visual language proficiency in English. Individual states have developed language assessments that are aligned with their English language proficiency standards; for example, the New York State English as a Second Language Achievement Test and the California English Language Development Test.

An authentic assessment tool that many teachers use is the Student Oral Language Observation Matrix (SOLOM), developed by the San Jose (CA) Area Bilingual Consortium. It's not a test per se; rather, the SOLOM is a rating scale that teachers use to assess students' command of English as they observe them talking and listening in real, day-to-day classroom activities. The SOLOM addresses five components of oral language:

Listening. Teachers score students along a continuum from unable to comprehend simple statements to understanding everyday conversations.

Fluency. Teachers score students along a continuum from halting, fragmentary speech to fluent speech, approximating that of native speakers.

Vocabulary. Teachers score students along a continuum from extremely limited word knowledge to using words and idioms skillfully.

Pronunciation. Teachers score students along a continuum from virtually unintelligible speech to using pronunciation and intonation proficiently, similar to native speakers.

Grammar. Teachers score students along a continuum from excessive errors that make speech unintelligible to applying word order, grammar, and usage rules effectively.

Each component has a 5-point range that's scored 1 to 5; the maximum score on the matrix is 25, and a score of 20 or higher indicates that students are fluent speakers of English. The SOLOM is available free of charge online at the Center for Applied Linguistics website, at other websites, and in many professional books.

READING ASSESSMENT. English learners face two challenges: learning to speak English at the same time they're learning to read. They learn to read the same way that native English speakers do, but they face additional challenges because their knowledge of English phonology, semantics, syntax, and pragmatics is limited and their background knowledge is different. English learners who are fluent readers in their home language already have substantial funds of knowledge about how written language works that they build on as they learn to read in English (Garcia, 2000; Peregoy & Boyle, 2013). Having this knowledge gives them a head start, but students also have to learn what transfers to English reading and what doesn't.

Teachers use the same assessments that they use for native English speakers to identify English learners' reading levels, monitor their growth, and document their learning. Peregoy and Boyle (2013) recommend using data from running records or informal reading inventories along with classroom-based informal assessments, such as observing and conferencing with students.

Because many English learners have less background knowledge about topics in books they're reading, it's important that teachers take stock of ELs' background knowledge before instruction so they can modify their teaching to meet students' needs. One of the best ways to accomplish this is with a **KWL chart**. As they work with students to complete the first two sections of the chart, teachers learn what students know about a topic and have an opportunity to build additional background knowledge and introduce related vocabulary. Later, when students complete the chart, teachers get a clear picture of what they've learned and which vocabulary words they can use.

Another way teachers learn about ELs' development is by asking them to assess themselves as readers (Peregoy & Boyle, 2013). Teachers ask students, for example, what they do when they come to an unfamiliar word, what differences they've noticed between narrative and expository texts, which reading strategies they use, and what types of books they prefer. These quick assessments, commonly done during conferences at the end of a grading period, shed light on students' growth in a way that other assessments can't.

WRITING ASSESSMENT. English learners' writing develops as their oral language grows and as they become more fluent readers (Riches & Genesee, 2006). For beginning writers, fluency is the first priority. They move from writing strings of familiar words to grouping words into short sentences that often follow a pattern, much like young native English speakers do. As they develop some writing fluency, ELs begin to stick to a single focus, often repeating words and sentences to make their writing longer. Once they become fluent writers, ELs are usually able to organize their ideas more effectively and group them into paragraphs. They incorporate more specific vocabulary and increase the length and variety of sentences. Their mechanical errors become less serious, and their writing is much easier to read. At this point, teachers begin teaching the writer's craft and choosing writing strategies and skills to teach based on the errors that students make.

Peregoy and Boyle (2013) explain that ELs' writing involves fluency, form, and correctness, and that teachers' assessment of students' writing should incorporate these components:

- Teachers monitor students' ability to write quickly, easily, and comfortably.
- Teachers assess students' ability to apply writing genres, develop their topic, organize the presentation of ideas, and use sophisticated vocabulary and a variety of sentence structures.
- Teachers check that students control Standard English grammar and usage, spell most words correctly, and use capitalization and punctuation conventions appropriately.

Teachers use **rubrics** to assess ELs' writing that address the writing process and the six traits that teachers have taught. They also conference with students about their writing and provide quick minilessons, as needed. To learn about students as writers, teachers observe them as they write, noticing how they move through the writing process, interact in **revising groups**, and share their writing from the author's chair. In addition, students document writing development by placing their best writing in portfolios.

ALTERNATIVE ASSESSMENTS. Because of the difficulties inherent in assessing English learners, it's important to use varied types of assessment that involve different language and literacy tasks and ways of demonstrating proficiency (Huerta-Macías, 1995). In addition to commercial tests, teachers use authentic assessment tools, including oral performances, story retellings, oral interviews, writing samples, illustrations, diagrams, posters, and multigenre projects.

Assessment is especially important for students who are learning to speak English at the same time they're learning to read and write in English. Teachers use many of the same assessment tools that they use for their native English speakers, but they also depend on more authentic alternative assessments because it's difficult to accurately measure these students' growth. Assessment results must be valid because teachers use them to make placement decisions, modify instruction, evaluate learning, and reflect on instructional effectiveness.

 MONITOR: Check Your Understanding 3.2

High-Stakes Testing

Annual high-stakes testing is emphasized in American schools with the goal of improving the quality of reading instruction. These tests are designed to objectively measure students' knowledge according to grade-level standards. The current emphases on testing and grade-level standards are reform efforts that began in response to The National Commission on Excellence in Education report *A Nation at Risk* (1983), which argued that American schools were failing miserably. The report stated that American students' test scores were dropping, comparing unfavorably with students' scores in other industrialized countries, and it concluded that the United States was in jeopardy of losing its global superiority. The No Child Left Behind (NCLB) Act of 2001, which promoted an increased focus on reading instruction to improve students' reading performance and narrow the racial and ethnic gaps in achievement, reinforced the call for annual standardized testing.

Researchers have repeatedly refuted these arguments (Bracey, 2004; Meier, Kohn, Darling-Hammond, Sizer, & Wood, 2004). Allington (2012) explained that average test scores have remained stable for many years despite the dramatic increases in federal funding over the past two decades. He goes on to explain that reporting average scores obscures important findings, and it's necessary to examine subgroup data to discover that most students from middle-class families read well even though many students from low-income families lag behind. He also notes that despite a gap, significant progress has been made in closing the achievement gap between white and minority students at the same time the number of minority students has grown tremendously. Finally, he points out that grade-level standards of achievement have increased in the last 50 years so that what was considered fifth grade level is now fourth grade level, and older readability formulas have been renormed to reflect today's higher grade-level standards. Nonetheless, the public's perception that schools are failing persists.

High-stakes testing is different than classroom assessment. The test scores typically provide little information for making day-to-day instructional decisions, but students, teachers, administrators, and schools are judged and held accountable by the results. The scores are used to make important educational decisions for students—to determine school placement and high school graduation, for example. These scores influence administrators' evaluations of teachers' effectiveness and even their salaries in some states, and they result in rewards or sanctions for administrators, schools, and school districts.

Standardized tests are comprehensive, with batteries of subtests covering decoding, vocabulary, comprehension, writing mechanics, and spelling. Figure 3–2 presents an overview of the most commonly used tests. Most tests use multiple-choice test items, although a few are introducing open-ended questions that require students to write responses. Beginning in second grade, classroom teachers administer the tests to their students, typically in the spring. Most require multiple testing periods to administer all of the subtests.

Problems With High-Stakes Testing

A number of problems are associated with high-stakes testing (IRA, 1999). Students feel the pressure of these tests, and researchers have confirmed what many teachers have noticed: Students don't try harder because of them (Hoffman, Assaf, & Paris, 2005). Struggling students, in particular, get discouraged and feel defeated, and over time, test pressure destroys their motivation and actually harms their achievement. In addition, student dropout rates are rising.

Teachers complain that they feel compelled to improve students' test scores at any price, and they lose valuable instructional time to testing and practice sessions (Hollingworth, 2007). Overemphasizing the test often leads teachers to abandon a balanced approach to instruction: Sometimes students spend more time practicing for the test than doing authentic reading and writing. One of the most insidious side effects is that teachers are often directed to focus on certain groups of students, especially those scoring just below a cutoff point, in hopes of improving test scores.

| FIGURE 3–2 | Standardized Achievement Tests |

TEST	DESCRIPTION	COMPONENTS	SPECIAL FEATURES	PUBLISHER
Iowa Test of Basic Skills (ITBS)	The ITBS provides information to improve instruction.	Vocabulary Comprehension Oral language Mechanics Spelling	The ITBS is the oldest statewide assessment program. It can be administered in the fall or spring.	Iowa schools are served by the Iowa Testing Program; outside Iowa, the ITBS is available from Riverside.
Metropolitan Achievement Test (MAT)	The MAT measures K–8 students using real-world content. Some items are multiple choice; others are performance-based.	Vocabulary Comprehension Mechanics Writing Spelling	The MAT provides a Lexile measure of students' reading levels.	The MAT can be ordered from Pearson.
Stanford Achievement Test (SAT)	The SAT measures K–8 students' progress toward meeting the challenges set forth by the Common Core State Standards.	Phonemic awareness Phonics Vocabulary Comprehension Mechanics Spelling	The SAT provides a Lexile measure of students' reading levels.	The SAT is published by Pearson.
TerraNova Test (TNT)	This innovative test uses both multiple-choice and constructed-response items that allow students to write responses.	Word analysis Vocabulary Comprehension Mechanics Spelling	Lexile scores are reported, and one version of the TNT is available as an online test.	The TNT is published by CTB/McGraw-Hill.

Preparing for Standardized Tests

Standardized tests are a unique text genre that requires readers and writers to do different things than they would normally, so teachers can't assume that students already know how to take reading tests. It's essential that teachers prepare students to take high-stakes tests without abandoning a balanced approach to instruction that's aligned to state standards (Kontovourki & Campis, 2010). Greene and Melton (2007) agree; they maintain that teachers must prepare students for high-stakes tests without sacrificing their instructional program. Unfortunately, with the pressure of data-driven school reform to raise test scores, some teachers are having students take many more multiple-choice practice tests while writing fewer essays and creating fewer projects (Shanahan, 2014).

Hollingworth (2007) recommends these five ways to prepare students for high-stakes tests without sacrificing the instructional program:

ⓔ Teachers check that their instructional program aligns with their state's standards and make any needed adjustments to ensure that they're teaching the concepts that the test addresses.

ⓔ Teachers set goals with students and use informal assessments to regularly monitor their progress.

ⓔ Teachers actively engage students in authentic literacy activities so that they become capable readers and writers.

ⓔ Teachers explain the purpose of the tests and how the results will be used, without making students anxious.

ⓔ Teachers stick with a balanced approach that combines explicit instruction and authentic application.

Other researchers advise that in addition to these recommendations, teachers prepare students to take standardized tests by teaching them how to read and answer test items and having them take practice tests to hone their test-taking strategies (McCabe, 2003). Preparing for tests involves explaining their purpose, examining the genre and format of multiple-choice tests, teaching the formal language of tests and test-taking strategies, and providing opportunities for students to take practice tests; and these lessons should be folded into the existing instructional program, not replace it. Greene and Melton (2007) organized test preparation into **minilessons** that they taught as part of reading workshop.

THE GENRE OF STANDARDIZED TESTS. Students need opportunities to examine old test forms to learn about the genre of standardized tests and how test questions are formatted (Hornof, 2008). They'll notice that tests look different than other texts they've read; they're typically printed in black and white, the text is dense, and few illustrations are included. Sometimes words, phrases, and lines in the text are numbered, bolded, or underlined. Through this exploration, students begin to think about what makes one type of text harder to read than others, and with practice, they get used to how tests are formatted so that they're better able to read them. Kontovourki and Campis (2010) recommend teaching a genre unit about standardized tests.

THE LANGUAGE OF TESTING. Standardized reading tests use formal language that's unfamiliar to many students. For example, some tests use the word *passage* instead of *text* and *author's intent* instead of *main idea*. Test makers also use *locate*, *except*, *theme*, *reveal*, *inform*, *reason*, *in order to*, *provide suspense*, and other words that students may not understand. Greene and Melton (2007) call the language of testing "test talk" and explain that "students are helpless on standardized reading tests if they can't decipher test talk" (p. 8). Students need help understanding test talk so that high-stakes tests really measure what they know.

TEST-TAKING STRATEGIES. Students learn to use test-taking strategies, and they vary the strategies they use according to the type of test they're taking. Most standardized tests employ multiple-choice questions, so it's important to teach students to use these test-taking strategies:

Read the entire question first. Students read the entire question first to make sure they understand what it's asking. For questions about a reading passage, students read the questions first to guide their reading.

Look for key words in the question. Students identify key words in the question, such as *compare*, *except*, and *author's intent*, that will guide them to choose the correct answer.

Read all answer choices before choosing the correct answer. After students read the question, they stop and think about the answer before reading all the possible answers. Then they eliminate the unlikely answer choices and identify the correct answer.

Answer easier questions first. Students answer the questions they know, skipping the difficult ones, and then they go back and answer the questions they skipped.

Make smart guesses. When students don't know the answer to a question, they make a smart guess, unless there's a penalty for guessing. To make a smart guess, students eliminate the answer choices they're sure are wrong, think about what they know about the topic, and then pick the best remaining answer choice. The correct answer is often the longest one.

Stick with your first answer. Students shouldn't second-guess themselves; their first answer is probably right. They shouldn't change answers unless they're certain that their first answer was wrong.

Pace yourself. Students budget their time so they'll be able to finish the test. They don't spend too much time on any one question.

Check your work carefully. Students check that they've answered every question, if they finish early.

Students use these test-taking strategies along with reading strategies, including determining importance, questioning, and re-reading, when they're taking standardized tests. Teaching students about **Question-Answer-Relationships** helps them to understand that sometimes answers to test questions can be found in a passage they've just read, or they may have to use their own knowledge.

Preparing for tests should be embedded in literacy activities and not take up a great deal of instructional time. Teachers often teach test-taking strategies through minilessons where they explain the strategy, model its use, and provide opportunities for guided practice and discussion. Researchers recommend teaching minilessons on test-taking strategies as well as the standardized-test genre, test formats, and the language of tests as part of reading workshop (Greene & Melton, 2007; Hornof, 2008; Kontovourki & Campis, 2010). They've reported that students, many of whom are English learners and struggling readers and writers, became more confident and empowered test-takers through test-preparation minilessons, and their test scores improved!

PRACTICE TESTS. Teachers design practice tests with the same types of items used on the standardized tests students will take. They choose easy-to read materials for practice tests so students can focus on practicing test-taking strategies without being challenged by the difficulty level of the text or the questions. They include a combination of unrelated narrative, poetic, and informational passages because all three types of texts are used on high-stakes tests. Once in a while teachers also provide answer sheets similar to those used on the standardized test so that students gain experience with them. So students will be familiar with the testing conditions, teachers simulate them in the classroom or take students to the location where the test will be administered for practice sessions. Through these practice tests, students develop confidence in their test-taking abilities and the stamina to persist through long tests.

Nurturing English Learners

How do teachers handle high-stakes testing? When students aren't familiar with multiple choice tests, preparation for achievement tests is especially important; otherwise, students won't fully demonstrate their knowledge. Don't confuse test preparation with teaching to the test: Preparing for a test involves teaching students how to take a test, but teaching to the test is the unethical practice of drilling students on actual questions from old tests. The term "teaching to the test" is also used in a less pejorative way to describe when teachers tailor instruction to meet state-mandated standards. Researchers question the use of standardized achievement tests with English learners because these tests are often invalid, underestimating students' achievement (Peregoy & Boyle, 2013). It seems obvious that when students have limited English proficiency, their test performance would be affected; however, even students who do well in the classroom often score poorly on standardized achievement tests (Lindholm-Leary & Borsato, 2006). There are several reasons for this dichotomy. First, test-taking procedures are less

---

Teach Kids to BE STRATEGIC

Test-Taking Strategies

Teach students how to use these test-taking strategies to answer multiple-choice questions on standardized tests:

- Read the entire question first.
- Look for key words in the question.
- Read all answer choices before choosing the correct one.
- Answer easier questions first.
- Make smart guesses.
- Stick with your first answer.
- Pace yourself.
- Check your work carefully.

Students learn to use these strategies through test-prep minilessons and practice tests.

familiar than comfortable classroom routines, and ELs may be more stressed by their unfamiliarity than native English speakers are. A second reason is that the language used in directions and test items is often complex, academic English, making comprehension more difficult for ELs. Another reason is cultural differences: English learners often lack background knowledge about the topics (e.g., folk legend Johnny Appleseed, Florida everglades, Panama Canal, and Russian Iron Curtain) addressed in the reading passages and test questions.

Researchers believe that the best way to assess English learners more fairly is to provide accommodations, by modifying either the test or the testing procedure (Lindholm-Leary & Borsato, 2006). They've experimented with both modifying tests, by simplifying the language, translating the test into students' home language, or adding visual supports, and modifying the testing procedure, by providing additional time, allowing students to use bilingual dictionaries, or translating or explaining the directions. Unfortunately, data are inconclusive about the effectiveness of these accommodations. Currently, there's renewed interest in rewriting test questions on high-stakes tests to avoid unnecessarily complex English syntactic structures and academic vocabulary so that ELs can actually demonstrate their knowledge.

Probably the best way to ameliorate the effects of ELs' potentially invalid test results is to use multiple measures, including some authentic assessments, to document English learners' language proficiency and literacy achievement. This accommodation, however, is unlikely to be implemented in today's educational climate where both students and teachers are being held accountable using the results from a single test.

The Politics of High-Stakes Testing

High-stakes testing is a politically charged issue (Casbarro, 2005). Test scores are being used as a means to reform schools, and although improving the quality of instruction and ensuring that all students have equal access to educational opportunities are essential, there are unwanted consequences for both students and teachers. Does high-stakes testing work? Proponents claim that schools are being reformed; however, although some gains in test scores for minority groups have been reported, many teachers believe that the improvement is the result of "teaching to the test." So far, no results indicate that students have actually become better readers and writers because of standardized achievement tests.

The goal of NCLB was admirable, but test experts have argued that a single evaluation shouldn't be used to judge either students' learning or teachers' effectiveness. Braunger and Lewis (2006) point out that "ironically, the national focus on accountability . . . may leave little room for assessment linked to instruction that could actually improve literacy outcomes for students who are being left behind" (p. 130).

🔄 **MONITOR: Check Your Understanding 3.3**

Portfolio Assessment

Students collect their work in portfolios and use them to evaluate their progress and showcase their best work (Afflerbach, 2012; Johnson & Mims-Cox, 2009). These systematic and meaningful collections of artifacts document students' literacy development over a period of time (Hebert, 2001). Students select the pieces to be placed in their portfolios, and in the process they learn to establish criteria for their selections. Because of students' involvement in selecting pieces for their portfolios and reflecting on them, portfolio assessment respects students and their abilities.

Portfolios help students, teachers, and parents see patterns of growth from one literacy milestone to another in ways that aren't possible with other types of assessment. There are other benefits, too:

- Students feel ownership of their work.
- Students become more responsible about their work.
- Students set goals and are motivated to work toward accomplishing them.
- Students make connections between learning and assessing.

Teachers use portfolios in parent conferences and to supplement the information provided on report cards. In schools where portfolios are used schoolwide, students overwhelmingly report that they're better able to show their parents what they're learning and also to set goals for themselves (Kuhs, Johnson, Agruso, & Monrad, 2001).

Collecting Work in Portfolios

Portfolios are folders or boxes that hold students' work. Teachers often have students label and decorate large folders and then store them in plastic crates or cardboard boxes. Students date and label items as they place them in their portfolios, and they often attach notes to the items to explain the context for the activity and why they selected a particular item. Portfolios should be stored in the classroom in a place where they are readily accessible, because students like to review their portfolios periodically and add new pieces to them.

Students usually choose the items to place in their portfolios within the guidelines the teacher provides. Some students submit the original piece of work; others want to keep the original, so they place a copy in the portfolio instead. In addition to the reading and writing samples that go directly into portfolios, students can record oral language and drama samples on audiotapes and videotapes to place in their portfolios. Large-size art and writing projects can be photographed, and the photos can be placed in the portfolio. Student work might include books, choral readings on podcasts, learning logs, graphic organizers, multigenre projects, lists of books read, and compositions; this variety of work samples reflects the students' literacy programs. Samples from literature focus units, literature circles, reading and writing workshop, basal reading programs, guided reading, and content area units can be included.

Many teachers collect students' work in folders, but the two types of collections differ in several important ways. Perhaps the most important difference is that portfolios are student oriented and work folders are usually teachers' collections—students choose which samples will be placed in portfolios, but teachers often place all completed assignments in work folders. Next, portfolios focus on students' strengths, not their weaknesses. Because students decide what to put in their portfolios, they choose samples that best represent their literacy development. Another difference is that portfolios involve reflection (Johnson & Mims-Cox, 2009); through reflection, students pause and become aware of their strengths as readers and writers. They also use their work samples to identify the literacy procedures, strategies, and skills they already know and the ones they need to focus on.

Involving Students in Self-Assessment

Portfolios are a tool for engaging students in self-assessment and goal setting. Students learn to reflect on and assess their own reading and writing activities and their development as readers and writers. Teachers begin by asking students to think about their reading and writing in terms of contrasts. For reading, students identify the books they've read that they liked most and least, and they ask themselves what these

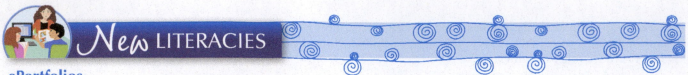

New LITERACIES

ePortfolios

Electronic portfolios are similar to paper portfolios, but instead of collecting writing samples, cassette tapes with oral reading samples, photos of projects, and other artifacts in bulky folders that take up lots of space, all artifacts are stored digitally. Increasingly, students create ePortfolios to showcase their best work and document their learning (Light, Chen, & Ittelson, 2012). They learn to use digital tools as they collect work for their portfolios:

- Scan writing samples
- Photograph art and multigenre projects with a digital camera
- Insert blogs, PowerPoint presentations, and wikis
- Have classmates video their oral projects

Students add text boxes or video clips to provide context for the samples, reflect on their achievement, and explain how their work demonstrates mastery of grade-level standards. They also insert hyperlinks to connect sections and enhance their ePortfolios by adding music and graphics.

Teachers create a template that lays out the design, including a title, table of contents, and collections of artifacts, and students use it to organize their portfolios. Sometimes rubrics are included to show how the artifacts were assessed. Collections of work samples from each grade are saved in separate files within students' portfolios.

When students have opportunities to showcase their achievement, they take more ownership of their learning. The key is reflection (Barrett, 2007): As they reflect on their portfolios, students explain why they selected each artifact and how it documents their learning and meets grade-level standards. ePortfolios are dynamic learning records that students can reorganize, and they can create links to highlight growth from one artifact to another.

ePortfolios are versatile assessment tools: They accept multimodal items, incorporate a hierarchical organization, make searching for and retrieving items easy, and can be displayed for a wide range of audiences to view. They're practical, too, especially once teachers and students are comfortable using software and digital tools, and if they're willing to devote the time needed to start up the portfolio system. These digital repositories are quick and easy to access because they're stored online, and they don't take up space on bookcase shelves or in teachers' file cabinets.

The 21st century has a knowledge-based economy, and K–8 students who document their learning in ePortfolios are likely to continue using them in adult life to document and showcase their accomplishments.

---

choices suggest about them as readers. They also identify what they do well in reading and what they need to improve. In writing, students make similar contrasts: They identify their best compositions and others that weren't as good, and they think about what they do well when they write and what to improve. By making these comparisons, students begin to reflect on their literacy development.

Teachers use minilessons and conferences to teach about the characteristics of good readers and writers. In particular, they discuss these topics:

- What fluent reading is
- Which reading and writing strategies students use
- How students demonstrate comprehension
- How students value books they've read
- What makes an effective piece of writing
- How to use writing rubrics
- Why correcting mechanical errors is a courtesy to readers

As students learn about what it means to be effective readers and writers, they acquire the tools they need to reflect on and evaluate their own reading and writing. They learn how to think about themselves as readers and writers and acquire the vocabulary to use in their reflections, such as *goal*, *strategy*, and *rubric*.

Students write notes on items they choose to put into their portfolios. In these self-assessments, students explain the reasons for their choices and identify strengths and accomplishments in their work. In some classrooms, students write their reflections and other comments on index cards, and in other classrooms, they design special comment sheets that they attach to the items in their portfolios.

Teachers usually collect baseline reading and writing samples at the beginning of the school year and then conduct portfolio review conferences with students at the end of each grading period. At these conferences, the teacher and the student talk about the items being placed in the portfolio and the student's self-assessments. Students also talk about what they want to improve or what they want to accomplish next, and these points become their goals for the next grading period.

Showcasing Students' Portfolios

At the end of the school year, many teachers organize "Portfolio Share Days" to celebrate students' accomplishments and to provide an opportunity for students to share their portfolios with classmates and the wider community. Often family members, local businesspeople, school administrators, local politicians, college students, and others are invited to attend. Students and community members form small groups, and students share their portfolios, pointing out their accomplishments and strengths. This activity is especially useful in involving community members in the school and showing them the types of literacy activities students are engaged in as well as how students are becoming effective readers and writers.

These sharing days also help students accept responsibility for their own learning—especially those who haven't been as motivated as their classmates. When less motivated students listen to their classmates talk about their work and how they've grown as readers and writers, they often decide to work harder the next year.

To examine the effectiveness of your program, use the Teacher Checklist: How do I assess students' learning?

 MONITOR: Check Your Understanding 3.4

TEACHER *Checklist*

How do I assess students' learning?

- O Do I determine students' independent, instructional, and frustration reading levels?
- O Do I consider the reading level of my instructional materials?
- O Do I use the instruction–assessment cycle?
- O Do I monitor students' progress during instruction?
- O Do I choose authentic assessment activities as well as tests to measure students' achievement?
- O Do I use checklists and rubrics to assess students' work?
- O Do I have students self-assess their work and reflect on their achievement?
- O Do I teach students how to take high-stakes tests?
- O Do students keep portfolios to highlight their literacy achievements and milestones?

Review

ASSESSING LITERACY DEVELOPMENT

Effective teachers use the instruction–assessment cycle to assess students' literacy development following the guidelines presented in this chapter, these points in particular:

3.1 Teachers link assessment with instruction through planning, monitoring, evaluating, and reflecting.

3.2 Teachers use diagnostic assessments to identify students' strengths and weaknesses and then provide instruction to address problem areas.

3.3 Teachers prepare students for high-stakes tests without sacrificing their instructional programs.

3.4 Teachers have students document their learning in portfolios.

✔ EVALUATE & REFLECT

Apply your understanding about assessing students' literacy development. The questions ask you to collect and analyze data, and report the results. Your response should meet academic standards and adhere to Standard English conventions.

1. Observe in a K–8 literacy classroom, and use the Teacher Checklist presented in this chapter to examine how the teacher assesses students' learning. In your response, describe the classroom, and address these points:

   ℮ What is this teacher's classroom assessment plan?
   ℮ Which items on the Teacher Checklist did you observe?
   ℮ How could this teacher become more effective?

2. Interview a K–8 teacher to learn how he or she uses diagnostic tests to inform instruction. Ask questions to examine these points:

   ℮ how the teacher determines students' reading levels
   ℮ how the teacher diagnoses students' strengths and weaknesses
   ℮ how the teacher differentiates instruction based on the results of diagnostic tests

   In your response, describe the teacher and his or her teaching assignment and explain what you've learned about how the teacher addresses the three points.

3. Examine a set of 10 books, representing a variety of genres, that are appropriate for one grade level, K–8. Use either the Fountas and Pinnell classification system or the Lexile Framework to level the books. Compare the books using these readability criteria from the chapter:

   ℮ Genre and format of the book
   ℮ Organization and use of text structures
   ℮ Familiarity and interest level of the content
   ℮ Complexity of ideas and themes
   ℮ Language and literary features
   ℮ Sentence length and complexity
   ℮ Sophistication of the vocabulary
   ℮ Word length and ease of decoding
   ℮ Relationship of illustrations to the text
   ℮ Length of the book, its layout, and other print features

   In your response, identify the grade level you've focused on and the reading level of each of the 10 books. Briefly summarize each book and discuss the readability criteria that make it easier or more difficult to read. Finally, summarize what you've learned about readability and explain how the criteria influence reading difficulty.

4. Administer the Concepts About Print Test to a kindergartner, a running record to a K–3 student, or an informal reading inventory to a grades 4–8 student. In your response, describe the student who was tested, the test you administered, and the test results. Then draw conclusions about the student's strengths and weaknesses, and make instructional recommendations.

5. Participate in a portfolio showcase celebration at a local K–8 school, and talk to two students about their portfolios and the artifacts they've collected. Ask the students and the teacher about how they collect artifacts for their portfolios and how they use the collections to reflect on their growth as readers and writers. In your response, describe the classroom, the teacher and students, and how their showcase was organized. Also, summarize the artifacts in each student's portfolio and how they use them to reflect on their academic development.

REFERENCES

Afflerbach, P. (2007). Best practices in literacy assessment. In L. B. Gambrell, L. M. Morrow, & M. Pressley (Eds.), *Best practices in literacy instruction* (3rd ed., pp. 264–282). New York: Guilford Press.

Afflerbach, P. (2012). *Understanding and using reading assessment, K–12* (2nd ed.). Newark, DE: International Reading Association.

Allington, R. L. (2012). *What really matters for struggling readers: Designing research-based programs* (3rd ed.). Boston: Pearson.

Barrett, H. (2007). Researching electronic portfolios and learner engagement: The REFLECT Initiative. *Journal of Adolescent & Adult Literacy, 50,* 436–449.

Boyd-Batstone, P. (2004). Focused anecdotal records assessment: A tool for standards-based, authentic assessment. *The Reading Teacher, 58,* 230–239.

Bracey, G. W. (2004). *Setting the record straight: Responses to misconceptions about public education in the United States.* Portsmouth, NH: Heinemann.

Braunger, J., & Lewis, J. P. (2006). *Building a knowledge base in reading* (2nd ed.). Newark, DE: International Reading Association/ National Council of Teachers of English.

Casbarro, J. (2005, February). The politics of high-stakes testing. *Education Digest, 70*(6), 20–23.

Clay, M. M. (2015). *An observation survey of early literacy achievement* (3rd ed.). Portsmouth, NH: Heinemann.

Cole, J. (1993). *The magic school bus lost in the solar system.* New York: Scholastic.

Danielson, L. M. (2009, February). Fostering reflection. *Educational Leadership, 66*(5). Retrieved from http://www.ascd.org/publications/educational-leadership/feb09/vol66/num05/Fostering-Reflection.aspx

Fountas, I. C., & Pinnell, G. S. (2007). *The Fountas and Pinnell benchmark assessment system.* Portsmouth, NH: Heinemann.

Fountas, I. C., & Pinnell, G. S. (2013). *The Fountas & Pinnell leveled book list, K–8+* (2013–2015 ed., Vols. 1 & 2). Portsmouth, NH: Heinemann.

Fry, E. (1968). A readability formula that saves time. *Journal of Reading, 11,* 587.

Garcia, G. E. (2000). Bilingual children's reading. In M. Kamil, P. Mosenthal, P. D. Pearson, & R. Barr (Eds.), *Handbook of reading research* (Vol. 3, pp. 813–834). Mahwah, NJ: Erlbaum.

Goodman, Y. M. (1978). Kid watching: An alternative to testing. *The National Elementary Principal, 57,* 41–45.

Greene, A. H., & Melton, G. D. (2007). *Test talk: Integrating test preparation into reading workshop.* Portsmouth, ME: Stenhouse.

Hebert, E. A. (2001). *The power of portfolios: What children can teach us about learning and assessment.* San Francisco: Jossey-Bass.

Hoffman, J. V., Assaf, L. C., & Paris, S. G. (2005). High-stakes testing in reading: Today in Texas, tomorrow? In S. J. Barrentine & S. M. Stokes (Eds.), *Reading assessment: Principles and practices for elementary teachers* (2nd ed., pp. 108–120). Newark, DE: International Reading Association.

Hollingworth, L. (2007). Five ways to prepare for standardized tests without sacrificing best practice. *The Reading Teacher, 61,* 339–342.

Hornof, M. (2008). Reading tests as a genre study. *The Reading Teacher, 62,* 69–73.

Howe, D., & Howe, J. (2006). *Bunnicula: A rabbit-tale of mystery.* New York: Aladdin Books.

Huerta-Macías, A. (1995). Alternative assessment: Responses to commonly asked questions. *TESOL Journal, 5,* 8–10.

International Reading Association. (1999). *High-stakes assessments in reading: A position statement.* Newark, DE: Author.

International Reading Association & National Council of Teachers of English. (2009). *Standards for the assessment of reading and writing* (Rev. ed.). Newark, DE: Author.

Johnson, R. S., & Mims-Cox, J. S. (2009). *Developing portfolios in education: A guide to reflection, inquiry, and assessment* (2nd ed.). Newbury Park, CA: Sage Publisher.

Kame'enui, E. (2000). *A practical guide to reading assessments.* Newark, DE: International Reading Association.

Kellogg, S. (2008). *Johnny Appleseed.* New York: HarperCollins.

Kontovourki, S., & Campis, C. (2010). Meaningful practice: Test prep in a third-grade public school classroom. *The Reading Teacher, 64,* 236–245.

Kress, J. E., & Fry, E. B. (2015). *The reading teacher's book of lists: Grades K–12* (6th ed.). Hoboken, NJ: Jossey-Bass.

Kuhs, T. M., Johnson, R. L., Agruso, S. A., & Monrad, D. M. (2001). *Put to the test: Tools and techniques for classroom assessment.* Portsmouth, NH: Heinemann.

Light, T. P., Chen, H. L., & Ittelson, J. C. (2012). *Documenting learning with ePortfolios.* San Francisco: Jossey-Bass.

Lindholm-Leary, K., & Borsato, G. (2006). Academic achievement. In F. Genesee, K. Lindholm-Leary, W. M. Saunders, & D. Christian (Eds.), *Educating English language learners: A synthesis of research evidence* (pp. 176–222). New York: Cambridge University Press.

Lowry, L. (2011). *Number the stars.* New York: Sandpiper.

MacLachlan, P. (2005). *Sarah, plain and tall.* New York: Scholastic.

McCabe, P. P. (2003). Enhancing self-efficacy for high-stakes reading tests. *The Reading Teacher, 57,* 12–20.

McLaughlin, M., & Overturf, B. J. (2012). *The Common Core: Teaching K–5 students to meet the reading standards.* Newark, DE: International Reading Association.

McLaughlin, M., & Overturf, B. J. (2013). *The Common Core: Teaching students in grades 6–12 to meet the reading standards.* Newark, DE: International Reading Association.

Meier, D., Kohn, A., Darling-Hammond, L., Sizer, T. R., & Wood, G. (Eds.). (2004). *Many children left behind.* Boston: Beacon Press.

National Commission on Excellence in Education. (1983). *A nation at risk: The imperative for educational reform.* Washington, DC: U.S. Government Printing Office.

Nilsson, N. L. (2008). A critical analysis of eight informal reading inventories. *The Reading Teacher, 61,* 526–536.

Peregoy, S. F., & Boyle, O. F. (2013). *Reading, writing, and learning in ESL: A resource book K–12 teachers* (6th ed.). Boston: Pearson.

Peverini, S. (2009). The value of teacher expertise and good judgment: Recent inspiring reading about assessment. *Language Arts, 86,* 44–47.

Riches, C., & Genesee, F. (2006). Literacy: Crosslinguistic and crossmodal issues. In F. Genesee, K. Lindholm-Leary, W. M. Saunders, & D. Christian (Eds.), *Educating English language learners: A synthesis of research evidence* (pp. 64–108). New York: Cambridge University Press.

Risko, V. J., & Walker-Dalhouse, D. (2010). Making the most of assessments to inform instruction. *The Reading Teacher, 63,* 420–422.

Sachar, L. (2008). *Holes.* New York: Farrar, Straus & Giroux.

Shanahan, T. (2014). How and how not to prepare students for the new tests. *The Reading Teacher, 68,* 184–188.

Skillings, M. J., & Ferrell, R. (2000). Student-generated rubrics: Bringing students into the assessment process. *The Reading Teacher, 53,* 452–455.

Stevens, D. D., Levi, A. J., & Walvoord, B. E. (2012). *Introduction to rubrics: An assessment tool to save grading time, convey effective feedback, and promote student learning* (2nd ed.). Sterling, VA: Stylus Publications.

Taylor, M. D. (2004). *Roll of thunder, hear my cry.* New York: Puffin Books.

The pot of gold (an Irish folk tale). (2001). Upper Saddle River, NJ: Celebration Press/Pearson.

Components of Literacy Development

Researchers have identified these components of literacy development that students need to learn to become effective readers and writers:

- **Alphabetic Code**
  Students learn phonemic awareness, phonics, and spelling to understand the English sound–symbol system.

- **Fluency**
  Students learn to read words fluently so that they have cognitive resources available for comprehension and writing.

- **Vocabulary**
  Students acquire a wide vocabulary and learn how to unlock the meaning of new words and choose specific words in writing.

- **Comprehension**
  Students learn to use strategies to direct and deepen their comprehension.

In this part opener, I introduce you to five students in Ms. Janusz's second grade class. You'll learn about them and how they develop as readers and writers. Four of these students—Rakie, Curt'Lynn, Michael, and Rhiannon—began second grade not meeting grade-level expectations, but the fifth student, Jimmy, exemplifies second grade standards and provides a grade-level comparison.

At the beginning of the school year, effective teachers like Ms. Janusz use their own observations, school records, and conversations with parents to identify the learning needs of their students. Ms. Janusz and I talked in early October about her students' literacy learning needs. Click on the play buttons for Rakie, Rhiannon, Michael, Jimmy, and Curt'Lynn and listen to my interviews with Ms. Janusz as she shares her wealth of knowledge about each student.

Rakie

Rakie's favorite color is pink, and she loves her cat, JoJo. She came to America from Africa when she was very young, and she's currently enrolled in the school's pull-out ESL program. Rakie enjoys reading books with her friends in the library area. Her favorite book is Doreen Cronin's *Click Clack Moo: Cows That Type* because she appreciates that troublesome duck. Rakie's a fluent reader, but she has difficulty understanding what she reads, mainly because of unfamiliar vocabulary, a common problem for English learners. Rakie's bright, and Ms. Janusz is pleased that she's making great strides!

A minte leter I opened the door and Jojo was foze in a ice cobe.

Beep beep beep beep it was 9:00 am. I new I had to wacke up. I toock my first Step, Slip the flors were frozen Solid.

Michael is gregarious and loves fun in any size or shape. He takes karate lessons, and his Xbox video gaming system is a prized possession. In September, Michael, who is bilingual, was reading below grade level and couldn't stay on task, but after Ms. Janusz encouraged him to choose books that he wanted to read and to identify topics for writing, his motivation began to grow. Now, he's making rapid progress! He's not crazy about reading except for The Magic Tree House series of chapter books, but he really enjoys writing. He says that his stories are good because he uses wordplay effectively.

Rhiannon

Rhiannon, the youngest in Ms. Janusz's class, is a charmer. Her gusto for life is contagious! In September, she held books upside down, but she's made tremendous progress since then. Mo Willems is her favorite author; she loves his stories, including *Don't Let the Pigeon Drive the Bus!* She struggles to decode unfamiliar words, usually depending on the "sound it out" strategy. Rhiannon's passionate about writing. She creates inventive stories about her dogs, Taco and Tequila, and gets very animated when sharing them with classmates, but abbreviated spellings make her writing difficult to read.

I soDit to my DaD. B u D up! So I pot Logr clos onanD Pas anD soD It to my DaD. B u D u p!

TRANSLATION:
I showed it to my Dad.
Bundle up! So I
put longer clothes on and
pants and showed it to my
Dad. Bundle up!

Curt'Lynn

Curt'Lynn enjoys playing with her buddies Leah and Audri at recess and spending time with her Granny. Her reading was at early first grade level at the beginning of second grade; she often "read" books to herself, telling the story through the illustrations. Now Curt'Lynn loves to read Dr. Seuss books because they're funny. Her focus is on decoding words, but she's beginning to think about whether the words she's reading make sense. Curt'Lynn recognizes that her reading has been improving this year because, as she explains, it's becoming easier to get the words right.

> When I was just 4 years old, I was a CherLeedre Because I rill wueted to be a cherLeedre.

> It was a haunted house! The door creKed opin. "BOO!" said a ghost. And Lady was gone! "AAAA!" said Jim.

Jimmy's a big sports fan—he likes the Cleveland Indians and the Ohio State Buckeyes, in particular—but his real passion is World War II. He likes to play Army with his best friend, Sam. Jimmy often chooses nonfiction books on varied topics to read; recently, he read a biography about rock-and-roll idol Elvis Presley. Jimmy's a bright student who achieves at or above grade level in all subjects. He's eager to please and worries about making a mistake when he's sharing his writing or reading aloud. In September, Jimmy had trouble with comprehension, but now he's a confident, strategic reader.

These students appear in the Literacy Portraits in this text. You can track their development in phonics, fluency, vocabulary, and comprehension, and you'll see the tremendous growth that they've made during second grade. All five students have become more capable readers and writers.

Chapter 4

The Youngest Readers and Writers

PLAN: Preview the Learning Outcomes

After studying this chapter, you'll be prepared to respond to these points:

4.1 Explain how children develop oral language.

4.2 Discuss ways teachers foster children's interest in literacy.

4.3 Describe the three stages that children move through as they develop as readers and writers.

4.4 List instructional practices that teachers use with young readers and writers.

K–3 Students' Literacy Development. Kindergarten through third grade students sit together on the carpet for a shared reading lesson. They watch and listen intently as Ms. McCloskey prepares to read *Make Way for Ducklings* (McCloskey, 2004), the big-book version of an award-winning story about the dangers facing a family of ducks living in the city of Boston. She reads the title and the author's name, and some children recognize that the author's last name is the same as hers, but she points out that they aren't related. She reads the first page and asks the class to make predictions about what will happen in the story. During this first reading, Ms. McCloskey reads each page expressively and tracks the text, word by word, with a pointer as she reads. She clarifies the meaning as she talks about the illustrations on each page. A child helps balance the book on the easel and turn the pages for her. After she finishes, they talk about the story. Some of the English learners are initially hesitant, but others eagerly relate their own experiences to the story and ask questions to learn more.

The next day, Ms. McCloskey begins by asking for volunteers to retell *Make Way for Ducklings*. Children take turns retelling each page, using the illustrations as clues. Ms. McCloskey includes this oral language activity because many of her students are English learners. The class is multilingual and multicultural: Approximately 45% are Asian Americans who speak Hmong, Khmer, or Lao; 45% are Hispanics who speak Spanish or English at home; and the remaining 10% are African Americans and whites who speak English.

Next, Ms. McCloskey rereads the story, stopping several times to ask the class to think about the characters, draw inferences, and reflect on the theme. Her questions include: Why did the police officer help the ducks? What would have happened to the ducks if the police officer didn't help? Do you think that animals should live in cities? What was Robert McCloskey trying to say to us in this story? On the third day, Ms. McCloskey reads the story again, and the children take turns using the pointer to track the text and join in reading familiar words. After they finish, the children clap because rereading the now familiar story provides a sense of accomplishment.

Ms. McCloskey understands that her students are moving through three developmental stages—emergent, beginning, and fluent—as they learn to read and write. She monitors each child's development to provide instruction that meets his or her needs. As she reads the big book aloud, she uses a pointer to show the direction of print, from left to right and top to bottom on the page. She also moves the pointer across the lines of text, word by word, to demonstrate the relationship between the words on the page and the words she's reading aloud. These are concepts that many of the youngest, emergent-stage readers are learning.

Others are beginning readers who are learning to recognize high-frequency words and decode phonetically regular words. One day after rereading the story, Ms. McCloskey turns to one of the pages and asks the children to identify familiar high-frequency words (e.g., *don't*, *make*) and decode other CVC words (e.g., *run*, *big*). She also asks children to isolate individual sentences on the page and note the capital letter at the beginning and the punctuation that marks the end of the sentence.

The children in the third group are fluent readers. Ms. McCloskey addresses their needs, too, as she rereads a page from the story: She asks several children to identify adjectives and notice inflectional endings on verbs. She also rereads the last sentence on the page and asks a child to explain why commas are used in it.

Ms. McCloskey draws the children's attention to the text as a natural part of **shared reading**. She demonstrates concepts; points out letters, words, and punctuation marks; models strategies; and asks questions about concepts of print. As they watch Ms. McCloskey and listen to their classmates, the children think about letters, words, and sentences and learn more about literacy.

Ms. McCloskey and her teaching partner, Mrs. Papaleo, share a large classroom and 40 students; despite the number of children present, the room feels spacious. Children's desks are arranged in clusters around the large, open area in the middle where children meet for whole-class activities. An easel to display big books is placed next to the teacher's chair. Several chart racks stand nearby; one rack holds Ms. McCloskey's morning messages and **interactive writing** texts that children have written, a second one holds charts with poems that the children use for **choral reading**, and a third rack holds a pocket chart with word cards and sentence strips.

On one side of the classroom is the library, with books arranged in crates by topic. One crate has frog books, and others have books about the ocean, plants, and the five senses. Some crates contain books by authors who have been featured in author studies, including Eric Carle, Kevin Henkes, and Paula Danziger. Picture books and chapter books are arranged in the crates; children take turns keeping the area neat. Sets of leveled books are arranged on a shelf above the children's reach for the teachers to use in guided reading lessons. A child-size sofa, a table and chairs, pillows, and rugs make the library area cozy and inviting. A listening center is set up at a nearby table with a tape player and headphones that accommodate six children at a time.

A **word wall** with high-frequency words fills a partition separating instructional areas; it's divided into sections for each letter of the alphabet. Arranged on it are nearly 100 words written on small cards cut into the shape of the words. The teachers introduce new words each week and post them on the word wall. The children often practice reading and writing the words as a center activity, and they refer to the word wall to spell words when they're writing.

A bank of computers with a printer are located on another side of the classroom. Everyone uses them, even the youngest children; those who have stronger computer skills assist their classmates. They use word processing to publish their writing during writing workshop and monitor their independent reading practice on the computer using the Accelerated Reader program. At other times, they search the Internet to find information related to topics they're studying in science and social studies, and use software programs to learn typing skills.

Literacy center materials are stored in another area. Clear plastic boxes hold sets of magnetic letters, puppets and other props, whiteboards and pens, puzzles and games, flash cards, and other manipulatives. The teachers choose materials to use during **minilessons**, and they also set boxes of materials out for children to use during center time.

Ms. McCloskey spends the morning teaching reading and writing using a variety of teacher-directed and student-choice activities; check the figure Ms. McCloskey's Schedule. After shared reading and a minilesson, the children participate in reading and writing workshop.

The children write books during writing workshop. They pick up their writing folders and write independently at their desks. While most of them are working, Ms. McCloskey brings together a small group for a special activity: She conducts interactive writing lessons with emergent writers and teaches the writing process and revision strategies to more fluent writers.

MS. McCLOSKEY'S SCHEDULE

TIME	ACTIVITY	DESCRIPTION
8:10–8:20	Class Meeting	Children participate in opening activities, read the morning message from their teachers, and talk about plans for the day.
8:20–8:45	Shared Reading	The teachers read big books and poems written on charts; this activity often serves as a lead-in to the minilesson.
8:45–9:00	Minilesson	The teachers teach minilessons on literacy procedures, concepts, strategies, and skills.
9:00–9:45	Writing Workshop	Children write books while the teachers conference with individual children and small groups. They also do interactive writing activities.
9:45–10:00	Recess	
10:00–11:15	Reading Workshop	Children read self-selected books independently while the teachers do guided reading lessons with small groups.
11:15–11:30	Class Meeting	Children share their writing from the author's chair, and they review the morning's activities.
11:30–12:10	Lunch	
12:10–12:30	Read-Aloud	Teachers read aloud picture books and chapter books, and children discuss them in grand conversations.

Today, she's conferencing with six children who are beginning writers; because they're writing longer compositions, Ms. McCloskey has decided to introduce revising. After each child reads his or her rough draft aloud to the group, classmates ask questions and offer compliments, and Ms. McCloskey encourages them to make a change in their writing so that their readers will understand it better. Anthony reads aloud a story about his soccer game, and after a classmate asks a question, he realizes that he needs to add more about how he scored a goal. He moves back to his desk to revise. The group continues with children sharing their writing and beginning to make revisions. At the end of writing workshop, the children come together for author's chair: Each day, three children take turns sitting in the author's chair to read their writing to classmates.

During reading workshop, children read independently or with a buddy while Ms. McCloskey and her teaching partner conduct guided reading lessons. The children have access to a wide variety of books in the classroom library, including predictable books for emergent readers, decodable books for beginning readers, and easy-to-read chapter books for fluent readers. The children know how to choose books that they can read successfully so they're able to spend their time really reading. The children keep lists of the books they read in their workshop folders so that their teachers can monitor their progress.

Ms. McCloskey is working with a group of four emergent readers, and today they'll read *Playing* (Prince, 1999), a seven-page predictable book with one line of text on each page that uses the pattern "I like to ___." She begins by asking children what they like to do when they're playing. Der says, "I like to play with my brother," and Ms. McCloskey writes that on a strip of paper. Some children say only a word or two, so she expands the words into a sentence for the child to repeat; then she writes the expanded sentence and reads it with the child. Next, she introduces the book and reads the title and the author's name. Ms. McCloskey does a picture walk, talking about the picture on each page and naming the activity the child is doing—running, jumping, sliding, and so on. She reviews the "I like to ___" pattern, and then the children read the book independently while Ms. McCloskey supervises and provides assistance as needed. The children eagerly reread the book several times, becoming more confident and excited with each reading.

Ms. McCloskey reviews the high-frequency words *I*, *like*, and *to*, and the children point them out on the classroom word wall. They use magnetic letters to spell the words and then write sentences that begin with "I like to" on whiteboards. Then Ms. McCloskey cuts their sentence strips apart for them to sequence; afterward the children put their sentences into envelopes to practice another day. At the end of the lesson, the teacher suggests that the children might want to write "I like to ___" books during writing workshop the next day.

During the last 30 minutes before lunch, the children work at literacy centers. Ms. McCloskey and Mrs. Papaleo have set out 12 centers, and the children are free to work at any one they choose. Check the figure Literacy Centers. They're familiar with the routine and know what's expected of them at each center. The two teachers circulate around the classroom, monitoring children's work and taking advantage of teachable moments to clarify misunderstandings, reinforce previous lessons, and extend children's learning.

After lunch, Ms. McCloskey reads aloud picture books and easy-to-read chapter books. Sometimes she reads books by a particular author, but at other times, she reads books related to a thematic unit. She uses these read-alouds to teach predicting, visualizing, and other reading strategies. This week, she's reading award-winning books, and today she reads aloud *The Stray Dog* (Simont, 2001), the story of a homeless dog that's taken in by a loving family. She uses the **interactive read-aloud** procedure to involve children in the book as she reads, and afterward they talk about it in a **grand conversation**. Ms. McCloskey asks them to share their connections to the story, which the teachers record on a chart divided into three sections. Most comments are text-to-self connections, but several children make other types of connections. Rosario says, "I am thinking of a movie. It was *101 Dalmatians*. It was about dogs, too." That's a text-to-text connection. Angelo offers a text-to-world connection: "You got to stay away from stray dogs. They can bite you, and they might have this bad disease called rabies—it can kill you."

LITERACY CENTERS

CENTER	DESCRIPTION
Bag a Story	Children use objects in a paper bag to create a story. They draw pictures or write sentences to tell the story they've created.
Clipboards	Children search the classroom for words beginning with a particular letter or featuring a spelling pattern and write them on paper attached to clipboards.
Games	Children play alphabet, phonics, and other literacy card and board games with classmates.
Library	Children read books related to a thematic unit and write or draw about the books in reading logs.
Listening	Children listen to a tape of a story or informational book while they follow along in a copy of the book.
Making Words	Children practice a making words activity that they've previously done together as a class with teacher guidance.
Messages	Children write notes to classmates and the teachers and post them on a special "Message Center" bulletin board.
Poetry Frames	Children arrange word cards on a chart-sized poetry frame to create a poem and then practice reading it.
Reading the Room	Children use pointers to point to and reread big books, charts, signs, and other texts posted in the classroom.
Research	Children use the Internet, informational books, photos, and realia to learn more about topics in literature focus units and thematic units.
Story Reenactment	Children use small props, finger puppets, or flannel board figures to reenact familiar stories with classmates.
Word Sort	Children categorize high-frequency or thematic word cards displayed in a pocket chart.

 STANDARDS CHECK!

Ms. McCloskey addressed the Common Core State Standards as she used the reading and writing processes in the vignette you've just read. Review the first grade literacy Standards document online at http://www.corestandards.org/ELA-Literacy, and identify the Standards that Ms. McCloskey and her students addressed. Create your list, and compare it with Ms. McCloskey's.

L iteracy is a process that begins in infancy and continues into adulthood, if not throughout life. It used to be that 5-year-olds came to kindergarten to be "readied" for reading and writing instruction, which formally began in first grade. The implication was that there's a point in children's development when it's time to teach them to read and write, and for those not ready, a variety of "readiness"

activities would prepare them. Since the 1970s, this view has been discredited because preschoolers have demonstrated that they can recognize signs and other environmental print, retell stories, scribble letters, invent printlike writing, and listen to stories read aloud (Morrow & Tracey, 2007). Some young children even teach themselves to read!

This perspective on how children become literate—that is, how they learn to read and write—is known as **emergent literacy**, a term that New Zealand educator Marie Clay coined. Studies from 1966 on have shaped the current outlook (McGee & Richgels, 2003; Morrow & Tracey, 2007). Now, researchers are looking at literacy learning from the child's point of view. Literacy development has been broadened to incorporate the cultural and social aspects of language learning, and children's experiences with and understandings about written language—both reading and writing—are included as part of emergent literacy.

Nurturing Children's Oral Language Development

Young children develop oral language through everyday experiences and interaction with parents and others; they learn words at the grocery store, on the playground, during swimming lessons, and from the guide at the zoo, for example. Children who go fishing with their grandpas, plant gardens with their moms, or collect Thomas trains or Disney princesses learn new words along the way, too. They learn even more words listening to adults read aloud picture books and watching *Blue's Clues*, *Dora the Explorer*, *Daniel Tiger's Neighborhood*, and other TV programs designed for young children.

Through these experiences, children develop expertise in all four language modes:

Phonology. Children learn to produce the sounds of English and to manipulate language in playful ways.

Syntax. Children learn to combine words into different types of sentences and to use irregular verb forms, pronouns, and plural markers and other inflectional endings.

Semantics. Children acquire knowledge about the meanings of words and add several thousand words to their vocabularies each year.

Pragmatics. Children learn to use language socially—to carry on a conversation, tell stories, and use social conventions, including "please" and "thank you."

By age 5, children have acquired the oral language of their home culture. They learn to converse with individuals and in groups to tell stories, and to listen to and follow directions, and they acquire vocabulary related to concepts they're learning.

Oral Language Activities

Children continue to develop oral language competence at school, especially as they participate in literacy activities. Probably the most valuable activity is the instructional procedure teachers use to read stories and other books aloud that's known as **interactive read-alouds**. As they listen, children learn new vocabulary and acquire more sophisticated sentence structures. Booklist: Books That Develop Oral Language presents popular picture books that introduce new vocabulary and develop young children's talking and listening abilities. After reading, children use words and phrases

Check the Compendium of Instructional Procedures, which follows Chapter 12.

Booklist   Books That Develop Oral Language

GRADE	BOOKS
K	Carle, E. (2002). *The very hungry caterpillar.* New York: Puffin Books.
	Fleming, D. (2007). *In the small, small pond.* New York: Henry Holt.
	Logue, M. (2012). *Sleep like a tiger.* Boston: Houghton Mifflin.
	Martin, B., Jr., & Archambault, J. (2009). *Chicka chicka boom boom.* New York: Beach Lane Books.
	Root, P. (2004). *Rattletrap car.* Cambridge, MA: Candlewick Press.
	Taback, S. (1997). *There was an old lady who swallowed a fly.* New York: Viking.
	Wood, A. (2005). *The napping house.* San Diego: Harcourt.
1	Gray, M. (1995). *My mama had a dancing heart.* New York: Orchard Books.
	Hoban, T. (2008). *Over, under, and through.* New York: Aladdin Books.
	Most, B. (1996). *Cock-a-doodle-moo!* Orlando: Harcourt.
	Rathmann, P. (1995). *Officer Buckle and Gloria.* New York: Putnam.
	Reynolds, A. (2012). *Creepy carrots.* New York: Simon & Schuster.
	Scieszka, J. (1999). *The true story of the 3 little pigs!* New York: Viking.
	Seeger, L. V. (2012). *Green.* New York: Roaring Brook Press.
2	Bunting, E. (1999). *Smoky night.* San Diego: Voyager.
	Di Pucchio, K. (2014). *Gaston.* New York: Atheneum.
	Fosberry, J. (2010). *My name is not Isabella.* Naperville, IL: Sourcebooks.
	Fox, M. (1998). *Tough Boris.* Orlando: Voyager.
	Hurd, T. (2003). *Moo cow kaboom.* New York: HarperCollins.
	St. George, J. (2004). *So you want to be president?* New York: Philomel.
	Yolen, J. (1987). *Owl moon.* New York: Scholastic.
3	Levine, E. (2007). *Henry's freedom box: A true story from the Underground Railroad.* New York: Scholastic Press.
	Obama, B. (2010). *Of thee I sing: A letter to my daughters.* New York: Knopf.
	Ryan, P. M. (1999). *Amelia and Eleanor go for a ride.* New York: Scholastic.
	Scieszka, J. (1995). *Math curse.* New York: Viking.
	Steig, W. (2009). *Amos & Boris.* New York: Square Fish Books.
	Van Allsburg, C. (1986). *The stranger.* Boston: Houghton Mifflin.
	Zelinsky, P. O. (1997). *Rapunzel.* New York: Dutton.

from the text as they participate in **grand conversations**, do **story retellings**, and use **story boards** to sequence events.

Figure 4–1 lists literacy activities that develop children's oral language; these activities are described in the Compendium of Instructional Procedures, which follows Chapter 12. In addition, whenever children work together in small groups, they have opportunities to use new vocabulary to talk about things they're learning.

Learning a Second Language

Children learn a second language much the same way they learn their first language: Both are developmental processes that require time and opportunity. Young children learn a second language best in a classroom where talk is encouraged and where the teacher and classmates serve as English language models. They hear English spoken in meaningful contexts and associated with physical actions, artifacts, and pictures. Children acquire conversational English, known as **Basic Interpersonal Communicative**

FIGURE 4–1 Activities to Develop Oral Language

COMPONENT	KINDERGARTEN	GRADES 1–3	GRADES 4–8
Expressiveness	Grand conversations Interactive read-alouds Interactive writing Language Experience Approach Story boards Story retelling	Book talks Grand conversations Interactive read-alouds Interactive writing Shared reading Story boards Story retelling Tea party	Book talks Grand conversations Hot seat Interactive read-alouds Possible sentences Quickwriting Shared reading Tea party
Wordplay	Interactive read-alouds Shared reading	Choral reading Interactive read-alouds Shared reading	Choral reading
Word Knowledge	Interactive read-alouds Interactive writing KWL charts	Interactive read-alouds KWL charts Semantic feature analysis Tea party Word sorts Word walls	Interactive read-alouds KWL charts Learning logs Open-mind portraits Possible sentences Question-Answer-Relationships Quickwriting Semantic feature analysis Tea party Word sorts Word walls

Skills (BICS), quickly, in 2 years or less, but academic English, known as **Cognitive Academic Language Proficiency** (CALP), can take 7 or 8 years to acquire (Cummins, 1979). Even though English learners in third or fourth grade may appear fluent in conversational settings, they may still struggle academically because they haven't learned more formal, academic English.

Societal and cultural factors influence language acquisition; children's personalities, the attitudes of their cultural group, and teacher expectations all play a role (Otto, 2014; Samway & McKeon, 2007). Children's level of proficiency in their first language also affects their second language development: Those who continue to develop their first language proficiency become better English speakers than those who stop learning their native language (Tabors, 2008).

The Link Between Oral Language and Literacy

Developing children's oral language is essential because it provides the foundation for literacy learning (Roskos, Tabors, & Lenhart, 2009). Children who don't develop strong oral language before first grade have difficulty keeping pace with classmates (Hart & Risley, 2003; Snow, Burns, & Griffin, 1998). Researchers have found that vocabulary knowledge is an important predictor of beginning reading success (Roth, Speece, & Cooper, 2002). Interestingly, children's ability to orally define words was found to be an important predictor of how well they'd be able to decode words and comprehend text in the primary grades. Other significant factors, such as phonemic awareness and letter knowledge, are related to children's ability to decode words but not to their comprehension.

Teachers use a variety of procedures to expand children's vocabulary. How does the teacher in this video develop children's oral language?

Assessing Children's Oral Language

Teachers monitor young children's oral language development because they understand its importance for academic achievement. They use informal assessment techniques to check that children demonstrate these talk skills:

- ❧ Speak clearly in complete sentences
- ❧ Respond to questions
- ❧ Initiate conversations
- ❧ Take turns
- ❧ Ask questions
- ❧ Participate in discussions
- ❧ Sing songs and recite fingerplays
- ❧ Tell about experiences

Teachers use observations, anecdotal notes, checklists, and video clips (Otto, 2014). They also monitor that children listen during conversations and discussions about books and to follow directions. They notice whether children play with words, connect new words to technical concepts they're learning, and use new vocabulary words appropriately as they talk and write.

🔄 **MONITOR: Check Your Understanding 4.1**

Fostering an Interest in Literacy

Young children's introduction to written language begins before they come to school. Parents and other caregivers read to them, and they learn to read signs and other environmental print in their community. They experiment with writing and have their parents write messages for them; they also observe adults writing. When young children come to school, their knowledge about written language expands quickly as they learn concepts about print and participate in meaningful experiences with reading and writing. The Common Core State Standards for English Language Arts emphasize the importance of fostering children's interest in reading and writing and developing their understanding of concepts about written language. Check the feature Common Core State Standards: Concepts About Written Language to learn more about the Standards for the youngest readers and writers.

Concepts About Print

Through experiences in their homes and communities, young children learn that print carries meaning and that reading and writing are used for a variety of purposes (Clay, 2000a). They notice menus in restaurants, write and receive postcards and letters to communicate with friends and relatives, and listen to stories read aloud for enjoyment. Children also observe parents and teachers using written language for all these reasons.

Children's understanding about the purposes of reading and writing reflects how written language is used in their community. Although reading and writing are part of daily life for almost every family, in different communities, families vary how they use written language (Heath, 1983). Young children have a wide range of literacy experiences in both middle-class and working-class families, even though those experiences might not be the same (Taylor & Dorsey-Gaines, 1987). In some communities, written language is used mainly as a tool for practical purposes such as paying bills, and in others, reading and writing are also used for leisure-time activities. In still other communities, written language serves even wider functions, such as debating social and political issues.

Preschool and kindergarten teachers demonstrate the purposes of written language and provide opportunities for children to experiment with reading and writing in many ways:

Posting signs in the classroom
Making a list of classroom rules
Using reading and writing materials in literacy play centers
Exchanging messages with classmates
Reading and writing stories
Labeling classroom items
Drawing and writing in journals
Writing notes to parents

Young children learn other concepts about print through these activities, too: They learn book-orientation concepts, including how to hold a book and turn pages, and that the text, not the illustrations, carries the message. Children also learn directionality concepts—that print is written and read from left to right and from top to bottom on a page. They match voice to print, pointing word by word to the text as it is read aloud. Children also notice punctuation marks and learn their names and their purposes.

Concepts About Words

At first, young children have only vague notions of literacy terms, such as *word, letter, sound,* and *sentence,* that teachers use in talking about reading and writing, but they develop an increasingly sophisticated understanding of these terms. Papandropoulou and Sinclair (1974) identified four stages of word consciousness. At first, young children don't differentiate between words and things. At the next level, they describe words as labels for things; children consider words that stand for objects as words, but they don't classify articles and prepositions as words because words such as *the* and *with* can't be represented with objects. At the third level, children understand that words carry meaning and that stories are built from words. Finally, more fluent readers and writers describe words as autonomous elements having meanings of their own with definite semantic and syntactic relationships. Children might say, "You make words with letters." Also, children understand that words have different appearances: They can be spoken, listened to, read, and written. Invernizzi (2003) explains the importance of reaching the fourth level this way: "A concept of word allows children to hold onto the printed word in their mind's eye and scan it from left to right, noting every sound in the beginning, middle, and end" (p. 152).

Children develop concepts about words through active participation in literacy activities. They watch as teachers point to words in big books during shared reading, and they mimic the teacher, pointing to words as they reread familiar texts. After many, many shared reading experiences, children notice that word boundaries are marked with spaces, and they pick out familiar words. With experience, children's

Listen as a kindergarten teacher discusses the importance of environmental print to enhance her students' literacy development. How do children develop a concept of words in a print-rich environment?

pointing becomes more exact, and they become more proficient at picking out specific words in the text, noticing that words at the beginning of sentences are marked with capital letters and words at the end are followed with punctuation marks.

ENVIRONMENTAL PRINT. Young children begin reading by recognizing logos on fast-food restaurants, department stores, grocery stores, and commonly used household items within familiar contexts (Harste, Woodward, & Burke, 1984). They recognize the golden arches of McDonald's and say "McDonald's," but when they're shown the word *McDonald's* written on a sheet of paper without the familiar sign and restaurant setting, they can't read it. At first, young children depend on context to read familiar words and memorized texts, but slowly, they develop relationships linking form and meaning as they gain more reading and writing experience.

WRITING. As children begin to experiment with writing, they use scribbles and letterlike forms to represent words (Schickedanz & Casbergue, 2004). As they learn about letter names and phoneme–grapheme correspondences, they use one, two, or three letters to stand for words. At first, they run their writing together, but they slowly learn to mark word boundaries by segmenting writing into words and leaving spaces between words. They sometimes add dots or lines as markers between words or draw circles around words. They also progress from capitalizing words randomly to using capital letters at the beginning of sentences and to mark proper nouns and adjectives. Similarly, children move from using a period at the end of each line of writing to indicating the ends of sentences with periods.

LITERACY PLAY CENTERS. Young children learn about the purposes of reading and writing as they use written language in their play: As they construct block buildings, children write signs and tape them on the buildings; as they play doctor, children write prescriptions on slips of paper; and as they play teacher, children read stories aloud to stuffed animal "students" (McGee, 2007). Young children use these activities to reenact familiar, everyday activities and to pretend to be someone else. Through these literacy play activities, children use reading and writing for a variety of purposes.

Kindergarten teachers add literacy materials to play centers to enhance their value for literacy learning. Housekeeping centers are probably the most common play centers, and they can easily be transformed into a grocery store, a post office, or a medical center by changing the props. They become literacy play centers when materials for reading and writing are included: Food packages, price stickers, and play money are props in grocery store centers; letters, stamps, and mailboxes are props in post office centers; and appointment books, prescription pads, and folders for patient records are props in medical centers. A variety of literacy play centers can be set up in classrooms and coordinated with literature focus units and thematic units.

Concepts About the Alphabet

Young children also develop concepts about the alphabet and how letters are used to represent phonemes. Pinnell and Fountas (1998) identified these components of letter knowledge:

𝒪 The letter's name
𝒪 The formation of the letter in upper- and lowercase manuscript handwriting

- The features of the letter that distinguish it from other letters
- The direction the letter must be turned to distinguish it from other letters (e.g., *b* and *d*)
- The use of the letter in known words (e.g., names and common words)
- The sound the letter represents in isolation
- The sound the letter represents in combination with others (e.g., *ch*, *th*)
- The sound the letter represents in the context of a word (e.g., the *c* sounds in *cat*, *city*, and *chair*)

Children use this knowledge to decode unfamiliar words as they read and to create spellings for words as they write.

The most basic information children learn about the alphabet is how to identify and form the letters in handwriting. They notice letters in environmental print and learn to sing the ABC song. By the time children enter kindergarten, they usually recognize some letters, especially those in their own names, in names of family members and pets, and in common words in their homes and communities. Children also write some of these familiar letters.

Research suggests that children don't learn letter names in any particular order or by isolating letters from meaningful written language in skill-and-drill activities.

FIGURE 4–2 Routines to Teach the Alphabet

ROUTINE	ACTIVITY
Alphabet Books	Teachers read alphabet books aloud to build vocabulary, and later, children reread the books to find words when making books about a letter.
Alphabet Chart	Children point to letters and pictures on the alphabet chart as they recite the alphabet and the name of the picture, such as "A-airplane, B-baby, C-cat," and so on.
Environmental Print	Children sort food labels, toy traffic signs, and other environmental print to find examples of a letter being studied.
Letter Books and Posters	Children make letter books with pictures of objects beginning with a particular letter on each page. They add letter stamps, stickers, or pictures cut from magazines. For posters, the teacher draws a large letterform on a chart and children add pictures, stickers, and letter stamps.
Letter Containers	Teachers collect coffee cans or shoe boxes, one for each letter, and place several familiar objects that represent the letter in each container. Teachers use these containers to introduce the letters, and children use them for sorting and matching activities.
Letter Frames	Teachers make circle-shaped letter frames from tagboard, collect large plastic bracelets, or shape pipe cleaners or Wikki-Stix (pipe cleaners covered in wax) into circles for students to use to highlight particular letters on charts or in big books.
Letter Sorts	Children sort objects and pictures representing two or more letters and place them in containers marked with the specific letters.
Letter Stamps	Children use letter stamps and ink pads to print letters on paper or in booklets. They also use letter-shaped sponges to paint letters and letter-shaped cookie cutters to cut out clay letters.
Magnetic Letters	Children pick all examples of one letter from a collection of magnetic letters or match upper- and lowercase letterforms of magnetic letters. They also arrange the letters in alphabetical order and use them to spell familiar words.
Whiteboards	Children practice writing upper- and lowercase forms of a letter and familiar words on whiteboards.

ASSESSMENT TOOLS

Concepts About Written Language

Teachers monitor children's growing awareness of the concepts about written language as they observe them during shared reading and other reading and writing activities. The most widely used assessment is Marie Clay's Concepts About Print Test:

- **Concepts About Print (CAP) Test**
  The CAP Test (Clay, 2015a) assesses young children's understanding of three types of concepts about print: book-orientation concepts, directionality concepts, and letter and word concepts. The test has 24 items and is administered individually in about 10 minutes. The teacher reads a short book aloud while a child looks on; the child is asked to open the book, turn pages, and point out particular print features as the text is read. Four forms of the CAP Test booklet are available: *Sand* (Clay, 2015b), *Stones* (Clay, 2014), *Follow Me, Moon* (Clay, 2000b), and *No Shoes* (Clay, 2000c), as well as a Spanish version. Teachers carefully observe children as they respond, and then mark their responses on a scoring sheet. The test is available for purchase from Heinemann.

Instead of using the test booklets, teachers can also administer the test using other books available in the classroom.

McGee and Richgels (2011) conclude that learning letters of the alphabet requires many, many experiences with meaningful written language and recommend that teachers take these steps to encourage children's alphabet learning:

Capitalize on children's interests. Teachers provide letter activities that children enjoy, and they talk about letters when children are interested in talking about them. Teachers know what features to comment on because they observe children during reading and writing activities to find out which letters or features of letters children are exploring.

Talk about the role of letters in reading and writing. Teachers talk about how letters represent sounds and combine to spell words and point out capital letters and lowercase letters.

Provide a variety of opportunities for alphabet learning. Teachers use children's names and environmental print in literacy activities, do interactive writing, encourage children to use invented spelling, share alphabet books, and play letter games.

Teachers begin teaching letters of the alphabet using two sources of words—children's own names and environmental print. They teach the ABC song to provide children with a strategy for identifying the name of an unknown letter. Children learn to sing this song and point to each letter on an alphabet chart until they reach the unfamiliar one; this is a very useful strategy because it gives them a real sense of independence in identifying letters. Teachers also provide routines, activities, and games for talking about and manipulating letters. During these familiar, predictable activities, teachers and children say letter names, manipulate magnetic letters, and write letters on whiteboards. At first, the teacher structures and guides the activities, but with experience, the children internalize the routine and do it independently, often at a literacy center. Figure 4–2 presents 10 routines to teach the letters of the alphabet.

Being able to name the letters of the alphabet is a good predictor of beginning reading achievement, even though knowing the names of the letters doesn't directly

ASSESSMENT *Snapshot*

CAP Test Scoring Sheet

Name ___Adele___   Date ___Jan. 10___

Title of Book ___First the Egg___

Check the items that the child demonstrates.

1. Book-Orientation Concepts
   - ☑ Shows the front of a book.
   - ☑ Turns to the first page of the story.
   - ☑ Shows where to start reading on a page.

2. Directionality Concepts
   - ☑ Shows the direction of print across a line of text.
   - ☐ Shows the direction of print on a page with more than one line of print.
   - ☐ Points to track words as the teacher reads.

3. Letter and Word Concepts
   - ☑ Points to any letter on a page.
   - ☐ Points to a particular letter on a page.
   - ☑ Puts fingers around any word on a page.
   - ☐ Puts fingers around a particular word on a page.
   - ☐ Puts fingers around any sentence on a page.
   - ☐ Points to the first and last letters of a word.
   - ☐ Points to a period or other punctuation mark.
   - ☑ Points to a capital letter.

> **TEACHER'S NOTE**
>
> Adele is familiar with books and has learned book-orientation concepts. She's reached the point where her classmates were in September. She's working on tracking words and needs to learn more about letters, words, and sentences.

affect a child's ability to read (Adams, 1990; Snow, Burns, & Griffin, 1998). A more likely explanation for this relationship between letter knowledge and reading is that children who have been involved in reading and writing activities before entering first grade know the names of the letters, and they're more likely to begin reading quickly. Simply teaching children to name the letters without the accompanying reading and writing experiences doesn't have this effect.

Assessing Children's Concepts About Written Language

Teachers regularly observe children as they look at books and reread familiar ones to monitor their developing knowledge about written language concepts. They also watch as children do pretend writing and write their names and other familiar words and phrases. They notice which concepts children understand and which ones they need to continue to talk about and demonstrate during shared reading.

Teachers use Marie Clay's Concepts About Print (CAP) Test (2015a) to assess young children's understanding of written language concepts; the CAP Test is explained in Assessment Tools: Concepts About Print. Teachers also create their own versions of the test to use with any story they're reading with a child, as shown in Assessment Snapshot: CAP Test Scoring Sheet. As teachers read aloud a book, they ask the child to point out book-orientation concepts, directionality concepts, and letter and word concepts. In the Snapshot, a kindergarten teacher asks Adele to point out written language concepts in *First the Egg* (Seeger, 2007); the results indicate that midway through kindergarten, this 5-year-old is making progress but lags behind her classmates.

 MONITOR: Check Your Understanding 4.2

How Children Develop as Readers and Writers

Young children move through three stages as they learn to read and write: *emergent, beginning,* and *fluent* (Juel, 1991). During the emergent stage, young children gain an understanding of the communicative purpose of print, and they move from pretend reading to reading predictable books and from using scribbles to simulate writing to writing patterned sentences, such as *I see a bird. I see a tree. I see a car.* The focus of the second stage, beginning reading and writing, is on children's growing ability to use phonics to "crack the alphabetic code" to decode and spell words. Children also learn to read and write many high-frequency words and write several sentences to develop a story or other composition. In the fluent stage, children are automatic, fluent readers, and in writing, they develop good handwriting skills, spell many high-frequency words correctly, and organize their writing into multiple-paragraph compositions. Figure 4–3 summarizes children's accomplishments in reading and writing development at each stage.

Stage 1: Emergent Reading and Writing

Children gain an understanding of the communicative purpose of print and develop an interest in reading and writing during the emergent stage. They notice environmental print in the world around them and develop concepts about print as teachers read and write with them. As children dictate stories for the teacher to record, for example, they learn that their speech can be written down, and they observe how teachers write from left to right and top to bottom.

During the emergent stage, children accomplish the following:

- Develop an interest in reading and writing
- Acquire concepts about print
- Develop book-handling skills
- Learn to identify the letters of the alphabet
- Develop handwriting skills
- Learn to read and write some high-frequency words

Children are usually emergent readers and writers in kindergarten, but some children whose parents have read to them every day and provided a variety of literacy experiences do learn how to read and write before they come to school. Caroline, a 5-year-old emergent reader and writer in Ms. McCloskey's classroom, is profiled in the Differentiated Instruction feature.

Young children make scribbles to represent writing. These scribbles may appear randomly on a page at first, but with experience, children line up the letters or scribbles from left to right on a line and from top to bottom on a page. Children also begin to "read," or tell what their writing says (Schickedanz & Casbergue, 2004). At first, they can reread their writing only immediately after writing, but with experience, they learn to remember what their writing says, and as their writing becomes more conventional, they're able to decipher it more easily.

Emergent readers and writers participate in a variety of literacy activities ranging from modeled and shared reading and writing, during which they watch as teachers read and write, to independent reading and writing that they do themselves. Ms. McCloskey's students, for example, listened to her read aloud books

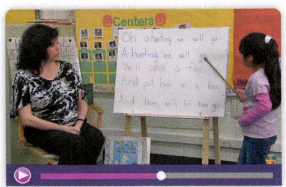

During the emergent reading stage, children acquire concepts about print. How do teachers help children develop this awareness?

FIGURE 4–3 Young Children's Literacy Development

STAGE	READING	WRITING
Emergent	Children: • notice environmental print • show interest in books • pretend to read • use picture cues and predictable patterns in books to retell the story • reread familiar books with predictable patterns • identify some letter names • recognize up to 20 high-frequency words	Children: • distinguish between writing and drawing • write letters and letterlike forms or scribble randomly on the page • develop an understanding of directionality • show interest in writing • write their first and last names • write up to 20 high-frequency words • use sentence frames to write a sentence
Beginning	Children: • identify letter names and sounds • match spoken words to written words • recognize 20–100 high-frequency words • use beginning, middle, and ending sounds to decode words • apply knowledge of the cueing systems to monitor reading • self-correct while reading • read slowly, word by word • read orally • point to words when reading • make reasonable predictions	Children: • write from left to right • print the upper- and lowercase letters • write one or more sentences • add a title • spell many words phonetically • spell 20–75 high-frequency words correctly • write single-draft compositions • use capital letters to begin sentences • use periods, question marks, and exclamation points to mark the end of sentences • can reread their writing
Fluent	Children: • identify most words automatically • read with expression • read at a rate of 100 words per minute or more • prefer to read silently • identify unfamiliar words using the cueing systems • recognize at least 100 high-frequency words • use a variety of strategies effectively • often read independently • use knowledge of text structure and genre to support comprehension • make inferences	Children: • use the writing process to write drafts and final copies • write compositions with one or more paragraphs • indent paragraphs • spell at least 75 of the 100 high-frequency words • use sophisticated and technical vocabulary • apply vowel patterns to spell words • add inflectional endings on words • apply capitalization rules • use commas, quotation marks, and other punctuation marks

and read big books using shared reading, and they also participated in reading and writing workshop. When working with children at the emergent stage, however, teachers often use modeled and shared reading and writing activities because they're demonstrating what readers and writers do and teaching concepts about print.

Stage 2: Beginning Reading and Writing

This stage marks children's growing awareness of the alphabetic principle. Children learn about phoneme–grapheme correspondences; phonics rules in words such as *run*, *hand*, *this*, *make*, *day*, and *road*; and word families, including -*ill* (*fill*, *hill*, *will*) and -*ake* (*bake*, *make*, *take*). They also apply (and misapply) their developing phonics knowledge to spell words. For example, they spell *night* as NIT and *train* as TRANE. At the same time, they're learning to read and write high-frequency words, many of which can't be sounded out, such as *what*, *are*, and *there*.

During the beginning stage of reading and writing development, children accomplish the following:

- Learn phonics skills
- Recognize 100 high-frequency words
- Apply reading strategies, including cross-checking, predicting, and repairing
- Write five or more sentences, sometimes organized into a paragraph
- Spell phonetically
- Spell 50 high-frequency words
- Use capital letters to begin sentences
- Use punctuation marks to indicate the ends of sentences
- Reread their writing

First grade teachers ensure their students know the sounds that letters represent. How does this teacher help students recognize and practice short *e*, short *o*, and short *u*?

Most first and second graders are beginning readers and writers, and with instruction in literacy strategies and skills and daily opportunities to read and write, children move through this stage to reach the fluent stage. Anthony, a 6-year-old beginning reader and writer in Ms. McCloskey's classroom, is also profiled in the Differentiated Instruction feature.

Children usually read aloud slowly, in a word-by-word fashion, stopping often to sound out unfamiliar words. They point at each word as they read, but by the end of this stage, their reading becomes smoother and more fluent, and they point at words only when the text is especially challenging.

Although the emphasis in this stage is on decoding and recognizing words, children also learn that reading involves comprehension. They make predictions to guide their thinking about events in stories they read, and they make connections between what they're reading and their own lives and the world around them as they personalize the reading experience. They monitor their reading to recognize when it doesn't make sense, cross-check using phonological, semantic, syntactic, and pragmatic information in the text to figure out the problem, and repair or self-correct it (Fountas & Pinnell, 1996). They also learn about story structure, particularly that stories have a beginning, middle, and end, and use this knowledge to guide their reading and retelling.

By the end of this stage, children move from writing one or two sentences to developing longer compositions, with five, eight, or more sentences organized into paragraphs. Their writing is better developed, too, because they're acquiring a sense of audience, and they want their classmates to like what they've written. Children continue to write single-draft compositions but begin to make a few revisions and editing corrections as they learn about the writing process toward the end of the stage.

Children apply what they're learning about phonics in their spelling; they correctly spell many of the high-frequency words that they've learned to read and can locate others on word walls posted in the classroom. They learn to use capital letters to mark the beginnings of sentences and punctuation to mark the ends. Children are more adept at rereading their writing, both immediately afterward and days later, because they're able to read many of the words they've written.

Teach Kids to
BE STRATEGIC

Beginning Reading Strategies

Introduce these first reading strategies in kindergarten and first grade:

- Cross-check
- Predict
- Connect
- Monitor
- Repair

Children practice them when they participate in shared and guided reading activities as well as interactive read-alouds. Look for children to use these strategies during guided practice and independent reading activities. If they struggle, reteach the strategies, making sure to name them, model their use, and think aloud and talk about their application.

Teachers plan activities for children at the beginning stage that range from modeled to independent reading and writing activities, but the emphasis is on interactive and guided activities. Through **interactive writing**, **choral reading**, and guided reading, teachers scaffold children as they read and write and use **minilessons** to provide strategy and skill instruction. For example, Ms. McCloskey's students were divided into small, homogeneous groups for guided reading lessons. The children met to read books at their reading levels, and Ms. McCloskey introduced new vocabulary words, taught reading strategies and skills, and assessed their comprehension.

Teachers introduce the writing process to beginning-stage writers once they develop a sense of audience and want to make their writing better so their classmates will like it. Children don't immediately begin writing rough drafts and final copies or doing both revising and editing: They often begin the writing process by rereading their compositions and adding a word or two, correcting a misspelled word, or capitalizing a lowercase letter. These changes are cosmetic, but the idea is established that the writing process doesn't end after the first draft. Next, children show interest in making a final copy that really looks good: They either recopy the composition by hand or use word processing and print out the final copy. Once children understand that writing involves a rough draft and a final copy, they're ready to learn more about revising and editing, and they usually reach this point at about the same time they become fluent writers.

Stage 3: Fluent Reading and Writing

The third stage marks children's move into fluent reading and writing. Fluent readers recognize hundreds and hundreds of words automatically and have the tools to identify unfamiliar words when reading. Fluent writers use the writing process to draft, revise, and publish their writing and participate in **revising groups**. They're familiar with a variety of genres and know how to organize their writing. They use conventional spelling and other written language conventions, including capital letters and punctuation marks.

Fluent readers and writers accomplish the following:

- Read fluently and with expression
- Recognize most one-syllable words automatically and can decode other words efficiently
- Use decoding and comprehension strategies effectively
- Write well-developed, multiparagraph compositions
- Use the writing process to draft and refine their writing
- Write stories, reports, letters, and other genres
- Spell most high-frequency and other one-syllable words correctly
- Use capital letters and punctuation marks correctly most of the time

Some second graders reach this stage, and all children should be fluent readers and writers by the end of third grade. Reaching this stage is an important milestone because it indicates that children are ready for the increased literacy demands of fourth grade, when they're expected to read longer chapter-book stories, use writing to respond to literature, read content area textbooks, and write essays and reports. Jazmen, an 8-year-old fluent reader and writer in Ms. McCloskey's classroom, is also profiled in the Differentiated Instruction feature.

Fluent readers have learned to read with expression. What knowledge do students need to read expressively?

The distinguishing characteristic of fluent readers is that they read words accurately, rapidly, and expressively. Fluent readers automatically recognize many words and can decode unfamiliar words efficiently. Their reading rate has increased to 100 words or more per minute; in addition, they can vary their speed according to the demands of the text they're reading.

Most fluent readers prefer to read silently because they can read more quickly than when they read orally. No longer do they point at words as they read. Children can read many books independently, actively making predictions, visualizing, monitoring their understanding, and making repairs when necessary. They have a range of strategies available and use them to enhance their comprehension.

Fluent readers' comprehension is stronger, and they think more deeply about their reading than emergent and beginning readers do. It's likely that children's comprehension improves at this stage because they have more cognitive energy available for comprehension now; in contrast, beginning readers use much more cognitive energy to decode words. So, as children become fluent, they use less energy for word identification and have more cognitive resources available for comprehending what they read.

During this stage, children read longer, more sophisticated picture books and chapter books, but they generally prefer chapter books because they enjoy really getting into a story or digging deeply in a nonfiction book. They learn more about the literary genres and their structural patterns, and literary devices, such as alliteration, personification, and symbolism. They participate in literature focus units featuring an author, genre, or book; in small-group literature circles where children read and discuss a book together; and in author studies where they read and compare several books by the same author and examine that author's writing style. They're able to explain why they liked a particular book and make recommendations to classmates.

Fluent writers understand that writing is a process, and they use the writing process stages—*prewriting, drafting, revising, editing,* and *publishing.* They make plans for writing and write both rough drafts and final copies. They reread their rough drafts and make revisions and editing changes that reflect their understanding of writing forms and their purpose for writing. They increasingly share their rough drafts with classmates and turn to them for advice on how to make their writing better.

Children get ideas for writing from books they've read and from TV programs and movies they've viewed. They organize their writing into paragraphs, indent paragraphs, and focus on a single idea in each paragraph. They develop ideas more completely and use more sophisticated vocabulary to express their ideas.

Fluent writers are aware of writing genres and organize their writing into stories, reports, letters, and poems. Their stories have a beginning, middle, and end, and the reports they write are structured using sequence, comparison, or cause-and-effect structures. Their letters reflect an understanding of the parts of a letter and how they're arranged on a page. Their poems incorporate alliteration, symbolism, rhyme, or other poetic devices to create vivid impressions.

Children's writing looks more conventional. They spell most of the 100 high-frequency words correctly and use phonics to spell other one-syllable words correctly. They add inflectional endings (e.g., *-s, -ed, -ing*) and experiment with spelling two-syllable and longer words. They've learned to capitalize the first word in sentences and names and to use punctuation marks correctly at the ends of sentences, although they're still experimenting with punctuation marks within sentences.

A list of instructional recommendations for each of the three stages of reading and writing development is presented in Figure 4–4.

FIGURE 4–4 Instructional Recommendations

STAGE	READING	WRITING
Emergent	• Use environmental print. • Include literacy materials in play centers. • Read aloud to children. • Read big books and poems on charts using shared reading. • Introduce the title and author of books before reading. • Teach directionality and letter and word concepts using big books. • Encourage children to make predictions and text-to-self connections. • Have children retell and dramatize stories. • Have children respond to literature through talk and drawing. • Have children manipulate sounds using oral phonemic awareness activities. • Use alphabet-learning routines. • Take children's dictation using the Language Experience Approach. • Teach 20–24 high-frequency words. • Post words on a word wall.	• Have children use crayons for drawing and pencils for writing. • Encourage children to use scribble writing or write random letters if they can't do more conventional writing. • Teach handwriting skills. • Use interactive writing for whole-class and small-group writing projects. • Have children write their names on sign-in sheets each day. • Have children write their own names and names of classmates. • Have children inventory or make lists of words they know how to write. • Have children "write the classroom" by making lists of familiar words in the classroom. • Have children use frames such as "I like _____" and "I see a _____" to write sentences. • Encourage children to remember what they write so they can read it.
Beginning	• Read charts of poems and songs using choral reading. • Read leveled books using guided reading. • Provide daily opportunities to read and reread books independently. • Teach phonics concepts and rules. • Teach children to cross-check using the cueing systems. • Teach the 100 high-frequency words. • Point out whether texts are stories, informational books, or poems. • Teach predicting, connecting, cross-checking, and other strategies. • Teach the elements of story structure, particularly beginning, middle, and end. • Have children write in reading logs and participate in grand conversations. • Have children take books home to read with parents.	• Use interactive writing to teach concepts about print and spelling rules. • Provide daily opportunities to write for a variety of purposes and using different genres. • Introduce the writing process. • Teach children to develop a single idea in their compositions. • Teach children to proofread their compositions. • Teach children to spell the 100 high-frequency words. • Teach contractions. • Teach capitalization and punctuation skills. • Have children use computers to publish their writing. • Have children share their writing from the author's chair.
Fluent	• Have children participate in literature circles. • Have children participate in reading workshop. • Teach about genres and literary features. • Involve children in author studies. • Teach children to make text-to-self, text-to-world, and text-to-text connections. • Have children respond to literature through talk and writing.	• Have children participate in writing workshop. • Teach children to use the writing process. • Teach children to revise and edit their writing. • Teach paragraphing skills. • Teach spelling rules. • Teach homophones. • Teach synonyms. • Teach root words and affixes. • Teach children to use a dictionary and a thesaurus.

MONITOR: Check Your Understanding 4.3

Young Children Develop as Readers and Writers

The Differentiated Instruction feature in this chapter highlights three students from Ms. McCloskey's K–3 multigrade classroom. Each child exemplifies the characteristics of one of the three stages of early literacy development; they vary in their knowledge of concepts about print and their ability to read and write words and longer texts. As you read, think about what the students know about literacy and how you'd personalize instruction for them in developmentally appropriate ways.

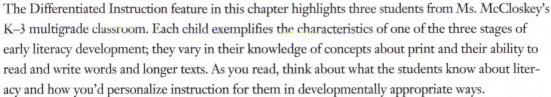

Meet Caroline, an Emergent Reader and Writer

Five-year-old Caroline is a friendly, eager child who is learning to speak English as she learns to read and write. Her grandparents emigrated from Thailand to the United States; her family speaks Hmong at home, and she speaks English only at school. When Caroline's Hmong-speaking classmates start to talk in their native language, she admonishes them to speak English because "we learn English school."

When she began kindergarten, Caroline couldn't identify any letters of the alphabet and had never held a pencil. She hadn't listened to stories read aloud and had no book-handling experience. She spoke very few words of English. The classroom culture and language were very different than those of her home, but Caroline was eager to learn. For the first few days, she stood back, observing her classmates; then she said "I do" and joined them.

Reading

Caroline has made remarkable progress in 5 months. She's been reading books with repetitive sentences on each page, and now at level 3, she's beginning to use phonics to sound out unfamiliar words. She knows the names of most letters and the sounds that they represent. She can also read almost 20 high-frequency words. Caroline's developed good book-handling skills and follows the line of words on a page. She reads word by word and points at the text as she reads. She's learning consonant and vowel sounds, but because of her pronunciation of English sounds and lack of vocabulary, she has difficulty decoding words.

Caroline demonstrates that she understands the books she reads, and she makes text-to-self connections. Recently, she was reading a book about a child having a birthday, and she pointed to the picture of a young, blond mother wrapping a child's birthday present. She looked up at Ms. McCloskey and said, "She no mom, she sister. This wrong." The woman in the picture looks nothing like her mother!

Writing

Caroline has participated in writing workshop since the first day of school. For several weeks, she scribbled, but within a month, she learned how to print some letters because she wanted her writing to look like her classmates'. Soon she wrote her own name, copied classmates' names, and wrote words she saw posted in the classroom.

A month ago, Ms. McCloskey gave Caroline a ring for key words. Every few days, Caroline chooses a new word to add to her ring; Ms. McCloskey writes the word on a word card that's added to the ring. Caroline has 31 words now, including *you* and *birthday*, and she flips through the cards to practice reading and uses the words to write sentences.

After 4 months of instruction, Caroline began writing sentences. Ms. McCloskey introduced the frame "I see a _____" and Caroline wrote sentences using familiar words, including some from her key words ring. Then, to make her writing longer, she wrote the same sentence over and over.

Next, she began reading and writing color words and expanded her writing to two- and three-sentence texts; for example, "I see a horse. It is black. It is fast." Most of the words that Caroline writes are spelled correctly because she uses key words and words she locates in a picture dictionary. Caroline puts a period at the end of each sentence, but recently she's noticed that some of her classmates put a period at the end of each line so she sometimes does the same. When she draws a picture to accompany a sentence, Caroline can usually read her writing immediately afterward, but by the next day, she doesn't remember what she's written.

Caroline has one of the thickest writing folders in the class, and she's very proud of her writing. Nearly 100 pages of writing are stuffed into the folder, tracing her development as a writer since the beginning of the school year.

Instructional Implications

Ms. McCloskey explains, "Caroline is an emergent-stage reader and writer. She's making excellent progress because she can read books with repetitive patterns and is learning phonics and high-frequency words and can write words and craft sentences." Check the chart Emergent Reader and Writer Characteristics That Caroline Exemplifies.

Now Ms. McCloskey is asking Caroline to begin reading books without repetitive patterns during guided reading; in these books, she has to recognize high-frequency words and use phonics to identify unfamiliar words rather than rely on repetitive sentence patterns. Similarly, during writing workshop, Ms. McCloskey is encouraging Caroline to write books about events in her life without using repetitive patterns. Working without the support the repetitive patterns provide is difficult for Caroline because her knowledge of English is limited. Ms. McCloskey concludes, "Even though Caroline is learning to speak English at the same time she's learning to read and write, I'm confident that she's up to the challenge."

EMERGENT READER AND WRITER CHARACTERISTICS THAT CAROLINE EXEMPLIFIES

Reading
- Shows great interest in reading
- Has developed book-handling skills
- Identifies most of the letters of the alphabet
- Knows some letter sounds
- Sounds out a few CVC words
- Reads almost 20 high-frequency words
- Uses predictable patterns in text to reread familiar books
- Makes text-to-self connections

Writing
- Shows great interest in writing
- Writes from left to right and top to bottom on a page
- Prints most of the letters of the alphabet
- Writes almost 20 high-frequency words
- Leaves spaces between words
- Writes sentences
- Begins sentences with a capital letter
- Puts periods at the ends of sentences
- Rereads what she has written immediately afterward

Meet Anthony, a Beginning Reader and Writer

Anthony, a first grader with a ready smile, is a beginning reader and writer. He's 6 years old and says that he likes to read and write. He's a well-behaved child who's extremely competitive. He reads at level 12 now, and recently he announced to Ms. McCloskey that he wants to read at level 15. She explained that to do that, Anthony needs to practice reading at home with his mom, so he's been taking several books home each night to practice. Ms. McCloskey predicts that by the end of the year, Anthony will be reading at level 18, the school's benchmark for the end of first grade.

Angel is Anthony's best friend, and he's in Ms. McCloskey's classroom, too. They often sit together to read and write, and they spur each other on, striving to read more books and write longer, more exciting stories. The boys eat together in the lunchroom and always play together outside, too.

Reading

Ms. McCloskey's assessment of Anthony's reading at the end of the second quarter shows that he recognizes 80 of the 100 high-frequency words taught in first grade, and he can decode most one-syllable words with short and long vowel sounds, including words with consonant blends and digraphs, such as *shock*, *chest*, and *spike*. He's beginning to try to sound out some of the more complex vowel digraphs and diphthongs (e.g., *loud*, *boil*, *soon*) and *r*-controlled vowels (e.g., *chart*, *snore*), and in the past month, Ms. McCloskey has noticed that his ability to decode words is growing and that about two thirds of the time, he can identify these words with more complex vowel sounds in the context of a sentence. He also is decoding some two- and three-syllable words, such as *dinner*, *parents*, and *hospital*, in books he's reading.

Anthony reads orally, and points only when he reads challenging texts. He's beginning to chunk words into phrases as he reads, and he notices when something he's reading doesn't make sense. He uses the cross-checking strategy to make corrections and get back on track.

According to his reading workshop log, Anthony has read 17 books this month. He's increasingly choosing easy-to-read chapter books, including Syd Hoff's *Sammy the Seal* (2000b) and *Oliver* (2000a). After he reads, he often shares his books with his friend Angel, and they reread them together and talk about their favorite parts. He regularly uses the connecting strategy and shares his text-to-self and text-to-world connections with Angel and Ms. McCloskey. When he reads two or more books by the same author, he shares text-to-text comparisons and can explain to his teacher how these comparisons make him a better reader: "Now I think and read at the same time," he explains.

Writing

Anthony likes to write during writing workshop. He identified his "I Was Sick" story as the very best one he's written, and Ms. McCloskey agrees. Anthony tells an interesting and complete story with a beginning, middle, and end; you can hear his voice clearly in the story. Here's his story:

I Was Sick
I went out sid [outside] with no! jaket [jacket] on and my throt [throat] started to hrt [hurt]. It rele [really] hrt and I was geting sick. I went to finde my

---

BEGINNING READER AND WRITER CHARACTERISTICS THAT ANTHONY EXEMPLIFIES

Reading
- Likes to read
- Reads orally
- Points to words when he reads challenging texts
- Recognizes 80 high-frequency words
- Uses phonics knowledge to decode unfamiliar words
- Makes good predictions
- Uses the cross-checking strategy
- Retells what he reads
- Makes text-to-self and text-to-world connections

Writing
- Likes to write
- Writes single-draft compositions
- Adds a title
- Writes organized compositions on a single topic
- Writes more than five sentences in a composition
- Has a beginning, middle, and end in his story
- Refers to the word wall to spell high-frequency words
- Uses his knowledge of phonics to spell words
- Uses capital letters to mark the beginnings of sentences
- Uses periods to mark the ends of sentences
- Reads his writing to classmates

Mom and I tolde her I was sick. My Mom gav me some Medisin [medicine] and she mad Cambell's chickn newdl [noodle] soup for me to eat. Then I got all betr [better].

Anthony's spelling errors are characteristic of phonetic spellers. He sounds out the spelling of many words, such as HRT (*hurt*), MEDISIN (*medicine*), and BETR (*better*), and he's experimenting with the final *e* marker at the end of TOLDE and FINDE but ignores it on other words, such as OUT SID (*outside*) and GAV (*gave*). He uses the word wall in the classroom and spells many high-frequency words correctly (e.g., *with*, *went*, *have*).

Anthony writes single-draft compositions in paragraph form, and he creates a title for his stories. He writes in sentences and includes simple, compound, and complex sentences in his writing. He uses capital letters to mark the beginnings of sentences and periods to mark the ends of sentences well, but he continues to randomly capitalize words.

Instructional Implications

"Anthony is a very motivated student: He's eager to read because he has a goal in mind," Ms. McCloskey explains. "I'm confident that he'll reach level 18 by the end of the year. I am encouraging Anthony to read increasingly difficult chapter books and practice using the strategies he's learned when he's reading independently." Check the chart Beginning Reader and Writer Characteristics that Anthony Exemplifies.

Ms. McCloskey plans to teach Anthony about complex vowel patterns and consonant blends and digraphs so he'll be able to decode unfamiliar words while he's reading. She's also noticed that it's time for Anthony to move beyond single-draft compositions and learn to use the writing process to revise and edit his writing.

Meet *Jazmen*, a Fluent Reader and Writer

Jazmen is a confident and articulate African American third grader with an easy smile. She's 8 years old, and she celebrated her birthday last fall with a family trip to the Magic Mountain amusement park in Southern California. Jazmen is a computer geek, often providing assistance to her classmates. When asked about her favorite school activity, Jazmen says that she likes using the computer best of all; in fact, she's interested in learning more about careers that involve computers because she knows that she always wants to work with them.

Ms. McCloskey identified Jazmen for this feature because she's made such remarkable progress this year. This is the second year that Jazmen's been in Ms. McCloskey's class. Last year, she seemed stuck in the beginning stage, not making too much progress, according to Ms. McCloskey, "but this year, it's like a lightbulb has been turned on!" She's now a fluent reader and writer.

Reading

Jazmen likes to read, and she reports that she has lots of books at home. According to the Accelerated Reader program, she's reading at 3.8 (third grade, eighth month) level, which means she's reading at or slightly above grade level. She enjoys reading the Marvin Redpost (e.g., *Marvin Redpost: A Magic Crystal?* by Louis Sachar, 2000) and Zack Files (e.g., *Never Trust a Cat Who Wears Earrings,* by Dan Greenburg, 1997) series of easy-to-read paperback chapter books. She says that she likes these books because they're funny.

Currently she's reading Paula Danziger's series of chapter-book stories about a third grader named Amber Brown who deals with the realities of contemporary life, including adjusting to her parents' divorce. The first book in the series is *Amber Brown Is Not a Crayon* (2006), about Amber and her best friend, Justin, who moves away at the end of the book; other chapter books in this "colorful" series are *Amber Brown Goes Fourth* (2007), *Amber Brown Is Feeling Blue* (1999), *Amber Brown Sees Red* (1998), and *Amber Brown Is Green With Envy* (2004).

Jazmen reads fluently. She recognizes words automatically and reads with expression. She says that when you're reading to someone, you have to be interesting, and that's why she reads the way she does. Her most outstanding achievement, according to Ms. McCloskey, is that she thinks inferentially: She can juggle thinking about plot, characters, setting, and theme in order to make thoughtful connections and interpretations. She knows about various genres and literary elements, and she uses this knowledge as she reflects on stories she's reading.

Writing

Jazmen likes to write. She gets her ideas for stories from television programs. She explains, "When I'm watching TV, I get these ideas and I draw pictures of them and that's how I think of a story." She's currently working on a story entitled "Lucky and the Color Purple," about a princess named Lucky who possesses magical qualities. Why are her stories interesting? Jazmen says, "Most important is that they are creative." She shares her stories with her classmates, and they agree that Jazmen is a good writer.

The story Jazmen particularly likes is "The Super Hero With Curly Hair." It has a strong voice. Jazmen wanted her story to sound interesting, she explained, so she substituted *whined* and *grouched* for *said*. Ms. McCloskey praised the story because it's complete with a beginning, middle, and end, and because Jazmen uses dialogue as well as quotation marks effectively. The errors remaining on the final draft of the paper also suggest direction for future instruction. Jazmen spelled 95% of the words in her composition correctly. In particular, Jazmen appears ready to learn more about plurals and possessives and using commas within sentences.

FLUENT READER AND WRITER CHARACTERISTICS THAT JAZMEN EXEMPLIFIES

Reading
- Recognizes most words automatically
- Reads with expression
- Reads more than 100 words per minute
- Reads independently
- Uses a variety of strategies
- Makes connections when reading
- Thinks inferentially
- Applies knowledge of story structure and genre when reading

Writing
- Uses the writing process
- Has a sense of audience and purpose
- Writes a complete story with a beginning, middle, and end
- Writes in paragraphs
- Indents paragraphs
- Uses sophisticated language
- Spells most words correctly
- Uses capital letters and punctuation to mark sentence boundaries

Instructional Implications

"Jazmen is a fluent reader," says Ms. McCloskey, "so she's ready to tackle more challenging fiction and nonfiction books, both during guided reading lessons and when she's reading independently." When she reads, Jazmen's focus has changed from decoding the words to comprehending the author's message. Ms. McCloskey plans to teach minilessons about asking questions, making inferences, and using other reading strategies to encourage Jazmen to think more deeply about the books she's reading. Check the chart Fluent Reader and Writer Characteristics That Jazmen Exemplifies.

Jazmen has begun to use the writing process to refine her compositions, but most of her pieces have been stories. Ms. McCloskey is encouraging Jazmen to write nonfiction books, poems, letters, and other genres. After reading *Hate That Cat* (Creech, 2010), a novel written in verse, Jazmen decided to imitate the genre and draft her own novel in verse, expanding on an encounter she had with a squirrel. Ms. McCloskey also plans to carefully monitor Jazmen's progress and teach minilessons on concepts and skills that she's attempting to use, including plurals and possessives and commas within sentences.

Instructional Practices

Teachers who work with young readers and writers use many of the same instructional practices used with older students, such as reading aloud, doing guided reading with leveled books, teaching from basal readers, and providing opportunities for independent reading and writing through reading and writing workshop. Teachers adapt these approaches to provide enough scaffolding so that young children are successful, but other instructional practices have been developed specifically for young children and other novice readers and writers. To assess how effectively you teach young readers and writers, use the Teacher Checklist: How do I support young children's literacy development?

Morning Message

Morning message is a daily literacy routine that teachers use to teach literacy concepts, strategies, and skills (Payne & Schulman, 1999). Before the children arrive, teachers write a brief message on chart paper, usually in the form of a friendly letter, about what will happen that day; then the message is read at the beginning of the school day. Afterward, children reread it and count the letters, words, and sentences in the message. Depending on their level of literacy development, they also pick out familiar letters and words, words following a particular phonics pattern, high-frequency words, or capital letters and punctuation marks.

Teachers usually follow a predictable pattern in their messages each day to make it easier for children to read, as these two morning messages show:

Dear Kindergartners,

Today is Monday.

We will *plant* seeds.

We will *make* books

about plants.

    Love,

      Ms. Thao

Dear Kindergartners,

Today is *Thursday*.

We will *measure* the plants.

We will *write* about how

plants grow.

    Love,

      Ms. Thao

The morning messages that teachers write for first and second graders become gradually more complex, as this second grade teacher's message demonstrates:

Good Morning!

Today is Monday, February 9, 2015. New literature circles begin on Wednesday. I'll tell you about the new book choices this morning, and then you can sign up for your favorite book. Who remembers what a <u>synonym</u> is? Can you give an example?

    Love,

    Ms. Salazar

Teachers usually choose children to take the messages home to share with their families, either day by day or at the end of each week.

Teachers have adapted the morning message routine in a variety of ways to support their literacy programs.

FILL-IN-THE-BLANK MORNING MESSAGE. The teacher writes the morning message, omitting some words for children to fill in. The teacher reads the entire message once, and then during the second reading, children identify the missing words and write them in the blanks. Sometimes teachers write the missing words on cards and display them in a pocket chart to simplify the activity. Here's a first grade class's morning message:

Mr. Diaz's Morning Message

Today is _____ , October 17, 2014. It is the _____ day of

school. We love to _____ The Cat in the Hat by Dr. _____ .

We can read words that rhyme with <u>cat</u>: _____ , _____ , and

_____ .

The missing words are *Wednesday*, *37th*, *read*, *Seuss*, *bat*, *hat*, and *rat*. After completing the chart, the children reread the message, count the sentences, circle high-frequency words they've learned, and think of additional rhyming words.

ONE CHILD DICTATES A MESSAGE TO SHARE WITH CLASSMATES. Children take turns dictating a message to share personal news with classmates, which the teacher writes on chart paper. Children usually read their own messages aloud to

---

TEACHER *Checklist*

How do I support young children's literacy development?

○ Do I foster young children's interest in literacy by reading books aloud?

○ Do I demonstrate the purposes of written language?

○ Do I teach concepts about print using environmental print and other activities?

○ Do I provide opportunities for children to experiment with reading and writing?

○ Do I teach literacy terms, such as *word*, *letter*, and *sound*, through children's active participation in literacy activities?

○ Do I teach concepts about words using literacy play centers and other activities?

○ Do I develop children's knowledge about the alphabet through meaningful literacy activities and routines?

○ Do I teach children handwriting skills, including how to form upper- and lowercase manuscript letters?

○ Do I assess children to determine their stage of literacy development?

○ Do I plan instruction based on children's developmental stage and on Standards?

𝒩ew LITERACIES

Interactive Books

Young children use interactive books to learn concepts about print, read high-frequency words, develop reading fluency, expand vocabulary knowledge, and practice comprehension strategies. These electronic books have text and illustrations similar to traditional picture books but incorporate computer technology to enhance children's reading experience (Lefever-Davis & Pearman, 2005): They provide audio renditions of the entire text as children read along, pronunciations of individual words when children highlight them, and hotspots that children click to produce sound effects and graphic animations where characters talk and settings spring to life.

Many interactive books, based on high-quality books of children's literature, are available on CD-ROM. Here are some of the best:

- Dr. Seuss's rhyming stories *The Cat in the Hat* and *Green Eggs and Ham,* from The Learning Company
- H. A. Rey's Curious George stories about a hilarious little monkey, from Simon & Schuster
- Norman Bridwell's stories about a big red dog named Clifford, from Scholastic
- Stan and Jan Berenstain's adventures about a bear family, from Broderbund
- Marc Brown's series about an aardvark named Arthur, from The Learning Company
- Janell Cannon's charming story about a bat named Stellaluna, from Living Books
- Mercer Mayer's *Just Grandma and Me*, a story about a little critter who takes a trip to the beach, from The Learning Company

Other interactive books for K–5 students are available from LeapFrog SchoolHouse: The Leveled Reading Series provides interactive books for independent reading practice, and the Language First! Program includes books for English learners at four levels of English proficiency with native-language audio support in Spanish, Vietnamese, Cantonese, Haitian Creole, and Hmong.

In addition to interactive books on CD-ROM, others are available at these websites:

Dora the Explorer. These interactive stories feature Dora the Explorer, from her Nickelodeon cable series.

PBS Kids. These interactive books are from the Between the Lions series on PBS.

Storia School Edition. Scholastic's K–6 digital library contains more than 2,000 eBooks in English and Spanish and is available by subscription. Teachers use the eBooks for guided reading and other instructional approaches. Plus, the library can be customized for individual students.

Storyline Online. These streaming video programs feature Screen Actors Guild members reading aloud books, including Mem Fox's *Wilfred Gordon McDonald Partridge.*

Children appreciate the control they have in choosing how much support the interactive book provides while they're reading, and researchers have documented that children's word knowledge and comprehension are enhanced by these reading experiences (Lefever-Davis & Pearman, 2005). There's a potential drawback, however: Children can become dependent on the electronic support that interactive books provide.

---

classmates, pointing to each word as they read, just like their teacher does. In this example, Ivan shares some big news:

Ivan's News

I have a new baby sister. Her name is Ava. She sleeps all the time, and I have to be very quiet so I won't wake her up.

After reading and rereading the message and examining individual words and punctuation marks, the children decide to write a welcome message to Ivan's sister at the bottom of the chart paper. They dictate it for the teacher to record and sign their names; then Ivan takes the chart paper home to share with his family.

CHILDREN CREATE A MESSAGE COLLABORATIVELY. Instead of morning messages, some teachers write class news at the end of the school day. They discuss the day's activities with the children and decide together what to write. Teachers use interactive writing so that children can do most of the writing. Here's an example of a first grade class's news:

Room 3 News

We are studying insects. Today we read <u>Diary of a Fly</u> by Doreen Cronin. It's a totally hilarious book! We learned that flies walk on walls, and they eat regurgitated food. That's so yucky!

Through these adaptations, children learn about the format of friendly letters and other writing genres and the relationships between reading and writing. The writing is authentic, and children learn how to use writing to share information with others.

Shared Reading

Teachers use **shared reading** to read aloud books that are appropriate for children's interest level but too difficult for them to read for themselves (Parkes, 2000). Teachers use the five stages of the reading process in shared reading, as Ms. McCloskey did in the vignette at the beginning of the chapter. The steps in shared reading are presented in Figure 4–5, showing how the activities fit into the five stages of the reading process. Through the reading process, teachers model what fluent readers do as they involve children in enjoyable reading activities (Fountas & Pinnell, 1996). After the text is read several times, teachers use it to teach phonics and high-frequency words. Children also read small versions of the book with partners or independently, and the pattern or structure found in the text can be used for writing activities.

FIGURE 4–5 How Shared Reading Fits Into the Reading Process

1. Prereading
- Activate or build background knowledge on a topic related to the book.
- Show the cover of the book and read the title.
- Talk about the author and the illustrator.
- Have students make predictions.

2. Reading
- Use a big book or text printed on a chart.
- Use a pointer to track during reading.
- Read expressively, with very few stops during the first reading.
- Highlight vocabulary and repetitive patterns.
- Reread the book once or twice, and encourage students to join in the reading.

3. Responding
- Discuss the book in a grand conversation.
- Ask inferential and higher level questions, such as "What would happen if . . . ?" and "What did this book make you think of?"
- Share the pen to write a sentence interactively about the book.
- Have students draw and write in reading logs.

4. Exploring
- Reread the book using small books.
- Add important words to the word wall.
- Teach minilessons on strategies and skills.
- Present more information about the author and the illustrator.
- Provide a text set with other books by the author or on the same topic.

5. Applying
- Have students write a collaborative book to retell the story.
- Have students write an innovation imitating the pattern used in the book.

The books chosen for shared reading are available as big books and are close to children's reading level, but still beyond their ability to read independently. As an instructional strategy, shared reading differs from **interactive read-alouds** because children see the text as the teacher reads. Also, they often join in the reading of predictable refrains and rhyming words, and after listening to the teacher read the text several times, children often remember enough of the text to read along with the teacher. Through shared reading, teachers also demonstrate how print works, provide opportunities for children to make predictions, and increase children's confidence in their ability to read.

Big books are greatly enlarged picture books that teachers use in shared reading, most commonly with primary grade students. In this technique, developed in New Zealand, teachers place an enlarged picture book on an easel or chart stand where all children can see it. They read it aloud, pointing to every word. Before long, children join in the reading, especially in repeating the refrain. Then teachers reread the book, inviting children to help with the reading. The next time the book is read, teachers read to the point that the text becomes predictable, such as the beginning of a refrain, and children supply the missing text; having them supply the missing words is important because it leads to independent reading. Once children are familiar with the text, they're invited to read the big book independently (Parkes, 2000).

PREDICTABLE BOOKS. The stories and other books that teachers use for shared reading with young children often have repeated sentences, rhyme, or other patterns; books that incorporate these patterns are called *predictable books*. These are the four most common patterns:

Repetition. Authors repeat sentences to create a predictable pattern in many picture books. In *Barnyard Banter* (Fleming, 1997), for example, a white goose chases an elusive butterfly around a farm as the cows, roosters, and other animals call out their greetings using a predictable pattern.

Cumulative Sequence. Sentences are repeated and expanded in each episode in these books. For example, in *The Gingerbread Boy* (Galdone, 2008), the cookie repeats and expands his boast as he meets each character during his escape from the Little Old Man and the Little Old Woman.

Rhyme and Rhythm. Rhyme and rhythm are two poetic devices that authors use to add a musical quality to their writing. Many of the popular Dr. Seuss books, such as *Fox in Socks* (1965), use rhyme and rhythm. The sentences have a strong beat, and rhyme is used at the end of lines. Other books that incorporate rhyme and rhythm include familiar songs, such as *Shoo Fly!* (Trapani, 2000), and book-long verses, such as *Pattern Fish* (Harris, 2000).

Sequential Patterns. Some authors use a familiar sequence—such as the months of the year, days of the week, numbers 1 to 10, or letters of the alphabet—to structure their books. For example, in *The Very Hungry Caterpillar* (Carle, 2002), the author uses number and day-of-the-week sequences as the caterpillar eats through an amazing array of foods.

Books representing each category can be found in Booklist: Predictable Books. These books are valuable for emergent readers because the repeated sentences, patterns, and sequences make it easier for children to predict the next sentence or episode (Tompkins & Webeler, 1983).

Language Experience Approach

The **Language Experience Approach** (LEA) is based on children's language and experiences (Ashton-Warner, 1986). In this approach, teachers do shared writing: Children dictate words and sentences about their experiences, and the teacher writes down what

Booklist — Predictable Books

TYPE	BOOKS
Repetition	Carle, E. (1997). *Have you seen my cat?* New York: Aladdin Books. Guarino, D. (2004). *Is your mama a llama?* New York: Scholastic. Martin, B., Jr. (2007). *Baby bear, baby bear, what do you see?* New York: Henry Holt. Rathmann, P. (2000). *Good night, gorilla.* New York: Puffin Books. Rosen, M. (2004). *We're going on a bear hunt.* New York: Candlewick Press.
Cumulative Sequence	Aylesworth, J. (1996). *The gingerbread man.* New York: Scholastic. Fleming, D. (2006). *The cow who clucked.* New York: Henry Holt. Pinkney, J. (2006). *The little red hen.* New York: Dial Books. Taback, S. (2004). *The house that Jack built.* New York: Puffin Books. Wood, A. (2007). *Silly Sally.* San Diego: Harcourt.
Rhyme and Rhythm	Fleming, D. (1995). *In the tall, tall grass.* New York: Henry Holt. Hoberman, M. A. (2003). *Miss Mary Mack: A hand-clapping rhyme.* Boston: Little, Brown. Hoberman, M. A. (2004). *The eensy-weensy spider.* Boston: Little, Brown. Martin, B., Jr., & Archambault, J. (2009). *Chicka chicka boom boom.* New York: Beach Lane Books. Shaw, N. (2006). *Sheep in a jeep.* Boston: Houghton Mifflin.
Sequential Patterns	Baker, K. (2007). *Hickory dickory dock.* San Diego: Harcourt. Carle, E. (1997). *Today is Monday.* New York: Putnam. Carle, E. (2005). *A house for hermit crab.* New York: Aladdin Books. Christelow, E. (2006). *Five little monkeys jumping on the bed.* New York: Clarion Books. Wood, A. (2004). *Ten little fish.* New York: Blue Sky Press/Scholastic.

the children say; the text they develop becomes the reading material. Because the language comes from the children themselves and because the content is based on their experiences, they're usually able to read the text easily. Reading and writing are connected, because children are actively involved in reading what they've written.

Using this approach, children create individual booklets. They draw pictures on each page or cut pictures from magazines to glue on each page, and then they dictate the text that the teacher writes beside each illustration. Children can also make **collaborative books**, where each child creates one page to be added to a class book. For example, as part of a unit on "The Three Bears," a kindergarten class made a collaborative book on bears. Children each chose a fact about bears for their page; they drew an illustration and dictated the text for their teacher to record. One page from this class book is shown in Figure 4–6. The teacher took the children's dictation rather than having them write the book themselves because she wanted it to be written in conventional spelling so everyone in the classroom could read and reread the book.

When taking dictation, it's a great temptation to change the child's language to the teacher's own, in either word choice or grammar, but editing should be kept to a minimum so that children don't get the impression that their language is inferior or inadequate. Also, as children become familiar with dictating to the teacher, they learn to pace their dictation to the teacher's writing speed. At first, children dictate as they think of ideas, but with experience, they watch as the teacher writes and supply the text word by word. This change also provides evidence of children's developing concepts about print.

Watch how Ms. McCloskey uses interactive writing to engage her young students in a writing activity. What steps does the interactive writing lesson involve?

Interactive Writing

Children and the teacher create a text together during **interactive writing**, "sharing the pen" as they write the text on chart paper (Button, Johnson, & Furgerson, 1996; McCarrier, Pinnell, & Fountas, 2000). The children compose the message together, and then the teacher guides them as they write it word by word on chart paper. Children take turns writing known letters and familiar words, adding punctuation marks, and leaving spaces between words. All children participate in creating and writing the text on chart paper, and they also write the text on small whiteboards or on paper as it's written on the chart paper. Afterward, children read and reread the text together with classmates and on their own.

Children use interactive writing to write class news, predictions before reading, retellings of stories, thank-you letters, reports, math story problems, and many other types of group writings (Tompkins & Collom, 2004). Figure 4–7 presents a math story problem written by a first grade class using interactive writing; children took turns writing entire words. The boxes drawn around some of the letters and words represent correction tape that was used to correct misspellings or poorly formed letters. After writing this story problem, children wrote other subtraction problems individually.

Through interactive writing, children learn concepts about print, letter–sound relationships and spelling patterns, handwriting concepts, and capitalization and punctuation skills. Teachers model correct spelling and use of conventions of print, and children practice segmenting the sounds in words and spelling familiar words.

Teachers help children spell all words conventionally. They teach high-frequency words such as *the* and *of*, assist children in segmenting sounds and syllables in other words, point out unusual spelling patterns such as *pieces* and *germs*, and teach other conventions of print. Whenever children misspell a word or form a letter incorrectly, teachers cover the mistake with correction tape and help them make the correction. For example, when a child wrote the numeral *8* to spell *ate* in Figure 4–7, the teacher explained the *eight–ate* homophones, covered the numeral with correction tape, and helped the child spell the word, including the silent *e*. Teachers emphasize the importance of using conventional spelling as a courtesy to readers, not that a child made a mistake. In contrast to the emphasis on conventional spelling in interactive writing, children are encouraged to use invented spelling and other spelling strategies when writing independently. They learn to look for familiar words posted on classroom **word walls** or

FIGURE 4–6   A Page From a Class Book

FIGURE 4–7   A Math Story Problem

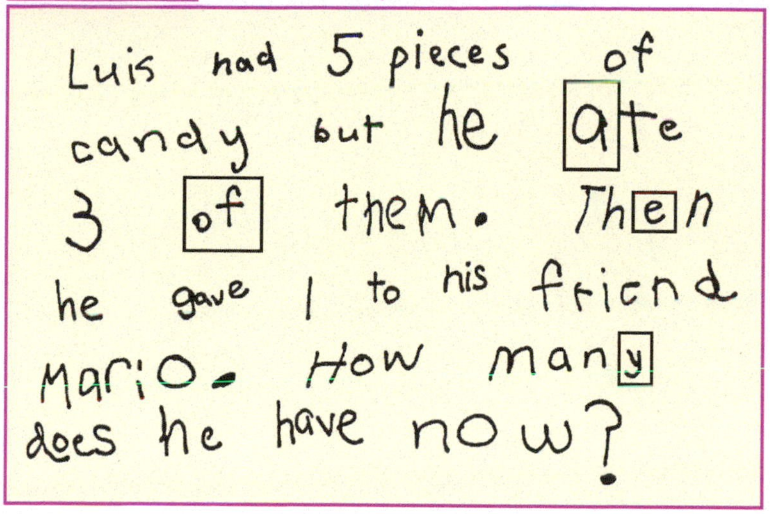

Luis had 5 pieces of candy but he [a]te 3 [of] them. Th[e]n he gave 1 to his friend Mario. How man[y] does he have now?

in books they've read, think about spelling patterns, or ask a classmate for help. Teachers also talk about purpose and explain that in personal writing and rough drafts, children do use invented spelling. Increasingly, however, children want to use conventional spelling and even ask to use the correction tape to fix errors they make as they write.

Manuscript Handwriting

Children enter kindergarten with different backgrounds of handwriting experience. Some 5-year-olds have never held a pencil, but many others have written cursivelike scribbles or manuscript letterlike lines and circles. Some have learned to print their names and even a few other letters. Handwriting instruction in kindergarten typically includes developing children's ability to hold pencils, refining their fine-motor control, and focusing on letter formation. Some people might argue that kindergartners are too young to learn handwriting skills, but young children should be encouraged to write from the first day of school. They write letters and words on labels, draw and write stories, keep journals, and write other types of messages. The more they write, the greater their need becomes for instruction in handwriting. Instruction is necessary so that children don't learn bad habits that later must be broken.

To teach children how to form letters, many kindergarten and first grade teachers create brief directions for forming letters that they sing to a familiar tune; for example, to form a lowercase letter *a*, try "All around and make a tail" sung to the tune of "Row, Row, Row Your Boat." As teachers sing the directions, they model the formation of the letter in the air or on the whiteboard using large arm motions. Then children sing along and practice forming the letter in the air.

Handwriting research indicates that moving models are much more effective than still models, which suggests that worksheets on the letters aren't very useful and explains why children often don't form the letters correctly. Researchers recommend that children watch teachers to see how letters are formed and then practice forming them themselves. Also, teachers supervise children as they write so that they can correct those who form letters incorrectly. It's important that children write circles counterclockwise, starting from 1:00, and form most lines from top to bottom and left to right across the page. When children follow these guidelines, they're less likely to tear their paper, and they'll have an easier transition to cursive handwriting.

FIGURE 4–8 A Reading Log Entry

Writing Centers

Writing centers are set up in kindergarten and first grade classrooms so that children have a special place where they can go to write. The center should be located at a table with chairs, and a box of supplies, including pencils, crayons, a date stamp, different kinds of paper, journal notebooks, a stapler, blank books, notepaper, and envelopes, should be stored nearby. The alphabet, printed in upper- and lowercase letters, should be available on the table for children to refer to as they write. In addition, there should be a crate where children can file their work. When children come to the writing center, they draw and write in journals, compile books, and write messages to classmates (Tunks & Giles, 2007). Teachers assist children and provide information about letters, words, and sentences as needed, or aides, parent-volunteers, or older students can assist. Figure 4–8 presents a reading log entry; it shows a kindergartner's response to *If You Give a Mouse a Cookie* (Numeroff, 2000). The child's writing says, "I love chocolate chip cookies."

Young children also make books at the writing center based on the books they've read. For example, they can use the same patterns as in *Baby Bear, Baby Bear, What Do You See?* (Martin, 2007), *If You Give a Mouse a Cookie* (Numeroff, 2000), and *Lunch* (Fleming, 1996) to create innovations, or new versions of familiar stories. A first grader's four-page book about a bee named Bumble, written after reading *If You Give a Mouse a Cookie*, is shown in Figure 4–9. In these writing projects, children often use invented spelling, but they're encouraged to spell familiar words and words from the story correctly.

Children also write notes and letters to classmates at the writing center. They learn about the format of friendly letters and how to phrase the greeting and the closing. Then they apply what they're learning as they write to classmates to say hello, offer a compliment, share news, trade telephone numbers, and offer birthday wishes. As they write messages, the children practice writing their names, their classmates' names, and the words they're learning to read and spell. The classmates who receive the messages also gain practice reading them. Teachers participate, too, by regularly writing brief messages to children. Through these activities, they model how to write messages and how to read and respond to the messages they receive. To facilitate the sharing of these messages, teachers often set up a message bulletin board or individual

mailboxes made from milk cartons or shoe boxes. This activity is especially valuable because children discover the social purposes of reading and writing as they write and receive notes and letters.

MONITOR: Check Your Understanding 4.4

Review

TEACHING THE YOUNGEST READERS AND WRITERS

Effective teachers understand that students move through three stages of reading and writing development—*emergent*, *beginning*, and *fluent*—during the primary grades, and they demonstrate their commitment to ensuring that their students are successful by organizing instruction according to children's level development as presented in this chapter, these points in particular:

4.1 Teachers nurture young children's oral language development.

4.2 Teachers foster young children's interest in literacy.

4.3 Teachers guide students through three stages of literacy development.

4.4 Teachers match instructional activities to children's stage of reading and writing development.

EVALUATE & REFLECT

Apply your understanding of young children's literacy development. The questions ask you to collect and analyze data, and report the results. Your response should meet academic standards and adhere to Standard English conventions.

1. Reread the vignette at the beginning of the chapter and identify activities for emergent, beginning, and fluent readers and writers. In your response, summarize the data you've collected, and based on the results of your data analysis, make suggestions about additional ways Ms. McCloskey could meet the needs of students working at all three levels of development in a multigrade classroom.

2. Administer the Concepts About Print Test to a kindergartner or struggling first grader and evaluate the child's progress in learning about written language. In your response, describe the child, report the test results, draw conclusions, and make recommendations.

3. Prepare materials to teach two of the alphabet routines described in Figure 4–2, and after teaching them in a kindergarten class, compare their effectiveness. For example, was one routine easier to teach, was one more effective, or did the children like one better? In your response, describe the classroom and the routines you prepared and taught, and summarize your teaching experience and the conclusions you drew. Then make recommendations about using the ABC routines in kindergarten classrooms.

4. Determine a third grader's stage of literacy development though observation and interview using the guidelines in Figure 4–3. In your response, describe the student's reading and writing achievement, identify the stage of development, explain how you analyzed the student's achievement, and make instructional recommendations.

5. Observe a K–3 teacher teach a lesson using interactive writing. Watch as the children contribute to the message and how the teacher supports them. In your response, explain the interactive writing lesson, with attention to the children's contributions and the support the teacher provided. What did you learn about interactive writing, and how might you use this procedure with young children or older struggling students?

REFERENCES

Adams, M. J. (1990). *Beginning to read: Thinking and learning about print*. Cambridge, MA: MIT Press.

Ashton-Warner, S. (1986). *Teacher*. New York: Simon & Schuster.

Button, K., Johnson, M. J., & Furgerson, P. (1996). Interactive writing in a primary classroom. *The Reading Teacher, 49*, 446–454.

Carle, E. (2002). *The very hungry caterpillar*. New York: Puffin Books.

Clay, M. M. (2000a). *Concepts about print: What have children learned about the way we print language?* Portsmouth, NH: Heinemann.

Clay, M. M. (2000b). *Follow me, moon*. Portsmouth, NH: Heinemann.

Clay, M. M. (2000c). *No shoes*. Portsmouth, NH: Heinemann.

Clay, M. M. (2014). *Stones* (New ed.). Portsmouth, NH: Heinemann.

Clay, M. M. (2015a). *An observation survey of early literacy achievement* (3rd ed.). Portsmouth, NH: Heinemann.

Clay, M. M. (2015b). *Sand* (New ed.). Portsmouth, NH: Heinemann.

Creech, S. (2010). *Hate that cat*. New York: HarperCollins.

Cronin, D. (2007). *Diary of a fly*. New York: HarperCollins.

Cummins, J. (1979). Linguistic interdependence and the educational development of bilingual children. *Review of Educational Research, 49*, 222–251.

Danziger, P. (1998). *Amber Brown sees red*. New York: Scholastic.

Danziger, P. (1999). *Amber Brown is feeling blue*. New York: Scholastic.

Danziger, P. (2004). *Amber Brown is green with envy*. New York: Scholastic.

Danziger, P. (2006). *Amber Brown is not a crayon*. New York: Scholastic.

Danziger, P. (2007). *Amber Brown goes fourth*. New York: Puffin Books.

Fleming, D. (1996). *Lunch*. New York: Henry Holt.

Fleming, D. (1997). *Barnyard banter*. New York: Henry Holt.

Fountas, I. C., & Pinnell, G. S. (1996). *Guided reading: Good first teaching for all children*. Portsmouth, NH: Heinemann.

Galdone, P. (2008). *The gingerbread boy*. New York: Clarion Books.

Greenburg, D. (1997). *Never trust a cat who wears earrings*. New York: Grosset & Dunlap.

Harris, T. (2000). *Pattern fish*. Brookfield, CT: Millbrook Press.

Harste, J., Woodward, V., & Burke, C. (1984). *Language stories and literacy lessons*. Portsmouth, NH: Heinemann.

Hart, B., & Risley, T. (2003). The early catastrophe: The 30 million word gap. *American Educator, 27*(1), 4–9.

Heath, S. B. (1983). *Ways with words*. New York: Oxford University Press.

Hoff, S. (2000a). *Oliver*. New York: Harper Trophy.

Hoff, S. (2000b). *Sammy the seal*. New York: Harper Trophy.

Invernizzi, M. (2003). Concepts, sounds, and the ABCs: A diet for a very young reader. In D. M. Barone & L. M. Morrow (Eds.), *Literacy and young children: Research-based practices* (pp. 140–156). New York: Guilford Press.

Juel, C. (1991). Beginning reading. In R. Barr, M. L. Kamil, P. Mosenthal, & P. D. Pearson (Eds.), *Handbook of reading research* (Vol. 2, pp. 759–788). Mahwah, NJ: Erlbaum.

Lefever-Davis, S., & Pearman, C. (2005). Early readers and electronic texts: CD-ROM storybook features that influence reading behaviors. *The Reading Teacher, 58,* 446–454.

Martin, B., Jr. (2007). *Baby bear, baby bear, what do you see?* New York: Henry Holt.

McCarrier, A., Pinnell, G. S., & Fountas, I. C. (2000). *Interactive writing: How language and literacy come together, K–2*. Portsmouth, NH: Heinemann.

McCloskey, R. (2004). *Make way for ducklings*. New York: Square Fish Books.

McGee, L. M. (2007). *Transforming literacy practices in preschool: Research-based practices that give all children the opportunity to reach their potential as learners*. New York: Scholastic.

McGee, L. M., & Richgels, D. J. (2003). *Designing early literacy programs: Strategies for at-risk preschool and kindergarten children*. New York: Guilford Press.

McGee, L. M., & Richgels, D. J. (2011). *Literacy's beginnings: Supporting young readers and writers* (6th ed.). Boston: Pearson.

Morrow, L. M., & Tracey, D. H. (2007). Best practices in early literacy development in preschool, kindergarten, and first grade. In L. B. Gambrell, L. M. Morrow, & M. Pressley (Eds.), *Best practices in literacy instruction* (3rd ed., pp. 57–82). New York: Guilford Press.

Numeroff, L. J. (2000). *If you give a mouse a cookie*. New York: HarperCollins.

Otto, B. (2014). *Language development in early childhood education* (4th ed.). Boston: Pearson.

Papandropoulou, I., & Sinclair, H. (1974). What is a word? Experimental study of children's ideas on grammar. *Human Development, 17,* 241–258.

Parkes, B. (2000). *Read it again! Revisiting shared reading*. Portland, ME: Stenhouse.

Payne, C. D., & Schulman, M. B. (1999). *Getting the most out of morning messages and other shared writing lessons*. New York: Scholastic.

Pinnell, G. S., & Fountas, I. C. (1998). *Word matters: Teaching phonics and spelling in the reading/writing classroom*. Portsmouth, NH: Heinemann.

Prince, S. (1999). *Playing*. Littleton, MA: Sundance.

Roskos, K. A., Tabors, P. O., & Lenhart, L. A. (2009). *Oral language and early literacy in preschool* (2nd ed.). Newark, DE: International Reading Association.

Roth, F. P., Speece, D. L., & Cooper, D. H. (2002). A longitudinal analysis of the connection between oral language and early reading. *Journal of Educational Research, 95,* 259–274.

Sachar, L. (2000). *Marvin Redpost: A magic crystal?* New York: Random House.

Samway, K. D., & McKeon, D. (2007). *Myths and realities: Best practices for English language learners* (2nd ed.). Portsmouth, NH: Heinemann.

Schickedanz, J., & Casbergue, R. (2004). *Writing in preschool: Learning to orchestrate meaning and marks*. Newark, DE: International Reading Association.

Seeger, L. V. (2007). *First the egg*. New York: Roaring Brook Press.

Seuss, Dr. (1965). *Fox in socks*. New York: Random House.

Simont, M. (2001). *The stray dog*. New York: HarperCollins.

Snow, C. E., Burns, M. S., & Griffin, P. (Eds.). (1998). *Preventing reading difficulties in young children*. Washington, DC: National Academy Press.

Tabors, P. O. (2008). *One child, two languages: A guide for early childhood educators of children learning English as a second language* (2nd ed.). Baltimore: Paul H. Brookes.

Taylor, D., & Dorsey-Gaines, C. (1987). *Growing up literate: Learning from inner-city families*. Portsmouth, NH: Heinemann.

Tompkins, G. E., & Collom, S. (2004). *Sharing the pen: Interactive writing with young children*. Upper Saddle River, NJ: Merrill/Prentice Hall.

Tompkins, G. E., & Webeler, M. (1983). What will happen next? Using predictable books with young children. *The Reading Teacher, 36,* 498–502.

Trapani, I. (2000). *Shoo fly!* Watertown, MA: Charlesbridge.

Tunks, K. W., & Giles, K. M. (2007). *Write now! Publishing with young authors, preK–grade 2*. Portsmouth, NH: Heinemann.

Chapter 5

Cracking the Alphabetic Code

PLAN: Preview the Learning Outcomes

After studying this chapter, you'll be prepared to respond to these topics:

5.1 Explain how children develop phonemic awareness.

5.2 Describe the phonics concepts that students learn.

5.3 Discuss how students develop as spellers.

First Grade Phonics Instruction. It's 8:10 on Thursday morning, and the 19 first graders in Mrs. Firpo's classroom are gathered on the carpet for their phonics lesson that she calls "word work." This week's topic is the long *i* and long *e* sounds for *y*: For example, in *my* and *multiply*, the *y* is pronounced as long *i*, and in *baby* and *sunny*, it's pronounced as long *e*. She shows pictures representing words that end with *y*: *fly, baby, jelly, bunny,* and *sky*. The children identify each object and say its name slowly to isolate the final sound. Saleena goes first. She picks up the picture of a fly and says, "It's a fly: /f/ /l/ /ī/. It ends with the /ī/ sound." Vincent is confused when it's his turn to identify the long *e* sound at the end of *bunny* so Mrs. Firpo demonstrates how to segment the sounds in the word: /b/ /ŭ/ /n/ /ē/. Then Vincent recognizes the long *e* sound at the end of the word. Next, the first graders sort the picture cards according to the final sound and place them in two columns in a nearby pocket chart. They add labels to the columns: *y* = ī and *y* = ē.

Mrs. Firpo begins her phonics lessons with an oral activity because she knows it's important to integrate phonemic awareness with phonics. In the oral activities, children focus on segmenting and blending the sounds they hear in words—without worrying about phoneme–grapheme cor-

respondences. Next, she introduces a set of cards with words ending in *y* for the children to read and classify. They take turns using phonics to sound out these words: *funny, my, try, happy, why, fussy, very, sticky, shy,* and *cry*. They add the word cards to the columns on the pocket chart. Then the teacher asks the children to suggest other words that end in *y*; Fernando names *yucky*, Crystal says *crunchy*, and Joel adds *dry*. Mrs. Firpo writes these words on small cards, too, and adds them to the pocket chart. Then Austin uses the pointer to point to each card in the pocket chart for the class to read aloud.

At the end of this 15-minute lesson, the children return to their desks and get out their whiteboards for spelling practice. This week's spelling words end in *y* pronounced as long *i*. Mrs. Firpo calls out each word, and the children practice writing it three times on their small whiteboards. If they need help spelling the word, they check the list of spelling

In this chapter, you'll learn about the alphabetic code and how children develop phonological awareness by manipulating sounds in words, matching letters and sounds to decode words, and representing sounds using letters as they spell words. As you read this vignette, notice how Mrs. Firpo teaches phonics. She engages students in a combination of oral and written activities as they develop phonemic awareness, phonics, and spelling knowledge, the three components of phonological awareness.

words on the Focus Wall. As they write, Mrs. Firpo circulates around the classroom, modeling how to form letters, reminding Jordan and Kendra to leave a "two-finger" space between words, and checking that their spellings are correct.

Check the figure Focus Wall. Each week, Mrs. Firpo posts the strategies and skills she'll be teaching, and the vocabulary words and spelling words are listed there, too. The vocabulary words are written on cards and displayed in a pocket chart attached to the Focus Wall so that they can be rearranged and used for various activities. Mrs. Firpo uses *Houghton Mifflin Reading* (Cooper & Pikulski, 2006), a basal reader series; each week's topics are identified for her in the teacher's edition of the textbook. The reason why she posts these topics is to emphasize what she's teaching and what children are learning. In addition, Mrs. Firpo has her state's reading and writing standards for first grade listed on a chart beside the wall.

Next, Mrs. Firpo guides children as they complete several pages in the workbook that accompanies the basal reader; some pages reinforce phonics and spelling concepts, and others focus on comprehension, vocabulary, grammar, and writing. Today, they begin on page 201. First the children examine the illustration at the top of the page, and then on the lines at the

FOCUS WALL

Theme 9: Special Friends	Week: 1	Reading Level: 1.5

PHONICS FOCUS: Long i and long e sounds for y

WORD PATTERN: -ay

say	day	way	bay	stay	gray
pay	may	lay	ray	pray	spray

SPELLING CONCEPT: Long i sound at the end of a
                              word spelled with y

COMPREHENSION STRATEGY: Monitoring

COMPREHENSION SKILL: Noting Details

GRAMMAR CONCEPT: is/are

WRITING GENRE: Friendly Letters

VOCABULARY WORDS

ocean	though	by
dance	talk	my
open	else	cry
ever	around	any
	Grandaddy	

SPELLING WORDS

1. by	5. cry
2. my	6. why
3. fly	7. pry
4. try	8. multiply

bottom of the page, they write two sentences about the silly things they see in the picture. They talk about the illustration, identifying the silly things they see. Felicia says, "I see a bunny reading a book, and I think that's silly." Mrs. Firpo gives Felicia a "thumbs up" to compliment her. And Fernando comments, "I see something else. It's a bear up in a balloon." "Is the balloon up in the sky?" Mrs. Firpo asks because she wants to emphasize the phonics pattern of the week. Fernando agrees that it is, and he repeats, "I see a bear up in a balloon in the sky." He, too, gets a "thumbs up."

After children identify five or six silly things, they get ready to write. Mrs. Firpo reminds them to begin their sentences with capital letters and end them with periods. As they write their sentences, Alicia notices that she has written *bunny*—a word that ends in *y* and has an /ē/ sound. Mrs. Firpo congratulates her and encourages other children to point out when they write words that end in *y*. Joel waves his hand in the air, eager to report that he has written *sky*—a word that ends in *y* and has an /ī/ sound.

Then the children move on to page 202. On this page, there's a word bank with words that end in *y* and represent the /ī/ sound at the top and sentences with blanks at the bottom. The children practice reading the words in the word bank. After reading the words several times, Vincent volunteers, "I get it! Look at these words: They all have *y* and they say /ī/." Mrs. Firpo is pleased and gives him a "thumbs up." Next, the teacher reads aloud the sentences at the bottom of the page and asks children to supply the missing words. Then they work independently to reread the sentences and complete them by filling in the missing words. Mrs. Firpo moves from one group of desks to the next as the children work, monitoring their work and providing assistance as needed.

Each week, the children receive take-home books that Mrs. Firpo has duplicated and stapled together; these books reinforce the week's phonics lesson and the vocabulary introduced in the reading textbook. The first graders read the books at school and use them for a phonics activity; then they take them home to practice reading with their families. Today's book is *I Spy*: It's eight pages long, with illustrations and text on each page. Mrs. Firpo introduces the book and reads it aloud once while the children follow along in their copies. They keep their books at their desks to use for a seatwork activity, and later they put the books in book bags that they take home each day. Already they've collected more than 75 books!

During the last 40 minutes of the reading period, Mrs. Firpo conducts guided reading groups. Her students' reading levels range from beginning first grade to the middle of second grade, with about half of them reading at grade level. She has grouped the first graders into four guided reading groups, and she meets with two groups each day. Children reading below grade level read leveled books, and those reading at and above grade level read easy-to-read chapter books, including Barbara Park's series of funny stories about a girl named Junie B. Jones (e.g., *Junie B., First Grader: Boss of Lunch* [2003]) and Mary Pope Osborne's Magic Tree House series of adventure stories (e.g., *High Tide in Hawaii* [2003]). Mrs. Firpo calls this period *differentiated instruction* because children participate in a variety of activities based on their reading levels.

While Mrs. Firpo does guided reading with one group, the others are involved in seatwork and center activities. For the seatwork activity, children read their take-home book and highlight all the words in it ending in *y* pronounced as /ī/; they don't highlight *bunny*, *play*, and other words where the *y* is not pronounced as /ī/. They also work in small groups to cut out pictures and words that end in *y*; sort into *y* = ē, *y* = ī, and *y* = *other* categories; and paste them on a sheet of paper. The pictures and words for the activity include *puppy, city, they, buy, pretty, play, funny, dry, party, fifty, boy, sky, fly, today,* and *yummy*.

The first graders practice their spelling words using magnetic letters at the spelling center, practice the phonics focus and word pattern using letter cards and flip books at the phonics center, make books at the writing center, listen to the take-home books read aloud at the listening center, and read eBooks interactively at the computer center. The centers are arranged around the perimeter of the classroom; children know how to work at centers and understand what they're expected to do at each one.

After a 15-minute recess, children spend the last 55 minutes of literacy instruction in writing workshop. Each week, the class focuses on the genre specified in the basal reading program; this week's focus is on writing personal letters. First, Mrs. Firpo teaches a **minilesson** and guides children as they complete more pages in their workbooks; today, she reviews how to use commas in a friendly letter. The children examine several letters hanging in the classroom that the class wrote earlier in the school year using **interactive writing**. After the class rereads each letter, Mrs. Firpo asks the children to mark the commas used in the letters with Vis-à-Vis pens (so their marks can be cleaned off afterward). Crystal points out that commas are used in the date, Saleena notices that a comma is used at the end of the greeting, and Luis marks the comma used after the closing. Next, children practice adding commas in the sample friendly letters on page 208 in their workbooks.

Then children spend the remaining 35 minutes of writing workshop working on the letters they're writing to their families this week. Mrs. Firpo works with five children on their letters while the others work independently. At the end of the writing time, Joel and Angelica sit in the author's chair to read their letters aloud to their classmates. Check the figure Angelica's Letter.

ANGELICA'S LETTER

April 29, 2015

Dear Nanna Isabel,

I am writting you a letter. My birthday is in 35 days! Did you no that? I wud like to get a present. I want you to come to my party. It will be very funny.

Love,
Angelica

Mrs. Firpo's students spend 3 hours each morning involved in literacy instruction. Most of the goals, activities, and instructional materials come from the basal reading program, but Mrs. Firpo adapts some activities to meet her students' varied instructional needs. Through these phonemic awareness, phonics, and spelling activities, these first graders are learning to crack the alphabetic code.

 STANDARDS CHECK!

Mrs. Firpo addressed the Common Core State Standards as she taught phonics in the vignette you've just read. Review the first grade literacy Standards document online at http://www .corestandards.org/ELA-Literacy, and identify the Standards that Mrs. Firpo addressed through her instruction. Create your list, and compare it with Mrs. Firpo's.

Children's level of phonological awareness is a strong predictor of their reading success. Why is phoneme–grapheme knowledge critical in learning to read and write?

$\mathcal{E}$nglish is an alphabetic language, and children crack this code as they learn about **phonemes**, **graphemes**, and **graphophonemic** relationships. They learn about phonemes as they notice rhyming words, segment words into individual sounds, and invent silly words by playing with sounds, much like Dr. Seuss did. They learn about letters as they sing the ABC song, name the letters of the alphabet, and spell their own names. They learn graphophonemic relationships as they match letters and letter combinations to sounds, blend sounds to form words, and decode and spell vowel patterns. By third grade, most students have figured out the alphabetic code, and in fourth through eighth grades, students apply what they've learned to decode and spell multisyllabic words. You may think of all of this as phonics, but children actually develop three separate but related types of alphabetic code knowledge:

🐛 **Phonemic Awareness.** Children learn to notice and manipulate the sounds of oral language. Those who are phonemically aware understand that spoken words are made up of sounds, and they can segment and blend sounds in spoken words.

🐛 **Phonics.** Children learn to convert letters into sounds and blend them to recognize words. Those who can apply phonics concepts understand that there are predictable **phoneme–grapheme correspondences** in English, and they can use decoding strategies to figure out unfamiliar written words.

🐛 **Spelling.** Children learn to segment spoken words into sounds and convert the sounds into letters to spell words. Those who have learned to spell conventionally understand English phoneme–grapheme correspondences and spelling patterns, and they can use spelling strategies to spell unfamiliar words.

In the vignette, Mrs. Firpo incorporated all three components into her literacy program. She began the word work lesson on the long *e* and long *i* sounds of *y* with an oral phonemic awareness activity; next, she moved to a phonics activity where children read words that ended in *y* and categorized them on a pocket chart. Later, they practiced spelling words that end with *y* on whiteboards. Teaching these graphophonemic relationships is not a complete reading program, but phonemic awareness, phonics, and spelling are integral to effective literacy instruction, especially for young children (National Reading Panel, 2000).

The feature Common Core State Standards: Phonological Awareness presents an overview of the phonemic awareness, phonics, and spelling Standards.

COMMON CORE STATE STANDARDS

Phonological Awareness

The Reading Standards: Foundational Skills and the Language Standards focus on developing students' knowledge of phonemic awareness, phonics, and spelling so they'll become capable readers and writers. The Standards specify these ways for students to demonstrate their understanding of words, phonemes, and syllables:

● Students blend and segment sounds in spoken words.

● Students apply phonics and word-analysis skills to decode one-syllable words in first grade, two-syllable words in second grade, and multisyllabic words in third grade and beyond.

● Students spell grade-appropriate words correctly.

● Students consult dictionaries to check spellings.

By fifth grade, students must be able to use their knowledge of phoneme–grapheme correspondences, syllabication patterns, and morphology to read unfamiliar multisyllabic words. Similarly, they need to be able to spell grade-appropriate words correctly. To learn more about the Standards, go to http://www.corestandards.org/ELA-Literacy, or check your state's educational standards website.

Phonemic Awareness

Phonemic awareness is children's basic understanding that speech is composed of a series of individual sounds, and it provides the foundation for phonics and spelling (Armbruster, Lehr, & Osborn, 2001). When children can choose a duck as the animal whose name begins with /d/ from a collection of toy animals, identify *duck* and *luck* as rhyming words in a song, and blend the sounds /d/ /ŭ/ /k/ to pronounce *duck*, they're phonemically aware. Cunningham and Allington (2016) describe phonemic awareness as children's ability to take words apart and put them back together again. The emphasis is on the sounds of spoken words, not on reading letters or pronouncing letter names. Developing phonemic awareness enables children to use phoneme–grapheme correspondences to read and spell words (Gillon, 2004).

Phonemes are the smallest units of speech, and they're written as graphemes, or letters of the alphabet. In this book, phonemes are marked using diagonal lines (e.g., /d/) and graphemes are italicized (*d*). Sometimes phonemes (e.g., /k/ in *duck*) are spelled with two graphemes (*ck*).

Understanding that words are composed of smaller units—phonemes—is a significant achievement for young children because phonemes are abstract language units. Phonemes carry no meaning, and children think of words according to their meanings, not their linguistic characteristics (Griffith & Olson, 1992). When children think about ducks, for example, they think of feathered animals that swim in ponds, fly through the air, and make noises we describe as "quacks"; they don't think of "duck" as a word with three phonemes or four graphemes, or as a word beginning with /d/ and rhyming with *luck*. Phonemic awareness requires that children treat speech as an object and that they shift their attention away from the meaning of words to the linguistic features of speech. This focus on phonemes is even more complicated because phonemes aren't discrete units in speech: Often they're slurred or clipped—think about the blended initial sound in *tree* and the ending sound in *eating*.

Phonemic Awareness Strategies

Children learn to manipulate spoken language in these ways:

Identifying Sounds in Words. Children identify a word that begins or ends with a particular sound. For example, when shown a brush, a car, and a doll, they can identify *doll* as the word that ends with /l/.

Categorizing Sounds in Words. Children recognize the "odd" word in a set of three words; for example, when the teacher says *ring*, *rabbit*, and *sun*, they recognize that *sun* doesn't belong.

Substituting Sounds to Make New Words. Children remove a sound from a word and substitute a different sound. Sometimes they substitute the beginning sound, changing *bar* to *car*, for example. Or, they change the middle sound, making *tip* from *top*, or substitute the ending sound, changing *gate* to *game*.

Blending Sounds to Form Words. Children blend two, three, or four individual sounds to form a word; for example, the teacher says /b/ /ĭ/ /g/, and the children repeat the sounds, blending them to form the word *big*.

Segmenting a Word Into Sounds. Children break a word into its beginning, middle, and ending sounds. For example, they segment the word *feet* into /f/ /ē/ /t/ and *go* into /g/ /ō/.

Children use these strategies, especially blending and segmenting, to decode and spell words. When they use phonics to sound out a word, for example, they say the sounds represented by each letter and blend them to read the word. Similarly, to spell a word, children say the word slowly to themselves, segmenting the sounds.

Teaching Phonemic Awareness

Teachers nurture children's phonemic awareness through the language-rich environments they create in the classroom. As

Teach Kids to BE STRATEGIC

Phonemic Awareness Strategies

Introduce these two strategies as students manipulate sounds orally:

- Blend
- Segment

Children practice these strategies orally as they play with words, identify rhyming words, and invent nonsense words. Look for children to apply the strategies to written language when they decode and spell words. If students struggle, reteach the strategies, making sure to name them, model their use with both oral and written language, and talk about their application in reading and writing.

they sing songs, chant rhymes, read aloud wordplay books, and play games, children have many opportunities to orally match, isolate, blend, and substitute sounds and to segment words into sounds (Griffith & Olson, 1992). Teachers often incorporate phonemic awareness into other oral language and literacy activities, but it's also important to teach lessons that focus specifically on the phonemic awareness strategies.

Phonemic awareness instruction should meet three criteria. First, the activities should be appropriate for 5- and 6-year-olds. Activities involving songs, rhymes, riddles, and wordplay books are good choices because they encourage children's playful experimentation with oral language. Second, the instruction should be planned and purposeful, not just incidental. Teachers need to choose instructional materials and plan activities that focus children's attention on the sound structure of oral language. Third, phonemic awareness activities should be integrated with other components of

Booklist   Wordplay Books

TYPE	BOOKS
Invented Words	Degan, B. (1985). *Jamberry*. New York: Harper Trophy. Hutchins, P. (2002). *Don't forget the bacon!* New York: Red Fox Books. Martin, B., Jr., & Archambault, J. (2009). *Chicka chicka boom boom*. New York: Beach Lane Books. Most, B. (1996). *Cock-a-doodle-moo!* San Diego: Harcourt Brace. Slate, J. (1996). *Miss Bindergarten gets ready for kindergarten*. New York: Dutton. Slepian, J., & Seidler, A. (2001). *The hungry thing*. New York: Scholastic.
Repetitive Lines	Deming, A. G. (1994). *Who is tapping at my window?* New York: Penguin. Downey, L. (2000). *The flea's sneeze*. New York: Henry Holt. Fleming, D. (2007). *In the small, small pond*. New York: Henry Holt. Hoberman, M. A. (2003). *The lady with the alligator purse*. Boston: Little, Brown. Taback, S. (1997). *There was an old lady who swallowed a fly*. New York: Viking. Taback, S. (2004). *This is the house that Jack built*. New York: Puffin Books. Westcott, N. B. (2003). *I know an old lady who swallowed a fly*. Boston: Little, Brown. Wilson, K. (2003). *A frog in a bog*. New York: McElderry.
Rhyming Words	Ehlert, L. (1993). *Eating the alphabet: Fruits and vegetables from A to Z*. San Diego: Voyager. McPhail, D. (1996). *Pigs aplenty, pigs galore*. New York: Puffin Books. Root, P. (2003). *One duck stuck*. Cambridge, MA: Candlewick Press. Seuss, Dr. (1963). *Hop on pop*. New York: Random House. Shaw, N. (2006). *Sheep in a jeep*. Boston: Houghton Mifflin.
Songs and Verse	Crebbin, J. (1998). *Cows in the kitchen*. Cambridge, MA: Candlewick Press. Gollub, M. (2000). *The jazz fly*. Santa Rosa, CA: Tortuga Press. Hillenbrand, W. (2002). *Fiddle-i-fee*. San Diego: Gulliver Books. Hoberman, M. A. (2003). *The eensy-weensy spider*. Boston: Little, Brown. Prelutsky, J. (1989). *The baby uggs are hatching*. New York: Mulberry Books. Raffi. (1988). *Down by the bay*. New York: Crown. Raffi. (1990). *The wheels on the bus*. New York: Crown.
Sounds	Ehlert, L. (2011). *RRRalph*. San Diego: Beach Lane Books. Most, B. (1991). *A dinosaur named after me*. San Diego: Harcourt Brace. Most, B. (2003). *The cow that went oink*. San Diego: Voyager. Seuss, Dr. (1974). *There's a wocket in my pocket*. New York: Random House.

a balanced literacy program. It's crucial that children perceive the connection between oral and written language (Yopp & Yopp, 2000).

Many wordplay books have been developed for young children; to see a selection, check Booklist: Wordplay Books. *Cock-a-Doodle-Moo!* (Most, 1996) and *Rattletrap Car* (Root, 2004), for instance, stimulate children to experiment with sounds and to invent nonsense words. Teachers often read wordplay books aloud more than once. During the first reading, children focus on comprehension or what interests them in the book. During a second reading, however, children's attention shifts to the wordplay elements, and teachers direct their attention to the way the author manipulated words and sounds by making comments and asking questions—"Did you notice how ____ and ____ rhyme?"—and encourage children to make similar observations themselves.

Teachers often incorporate wordplay books, songs, and games into the minilessons they teach. Check Minilesson: Blending Sounds Into Words to see a kindergarten teacher's phonemic awareness lesson. The teacher reread Dr. Seuss's *Fox in Socks* (1965) and then asked children to identify words from the book that she pronounced sound by sound. This book is rich in wordplay: rhyming (e.g., *do, you, goo, chew*), initial consonant substitution (e.g., *trick, quick, slick*), vowel substitution (e.g., *blabber, blibber, blubber*), and alliteration (e.g., *Luke Luck likes lakes*).

SOUND-MATCHING ACTIVITIES. Children choose one of several words beginning with a particular phoneme or say a word that begins with a particular sound (Yopp, 1992). For these games, teachers use familiar objects (e.g., feather, toothbrush, book) and toys (e.g., small plastic animals, toy trucks, artificial fruits and vegetables), as well as pictures of familiar objects.

Teachers can play a sound-matching guessing game (Lewkowicz, 1994). For this game, teachers collect two boxes and pairs of objects to place in the boxes (e.g., forks, mittens, erasers, combs, and books); one item from each pair is placed in each box. After the teacher shows children the objects in the boxes and they name them together, two children play the game. One child selects an object, holds it, and pronounces the initial (or medial or final) sound. The second child chooses the same object from the second box and holds it up. Classmates check to see if the two players are holding the same object.

Children also identify rhyming words as part of sound-matching activities: They name a word that rhymes with a given word and identify rhyming words from familiar songs and stories. As children listen to parents and teachers read Dr. Seuss books, such as *Fox in Socks* (1965) and *Hop on Pop* (1963), and other wordplay books, they refine their understanding of rhyme.

SOUND-ISOLATION ACTIVITIES. Teachers say a word and then children identify the sounds at the beginning, middle, or end of the word, or teachers and children isolate sounds as they sing familiar songs. Yopp (1992) created these new verses to the tune of "Old MacDonald Had a Farm":

What's the sound that starts these words:
Chicken, chin, and cheek?
(wait for response)
/ch/ is the sound that starts these words:
Chicken, chin, and cheek.
With a /ch/, /ch/ here, and a /ch/, /ch/ there,
Here a /ch/, there a /ch/, everywhere a /ch/, /ch/.
/ch/ is the sound that starts these words:
Chicken, chin, and cheek. (p. 700)

Watch as kindergartners look for objects whose names sound alike. How does this activity develop phonemic awareness?

Minilesson

TOPIC: Blending Sounds Into Words
GRADE: Kindergarten
TIME: One 20-minute period

Ms. Lewis regularly includes a 20-minute lesson on phonemic awareness in her literacy block. She usually rereads a familiar wordplay book and plays a phonemic awareness game with the kindergartners that emphasizes one of the phonemic awareness strategies.

1 Introduce the Topic

Ms. Lewis brings her 19 kindergartners together on the rug and explains that she's going to reread Dr. Seuss's *Fox in Socks* (1965). It's one of their favorite books, and they clap their pleasure. She explains that after reading, they're going to play a word game.

2 Share Examples

Ms. Lewis reads aloud *Fox in Socks*, showing the pictures on each page as she reads. She encourages the children to read along. Sometimes she stops and invites them to fill in the last rhyming word in a sentence or to echo read (repeating after her like an echo) the alliterative sentences. After they finish reading, she asks what they like best about the book. Pearl replies, "It's just a really funny book. That's why it's so good." "What makes it funny?" Ms. Lewis asks. Teri explains, "The words are funny. They make my tongue laugh. You know—*fox–socks–box–Knox*. That's funny on my tongue!" "Oh," Ms. Lewis clarifies, "your tongue likes to say rhyming words. I like to say them, too." Other children recall other rhyming words in the book: *clocks–tocks–blocks–box, noodle–poodle*, and *new–do–blue–goo*.

3 Provide Information

"Let me tell you about our game," Ms. Lewis explains. "I'm going to say some of the words from the book, but I'm going to say them sound by sound, and I want you to blend the sounds together and guess the word." "Are they rhyming words?" Teri asks. "Sure," the teacher agrees. "I'll say two words that rhyme, sound by sound, for you to guess." She says the sounds /f/ /ŏ/ /ks/ and /b/ /ŏ/ /ks/ and the children correctly blend the sounds and say the words *fox* and *box*. She repeats the procedure for *clock–tock, come–dumb, big–pig, new–blue, rose–hose, game–lame*, and *slow–crow*. Ms. Lewis stops and talks about how to "bump" or blend the sounds to figure out the words. She models how she blends the sounds to form the word. "Make the words harder," several children say, and Ms. Lewis offers several more difficult pairs of rhyming words, including *chick–trick* and *beetle–tweedle*.

4 Guide Practice

Ms. Lewis continues playing the guessing game, but now she segments individual words. As each child identifies a word, that child leaves the group and goes to work with the aide. Finally, six children remain who need additional practice. They continue blending *do, new*, and other two-sound words and some of the easier three-sound words, including *box, come*, and *like*.

5 Assess Learning

Through the guided practice part of the lesson, Ms. Lewis informally checks to see which children need more practice blending sounds into words and provides additional practice for them.

Teachers change the question at the beginning of the verse to focus on medial sounds. For example:

> What's the sound in the middle of these words?
> Whale, game, and rain. (p. 700)

And for final sounds:

> What's the sound at the end of these words?
> Leaf, cough, and beef. (p. 700)

Teachers also set out trays of objects and ask children to choose the one object that doesn't belong because it begins with a different sound. For example, from a tray with a toy pig, a puppet, a teddy bear, and a pen, the teddy bear doesn't belong.

SOUND-BLENDING ACTIVITIES. Children blend sounds in order to combine them to form a word. For example, children blend the sounds /d/ /ŭ/ /k/ to form the word *duck*. Teachers play the "What am I thinking of?" guessing game with children by identifying several characteristics of the item and then saying its name, articulating each of the sounds slowly and separately (Yopp, 1992). Then children blend the sounds and identify the word, using the phonological and semantic information that the teacher provided. For example:

> *I'm thinking of a small animal that lives in the pond when it's young. When it's an adult, it lives on land and it's called a /f/ /r/ /ŏ/ /g/. What is it?*

The children blend the sounds to pronounce the word *frog*. Then the teacher can move into phonics and spelling by setting out magnetic letters for children to arrange to spell *frog*. In this example, the teacher connects the game with a thematic unit, thereby making the game more meaningful for children.

SOUND-ADDITION AND -SUBSTITUTION ACTIVITIES. Children play with words and create nonsense words as they add or substitute sounds in words from songs they sing or from books read aloud to them. Teachers read wordplay books such as Pat Hutchins's *Don't Forget the Bacon!* (1989), in which a boy leaves for the store with a mental list of four items to buy. As he walks, he repeats his list, substituting words each time: "A cake for tea" changes to "a cape for me" and then to "a rake for leaves." Children suggest other substitutions, such as "a game for a bee."

Students substitute sounds in refrains of songs (Yopp, 1992). For example, they can change the "Ee-igh, ee-igh, oh!" refrain in "Old MacDonald Had a Farm" to "Bee-bigh, bee-bigh, boh!" to focus on the initial /b/ sound. Teachers can choose one sound, such as /sh/, and have children substitute it for the beginning sound in their names and in words for items in the classroom. For example, *Jimmy* becomes *Shimmy*, *José* becomes *Shosé*, and *clock* becomes *shock*.

SOUND-SEGMENTATION ACTIVITIES. One of the more difficult phonemic awareness activities is *segmentation*, in which children isolate the sounds in a spoken word (Yopp, 1988). An introductory segmentation activity is to draw out the beginning sound in words. Children enjoy exaggerating the initial sound in their own names and other familiar words. For example, a pet guinea pig named Popsicle lives in Mrs. Firpo's classroom, and the children exaggerate the beginning sound of her name so that it's pronounced as "P-P-P-Popsicle." Children can also pick up objects or pictures of objects and identify the initial sound; a child who picks up a toy truck says, "This is a truck and it starts with /t/."

From that beginning, children move to identifying all the sounds in a word. Using a toy truck again, the child would say, "This is a truck, /t/ /r/ /ŭ/ /k/." Yopp (1992) suggests singing a song to the tune of "Twinkle, Twinkle, Little Star" in which children segment entire words. Here's one example:

Listen, listen to my word
Then tell me all the sounds you heard: coat
(slowly)
/k/ is one sound
/ō/ is two
/t/ is last in coat
It's true. (p. 702)

After several repetitions of the verse segmenting other words, the song ends this way:

Thanks for listening to my words
And telling all the sounds you heard! (p. 702)

Teachers also use **Elkonin boxes** to teach students to segment words; this activity comes from the work of Russian psychologist D. B. Elkonin (Clay, 2005). As seen in Figure 5–1, the teacher shows an object or a picture of an object and draws a row of boxes, with one box for each phoneme in the name of the object or picture. Then the teacher or a child moves a marker into each box as the sound is pronounced. Children can move small markers onto cards on their desks, or the teacher can draw the boxes on the chalkboard and use tape or small magnets to hold the larger markers in place. Elkonin boxes can also be used for spelling activities: When a child is trying to spell a word, such as *duck*, the teacher can draw three boxes, do the segmentation activity, and then have the child write the letters representing each phoneme in the boxes.

Children are experimenting with oral language in these activities, which stimulate their interest in language and provide valuable experiences with books and words. Effective teachers recognize the importance of building this foundation as children are beginning to read and write. To assess the effectiveness of your instruction, use the Teacher Checklist: How do I teach phonemic awareness?

Nurturing English Learners

How do teachers teach phonemic awareness? It's more difficult to develop English learners' phonemic awareness than native English speakers' because they're just learning to speak English; however, this training is worthwhile for ELs as long as familiar and meaningful words are used (Riches & Genesee, 2006). Teachers create a rich literacy environment and begin by reading books and poems aloud and singing songs so children can learn to recognize and pronounce English sound patterns.

To plan effective phonemic awareness instruction, teachers need to be familiar with English learners' home languages and understand how they differ from English (Peregoy & Boyle, 2013). Instruction should begin with sounds that children can pronounce easily and that don't conflict with those in their home language. Sounds that aren't present in children's home language or those that they don't perceive as unique, such as /ch/–/sh/ or /ĕ/–/ĭ/ for Spanish speakers, are more difficult; children may need more time to practice producing and manipulating these difficult sounds.

FIGURE 5–1 Ways to Use Elkonin Boxes

TYPE	PURPOSES	STEPS
Phonemic Awareness	Segmenting sounds in a one-syllable word	1. Show children an object or a picture of an object with a one-syllable name, such as a duck, game, bee, or cup. 2. Prepare a diagram with a row of boxes, side by side, corresponding to the number of sounds heard in the name of the object. Draw the row of boxes on the chalkboard or on a small white board. For example, draw two boxes to represent the two sounds in *bee* or three boxes for the three sounds in *duck*. 3. Distribute coins or other small items to use as markers. 4. Say the name of the object slowly and move a marker into each box as the sound is pronounced. Then have children repeat the procedure.
	Segmenting a multisyllabic word into syllables	1. Show children an object or a picture of an object with a multisyllabic name, such as a butterfly, alligator, cowboy, or umbrella. 2. Prepare a diagram with a row of boxes, corresponding to the number of syllables in the name of the object. For example, draw four boxes to represent the four syllables in *alligator*. 3. Distribute markers. 4. Say the name of the object slowly and move a marker into each box as the syllable is pronounced. Then have children repeat the procedure.
Spelling	Representing sounds with letters	1. Draw a row of boxes corresponding to the number of sounds heard in a word. For example, draw two boxes for *go*, three boxes for *ship*, and four boxes for *frog*. 2. Pronounce the word, pointing to each box as the corresponding sound is pronounced. 3. Have the child write the letter or letters representing the sound in each box.
	Applying spelling patterns	1. Draw a row of boxes corresponding to the number of sounds heard in a word. For example, draw three boxes for the word *duck, game,* or *light*. 2. Pronounce the word, pointing to each box as the corresponding sound is pronounced. 3. Have the child write the letter or letters representing the sound in each box. 4. Pronounce the word again and examine how each sound is spelled. Insert additional unpronounced letters to complete the spelling patterns. d | u | ck

Watch as a kindergarten teacher presents a lesson on phoneme–grapheme correspondences. Which phonemic awareness concepts are the English learners practicing?

Researchers recommend explicit instruction on phonemic awareness and practice opportunities for English learners (Snow, Burns, & Griffin, 1998). They sing familiar songs and play language games like native speakers do, but teachers also draw ELs' attention to pronouncing English sounds and words. Teachers often integrate phonemic awareness training, vocabulary instruction, and reading and writing activities to show how oral language sounds are represented by letters in written words (Peregoy & Boyle, 2013).

Phonemic awareness is a common underlying linguistic ability that transfers from one language to another (Riches & Genesee, 2006). Children who have learned to read in their home language are phonemically aware, and this knowledge supports their reading and writing development in English. ᲂᎮ

Assessing Children's Phonemic Awareness

Through phonemic awareness instruction, children learn strategies for segmenting, blending, and substituting phonemes in words. Teachers often monitor their learning

ASSESSMENT TOOLS

Phonemic Awareness

Kindergarten and first grade teachers monitor children's learning by observing them during classroom activities, and they screen, monitor, diagnose, and document their growing phonemic awareness by administering these tests:

- **Dynamic Indicators of Basic Early Literacy Skills (DIBELS): Phoneme Segmentation Fluency Subtest**
  This individually administered subtest (Kaminski & Good, 1996) assesses children's ability to segment words with two and three phonemes. Multiple forms are available so that this test can be used periodically to monitor children's progress. The test is available free of charge on the DIBELS website, but there is a charge for analyzing and reporting the test results.

- **Phonological Awareness Literacy Screening (PALS) System: Rhyme Awareness and Beginning Sound Subtests**
  The kindergarten level of PALS (Invernizzi, Meier, & Juel, 2003) includes brief subtests to assess young children's phonemic awareness. Children look at pictures and supply rhyming words or produce the beginning sounds for picture names. The grades 1–3 tests also include phonemic awareness subtests for children who score below grade level on other tests. PALS is available from the University of Virginia; it's free for Virginia teachers, but teachers in other states pay a fee to use it.

- **Test of Phonological Awareness (TPA)**
  This 40-minute group test (Torgesen & Bryant, 2004) designed for children ages 5–8 measures their ability to isolate individual phonemes in spoken words and understand the relationship between phonemes and graphemes. The TPA is available from LinguiSystems.

- **Yopp-Singer Test of Phonemic Segmentation**
  This individually administered oral test (Yopp, 1995) for kindergartners measures their ability to segment the phonemes in words; it contains 22 items and is administered in less than 10 minutes. The test is free; it can be found in the September 1995 issue of *The Reading Teacher* or online. A Spanish version is also available.

Information gained from classroom observations and these assessments is used to identify students who aren't yet phonemically aware, plan appropriate instruction, and monitor students' progress.

as they participate in phonemic awareness activities: When children sort picture cards according to beginning sounds or identify rhyming words in a familiar song, they're demonstrating their ability to manipulate sounds. Teachers also administer one of several readily available phonemic awareness tests to screen children's ability to use phonemic awareness strategies, monitor their progress, and document their learning. Four tests are described in Assessment Tools: Phonemic Awareness.

Why Phonemic Awareness Is Important

A clear connection exists between phonemic awareness and learning to read; researchers have concluded that phonemic awareness is a prerequisite for reading development. As they become phonemically aware, children recognize that speech can be segmented into smaller units; this knowledge is very useful as they learn about phoneme–grapheme correspondences and spelling patterns (Cunningham, 2015).

Watch as a teacher administers phonemic awareness tests and discusses how children's ability to manipulate words affects their literacy achievement. How does children's phonemic awareness influence their writing development?

Children can be explicitly taught to segment and blend speech, and those who receive approximately 20 hours of training in phonemic awareness do better in both reading and spelling (Juel, Griffith, & Gough, 1986). Phonemic awareness is also nurtured in spontaneous ways by providing children with language-rich environments and emphasizing wordplay as teachers read books aloud and engage children in singing songs, chanting poems, and telling riddles.

Moreover, phonemic awareness has been shown to be the most powerful predictor of later reading achievement. Klesius, Griffith, and Zielonka (1991) found that children who began first grade with strong phonemic awareness did well regardless of the kind of reading instruction they received, and no one type of instruction was better for children who were low in phonemic awareness at the beginning of first grade.

 MONITOR: Check Your Understanding 5.1

Phonics

Phonics is the set of relationships between phonology, the sounds in speech, and orthography, the spelling patterns of written language. The emphasis is on spelling patterns, not individual letters, because there isn't a one-to-one correspondence between phonemes and graphemes in English. Phonemes are spelled in different ways. There are several reasons for this variety; one is that sounds, especially vowels, vary according to their location in a word (e.g., *go–got*). Adjacent letters often influence how letters are pronounced (e.g., *bed–bead*), as do vowel markers such as final *e* (e.g., *bit–bite*) (Shefelbine, 1995).

Etymology, or language origin, of words also influences their pronunciation. For example, the *ch* digraph is pronounced in several ways; the three most common are /ch/ as in *chain* (English), /sh/ as in *chauffeur* (French), and /k/ as in *chaos* (Greek). Neither the location of the digraph within the word nor adjacent letters account for these pronunciation differences: In all three words, the *ch* digraph is at the beginning of the word and is followed by two vowels, the first of which is *a*. Some letters in words aren't pronounced, either. In words such as *write*, the *w* isn't pronounced, even though it probably was at one time; the same is true for the *k* in *knight*, *know*, and *knee*. "Silent" letters in words such as *sign* and *bomb* reflect their parent words, *signature* and *bombard*, and have been retained for semantic, not phonological, reasons (Venezky, 1999).

Phonics Concepts

Phonics explains the relationships between phonemes and graphemes. There are 44 phonemes in English, and they are represented by the 26 letters. The **alphabetic principle** suggests that there should be a one-to-one correspondence between phonemes and graphemes, so that each sound is consistently represented by one letter. English, however, isn't a perfect phonetic language, and there are more than 500 ways to represent the 44 phonemes using single letters or combinations of letters. Consider the word *day*: The two phonemes, /d/ and /ā/, are represented by three letters. The letter *d* is a consonant, and *a* and *y* are vowels. Interestingly, *y* isn't always a vowel; it's a consonant at the beginning of a word and a vowel at the end. When two vowels are side by side at the end of a word, they represent a long vowel sound. In *day*, the vowel sound is long *a*. Primary grade students learn these phonics concepts to decode unfamiliar words.

CONSONANTS. Phonemes are classified as either consonants or vowels. The **consonants** are *b, c, d, f, g, h, j, k, l, m, n, p, q, r, s, t, v, w, x, y,* and *z*. Most consonants represent a single sound consistently, but there are some exceptions. *C*, for example, doesn't represent a sound of its own: When it's followed by *a, o,* or *u*, it's pronounced /k/ (e.g., *castle, coffee, cut*), and when it's followed by *e, i,* or *y*, it's pronounced /s/ (e.g., *cell, city, cycle*). *G* represents two sounds, as the word *garbage* illustrates: It's usually pronounced /g/ (e.g., *glass, go, green, guppy*), but when *g* is followed by *e, i,* or *y*, it's pronounced /j/, as in *giant*. *X* is also pronounced differently according to its location in a word. At the beginning of a word, it's often pronounced /z/, as in *xylophone*, but sometimes the letter name is used, as in *x-ray*. At the end of a word, *x* is pronounced /ks/, as in *box*. The letters *w* and *y* are particularly interesting: At the beginning of a word or a syllable, they're consonants (e.g., *wind, yard*), but when they're in the middle or at the end, they're vowels (e.g., *saw, flown, day, by*).

Two kinds of combination consonants are blends and digraphs. **Consonant blends** occur when two or three consonants appear next to each other in words and their individual phonemes are "blended" together, as in *grass, belt,* and *spring*. **Consonant digraphs** are letter combinations representing single sounds that aren't represented by either letter; the four most common are *ch* as in *chair* and *each*, *sh* as in *shell* and *wish*, *th* as in *father* and *both*, and *wh* as in *whale*. Another consonant digraph is *ph*, as in *photo* and *graph*.

VOWELS. The remaining five letters—*a, e, i, o,* and *u*—represent **vowels**, and *w* and *y* are vowels when used in the middle and at the end of syllables and words. Vowels often represent several sounds. The two most common are short (marked with the symbol ˘, called a **breve**) and long sounds (marked with the symbol ¯, called a **macron**). The **short vowel** sounds are /ă/ as in *cat*, /ĕ/ as in *bed*, /ĭ/ as in *win*, /ŏ/ as in *hot*, and /ŭ/ as in *cup*. The **long vowel** sounds—/ā/, /ē/, /ī/, /ō/, and /ū/—are essentially the same as the letter names, and they're illustrated in the words *make, feet, bike, coal,* and *rule*. Long vowel sounds are usually spelled with two vowels, except when the long vowel is at the end of a one-syllable word or a syllable, as in *she* or *secret* and *try* or *tribal*. When *y* is a vowel by itself at the end of a word, it's pronounced as long *e* or long *i*, depending on the length of the word. In one-syllable words such as *by* and *cry*, the *y* is pronounced as long *i*, but in longer words such as *baby* and *happy*, the *y* is usually pronounced as long *e*.

Literacy Portraits

Beginning readers and writers usually depend on the "sound it out" strategy to decode and spell words: It's effective for phonetically regular words, such as *bus* and *feet*, but not for figuring out *chair, now,* or *said*. Recall that Ms. Janusz teaches the second graders about other ways to decode and spell words in her minilesson on the "think it out" strategy. Click here to watch her minilesson. Also, check my interviews with Rakie, Curt'Lynn, and Rhiannon. These children still rely on the "sound it out" strategy: They describe reading as a process of decoding words and emphasize that good writers spell words correctly. Think about the phonics concepts and the stages of spelling development presented in this chapter. How do you expect these children's views to change once they become fluent readers and writers?

Rakie

Curt'Lynn

Rhiannon

Vowel sounds are more complicated than consonant sounds, and there are many vowel combinations representing long vowels and other vowel sounds. Consider these combinations:

ai as in *nail*	*oa* as in *soap*
au as in *laugh* and *caught*	*oi* as in *oil*
aw as in *saw*	*oo* as in *cook* and *moon*
ea as in *peach* and *bread*	*ou* as in *house* and *through*
ew as in *sew* and *few*	*ow* as in *now* and *snow*
ia as in *dial*	*oy* as in *toy*
ie as in *cookie*	

Most vowel combinations are vowel digraphs or diphthongs: When two vowels represent a single sound, the combination is a **vowel digraph** (e.g., *nail*, *snow*), and when the two vowels represent a glide from one sound to another, the combination is a

New LITERACIES

Digital Games

Students practice phonics and spelling concepts they're learning as they play online games on computers, tablets, and Kindles. These interactive games provide opportunities for students to match letters to pictures of objects illustrating their sounds, identify rhymes, sort words according to vowel pattern, and spell words, for example. They provide engaging practice opportunities because the colorful screen displays, sound effects, fast-paced action, and feedback about game performance grab students' attention, maintain their enthusiasm, and scaffold their learning (Chamberlain, 2005; Kinzer, 2005).

Teachers choose games based on concepts they're teaching and students' achievement levels. They preview the games and bookmark those they want to use, and then students use the bookmarks to quickly access the game they'll play at the computer center. They play the games individually or with partners. Because most young children are experienced game players and because many games have tutorial features, teachers don't have to spend much time introducing them, but it's helpful to have a parent-volunteer or an older student available to assist when there are problems.

Websites. These websites offer phonics and spelling games:

Gamequarium. Check this mega website with links to alphabet, phonics, and spelling games at other websites. Although hundreds of literacy-related games can be accessed through this site, Gamequarium is only a portal, so the quality of the games and computer requirements vary.

PBS Kids. Play games and view video clips from the popular PBS series *Between the Lions, Sesame Street, Reading Rainbow, Word World,* and *Super Why!* to learn letters of the alphabet, rhyming words, phonics, and spelling concepts.

RIF's Reading Planet Club. To reach the Reading Planet, click on the Kids box on the homepage and then on the Reading Planet link

as you scroll down. Kids can join the Reading Planet Club at the Reading Is Fundamental website to play a variety of phonics and vocabulary games at the Game Station. Be sure to check out the Book Zone and Express Yourself to read about featured authors and books and learn more about writing.

Scholastic Kids. Click on the Kids tab on the homepage, and go to the Family Playground Home for K–2 students or The Stacks Home for grades 2–6 students to play Concentration, make a word, word scrabble, and word find games featuring Clifford the Big Red Dog and other book characters.

Sesame Street. Try these interactive games about letters, consonant sounds, and rhyming words featuring Big Bird, Elmo, Grover, and the other familiar Sesame Street characters. These easy-to-play games engage young children without overwhelming them.

All of the games are free, but advertisements pop up at some sites.

There's an App for That! Hundreds of reading and writing apps are available today, and more become available every week at the iTunes store, Best Buy, and other outlets. Many address teaching the alphabet, rhyming words, phonics, word families, spelling, and handwriting. These apps are recommended because they're engaging, apply learning theory, and provide support:

Avokiddo ABC Ride	iSort Words
Clickity-Clack Alphabet	Sky Fish Phonics
Hairy Letters	Spooky Letters

Teachers don't need a classroom set of tablets to use apps effectively. If only a small set is available, they use the tablets in a literacy center.

diphthong. Two vowel combinations that are consistently diphthongs are *oi* and *oy*, but other combinations, such as *ou* as in *house* (but not in *through*) and *ow* as in *now* (but not in *snow*), are diphthongs when they represent a glided sound. In *through*, *ou* represents the /ū/ sound as in *moon*, and in *snow*, *ow* represents the /ō/ sound.

When one or more vowels in a word are followed by an *r*, it's called an **r-controlled vowel** because the *r* influences the pronunciation of the vowel sound. For example, read these words aloud: *start, award, nerve, squirt, horse, word, surf, square, stairs, pearl, beard, cheer, where, here, pier, wire, board, floor, scored, fourth,* and *cure*. Some words have a single vowel plus *r* and others have two vowels plus *r*, or the *r* is in between the vowels. Single vowels with *r* are more predictable than the other types. The most consistent *r*-controlled vowels are *ar* as in *car* and *shark* and *or* as in *fork* and *born*. The remaining single vowel + *r* combinations, *er, ir,* and *ur*, are difficult to spell because they're often pronounced /ûr/ in words, including *herd, father, girls, first, burn,* and *nurse.*

Three-letter spellings of *r*-controlled vowels are more complicated; they include *-are* (*care*), *-ear* (*fear*), *-ere* (*here*), *-oar* (*roar*), and *-our* (*your*). Consider these *-ear* words, where the vowel sound is pronounced in four ways: *bears, beard, cleared, early, earth, hear, heard, heart, learner, pear, pearls, spear, wearing, yearly,* and *yearn*. The most common pronunciation for *ear* is /ûr/, as in *earth, learner,* and *pearls*; this pronunciation is used when *ear* is followed by a consonant, except in *heart* and *beard*. The next most common pronunciation is found in *cleared* and *spear*, where the vowel sounds like the word *ear*. In several words, including *bear* and *wearing*, the vowel sound is pronounced as in the word *air*. Finally, in *heart*, *ear* is pronounced as in *car*. Teachers usually introduce the more predictable ways to decode *r*-controlled vowels, but students learn words with less common pronunciations, including *award, courage, flour, heart, here, very,* and *work*, in other ways.

The vowels in the unaccented syllables of multisyllabic words are often softened and pronounced "uh," as in the first syllable of *about* and *machine*, and the final syllable of *pencil, tunnel, zebra,* and *selection*. This vowel sound is called **schwa** and is represented in dictionaries with ə, which is an inverted *e*.

BLENDING INTO WORDS. Readers blend or combine phonemes to decode words. Even though children may identify each phoneme, one by one, they must also be able to blend them into a word. For example, to read the short-vowel word *best*, children identify /b/ /ĕ/ /s/ /t/ and then combine the sounds to form the word. For long-vowel words, children must identify the vowel pattern as well as the surrounding letters. In *pancake*, for example, children identify /p/ /ă/ /n/ /k/ /ā/ /k/ and recognize that the *e* at the end of the word is silent and marks the preceding vowel as long. Shefelbine (1995) emphasizes the importance of blending and explains that students who have difficulty decoding words usually know the phoneme–grapheme correspondences but can't blend the phonemes into recognizable words. The ability to blend sounds into words is part of phonemic awareness, and students who haven't had this practice are likely to have trouble decoding unfamiliar words.

PHONOGRAMS. One-syllable words and syllables in longer words can be divided into two parts, the onset and the rime: The **onset** is the consonant sound, if any, that precedes the vowel, and the **rime** is the vowel and any consonant sounds that follow it. For example, in *show*, *sh* is the onset and *ow* is the rime, and in

Classroom INTERVENTIONS

Phonics

Struggling readers need to learn to decode words, and phonics is a very useful tool. Most struggling students already know phoneme–grapheme relationships, but they guess at words based on the first letter or they sound out the word, letter by letter, without blending them together or considering spelling patterns. Instruction for students who can't decode words includes two components (Cunningham, 2013; McKenna, 2002): First, review word families. Teachers create a word wall divided into sections for words representing each phonogram, and they teach students to decode by analogy. Second, teach spelling patterns and have students practice them using word sorts. Regrettably, some teachers have students read textbooks with decodable texts to practice particular phonics patterns. For example, this passage emphasizes /ă/ and the CVC pattern:

The cat sat on a mat. The cat was black. He sat and sat. The black cat was sad. Too bad!

Even though publishers of these texts often tout their research base, Allington (2012) found no research to support their claims. Trade books at students' independent reading levels are more effective for decoding practice. Sometimes teachers skip phonics instruction because they believe that struggling readers have been taught phonics without much benefit, but McKenna (2002) counters: "Unfortunately, there is no way to . . . bypass the decoding stage of reading development" (p. 9). Here's the reasoning: If students can't decode words, they won't become fluent readers; if they can't read fluently, they won't comprehend what they're reading; and if they can't comprehend, they won't become successful readers.

FIGURE 5–2 The 37 Rimes and Common Words Using Them

RIME	EXAMPLES	RIME	EXAMPLES
-ack	black, pack, quack, stack	-ide	bride, hide, ride, side
-ail	mail, nail, sail, tail	-ight	bright, fight, light, might
-ain	brain, chain, plain, rain	-ill	fill, hill, kill, will
-ake	cake, shake, take, wake	-in	chin, grin, pin, win
-ale	male, sale, tale, whale	-ine	fine, line, mine, nine
-ame	came, flame, game, name	-ing	king, sing, thing, wing
-an	can, man, pan, than	-ink	pink, sink, think, wink
-ank	bank, drank, sank, thank	-ip	drip, hip, lip, ship
-ap	cap, clap, map, slap	-it	bit, flit, quit, sit
-ash	cash, dash, flash, trash	-ock	block, clock, knock, sock
-at	bat, cat, rat, that	-oke	choke, joke, poke, woke
-ate	gate, hate, late, plate	-op	chop, drop, hop, shop
-aw	claw, draw, jaw, saw	-ore	chore, more, shore, store
-ay	day, play, say, way	-ot	dot, got, knot, trot
-eat	beat, heat, meat, wheat	-uck	duck, luck, suck, truck
-ell	bell, sell, shell, well	-ug	bug, drug, hug, rug
-est	best, chest, nest, west	-ump	bump, dump, hump, lump
-ice	mice, nice, rice, slice	-unk	bunk, dunk, junk, sunk
-ick	brick, pick, sick, thick		

Based on Wylie and Durrell, (1970). Teaching vowels through phonograms. *Elementary English, 47,* 787–791

ball, b is the onset and *all* is the rime. For *at* and *up,* there is no onset; the entire word is the rime. Research has shown that children make more errors decoding and spelling the rime than the onset and more errors on vowels than on consonants (Caldwell & Leslie, 2012). In fact, rimes may provide an important key to word identification.

Wylie and Durrell (1970) identified 37 rimes, including *-ay, -ing, -oke,* and *-ump,* that are found in nearly 500 common words; these rimes and some words using each one are presented in Figure 5–2. Knowing these rimes and recognizing common words made from them are very helpful for beginning readers because they can use the words to de-code other words (Cunningham, 2013). For example, when children know the *-ay* rime and recognize *say,* they use this knowledge to pronounce *clay:* They identify the *-ay* rime and blend *cl* with *ay* to decode the word. This strategy is called *decoding by analogy,* which you'll read more about in Chapter 6, "Developing Fluent Readers and Writers."

Teachers refer to rimes as **phonograms** or word families when they teach them, even though *phonogram* is a misnomer; by definition, a *phonogram* is a letter or group of letters that represent a single sound. Two of the rimes, *-aw* and *-ay,* represent single sounds, but the other 35 don't.

Beginning readers often read and write words using each phonogram. First and second graders can read and write these words made using *-ain: brain, chain, drain, grain, main, pain, plain, rain, sprain, stain,* and *train.* Students must be familiar with consonant blends and digraphs to read and spell these words. Teachers often post these word lists on a word families **word wall,** as shown in Figure 5–3. Each phonogram and the words made using it are listed in a separate section of the word wall. Teachers use the words on the word wall for a variety of phonics activities, and students refer to it to spell words when they're writing.

Check the Compendium of Instructional Procedures, which follows Chapter 12.

PHONICS RULES. Because English doesn't have a one-to-one correspondence between phonemes and graphemes, linguists have created rules to clarify English spelling patterns. One rule is that *q* is followed by *u* and pronounced /kw/, as in *queen, quick,* and *earthquake; Iraq, Qantas,* and other names are exceptions. Another rule that has few exceptions relates to *r*-controlled vowels: *r* influences the preceding vowels so that they're neither long nor short. Examples are *car, wear,* and *four.* There are exceptions, however; one is *fire.*

FIGURE 5–3 **Excerpt From a Word Wall of Phonograms**

-ock		-oke		-old	
block	lock	broke	poke	bold	hold
clock	rock	Coke	smoke	cold	sold
dock	sock	choke	woke	fold	told
flock		joke		gold	
		*soak			

-op		-ore			-ot	
cop	pop	more		store	dot	lot
chop	plop	sore		tore	got	not
drop	shop	shore		wore	hot	shot
hop	stop	snore			knot	spot
mop	top					
		*door	*pour	*soar		
		*floor	*your	*war		

* = exceptions

Many rules aren't very useful because there are more exceptions than words that conform (Clymer, 1963). A good example is this long-vowel rule: When there are two adjacent vowels, the long vowel sound of the first one is pronounced and the second is silent; teachers sometimes call this the "when two vowels go walking, the first one does the talking" rule. Examples of conforming words are *meat, soap,* and *each.* There are many more exceptions, however, including *food, said, head, chief, bread, look, soup, does, too,* and *again.*

Only a few phonics rules have a high degree of utility. Students should learn the ones that work most of the time because they're the most useful (Adams, 1990). Eight useful rules are listed in Figure 5–4. Even though they're fairly reliable, very few of them approach 100% utility. The rule about *r*-controlled vowels just mentioned has been calculated to be useful in 78% of words in which the letter *r* follows the vowel (Adams, 1990). Other commonly taught, useful rules have even lower percentages of utility. The CVC pattern rule—which says that when a one-syllable word has only one vowel and the vowel comes between two consonants, it's usually short, as in *bat, land,* and *cup*—is estimated to work only 62% of the time. Exceptions include *told, fall, fork,* and *birth.* The CVCe pattern rule—which says that when there are two vowels in a one-syllable word and one vowel is an *e* at the end of the word, the first vowel is long and the final *e* is silent—is estimated to work in 63% of CVCe words. Examples of conforming words are *came, hole,* and *pipe;* but three very common words—*have, come,* and *love*—are exceptions.

Teaching Phonics

The best way to teach phonics is through a combination of explicit instruction and authentic application activities. The National Reading Panel (2000) reviewed the research about phonics instruction and concluded that the most effective programs were systematic; that is, the most useful phonics skills are taught in a predetermined sequence. Most teachers begin with consonants and then introduce the short vowels so that children can read and spell consonant-vowel-consonant or CVC-pattern words, such as *dig* and *cup.* Then children learn about consonant blends and digraphs and long vowels so that they can read and spell consonant-vowel-consonant-*e* or CVCe-pattern words, such as *broke* and *white*, and consonant-vowel-vowel-consonant or CVVC-pattern words, such as *clean*, *wheel*, and *snail*. Finally, children learn about the less common vowel digraphs and diphthongs, such as *claw*, *bought*, *shook*, and *boil*, and *r*-controlled vowels, including *square*, *hard*, *four*, and *year*. Figure 5–5 details this sequence of phonics skills.

Children also learn strategies to use in identifying unfamiliar words (Mesmer & Griffith, 2005). Three of the most useful strategies are sounding out words, decoding by analogy, and applying phonics rules. When children sound out words, they convert letters and patterns of letters into sounds and blend them to pronounce the word; it's most effective when children are reading phonetically regular one-syllable words. In

FIGURE 5–4 The Most Useful Phonics Rules

PATTERN	DESCRIPTION	EXAMPLES	
Two sounds of *c*	The letter *c* can be pronounced as /k/ or /s/. When c is followed by *a, o,* or *u,* it's pronounced /k/—the hard *c* sound. When *c* is followed by *e, i,* or *y,* it's pronounced /s/—the soft *c* sound.	cat cough cut	cent city cycle
Two sounds of *g*	The letter *g* can be pronounced /g/ or /j/. When *g* is followed by *a, o,* or *u,* it's pronounced /g/—the hard *g* sound. When g is followed by *e, i,* or *y,* it's usually pronounced /j/—the soft g sound. Exceptions include *get* and *give.*	gate go guess	gentle giant gypsy
CVC pattern	When a one-syllable word has only one vowel and the vowel comes between two consonants, it's usually short. One exception is *told.*	bat cup land	
Final *e* or CVCe pattern	When there are two vowels in a one-syllable word and one of them is an *e* at the end of the word, the first vowel is long and the final *e* is silent. Three exceptions are *have, come,* and *love.*	home safe cute	
CV pattern	When a vowel follows a consonant in a one-syllable word, the vowel is long. Exceptions include *the, to,* and *do.*	go be	
r-controlled vowels	Vowels that are followed by the letter *r* are overpowered and are neither short nor long. One exception is *fire.*	car dear	birth pair
-igh	When *gh* follows *i,* the *i* is long and the *gh* is silent. One exception is *neighbor.*	high night	
kn- and wr-	In words beginning with *kn-* and *wr-,* the first letter is not pronounced.	knee write	

Based on Clymer (1963). The utility of phonic generalizations in the primary grades. The *Reading Teacher, 16,* 252–258.

FIGURE 5–5 Sequence of Phonics Instruction

GRADES	SKILL	DESCRIPTION	EXAMPLES
K	More common consonants	Children identify consonant sounds, match sounds to letters, and substitute sounds in words.	/b/, /d/, /f/, /m/, /n/, /p/, /s/, /t/
K–1	Less common consonants	Children identify consonant sounds, match sounds to letters, and substitute sounds in words.	/g/, /h/, /j/, /k/, /l/, /q/, /v/, /w/, /x/, /y/, /z/
	Short vowels	Children identify the five short vowel sounds and match them to letters.	/ă/ = cat, /ĕ/ = bed, /ĭ/ = pig, /ŏ/ = hot, /ŭ/ = cut
	CVC pattern	Children read and spell CVC-pattern words.	dad, men, sit, hop, but
1	Consonant blends	Children identify and blend consonant sounds at the beginning and end of words.	/pl/ = plant /str/ = string
	Phonograms	Children break CVC words into onsets and rimes and use phonograms to form new words.	not: dot, shot, spot will: still, fill, drill
	Consonant digraphs	Children identify consonant diagraphs, match sounds to letters, and read and spell words with consonant digraphs.	/ch/ = chop /sh/ = dash /th/ = with /wh/ = when
	Long vowel sounds	Children identify the five long vowel sounds and match them to letters.	/ā/ = name, /ē/ = bee, /ī/ = ice, /ō/ = soap, /ū/ = tune
	CVCe pattern	Children read and spell CVCe-pattern words.	game, ride, stone
	Common long vowel digraphs	Children identify the vowel sound represented by common long vowel digraphs and read and spell words using them.	/ā/ = ai (rain), ay (day) /ē/ = ea (reach), ee (sweet) /ō/ = oa (soap), ow (know)
1–2	w and y	Children recognize when w and y are consonants and when they're vowels, and identify the sounds they represent.	window, yesterday y = /ī/ (by) y = /ē/ (baby)
	Phonograms	Children divide long-vowel words into onsets and rimes and use phonograms to form new words.	woke: joke, broke, smoke day: gray, day, stay
	Hard and soft consonant sounds	Children identify the hard and soft sounds represented by c and g, and read and spell words using them.	g = girl (hard), gem (soft) c = cat (hard), city (soft)
2–3	Less common vowel digraphs	Children identify the sounds of less common vowel digraphs and read and spell words using them.	/ô/ = al (walk), au (caught), aw (saw), ou (bought) /ā/ = ei (weigh) /ē/ = ey (key), ie (chief) /ī/ = ie (pie) /o͝o/ = oo (good), ou (could) /ū/ = oo (moon), ew (new), ue (blue), ui (fruit)
	Vowel diphthongs	Children identify the vowel diphthongs and read and write words using them.	/oi/ = oi (boil), oy (toy) /ou/ = ou (cloud), ow (down)
	Less common consonant digraphs	Children identify the sounds of less common consonant digraphs and read and write words using them.	ph = phone ng = sing gh = laugh tch = match
	r-controlled vowels	Children identify r-controlled vowel patterns and read and spell words using them.	/âr/ = hair, care, bear, there, their /ar/ = heart, star /er/ = clear, deer, here /or/ = born, more, warm /ûr/ = learn, first, work, burn

the second strategy, decoding by analogy, children apply their knowledge of phonograms to analyze the structure of an unfamiliar word (White, 2005). They use known words to recognize unfamiliar ones. For example, if children are familiar with *will*, they can use it to identify *grill*. They also apply phonics rules to identify unfamiliar words, such as *while* and *clean*. These strategies are especially useful when children don't recognize many words, but they become less important as readers gain more experience and can recognize most words automatically.

The second component of phonics instruction is daily opportunities for children to apply the phonics strategies and skills they're learning in authentic reading and writing activities (National Reading Panel, 2000). Cunningham and Cunningham (2002) estimate that the ratio of time spent on real reading and writing to time spent on phonics instruction should be 3 to 1. Without this meaningful application of what they're learning, phonics instruction is often ineffective (Dahl, Scharer, Lawson, & Grogan, 2001).

Phonics instruction begins in kindergarten when children learn to connect consonant and short vowel sounds to the letters, and it's completed by third grade because older students rarely benefit from it (Ivey & Baker, 2004; National Reading Panel, 2000). To assess your knowledge about phonics instruction, use the Teacher Checklist: How do I teach phonics?

EXPLICIT INSTRUCTION. Teachers present **minilessons** on phonics concepts to the whole class or to small groups of students, depending on their instructional needs. They follow the minilesson format, explicitly presenting information about a phonics strategy or skill, demonstrating how to use it, and presenting words for students to use in guided practice, as Mrs. Firpo did in the vignette at the beginning of the chapter. During the minilesson, teachers use these activities to provide guided practice opportunities for students to manipulate sounds and read and write words:

- Sort objects, pictures, and word cards according to a phonics concept
- Write letters or words on small whiteboards
- Arrange magnetic letters or letter cards to spell words
- Make class charts of words representing phonics concepts, such as the two sounds of *g* or the *-ore* phonogram
- Make a poster or book of words representing a phonics concept
- Locate other words exemplifying the spelling pattern in books students are reading

Minilesson: Decoding CVC Words With Final Consonant Blends shows how a first grade teacher presents phonics instruction.

APPLICATION ACTIVITIES. Children apply the phonics concepts they're learning as they read and write and participate in teacher-directed activities. In **interactive writing**, for example, children segment words into sounds and take turns writing letters and sometimes whole words on the chart (McCarrier, Pinnell, & Fountas, 2000; Tompkins & Collom,

Teach Kids to BE STRATEGIC

Phonics Strategies

Teach students to use these strategies to decode words:

- Sound it out
- Decode by analogy
- Apply phonics rules

They practice the strategies as they participate in guided reading, word wall activities, and other reading activities. Look for students to apply them during reading workshop and other types of independent reading. If they struggle, reteach the developmentally appropriate strategy, making sure to name it, model its use, and talk about its application.

TEACHER *Checklist*

How do I teach phonics?

- ○ Do I address Standards in my instruction?
- ○ Do I teach the most useful phonics concepts?
- ○ Do I follow a developmental continuum for systematic phonics instruction, beginning with rhyming and ending with phonics rules?
- ○ Do I provide explicit instruction on phonics?
- ○ Do I provide opportunities for students to apply what they're learning about phonics?
- ○ Do I take advantage of teachable moments to clarify misunderstandings, and infuse phonics instruction into literacy activities?
- ○ Do I use oral activities to reinforce phonemic awareness strategies during phonics and spelling instruction?
- ○ Do I review phonics as part of spelling, when necessary, in the upper grades?

Minilesson

TOPIC: Decoding CVC Words With Final Consonant Blends
GRADE: First Grade
TIME: One 30-minute period

Mrs. Nazir is teaching her first graders about consonant blends. She introduced initial consonant blends to the class, and children practiced reading and spelling words, such as *club*, *drop*, and *swim*, that were chosen from the selection they were reading in their basal readers. Then, in small groups, they completed workbook pages and made words using plastic tiles with onsets and rimes printed on them. For example, using the *-ip* phonogram, they made *clip*, *drip*, *flip*, *skip*, and *trip*. This is the fifth whole-class lesson in the series. Today, Mrs. Nazir is introducing final consonant blends.

1 Introduce the Topic

Mrs. Nazir explains that blends are also used at the end of words. She writes these words on the whiteboard: *best*, *rang*, *hand*, *pink*, and *bump*. Together the children sound them out: They pronounce the initial consonant sound, the short vowel sound, and the final consonants. They blend the final consonants, then they blend the entire word and say it aloud. Children use the words in sentences to ensure that everyone understands them, and Dillon, T.J., Pauline, Cody, and Brittany circle the blends in the words on the whiteboard. The teacher points out that *st* is a familiar blend also used at the beginning of words, but that the other blends are used only at the end of words.

2 Share Examples

Mrs. Nazir says these words: *must*, *wing*, *test*, *band*, *hang*, *sink*, *bend*, and *bump*. The first graders repeat each word, isolate the blend, and identify it. Carson says, "The word is *must*—/m/ /ŭ/ /s/ /t/—and the blend is *st* at the end." Bryan points out that Ng is his last name, and everyone claps because his name is so special. Several children volunteer additional words: Dillon suggests *blast*, and Henry adds *dump* and *string*. Then the teacher passes out word cards and children read the words, including *just*, *lamp*, *went*, and *hang*. They sound out each word carefully, pronouncing the initial consonant, the short vowel, and the final consonant blend. Then they blend the sounds and say the word.

3 Provide Information

Mrs. Nazir posts a piece of chart paper and labels it "The *-ink* Word Family." The children brainstorm these words with the *-ink* phonogram: *blink*, *sink*, *pink*, *rink*, *mink*, *stink*, and *wink*, and they take turns writing the words on the chart. They also suggest *twinkle* and *wrinkle*, and Mrs. Nazir adds them to the chart.

4 Guide Practice

Children create other word family charts using *-and*, *-ang*, *-ank*, *-end*, *-ent*, *-est*, *-ing*, *-ump*, and *-ust*. Each group brainstorms at least five words and writes them on the chart. Mrs. Nazir monitors children's work and helps them think of additional words and correct spelling errors. Then children post their word family charts and share them with the class.

5 Assess Learning

Mrs. Nazir observes the first graders as they brainstorm words, blend sounds, and spell the words. She notices several children who need more practice and will call them together for a follow-up lesson.

2004). Teachers help children correct errors, and they take advantage of teachable moments to review consonant and vowel sounds and spelling patterns, as well as handwriting skills and rules for capitalization and punctuation. **Making words** and **word sorts** are other activities that children do to apply what they're learning about phoneme–grapheme correspondences, word families, and phonics rules.

Assessing Students' Phonics Knowledge

Primary grade teachers assess children's developing phonics knowledge using a combination of tests, observation, and reading and writing samples. They often use a test to screen children at the beginning of the school year, monitor their progress at midyear, and document their achievement at the end of the year. When children aren't making expected progress, teachers administer a test to diagnose the problem and plan for instruction. Four tests that evaluate children's phonics knowledge, including one designed for older, struggling readers, are described in Assessment Tools: Phonics.

ASSESSMENT TOOLS

Phonics

Teachers monitor students' developing phonics knowledge by observing them during classroom activities and by administering these tests:

- **Observation Survey of Early Literacy Achievement (OS): Word Reading and Hearing and Recording Sounds in Words Subtests**
  The OS (Clay, 2015) includes six subtests. The Word Reading and Hearing and Recording Sounds in Words subtests are used to assess young children's ability to apply phonics concepts to decode and spell words. The subtests are administered individually, and children's scores for each subtest can be standardized and converted to stanines. The OS is published by Heinemann.

- **Dynamic Indicators of Basic Early Literacy Skills (DIBELS): Nonsense Word Fluency Subtest**
  This individually administered subtest (Kaminski & Good, 1996) assesses young children's ability to apply phonics concepts to read two- and three-letter nonsense words (e.g., *ap, jid*). Multiple forms are available, so this test can be used to monitor children's progress during kindergarten and first grade. The test is available at the DIBELS website free of charge, but there's a charge for scoring tests and for reporting scores.

- **The Tile Test**
  This individually administered test (Norman & Calfee, 2004) assesses K–2 students' knowledge of phonics. Children manipulate letter tiles to make words, and teachers also arrange tiles to spell words for them to read. The Tile Test can easily be administered in 10 to 15 minutes. It's available online, free of charge.

- **The Names Test: A Quick Assessment of Decoding Ability**
  The Names Test (Cunningham, 1990; Duffelmeyer et al., 1994; Mather, Sammons, & Schwartz, 2006) measures older students' (grades 3–8) ability to decode words. The test is a list of names that illustrate phoneme–grapheme correspondences and phonics rules. As students read the names, teachers mark which ones they read correctly and which they mispronounce. Then teachers analyze the errors to determine which phonics concepts students haven't learned. This free assessment is available online.

These tests are useful assessment tools that teachers use to screen, monitor, diagnose, and document children's phonics knowledge and to make instructional decisions.

Teachers observe children as they participate in phonics activities and when they're reading and writing to see how they're applying the phonics strategies and skills they're learning. For example, when children use magnetic letters to write words with the *-at* phonogram, such as *bat, cat, hat, mat, rat,* and *sat,* they're demonstrating their phonics knowledge. They also show what they've learned during interactive writing, making words, and word sort activities. Similarly, as teachers listen to children read aloud or read children's writing, they analyze their errors to determine which phonics concepts children are confusing or those they don't yet understand.

The Role of Phonics in a Balanced Literacy Program

Phonics is a controversial topic. Some parents and politicians, as well as even a few teachers, believe that most of our educational ills could be solved if children were taught to read using phonics. A few people still argue that phonics is a complete reading program, but that view ignores what we know about the interrelatedness of the four cueing systems. Reading is a complex process, and the phonological system works in conjunction with the semantic, syntactic, and pragmatic systems, not in isolation.

The controversy centers on the best way to teach phonics. In her landmark review of the research on phonics instruction, Marilyn Adams (1990) recommends that phonics be taught within a balanced approach that integrates instruction in reading strategies and skills with meaningful opportunities for reading and writing. She emphasizes that phonics instruction should focus on the most useful information for identifying words, that it should be systematic and intensive, and that it should be completed by third grade.

 MONITOR: Check Your Understanding 5.2

Spelling

Learning to spell is also part of "cracking the code." As children learn about phonics, they apply what they're learning through both reading and writing. Children's early spellings reflect what they know about phoneme–grapheme relationships, phonics rules, and spelling patterns. As their knowledge grows, their spelling increasingly approximates conventional spelling.

Students need to learn to spell words conventionally so that they can communicate effectively through writing. Learning phonics during the primary grades is part of spelling instruction, but students also need to learn other strategies and information about English orthography. In the past, weekly spelling tests were the main instructional approach; now, they're only one part of a comprehensive spelling program. To analyze your instructional program, use the Teacher Checklist: How do I teach spelling?

Stages of Spelling Development

As young children begin to write, they create unique spellings, called **invented spelling**, based on their knowledge of phonology (Read, 1975). The children in Read's studies used letter names to spell words, such as U (*you*) and R (*are*), and they used consonant sounds rather consistently: GRL (*girl*), TIGR (*tiger*), and NIT (*night*). They used several unusual but phonetically based spelling patterns to represent affricates; for example, they replaced *tr* with *chr* (e.g., CHRIBLES for *troubles*) and *dr* with *jr* (e.g., JRAGIN for *dragon*). Words with long vowels were spelled using letter names:

MI (*my*), LADE (*lady*), and FEL (*feel*). The children used several ingenious strategies to spell words with short vowels: The preschoolers selected letters to represent short vowels on the basis of place of articulation in the mouth: Short *i* was represented with *e*, as in FES (*fish*), short *e* with *a*, as in LAFFT (*left*), and short *o* with *i*, as in CLIK (*clock*). These spellings may seem odd to adults, but they're based on phonetic relationships.

Based on examinations of children's spellings, Bear, Invernizzi, Templeton, and Johnson (2016) identified these five stages that students move through on their way to becoming conventional spellers:

- Emergent spelling
- Letter name-alphabetic spelling
- Within-word pattern spelling
- Syllables and affixes spelling
- Derivational relations spelling

At each stage, students use different strategies and focus on particular aspects of spelling. The characteristics of the five stages are summarized in Figure 5–6.

STAGE 1: EMERGENT SPELLING. Children string scribbles, letters, and letterlike forms together, but they don't associate the marks they make with any specific phonemes. Spelling at this stage represents a natural, early expression of the alphabet and other written language concepts. Children may write from left to right, right to left, top to bottom, or randomly across the page, but by the end of the stage, they have an understanding of directionality. Some emergent spellers have a large repertoire of letterforms to use in writing, but others repeat a small number of letters over and over. They use both upper- and lowercase letters but show a distinct preference for uppercase letters. Toward the end of the stage, children are beginning to discover how spelling works and that letters represent sounds in words. This stage is typical of 3- to 5-year-olds. During the emergent stage, children learn these concepts:

- The distinction between drawing and writing
- How to make letters
- The direction of writing on a page
- Some letter–sound matches

STAGE 2: LETTER NAME-ALPHABETIC SPELLING. Children learn to represent phonemes in words with letters. They develop an understanding of the alphabetic principle, that a link exists between letters and sounds. At first, the spellings are quite abbreviated and represent only the most prominent features in words; children use only several letters to represent an entire word. Examples of early Stage 2 spelling are D (*dog*) and KE (*cookie*), and children may still be writing mainly with capital letters. They slowly pronounce the word they want to spell, listening for familiar letter names and sounds.

In the middle of the letter name-alphabetic stage, children use most beginning and ending consonants and include a vowel in most syllables; they spell *like* as LIK and *bed* as BAD. By the end of the stage, they use consonant blends and digraphs and short-vowel patterns to spell *hat*, *get*, and *win*, but some still spell *ship* as SEP. They can also

TEACHER *Checklist*

How do I teach spelling?

- ○ Do I address Standards in my instructional program?
- ○ Do I analyze students' spelling errors to provide appropriate instruction based on their developmental stage?
- ○ Do I connect phonemic awareness, phonics, and spelling during minilessons by having students manipulate words orally and read and spell them?
- ○ Do I guide students to use strategies to spell unfamiliar words?
- ○ Do I teach students to spell high-frequency words?
- ○ Do I post words on word walls and use them in activities?
- ○ Do I involve students in making words, word sorts, and other hands-on spelling activities?
- ○ Are spelling tests only one part of my instructional program?
- ○ Do I involve students in authentic literacy activities every day?

Watch as kindergartners match words and pictures for the *-ad* and *-an* word families. Which letter name-alphabetic stage concepts are these children learning?

FIGURE 5–6 Stages of Spelling Development

Stage 1: Emergent Spelling
Children string scribbles, letters, and letterlike forms together, but they don't associate the marks they make with any specific phonemes. This stage is typical of 3- to 5-year-olds. Children learn these concepts:

- The distinction between drawing and writing
- How to make letters
- The direction of writing on a page
- Some letter–sound matches

Stage 2: Letter Name-Alphabetic Spelling
Children learn to represent phonemes in words with letters. At first, their spellings are quite abbreviated, but they learn to use consonant blends and digraphs and short-vowel patterns to spell many short-vowel words. Spellers are 5- to 7-year-olds. Children learn these concepts:

- The alphabetic principle
- Consonant sounds
- Short vowel sounds
- Consonant blends and digraphs

Stage 3: Within-Word Pattern Spelling
Students learn long-vowel patterns and *r*-controlled vowels, but they may confuse spelling patterns and spell *meet* as METE, and they reverse the order of letters, such as FORM for *from* and GRIL for *girl*. They also confuse homophones, such as *your–you're*. Spellers are 7- to 9-year-olds, and they learn these concepts:

- Long-vowel spelling patterns
- *r*-controlled vowels
- More complex consonant patterns
- Diphthongs and other less common vowel patterns
- Homophones

Stage 4: Syllables and Affixes Spelling
Students apply what they've learned about one-syllable words to spell longer words, and they learn to break words into syllables. They also learn to add inflectional endings (e.g., *-es*, *-ed*, *-ing*) and to spell compound words and contractions. Spellers are often 9- to 11-year-olds, and they learn these concepts:

- Inflectional endings
- Rules for adding inflectional endings
- Syllabication
- Contractions

Stage 5: Derivational Relations Spelling
Students explore the relationship between spelling and meaning and learn that words with related meanings are often related in spelling despite changes in sound (e.g., *wise–wisdom*, *sign–signal*, *nation–national*). They also learn about Latin and Greek root words and derivational affixes (e.g., *amphi-*, *pre-*, *-able*, *-tion*). Spellers are 11- to 14-year-olds. Students learn these concepts:

- Consonant alternations
- Vowel alternations
- Latin affixes and root words
- Greek affixes and root words
- Etymologies

Based on Bear et al., 2012. *Words their way: Word study for phonics, vocabulary, and spelling instruction* (5th ed.).

spell some CVCe words such as *name* correctly. Spellers at this stage are usually 5- to 7-year-olds. During the letter name-alphabetic stage, children learn these concepts:

- The alphabetic principle
- Consonant sounds
- Short vowel sounds
- Consonant blends and digraphs

STAGE 3: WITHIN-WORD PATTERN SPELLING. Students begin the within-word pattern stage when they can spell most one-syllable short-vowel words, and during this stage, they learn to spell long-vowel patterns and *r*-controlled vowels. They experiment with long-vowel patterns and learn that words such as *come* and *bread* are exceptions that don't fit the vowel patterns. Students may confuse spelling patterns and spell *meet* as META, and they reverse the order of letters, such as FORM for *from* and GRIL for *girl*. They also learn about complex consonant sounds, including *-tch* (*match*) and *-dge* (*judge*), and less frequent vowel patterns, such as *oi/oy* (*boy*), *au* (*caught*), *aw* (*saw*), *ew* (*sew, few*), *ou* (*house*), and *ow* (*cow*). Students also become aware of homophones and compare short- and long-vowel combinations (e.g., *hop–hope*) as they experiment with vowel patterns. Students at this stage are 7- to 9-year-olds, and they learn these spelling concepts:

- Long-vowel spelling patterns
- *r*-controlled vowels
- More complex consonant patterns
- Diphthongs and other less common vowel patterns
- Homophones

STAGE 4: SYLLABLES AND AFFIXES SPELLING. Students focus on syllables in this stage and apply what they've learned about one-syllable words to longer, multisyllabic words. They learn about inflectional endings (*-s, -es, -ed,* and *-ing*) and rules about consonant doubling, changing the final *y* to *i,* or dropping the final *e* before adding an inflectional suffix. They also learn about compound words, contractions, and some of the more common prefixes and suffixes. Spellers in this stage are generally 9- to 11-year-olds. Students learn these concepts during the syllables and affixes stage of spelling development:

- Inflectional endings (*-s, -es, -ed, -ing*)
- Rules for adding inflectional endings
- Syllabication
- Compound words
- Contractions

STAGE 5: DERIVATIONAL RELATIONS SPELLING. Students explore the relationship between spelling and meaning during the derivational relations stage, and they learn that words with related meanings are often related in spelling despite changes in vowel and consonant sounds (e.g., *wise–wisdom, sign–signal, nation–national*). The focus in this stage is on **morphemes**, and students learn about Greek and Latin root words and affixes. They also begin to examine etymologies and the role of history in shaping how words are spelled. They learn about words from people's names, called **eponyms**, such as *maverick* and *sandwich*. Spellers at this stage are 11- to 14-year-olds. Students learn these concepts at this stage of spelling development:

- Consonant alternations (e.g., *soft–soften, magic–magician*)
- Vowel alternations (e.g., *please–pleasant, define–definition, explain–explanation*)
- Greek and Latin affixes and root words
- Etymologies

Children's spelling provides valuable evidence of their growing understanding of English **orthography**. The words they spell correctly show which phonics concepts, spelling patterns, and other written language features they've learned to apply, and the words they invent and misspell show what they're still learning to use and those features of spelling that they haven't noticed or learned about. Invented spelling is sometimes criticized because it appears that students are learning bad habits by misspelling words, but researchers have confirmed that students grow more quickly in phonemic awareness, phonics, and spelling when they use invented spelling as long as they're also receiving spelling instruction (Snow, Burns, & Griffin, 1998). As students learn more about spelling, their invented spellings become more sophisticated to reflect their new knowledge, even if the words are still misspelled, and increasingly students spell more and more words correctly as they move through the stages of spelling development.

Nurturing English Learners

How do teachers teach spelling? English learners progress through the same five developmental stages that native English speakers do, but they move more slowly because they're less familiar with the phoneme–grapheme correspondences, spelling patterns, and grammar of English (Helman, Bear, Templeton, Invernizzi, & Johnston, 2012). Students' spelling development reflects their reading achievement, but it lags behind reading: When ELs learn a word, they begin by learning its meaning and how to pronounce it. Almost immediately, they're introduced to the word's written form, and with practice, they learn to recognize and read it. Soon they're writing the word, too. At first their spellings reflect what they know about the English spelling system, but with spelling instruction and reading and writing practice, they learn to spell words correctly. Because spelling is more demanding than reading, it's not surprising that students' knowledge about spelling grows this way.

It's essential that teachers learn about English learners' home language, especially about the ways it differs from English, and then explicitly teach students about the contrasts because they're harder to learn than the similarities (Helman et al., 2012). Consider these written language differences, for example: Chinese uses syllable-length characters instead of letters; Arabic is written from right to left, and the way letters are formed varies according to their location within a word; and vowels aren't used in Croatian and Czech. Some languages, including Arabic, Spanish, Kiswahili (Swahili), and Russian, are more phonetically consistent than English; students who speak these languages are often confused by the number of ways a sound can be spelled in English. There are phonological differences, too: Many languages, including Korean, don't have the /th/ sound; there's no /p/ in Arabic, so Arabic speakers often substitute /b/ in English; and /l/ and /r/ sound alike to speakers of Asian languages. Vowels are particularly difficult for English learners because they're often pronounced differently in their home language. For example, Russian speakers don't differentiate between short and long vowels, and Spanish speakers often substitute /ĕ/ for /ā/ and /ō/ for /ŏ/. Many African and Asian languages, including Kiswahili, Punjabi, Chinese, and Thai, as well as Navajo, a Native American language, are tonal; in these languages, pitch, not spelling differences, is used to distinguish between words. In addition, there are syntactic differences that affect spelling: Hmong speakers don't add plural markers to nouns; Korean speakers add grammatical information to the end of verbs instead of using auxiliary verbs; and Chinese speakers aren't familiar with prefixes or suffixes because they're not used in their language.

Teachers base their instruction on English learners' stage of spelling development, and they emphasize the contrasts between students' home languages and English. At each developmental stage, teachers focus their instruction on concepts that confuse English learners, according to Helman and her colleagues (2012).

EMERGENT STAGE. Students learn English letters, sounds, and words, and they learn that English is written from left to right and top to bottom, with spaces between words. Developing this awareness is more difficult for students whose home languages are not alphabetic.

LETTER NAME-ALPHABETIC STAGE. Students learn that letters represent sounds, and the sounds that are the same in ELs' home languages and English are the easiest to learn. They learn both consonant and vowel sounds. Those consonant sounds that are more difficult include /d/, /j/, /r/, /sh/, and /th/. English learners often have difficulty pronouncing and spelling final consonant blends (e.g., -*st* as in *fast*, -*ng* as in *king*, -*mp* as in *stomp*, and -*rd* as in *board*). Long and short vowel sounds are especially hard because they're often pronounced differently than in students' home languages.

WITHIN-WORD PATTERN STAGE. Students move from representing individual sounds in words to using spelling patterns. They practice CVCe and CVVC spelling patterns and words that are exceptions to these rules; *r*-controlled vowels are especially tricky because they're found in common words, and sound often doesn't predict spelling (e.g., *bear/care/hair, bird/heard/fern/burst*).

SYLLABLES AND AFFIXES STAGE. Students learn spelling and grammar concepts together as they investigate verb forms (e.g., *talk–talked, take–took–taken, think–thought*), change adjectives to adverbs (e.g., *quick–quickly*), and add inflectional endings (e.g., *walks–walked–walking*) and comparatives and superlatives (e.g., *sunny–sunnier–sunniest*). They also learn to pronounce accented and unaccented syllables differently and to use the schwa sound in unaccented syllables. English learners also learn to spell homophones (e.g., *wear–where, to–too–two*) and contractions during this stage.

DERIVATIONAL RELATIONS STAGE. Students learn about Latin and Greek root words and vowel alternations in related words (e.g., *define–definition*). Some ELs use tonal changes to signal these relationships in their home languages, but they must learn that related words in English are signaled by similar spelling and changes in how the vowels are pronounced.

Spelling instruction for English learners is similar to that for native speakers: Teachers use a combination of explicit instruction, word sorts and other practice activities, and authentic reading and writing activities. The biggest difference is that ELs need more instruction on the English spelling concepts that confuse them, often because these features don't exist in their home languages.

Watch as a small group of English learners and their native English-speaking classmates participate in a word sort to investigate the -*ed* inflectional ending. What concepts are these students learning about inflectional endings?

Teaching Spelling

Perhaps the best known way to teach spelling is through weekly spelling tests, but tests should never be considered a complete spelling program. To become good spellers, students need to learn about the English orthographic system and move through the stages of spelling development. They develop strategies to use in spelling unknown words and gain experience in using dictionaries and other resources. A complete spelling program includes these components:

- Teaching spelling strategies
- Matching instruction to students' stage of spelling development

Teach Kids to BE STRATEGIC

Spelling Strategies

Teach students to use these strategies to spell words and to verify that words they've written are spelled correctly:

- Sound it out
- Spell by analogy
- Apply affixes
- Proofread
- Check a dictionary

Students learn to sound out spellings for phonetically regular words in first grade; later, they learn to think out spellings for multisyllabic words. Teach minilessons and then monitor that students apply what they've learned during writing workshop. If students struggle, reteach developmentally appropriate strategies.

- Providing daily reading and writing opportunities
- Teaching students to spell high-frequency words

Students learn spelling strategies that they can use to figure out the spelling of unfamiliar words. As they move through the stages of spelling development, they become increasingly more sophisticated in their use of phonological, semantic, and historical knowledge to spell words; that is, they become more strategic. Important spelling strategies include the following:

- Segmenting the word and spelling each sound, often called "sound it out"
- Spelling unknown words by analogy to familiar words
- Applying affixes to root words
- Proofreading to locate spelling errors in a rough draft
- Locating the spelling of unfamiliar words in a dictionary

Teachers often give the traditional "sound it out" advice when young children ask how to spell an unfamiliar word, but they provide more useful information when they suggest that students use a strategic "think it out" approach. This advice reminds students that spelling involves more than phonological information and encourages them to think about spelling patterns, root words and affixes, and what the word looks like.

Two of the most important ways that students learn to spell are through daily reading and writing activities. Students who are good readers tend to be good spellers, too: As they read, students visualize words—the shape of the word and the configuration of letters within it—and they use this knowledge to spell many words correctly and to recognize when a word they've written doesn't look right. Through writing, of course, students gain valuable practice using the strategies they've learned to spell words. And, as teachers work with students to proofread and edit their writing, they learn more about spelling and other writing conventions.

In addition to reading and writing activities, students learn about the English orthographic system through minilessons about phonics, high-frequency words, spelling rules, and spelling strategies. Minilesson: Spelling -at Family Words shows how Mr. Cheng teaches his first graders about phonograms. In addition to minilessons, teachers involve students in a variety of activities to expand their knowledge and help them move through the stages of spelling development.

Watch as a third grade teacher teaches a making words lesson. How does this procedure give students opportunities to apply the spelling concepts they're learning?

WORD WALLS. Teachers use two types of **word walls** in their classrooms. One word wall features "important" words from books students are reading or from thematic units. Words may be written on a large sheet of paper hanging in the classroom or on word cards and placed in a large pocket chart. Then students refer to these word walls when they're writing. Seeing the words posted on word walls and other charts in the classroom and using them in their writing help students learn to spell the words.

The second type of word wall displays high-frequency words. Researchers have identified the most commonly used words and recommend that students learn to spell 100 of these words because of their usefulness. The most frequently used words represent more than 50% of all the words children and adults write! Figure 5–7 lists the 100 most frequently used words.

MAKING WORDS. Teachers choose a five- to eight-letter word (or longer words for older students) and prepare sets of letter cards for a **making words** activity (Cunningham

Minilesson

TOPIC: Spelling -at Family Words
GRADE: First Grade
TIME: One 10-minute period

Mr. Cheng teaches phonics skills during guided reading lessons. He introduces, practices, and reviews phonics concepts using words from selections his first graders are reading. The children decode and spell words using letter and word cards, magnetic letters, and small whiteboards and pens.

1 Introduce the Topic

Mr. Cheng holds up a copy of *At Home*, the small paperback level E book the children read yesterday, and asks them to reread the title. Then he asks the children to identify the first word, *at*. After they read the word, he hands a card with the word *at* written on it to each of the six children in the guided reading group. "Who can read this word?" he asks. Several children recognize it immediately, and others carefully sound out the two-letter word.

2 Share Examples

Mr. Cheng asks children to think about rhyming words: "Who knows what rhyming words are?" Mike answers that rhyming words sound alike at the end—for example, *Mike, bike,* and *like*. The teacher explains that there are many words in English that rhyme, and that today, they're going to read and write words that rhyme with *at*. "One rhyming word is *cat*," he explains. Children name rhyming words, including *hat, fat*, and *bat*. Mr. Cheng helps each child in the group to name at least three rhyming words.

3 Provide Information

Mr. Cheng explains that children can spell these *at* words by adding a consonant in front of *at*. For example, he places the foam letter *c* in front of his *at* card, and the children blend *c* to *at* to decode *cat*. Then he repeats the procedure by substituting other foam letters for the *c* to spell *bat, fat, hat, mat, pat, rat*, and *sat*. He continues the activity until every child successfully decodes one of the words.

4 Guide Practice

Mr. Cheng passes out small plastic trays with foam letters to the children and asks them to add one of the letters to their *at* cards to spell the words as he pronounces them. He continues the activity until children have had several opportunities to spell each word, and they can quickly choose the correct initial consonant to spell it. Then Mr. Cheng collects the *at* cards and trays with foam letters.

5 Assess Learning

Mr. Cheng passes out small whiteboards and pens. He asks the first graders to write the words as he says each one aloud: *cat, hat, mat, pat, rat, sat, bat, fat*. He carefully observes as each child segments the onset and rime to spell the word. The children hold up their boards to show him their spellings. Afterward, children erase the word and repeat the process, writing the next word. After children write all eight words, Mr. Cheng quickly jots a note about which children need additional practice with the -at word family before continuing with the guided reading lesson.

FIGURE 5–7 The 100 Most Frequently Used Words

A		B		C		D E	
a	and	back		came		day	do
about	are	be		can		did	don't
after	around	because		could		didn't	down
all	as	but					
am	at	by					
an							

F G		H		I J		K L	
for		had	his	I	is	know	
from		have	home	if	it	like	
get		he	house	in	just	little	
got		her	how	into			
		him					

M N		O		P Q R		S	
man	no	of	our	people		said	she
me	not	on	out	put		saw	so
mother	now	one	over			school	some
my		or				see	

T		U V		W X		Y Z	
that	think	up		was	when	you	
the	this	us		we	who	your	
them	time	very		well	will		
then	to			went	with		
there	too			were	would		
they	two			what			
things							

Watch as sixth graders complete a word sort based on the novel *The Cay*. How does this sort engage students in conversation about the novel?

& Cunningham, 1992). Then students use the cards to practice spelling words and to review spelling patterns and rules. They arrange and rearrange the cards to spell one-letter words, two-letter words, three-letter words, and so forth, until they use all the letters to spell the original word. Second graders, for example, can create these words using the letters in *weather: a, at, we, he, the, are, art, ear, eat, hat, her, hear, here, hate, heart, wheat, there,* and *where.*

WORD SORTS. Students use **word sorts** to explore, compare, and contrast word features in a pack of word cards. Teachers prepare word cards for students to sort into two or more categories according to their spelling patterns or other criteria (Bear et al., 2016). Sometimes teachers tell students what categories to use, which makes the sort a closed sort; when students determine the categories themselves, the sort is an open sort. Students can sort word cards and then return them to an envelope for future use, or they can glue the cards onto a sheet of paper.

INTERACTIVE WRITING. Teachers use **interactive writing** to teach spelling concepts as well as other concepts about written language. Because correct spelling and legible handwriting are courtesies for readers, they emphasize correct spelling as students take turns to collaboratively write a message. It's likely that students will misspell a few words as they write, so teachers take advantage of these teachable moments to clarify students' misunderstandings. Through interactive writing, students learn to use a variety of resources to correct misspelled words, including classroom word walls, books, classmates, and the dictionary.

PROOFREADING. Proofreading is a special kind of reading that students use to locate misspelled words and other mechanical errors in rough drafts. As students learn about the writing process, they're introduced to proofreading in the editing stage. More in-depth instruction about how to use proofreading to locate spelling errors and then correct these misspelled words is part of spelling instruction (Cramer, 1998). Through a series of minilessons, students can learn to proofread sample student papers and mark misspelled words. Then, working in pairs, students can correct the misspellings.

Proofreading should be introduced in the primary grades. Young children and their teachers proofread **collaborative books** and dictated stories together, and students can be encouraged to read over their own compositions and make necessary corrections soon after they begin writing. This way, students accept proofreading as a natural part of writing. Proofreading activities are more valuable for teaching spelling than are dictation activities, in which teachers dictate sentences for students to write and correctly capitalize and punctuate. Few people use dictation in their daily lives, but we use proofreading skills every time we polish a piece of writing.

DICTIONARY USE. Students need to learn to locate the spelling of unfamiliar words in the dictionary. Although it's relatively easy to find a "known" word in the dictionary, it's hard to locate unfamiliar words, and students need to learn what to do when they don't know how to spell a word. One approach is to predict possible spellings for unknown words, then check the most probable ones in a dictionary.

Students should be encouraged to check the spelling of words in a dictionary as well as to use a dictionary to check multiple meanings or etymology. Too often, students view consulting a dictionary as punishment; teachers must work to change this view. One way to do this is to appoint several students as dictionary checkers: These students keep dictionaries on their desks, and they're consulted whenever questions arise about spelling, a word's meaning, or word usage.

SPELLING OPTIONS. In English, alternate spellings occur for many sounds because so many words borrowed from other languages retain their native spellings. There are many more options for vowel sounds than for consonants. Spelling options sometimes vary according to the letter's position in the word. For example, *ff* is found in the middle and at the end of words but not at the beginning (e.g., *muffin, cuff*), and *gh* represents /f/ only at the end of a syllable or word (e.g., *cough, laughter*).

Teachers point out spelling options as they write words on word walls and when students ask about the spelling of a word. They also can teach upper grade students about these options in a series of minilessons. During each lesson, students focus on one phoneme, such as /ō/ or /k/, and as a class or small group they develop a list of the various ways the sound is spelled, giving examples of each spelling.

Weekly Spelling Tests

Many teachers question the usefulness of spelling tests, because research on invented spelling suggests that spelling is best learned through reading and writing (Gentry & Gillet, 1993). In addition, teachers complain that lists of spelling words are unrelated to the words students are reading and writing and that the 30 minutes of valuable instructional time spent each day in completing spelling activities is excessive. Even so, parents and school board members value spelling tests as evidence that spelling is being taught. Weekly spelling tests, when they're used, should be individualized so that students learn to spell the words they need for writing.

In the individualized approach to spelling instruction, students choose the words they'll study, many of which are words they use in their writing projects. Students study 5 to 10 words during the week using this procedure for studying spelling words:

1. **Say the word.** Students look at the first word on their spelling list and say it to themselves.

2. **Read the letters.** Students pronounce each letter in the word to spell it aloud.

3. **Spell the word.** Students close their eyes, visualize the word, and spell it aloud.

4. **Write the word.** Students write the word and check that it's spelled correctly. If the word is correct, they continue to the next step, but if it's misspelled, students repeat this step.

5. **Write the word again.** Students write the word again and check that it's spelled correctly. If it is, students repeat the steps with the next word on their list, but if it's misspelled, they repeat the procedure with the same word.

This approach places more responsibility on students for their own learning. Teachers develop a weekly word list of 20 or more words of varying difficulty from which students select words to study. Words for the master list include high-frequency words, words from the word wall related to literature focus units and thematic units, and words students needed for their writing projects during the previous week. Words from spelling programs can also be added to the list.

On Monday, the teacher administers a pretest using the master list of words, and students spell as many of the words as they can. Students correct their own pretests, and from the words they misspell they create individual spelling lists. They make two copies of their study list, using the numbers on the master list to make it easier to take the final test on Friday. Students use one copy of the list for study activities, and the teacher keeps the second copy.

Students spend approximately 5 to 10 minutes studying the words on their study lists each day during the week. Research shows that instead of "busy-work" activities such as using their spelling words in sentences or gluing yarn in the shape of the words, it's more effective for students to use a study strategy. The procedure just described focuses on the whole word rather than on breaking the word apart into sounds or syllables. Teachers explain how to use the procedure during a minilesson at the beginning of the school year and then post a copy of it in the classroom. In addition, students often trade word lists on Wednesday to give each other a practice test.

A final test is administered on Friday. The teacher reads the master list, and students write only those words they've practiced during the week. To make the test easier to administer, students first list the numbers of the words they've practiced from their study lists on their test papers. Any words that students misspell should be included on their lists the following week.

GO DIGITAL! **Spelling Games.** Students play spelling games at these websites, and at several sites, teachers and students can create their own games to practice the words on the weekly spelling lists:

Houghton Mifflin's Spelling Games. Go to the website's homepage, and click on the "Students" tab and then on the "Games" button to locate spelling games coordinated with Houghton Mifflin's spelling program. The games reinforce phonics and root words; they're useful for all students, not just those using this spelling program.

Kids Spell. This website offers a variety of spelling games for K–8 students, including Spellasaurus, Cast a Spell, and Defender.

Puzzle Maker. Teachers and students can turn spelling lists into a variety of games at this free site.

Spelling City. This website allows teachers and students to type in spelling lists and use them to make spelling tests, flash cards, and word-search games. A variety of other spelling games are also available.

Spelling Wizard. At the Scholastic website, search for the Spelling Wizard at the Homework Hub. At this activity center, students type in their spelling words and the website turns them into spelling-scramble and word-search games.

Assessing Students' Spelling

The choices students make as they spell words are important indicators of their knowledge of both phonics and spelling. For example, a student who spells phonetically might spell *money* as MUNE, and others who are experimenting with long vowels might spell the word as MONYE or MONIE. Teachers classify and analyze the words students misspell in their writing to gauge their level of spelling development

ASSESSMENT TOOLS

How to Determine a Student's Stage of Spelling Development

1. Choose a Writing Sample
Teachers choose a student's writing sample to analyze. In the primary grades, the sample should total at least 50 words, in the middle grades 100 words, and in the upper grades 200 words. Teachers must be able to decipher most words in the sample to analyze it.

2. Identify Spelling Errors
Teachers read the writing sample to note the errors and identify the words the student was trying to spell. If necessary, teachers check with the writer to determine the intended word.

3. Make a Spelling Analysis Chart
Teachers draw a chart with five columns, one for each stage of spelling development.

4. Categorize the Spelling Errors
Teachers classify the student's spelling errors according to the stage of development. They list each error in one of the stages, ignoring proper nouns, capitalization errors, and grammar errors. Teachers ignore poorly formed letters or reversed letterforms in kindergarten and first grade, but these are significant errors when older students make them. To simplify the analysis, teachers write both the student's error and the correct spelling in parentheses.

5. Tally the Errors
Teachers count the errors in each column, and the one with the most errors indicates the student's current stage of development.

6. Identify Topics for Instruction
Teachers examine the student's errors to identify topics for instruction.

ASSESSMENT *Snapshot*

Spelling Analysis

I worked hard as a reasearcher. I took my time on pickers and handwriting. I read books too. After that I wrote the facks down on indecks cards. I laid them owt and then numberd them. My favorit part was when I figred owt I was stdying my first choyce.

Classification of Errors

Letter Name-Alphabetic	Within-Word Pattern	Syllables and Affixes	Derivational Relations
	pickers	reasearcher	
	facks	numberd	
	indecks	favorit	
	owt	figred	
	owt		
	stdying		
	choyce		

TEACHER'S NOTE

Tatum spelled 88% of words correctly, and most errors were in the within-word pattern stage. These errors indicate that she's investigating ways to spell complex consonant and vowel sounds. She also wrote 10 2- and 3-syllable words, and spelled 3 correctly. Tatum's moving into the syllables and affixes stage; her development meets grade-level standards.

and to plan for instruction. The procedure is explained in Assessment Tools: How to Determine a Student's Stage of Spelling Development. An analysis of a first grader's spelling development is shown in Assessment Snapshot: Spelling Analysis.

Teachers analyze the errors in students' compositions and on weekly spelling tests, and administer diagnostic tests. Assessment Tools: Spelling lists tests that teachers use to determine their students' stage of spelling development.

The Controversy About Spelling Instruction

The press and concerned parent groups periodically raise questions about invented spelling and the importance of weekly spelling tests. There's a misplaced public perception that today's children can't spell: Researchers who have examined the types of errors students make have noted that the number of misspellings increases in grades 1 through 4, as students write longer compositions, but that the percentage of errors

ASSESSMENT TOOLS

Spelling

Teachers assess students' spelling development by examining misspelled words in the compositions that students write. They classify students' spelling errors according to the stages of spelling development and plan instruction based on their analysis. Teachers also examine students' misspellings on weekly spelling tests and diagnostic tests. These three tests were designed for classroom teachers to screen, monitor, diagnose, and document students' spelling development:

- **Developmental Spelling Analysis (DSA)**
  The Developmental Spelling Analysis is a dictated spelling inventory with two components: a Screening Inventory for determining students' stage of spelling development, and Feature Inventories to highlight students' knowledge of specific spelling concepts. The DSA with detailed guidelines is available in Ganske's book, *Word Journeys: Assessment-Guided Phonics, Spelling, and Vocabulary Instruction* (2013).

- **Phonological Awareness Literacy Screening (PALS) System: Spelling Subtest**
  The kindergarten-level battery of tests (Invernizzi, Meier, & Juel, 2003) includes a brief spelling subtest in which children write the sounds they hear in CVC words. In the grades 1–3 tests, the spelling subtest includes words that exemplify phonics features that are appropriate for that grade level. Children receive credit for spelling the specific feature correctly and additional points for spelling the word correctly. The PALS test is available free for Virginia teachers from the University of Virginia, and it can be purchased by teachers in other states.

- **Qualitative Spelling Inventory (QSI)**
  The QSI has two forms, one for grades K–6 and another for grades 6–8. These tests each include 20 or 25 spelling words listed according to difficulty and can easily be administered to small groups or whole classes. The QSI is available in *Words Their Way: Word Study for Phonics, Vocabulary, and Spelling Instruction* (Bear et al., 2016).

Through these tests, teachers identify students' stage of spelling development and use this information to monitor their progress and plan for instruction.

decreases. The percentage continues to decline in the upper grades, although some students continue to make errors.

 MONITOR: Check Your Understanding 5.3

ASSISTING STUDENTS IN CRACKING THE ALPHABETIC CODE

Effective teachers teach their students to use phonemic awareness, phonics, and spelling to decode and spell words. They ensure that their students are successful in "cracking the code" when they use the guidelines presented in this chapter, these points in particular:

5.1 Teachers develop students' phonemic awareness by teaching them to manipulate words.

5.2 Teachers teach high-utility phonics concepts, rules, phonograms, and spelling patterns.

5.3 Teachers understand that students follow a series of developmental stages as they learn to spell words conventionally.

EVALUATE & REFLECT

Apply your understanding about how students learn to "crack the code." The questions ask you to collect and analyze data, and report the results. Your response should meet academic standards and adhere to Standard English conventions.

1. Observe a kindergarten teacher teach several lessons on phonemic awareness, and use the Teacher Checklist on phonemic awareness presented in this chapter to examine how the teacher helps the 5-year-olds crack the alphabetic code. In your response, describe the teacher, students, and the classroom environment. Address these points:

   - How did the teacher teach phonemic awareness?
   - Which items on the Teacher Checklist did you observe?
   - How could this teacher become more effective?

2. Teach a phonemic awareness lesson to a child or small group of kindergartners using a word play book listed in the Booklist in this chapter. In your response, describe the children and their phonemic awareness knowledge and the lesson you taught. Address these points:

   - Which phonemic awareness strategy did you teach?
   - What did you learn about using mentor texts?
   - How could you have made your lesson more effective?

3. Observe a first, second, or third grade teacher teach several lessons on phonics, and use the Teacher Checklist on phonics presented in this chapter to examine how the teacher teaches students to crack the alphabetic code. In your response, describe the teacher, students, and the classroom environment. Address these points:

   - How did the teacher teach phonics?
   - Which items on the Teacher Checklist did you observe?
   - How could this teacher become more effective?

4. Collect a set of four writing samples from a K–8 student. Analyze the student's misspelled words and classify them using the stages of spelling development described in this chapter. From the results of your analysis, identify the student's strengths and weaknesses, determine the student's level of spelling development, and recommend appropriate spelling instruction.

5. Interview a student about phonemic awareness, phonics, or spelling, depending on grade level. Ask questions to probe the student's understanding of the concept and determine the student's ability to use phonemic awareness, phonics, or spelling to crack the alphabetic code. In your response, address these points:

   - Describe the student.
   - Explain the student's ability to talk about the chosen concept.
   - Discuss the student's ability to apply the concept in reading and/or writing.
   - Recommend appropriate instructional activities to extend or apply the student's understanding.

REFERENCES

Adams, M. J. (1990). *Beginning to read: Thinking and learning about print.* Cambridge, MA: MIT Press.

Allington, R. L. (2012). *What really matters for struggling readers: Designing research-based programs* (3rd ed.). Boston: Pearson.

Armbruster, B. B., Lehr, F., & Osborn, J. (2001). *Put reading first: The research building blocks for teaching children to read.* Urbana, IL: Center for the Improvement of Early Reading Achievement.

Bear, D. R., Invernizzi, M., Templeton, S., & Johnston, F. (2016). *Words their way: Word study for phonics, vocabulary, and spelling instruction* (6th ed.). Boston: Pearson.

Caldwell, J. S., & Leslie, L. (2012). *Intervention strategies to follow informal reading inventory assessment: So what do I do now?* (3rd ed.). Boston: Pearson.

Chamberlain, C. J. (2005). Literacy and technology: A world of ideas. In R. A. Karchmer, M. H. Mallette, J. Kara-Soteriou, & D.

J. Leu, Jr. (Eds.), *Innovative approaches to literacy education: Using the Internet to support new literacies* (pp. 44–64). Newark, DE: International Reading Association.

Clay, M. M. (2005). *Literacy lessons: Designed for individuals, part 2: Teaching procedures*. Portsmouth, NH: Heinemann.

Clay, M. M. (2015). *An observation survey of early literacy achievement* (3rd ed.). Portsmouth, NH: Heinemann.

Clymer, T. (1963). The utility of phonic generalizations in the primary grades. *The Reading Teacher, 16*, 252–258.

Cooper, J. D., & Pikulski, J. J. (2006). *Houghton Mifflin reading* (California ed.). Boston: Houghton Mifflin.

Cramer, R. L. (1998). *The spelling connection: Integrating reading, writing, and spelling instruction*. New York: Guilford Press.

Cunningham, P. (1990). The Names Test: A quick assessment of decoding ability. *The Reading Teacher, 44*, 124–129.

Cunningham, P. M. (2013). *Phonics they use: Words for reading and writing* (6th ed.). Boston: Allyn & Bacon/Pearson.

Cunningham, P. M. (2015). Best practices in teaching phonological awareness and phonics. In L. B. Gambrell, L. M. Morrow, & M. Pressley (Eds.), *Best practices in literacy instruction* (5th ed., pp. 169–194). New York: Guilford Press.

Cunningham, P. M., & Allington, R. L. (2016). *Classrooms that work: They can all read and write* (6th ed.). Boston: Pearson.

Cunningham, P. M., & Cunningham, J. W. (1992). Making words: Enhancing the invented spelling-decoding connection. *The Reading Teacher, 46*, 106–115.

Cunningham, P. M., & Cunningham, J. W. (2002). What we know about how to teach phonics. In A. E. Farstrup & S. J. Samuels (Eds.), *What research has to say about reading instruction* (3rd ed., pp. 87–109). Newark, DE: International Reading Association.

Dahl, K. L., Scharer, P. L., Lawson, L. L., & Grogan, P. R. (2001). *Rethinking phonics: Making the best teaching decisions*. Portsmouth, NH: Heinemann.

Duffelmeyer, F. A., Kruse, A. E. Merkley, D. J., & Fyfe, S. A. (1994). Further validation and enhancement of the Names Test. *The Reading Teacher, 48*, 118–128.

Ganske, K. (2013). *Word journeys: Assessment-guided phonics, spelling, and vocabulary instruction* (2nd ed.). New York: Guilford Press.

Gentry, J. R., & Gillet, J. W. (1993). *Teaching kids to spell*. Portsmouth, NH: Heinemann.

Gillon, G. T. (2004). *Phonological awareness: From research to practice*. New York: Guilford Press.

Griffith, F., & Olson, M. (1992). Phonemic awareness helps beginning readers break the code. *The Reading Teacher, 45*, 516–523.

Helman, L., Bear, D. R., Templeton, S., Invernizzi, M., & Johnston, F. (2012). *Words their way with English learners: Word study for phonics, vocabulary, and spelling* (2nd ed.). Upper Saddle River, NJ: Pearson Education.

Hutchins, P. (1989). *Don't forget the bacon!* New York: HarperCollins.

Invernizzi, M., Meier, J. D., & Juel, C. (2003). *Phonological Awareness Literacy Screening System*. Charlottesville: University of Virginia Press.

Ivey, G., & Baker, M. I. (2004). Phonics instruction for older students? Just say no. *Educational Leadership, 61*(6), 35–39.

Juel, C., Griffith, P. L., & Gough, P. B. (1986). Acquisition of literacy: A longitudinal study of children in first and second grade. *Journal of Educational Psychology, 78*, 243–255.

Kaminski, R. A., & Good, R. H., III. (1996). *Dynamic Indicators of Basic Early Literacy Skills*. Eugene: University of Oregon Center on Teaching and Learning.

Kinzer, C. K. (2005). The intersection of schools, communities, and technology: Recognizing children's use of new literacies. In R. A. Karchmer, M. H. Mallette, J. Kara-Soteriou, & D. J. Leu, Jr. (Eds.), *Innovative approaches to literacy education: Using the Internet to support new literacies* (pp. 65–82). Newark, DE: International Reading Association.

Klesius, J. P., Griffith, P. L., & Zielonka, P. (1991). A whole language and traditional instruction comparison: Overall effectiveness and development of the alphabetic principle. *Reading Research and Instruction, 30*, 47–61.

Lewkowicz, N. K. (1994). The bag game: An activity to heighten phonemic awareness. *The Reading Teacher, 47*, 508–509.

Mather, N., Sammons, J., & Schwartz, J. (2006). Adaptations of the Names Test: Easy to use phonics assessments. *The Reading Teacher, 60*, 114–122.

McCarrier, A., Pinnell, G. S., & Fountas, I. C. (2000). *Interactive writing: How language and literacy come together, K–2*. Portsmouth, NH: Heinemann.

McKenna, M. C. (2002). *Help for struggling readers: Strategies for grades 3–8*. New York: Guilford Press.

Mesmer, H. A. E., & Griffith, P. L. (2005). Everybody's selling it—But just what is explicit, systematic phonics instruction? *The Reading Teacher, 59*, 366–376.

Most, B. (1996). *Cock-a-doodle-moo!* San Diego: Harcourt Brace.

National Reading Panel. (2000). *Teaching children to read: An evidence-based assessment of the scientific research literature on reading and its implications for reading instruction*. Washington, DC: National Institute of Child Health and Human Development.

Norman, K. A., & Calfee, R. C. (2004). Tile Test: A hands-on approach for assessing phonics in the early grades. *The Reading Teacher 58*, 42–52.

Osborne, M. P. (2003). *High tide in Hawaii*. New York: Random House.

Park, B. (2003). *Junie B., first grader: Boss of lunch*. New York: Random House.

Peregoy, S. F., & Boyle, O. F. (2013). *Reading, writing and learning in ESL: A resource book for K–12 teachers* (6th ed.). Boston: Pearson.

Read, C. (1975). *Children's categorization of speech sounds in English* (NCTE Research Report No. 17). Urbana, IL: National Council of Teachers of English.

Riches, C., & Genesee, F. (2006). Literacy: Crosslinguistic and crossmodal issues. In F. Genesee, K. Lindholm-Leary, W. M. Saunders, & D. Christian (Eds.), *Educating English language learners: A synthesis of research evidence* (pp. 64–108). New York: Cambridge University Press.

Root, P. (2004). *Rattletrap car*. Cambridge, MA: Candlewick Press.

Seuss, Dr. (1963). *Hop on pop*. New York: Random House.

Seuss, Dr. (1965). *Fox in socks*. New York: Random House.

Shefelbine, J. (1995). *Learning and using phonics in beginning reading* (Literacy research paper; volume 10). New York: Scholastic.

Snow, C. E., Burns, M. W., & Griffin, P. (1998). *Preventing reading difficulties in young children*. Washington, DC: National Academy Press.

Tompkins, G. E., & Collom, S. (2004). *Sharing the pen: Interactive writing with young children*. Upper Saddle River, NJ: Merrill/Prentice Hall.

Torgesen, J. K., & Bryant, B. R. (2004). *Test of Phonological Awareness* (2nd ed.). East Moline, IL: LinguiSystems.

Venezky, R. L. (1999). *The American way of spelling: The structure and origins of American English orthography*. New York: Guilford Press.

White, T. G. (2005). Effects of systematic and strategic analogy-based phonics on grade 2 students' word reading and reading comprehension. *Reading Research Quarterly, 40*, 234–255.

Wylie, R. E., & Durrell, D. D. (1970). Teaching vowels through phonograms. *Elementary English, 47*, 787–791.

Yopp, H. K. (1988). The validity and reliability of phonemic awareness tests. *Reading Research Quarterly, 23*, 159–177.

Yopp, H. K. (1992). Developing phonemic awareness in young children. *The Reading Teacher, 45*, 696–703.

Yopp, H. K. (1995). Read-aloud books for developing phonemic awareness: An annotated bibliography. *The Reading Teacher, 48*, 538–542.

Yopp, H. K., & Yopp, R. H. (2000). Supporting phonemic awareness development in the classroom. *The Reading Teacher, 54*, 130–143.

Chapter 6

Developing Fluent Readers and Writers

PLAN: Preview the Learning Outcomes

After studying this chapter, you'll be prepared to respond to these points:

6.1 Identify and explain the components of reading fluency.

6.2 Identify and explain the components of writing fluency.

6.3 Describe how to help older, dysfluent students.

High-Frequency Words. Ms. Williams's second graders are studying hermit crabs and their tide pool environments. A hermit crab living in a plastic habitat box sits in the center of each group of desks, and as children care for their crustaceans, they study them. They've examined hermit crabs up close using magnifying glasses and identified their body parts. Ms. Williams helped them draw a diagram of a hermit crab on a large chart and label the body parts. They've compared hermit crabs to true crabs and examined their exoskeletons. They've also learned how to feed hermit crabs and get them to come out of their shells, and how they molt. And, they've conducted experiments to determine which environment hermit crabs prefer.

These children use reading and writing as tools for learning. Eric Carle's *A House for Hermit Crab* (2005) is the featured book for this unit. Ms. Williams has read it aloud several times, and children are rereading it at the listening center. *Moving Day* (Kaplan, 1996), *Pagoo* (Holling, 1990), and other books are available on a special shelf in the classroom library. The teacher has read some aloud, and children read others independently or with buddies. Children also write about hermit crabs in **learning logs**.

Ms. Williams and her second graders also write interesting and important vocabulary words related to hermit crabs on a **word wall** made on a sheet of butcher paper, divided into boxes for each letter. These words appear on their word wall:

coral	larvae	sea urchins
crustacean	molting	seaweed
eggs	pebbles	shells
enemies	pincers	shrimp
exoskeleton	regeneration	snails
lantern fish	scavenger	starfish
larva	sea anemone	tide pool

The focus in this chapter is fluency; that is, students' ability to read and write accurately, quickly, and with expression. Primary grade teachers, like Ms. Williams in this vignette, develop their young students' reading and writing fluency through instruction, guided practice, and independent reading and writing. As you read this vignette, try to identify the specific activities Ms. Williams uses to develop her students' reading and writing fluency and ask yourself how she monitors their fluency development.

The children refer to the words as they write about hermit crabs, and Ms. Williams uses them for various word-study activities.

Ms. Williams integrates many components of reading instruction, including fluency instruction, into the unit on hermit crabs. To develop her second graders' ability to recognize high-frequency words, she uses another word wall. This one differs from the hermit crab word wall, which contains only words related to these ocean animals: Her high-frequency word wall is a brightly colored alphabet quilt with 26 paper blocks, one for each letter of the alphabet, displayed permanently on one wall of the classroom.

At the beginning of the school year, Ms. Williams and her students posted on the word wall the 70 high-frequency words that they learned in first grade. Each word is written clearly on a card, using print that's large enough for everyone to read. Then each week, Ms. Williams adds three to five new words. At first, the words she chose were from her list of the 100 high-frequency words, and after finishing that list, she's begun choosing words from a list of the second 100 high-frequency words. She doesn't introduce the words in alphabetical order; instead, she chooses words that she connects to phonics lessons and literature focus units, and words that children misspell in their writing.

This week, Ms. Williams adds *soon*, *house*, *your*, and *you're* to the word wall. She chooses *soon* and *house* because these words are used in *A House for Hermit Crab* and because several children have recently asked her how to spell *house*. She chooses the homophones *your* and *you're* because children are confusing and misspelling these words. She's also noticed that some children are confused about contractions, so she plans to review the topic, using *you're* as an example.

Ms. Williams's students sit on the floor near the word wall when she introduces and posts the words on it. To introduce each new word, she uses a cookie sheet and large magnetic letters. Ms. Williams explains that two of the new words—*house* and *soon*—are from *A House for Hermit Crab*. She scrambles the letters at the bottom of the cookie sheet and slowly builds the new word at the top of the sheet as children guess it. She begins with *h*, adds the *ou*, and several children call out "house." Ms. Williams continues adding letters, and when they're all in place, a chorus of voices says, "house." Kari places the new word card in the H square of the word wall, and children use the chant and clap procedure to spell the word. Ms. Williams begins, "House, house, h-o-u-s-e," and children echo her chant. She calls on Enrique to begin the chant, and children echo him. Then Ms. Williams repeats the procedure with the three remaining words.

The next day, Ms. Williams and the second graders use **interactive writing** to compose sentences using each of the new words. They write these sentences:

> The hermit crab has a good shell for a <u>house</u>. He likes it but <u>soon</u> he will move. "<u>You're</u> too small for me," he says. "I have to move, but I will always be <u>your</u> friend."

Children take turns writing these sentences on a chart, and after rereading them, they underline the four new words. Each week, the children write sentences using the new word wall words, and they often reread the sentences they've written during previous weeks.

The next day, after children practice the new word wall words, Ms. Williams takes a few minutes to review contractions so that they understand that *you're* is a contraction of *you* and *are* and that the apostrophe indicates that a letter has been omitted. Then children volunteer other contractions.

Michael identifies three: *I'm, can't,* and *don't.* The children use interactive writing to make a chart of contractions: They list the contractions and the two words that make up each one. Ms. Williams explains that she'll put the chart in the word work center and that they can use the information to make books about contractions.

After this practice with high-frequency words, children participate in activities at literacy centers while Ms. Williams meets with guided reading groups. Most of the center activities relate to the unit on hermit crabs and Eric Carle's book *A House for Hermit Crab,* but children also practice reading and writing high-frequency words at two of the centers. The figure Ms. Williams's Literacy Centers describes the eight centers in the classroom.

MS. WILLIAMS'S LITERACY CENTERS

CENTER	DESCRIPTION
Library Center	Children reread leveled books, including *Moving Day* (Kaplan, 1996) (Level 7), *Hermit Crab* (Randell, 1994) (Level 8), *Hermit's Shiny Shell* (Tuchman, 1997) (Level 10), and other books about hermit crabs located on a special shelf in the library.
Listening Center	Children use headphones to listen to an informational book about hermit crabs.
Retelling Center	Children sequence pictures of the events in *A House for Hermit Crab* and use them as a guide to retell the story.
Science Center	Children observe their hermit crab and make notes in their learning logs about its physical characteristics and eating habits.
Word Sort Center	Children sort a pack of cards with words from *A House for Hermit Crab* into categories and then copy their sort onto papers available at the center.
Word Wall Center	Children practice reading both word walls in the classroom using pointers.
Word Work Center	Children use magnetic letters to spell this week's high-frequency words—*house, soon, your,* and *you're*—and the words from the last 2 weeks.
Writing Center	Children write "I Am a Hermit Crab" poems following the model posted at the center. Or, they write other books about hermit crabs.

Each morning, a sixth grade student aide comes to the classroom to monitor the children's work at the centers and provide assistance as needed. Ms. Williams worked with two sixth grade teachers to train 10 students to serve as student aides, and they come to the classroom once every week or two on a rotating basis.

The second graders keep track of their work in centers using small booklets with eight sheets of paper that Ms. Williams calls their "center passports." The student aide marks their passports with stickers or stamps at each center after they finish an assignment, and children leave their written work in a basket at the center.

As a culminating activity, Ms. Williams and her students write a retelling of *A House for Hermit Crab.* The children compose the text, and Ms. Williams uses the **Language Experience Approach** to write their rough draft on chart paper so that everyone can see it. Children learn revision strategies as they fine-tune their retelling, and then Ms. Williams types the text on five sheets of paper, makes copies, and compiles booklets. Children each receive a copy of the booklet to read and illustrate. Later they'll take their booklets home to read to their families.

Ms. Williams reads their retelling aloud as children follow along and then join in the reading. They do **choral reading** as they read in small groups. The numbers on the left side indicate which group reads each sentence. As children read and reread the text aloud, they become increasingly fluent readers. Here's the last section of the class's retelling:

1 Soon it was January again.
2 The big Hermit Crab moved out of his house and the little crab moved in.
3 Hermit Crab said, "Goodbye. Be good to my friends."
4 Soon Hermit Crab saw the next perfect house for him.
5 It was empty.
1 It was a little plain but Hermit Crab didn't care.
2 He will decorate it
3 with starfish,
4 with coral,
5 with sea anemones,
1 with sea urchins,
2 and with snails.
All There are so many possibilities!

The underlined words are high-frequency words that are posted on the word wall in Ms. Williams's classroom; of the 75 words in this excerpt, 42 are high-frequency words! Also, two of the new words for this week, *soon* and *house*, are used twice.

STANDARDS CHECK!

Ms. Williams addressed the Common Core State Standards as she taught high-frequency words in the vignette you've just read. Review the second grade literacy Standards document online at http://www.corestandards.org/ELA-Literacy, and identify the Standards that Ms. Williams addressed through her assessment activities. Create your list, and compare it with Ms. Williams's.

Fluency is the ability to read and write effortlessly and efficiently; becoming fluent readers and writers is a developmental milestone. Most students reach the fluent stage during the second or third grade through a combination of explicit instruction and lots of authentic reading and writing. This achievement is crucial because both readers and writers must be able to focus attention on meaning, not on decoding and spelling words. Researchers have found that fluent readers comprehend what they're reading better than less fluent readers do (National Reading Panel, 2000). The same is true about writers: Fluent writers are more successful in crafting effective compositions than less fluent writers are.

The Common Core State Standards for English Language Arts address reading fluency as an essential foundational skill that students must develop by fourth grade to become proficient readers. The Standards focus on teaching students to use phonics and other word-identification strategies to decode unfamiliar words and on ensuring that students read fluently. The feature Common Core State Standards: Reading Fluency provides additional information.

COMMON CORE STATE STANDARDS

Reading Fluency

Reading Standards: Foundational Skills foster K–5 students' understanding of the basic conventions of the English writing system so that they'll become proficient readers who can comprehend fiction and nonfiction texts. They address these fluency requirements:

- Students know and apply grade-level phonics and word-analysis skills to decode words.
- Students read with sufficient accuracy and fluency to support comprehension.
- Students use word-identification strategies to decode unfamiliar words.

The Standards emphasize that foundational skills aren't an end in themselves but are essential for reading comprehension, and they direct teachers to differentiate instruction because capable readers need less practice to become fluent readers than struggling students do. To learn more about the fluency Standards, go to http://www.corestandards.org/ELA-Literacy, or check your state's educational standards website.

Reading Fluency

Reading fluency is the ability to read quickly, accurately, and with expression, and to read fluently, students must recognize most words automatically and be able to identify unfamiliar words easily (Caldwell & Leslie, 2012). Pikulski and Chard (2005) explain that reading fluency is a bridge between decoding and comprehension. Fluent readers are better able to comprehend what they're reading because they automatically recognize most of the words and apply word-identification strategies to read unfamiliar words. Their reading is faster and more expressive (Kuhn & Rasinski, 2011). Reading fluency involves these three components:

Automaticity. Fluent readers recognize familiar words automatically without conscious thought, and they identify unfamiliar words almost as quickly. It's critical that students know most of the words they're reading because when they have to stop to decode words, their reading slows down. The conventional wisdom is that students can read a text successfully when they know at least 95% of the words; that's 19 of every 20 words or 95 of every 100 words. Allington (2009) challenges this notion, however, suggesting that students need to know 98 or 99% of the words to read fluently; otherwise, they're stopping too often to figure out unfamiliar words.

Speed. Fluent readers read at least 100 words per minute. Most students reach this speed by third grade, and their reading rate continues to grow each year. By eighth grade, most students read 150 words per minute, and many adults read 250 words per minute or more. In addition, fluent readers vary their reading speed, depending on the selection—its topic, genre, and text complexity—and their purpose for reading.

Prosody. Fluent readers read sentences expressively, with appropriate phrasing and intonation; this ability is called **prosody**. Dowhower (1991) describes prosody as "the ability to read in expressive rhythmic and melodic patterns" (p. 166). Beginning readers read word by word with little or no expression, but with experience, they chunk words into phrases, attend to punctuation, and apply appropriate syntactic emphases. Once students become fluent readers, their oral reading approximates speech. Too often, reading speed is equated with fluency, and some assessment tools use speed as the only measure of fluency, but accurately identifying words and reading expressively are also critical components. Figure 6–1 summarizes the characteristics of fluent readers.

Watch this video to learn about the importance of modeling fluent reading. What materials could you use to model fluent reading?

Automatic Reading

Students acquire a large stock of words that they recognize automatically and read correctly because it's impossible to analyze every word they encounter when reading. Through repeated reading and writing experiences, students develop **automaticity**, the ability to quickly recognize words (Samuels, 2004). The vital element in word recognition is learning each word's unique letter sequence.

HIGH-FREQUENCY WORDS. The most common words that readers use again and again are high-frequency words. There have been numerous attempts to identify these words and to calculate their frequency in reading materials. Pinnell and

FIGURE 6–1	Fluent Readers
COMPONENT	**CHARACTERISTICS**
Automaticity	• Students recognize many high-frequency words. • Students apply phonics knowledge to decode unfamiliar words. • Students decode new words by making analogies to familiar words. • Students break longer words into syllables to decode them.
Speed	• Students read at least 100 words per minute. • Students vary their speed depending on their purpose and text complexity.
Prosody	• Students chunk words into phrases. • Students read smoothly, with few pauses or breakdowns. • Students read with expression. • Students' reading pace approximates speech.

Fountas (1998, p. 89) identify these 24 common words that kindergartners learn to read:

a	at	he	it	no	the
am	can	I	like	see	to
an	do	in	me	she	up
and	go	is	my	so	we

They also learn to spell many of these words.

These words are part of the 100 high-frequency words, which account for more than half of the words people read and write. Eldredge (2005) has identified the 300 high-frequency words that make up nearly three quarters of the words people read and write; in fact, these 300 words account for 72% of the words that beginning readers read. Figure 6–2 presents Eldredge's list; the 100 most common ones are printed in red. Students learn most of the 100 highest frequency words in first grade and the rest during second and third grades. If fourth graders don't know all 300 of these words, it's crucial that they learn them to become automatic readers.

Many high-frequency words are tough to learn because they're difficult to decode (Cunningham, 2009); try sounding out the words *to*, *what*, and *could* and you'll see how difficult they are. A further complication is that many of these words are function words, so they don't carry much meaning. It's easier to learn to recognize the word *whale* than *what*, because *whale* conjures up the image of a huge aquatic mammal, but *what* is abstract; however, *what* is used much more frequently, and students must learn to read it.

Teachers teach the high-frequency words using explicit instruction. Each week they introduce three to five words, and then involve students in a variety of practice activities each day, as Ms. Williams did in the vignette. Even though the words are listed alphabetically in Figure 6–2, they aren't taught in that order; instead, teachers choose words that they can connect with ongoing literacy activities or words students are using but confusing.

Teachers create **word walls** with high-frequency words. They prepare word walls at the beginning of the school year and then add to them as they introduce new

Watch this first grade class practice reading and writing high-frequency words. What procedure does the teacher use?

Check the Compendium of Instructional Procedures, which follows Chapter 12.

FIGURE 6–2 **The 300 High-Frequency Words**

a	children	great	looking	ran	through
about	city	green	made	read	time
after	come	grow	make	red	to
again	could	had	man	ride	toad
all	couldn't	hand	many	right	together
along	cried	happy	may	road	told
always	dad	has	maybe	room	too
am	dark	hat	me	run	took
an	day	have	mom	said	top
and	did	he	more	sat	tree
animals	didn't	head	morning	saw	truck
another	do	hear	mother	say	try
any	does	heard	mouse	school	two
are	dog	help	Mr.	sea	under
around	don't	hen	Mrs.	see	until
as	door	her	much	she	up
asked	down	here	must	show	us
at	each	hill	my	sister	very
ate	eat	him	name	sky	wait
away	end	his	need	sleep	walk
baby	even	home	never	small	walked
back	ever	house	new	so	want
bad	every	how	next	some	wanted
ball	everyone	I	nice	something	was
be	eyes	I'll	night	soon	water
bear	far	I'm	no	started	way
because	fast	if	not	stay	we
bed	father	in	nothing	still	well
been	find	inside	now	stop	went
before	fine	into	of	stories	were
began	first	is	off	story	what
behind	fish	it	oh	sun	when
best	fly	it's	old	take	where
better	for	its	on	tell	while
big	found	jump	once	than	who
bird	fox	jumped	one	that	why
birds	friend	just	only	that's	will
blue	friends	keep	or	the	wind
book	frog	king	other	their	witch
books	from	know	our	them	with
box	fun	last	out	then	wizard
boy	garden	left	over	there	woman
brown	gave	let	people	these	words
but	get	let's	picture	they	work
by	girl	like	pig	thing	would
called	give	little	place	things	write
came	go	live	play	think	yes
can	going	long	pulled	this	you
can't	good	look	put	thought	your
cat	got	looked	rabbit	three	you're

From Eldredge, J. Lloyd, *Teach Decoding: Why and How*, 2nd Ed., ©2005, pp.119-120. Reprinted and Electronically reproduced by permission of Pearson Education, Inc., New York, NY.

The words in red are the first 100 most frequently used words, as shown in Figure 5–7.

words. Kindergarten teachers begin by listing children's names and other common words (e.g., *love, Mom*) and then add the 24 highest frequency words, 1 or 2 per week. First grade teachers begin with the 24 words introduced in kindergarten and add new words each week. In second grade, teachers begin with the easier half of the first 100 words and introduce 100 more words during the school year. Third grade teachers check students' knowledge of the 100 or 200 high-frequency words at the beginning of the school year, add any words they don't know, and then teach the rest of the high-frequency words so that everyone learns most of the 300 high-frequency words by the end of the year. Fourth grade teachers and teachers in higher grades continue to use high-frequency word walls if their students aren't fluent readers and writers. They test students' ability to read and write the 300 high-frequency words and teach any words they don't know.

Teaching high-frequency words isn't easy, because many of them have little or no meaning when they're used in isolation. Cunningham (2009) recommends using this chant and clap procedure to practice reading and spelling the words being placed on the word wall:

1. **See and hear the word.** Teachers point to a new word on a high-frequency word wall and pronounce it as students look at it.

2. **Say the word.** Students pronounce the word.

3. **Spell the word.** Students spell the word aloud, clapping their hands as they say each letter. Teachers remind students to check the word wall if they're unsure about the spelling.

4. **Spell the word again.** Students repeat the third step.

5. **Write the word.** Students write the word on a small whiteboard or a sheet of paper, making sure to spell it correctly.

6. **Check the word.** Students hold up their whiteboards or sheets of paper so teachers can quickly check the spelling.

7. **Say the word again.** Students repeat the second step.

Depending on students' familiarity with the words, teachers shorten or lengthen the procedure. Children practice high-frequency words and clarify easily confused words using this procedure. To learn more, see Minilesson: Teaching High-Frequency Words.

WORD-IDENTIFICATION STRATEGIES. Students use four word-identification strategies to decode unfamiliar words: *phonic analysis, decoding by analogy, syllabic analysis,* and *morphemic analysis.* Beginning readers depend on phonics to sound out unfamiliar words, but students gradually learn to decode words by analogy and to use syllabic and morphemic analysis effectively. These strategies are summarized in Figure 6–3.

Phonic Analysis. Students apply what they've learned about **phoneme–grapheme correspondences** and phonics rules to decode words using the phonic analysis strategy. Even though English isn't a perfectly phonetic language, this strategy is very useful because almost every word has some phonetically regular parts. Researchers report that the biggest difference between students who identify words effectively and those who don't is whether they notice almost all the letters in a word and analyze the letter sequences (Stanovich, 1992). Young children often try to decode a word by guessing at it based on the beginning sound. As you might imagine, their guesses are usually wrong; sometimes they don't even make sense in the sentence.

Minilesson

TOPIC: Teaching High-Frequency Words
GRADE: First Grade
TIME: One 15-minute period

Miss Shapiro's goal is for her first graders to learn at least 75 of the 100 high-frequency words. She has a large word wall that's divided into sections for each letter. Each week, she introduces three new words and adds them to the word wall; she chooses words from the big book she's using for shared reading. On Monday, she introduces the new words and over the next 4 days, she focuses on them and reviews those she's introduced previously. To make the word study more authentic, the children often hunt for the word in reading materials available in the classroom; sometimes they look in familiar big books, in small books they're rereading, on charts of familiar poems and songs, or on Language Experience and interactive writing charts. On other days, the children create sentences using the words, which the teacher writes on sentence strips and displays in the classroom.

① Introduce the Topic

"Let's read the D words on the word wall," Miss Shapiro says. As she points to the words, the class reads them aloud. "Which word is new this week?" she asks. The children respond, "do." Next, they read the H words and identify *here* as a new word, and then the M words and identify *my* as a new word. She asks individual children to reread the D, H, and M words on the word wall.

② Share Examples

"Who can come up and point to our three new words for this week?" Miss Shapiro asks. Aaron eagerly comes to the word wall to point out *do, here*, and *my*. As he points to each word, Miss Shapiro writes it on the whiteboard, pronounces it, and spells it aloud. She and Aaron lead the class as they chant and clap the words: "Do, do, d-o, do!" "Here, here, h-e-r-e, here!" "My, my, m-y, my!"

③ Provide Information

"Let's look for *do, here,* and *my* in these books," Miss Shapiro suggests as she passes out a familiar big book to the children at each table. In each group, the children reread the book, pointing out *do, here,* and *my* each time they occur. The teacher circulates around the classroom, checking that the children notice the words.

④ Guide Practice

Miss Shapiro asks Aaron to choose three classmates to come to the whiteboard to spell the words with large magnetic letters; Daniel, Elizabeth, and Wills spell the words and read them aloud. Then Aaron passes out plastic bags with small magnetic letters and word cards to each pair of children. They read the word cards and spell the three words at their desks.

⑤ Assess Learning

On Friday, Miss Shapiro works with the first graders in small groups, asking them to locate the words in sentences they've written and to read the words individually on word cards.

FIGURE 6–3 Word-Identification Strategies

STRATEGY	DESCRIPTION	EXAMPLES
Phonic Analysis	Students apply their knowlege of phoneme–grapheme correspondences, phonics, rules, and spelling patterns to read or write a word.	*blaze* *chin* *peach* *spring*
Decoding by Analogy	Students use their knowledge of phonograms to deduce the pronunciation or spelling of an unfamiliar word.	*claw* from *saw* *flat* from *cat* *stone* from *cone* *think* from *pink*
Syllabic Analysis	Students break a multisyllabic word into syllables and then apply their knowledge of phonics to decode the word, syllable by syllable.	*drag-on* *fa-mous* *mul-ti-ply* *vol-ca-no*
Morphemic Analysis	Students use their knowledge of root words and affixes to read or write an unfamiliar word.	*astro-naut* *bi-cycle* *centi-pede* *trans-port*

Decoding by Analogy. Students use the decoding by analogy strategy to identify words by associating them with words they already know (Cunningham, 2009). When readers come to *small*, for example, they might notice the **phonogram** *-all*, think of the word *ball*, and decode the word by analogy. Students learn to apply this strategy when they read and write "word families," using *-at*, *-ell*, *-ice*, *-own*, *-unk*, and other phonograms. To apply the strategy, they must be familiar with consonant blends and digraphs and be able to manipulate sounds. Using *-ill*, for example, students can read and spell these words: *bill, chill, fill, gill, grill, hill, kill, pill, spill, still,* and *will*. They can decode longer words, too, including *hills, chilly, spilled, killers, grilling, hilltop, silly,* and *pillow*. Teachers also share picture books that include several words containing a particular phonogram (Caldwell & Leslie, 2012). In Fleming's *In the Tall, Tall Grass* (1995), for example, students can locate these *-um* words: *drum, hum,* and *strum*. See Booklist: Books With Phonograms for additional books with words representing word families. It's a big step, however, for students to move from a structured activity to using this strategy independently to identify unfamiliar words.

Syllabic Analysis. More experienced readers divide longer words, such as *angry, pioneer,* and *yogurt,* into **syllables** to identify them. There's one vowel sound in each syllable of a word, but sometimes there's more than one vowel letter in a syllable. Consider the two-syllable words *target* and *chimney*: *Target* has a single vowel letter representing a short vowel sound in each syllable; *chimney* has one vowel in the first syllable but two vowel letters (*ey*) representing a long vowel

Teach Kids to **BE STRATEGIC**

Word-Identification Strategies

Teach students to use these strategies to identify unfamiliar words when they're reading:

- Phonic analysis
- Decode by analogy
- Divide into syllables
- Morphemic analysis

Students practice these strategies when they participate in guided reading activities and as they read during reading workshop. Their choice of strategy depends on their knowledge about words and the complexity of the unfamiliar word. If students struggle, reteach the strategies, demonstrate their use, and think aloud about their application.

Booklist — Books With Phonograms

PHONOGRAM	BOOK
-ack	Shaw, N. E. (1996). *Sheep take a hike*. Boston: Houghton Mifflin.
-ail	Shaw, N. E. (1992). *Sheep on a ship*. Boston: Houghton Mifflin.
-are	Fleming, D. (1998). *In the small, small pond*. New York: Henry Holt.
-ash	Shaw, N. E. (2005). *Sheep eat out*. Boston: Houghton Mifflin.
-ay	Fleming, D. (1998). *In the small, small pond*. New York: Henry Holt.
-eep	Shaw, N. E. (1997). *Sheep in a jeep*. Boston: Houghton Mifflin.
-eet	Heiligman, D. (2005). *Fun dog, sun dog*. New York: Marshall Cavendish.
-ip	Fleming, D. (1995). *In the tall, tall grass*. New York: Henry Holt.
-og	Wood, A. (1992). *Silly Sally*. San Diego: Harcourt Brace.
-oose	Numeroff, L. J. (1991). *If you give a moose a muffin*. New York: HarperCollins.
-op	Shaw, N. E. (2005). *Sheep eat out*. Boston: Houghton Mifflin.
-ouse	Hoberman, M. A. (2007). *A house is a house for me*. New York: Puffin Books.
-own	Wood, A. (1992). *Silly Sally*. San Diego: Harcourt Brace.
-uck	Root, R. (2003). *One duck stuck*. Cambridge, MA: Candlewick Press.
-ug	Edwards, P. D. (1996). *Some smug slug*. New York: HarperCollins.
-um	Fleming, D. (1995). *In the tall, tall grass*. New York: Henry Holt.
-un	Heiligman, D. (2005). *Fun dog, sun dog*. New York: Marshall Cavendish.

sound in the second syllable. The most common guidelines for dividing words into syllables are presented in Figure 6–4. The first rule about dividing syllables between two consonants is the easiest one; examples include *mer-maid* and *pic-nic*. The second rule deals with words where three consonants appear together, such as *ex-plore*: The word is divided between *x* and *p* to preserve the *pl* blend. The third and fourth rules involve the VCV pattern. Usually the syllable boundary comes after the first vowel, as in *ho-tel* and *shi-ny*; however, in words such as *riv-er*, the division comes after the consonant because *ri-ver* isn't a recognizable word.

FIGURE 6–4 Syllabication Rules

RULE	EXAMPLES	
When two consonants come between two vowels in a word, divide the syllables between the consonants.	mer-maid pic-nic	soc-cer win-dow
When more than two consonants come together in a word, divide the syllables keeping the blends together.	bank-rupt com-plete	ex-plore mon-ster
When one consonant comes between two vowels in a word, divide the syllables after the first vowel.	ca-jole bo-nus	plu-ral gla-cier
If the previous rule doesn't make a recognizable word, divide the syllables after the consonant that comes between the vowels.	doz-en ech-o	meth-od cour-age
When two vowels together don't represent a long vowel sound or a diphthong, divide the syllables between the vowels.	cha-os po-em	li-on qui-et

According to the fifth rule, syllables are divided between two vowels when they don't represent a digraph or diphthong; one example is *li-on*.

Morphemic Analysis. Students use morphemic analysis to identify multisyllabic words. They locate the root word by peeling off prefixes and suffixes. A root word is a **morpheme**, the basic, most meaningful part of a word. **Prefixes** are added to the beginning of a root word, as in *replay*, and **suffixes** are added to the end, as in *playing*, *playful*, and *player*. Two types of suffixes are inflectional and derivational. *Inflectional suffixes* are endings that indicate verb tense, person, plurals, possession, and comparison:

the -*s* in *dogs*	the -*ed* in *walked*	the -*er* in *faster*
the -*es* in *beaches*	the -*s* in *eats*	the -*est* in *sunniest*
the -*'s* in *girl's*	the -*ing* in *singing*	

In contrast, *derivational suffixes* show the relationship of the word to its root word. Consider how derivational suffixes affect the meaning of these words that contain the root word *friend*: *friendly*, *friendship*, and *friendless*. When students recognize roots and affixes, they can more easily break apart and identify multisyllabic words:

astronaut (*astro* = star; *naut* = sailor)
microscope (*micro* = small; *scope* = see)
scribble (*scrib* = write)
synonym (*syn* = same; *onym* = name)
vitamin (*vita* = life)

In addition, knowing the meaning of word parts provides context and facilitates word identification.

Fluent readers recognize most words automatically and apply word-identification strategies effectively to decode unfamiliar words. Less fluent readers depend on explicit instruction to learn how to identify words (Gaskins, Gaskins, & Gaskins, 1991). To evaluate how effectively you teach word identification, see Teacher Checklist: How do I teach students to identify unfamiliar words?

Reading Speed

Students must develop an adequate reading speed or rate to have the cognitive resources available to focus on meaning (Allington, 2009; Rasinski & Padak, 2013). Researchers have identified target reading speeds for each grade level, and they're shown in Figure 6–5; however, teachers should use these numbers cautiously because many factors affect reading speed. Fountas and Pinnell (2013) identified these factors affecting students' reading speed:

🍥 Students who have background knowledge about the topic can read more quickly and connect the ideas they're reading to what they already know.

🍥 Students who are knowledgeable about the genre, text structure, and text layout can anticipate what they're reading.

🍥 Students who speak English fluently have an advantage in developing reading speed because they know more words, are familiar with English sentence structure, and recognize metaphors and other literary features.

TEACHER CHECKLIST

How do I teach students to identify unfamiliar words?

○ Do I post high-frequency words on word walls?
○ Do I teach students to read and spell high-frequency words?
○ Do I address the Standards through my instruction?
○ Do I have students practice reading and writing high-frequency words through authentic literacy activities?
○ Do I introduce key words before reading and teach other words during and after reading?
○ Do I model how to use word-identification strategies?
○ Do I teach students to use phonic analysis, decoding by analogy, syllabic analysis, and morphemic analysis word-identification strategies?
○ Do I use words from reading selections as examples in minilessons on word-identification strategies?
○ Do I encourage students to apply word-identification strategies to both reading and spelling?

FIGURE 6–5 Oral Reading Speeds

GRADE	END-OF-YEAR
1	60–75 wcpm*
2	75–100
3	100–120
4	120–140
5	130–150
6	140–160
7	150–170
8	160–180

*wcpm = words correct per minute

Students become more strategic readers as they learn to use speed appropriately and vary their reading rate depending on the text.

Teachers provide daily practice opportunities to develop students' reading speed and stamina. To increase reading volume, teachers offer a combination of teacher-guided and independent reading practice:

Choral Reading. Students work in small groups or together as a class for **choral reading**. They experiment with different ways to read poems and other short texts aloud (Rasinski, 2010). More fluent classmates serve as models and set the reading speed.

Readers Theatre. Students practice reading a story script to develop speed and expressiveness before performing it for classmates. Researchers have found that **readers theatre** significantly improves students' reading fluency (Martinez, Roser, & Strecker, 1998/1999).

Listening Centers. Students read along in a book at their instructional reading level while listening to it being read aloud at a listening center (Kuhn & Stahl, 2004).

Partner Reading. Classmates read or reread books together (Griffith & Rasinski, 2004). They choose a book that interests them and decide how they'll read it; they may read aloud in unison or take turns reading aloud while the partner follows along.

To develop fluency through these practice activities, books must be appropriate; that is, students must be interested in the topics and be able to read them with 98–99% accuracy.

Once students become fluent readers, the focus shifts to helping them develop reading stamina so they can read for 30 minutes or more. Students develop this strength through daily opportunities to read independently for increasingly longer periods. When students' reading is limited to basal reader selections or leveled books that can be completed in 15 minutes or less, they won't develop the endurance they need to become fluent readers. Teachers include extended opportunities each day for independent reading of self-selected texts, and students also benefit from doing additional independent reading at home.

Prosody

When students read expressively, they use their voices to add meaning to the words. Rasinski and Padak (2013) identified these components of prosody:

Expression. Students read with enthusiasm and vary their expression to match their interpretation of the text.

Phrasing. Students chunk words into phrases as they read and apply stress and intonation appropriately.

Volume. Students vary the loudness of their voices to add meaning to the text.

Smoothness. Students read with a smooth rhythm and quickly self-correct any breakdowns.

Pacing. Students read at a conversational speed.

Literacy Portraits

Most second graders move toward fluent reading, and Ms. Janusz spends a great deal of time talking about fluent reading, explaining its importance, teaching the components, and listening to her students read aloud to monitor their growth. Listen as Ms. Janusz explains reading fluency during a guided reading lesson. Does she include the three components of fluency addressed in this chapter? Why do you think that she asks students to retell what they've just read?

Rakie

New LITERACIES

eReaders

eReaders are popular hi-tech devices that adults use to read digital books. They're lightweight, portable devices with wireless connectivity for downloading books, magazines, and newspapers. They employ e-ink technology that mimics the appearance of ink on paper to display text, which gives readers the feeling of reading actual books. eReaders incorporate touchscreen navigation tools so readers turn pages easily. Capacity is another important feature: Most eReaders can store thousands of texts.

Children like eReaders as much as adults do, and these devices are useful in developing reading fluency. Two popular eReaders designed for young children, ages 3–8, are the V.Reader Interactive eReading System and LeapFrog's LeapReader. These devices come with their own collections of stories and interactive games and incorporate these features:

- A kid-friendly design that makes the device easy for children to hold and use
- A colorful touchscreen with controls that make navigation easy
- A downloadable library of entertaining eBooks
- A text-to-speech feature so children can listen to the text as it's read aloud or identify unfamiliar words
- A stylus that children use to draw and write on the screen

As children use these educational toys, they're learning high-frequency words, increasing their reading speed, and developing prosody. The text-to-speech feature that allows children to hear individual words or sentences read aloud is especially helpful in developing reading fluency. As they play with these devices, children also acquire the navigational skills they'll need to read books on eReaders designed for adults.

By third grade, students are ready for adult eReaders, such as Amazon's Kindle, Barnes & Noble's Nook, and Apple's iPad. These devices have large touchscreen displays with controls that make page turns, navigation, and note taking easy; virtual QWERTY keyboards; and built-in dictionaries. Children can download hundreds of fiction and nonfiction books at their reading levels, including eBooks from online bookstores and from school and public libraries.

eReaders are "cool." Because kids like them, they may spend more time reading with these digital devices than they would with print texts, and they're especially valuable for unmotivated and struggling readers. The ways children read in the 21st century are changing; some people complain that the reading experience is altered when children read digital texts, but kids eagerly embrace new technologies.

These components seem more related to oral reading, but prosody plays an important role during silent reading, too, because students' internal voice affects comprehension.

Teachers emphasize prosody by modeling expressive reading every time they read aloud and using the **think-aloud** procedure to reflect on how they varied their expression, chunked words into phrases, modulated the loudness of their voice, or varied the pacing. They talk about the importance of prosody for both fluency and comprehension and show students how meaning is affected when they read in a monotone or slow down their reading speed.

Assessing Reading Fluency

Teachers informally monitor students' reading fluency by listening to them read aloud during guided reading lessons, reading workshop, or other reading activities. At the beginning of the school year and at the end of each month or quarter, teachers collect data about students' accuracy, speed, and prosody to document their progress and provide evidence of their growth over time:

Automaticity. Teachers check students' knowledge of high-frequency words and their ability to use word-identification strategies to decode other words in grade-level texts. Kindergartners are expected to read 24 high-frequency words, first graders 100 words, second graders 200 words, and third graders 300 words. In addition to the list of high-frequency words presented in this chapter, teachers can

Watch this third grade teacher teach a lesson on reading with expression. How does prosody support comprehension?

ASSESSMENT *Snapshot*

Prosody Rubric

	1	2	3	4
Expression	Monotone	Some expressiveness ✓	Reasonable expressiveness	Expression matches interpretation
Phrasing	Word-by-word reading	Choppy reading	Reasonable chunking and intonation ✓	Effective phrasing
Loudness	Very quiet voice	Quiet voice ✓	Appropriate volume	Volume matches interpretation
Smoothness	Frequent extended pauses or breakdowns	Some pauses or breakdowns	A few pauses or breakdowns ✓	Smooth rhythm
Pacing	Very laborious reading	Slow reading	Uneven combination of fast and slow reading	Appropriate conversational pace ✓

TEACHER'S NOTE

Jesse is a shy second grader, and in the spring of the year, he's reading at grade level. On this prosody rubric, Jesse scored a 3, indicating that he's making good progress toward fluency. I plan to show Jesse how to read with more expression and encourage him to read a little louder.

use the Dolch list of 220 sight words and Fry's list of 300 instant words, both of which are widely available in professional books, such as *Assessment for Reading Instruction* (McKenna & Dougherty Stahl, 2015), and online.

Speed. Teachers time students as they read an instructional-level passage aloud and determine how many words they read correctly per minute. Teachers can use the speeds listed in Figure 6–5 to compare their students' reading speeds to national norms.

Prosody. Teachers choose excerpts for students to read from both familiar and unfamiliar instructional-level texts. As they listen, teachers judge whether students read with appropriate expression. **Rubrics** can also be used; the one presented in Assessment Snapshot: Prosody Rubric shows how a second grade teacher scored a student reading at grade level.

This assessment information is also useful for teachers as they make instructional decisions.

Teachers use **running records**, informal reading inventories, and classroom texts to document students' reading fluency. Assessment Tools: Oral Reading Fluency (Grades K–3) lists the tests that evaluate fluency—reading speed, in particular. Until students become fluent readers, it's crucial that teachers regularly monitor their developing accuracy, speed, and prosody to ensure that they're making adequate progress and identify those students who are struggling.

ASSESSMENT TOOLS

Oral Reading Fluency (Grades K–3)

Teachers use these assessment tools as well as running records and IRIs to monitor and document children's reading fluency:

- **aimsweb**

  Teachers screen students' oral reading fluency at the beginning of the school year and periodically monitor their progress during the year using **aims**web, an online assessment system. As students read a text aloud, teachers click on their errors on the online scoring sheet, and afterward the system automatically scores the test. This assessment system for K–8 students is available from Pearson.

- **Dynamic Indicators of Basic Early Literacy Skills (DIBELS): Oral Reading Fluency Subtest**

  The Oral Reading Fluency Subtest (Kaminski & Good, 1996) is a collection of graded passages used to measure first through third graders' reading speed. In this individually administered test, children read aloud for one minute, and teachers mark errors; children's speed is the number of words read correctly. This test is available on the DIBELS website.

- **Fluency Formula Kits**

  Teachers use these grade-level kits, developed by Scholastic, to quickly assess individual children's reading fluency three times a year and interpret their scores using national norms. Each grade-level kit (grades 1–4) contains 3 benchmark passages, 24 progress-monitoring passages, an assessment handbook, a student timer, and progress charts. Scholastic sells each grade-level kit separately.

- **Observation Survey of Early Literacy Achievement (OS): Word Reading and Writing Vocabulary Subtests**

  These two OS subtests (Clay, 2015) assess children's knowledge of high-frequency words. In the Word Reading Subtest, children read 15 high-frequency words, and in the Writing Vocabulary Subtest, they write all the words they know (with a 10-minute time limit). The Word Reading Subtest is administered individually, but children take the Writing Vocabulary Subtest together. The tests and directions for administering and scoring them are included in Marie Clay's *An Observation Survey of Early Literacy Achievement*, which is available from Heinemann.

- **Phonological Awareness Literacy Screening (PALS) System: Word Recognition in Isolation Subtest**

  The Word Recognition in Isolation Subtest (Invernizzi, Meier, & Juel, 2003) consists of graded word lists that children read aloud; the highest level at which children read 15 words correctly is their instructional level. First through third grade teachers use this subtest to monitor children's automatic word recognition. The PALS test is free for Virginia teachers from the University of Virginia, and it's available for purchase in other states.

- **Reading Fluency Benchmark Assessor (RFBA)**

  Teachers use the RFBA to regularly monitor children's progress and identify those readers who aren't making adequate progress. This quick and easy-to-use assessment tool includes 30 fiction and nonfiction passages at each grade level, and software is available for recording data and generating reports. Teachers measure children's fluency by listening to them read a passage aloud for one minute and calculating the number of words they read correctly. The RFBA is available for purchase at the Read Naturally website.

Although many of these tests use reading speed to measure fluency, it's important to remember that fluency also requires children to recognize high-frequency words automatically, apply word-identification strategies to decode unfamiliar words, and read expressively.

Monitor: Check Your Understanding 6.1

Writing Fluency

Fluent writers spell words automatically and write quickly so that they can focus on developing their ideas. Their writing seems to flow effortlessly, and it's distinctive. Fluent writing sounds like talking—it has "voice." Fluency is as crucial for writers as it is for readers, and the components are similar:

Watch as students write in journals, including dialogue journals. How does journal writing develop writing fluency?

Automaticity. Fluent writers write most words automatically and accurately, without having to stop and think about how to spell them. Students must know how to spell high-frequency words and be able to apply strategies to spell other words; otherwise, they get so bogged down in spelling a word that they forget the sentence they're writing or the one that comes next.

Speed. Students need to write quickly enough to keep pace with their thinking. Researchers have examined the number of words students write per minute, compared their speed to the quality of their compositions, and concluded that students need to write 10 words per minute to be considered fluent writers (Graham, Weintraub, & Berninger, 1998). Most third graders reach this rate, and because girls usually do more writing than boys do, it isn't surprising that they write 1 or 2 words per minute faster than boys. Sometimes legibility is an issue because students can't sacrifice neatness for speed: It doesn't do any good to write quickly if readers can't decipher their writing.

Writer's Voice. Writers develop distinctive voices that reflect their individuality (Spandel, 2009). *Voice*, which is similar to prosody, is the tone or emotional feeling of a piece of writing. Writers develop their voices through the words they choose and how they string them into sentences. Each student's voice is unique, and teachers can usually identify who wrote a composition according to its voice, just as many of us can identify books written by our favorite authors by their voice.

The characteristics of fluent writers are summarized in Figure 6–6.

Automatic Writing

To become fluent writers, students need to be able to spell most high-frequency words automatically and apply spelling strategies to write other words. Teachers

FIGURE 6–6 Fluent Writers

COMPONENT	CHARACTERISTICS
Automaticity	• Students spell most high-frequency words correctly. • Students apply spelling patterns and rules to spell words correctly. • Students' spelling becomes increasingly more conventional.
Speed	• Students write quickly. • Students write easily, without discomfort. • Students write legibly. • Students develop keyboarding skills to word process quickly.
Writer's Voice	• Students use alliteration, onomatopoeia, repetition, and other literary devices. • Students make their writing distinctive.

teach students to write high-frequency words the same way they teach them to read the words. Each week they introduce five or six words and provide daily opportunities for students to practice reading and writing them through these activities:

- Students write the words and sentences they compose on whiteboards.
- Students use letter cards or magnetic letters to spell the words.
- Students write the words during interactive writing activities.

Teachers direct some of these activities, and students participate in others at centers.

At first, students sound out the words they're trying to spell. They segment the word into sounds and write a letter for each sound they recognize. They might spell *baby* as BABE or *house* as HUS, for example, using their knowledge of phoneme–grapheme correspondences, but through phonics and spelling instruction and more experience with reading and writing, students spell words more accurately. They also learn to use the "think it out" strategy to spell words. Students apply their knowledge of phonics rules, spelling patterns, word families, syllables, and morphemes. They also develop a visual image of words they can read, and they're more likely to recognize when a spelling doesn't look right and ask a classmate, check a word wall, or consult a dictionary to get the correct spelling.

Writing Speed

For students to become fluent writers, their transcription of ideas onto paper must be automatic; that means they spell most words automatically and use legible handwriting without thinking about how to form letters or keyboard without hunting for letter keys. Students need to know how to hold pencils comfortably, so their hands and arms don't hurt, and they need to learn how to form manuscript letters in kindergarten through second grade and cursive letters in third and fourth grades to improve their speed and legibility. Sometimes teachers require third and fourth graders to write only in cursive, but students should be allowed to use either form, as long as it's easy to read and can be written quickly.

Left-handed writers face unique handwriting problems. The basic difference between right- and left-handed writers is physical orientation: Righties pull their hand and arm away from the body, but lefties move their hand across what has just been written, often covering it. Unfortunately, some students adopt a "hook" position to avoid covering what they've just written. To address that problem, left-handed writers should hold pencils and pens an inch or more farther back from the tip than others do so they can see what they've just written. The tilt of their papers is a second issue: Left-handed students should tilt their papers slightly to the right, in contrast to right-handed writers, who tilt their papers to the left to more comfortably form letters. Slant is a third concern: Lefties should slant their letters in a way that allows them to write comfortably. It's acceptable for them to write cursive letters vertically or even slightly backward, in contrast to righties, who slant cursive letters to the right.

Students develop writing speed through practice. They need to use writing throughout the school day—for example, to contribute to class charts, to make entries in reading logs, to write words and sentences on whiteboards, to add pages to class books, to write books at the writing center or during writing workshop, and to create projects during literature focus units and thematic units. When students use writing three or four times a day or write for extended periods each day, their writing speed will increase.

For students with legibility problems, teachers check that they know how to hold writing instruments and how to form manuscript or cursive letters. It may be necessary to have students slow down their writing at first and concentrate on forming letters carefully and including every letter in a word before they try to increase their writing speed. **Interactive writing** is a useful procedure for examining young children's handwriting skills and demonstrating how to form letters legibly.

GO DIGITAL! **Keyboarding.** Keyboarding is an essential 21st-century literacy skill; most schools use tutorial programs to teach typing skills, beginning with the location of the home keys and correct fingering on the keyboard. Software programs as well as easy-to-use online keyboarding programs and games are available for students of all ages. Students like these programs because they're fun and engaging:

- Ainsworth Keyboard Trainer
- All the Right Type
- Garfield's Typing Pal
- Type to Learn
- Typing Instructor for Kids
- Typing Quick & Easy
- Ultra Key

Students practice using the keys to write words and sentences in these programs, and they receive feedback about their accuracy and speed. Students usually learn keyboarding in second or third grade, and this instruction is critical, because when they don't know how to keyboard, they use the inefficient hunt-and-peck technique and their writing speed is very slow. 🐌

Writer's Voice

The writer's voice reflects the person doing the writing. It sounds natural, not stilted. Pulitzer prize–winning author and teacher Donald Murray (2012) said that a writer's voice is the person in the writing. As students gain experience as readers and writers, their voices will emerge, especially when they're writing about topics they know well.

As students develop their writers' voices, they learn to vary their tone when they're writing to entertain, inform, or persuade. They also learn that some writing forms require a more informal or formal voice: Think about the difference when you're writing an email message and a business letter. Similarly, students' voices are more casual and relaxed when they're writing for classmates than when they're writing for adults.

Doing lots of reading and writing helps students develop their voices. As they read books and listen to the teacher read others aloud, students develop an awareness of voice. Teachers highlight the lyrical tone in *Owl Moon* (Yolen, 2007) and *My Mama Had a Dancing Heart* (Gray, 2001), the lively spirit in *Barn Dance!* (Martin & Archambault, 1988), and repetitive sentences in *The Napping House* (Wood, 2005) and *Alexander and the Terrible, Horrible, No Good, Very Bad Day* (Viorst, 2009). As students become aware of these techniques, they begin applying them in their own writing.

At the same time they're examining authors' voices in books they're reading, students do lots of informal writing to develop their own voices. They need to write every day to become fluent. Keeping a personal journal is a good way to begin, or students write in **reading logs** on topics they choose or on topics the teacher provides. They can try writing from varied viewpoints to experiment with voice. For example, if students retold "Goldilocks and the Three Bears" from Goldilocks's viewpoint, the tone would be quite different.

Assessing Writing Fluency

Teachers assess writing fluency as they observe students writing and examine their compositions. They consider these questions:

- Do students spell most words automatically, or do they stop to figure out how to spell many words?
- Do students write quickly enough to complete the assignment, or do they write slowly or try to avoid writing?
- Is students' writing legible?
- Do students write easily, or do they write laboriously, complaining that their hands hurt?

These questions help teachers quickly identify students who aren't fluent writers. If their observation suggests that students are struggling, teachers conduct additional testing to diagnose fluency problems:

Automaticity. Teachers assess students' ability to spell the high-frequency words and use strategies to spell other words on spelling tests or by examining their writing samples. Fluent writers spell most words correctly, so it's essential that students know how to spell high-frequency words automatically and efficiently figure out the spelling of most other words they want to write.

Speed. Teachers time students as they write a paragraph or two to assess their writing speed. Students write for 1 to 5 minutes about a familiar topic, and then teachers count the number of words they've written and divide that number by the number of minutes to determine students' writing rates. For example, second grade Amie writes 43 words in 5 minutes; her speed is nearly 9 words per minute, and she's almost reached the threshold fluency rate of 10 words per minute. Teachers repeat this assessment several times a year using a different, but equally familiar, topic. Each topic must be accessible because the purpose of the assessment is to monitor students' writing speed, not their knowledge about the topic. Teachers also carefully observe students as they write because their behavior may indicate handwriting problems.

Writer's Voice. Teachers reread several compositions students have written to evaluate their unique style. There aren't standards to use in assessing voice, so teachers often compare one student's writing to classmates' to rate it as comparable or above or below average.

Commercial tests aren't available to assess students' writing fluency, but these informal assessments are useful in diagnosing writers with fluency problems.

Reading fluency typically precedes writing fluency, but the two are clearly linked. The more reading students do, the sooner they'll reach writing fluency; and the more writing students do, the sooner they'll achieve reading fluency.

⟲ Nurturing English Learners

How do teachers teach fluency? English learners need to read words accurately, quickly, and expressively, like native English speakers do; however, it's unlikely that they'll become fluent readers until they speak English fluently because their lack of oral language proficiency limits their recognition of high-frequency words and use of word-identification strategies, and it interferes with their ability to understand word meanings, string words together into sentences, and read expressively (Peregoy & Boyle, 2013).

It's also unlikely that ELs will become fluent writers before they develop oral language proficiency.

Teachers immerse students in oral activities at the same time they're learning to read and write. They help them to make connections between the oral and written language modes to accelerate their achievement and overcome the obstacles to becoming fluent readers and writers:

Automaticity. Becoming automatic readers and writers is challenging for many English learners, and the process takes longer than it does for native English speakers. High-frequency words are difficult to recognize because many of them are abstract (e.g., *about, this, which*), and they're hard to spell because many violate spelling rules (e.g., *could, said, what, who*). Many ELs speak with a native-language accent, which makes phonic analysis more arduous, but their pronunciation differences needn't hamper their reading fluency. For example, even though some Hispanic students, especially more recent immigrants, pronounce *check* as /shĕk/ because the *ch* digraph doesn't exist in Spanish, they're reading the word accurately. Everyone has an accent, even native English speakers, so ELs shouldn't be expected to eliminate their accents to be considered fluent readers. Applying syllabic analysis to identify words that aren't in their speaking vocabularies can be a formidable task, especially if they're not familiar with cognates or related words in their native language.

Speed. English learners' limited background knowledge and lack of English vocabulary affect their reading and writing speed. By building background knowledge and introducing new words beforehand, teachers can help ELs improve their reading speed. In addition, students need opportunities to reread familiar books. To develop their writing speed, teachers talk with ELs about topics before writing and create lists of words related to a topic. In addition, teachers shouldn't place too much importance on grammatical correctness, because if they do, students will stick with safe, grammatically correct sentences they already know how to write.

Expressiveness. Students' knowledge of spoken English plays a critical role in developing prosody and a writer's voice. ELs' intonation patterns usually reflect their native language. This common problem is due to their limited knowledge of English syntax, and to the fact that punctuation marks don't provide enough clues about chunking words (Allington, 2009). To remedy this problem, teachers teach about punctuation marks. They use echo reading, in which the teacher reads a sentence expressively and then students repeat it, trying to imitate the teacher's prosody. Developing a writer's voice is just as challenging: Students need to learn to use varied sentence structures, idioms, and figurative language. Teachers highlight the authors' voices in books they're reading aloud, and ELs often use books they've read as models for their writing. For example, the repetitive sentence structure from *If You Give a Mouse a Cookie* (Numeroff, 2000) provides a pattern for writing. ELs develop expressiveness through lots of reading and writing practice.

 MONITOR: Check Your Understanding 6.2

Dysfluent Students

By the time they reach fourth grade, most students have become fluent readers and writers; they've moved from word-by-word reading into fluent reading. Allington (2009) estimates, however, that 10–15% of older students have difficulty recognizing words, and their reading achievement is slowed. In some classrooms, the problem is more widespread: More than half of the students read 2 or more years below grade level, and they have difficulty decoding words, reading at an appropriate speed, or reading expressively. Many of these students also continue to struggle to get their ideas down on paper, form letters legibly, and spell common words correctly. It's crucial that teachers intervene to help students overcome these obstacles to reading and writing fluency because they must be able to focus their attention on meaning, not on decoding and spelling words. Researchers have found that fluent readers comprehend better than less fluent readers (National Reading Panel, 2000). The same conclusion can be drawn about writers: Fluent writers are more successful in creating effective compositions than less fluent writers.

Older Dysfluent Readers

Students in fourth grade and beyond who aren't fluent readers are dysfluent. They read hesitantly and without expression. They often try to sound out phonetically irregular words, such as *what* and *their*, and they complain that what they're reading doesn't make sense. Figure 6–7 summarizes the characteristics of dysfluent readers.

FIGURE 6–7	Dysfluent Readers and Writers

MODE	COMPONENT	CHARACTERISTICS
Reading	Automaticity	• Students don't recognize many high-frequency words. • Students guess at words based on the beginning sound. • Students don't break multisyllabic words into syllables to decode them. • Students don't peel off affixes to decode multisyllabic words. • Students don't remember a word the second or third time it's used.
	Speed	• Students point at words as they read. • Students repeat words and phrases as they're reading. • Students read slowly or too quickly.
	Prosody	• Students read in a word-by-word manner. • Students ignore punctuation marks. • Students read without expression.
	Other	• Students misbehave to avoid reading.
Writing	Automaticity	• Students misspell many words, including high-frequency ones. • Students leave out words.
	Speed	• Students write slowly. • Students write laboriously, shaking their arms, rubbing their fingers, or complaining of pain. • Students write illegibly. • Students lack keyboarding skills to word process quickly.
	Writer's Voice	• Students don't insert punctuation marks. • Students don't make their writing distinctive.
	Other	• Students write very little. • Students misbehave to avoid writing.

Many struggling readers don't read fluently, and their labored reading affects their comprehension. Allington (2012) examined the research about dysfluent readers and found no single common problem: Some readers have difficulty decoding words, but others read very slowly or in a monotone, ignoring phrasing and punctuation cues. Because struggling readers exhibit different fluency problems, it's essential to diagnose students and plan instruction that's tailored to their instructional needs.

By the time students reach fourth grade, they should be fluent readers. Teachers identify struggling readers, students whose instructional reading levels are more than a year below their grade placement, and screen them for fluency problems. They begin by listening to the struggling readers read aloud in instructional-level texts and considering these questions:

- Do students read most words automatically, or do they stop to decode many common words?
- Are students able to identify most grade-appropriate multisyllabic words?
- Do students read quickly enough to understand what they're reading, or do they read too slowly or too fast?
- Do students chunk words into phrases when they're reading, or do they read word by word?
- Do students read grade-level texts expressively, or do they read in a monotone?

Any of the fluency components—automaticity, speed, or expressiveness—can pose obstacles for dysfluent readers, and these questions help teachers quickly identify struggling readers with fluency problems.

If their observation suggests that students have difficulty with any of these components, teachers conduct additional testing to pinpoint fluency problems:

Automaticity. Teachers assess students' knowledge of high-frequency words and their ability to identify unfamiliar words. First, students read a list of high-frequency words, and teachers mark the ones they read correctly. Second, students read a list of words taken from grade-appropriate texts, and teachers check whether they use their knowledge of phonics, analogies, syllabication, and morphemic analysis to identify them.

Speed. Teachers assess students' reading speed by timing them as they read an instructional-level passage aloud and determining how many words they read per minute. To be considered fluent, students need to read at least 100 words per minute.

Prosody. The best way to gauge prosody is to listen to students read aloud. Teachers choose excerpts from both familiar and unfamiliar instructional-level texts for students to read. As they listen, teachers judge whether students read with appropriate expression.

Fourth through eighth grade teachers generally use informal assessment tools to diagnose struggling students' fluency problems, but they can also use classroom tests, especially the graded word lists and passages in informal reading inventories, to analyze students' fluency according to grade-level expectations. See Assessment Tools: Oral Reading Fluency (Grades 4–8) for a variety of tests.

Older Dysfluent Writers

Students in fourth grade and beyond who aren't fluent writers are dysfluent. They write slowly and hesitantly. They can't spell many high-frequency words, their handwriting is often difficult to decipher, and their writing lacks a voice or expressiveness. The characteristics of dysfluent writers are also summarized in Figure 6–7.

ASSESSMENT TOOLS

Oral Reading Fluency (Grades 4–8)

Teachers use these assessment tools as well as informal observation and teacher-made word lists to diagnose struggling readers' accuracy, reading speed, and prosody problems:

- **The Names Test: A Quick Assessment of Decoding Ability**

  The Names Test (Cunningham, 1990: Duffelmeyer et al., 1994; Mather, Sammons, & Schwartz, 2006), a list of names that students read aloud, measures young adolescents' ability to decode phonetically regular words. To plan for instruction, teachers record students' errors and then analyze them to determine which phonics concepts students know and which they don't. This free assessment is available online.

- **Fluency Checks**

  Teachers use these graded passages (Johns & Berglund, 2009) to assess students' fluent reading. They listen to students read aloud a narrative or expository passage for one minute and mark errors on a scoring sheet. They also ask comprehension questions. Afterward, teachers calculate students' reading speed and score it against grade-level standards, and they rate their prosody (phrasing, expression, and attention to punctuation marks).

- **Developmental Reading Assessment, 2nd Edition PLUS (DRA2+)**

  The DRA2+ kit for grades 4–8 contains a collection of leveled books that teachers use to assess students' reading fluency. Students read aloud books at their instructional levels while teachers take running records to examine their accuracy, speed, and prosody. The DRA2+ kit is available from Pearson.

- **Informal Reading Inventories (IRIs)**

  Teachers listen to students read aloud grade-level passages in an IRI and mark accuracy and prosody errors on scoring sheets. Accuracy errors include substituted, mispronounced, and skipped words; prosody errors include pauses, phrasing, and expressiveness. In addition, teachers use a stopwatch to record the time it takes students to read the passage and then calculate their reading rate (words read correctly per minute). They also examine students' accuracy errors to determine their knowledge of high-frequency words and their use of word-identification strategies. IRIs are recommended for students who read at the second grade level or higher; for students reading below second grade level, running records provide more useful information.

- **Running Records**

  Teachers use running records (Clay, 2015) to examine students' oral reading of authentic texts. Although they're more commonly used with children in the primary grades, running records can be used with older dysfluent readers, too (Lapp & Flood, 2003). As students read a passage orally, teachers time their reading, mark errors on a copy of the text, and evaluate their prosody. Afterward, students retell what they've read to provide a measure of their comprehension.

- **3-Minute Reading Assessments**

  This quick tool (Rasinski & Padak, 2005a, 2005b) measures students' oral reading fluency using 200- to 400-word passages. Students read the passages aloud and teachers time the reading and mark uncorrected word-identification errors; then students retell what they've read. Two versions of the 3-Minute Reading Assessments are available from Scholastic; one is for grades 1–4 and the other is for grades 5–8.

Teachers use these tests to diagnose struggling readers' fluency problems and regularly monitor students' developing accuracy, reading speed, and prosody until they become fluent.

It's easy to spot dysfluent writers in the classroom because these students write slowly and accomplish very little. They often complain that their hands and arms hurt. Their slow, laborious handwriting interferes with their expression of ideas, and they may not be able to reread what they've written or describe what they're planning to write next. Teachers assess writing fluency as they watch students write and examine their compositions. They consider these questions:

- Do students spell most words automatically, or do they stop to sound out spellings of many words?
- Do students write quickly enough to complete assignments, or do they write slowly or try to avoid writing?
- Is students' writing legible?
- Do students write laboriously, complaining that their hands hurt?

These questions help teachers quickly identify older students who may not be fluent writers.

If their observation suggests that students are struggling writers, teachers conduct additional testing to diagnose fluency problems:

Automaticity. Teachers assess struggling writers' ability to spell high-frequency words and use strategies to spell other words with spelling tests or by examining their writing samples. Fluent writers spell most words correctly, so it's essential that students know how to spell high-frequency words automatically and efficiently figure out the spelling of most other words they write.

Speed. Teachers time students as they write a composition, at least one or two paragraphs in length, to assess their writing speed. To be considered fluent, students should write at least 10 words per minute. Teachers also carefully observe students as they write because their behavior may indicate handwriting problems.

Writer's Voice. Teachers reread several compositions students have written to evaluate their unique style. There aren't standards to use in assessing voice, so teachers often compare one student's writing to classmates' to rate its voice as comparable or above or below average.

Commercial tests aren't available to assess students' writing fluency, but these informal assessments are useful in diagnosing students who have writing fluency problems.

Obstacles to Fluency

Students who struggle with fluency may have a single problem, such as slow reading speed or delayed spelling development, or they may face numerous obstacles in both reading and writing. Teachers need to intervene and help older students become more fluent readers, so they can comprehend what they're reading, and more fluent writers, so they can focus on creating meaning as they write. Providing targeted instruction is often necessary to help students overcome those obstacles; however, effective interventions require more than "fix-it" instruction. Mary Curtis (2004) and other researchers recommend these components for the most effective interventions:

- Providing explicit instruction on diagnosed fluency problems
- Increasing the time for students to read books at their independent level
- Modeling fluent reading and writing
- Clarifying the connections between reading fluency and comprehension and between writing fluency and effective compositions
- Increasing opportunities for writing

"Fix-it" intervention programs for older students usually aren't successful because they target one area and ignore the larger problem. Ivey (2008) explains that not being able to identify multisyllabic words, for example, may only be a symptom of a student's limited reading experience, and being a slow writer may similarly be a symptom of a student's limited writing experience.

The amount of reading and writing that students do makes a critical difference. Guthrie (2004) found that capable readers spend 500% more time reading than struggling readers do, and Allington (2009) warns that "older struggling readers will never become fluent and proficient readers unless teachers design interventions that dramatically increase the volume of reading that they do" (p. 99). Teachers can increase students' independent reading time in several ways, including reading workshop, Sustained Silent Reading, or a 15- or 20-minute reading period during interventions. Two ways that teachers can increase students' writing are through writing workshop and a 15- or 20-minute writing period during interventions.

OBSTACLE 1: Lack of Automaticity. Teachers use explicit instruction to teach students to read and write high-frequency words. Each week they focus on five words and involve students in these activities to practice them:

ᗧ Students locate examples of the words in books they're reading.
ᗧ Students practice reading flash cards with the words to partners.
ᗧ Students play games, such as Concentration, using the words.
ᗧ Students write the words and sentences they compose with them on whiteboards.
ᗧ Students spell the words with letter cards or magnetic letters.
ᗧ Students write the words during interactive writing activities.

These activities provide the practice that's necessary for students to learn to recognize and spell high-frequency words automatically.

Teachers create word walls with the high-frequency words that they post in the classroom when most students are learning them, or they make individual word lists for older dysfluent students. They type up an alphabetical list of words and make copies to cut into bookmarks or glue on file folders. Students practice reading the words and refer to the list when they're writing so that they can spell the words correctly.

Students also create word banks of high-frequency words that they've learned to read. When teachers introduce new words, they distribute small word cards and students practice reading them, often adding a checkmark on the back of the card each time they read it correctly. Once they can consistently identify the word, students add it to their word banks. Then they continue to practice reading the words and refer to them, if necessary, when they're writing. Students' confidence increases as their bank of word cards grows to 20, 50, or 100 words or more.

Targeted instruction on high-frequency words is only part of an effective intervention. It's equally important to increase the amount of time students are reading and writing: They need to spend at least 15 minutes reading books at their independent reading level and another 15 minutes quickwriting, writing in reading logs and other journals, and doing other writing activities each day. Authentic reading and writing activities are essential for building students' store of known words.

OBSTACLE 2: Unfamiliarity With Word-Identification Strategies. Teachers include these components in their intervention programs to develop students' ability to read and spell words:

ᗧ Develop students' background knowledge and introduce new vocabulary words before reading
ᗧ Teach word-identification strategies
ᗧ Provide more time for reading and writing practice

These components help dysfluent readers and writers develop automaticity.

Some fourth through eighth grade students continue to struggle to decode words. Too often struggling readers simply guess at words based on the first letter, but their guesses don't make sense when they lack adequate background knowledge. For example, if you were reading a passage about Abraham Lincoln and didn't know a five-letter word beginning with a capital *C* and followed by the capitalized word *War*, would you have any difficulty identifying the word *Civil*? A surprising number of older students would. It's essential that teachers build students' background knowledge and introduce new vocabulary words before reading so that struggling readers will have additional sources of information to apply while they're reading.

Students need to learn strategies for identifying unfamiliar words. Teachers use minilessons to teach phonic analysis, decoding by analogy, syllabic analysis, and morphemic analysis with words that students are attempting to read and write. Mary Curtis (2004) recommends focusing on spelling rather than on decoding because older students are often embarrassed that they can't identify words effectively. For example, when a student spells *lake* as *lack* or *jungle* as *jungul*, teachers have opportunities to review phonics and spelling concepts in a meaningful way. Minilesson: Using Morphemic Analysis to Identify Words describes how Mr. Morales teaches his sixth graders to figure out the meaning of multisyllabic words.

Dysfluent students need more time for reading books at their independent reading level and for writing on topics that interest them. Even though teachers often think that additional instruction, and phonics instruction in particular, will solve students' reading problems, researchers have concluded that older struggling students rarely benefit from it (Ivey & Baker, 2004; National Reading Panel, 2000). Instead, lots of reading and writing practice is more important in developing students' ability to identify and spell words without conscious effort, but struggling students who don't do as much reading and writing lack the necessary experience.

OBSTACLE 3: Slow Reading Speed. The most important way that teachers intervene is by providing daily practice opportunities to develop students' reading speed and stamina. Allington (2009) reports that "by fourth grade, struggling readers have read millions fewer words than their achieving classmates" (p. 101). Struggling readers typically don't read outside of school; in contrast, most grade-level students in the middle grades read 15 to 30 minutes a day in addition to doing homework assignments. To increase reading volume, teachers provide a combination of teacher-guided and independent reading practice, including choral reading, guided reading, readers theatre, listening center, and partner reading. To develop fluency through these practice activities, books must be appropriate; that is, students must be interested in their topics and be able to read them with 98 or 99% accuracy.

Another way to improve reading speed is the repeated readings procedure, in which students practice reading a text aloud three to five times, striving to improve their reading speed and reduce their errors with each reading (Samuels, 1979). Students time their reading and plot their speed on a graph so they can track their improvement. For years, researchers have advocated repeated readings as an effective way to increase students' reading fluency, but now researchers suggest that reading a variety of books is at least as effective and perhaps even more beneficial (Allington, 2009; Kuhn & Stahl, 2004). When teachers have students use the repeated readings procedure, it should be done one or two days a week for only for a month or two so that students have plenty of time for independent reading.

Once students reach the fluency level, the focus shifts to helping them develop reading stamina, or the strength to read silently for increasingly longer periods. Students develop this stamina through daily opportunities to read independently for extended periods. When students' reading is limited to basal reader selections or magazine articles that can be completed in 15 or 20 minutes, they won't develop the

Minilesson

As part of a thematic unit on ancient civilizations, Mr. Morales introduces the concepts *democracy, monarchy, oligarchy,* and *theocracy* and adds the words to the word wall; however, he notices that many of his sixth graders have difficulty pronouncing the words and remembering what they mean even though they've read about them in the social studies textbook.

1 Introduce the Topic

Mr. Morales looks over the ancient civilizations word wall and reads aloud these words: *democracy, monarchy, oligarchy,* and *theocracy.* Marcos volunteers that he thinks the words have something to do with kings or rulers, but he's not sure.

2 Share Examples

The teacher writes the words on the whiteboard, dividing them into word parts so that the sixth graders can pronounce them more easily. The students practice saying the words several times, but they're still puzzled about their meanings.

3 Provide Information

Mr. Morales explains that he can help them figure out the meaning of the words. "The words are Greek," he says, "and they have two word parts. If you know the meaning of the word parts, you'll be able to figure out the meaning of the words." He writes the four words and breaks them into word parts this way:

> *democracy = demo + cracy*   *monarchy = mono + archy*
> *oligarchy = olig + archy*   *theocracy = theo + cracy*

Then he explains that Marcos was right—the words have to do with kings and rulers: They describe different kinds of government. *Cracy* means *government* and *archy* means *leader.* The first word part tells more about the kind of government; one of them means *gods,* and the others mean *one, people,* and *few.* The students work in small groups to figure out that *democracy* means government by the people, *monarchy* means one leader, *oligarchy* means rule by a few leaders, and *theocracy* means government by the gods.

4 Guide Practice

The next day, Mr. Morales divides the class into four groups, and each group makes a poster to describe one of the four types of government. On each poster, students write the word, the two Greek word parts, and a definition. They also create an illustration based on what they've learned about this type of government. Afterward, students share their posters with the class and display them in the classroom.

5 Assess Learning

On the third day, Mr. Morales passes out a list of six sentences about the different types of government taken from the social studies textbook and asks students to identify the type. He encourages the sixth graders to refer to the posters the class made as they complete the assignment. Afterward, he reviews their papers to determine which students can use the words correctly to identify the four types of government.

endurance they need. Many teachers report that by sixth or seventh grade, their students can't read comfortably for more than 20 minutes. It's essential that they develop the stamina to read for longer periods so they can read novels and handle the lengthier texts they're expected to read. Teachers include extended opportunities each day for independent reading of self-selected texts through reading workshop or **Sustained Silent Reading**. In the middle grades, students' independent reading time begins at 40 to 45 minutes and increases to 60 minutes, if the schedule permits. Students also benefit from doing additional independent reading at home.

Another way of looking at how students develop stamina is by the number of words they're expected to read. Many school districts expect students to read 500,000 words in fourth grade and gradually increase the number of words until they read one million words in eighth grade. You may wonder how the number of words translates to books: Students in fourth, fifth, and sixth grades often read novels that are approximately 200 pages long, and these books typically have about 35,000 words; for example, *Esperanza Rising* (Ryan, 2002) and *Loser* (Spinelli, 2002). Therefore, students need to read approximately 14 books to reach 500,000 words. Those who read two novels each month will reach the 500,000-word mark.

Students in seventh and eighth grades usually read books with 250 pages or more. Books with 250 pages, such as *Bud, Not Buddy* (Curtis, 2004), *Holes* (Sachar, 2008), and *Crispin: The Cross of Lead* (Avi, 2004), contain at least 50,000 words. Books containing more than 300 pages, such as *Harry Potter and the Chamber of Secrets* (Rowling, 1999), range from 75,000 to 100,000 words. Students need to read 10 to 20 books, depending on length, to reach one million words. So, those who read two books with 250 to 350 pages each month will reach the one million–word mark.

OBSTACLE 4: Slow Writing Speed. The best way to improve students' writing speed is through lots of writing. Dysfluent writers often have trouble sustaining a writing project through the writing process, but these informal writing activities are productive ways to increase writing speed:

Quickwriting. Students choose a topic for **quickwriting** and write without stopping for 5 or 10 minutes to explore the topic and deepen their understanding. The writing is informal, and students are encouraged to pour out ideas without stopping to organize them.

Reading Logs. Students write entries in **reading logs** as they read a story or listen to the teacher read a novel aloud. In their entries, students share their predictions, write summaries, ask questions, collect quotes, and reflect on the reading experience.

Simulated Journals. Students assume the role of a book character and write entries from that character's viewpoint in simulated journals. They delve into the character's thoughts and actions to deepen their understanding of the novel they're reading or that the teacher is reading aloud.

Learning Logs. Students write entries in **learning logs** as part of thematic units. They're using writing as a tool for learning as they take notes, draw and label graphic organizers, summarize big ideas, and write answers to questions.

It's important to have available a list of high-frequency words as well as a word wall with vocabulary related to the book or the thematic unit for struggling writers to refer to while they're writing.

For students with legibility problems, teachers check that they know how to hold pens and form manuscript and cursive letters correctly. Before they focus on increasing their writing speed, students may need to slow down their writing at first and concentrate on forming letters carefully and including all letters in each word.

Interactive writing is a useful procedure for examining students' handwriting skills and demonstrating how to write legibly. For students with serious problems, developing keyboarding skills may be a better alternative.

OBSTACLE 5: Lack of Prosody. Teachers emphasize prosody by modeling expressive reading every time they read aloud and using the think-aloud procedure to reflect on how they varied their expression, chunked words into phrases, modulated the loudness of their voice, or varied their pacing. They talk about the importance of prosody for both fluency and comprehension and show students how meaning is affected when they read in a monotone or slow down their reading speed.

Schreider (1991) recommends teaching students to phrase or chunk words together to read with expression. Fluent readers understand how to chunk words into meaningful units, perhaps because they've been read to or have had numerous reading experiences themselves, but many dysfluent readers don't. Consider this sentence from *Sarah, Plain and Tall* (MacLachlan, 2005): "A few raindrops came, gentle at first, then stronger and louder, so that Caleb and I covered our ears and stared at each other without speaking" (p. 47). This sentence comes from the chapter describing a terrible storm that the pioneer family endured, huddled with their animals in their sturdy barn. Three commas help students read the first part of this sentence, but then they must decide how to chunk the second part.

Teachers work with dysfluent readers to break sentences into phrases and read the sentences expressively. They make copies of a page from a book students are reading so they can mark pauses in longer sentences, then students practice rereading the sentences. After practicing with one sentence, they work with a partner to chunk and read another sentence.

Two other ways to improve students' expressiveness are **choral reading** and **readers theatre**. The emphasis in both is on reading smoothly at a conversational pace and using expression so students' voices add meaning to the words.

OBSTACLE 6: Voiceless Writing. Doing lots of reading and writing helps dysfluent writers develop their voices. As they read books and listen to the teacher read others aloud, students develop an awareness of the writer's voice. While reading aloud the hilarious *My Dad's a Birdman* (Almond, 2008), a story about Lizzie and her dad who enter the Great Human Bird Competition, a fifth grade teacher pointed out how the author emphasized his voice through dialogue, onomatopoeia, lots of detail, alliteration, and British jargon. Even the character names—Jackie Crow, Mortimer "Missile" Mint, Doreen Doody, and Mr. Poop—are humorous. The fifth graders also collected alliterative phrases from the novel, including "the nits, the ninnies, the nincompoopy noodleheads" (n.p.), and made a list of words and phrases that emphasized David Almond's voice, including *tweakling and twockling, don't be daft, potty as a pancake*, and *blitheration*. Through minilessons and word-study activities, students become aware of techniques they can apply in their own writing so their voices will come through.

At the same time they're examining authors' voices in books they're reading, students do lots of informal writing to develop their own voices. To become fluent, students need to write every day for at least 15 or 20 minutes, and most intervention programs include writing components. Students can try writing from varied viewpoints to experiment with voice. For example, on the topic "what I'm thankful for," it's not hard to imagine how a criminal, parent, farm worker, police officer, or film star might respond. Another way to emphasize voice is by having students talk out their writing ideas with a partner before beginning to write; this prewriting conversation serves as a rehearsal and makes students' writing more effective.

Older students' fluency problems often reflect their limited reading and writing experiences. The amount of reading and writing that students do makes a critical difference in their literacy achievement. The most important recommendation for students who struggle with fluency is to dramatically increase the amount of reading and writing they do every day. Students need to spend at least 15 to 30 minutes reading books at their independent reading level in addition to their formal reading instruction and any intervention programs.

 **MONITOR: Check Your Understanding 6.3**

Review

DEVELOPING FLUENT READERS AND WRITERS

Effective teachers ensure that their students are fluent readers and writers by fourth grade, and they work with older dysfluent students to overcome obstacles to fluency using the guidelines presented in this chapter, these points in particular:

6.1 Teachers develop these three components of reading fluency: *automaticity*, *speed*, and *prosody*.

6.2 Teachers develop these three components of writing fluency: *automaticity*, *speed*, and *voice*.

6.3 Teachers address older struggling students' obstacles to fluency.

✔ EVALUATE & REFLECT

Apply your understanding about assessing students' fluency. The questions ask you to collect and analyze data, and report the results. Your response should meet academic standards and adhere to Standard English conventions.

1. Listen to a K–3 student read and evaluate his/her reading fluency using the three components of reading fluency. In your response, describe the student, report the results of your evaluation, and make instructional recommendations.

2. Observe a K–3 student write on several occasions and evaluate his/her writing fluency using the three components of writing fluency. In your response, describe the student, report the results of your evaluation, and make instructional recommendations.

3. Reflect on your own reading and writing fluency, both when you were an elementary student and today. Reflect on your fluency according to the three components of reading fluency and the three components of writing fluency. In your response, describe your reading and writing fluency as a child and as an adult, and explain how teachers supported you or how they could have been more effective.

4. Evaluate a dysfluent reader in grades 4–8 to determine the specific obstacles he/she faces in developing reading fluency. In your response, describe the student, explain his/her level of reading fluency according to the three components, and make recommendations for helping the student overcome obstacles.

5. Observe a dysfluent writer in grades 4–8 to determine the specific obstacles he/she faces in developing writing fluency. In your response, describe the student, explain his/her degree of writing fluency according to the three components, and make recommendations for helping the student overcome obstacles.

REFERENCES

Allington, R. L. (2009). *What really matters in fluency: Research-based best practices across the curriculum*. Boston: Allyn & Bacon/Pearson.

Allington, R. L. (2012). *What really matters for struggling readers: Designing research-based programs* (3rd ed.). Boston: Pearson.

Almond, D. (2008). *My dad's a birdman*. Somerville, MA: Candlewick Press.

Avi. (2004). *Crispin: The cross of lead*. New York: Hyperion Books.

Caldwell, J. S., & Leslie, L. (2012). *Intervention strategies to follow informal reading inventory assessment: So what do I do now?* (3rd ed.). Boston: Pearson.

Carle, E. (2005). *A house for hermit crab*. New York: Aladdin Books.

Clay, M. M. (2015). *An observation survey of early literacy achievement* (3rd ed.). Portsmouth, NH: Heinemann.

Cunningham, P. (1990). The Names Test: A quick assessment of decoding ability. *The Reading Teacher, 44*, 124–129.

Cunningham, P. M. (2009). *What really matters in vocabulary: Research-based practices across the curriculum*. Boston: Allyn & Bacon/Pearson.

Curtis, C. P. (2004). *Bud, not Buddy*. New York: Laurel Leaf.

Curtis, M. E. (2004). Adolescents who struggle with word identification: Research and practice. In T. L. Jetton & J. A. Dole (Eds.), *Adolescent literacy research and practice* (pp. 119–134). New York: Guilford Press.

Dowhower, S. L. (1991). Speaking of prosody: Fluency's unattended bedfellow. *Theory Into Practice, 30*, 165–173.

Duffelmeyer, F. A., Kruse, A. E., Merkley, D. J., & Fyfe, S. A. (1994). Further validation and enhancement of the Names Test. *The Reading Teacher, 48*, 118–128.

Eldredge, J. L. (2005). *Teach decoding: How and why* (2nd ed.). Upper Saddle River, NJ: Merrill/Prentice Hall.

Fleming, D. (1995). *In the tall, tall grass*. New York: Henry Holt.

Fountas, I. C., & Pinnell, G. S. (2013). *Fountas & Pinnell leveled book list, K–8+* (2013–2015 ed., vols. 1 & 2). Portsmouth, NH: Heinemann.

Gaskins, R. W., Gaskins, J. C., & Gaskins, I. W. (1991). A decoding program for poor readers—and the rest of the class, too! *Language Arts, 68*, 213–225.

Graham, S., Weintraub, N., & Berninger, V. W. (1998). The relationship between handwriting style and speed and legibility. *Journal of Educational Research, 91*, 290–296.

Gray, L. M. (2001). *My mama had a dancing heart*. New York: Scholastic.

Griffith, L. W., & Rasinski, T. V. (2004). A focus on fluency: How one teacher incorporated fluency with her reading curriculum. *The Reading Teacher, 58*, 126–137.

Guthrie, J. T. (2004). Teaching for literacy engagement. *Journal of Literacy Research, 36*(1), 1–28.

Holling, H. C. (1990). *Pagoo*. Boston: Houghton Mifflin.

Invernizzi, M., Meier, J. D., & Juel, C. (2003). *Phonological Awareness Literacy Screening System*. Charlottesville: University of Virginia Press.

Ivey, G. (2008). Intervening when older youth struggle with reading. In K. A. Hinchman & H. K. Sheridan-Thomas (Eds.), *Best practices in adolescent literacy instruction* (pp. 247–260). New York: Guilford Press.

Ivey, G., & Baker, M. I. (2004). Phonics instruction for older students? Just say no. *Educational Leadership, 61*(6), 35–39.

Johns, J. L., & Berglund, R. L. (2009). *Fluency: Strategies & assessments* (3rd ed.). Newark, DE: International Reading Association and Kendall Hunt.

Kaminski, R. A., & Good, R. H., III. (1996). *Dynamic Indicators of Basic Early Literacy Skills (DIBELS)*. Eugene: University of Oregon Center on Teaching and Learning.

Kaplan, R. (1996). *Moving day*. New York: Greenwillow.

Kuhn, M. R., & Rasinski, T. (2011). Best practices in fluency instruction. In L. M. Morrow & L. B. Gambrell (Eds.), *Best practices in literacy instruction* (4th ed., pp. 276–294). New York: Guilford Press.

Kuhn, M. R., & Stahl, S. A. (2004). Fluency: A review of developmental and remedial practices. In R. B. Ruddell & N. J. Unrau (Eds.), *Theoretical models and processes of reading* (5th ed., pp. 412–453). Newark, DE: International Reading Association.

Lapp, D., & Flood, J. (2003). Understanding the learner: Using portable assessment. In R. L. McCormack & J. R. Paratore (Eds.), *After early intervention, then what? Teaching struggling readers in grades 3 and up* (pp. 10–24). Newark, DE: International Reading Association.

MacLachlan, P. (2005). *Sarah, plain and tall*. New York: Scholastic.

Martin, B., Jr., & Archambault, J. (1988). *Barn dance!* New York: Henry Holt.

Martinez, M., Roser, N. L., & Strecker, S. (1998/1999). "I never thought I could be a star": A readers theatre ticket to fluency. *The Reading Teacher, 52*, 326–334.

Mather, N., Sammons, J., & Schwartz, J. (2006). Adaptations of the Names Test: Easy to use phonics assessments. *The Reading Teacher, 60*, 114–122.

McKenna, M. C., & Dougherty Stahl, K. A. (2015). *Assessment for reading instruction* (3rd ed.). New York: Guilford Press.

Murray, D. M. (2012). *The craft of revision* (Anniv. ed.). Belmont, CA: Wadsworth.

National Reading Panel. (2000). *Teaching children to read: An evidence-based assessment of the scientific research literature on reading and its implications for reading instruction*. Washington, DC: National Institute of Child Health and Human Development.

Numeroff, L. J. (2000). *If you give a mouse a cookie*. New York: HarperCollins.

Peregoy, S. F., & Boyle, O. F. (2013). *Reading, writing and learning in ESL: A resource book for K–12 teachers* (6th ed.). Boston: Pearson.

Pikulski, J. J., & Chard, D. J. (2005). Fluency: Bridge between decoding and reading comprehension. *The Reading Teacher, 58*, 510–519.

Pinnell, G. S., & Fountas, I. C. (1998). *Word matters: Teaching phonics and spelling in the reading/writing classroom*. Portsmouth, NH: Heinemann.

Randell, B. (1994). *Hermit crab*. Crystal Lake, IL: Rigby Books.

Rasinski, T. V. (2010). *The fluent reader: Oral and silent reading strategies for building fluency, word recognition, and comprehension* (2nd ed.). New York: Scholastic.

Rasinski, T., & Padak, N. (2005a). *3-minute reading assessments: Word recognition, fluency, and comprehension for grades 1–4*. New York: Scholastic.

Rasinski, T., & Padak, N. (2005b). *3-minute reading assessments: Word recognition, fluency, and comprehension for grades 5–8*. New York: Scholastic.

Rasinski, T. V., & Padak, N. D. (2013). *From phonics to fluency: Effective teaching of decoding and reading fluency in the elementary school* (3rd ed.). Boston: Pearson.

Rowling, J. K. (1999). *Harry Potter and the chamber of secrets*. New York: Scholastic.

Ryan, P. M. (2002). *Esperanza rising*. New York: Scholastic.

Sachar, L. (2008). *Holes*. New York: Farrar, Straus & Giroux.

Samuels, S. J. (1979). The method of repeated readings. *The Reading Teacher, 32*, 403–408.

Samuels, S. J. (2004). Toward a theory of automatic information processing in reading, revisited. In R. B. Ruddell & N. J. Unrau (Eds.), *Theoretical models and processes of reading* (5th ed., pp. 1127–1148). Newark, DE: International Reading Association.

Schreider, P. A. (1991). Understanding prosody's role in reading acquisition. *Theory Into Practice, 30,* 158–164.

Spandel, V. (2009). *Creating writers through 6-trait writing assessment and instruction* (5th ed.). Boston: Allyn & Bacon/Pearson.

Spinelli, J. (2002). *Loser.* New York: HarperCollins.

Stanovich, K. E. (1992). Speculations on the causes and consequences of individual differences in early reading acquisition. In P. B. Gough, L. C. Ehri, & R. Treiman (Eds.), *Reading acquisition* (pp. 307–342). Hillsdale, NJ: Erlbaum.

Tuchman, G. (1997). *Hermit's shiny shell.* New York: Macmillan/McGraw-Hill.

Viorst, J. (2009). *Alexander and the terrible, horrible, no good, very bad day.* New York: Atheneum.

Wood, A. (2005). *The napping house.* San Diego: Harcourt.

Yolen, J. (2007). *Owl moon.* New York: Philomel.

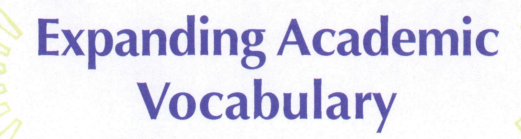

Chapter 7

Expanding Academic Vocabulary

PLAN: Preview the Learning Outcomes

After studying this chapter, you'll be prepared to respond to these points:

7.1 Explain what *academic vocabulary* means, and cite some examples.

7.2 Provide examples of word-study concepts.

7.3 Discuss how to teach academic vocabulary.

The Word Wizards Club. Mrs. Sanom, a K–6 literacy resource teacher, sponsors an after-school Word Wizards Club for fifth and sixth graders; the club meets for an hour every Wednesday afternoon. Nineteen students are club members this year, and many of them are struggling English learners. Mrs. Sanom teaches vocabulary lessons during the club meetings. She focuses on a different word-study topic each week; the topics have included writing alliterations, choosing synonyms carefully, applying context clues to figure out unfamiliar words, using a dictionary and a thesaurus, understanding multiple meanings of words, choosing between homophones, and adding prefixes and suffixes to words.

She devised this club because many students have limited vocabularies, which affects their reading achievement. She displays this banner in her classroom: "Knowing Words Makes You Powerful." In the reflections that club members write at the end of the school year, they report that they've learned to pay more attention to words an author uses, and they've become more effective at using context clues to figure out the meaning of unfamiliar words. Most importantly, the students say that participation in the Word Wizards Club gives them an appreciation for words that will last a lifetime. Rosie writes:

I love being a Word Wizard. I learned lots of new words and that makes me smart. I have a favorite word that is <u>hypothesis</u>. Did you know that I am always looking for more new words to learn? My Tío Mario gave me a dictionary because I wanted it real bad. I like looking for words in the dictionary and I like words with lots of syllables the best. I want to be in the club next year in 6th grade. Ok?

At the first club meeting, Mrs. Sanom read aloud *Miss Alaineus: A Vocabulary Disaster* (Frasier, 2007), a touching story of a girl named Sage who loves words. In the story, Sage misunderstands the meaning of *miscellaneous*, but what begins as embarrassment turns into victory when she wins an award for her costume in the school's annual vocabulary parade. The students talked about the story in a **grand conversation**, and they decided that they want to dress in costumes and have a vocabulary parade themselves, just as Mrs. Sanom knew they would. "I like to dress in vocabulary costumes, too," Mrs. Sanom explained. "In fact, I plan to dress up in clothes or a hat that represents a vocabulary word at each club meeting." With that introduction, she reached into a shopping bag and pulled out an oversized, wrinkled shirt and put it on over her clothes. "Here's my costume," she announced. "Can you guess the word?" She modeled the shirt, trying to smooth the wrinkles, until a student guessed the word *wrinkled*.

The students talked about *wrinkle*, forms of the word (*wrinkled, unwrinkled,* and *wrinkling*), and the meanings. They checked the definitions of *wrinkle* in the dictionary. They understood the first meaning, "a crease or fold in clothes or skin," but the second meaning—"a clever idea or trick"—was more difficult. Mrs. Sanom called their idea to have a vocabulary parade "a new wrinkle" in her plans for the club, and then the students began to grasp the meaning.

The borders of each page in *Miss Alaineus* are decorated with words beginning with a specific letter; the first page has words beginning with A, the second page B, and so on. To immerse students in words, Mrs. Sanom asked them each to choose a letter from a box of plastic letters, turn to that page in the book, and then choose a word beginning with that letter from the border to use in an activity. The words they chose included *awesome, berserk, catastrophe,* and *dwindle*. Students wrote the word on the first page of their Word Wizard Notebooks (small, spiral-bound notebooks that Mrs. Sanom purchased for them), checked its meaning in a dictionary and wrote it beside the word, and then drew a picture to illustrate the meaning. While they worked, Mrs. Sanom wrote the words on the alphabetized **word wall** she posted in the classroom. Afterward, the students shared their words and illustrations in a **tea party** activity.

At today's club meeting, Mrs. Sanom is wearing a broad-brimmed hat with two wrecked cars and a stop sign attached. The students check out Mrs. Sanom's costume because they know it represents a word—and that word is the topic of today's meeting. They quickly begin guessing words: "Is it *crash*?" Oscar asks. "I think the word is *accident*. My dad had a car accident last week," says Danielle. Ramon suggests, "Those cars are *wrecked*. Is that the word?" Mrs. Sanom commends the club members for their good guesses and says they're on the right track. To provide a little help, she draws a row of nine letter boxes on the whiteboard and fills in the first letter and the last four letters. Then Martha guesses it—*collision*. Next, the teacher begins a cluster with the word *collision* written in the middle circle and related words on each ray. Students compare the noun *collision* and the verb *collide*. They also check the dictionary and a thesaurus for more information and write *crash, accident, wreck, hit, smashup,* and *collide* on the rays to complete the cluster. They talk about how and when to use *collide* and *collision*. Ramon offers, "I know a sentence: On 9-11, the terrorists' airplanes collided with the World Trade Center."

Mrs. Sanom explains that ships can be involved in collisions, too: A ship can hit another ship, or it can collide with something else in the water—an iceberg, for example. Several students know about the *Titanic*, and they share what they know about that ship's fateful ocean crossing. Mrs. Sanom selects *Story of the Titanic* (Kentley, 2001) from her text set of books about the *Titanic* and shows photos and drawings of the ship to provide more background information. They make a **KWL** chart, listing what they know in the K column and questions they want to find answers for in the W column. The students also make individual charts in their Word Wizard Notebooks.

Next, Mrs. Sanom projects a list of words on a whiteboard—some about the *Titanic* article they'll read and some not—for an **exclusion brainstorming** activity; the words include *unsinkable*, *crew*, *liner*, *passengers*, *voyage*, *airplane*, *catastrophe*, *mountain*, *lifeboat*, and *general*. The students predict which words relate to the article and which don't. The word *general* stumps them because they think of it as an adjective meaning "having to do with the whole, not specific." A student checks the dictionary to learn about the second meaning—"a high-ranking military officer" (noun). The students are still confused, but after reading the article, they realize that the word *general* isn't related: The officer in charge of the *Titanic* (or any ship, for that matter) is called a *captain*.

Mrs. Sanom passes out copies of the one-page article and reads it aloud while students follow along. They discuss the article, talking and asking more questions about the tragedy. Then they complete the L section of the KWL chart and the exclusion brainstorming activity. Because the students are very interested in learning more about the disaster, Mrs. Sanom introduces her text set of narrative and nonfiction books about the *Titanic*, including *Inside the Titanic* (Brewster, 1997), *Tonight on the Titanic* (Osborne & Osborne, 1995), *Titanic: A Nonfiction Companion to Tonight on the Titanic* (Osborne & Osborne, 2002), *On Board the Titanic: What It Was Like When the Great Liner Sank* (Tanaka, 1996), and *Voyage on the Great Titanic: The Diary of Margaret Ann Brady* (White, 1998). She invites the students to spend the last few minutes of the club meeting choosing a book from the text set to take home to read before the next meeting.

Mrs. Sanom wears a different costume each week. Here are her favorites:

bejeweled:	A silky shirt with "jewels" glued across the front
champion:	Racing shorts, a tee shirt, and a medal on a ribbon worn around her neck
hocus-pocus:	A black top hat with a stuffed rabbit stuck inside, white gloves, and a magic wand
international:	A dress decorated with the flags of many countries and a globe cut in half for a hat
slick:	A black leather jacket, sunglasses, and hair slicked back with mousse
transparent:	A clear plastic raincoat, clear plastic gloves, and a clear shower cap
vacant:	A bird cage with a "for rent" sign worn as a hat with an artificial bird sitting on her shoulder

One week, however, she forgets to bring a costume, so after a bit of quick thinking, she decides to feature the word *ordinary*, and she wears her everyday clothes as her costume!

For their 17th weekly club meeting, Mrs. Sanom dressed as a queen with a flowing purple robe and a tiara on her head. The focus of the week was words beginning with Q, the 17th letter of the alphabet. They began by talking about queens—both historical queens such as Queen Isabella of Spain, who financed Christopher Columbus's voyage to the New World, and queens who are alive today. Next, Mrs. Sanom began a list of Q words with *queen*, and the students added words to it. They checked the Q page in alphabet books and examined dictionary entries for Q words. They chose interesting words, including *quadruped*, *quadruplet*, *qualify*, *quest*, *quarantine*, *quintet*, *quiver*, *quench*, and *quotation*. After they had more than 20 words on their list, Mrs. Sanom asked each student to choose a Q word, study it, and make a square poster to share what he or she learned. Afterward, Mrs. Sanom collected the posters, made a quilt from them, and hung the quilt on the wall outside the classroom. To see a student's square about *quadruped*, check the figure A Quilt Square; it documents that student's understanding of root words.

The Word Wizards make and wear word bracelets to highlight special words; in October, students made bracelets that spell the word they'd chosen to describe themselves, such as *genius*, *ornery*, or *sincere*. Mrs. Sanom's word was *sassy*, and she demonstrated how to make a bracelet using small alphabet beads strung on an elastic string. Then students followed her steps to make their own bracelets, which they proudly wear and show off to their classmates. In February, they studied patriotic words, such as *allegiance*, *citizen*, *equality*, *independence*, and *republic*, and chose a word for a second bracelet. They chose words after reading books with patriotic themes, such as Lynne Cheney's *America: A Patriotic Primer* (2002) and *A Is for America: An American Alphabet* (Scillian, 2001). For their third word bracelet, they chose the most interesting word they'd collected in their Word Wizard Notebooks, including *valiant*, *phenomenon*, *plethora*, *incredulous*, *mischievous*, and *razzle-dazzle*.

A QUILT SQUARE

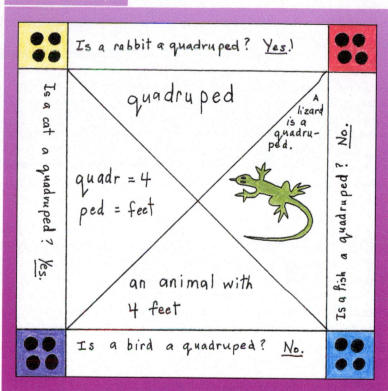

The vocabulary parade is the highlight of the year. Every club member creates a costume and participates in the parade. Mrs. Sanom dresses as a wizard—a word wizard, that is—and she leads the parade from classroom to classroom in the school's intermediate wing. The students dress as *camouflage, victory, shimmer, monarch, liberty, uncomfortable, fortune, emerald,* and *twilight,* for instance, and they carry word cards so that everyone will know the words they represent. As they tour each classroom, the students talk about their words. The club members' parents come to school to view the parade, and a local television station films it for the evening news.

 STANDARDS CHECK!

Mrs. Sanom addressed the Common Core State Standards as she developed her students' vocabulary knowledge in the vignette you've just read. Review the fifth grade literacy Standards document online at http://www.corestandards.org/ELA-Literacy, and identify the Standards that Mrs. Sanom addressed through her vocabulary activities. Create your list, and compare it with Mrs. Sanom's.

*C*apable students' vocabularies grow at an astonishing rate—about 3,000 to 4,000 words a year, or roughly 8 to 10 new words every day. By the time they graduate from high school, their vocabularies reach 25,000 to 50,000 words or more. These students learn the meanings of words by being immersed in a word-rich environment, through lots of daily independent reading, teacher read-alouds, and explicit instruction. They learn most words incidentally through reading and family activities, but teachers expand students' vocabulary by teaching specific words and word-learning strategies and by fostering students' interest in words (Graves, 2006). In the vignette, Mrs. Sanom engaged her fifth and sixth graders with words as they participated in lively Word Wizards Club activities.

Vocabulary knowledge and reading achievement are closely related: Students with larger vocabularies are more capable readers, and they know more strategies for figuring out the meanings of unfamiliar words than less capable readers do (Graves, 2006). One reason why capable readers have larger vocabularies is that they do more reading. This idea is an example of the Matthew effect, which suggests that "the rich get richer and the poor get poorer" (Stanovich, 1986): Capable readers get better because they read more, and the books they read are more challenging, with academic vocabulary words. The gulf between more capable and less capable readers grows each year because less capable readers do less reading and the books they read have fewer grade-level academic words.

Vocabulary learning can't be left to chance because students' word knowledge affects whether they comprehend what they're reading, write effectively, and learn content area information (Stahl & Nagy, 2006). Children come to school with varying levels of word knowledge, both in the number of words they know and in the depth of their understanding. Students from low-income homes have less than half of the vocabulary that more affluent children possess, and some researchers estimate that they know one quarter to one fifth of the words that their classmates do. To make matters worse, this gap widens each year (Cunningham, 2009). Therefore, it's essential that teachers recognize the impact of socioeconomic level on students' vocabulary knowledge, support all students' vocabulary growth, and emphasize word learning for students who know fewer words.

Academic Vocabulary

The words that are frequently used in language arts, social studies, science, and math are called **academic vocabulary** (Burke, 2008). These words are found in books and textbooks that students read; teachers use them in minilessons and discussions, and students use them in classroom assignments and are expected to understand them in high-stakes tests. Here's a sample of academic vocabulary:

Primary Grades	Middle Grades	Upper Grades
character	bias	apartheid
graph	colonial	biome
minus	idiom	irony
pattern	justify	jargon
pledge	parasite	perpendicular
sentence	prey	plagiarize
vote	semicolon	variable

Knowing these words is especially useful because they often have multiple forms and are used in different ways. Some are technical words that are limited to specific content areas, but others are used more broadly. In addition, a few are common words being used in new ways. Students' knowledge of academic vocabulary is part of their background knowledge, and it affects their school success (Marzano & Pickering, 2005).

Three Tiers of Words

Beck, McKeown, and Kucan (2002) have devised a tool to assist teachers in identifying academic vocabulary and choosing which words to study. The researchers divide vocabulary words into three tiers or levels:

Tier 1: Basic Words. These common words are used socially, in informal conversation at home and on the playground; examples include *animal*, *clean*, and *laughing*. Native English-speaking students rarely require instruction about the meanings of these words.

Tier 2: Academic Vocabulary. These words have wide application in school and are used more frequently in written than in oral language. Some are related to literacy concepts—*apostrophe*, *paragraph*, and *preposition*, for instance—or they're found in literature, such as *greedy*, *keen*, and *evidence*. Other academic vocabulary words are more sophisticated terms related to familiar concepts. For example, students understand the concept of *smell*, but they may not be not familiar with *scent*, *odor*, or *aroma*; teaching these words expands students' knowledge and has a powerful impact on learning.

Tier 3: Specialized Terms. These technical words are content-specific and often abstract; examples include *minuend*, *osmosis*, and *suffrage*. They aren't used frequently enough to devote time to teaching them when they come up during language arts, but they're the words that teachers explicitly teach during thematic units and in content area classes.

As teachers choose words for instruction and word-study activities, they focus on Tier 2 words even though words representing all three levels are written on word walls and explained when necessary.

During a fifth grade unit on America in the 20th century, students learned to sing Woody Guthrie's folk ballad "This Land Is Your Land" (Guthrie, 2008) and then read Bonnie Christensen's biography, *Woody Guthrie: Poet of the People* (2001). The students created a **word wall** that included these words:

Check the Compendium of Instructional Procedures, which follows Chapter 12.

ballads	Great Depression	nightmare	spirit
celebrate	guitar	ordinary	stock market
criss-cross	hardship	original	tragedy
depression	harmonica	rallies	unfair
desperate	hitchhiked	restless	unions
devastated	lonesome	scorn	unsanitary
drought	migrant	severe	wandering
Dust Bowl	migration	sorrow	worries

From this list, the teacher, Mr. Perez, identified some Tier 1, 2, and 3 words:

Tier 1 words: *guitar, harmonica, worries, nightmare, unfair, celebrate*
Tier 2 words: *ordinary, spirit, desperate, original, sorrow, tragedy*
Tier 3 words: *drought, Dust Bowl, stock market, Great Depression, unions, unsanitary*

Only one Tier 1 word—*harmonica*—needed to be taught, so Mr. Perez invited a friend who played the instrument to visit the classroom, and he focused on teaching both Tier 2 and Tier 3 words because this was a social studies unit.

Nurturing English Learners

How do teachers teach vocabulary? English learners often need more explicit instruction on words than native English speakers do. Sometimes English learners need only to have a word translated; but at other times, instruction is necessary because they're confused about a new meaning of a familiar word, or they're unfamiliar with both the underlying concept and words that describe it.

TIER 1 WORDS. Tier 1 words are easier for English learners to learn because they often know these words in their native language; what they don't know are the equivalent English words. If teachers speak students' native language, they can translate the words and help students learn these English equivalents. English-speaking teachers often use pictures, pantomime, and demonstration to explain the words. It's often helpful for teachers to put together collections of small objects and pictures to share with students during literature focus units and thematic units.

TIER 2 WORDS. To build background knowledge, teachers preteach some unfamiliar words, including essential Tier 2 words, before students read a book or study a topic. Later, through explicit instruction and a variety of word-study activities, they teach other Tier 2 words. In addition, Calderón (2007) points out that ELs need to understand transition words and phrases, words with multiple meanings, and English words with cognates. Transition words, such as *consequently*, *yet*, *likewise*, *against*, *meanwhile*, *afterward*, and *finally*, are used to bridge ideas in sentences, paragraphs, and longer texts; teachers can help ELs recognize these words and phrases, understand their meaning, and use them in their own writing.

Learning new meanings for familiar words is another Tier 2 activity. Some common words, such as *key*, *soft*, and *ready*, have less frequently used meanings that confuse English learners even though they're usually familiar with one or two of the meanings. Students also learn how to choose among related words. For example, *instrument* means a device for doing work; *tool* and *utensil* are also devices for doing work, but they don't mean exactly the same thing. *Instruments*, such as stethoscopes and scalpels, are used for doing complicated work; *tools*, such as hammers and screwdrivers, are used for skilled jobs, and *utensils* are simple devices, such as whisks and spoons, for working in the kitchen. Teachers also point out cognates, English words that are related to words in students' native language. Many Tier 2 words are Latin-based, so it's important to teach English learners who speak Spanish, Portuguese, Italian, and French to ask themselves whether an unfamiliar word is similar to a word in their native language.

TIER 3 WORDS. It's less important to teach these technical words because of their limited usefulness, and only a few words have cognates that students would know. Calderón (2007) recommends that teachers translate the words or briefly explain them. However, during thematic units, teachers do teach Tier 3 words that are important to understanding the big ideas being studied through a combination of instruction and word-study activities, including making word posters, doing **word sorts**, and completing **semantic feature analyses**. 🐌

Levels of Word Knowledge

Students develop knowledge about a word gradually, through repeated oral and written exposure to it. They move from not knowing a word at all to recognizing that they've seen the word before, and then to a level of partial knowledge where they have a general sense of the word or know one meaning. Finally, students know the word fully: They know multiple meanings of the word and can use it in a variety of ways (Nagy, 1988). Here are the levels:

Unknown Word. Students don't recognize the word.

Initial Recognition. Students have seen or heard the word or can pronounce it, but they don't know the meaning.

Partial Word Knowledge. Students know one meaning of the word and can use it in a sentence.

Full Word Knowledge. Students know more than one meaning of the word and can use it in several ways. (Allen, 1999)

Once students reach the third level, they can usually understand the word in context and use it in writing. In fact, they don't reach the fourth level with every word they learn, but when they do develop full word knowledge, they're described as flexible word users because they understand the core meaning of a word and how it changes in different contexts (Stahl, 1999).

Word Consciousness

Another component of vocabulary instruction is developing students' **word consciousness**, their interest in learning and using words (Graves & Watts-Taffe, 2002). According to Scott and Nagy (2004), word consciousness increases students' word knowledge and their interest in learning academic vocabulary. Students who have word consciousness exemplify these characteristics:

❧ Students use words skillfully, understanding the nuances of word meanings.
❧ Students gain a deep appreciation of words and value them.
❧ Students are aware of differences between social and academic language.
❧ Students understand the power of word choice.
❧ Students are motivated to learn the meaning of unfamiliar words.

Word consciousness is important because vocabulary knowledge is generative—that is, it transfers to and enhances students' learning of other words (Scott & Nagy, 2004).

The goal is for students to become more aware of words, manipulate them playfully, and appreciate their power. Teachers foster word consciousness in a variety of ways, as Mrs. Sanom did in the vignette. Most importantly, they model interest in words and precise use of vocabulary (Graves, 2006). To encourage students' interest in words, teachers share books about words, including *Miss Alaineus: A Vocabulary Disaster* (Frasier, 2007) and *Baloney (Henry P.)* (Scieszka, 2005). Booklist: Vocabulary presents more books about words and word-study concepts. Next, teachers call students' attention to words by highlighting words of the day, posting words on word walls, and having students collect words from books they're reading.

Teachers also promote wordplay by sharing riddles, jokes, puns, songs, and poems and encouraging students to experiment with these types of wordplay:

Alliteration. Students repeat words with the same beginning consonant or vowel sound in words within a phrase or sentence. For example: *now or never, do or die,* and *Peter Piper picked a peck of pickled peppers.* Alliterative sentences are often called *tongue twisters.*

Eponyms. Students recognize that people's names can become words. For example: *teddy bear, sandwich, maverick, pasteurization,* and *Ferris Wheel.*

Hyperbole. Students create exaggerated statements. For example: *I almost died laughing, my feet are killing me,* and *I'm so hungry I could eat a horse.*

Onomatopoeia. Students use words that imitate sounds. For example: *tick-tock, kerplunk,* and *sizzling.*

Oxymorons. Students combine two normally contradictory words to create a paradoxical image. For example: *jumbo shrimp, pretty ugly,* and *deafening silence.* Oxymorons are usually inadvertent errors, but sometimes they're used intentionally.

Palindromes. Students notice words and phrases that read the same forward and backward. For example: *mom, civic,* and *a man, a plan, a canal—Panama.*

Booklist Vocabulary

CATEGORY	BOOKS
Antonyms	Carle, E. (2007). *Eric Carle's opposites*. New York: Grosset & Dunlap. P
	Cleary, B. P. (2008). *Stop and go, yes and no: What is an antonym?* Minneapolis, MN: First Avenue Editions. PM
	Hoban, T. (1997). *Exactly the opposite*. New York: Greenwillow. P
	Scholastic dictionary of synonyms, antonyms, and homonyms. (2001). New York: Scholastic. MU
	Wilbur, R. (2006). *Opposites, more opposites, and a few differences*. New York: Sandpiper. PM
Figurative Meanings	Brennan-Nelson, D. (2011). *My teacher likes to say*. Ann Arbor, MI: Sleeping Bear Press. (And other books in the series.) PM
	Cleary, B. P. (2011). *Skin like milk, hair of silk. What are similes and metaphors?* Minneapolis, MN: Millbrook Press. M
	Gwynne, F. (1988). *A chocolate moose for dinner*. New York: Aladdin Books. MU
	Gwynne, F. (1988). *The king who rained*. New York: Aladdin Books. MU
	Leedy, L. (2002). *Crazy like a fox: A simile story*. New York: Holiday House. PM
	Leedy, L. (2003). *There's a frog in my throat! 440 animal sayings a little bird told me*. New York: Holiday House. PM
	Loewen, N. J. (2011). *You're toast and other metaphors we adore*. North Mankato, MN: Picture Window Books. M
	Terban, M. (1993). *It figures! Fun figures of speech*. New York: Sandpiper. MU
	Terban, M. (2006). *Scholastic dictionary of idioms*. New York: Scholastic. MU
	Terban, M. (2007). *In a pickle and other funny idioms*. New York: Sandpiper. M
	Terban, M. (2007). *Mad as a wet hen and other funny idioms*. New York: Sandpiper. M
History of English	Brook, D. (1998). *The journey of English*. New York: Clarion Books. M
	Gorrell, G. K. (2009). *Say what? The weird and mysterious journey of the English language*. Toronto, ON: Tundra Books. MU
Homonyms	Barretta, G. (2010). *Dear deer: A book of homophones*. New York: Square Fish Books. PM
	Cleary, B. P. (2007). *How much can a bare bear bear? What are homonyms and homophones?* Minneapolis, MN: First Avenue Editions. M
	Loewen, N. (2007). *If you were a homonym*. North Mankato, MN: Picture Window Books. M
	Scholastic dictionary of synonyms, antonyms, and homonyms. (2001). New York: Scholastic. MU
	Terban, M. (2007). *Eight ate: A feast of homonyn riddles*. New York: Sandpiper. MU
Root Words and Affixes	Aboff, M. (2008). *If you were a prefix*. North Mankato, MN: Picture Window Books. M
	Aboff, M. (2008). *If you were a suffix*. North Mankato, MN: Picture Window Books. M
	Fine, E. H. (2004). *Cryptomania! Teleporting into Greek and Latin with the Cryptokids*. Berkeley, CA: Tricycle Press. MU
Synonyms	Cleary, B. P. (2007). *Pitch and throw, grasp and know: What is a synonym?* Minneapolis, MN: Millbrook Press. PM
	Cleary, B. P. (2010). *Stroll and walk, babble and talk: More about synonyms*. Minneapolis, MN: Millbrook Press. PM
	Dahl, M. (2007). *If I were a synonym*. North Mankato, MN: Picture Window Books. M
	Scholastic dictionary of synonyms, antonyms, and homonyms. (2001). New York: Scholastic. MU
Word Fun	Banks, K. (2006). *Max's words*. New York: Farrar, Straus & Giroux. P
	Clements, A. (1998). *Frindle*. New York: Atheneum. M
	Frasier, D. (2007). *Miss Alaineus: A vocabulary disaster*. New York: Sandpiper. MU
	Frasier, D. (2010). *A fabulous fair alphabet*. New York: Beach Lane Books. PM
	Herzog, B. (2004). *H is for home run: A baseball alphabet*. Ann Arbor, MI: Sleeping Bear Press. MU
	O'Connor, J. (2008). *Fancy Nancy's favorite fancy words: From accessories to zany*. New York: HarperCollins. PM
	Scieszka, J. (2005). *Baloney (Henry P.)*. New York: Puffin Books. M

P = primary grades (K–2); M = middle grades (3–5); U = upper grades (6–8)

Personification. Students endow inanimate objects with human traits or abilities. For example: *the old VW's engine coughed, raindrops danced on my umbrella,* and *fear knocked on the door.*

Portmanteau. Students commonly use words that were created by fusing two words to combine the meaning of both words. For example: *spork* (*spoon + fork*), *brunch* (*breakfast + lunch*), and *smog* (*smoke + fog*). Sometimes they also create their own portmanteau words. This wordplay form was invented by Lewis Carroll in *Jabberwocky*.

Spoonerisms. Students switch sounds in words, often with a humorous effect. For example: *butterfly–flutterby, take a shower–shake a tower,* and *save the whales–wave the sails.* These "slips of the tongue," named for Reverend William Spooner (1844–1930), usually occur when a person is speaking quickly.

As students learn about these types of wordplay, they become more powerful word users.

 MONITOR: Check Your Understanding 7.1

Word-Study Concepts

It's not enough to have students memorize one definition of a word; to develop full word knowledge, they need to learn more about a word (Stahl & Nagy, 2006). Consider the word *brave*: It can be used as an adjective, a noun, or a verb. It often means "showing no fear," but it can also mean an "American Indian warrior" or "to challenge or defy." These forms are related to the first meaning: *braver, bravest, bravely,* and *bravery.* Synonyms related to the first meaning include *courageous, bold, fearless, daring, intrepid, heroic,* and *valiant*; antonyms include *cowardly* and *frightened.* Our word *brave* comes from the Italian word *bravo.* Interestingly, the Italian word *bravo* and a related form—*bravissimo*—have entered English directly, and they're used to express great approval; these words mean "excellent," an obsolete meaning of *brave.* In addition, there's *bravado,* a Spanish word that means "a pretense of courage." As students learn some of this information about *brave,* they're better able to understand the word and use it orally and in writing.

As students learn about a word, they acquire a wide range of information. They learn one or more meanings for a word and synonyms and antonyms to compare and contrast meanings. Sometimes they confuse a word they're learning with a homonym that sounds or is spelled the same. Students also learn about idioms and figurative sayings that make our language more colorful. The results of a seventh grader's investigation of the word *vaporize* are shown in Figure 7–1.

Multiple Meanings of Words

Many words have more than one meaning. For some words, multiple meanings develop for the noun and verb forms, but sometimes additional meanings develop through wordplay and figurative language. Think about the word *sing*: The most common meaning is about musical sounds; both birds and people sing when they use their voices to make music. However, when criminals sing, the meaning is different: They sing when they provide evidence and information to the police. Multiple meanings develop in other ways, too. The word *bank,* for example, has these meanings:

a piled-up mass of snow or clouds
the slope of land beside a lake or river

FIGURE 7–1 A Word Map

Morphemic Analysis vapor + ize	Root Word vapor	Suffix ize
		It is used to change a noun into a verb.

VAPORIZE

To change from a solid into a vapor (gas) (verb)

Word History	Related Words	Figurative Use
It became a word in the 1600's. It came from the Latin word "steam".	evaporate vaporizer vaporous	The boy's thoughts vaporized and he couldn't remember the answer.

the slope of a road on a turn
the lateral tilting of an airplane in a turn
to cover a fire with ashes for slow burning
a business establishment that receives and lends money
a container money is saved in
a supply for use in emergencies (e.g., a blood bank)
a place for storage (e.g., a computer's memory bank)
to count on
similar things arranged in a row (e.g., a bank of elevators)
to arrange things in a row

You may be surprised that there are at least a dozen meanings for this common word. Some are nouns and others are verbs, but grammatical form alone doesn't account for so many meanings.

The meanings of *bank* come from three sources. The first five meanings come from a Viking word, and they're related because they all deal with something slanted or making a slanted motion. The next five come from the Italian word *banca*, a money changer's table. These meanings deal with financial banking except for the 10th meaning, "to count on," which requires a bit more thought. We use the saying "to bank on" figuratively to mean "to depend on," but it began more literally from the actual counting of money on a table. The last two meanings come from the French word *banc*, meaning "bench." Words acquired multiple meanings as society became more complex and finer shades of meaning were necessary; for example, the meanings of *bank* as an emergency supply and a storage place are fairly new. As with many words with multiple meanings, it's just a linguistic accident that three original words from different languages with related meanings came to be spelled the same way (Tompkins & Yaden, 1986). A list of other common words with more than five meanings is shown in Figure 7–2.

Students gradually acquire additional meanings for words, and they usually learn these new meanings through reading. When a familiar word is used in a new way, students often notice the new application and may be curious enough to check the meaning in a dictionary.

FIGURE 7-2 Common Words With Multiple Meanings

act	drive	lay	place	set	strike
air	dry	leave	plant	sharp	stroke
away	dull	line	plate	shine	strong
bad	eye	low	play	shoot	stuff
bar	face	make	point	short	sweep
base	fail	man	post	side	sweet
black	fair	mark	print	sight	swing
blow	fall	mind	quiet	sign	take
boat	fast	mine	rain	sing	thick
break	fire	natural	raise	sink	thing
carry	fly	new	range	slip	think
case	good	nose	rear	small	throw
catch	green	note	rest	sound	tie
change	hand	now	return	spin	tight
charge	have	off	rich	spread	time
check	head	open	ride	spring	touch
clear	heel	out	right	square	tough
color	high	paper	ring	stamp	train
count	hold	part	rise	star	trip
cover	hot	pass	roll	stay	turn
crack	house	pay	rule	step	under
cross	keep	pick	run	stick	up
crown	key	picture	scale	stiff	watch
cut	knock	piece	score	stock	way
draw	know	pitch	serve	stop	wear

Synonyms: Words With Similar Meanings

Words that have nearly the same meaning as other words are **synonyms**. English has so many synonyms because numerous words have been borrowed from other languages. Synonyms are useful because they're more precise. Think of all the synonyms for the word *cold*: *cool, chilly, frigid, icy, frosty,* and *freezing*. Each word has a different shade of meaning: *Cool* means moderately cold; *chilly* is uncomfortably cold; *frigid* is intensely cold; *icy* means very cold; *frosty* means covered with frost; and *freezing* is so cold that water changes into ice. English would be limited if we had only the word *cold*.

Teachers should carefully articulate the differences among synonyms. Nagy (1988) emphasizes that teachers should focus on teaching concepts and related words, not just provide single-word definitions using synonyms. For example, to tell a student that *frigid* means *cold* provides only limited information. And, when a student says, "I want my sweater because it's frigid in here," it shows that he or she doesn't understand the different degrees of cold; there's a big difference between *chilly* and *frigid*.

Antonyms: Words That Mean the Opposite

Words that express opposite meanings are **antonyms**. For the word *loud*, some antonyms are *soft, subdued, quiet, silent, inaudible, sedate, somber, dull,* and *colorless*. These antonyms express shades of meaning just as synonyms do, and some opposites are more appropriate for one meaning of *loud* than for another. When *loud* means *gaudy*, for instance, antonyms are *somber, dull,* and *colorless*; when *loud* means *noisy*, the opposites are *quiet, silent,* and *inaudible*.

Watch as a second grade teacher completes a graphic organizer called a "Word Snapshot" with a small group of children. How does this activity reinforce these children's understanding of a new vocabulary word?

To locate both synonyms and antonyms, students learn to use a thesaurus. Three excellent reference books are *A First Thesaurus* (Wittels & Greisman, 2001), *Scholastic Children's Thesaurus* (Bollard, 2006), and *The American Heritage Children's Thesaurus* (Hellweg, 2009). Students need to learn how to use these handy references to locate more effective words when they're revising their writing and during word-study activities. Teachers also share books about synonyms and antonyms; check Booklist: Vocabulary for recommendations.

Homonyms: Words That Confuse

Homonyms are confusing because even though these words have different meanings, they're either pronounced or spelled the same as other words. **Homophones** are words that sound alike but are spelled differently, such as *right–write*, *air–heir*, *to–too–two*, and *there–their–they're*. A list of homophones is presented in Figure 7–3. Sometimes students confuse the meanings of these words, but more often they confuse their spellings. Most homophones are linguistic accidents, but *stationary* and *stationery* share an interesting history: *Stationery*, meaning paper and books, developed

---

FIGURE 7–3 Homophones

air–heir	creak–creek	hour–our	peace–piece	chute–shoot
allowed–aloud	days–daze	knead–need	peak–peek–pique	side–sighed
ant–aunt	dear–deer	knew–new	peal–peel	slay–sleigh
ate–eight	dew–do–due	knight–night	pedal–peddle–petal	soar–sore
ball–bawl	die–dye	knot–not	plain–plane	soared–sword
bare–bear	doe–dough	know–no	pleas–please	sole–soul
be–bee	ewe–you	lead–led	pole–poll	some–sum
beat–beet	eye–I	leak–leek	poor–pore–pour	son–sun
berry–bury	fair–fare	lie–lye	praise–prays–preys	stairs–stares
billed–build	feat–feet	loan–lone	presence–presents	stake–steak
blew–blue	find–fined	made–maid	pride–pried	stationary–stationery
boar–bore	fir–fur	mail–male	prince–prints	steal–steel
board–bored	flair–flare	main–mane	principal–principle	straight–strait
bough–bow	flea–flee	manner–manor	profit–prophet	suite–sweet
brake–break	flew–flu	marshal–martial	quarts–quartz	tail–tale
brews–bruise	flour–flower	meat–meet–mete	rain–reign–rein	taught–taut
bridal–bridle	for–fore–four	medal–meddle–metal	raise–rays–raze	tear–tier
brows–browse	forth–fourth	might–mite	rap–wrap	their–there–they're
buy–by–bye	foul–fowl	mind–mined	read–red	threw–through
capital–capitol	gorilla–guerrilla	miner–minor	read–reed	throne–thrown
ceiling–sealing	grate–great	missed–mist	right–rite–write	tide–tied
cell–sell	grill–grille	moan–mown	ring–wring	to–too–two
cellar–seller	groan–grown	morning–mourning	road–rode–rowed	toad–toed–towed
cent–scent–sent	guessed–guest	muscle–mussel	role–roll	toe–tow
chews–choose	hair–hare	naval–navel	root–route	troop–troupe
chic–sheik	hall–haul	none–nun	rose–rows	vain–vane–vein
chili–chilly	hay–hey	oar–or–ore	rung–wrung	wade–weighed
choral–coral	heal–heel	one–won	sail–sale	waist–waste
chord–cord–cored	hear–here	pail–pale	scene–seen	wait–weight
cite–sight–site	heard–herd	pain–pane	sea–see	wares–wears
close–clothes	hi–high	pair–pare–pear	seam–seem	way–weigh
coarse–course	hoarse–horse	passed–past	serf–surf	weak–week
colonel–kernel	hole–whole	patience–patients	sew–so–sow	wood–would

from *stationary*. In medieval England, merchants traveled from town to town selling their wares. The merchant who sold paper goods was the first to set up shop in one town. His shop was "stationary" because it didn't move, and he came to be the "stationer." The spelling difference between the two words signifies the semantic difference. In contrast, words with identical spellings but different meanings and pronunciations, such as the noun and verb forms of *wind* and the noun and adjective forms of *minute*, are **homographs**. Other examples include *live*, *read*, *bow*, *conduct*, *present*, and *record*.

A variety of books for children highlight confusing homonyms; two of the best are Fred Gwynne's *The King Who Rained* (2006) and *A Chocolate Moose for Dinner* (2005). Check Booklist: Vocabulary for additional recommendations.

Primary grade teachers introduce homonyms and teach the easier pairs, including *see–sea*, *I–eye*, *right–write*, and *dear–deer*. In the upper grades, teachers focus on homographs and the homophones that students continue to confuse, such as *there–their–they're* and the more sophisticated pairs, including *morning–mourning*, *flair–flare*, and *complement–compliment*. Teachers teach minilessons to explain the concept of homophones and homographs and have students make charts of the homophones and homographs; calling students' attention to the differences in spelling, meaning, and pronunciation helps to clarify the words. This explicit instruction is especially important for English learners (Jacobson, Lapp, & Flood, 2007). Students can also make homonym posters, using drawings and sentences to contrast homonyms. Displaying these posters in the classroom reminds students of the differences between the words.

Root Words and Affixes

Teaching students about root words and affixes shows them how words work. Many words come from a single root word; for example, the related Latin words *portare* (to carry), *portus* (harbor), and *porta* (gate) are the sources of at least 12 English words: *deport*, *export*, *exporter*, *import*, *port*, *portable*, *porter*, *report*, *reporter*, *support*, *transport*, and *transportation*. Latin is the most common source of English root words; Greek and English are two other important sources.

Some root words are whole words, and others are word parts. Root words are **free morphemes** when they're words. For instance, the word *cent* comes from the Latin root word *cent*, meaning "hundred." English treats the word as a root word that's used independently and in combination with affixes, as in *century*, *bicentennial*, and *centipede*. The words *cosmopolitan*, *cosmic*, and *microcosm* come from the Greek root word *cosmo*, meaning "universe," which isn't an independent root. A list of Latin and Greek root words appears in Figure 7–4. Words such as *eye*, *tree*, and *water* are root words, too. New words are formed through compounding—for example, *eyelash*, *treetop*, and *waterfall*—and other roots, such as *read*, combine with affixes, as in *reader* and *unreadable*.

Affixes are **bound morphemes** that are added to words: **Prefixes** are placed at the beginning, as in *disrespect* and *refill*, and **suffixes** are located at the end, as in *fluently*, *elevator*, and *courageous*. Like roots, some affixes are English and others come from Latin and Greek. Affixes often change a word's meaning, such as adding *un-* to *happy* to make *unhappy*. Sometimes they change the part of speech, too; for instance, when *-tion* is added to *attract* to form *attraction*, the verb *attract* becomes a noun.

When a word's affix is "peeled off," the remaining word is usually a real word. For example, when the prefix *pre-* is removed from *preview* or the suffix *-er* is removed from *viewer*, the word *view* can stand alone. Sometimes, however, Latin and Greek roots can't stand alone. One example is *legible*: The *-ible* is a suffix, and *leg-* is a root word even though it can't stand alone. Of course, *leg*—meaning part of the body—is a word, but the root word *leg-* from *legible* isn't: It's a Latin root, meaning "to read."

A list of English, Greek, and Latin prefixes and suffixes is presented in Figure 7–5. White, Sowell, and Yanagihara (1989) researched affixes and identified the most

FIGURE 7–4   Root Words

ROOT	LANGUAGE	MEANING	SAMPLE WORDS
ann/enn	Latin	year	anniversary, annual, centennial, millennium, perennial, semiannual
arch	Greek	ruler	anarchy, archbishop, architecture, hierarchy, monarchy, patriarch
astro	Greek	star	aster, asterisk, astrology, astronaut, astronomy, disaster
auto	Greek	self	autobiography, automatic, automobile, autopsy, semiautomatic
bio	Greek	life	biography, biohazard, biology, biodegradable, bionic, biosphere
capit/capt	Latin	head	capital, capitalize, capitol, captain, decapitate, per capita
cent	Latin	hundred	bicentennial, cent, centennial, centigrade, centipede, century, percent
circ	Latin	around	circle, circuit, circular, circumference, circumspect, circumstance, circus
cosmo	Greek	universe	cosmic, cosmopolitan, cosmos, microcosm
cred	Latin	believe	credit, creed, creditable, discredit, incredulity
cycl	Greek	wheel	bicycle, cycle, cyclist, cyclone, recycle, tricycle
dict	Latin	speak	contradict, dictate, dictator, prediction, verdict
gram	Greek	letter	cardiogram, diagram, grammar, monogram, telegram
graph	Greek	write	autobiography, biographer, cryptograph, epigraph, graphic, paragraph
jud/jur/jus	Latin	law	injury, injustice, judge, juror, jury, justice, justify, prejudice
luc/lum/lus	Latin	light	illuminate, lucid, luminous, luster, translucent
man	Latin	hand	manacle, maneuver, manicure, manipulate, manual, manufacture
mar/mer	Latin	sea	aquamarine, marine, maritime, marshy, mermaid, submarine
meter	Greek	measure	centimeter, diameter, seismometer, speedometer, thermometer
mini	Latin	small	miniature, minibus, minimize, minor, minimum, minuscule, minute
mort	Latin	death	immortal, mortality, mortuary, postmortem
ped	Latin	foot	biped, impede, pedal, pedestrian, pedicure
phono	Greek	sound	earphone, microphone, phonics, phonograph, saxophone, symphony
photo	Greek	light	photograph, photographer, photosensitive, photosynthesis
pod/pus	Greek	foot	gastropod, octopus, podiatry, podium, tripod
port	Latin	carry	exporter, import, port, portable, porter, reporter, support, transportation
quer/ques/quis	Latin	seek	inquisitive, query, quest, question, request
scope	Latin	see	horoscope, kaleidoscope, microscope, periscope, telescope
scrib/scrip	Latin	write	describe, inscription, postscript, prescribe, scribble, scribe, script
sphere	Greek	ball	atmosphere, atmospheric, hemisphere, sphere, stratosphere
struct	Latin	build	construct, construction, destruction, indestructible, instruct, reconstruct
tele	Greek	far	telecast, telegram, telegraph, telephone, telescope, telethon, television
terr	Latin	land	subterranean, terrace, terrain, terrarium, terrier, territory
vers/vert	Latin	turn	advertise, anniversary, controversial, divert, reversible, versus
vict/vinc	Latin	conquer	convict, convince, evict, invincible, victim, victor, victory
vid/vis	Latin	see	improvise, invisible, revise, supervisor, television, video, vision, visitor
vit/viv	Latin	live	revive, survive, vital, vitamin, vivacious, vivid, viviparous
volv	Latin	roll	convolutions, evolve, evolution, involve, revolutionary, revolver, volume

FIGURE 7–5 Derivational Affixes

LANGUAGE	PREFIXES	SUFFIXES
English	*over- (too much): overflow self- (by oneself): self-employed *un- (not): unhappy *un- (reversal): untie under- (beneath): underground	-ful (full of): hopeful -ish (like): reddish -less (without): hopeless -ling (young): duckling *-ly (in the manner of): slowly *-ness (state or quality): kindness -ship (state of, art, or skill): friendship, seamanship -ster (one who): gangster -ward (direction): homeward *-y (full of): sleepy
Greek	a-/an- (not): atheist, anaerobic amphi- (both): amphibian anti- (against): antiseptic di- (two): dioxide hemi- (half): hemisphere hyper- (over): hyperactive hypo- (under): hypodermic micro- (small): microfilm mono- (one): monarch omni- (all): omnivorous poly- (many): polygon sym-/syn-/sys- (together): symbol, synonym, system	-ism (doctrine of): communism -ist (one who): artist -logy (the study of): zoology
Latin	bi- (two, twice): bifocal, biannual contra- (against): contradict de- (away): detract *dis- (not): disapprove *dis- (reversal): disinfect ex- (out): export *il-/im-/in-/ir- (not): illegible, impolite, inexpensive, irrational *in- (in, into): indoor inter- (between): intermission mille- (thousand): millennium *mis- (wrong): mistake multi- (many): multimillionaire non- (not): nonsense post- (after): postwar pre- (before): precede quad-/quart- (four): quadruple, quarter re- (again): repay *re-/retro- (back): replace, retroactive *sub- (under): submarine super- (above): supermarket trans- (across): transport tri- (three): triangle	-able/-ible (worthy of, can be): lovable, audible *-al/-ial (action, process): arrival, denial -ance/-ence (state or quality): annoyance, difference -ant (one who): servant -ary/-ory (person, place): secretary, laboratory -cule (very small): molecule -ee (one who is): trustee *-er/-or/-ar (one who): teacher, actor, liar -ic (characterized by): angelic -ify (to make): simplify -ment (state or quality): enjoyment -ous (full of): nervous *-sion/-tion (state or quality): tension, attraction -ure (state or quality): failure

Republished with the permission of John Wiley & Sons, Inc, from Teaching elementary students to use word-part clues by Thomas G White; Joanne Sowell; Alice Yanagihara, *The Reading Teacher*, 42, 302–308 © 1989; permission conveyed through Copyright Clearance Center, Inc.

common ones; these are marked with an asterisk in the figure. White and his colleagues recommend that teachers teach the commonly used affixes because they're useful. Some of the most commonly used prefixes can be confusing, however, because they have more than one meaning; the prefix *un-*, for instance, can mean "not" as in *unclear*, or it can reverse the meaning of a word, as in *tie–untie*.

Etymologies: Word Histories

Glimpses into the history of the English language offer fascinating information about word meanings and spellings (Tompkins & Yaden, 1986). The English language began in A.D. 447 when Angles, Saxons, and other Germanic tribes invaded England. This Anglo-Saxon English was first written down by Latin missionaries in approximately A.D. 750. The English of the period from 450 to 1100 is known as *Old English*. During this time, English was a very phonetic language and followed many German syntactic patterns. Many loan words, including *ugly, window, egg, they, sky,* and *husband*, were contributed by the marauding Vikings who plundered villages along the English coast.

The Norman Conquest in 1066 marks the beginning of Middle English (1100–1500). William, Duke of Normandy, invaded England and became the English king. William, his lords, and the royals who accompanied him spoke French, so it became the official language of England for nearly 200 years. Many French words entered the language, and their spellings replaced Old English spellings. For example, *night* was spelled *niht* and *queen* was spelled *cwen* in Old English to reflect their pronunciations; their modern spellings reflect changes by French scribes. Words from Dutch, Latin, and other languages entered English during this period, too.

The invention of the printing press initiated the transition from Middle English to Modern English (1500–present). William Caxton brought the first printing press to England in 1476, and soon books and pamphlets were being mass-produced. Soon after, spelling became standardized as Samuel Johnson and other lexicographers compiled dictionaries, even though English pronunciation of words continued to evolve. Words continued to flow into English from almost every language in the world. Exploration and colonization in North America and around the world accounted for many of the loan words. For example, *canoe* and *moccasin* are from Native American languages; *bonanza, chocolate,* and *ranch* are from Mexican Spanish; and *cafeteria, prairie,* and *teenager* are American English. Other loan words include *zero* (Arabic), *tattoo* (Polynesian), *robot* (Czech), *yogurt* (Turkish), *restaurant* (French), *dollar* (German), *jungle* (Hindi), and *umbrella* (Italian). Some words, such as *electric, democracy,* and *astronaut*, were created using Greek word parts. New words continue to enter English every year, and some of these words, such as *selfie*, *FLOTUS*, and *crowdsourcing*, reflect new inventions and cultural practices. Many new words today, such as *email* and *hotspot*, relate to the Internet. The word *Internet* is about 40 years old.

Students use etymological information in dictionaries to learn how particular words evolved and what the words mean. Etymological information is included in brackets at the beginning or end of dictionary entries. Here's the etymological information for three words:

> *democracy [1576, < MF < LL < Gr demokratia, demos (people) + kratia (cracy = strength, power)]*

The etymological information explains that the word *democracy* entered English in 1576 through French, and that the French word came from Latin and before that Greek. In Greek, the word *demokratia* means "power to the people."

> *house [bef. 900, ME hous, OE hus]*

According to the etymological information, *house* is an Old English word that entered English before 900. It was spelled *hus* in Old English and *hous* in Middle English.

> *moose [1603, < Algonquin, "he who strips bark"]*

The etymological information explains that the word *moose* is Native American—from an Algonquin tribe in the northeastern United States—and entered English in 1603. It comes from the Algonquin word for "he who strips bark."

Even though words have entered English from around the world, the three main sources of words are English, Latin, and Greek. Upper grade students can learn to identify the languages that these words came from; knowing the language backgrounds helps students to predict the spellings and meanings (Venezky, 1999). English words are usually one- or two-syllable common words that may or may not be phonetically regular, such as *fox, arm, Monday, house, match, eleven, of, come, week, horse, brother,* and *dumb.* Words with *ch* (pronounced as /ch/), *sh, th,* and *wh* digraphs are usually English, as in *church, shell, bath,* and *what.* Many English words are compound words or use comparative and superlative forms, such as *starfish, toothache, fireplace, happier,* and *fastest.*

Many words from Latin are similar to comparable words in French, Spanish, or Italian, such as *ancient, judicial, impossible,* and *officer.* Latin words have related words or derivatives, such as *courage, courageous, encourage, discourage,* and *encouragement.* Also, many Latin words have *-tion/-sion* suffixes: *imitation, corruption, attention, extension,* and *possession.*

Greek words are the most unusual. Many are long words, and their spellings seem unfamiliar. The digraph *ph* is pronounced /f/, and the digraph *ch* is pronounced /k/ in Greek loan words, as in *autograph, chaos,* and *architect.* Longer words with *th,* such as *thermometer* and *arithmetic,* are Greek. The suffix *-ology* is Greek, as in the words *biology, psychology,* and *geology.* The letter *y* is used in place of *i* in the middle of some words, such as *bicycle* and *myth.* Many Greek words are composed of two parts: *bibliotherapy, microscope, biosphere, hypodermic,* and *telephone.* Figure 7–6 presents lists of words from English, Latin, and Greek that teachers can use for **word sorts** and other vocabulary activities.

Conceptually related words have developed from English, Latin, and Greek sources. Consider the words *tooth, dentist,* and *orthodontist. Tooth* is an English word, which explains its irregular plural form, *teeth. Dentist* is a Latin word; *dent* means "tooth" in Latin, and the suffix *-ist* means "one who does." The word *orthodontist* is Greek. *Ortho* means "straighten" and *dont* means "tooth"; therefore, *orthodontist* means "one who straightens teeth." Other conceptually related triplets include the following:

book: bookstore (E), bibliography (Gr), library (L)
eye: eyelash (E), optical (Gr), binoculars (L)
foot: foot-dragging (E), tripod (Gr), pedestrian (L)
great: greatest (E), megaphone (Gr), magnificent (L)
see: foresee (E), microscope (Gr), invisible (L)
star: starry (E), astronaut (Gr), constellation (L)
time: time-tested (E), chronological (Gr), contemporary (L)
water: watermelon (E), hydrate (Gr), aquarium (L)

When students understand English, Latin, and Greek root words, they appreciate the relationships among words and their meanings.

Figurative Meanings

Many words have both literal and figurative meanings: **Literal meanings** are the explicit, dictionary meanings, and **figurative meanings** are metaphorical or use figures

FIGURE 7–6   Words From English, Latin, and Greek

ENGLISH	LATIN	GREEK
apple	addiction	ache
between	administer	arithmetic
bumblebee	advantage	astronomy
child	beautiful	atomic
cry	capital	biology
cuff	confession	chaos
earth	continent	chemical
fireplace	delicate	democracy
fourteen	discourage	disaster
freedom	erupt	elephant
Friday	explosion	geography
get	fraction	gymnastics
have	fragile	helicopter
horse	frequently	hemisphere
knight	heir	hieroglyphics
know	honest	kaleidoscope
ladybug	identify	myth
lamb	January	octopus
lip	journal	phenomenal
lock	junior	photosynthesis
mouth	nation	pseudonym
out	occupy	rhinoceros
quickly	organize	rhythm
ride	principal	sympathy
silly	procession	telescope
this	salute	theater
twin	special	thermometer
weather	uniform	trophy
whisper	vacation	zodiac
wild	vegetable	zoo

of speech. For example, to describe *winter* as the coldest season of the year is literal, but to say that "winter has icy breath" is figurative. Two types of figurative language are idioms and comparisons.

Idioms are groups of words, such as "in hot water," that have a special meaning. Idioms can be confusing because they must be interpreted figuratively. "In hot water" is an old expression meaning "to be in trouble." In the Middle Ages, people had to protect themselves from robbers. When a robber tried to break into a house, the homeowner might pour boiling water from a second-floor window onto the head of the robber, who would then be "in hot water." English has hundreds of idioms, which we use every day to create word pictures that make language more colorful. Some examples are "out in left field," "a skeleton in the closet," "raining cats and dogs," and "a chip off the old block." Booklist: Vocabulary includes a variety of books that explain idioms, such as the *Scholastic Dictionary of Idioms* (Terban, 2006).

Because idioms are figurative sayings, many students—and especially English learners—have difficulty understanding them (Palmer, Shackelford, Miller, & Leclere, 2006/2007). It's crucial that teachers provide explicit instruction so that

FIGURE 7–7 An Idiom Poster

students move beyond the literal meanings of phrases. One way to help students learn about figurative language is to have them create idiom posters showing both literal and figurative meanings, as illustrated in Figure 7–7.

Metaphors and similes are comparisons that liken something to something else. A **simile** is a comparison signaled by the use of *like* or *as*: "The crowd was as rowdy as a bunch of marauding monkeys" and "My apartment was like an oven after the air-conditioning broke" are two examples. In contrast, a **metaphor** compares two things by implying that one is the other, without using *like* or *as*: "The children were frisky puppies playing in the yard" is an example. Metaphors are stronger comparisons, as these examples show:

> She's as cool as a cucumber.
> She's a cool cucumber.

> In the moonlight, the dead tree looked like a skeleton.
> In the moonlight, the dead tree was a skeleton.

Differentiating between the terms *simile* and *metaphor* is less important than understanding the meaning of comparisons in books students read and having students use comparisons to make their writing more vivid. For example, a sixth grade student compared anger to a thunderstorm using a simile; she wrote, "Anger is like a thunderstorm, screaming with thunder-feelings and lightning-words." Another student used a metaphor to compare anger to a volcano: "Anger is a volcano, erupting with poisonous words and hot-lava actions."

Students begin by learning traditional comparisons such as "happy as a clam" and "high as a kite," and then they learn to notice and invent fresh, unexpected comparisons. To introduce traditional comparisons to young children, teachers often use

Audrey Wood's *Quick as a Cricket* (1982). Middle and upper grade students can invent new comparisons for stale expressions such as "butterflies in your stomach." In *Anastasia Krupnik* (1984), for example, Lois Lowry substituted "ginger ale in her knees" for the trite "butterflies in her stomach" to describe how nervous Anastasia felt when she stood in front of the class to read a poem she had written.

🔄 MONITOR: Check Your Understanding 7.2

Teaching Students to Unlock Word Meanings

Vocabulary instruction plays an important role in balanced literacy classrooms because of the crucial role it plays in both reading and writing achievement. Baumann, Kame'enui, and Ash (2003) and Graves (2006) identified these components of vocabulary instruction:

- Immerse students in words through listening, talking, reading, and writing
- Teach specific words through active involvement and multiple encounters with words
- Teach word-learning strategies so students can figure out the meanings of unfamiliar words
- Develop students' word consciousness, their awareness of and interest in words

Teachers address all of these components when they teach vocabulary. Too often, vocabulary instruction has emphasized only the second component, teaching specific words, without considering how to develop students' ability to learn words independently. To evaluate your effectiveness, use the Teacher Checklist: How do I teach vocabulary?

The Common Core State Standards for English Language Arts emphasize that learning grade-level academic vocabulary is essential for academic achievement. The Language Standards focus on teaching students to determine the meaning of unfamiliar words, to understand figurative language, and to acquire vocabulary needed for understanding books they're reading and for expressing ideas in their writing. The feature Common Core State Standards: Vocabulary provides additional information.

TEACHER Checklist

How do I teach vocabulary?

- ○ Do I address Standards in my teaching?
- ○ Do I choose words for instruction from books students are reading and from thematic units?
- ○ Do I highlight academic vocabulary on word walls?
- ○ Do I engage students in word-study activities?
- ○ Do I teach minilessons about the meanings of individual words, vocabulary concepts, and word-learning strategies?
- ○ Do I scaffold students as they develop full word knowledge by learning multiple meanings, how root words and affixes affect meaning, synonyms, antonyms, word histories, and figurative meanings?
- ○ Do I teach students to use word-learning strategies?
- ○ Do I develop students' word consciousness by demonstrating curiosity about words, teaching students about words, and involving them in wordplay activities?
- ○ Do I provide daily opportunities for independent reading—at least 15–30 minutes in grades 1–3 and 30–60 minutes in grades 4–8?

Word Walls

Teachers post **word walls** in the classroom; usually they're made from large sheets of butcher paper and divided into sections for each letter of the alphabet. Students and the teacher write interesting, confusing, and important words representing all three tiers on the word wall. Usually students choose the words to write and may even do the writing themselves; teachers add other important words that students haven't chosen. Words are added to the word wall as they come up in books students are reading or during a thematic unit, not in advance. Janet Allen (2007) says that word walls should be "a living part of the classroom with new words being added each day" (p. 120). Word walls are useful

FIGURE 7-8   A Word Wall for *Hatchet*

A	B	C	D
alone	bush plane	Canadian wilderness	divorce
absolutely terrified	Brian Robeson	controls	desperation
arrows	bruised	cockpit	destroyed
aluminum cookset	bow & arrow	crash	disappointment
		careless	devastating
		campsite	
E	**F**	**G**	**H**
engine	fire	gut cherries	hatchet
emergency	fuselage	get food	heart attack
emptiness	fish		hunger
exhaustion	foolbirds		hope
	foodshelf		
	54 days		
I J	**K L**	**M N**	**O P Q**
instruments	lake	memory	pilot
insane		mosquitoes	panic
incredible wealth		mistakes	painful
		matches	porcupine quills
		mental journal	patience
		moose	
R	**S T**	**U V**	**W X Y Z**
rudder pedals	stranded	visitation rights	wilderness
rescue	secret	viciously thirsty	windbreaker
radio	survival pack	valuable asset	wreck
relative comfort	search	vicious whine	woodpile
raspberries	sleeping bag	unbelievable riches	wolf
roaring bonfire	shelter		
raft	starved		

resources: Students locate words that they want to use during a grand conversation or check the spelling of a word they're writing, and teachers use the words for word-study activities.

Some teachers use large pocket charts and word cards instead of butcher paper for their word walls; this way, the word cards can easily be used for word-study activities, and they can be sorted and rearranged on the pocket chart. After the book or unit is completed, teachers punch holes in one end of the cards and hang them on a ring. Then the collection of word cards can be placed in the writing center for students to use when they're writing.

Students also make individual word walls by dividing a sheet of paper into 20–24 boxes and labeling the boxes with the letters of the alphabet; they can put several letters together in one box. Then students write important words and phrases in the boxes as they read and discuss a book. Figure 7–8 shows a sixth grader's word wall for *Hatchet* (2007), a wilderness survival novel by Gary Paulsen.

COMMON CORE STATE STANDARDS

Vocabulary

The Common Core State Standards for English Language Arts emphasize that students must expand their vocabularies and learn to determine the meaning of unknown words. They address these requirements:

- Students choose the most appropriate meaning of words with multiple meanings.
- Students use context clues.
- Students understand figurative language, word relationships, and nuances in word meanings.
- Students analyze root words and affixes to determine the meaning of words.

The Standards emphasize that vocabulary knowledge is inseparable from reading and writing instruction. To learn more about the vocabulary Standards, go to http://www.corestandards.org/ELA-Literacy, or check your state's educational standards website.

Watch as a teacher develops a content-specific vocabulary word wall with students. How do teachers engage students in creating this kind of word wall?

Even though 25, 50, or more words may be added to the word wall, not all of them are explicitly taught. As they plan, teachers create lists of words that will probably be written on word walls during the unit. From this list, they choose the words they'll teach—usually Tier 2 words that are critical to understanding the book or the unit.

Explicit Instruction

Teachers explicitly teach students about academic vocabulary, usually Tier 2 words. McKeown and Beck (2004) emphasize that instruction should be rich, deep, and extended. That means that teachers provide multiple encounters with words; present a variety of information, including definitions, contexts, examples, and related words; and involve students in word-study activities so that they have multiple opportunities to interact with words. The procedure is time-consuming, but researchers report that students are more successful in learning and remembering word meanings this way (Beck, McKeown, & Kucan, 2002).

As teachers plan for instruction, they consider what students already know about a word. Sometimes the word is unfamiliar, or it represents a new concept. At other times, the word is familiar and students know one meaning, but they need to learn a new meaning. A word representing an unfamiliar concept takes the most time to teach, and a new meaning for a familiar word, the least.

Teachers use **minilessons** to teach students about specific words. They provide information about words, including both definitions and contextual information, and they engage students in activities to get them to think about and use words orally and in reading and writing. Sometimes teachers present minilessons before reading; at other times, they teach them after reading. Minilesson: Introducing Content Area Vocabulary Words shows how one teacher introduces key words before reading a chapter in a social studies textbook.

View this video about the best ways to expand students' knowledge of word meanings. Why are these activities more effective than having students look up dictionary definitions?

Word-Study Activities

Students examine new words and think more deeply about them as they participate in word-study activities (Allen, 2007). In some activities, they create visual representations of words, and in others, they categorize words or learn related words. Teachers use these word-study activities to teach new academic vocabulary:

Word Posters. Students choose a word and write it on a small poster; then they draw a picture to illustrate it. They also write a sentence using the word on the poster. This is one way that students visualize the meaning of a word.

Word Maps. Students create a diagram to examine a word they're learning: They write the word, make a box around it, draw several lines from the box, and add information about the word in additional boxes they make at the end of each line. Three kinds of information typically included in a word map are a category for the word, examples, and characteristics or associations. Figure 7–9 shows a word map a fifth grader reading *Bunnicula: A Rabbit-Tale of Mystery* (Howe & Howe, 2006) made. Word maps are another way to visualize a word's meaning (Duffelmeyer & Banwart, 1992–1993).

Minilesson

Mrs. Cramer's fifth grade class is involved in a social studies unit on immigration. The class has already created a KWL chart on immigration to activate students' background knowledge, and students have written about how and when their families came to the United States. They've also marked their countries of origin on a world map in the classroom. In this 3-day minilesson, Mrs. Cramer introduces five key vocabulary words before students read a chapter in their social studies textbook. Because many of her students are English learners, she takes more time to practice vocabulary before reading the chapter.

① Introduce the Topic

Mrs. Cramer explains that after a week of studying immigration, the fifth graders are now getting ready to read the chapter about immigration in the social studies text. She places these five words written on word cards in a pocket chart and reads each one aloud: *culture, descendant, immigrant, prejudice,* and *pluralism.* She tells students that these words are used in the chapter and that it's important to be familiar with them before reading.

② Share Examples

Mrs. Cramer distributes anticipation guides for students to rate their knowledge of the new words. The guide has four columns; the new words are listed in the left column, and the other three columns have these headings: *I know the word well, I've heard of it, I don't know this word.* For each word, the students put a checkmark in the appropriate column. At the end of the unit, they'll again rate their knowledge of the words and compare the two ratings to assess their learning.

③ Provide Information

Mrs. Cramer divides the students into small groups for a word sort. Each group receives a pack of 10 cards; the new vocabulary words are written on five of the cards and their definitions on the other cards. Students work together to match the words and definitions, and then Mrs. Cramer reviews the meaning of each word.

④ Guide Practice

The next day, the students repeat the word sort activity to review the meanings of the words. Then they work with partners to complete a cloze activity: Mrs. Cramer has prepared a list of sentences taken from the chapter with the new words omitted, and students write the correct word in each blank. Afterward she reviews the sentences, explaining any sentences completed incorrectly.

⑤ Assess Learning

On the third day, Mrs. Cramer adds the new words to the word wall on immigration displayed in the classroom. Next, she models writing a quickwrite using the new words and other words from the word wall. Following the teacher's model, students write quickwrites using at least three of the new words and three other words from the word wall. Afterward, students use highlighters to mark the immigration-related words they've incorporated in their quickwrites. Later, Mrs. Cramer reads the quickwrites to assess the students' vocabulary knowledge.

FIGURE 7–9 A Word Map

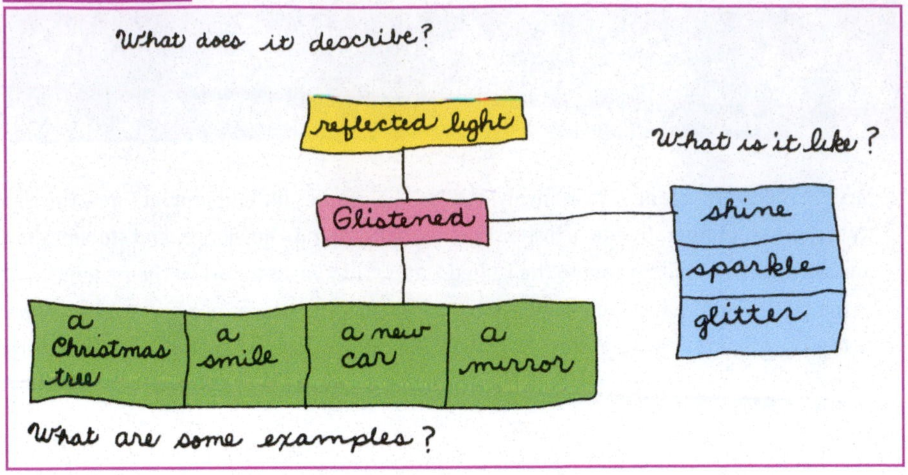

What does it describe?

reflected light

Glistened

What is it like?

shine
sparkle
glitter

a Christmas tree | a smile | a new car | a mirror

What are some examples?

Possible Sentences. To activate background knowledge about a topic and increase their curiosity before reading a book or a chapter in a content area textbook, students write **possible sentences** using vocabulary words (Stahl & Kapinus, 1991). After reviewing the definitions of a set of words, students work with classmates to craft sentences using the words and afterward share them. Then after reading or later in the unit, students review the sentences and revise those that aren't accurate.

Dramatizing Words. Students each choose a word and dramatize it for classmates, who then try to guess it. Sometimes an action is more effective than a verbal definition for explaining a word. For example, a teacher reading *Chrysanthemum* (Henkes, 1996), the story of a little girl who didn't like her name, dramatized the word *wilted* for her second graders when they didn't understand how a girl could wilt. Other words in *Chrysanthemum* that can easily be acted out include *humorous, sprouted, dainty,* and *wildly.* Dramatization is an especially effective activity for English learners.

Word Sorts. Students sort a collection of words taken from the word wall into two or more categories in a **word sort** (Bear, Invernizzi, Templeton, & Johnston, 2016). Usually students choose the categories they use for the sort, but sometimes the teacher chooses them. For example, words from a story might be sorted by character, or words from a thematic unit on machines might be sorted according to type of machine. The words are written on cards, and then students sort them into piles.

Word Chains. Students choose a word and then identify three or four words to sequence before or after it to make a chain. For example, the word *tadpole* can be chained this way: *egg, tadpole, frog*; and the word *aggravate* can be chained like this: *irritate, bother, aggravate, annoy.* Students can draw and write their chains on a sheet of paper, or they can make a chain out of construction paper and write a word on each link.

Semantic Feature Analysis. Students learn the meanings of conceptually related words by examining their characteristics in a **semantic feature analysis** (Allen, 2007). Teachers select a group of related words, such as animals and plants in the rain forest or planets in the solar system, and then make a grid to classify them according to distinguishing characteristics (Pittelman, Heimlich, Berglund, & French, 1991; Rickelman & Taylor, 2006). Students analyze each word, characteristic by characteristic, and they put checkmarks, circles, and question marks in each cell to indicate whether the word represents that characteristic. For example, on a semantic feature analysis about the rain forest, animals, plants, and people living in the rain forest are listed on one side of the grid and characteristics on the top. For the word *sloth*, students would add checkmarks in the grid to indicate that it's a mammal, lives in the canopy, goes to the forest floor, and has camouflage. They would add circles to indicate that a sloth is not colorful, not dangerous to people, not a plant, and not a bird or insect. If they aren't sure whether sloths are used to make medicine, they use a question mark.

These word-study activities provide opportunities for students to deepen their understanding of words listed on word walls, other words related to books they're reading, and words they're learning during thematic units. Students develop concepts, learn one or more meanings of words, and make associations among words through these activities. None of them require students to simply write words and their definitions or to use the words in sentences or a contrived story.

Word-Learning Strategies

When students come across an unfamiliar word while reading, they can do a variety of things: for example, reread the sentence, analyze root words and affixes in the word, check a dictionary, sound out the word, look for context clues in the sentence, skip the word and keep reading, or ask the teacher or a classmate for help (Allen, 1999). Some techniques, however, work better than others. After studying the research on ways to deal with unfamiliar words, Michael Graves (2006) has identified these three effective word-learning strategies:

- Using context clues
- Analyzing word parts
- Checking a dictionary

Capable readers know and use these strategies to figure out the meaning of unfamiliar words as they read. In contrast, less capable readers have fewer strategies available: They often depend on just one or two less effective strategies, such as sounding out the word or skipping it.

Graves (2006) recommends teaching students what to do when they encounter an unfamiliar word. They need to recognize when a word they're reading is unfamiliar and decide how important it is to know its meaning. If the word isn't important to the text, students skip it and continue reading, but if it is important, they need to take action. He recommends that teachers teach students this procedure for figuring out the meaning of an unfamiliar word:

1. Students reread the sentence containing the word.
2. Students use context clues to figure out the meaning of the word, and if that doesn't work, they continue to the next step.
3. Students examine the word parts, looking for familiar root words and affixes to aid in figuring out the meaning. If they're still not successful, they continue to the next step.

Teach Kids to BE STRATEGIC

Word-Learning Strategies

Teach students to use these strategies to figure out the meaning of an unfamiliar word:

- Use context clues
- Analyze word parts
- Check a dictionary

Students practice these strategies through word-study activities, such as word maps and word sorts. Look for students to apply them when they're reading independently and studying social studies and science topics. If students struggle, reteach the strategies, making sure to model their use and think aloud about their application.

4. Students pronounce the word to see if they recognize it when they say it. If they still can't figure it out, they continue to the next step.
5. Students check the word in a dictionary or ask the teacher for help.

This procedure has the greatest chance of success because it incorporates all three word-learning strategies.

USING CONTEXT CLUES. Students learn many words from context as they read. The surrounding words and sentences offer context clues; some clues provide information about the meaning of the word, and others provide information about the part of speech and how the word is used in a sentence. This contextual information helps students infer the meaning of the unfamiliar word. Illustrations also provide contextual information that helps readers identify words. The types of context clues that readers use are presented in Figure 7–10. Interestingly, two or three types of contextual information are often found in the same sentence.

Nagy, Anderson, and Herman (1987) found that students who read books at their grade level have a 1 in 20 chance of learning the meaning of a word from context. Although that might seem insignificant, if students read 20,000 words a year and learn 1 of every 20 words from context, they'll learn 1,000 words, or one third of their annual vocabulary growth. That's significant! How much time does it take to read 20,000 words? Nagy (1988) estimated that if teachers provide 30 minutes of daily reading time, students will learn an additional 1,000 words a year! It's interesting to note that both capable and less capable readers learn from context at about the same rate (Stahl, 1999).

Modeling is the best way to teach students about context clues. When teachers read aloud, they stop at a difficult word and do a **think-aloud** to show students how they use context clues to figure out its meaning. When the context provides enough information, teachers use the information and continue reading, but when the rest of the sentence or paragraph doesn't provide enough information, teachers use another strategy to figure out the meaning of the word.

FIGURE 7–10 Context Clues

CLUE	DESCRIPTION	SAMPLE SENTENCE
Definition	Readers use the definition in the sentence to understand the unknown word.	Some spiders spin silk with tiny organs called *spinnerets*.
Example-Illustration	Readers use an example or illustration to understand the unknown word.	Toads, frogs, and some birds are *predators* that hunt and eat spiders.
Contrast	Readers understand the unknown word because it's compared or contrasted with another word in the sentence.	Most spiders live for about one year, but *tarantulas* sometimes live for 20 years or more!
Logic	Readers think about the rest of the sentence to understand the unknown word.	An *exoskeleton* acts like a suit of armor to protect the spider.
Root Words and Affixes	Readers use their knowledge of root words and affixes to figure out the unknown word.	People who are terrified of spiders have *arachnophobia*.
Grammar	Readers use the word's function in the sentence or its part of speech to figure out the unknown word.	Most spiders *molt* five to ten times.

ANALYZING WORD PARTS. When students understand how word parts function, they use their knowledge of prefixes, suffixes, and root words to unlock many multi-syllabic words. For example, *omnivorous*, *carnivorous*, and *herbivorous* relate to the foods that animals eat: *Omni* means "all," *carn* means "flesh," and *herb* means "vegetation." The common word part *vorous* comes from the Latin *vorare*, meaning "to swallow up." When students know *carnivorous* or *carnivore*, they use morphemic analysis to figure out the other words.

Teaching derivational prefixes and suffixes and non-English root words in fourth through eighth grades improves students' ability to unlock the meaning of unfamiliar words (Baumann, Edwards, Font, Tereshinski, Kame'enui, & Olejnik, 2002; Baumann, Font, Edwards, & Boland, 2005). For example, when students recognize that the Latin roots *-ann* and *-enn* mean "year," they can figure out the meanings of many of these words: *annual*, *biennial*, *perennial*, *centennial*, *bicentennial*, *millennium*, and *sesqui-centennial*. Graves (2006) recommends that teachers teach morphemic analysis when non-English root words appear in books students are reading and during thematic units; teachers break apart the words and discuss the word parts when they're posted on the word wall and through minilessons.

CHECKING THE DICTIONARY. Looking up unfamiliar words in the dictionary is often frustrating because the definitions don't provide enough useful information or because words used in the definition are forms of the word being defined (Allen, 1999). Sometimes the definition that students choose—usually the first one—is the wrong one. Or, the definition doesn't make sense. For example, the word *pollution* is usually defined as "the act of polluting"—not a useful definition. Students could look for an entry for *polluting*, but they won't find it. They might notice an entry for *pollute*, where the first definition is "to make impure." The second definition is "to make unclean, especially with man-made waste," but even this definition may be difficult to understand.

Because dictionary definitions are most useful when a person is vaguely familiar with the word's meaning, teachers play an important role in dictionary work: They teach students how to read a dictionary entry and decide which definitions make sense, and they model the strategy when they're reading aloud and come across a word that's unfamiliar to most students. They also assist students by explaining the definitions that students locate, providing sample sentences, and comparing the word to related words and opposites.

Incidental Word Learning

Students learn words incidentally all the time, and because they learn so many words this way, teachers know that they don't have to teach the meaning of every unfamiliar word in a text. Students learn words from many sources, but researchers report that reading is the single largest source of vocabulary growth for students, especially after third grade (Swanborn & de Glopper, 1999). In addition, the amount of time students spend reading independently is the best predictor of vocabulary growth between second and fifth grades.

INDEPENDENT READING. Students need daily opportunities for independent reading in order to learn words, and they need to read books at their independent reading levels; if the books are too easy or too hard, students learn very few new words. The best way to provide opportunities for independent reading is reading workshop. Students choose books that they're interested in from age-appropriate and reading-level-suitable collections in their classroom libraries, and because they've chosen the books themselves, they're more likely to keep reading. **Sustained Silent Reading** (SSR) is another way to encourage wide reading. All students in a classroom or in the school spend 10 to 30 minutes or more silently reading appropriate books that they've chosen themselves. Even the teacher takes time to read, at the same time modeling how adults who enjoy reading make it part of their daily routine. Simply providing time for independent reading, however, doesn't guarantee that students will increase their vocabulary knowledge (Stahl & Nagy, 2006); students need to know how to use context clues and other word-learning strategies to figure out the meaning of unfamiliar words to increase their vocabulary.

READING ALOUD TO STUDENTS. Teachers also provide for incidental word learning when they read aloud stories, poems, and nonfiction books. Daily read-aloud activities are important for students at all grade levels, kindergarten through eighth grade. Teachers use the **interactive read-aloud** procedure and focus on a few key words in the book, model how to use context clues to understand new words, and talk about the words after reading. They use **think-alouds** when they model using context clues and other word-identification strategies. Two studies found that teachers enhance students' vocabulary knowledge and their comprehension when they add a focus on vocabulary to their read-alouds (Fisher, Frey, & Lapp, 2008; Santoro, Chard, Howard, & Baker, 2008).

Cunningham (2009) recommends that primary grade teachers choose one picture book each week to read aloud and teach key vocabulary. Teachers read the book aloud one time and then present three new words from it, each written on a word card. During the second reading, students listen for the words, and the teacher takes time to talk about each word's meaning using information available in the text and in the illustrations. Later, the teacher encourages students to practice using the new words when they talk and write about the book.

Although reading aloud is important for all students, it's especially important for struggling readers who typically read fewer books themselves, and because the books at their reading level have less sophisticated vocabulary words. In fact, researchers report that students learn as many words incidentally while listening to teachers read aloud as they do by reading themselves (Stahl, Richek, & Vandevier, 1991).

The Role of Oral Language

Oral language plays a crucial role in vocabulary development. Of course, parents nurture young children's knowledge of words as they talk with them, identifying objects, describing people, offering explanations, and telling stories. The amount of time that parents talk to young children and the quality of their interactions affect children's vocabulary development (Stahl & Nagy, 2006). Teachers play a similar role by creating a word-rich environment where students are immersed in talking, listening, reading, and writing activities using the decontextualized academic vocabulary they're learning (Blachowicz & Fisher, 2011). Posting new words on word walls and encouraging students to refer to the word wall and use the words as they collaborate in small groups, participate in discussions, and listen to the teacher read aloud stories and nonfiction books are examples of a word-rich environment.

Teachers link oral, written, and visual language as they teach vocabulary. For example, students talk about words and their meanings with classmates as they participate in **word sorts** and **possible sentence** activities, and they add a visual component when they dramatize words, make word posters, and draw and label

Watch a third grade teacher and a seventh grade teacher teach vocabulary lessons to their students. What oral and written activities do the teachers use to scaffold the English learners in their classrooms?

diagrams. Students also use the same words they used during **grand conversations** and other discussions when they write in **reading logs** and other journals. When the oral component is missing, students are far less likely to use the words in writing activities.

Assessing Students' Vocabulary Knowledge

Teachers follow the four-step instruction–assessment cycle as they teach vocabulary, particularly during literature focus units and thematic units. They identify academic vocabulary words, plan minilessons and instructional activities, monitor students' progress, and evaluate their achievement. Teachers also reflect on their teaching effectiveness at the end of the unit.

STEP 1: Planning. Teachers consider students' current level of vocabulary knowledge, identify the academic words they'll teach, and plan minilessons and word-study activities. Sometimes they also assess students' current knowledge of vocabulary related to the unit and plan ways to build students' background knowledge when necessary.

Students can self-assess their familiarity with key vocabulary at the beginning of a unit. Cunningham and Allington (2016) suggest having students assess their knowledge of specific words. Teachers develop a list of the levels of word knowledge using language that's appropriate for their students and post it in the classroom. Here's a sixth grade teacher's list:

1 = I don't know this word at all.
2 = I've heard this word before, but I don't know the meaning.
3 = I know one meaning for this word, and I can use it in a sentence.
4 = I know several meanings or other things about this word.

Teachers give students a list of key vocabulary words, and students assess their word knowledge by writing beside each word the number that indicates their level of knowledge. Teachers often have students repeat the assessment at the end of the unit to examine how their knowledge has grown. Or, before introducing a new word, teachers can informally ask students to raise their hands and show the number of fingers that corresponds with their level of knowledge about the word.

STEP 2: Monitoring. Teachers use these informal assessment tools to monitor students' progress:

Observations. Teachers watch how students use new words during word-study activities, minilessons, and discussions. They also notice how students apply word-learning strategies during guided reading and when they're reading aloud.

Conferences. Teachers talk with students about the words they've used in word-study activities and in their writing. They also ask what students do when they come across an unfamiliar word and talk about word-learning strategies.

Classroom INTERVENTIONS

More Word Knowledge

One of the biggest challenges facing struggling readers is their limited word knowledge. Even though independent reading is an important way most students acquire a large vocabulary, it isn't enough for struggling students (Allington, 2012). Students who exhibit reading difficulties don't do as much reading as their classmates, and the books they read don't introduce them to grade-level vocabulary words. To expand students' vocabularies, it's essential that teachers provide both daily activities to draw students' attention to words and instruction on academic vocabulary and word-learning strategies. Cooper, Chard, and Kiger (2006) offer these instructional recommendations:

- Nurture students' awareness of words using word walls, independent reading, and interactive read-alouds.
- Explicitly teach the meanings of 8–10 words each week by introducing key words before reading and providing worthwhile practice activities afterward.
- Develop students' ability to figure out the meaning of unfamiliar words.

Teachers can accelerate students' vocabulary development by implementing a more structured program with daily lessons based on these recommendations.

Sometimes teachers thwart students' vocabulary development. Allington (2012) identified three activities that waste instructional time: First, students shouldn't read books that are too difficult because they won't understand what they're reading. Next, teachers can't expect students to figure out the meaning of unfamiliar words when they're reading if they haven't been taught to use context clues or other word-learning strategies. Third, students shouldn't be given a list of words and asked to copy the definition for each word or write a sentence using it. These activities aren't recommended because they don't develop students' in-depth word knowledge.

Teachers also use these monitoring tools to check that their instruction is effective and then make modifications when necessary.

STEP 3: Evaluating. Teachers often choose more authentic measures to evaluate students' vocabulary knowledge because they provide more useful information than formal tests do (Bean & Swan, 2006). Teachers evaluate students' vocabulary knowledge using these authentic tools:

Rubrics. Teachers include items about vocabulary on rubrics to emphasize the importance of academic vocabulary. For oral-presentation rubrics, teachers emphasize the use of technical words related to the topic, and for writing, they emphasize precise vocabulary.

Quickwrites. Students quickwrite about a word listed on the word wall, explaining what they know about the word.

Word Sorts. Students complete a **word sort** activity to demonstrate that they can identify the connections among words related to a book they've read or to a thematic unit.

ASSESSMENT TOOLS

Vocabulary

Both informal assessments and standardized tests can be used to measure students' vocabulary knowledge, but tests often equate word knowledge with recognizing or being able to state a single definition of a word rather than assessing the depth of students' knowledge. Here are several norm-referenced vocabulary tests:

- **Peabody Picture Vocabulary Test-4 (PPVT-4)**
  The PPVT-4 (Dunn, Dunn, & Dunn, 2006) is an individually administered assessment to screen students' vocabulary knowledge. The test can be used with K–8 students, but it's most commonly used with K–2 students showing limited verbal fluency. The PPVT-4 measures receptive vocabulary: The teacher says a word and asks the student to look at four pictures and identify the one that best illustrates the meaning of the word. Unfortunately, this test takes 10–15 minutes, which makes it too time-consuming for regular use. The PPVT-4 is available for purchase from the American Guidance Service.

- **Expressive Vocabulary Test-2 (EVT-2)**
  The EVT-2 (Williams, 2006) is also an individual test that's used to screen K–8 students' knowledge of words. The EVT-2 is the expressive counterpart of the PPVT-4: The teacher points to a picture and asks the student to say a word that labels the picture or to provide a synonym for a word that's illustrated in the picture. This test is also very time-consuming to use. It's available from the American Guidance Service.

- **Informal Reading Inventories (IRIs)**
  Sometimes teachers in grades 2–8 use IRIs to assess students' vocabulary knowledge. One or two comprehension questions at each grade level focus on the meaning of words selected from the passage students have read. The usefulness of this assessment is limited, however, because so few questions deal with vocabulary and because students who read below grade level aren't tested on age-appropriate words.

Even though these tests aren't very useful in classroom settings, they can aid in diagnosing struggling readers and English learners with limited word knowledge.

Visual Representations. Students create a word map about a word, draw a picture to represent a word's meaning, or create some other visual representation of a word or a group of related words.

These evaluations require students to go beyond simply providing a definition or using a word in a sentence.

STEP 4: Reflecting. Teachers take time at the end of a unit to reflect on their teaching, including the effectiveness of their instruction. They can also ask students to reflect on their growing word knowledge. If students self-assessed their word knowledge using the levels of word knowledge at the beginning of the unit, they can complete the assessment again to gain insight on their learning.

DIAGNOSTIC ASSESSMENT. It's difficult to assess struggling students' vocabulary knowledge because there aren't any grade-level standards to indicate which words students should know or even how many words they need to learn. In addition, it's complicated because students learn words gradually, moving from grade to grade to deeper levels of "knowing" a word. Teachers typically use informal measures to monitor and evaluate students' knowledge of academic vocabulary, but several commercial tests are available to measure students' vocabulary; they're described in Assessment Tools: Vocabulary.

 **MONITOR: Check Your Understanding 7.3**

Review

EXPANDING STUDENTS' ACADEMIC VOCABULARY

Effective teachers demonstrate their responsibility and commitment to ensuring that their students are successful when they teach academic vocabulary using the guidelines presented in this chapter, these points in particular:

7.1 Teachers categorize unfamiliar words into three tiers—basic words, academic vocabulary, and specialized terms.

7.2 Teachers teach these vocabulary concepts: multiple meanings, synonyms, antonyms, homonyms, root words and affixes, etymologies, and figurative language.

7.3 Teachers teach academic vocabulary and word-learning strategies through a variety of activities.

✓ EVALUATE & REFLECT

Apply your understanding about teaching academic vocabulary. The questions ask you to collect and analyze data, and report the results. Your response should meet academic standards and adhere to Standard English conventions.

1. Choose a picture-book story that's appropriate for students in grades 2–4. Identify key words for the word wall and classify them according to the three tiers. In your response, provide bibliographic information and a brief summary of the book you choose, and list the words you've chosen for each of the three tiers.

2. Compare how teachers teach the three tiers of words to native English speakers with how they teach them to English learners. In your response, discuss the three tiers, the differences between native speakers and ELs in learning vocabulary, and the necessary adaptations.

3. Interview three students with differing reading and writing achievement levels in grades 3–8 to examine their knowledge about at least four of these word-study concepts: multiple meanings of words, synonyms, antonyms, homonyms, root words and affixes, etymologies, and figurative language. Ask students to explain the concepts and give examples. In your response, describe the students, the results of the interviews, and the implications for vocabulary instruction.

4. Imagine that you're establishing a Word Wizards Club like Mrs. Sanom's that was described in the vignette at the beginning of this chapter. Choose your key word and your costume, and plan your first week's lesson. In your response, identify the grade level, describe the students in your classroom, and explain your lesson plan.

5. Five students in your middle school language arts class are struggling readers, and you know that vocabulary knowledge plays a crucial role in reading achievement. Describe three ways you can help these students expand their vocabularies to support their reading development. (You may want to reread the Classroom Interventions feature in this chapter.) Also explain how you will implement these changes.

REFERENCES

Allen, J. (1999). *Words, words, words*. Portsmouth, NH: Heinemann.

Allen, J. (2007). *Inside words: Tools for teaching academic vocabulary, grades 4–12*. Portland, ME: Stenhouse.

Allington, R. L. (2012). *What really matters for struggling readers: Designing research-based programs* (3rd ed.). Boston: Pearson.

Baumann, J. F., Edwards, E. C., Font, G., Tereshinski, C. A., Kame'enui, E. J., & Olejnik, S. (2002). Teaching morphemic and contextual analysis to fifth grade students. *Reading Research Quarterly, 37*, 150–176.

Baumann, J. F., Font, G., Edwards, E. C., & Boland, E. (2005). Strategies for teaching middle-grade students to use word-part and context clues to expand reading vocabulary. In E. Hiebert & M. L. Kamil (Eds.), *Teaching and learning vocabulary: Bringing research to practice* (pp. 179–205). Mahwah, NJ: Erlbaum.

Baumann, J. F., Kame'enui, E. J., & Ash, G. (2003). Research on vocabulary instruction: Voltaire redux. In J. Flood, D. Lapp, J. R. Squire, & J. M. Jensen (Eds.), *Handbook of research on teaching the English language arts* (2nd ed., pp. 752–785). Mahwah, NJ: Erlbaum.

Bean, R. M., & Swan, A. (2006). Vocabulary assessment: A key to planning vocabulary instruction. In C. C. Block & J. N. Mangieri (Eds.), *The vocabulary-enriched classroom: Practices for improving the reading performance of all students in grades 3 and up* (pp. 164–187). New York: Scholastic.

Bear, D. R., Invernizzi, M., Templeton, S., & Johnston, F. (2016). *Words their way: Word study for phonics, vocabulary, and spelling instruction* (6th ed.). Boston: Pearson.

Beck, I. L., McKeown, M. G., & Kucan, L. (2002). *Bringing words to life: Robust vocabulary instruction*. New York: Guilford Press.

Blachowicz, C. L. Z., & Fisher, P. J. (2011). Best practices in vocabulary instruction revisited. In L. M. Morrow & L. B. Gambrell (Eds.), *Best practices in literacy instruction* (4th ed., pp. 224–249). New York: Guilford Press.

Bollard, J. K. (2006). *Scholastic children's thesaurus*. New York: Scholastic.

Brewster, H. (1997). *Inside the Titanic*. Boston: Little, Brown.

Burke, J. (2008). *The English teacher's companion: A complete guide to classroom, curriculum, and the profession*. Portsmouth, NH: Heinemann.

Calderón, M. (2007). *Teaching reading to English language learners, grades 6–12*. Thousand Oaks, CA: Corwin Press.

Cheney, L. (2002). *America: A patriotic primer*. New York: Simon & Schuster.

Christensen, B. (2001). *Woody Guthrie: Poet of the people*. New York: Knopf.

Cooper, J. D., Chard, D. J., & Kiger, N. D. (2006). *The struggling reader: Interventions that work*. New York: Scholastic.

Cunningham, P. M. (2009). *What really matters in vocabulary: Research-based practices across the curriculum*. Boston: Allyn & Bacon/Pearson.

Cunningham, P. M., & Allington, R. L. (2016). *Classrooms at work: They can all read and write* (6th ed.). Boston: Pearson.

Duffelmeyer, F. A., & Banwart, B. H. (1992–1993). Word maps for adjectives and verbs. *The Reading Teacher, 46*, 351–353.

Dunn, D. M., Dunn, L. W., & Dunn, L. M. (2006). *Peabody picture vocabulary test-4*. Bloomington, MN: American Guidance Service/Pearson.

Fisher, D., Frey, N., & Lapp, D. (2008). Shared readings: Modeling comprehension, vocabulary, text structures, and text features for older readers. *The Reading Teacher, 61*, 548–556.

Frasier, D. (2007). *Miss Alaineus: A vocabulary disaster*. New York: HarperCollins/Voyager.

Graves, M. F. (2006). *The vocabulary book: Learning and instruction.* New York: Teachers College Press.

Graves, M. F., & Watts-Taffe, S. M. (2002). The place of word consciousness in a research-based vocabulary program. In S. J. Samuels & A. E. Farstrup (Eds.), *What research has to say about reading instruction* (3rd ed., pp. 140–165). Newark, DE: International Reading Association.

Guthrie, W. (2008). *This land is your land.* New York: Little, Brown.

Gwynne, F. (2005). *A chocolate moose for dinner.* New York: Aladdin Books.

Gwynne, F. (2006). *The king who rained.* New York: Aladdin Books.

Hellweg, P. (2009). *The American Heritage children's thesaurus.* Boston: Houghton Mifflin.

Henkes, K. (1996). *Chrysanthemum.* New York: Harper Trophy.

Howe, D., & Howe, J. (2006). *Bunnicula: A rabbit-tale of mystery.* New York: Aladdin Books.

Jacobson, J., Lapp, D., & Flood, J. (2007). A seven-step instructional plan for teaching English-language learners to comprehend and use homonyms, homophones, and homographs. *Journal of Adolescent & Adult Literacy, 51,* 98–111.

Kentley, E. (2001). *Story of the Titanic.* London: Dorling Kindersley.

Lowry, L. (1984). *Anastasia Krupnik.* New York: Yearling.

Marzano, R. J., & Pickering, D. J. (2005). *Building academic vocabulary: Teacher's manual.* Alexandria, VA: Association for Supervision and Curriculum Development.

McKeown, M. G., & Beck, I. L. (2004). Direct and rich vocabulary instruction. In J. F. Baumann & E. J. Kame'enui (Eds.), *Vocabulary instruction: Research to practice* (pp. 13–27). New York: Guilford Press.

Nagy, W. E. (1988). *Teaching vocabulary to improve reading comprehension.* Urbana, IL: ERIC Clearinghouse on Reading and Communication Skills and the National Council of Teachers of English and the International Reading Association.

Nagy, W. E., Anderson, R. C., & Herman, P. A. (1987). Learning word meanings from context during normal reading. *American Educational Research Journal, 24,* 237–270.

Osborne, W., & Osborne, M. P. (1995). *Tonight on the Titanic.* New York: Random House.

Osborne, W., & Osborne, M. P. (2002). *Titanic: A nonfiction companion to Tonight on the Titanic.* New York: Random House.

Palmer, B. C., Shackelford, V. S., Miller, S. C., & Leclere, J. T. (2006/2007). Bridging two worlds: Reading comprehension, figurative language instruction, and the English-language learner. *Journal of Adolescent & Adult Literacy, 50,* 258–267.

Paulsen, G. (2007). *Hatchet.* New York: Simon & Schuster.

Pittelman, S. D., Heimlich, J. E., Berglund, R. L., & French, M. P. (1991). *Semantic feature analysis: Classroom applications.* Newark, DE: International Reading Association.

Rickelman, R. J., & Taylor, D. B. (2006). Teaching vocabulary by learning content-area words. In C. C. Block & J. N. Mangieri (Eds.), *The vocabulary-enriched classroom: Practices for improving the reading performance of all students in grades 3 and up* (pp. 54–73). New York: Scholastic.

Santoro, L. E., Chard, D. J., Howard, L., & Baker, S. K. (2008). Making the *very* most of classroom read-alouds to promote comprehension and vocabulary. *The Reading Teacher, 61,* 396–408.

Scieszka, J. (2005). *Baloney (Henry P.).* New York: Puffin Books.

Scillian, D. (2001). *A is for America: An American alphabet.* Chelsea, MI: Sleeping Bear Press.

Scott, J. A., & Nagy, W. E. (2004). Developing word consciousness. In J. F. Baumann & E. J. Kame'enui (Eds.), *Vocabulary instruction: Theory to practice* (pp. 210–217). New York: Guilford Press.

Stahl, S. A. (1999). *Vocabulary development.* Cambridge, MA: Brookline Books.

Stahl, S. A., & Kapinus, B. (1991). Possible sentences: Predicting word meanings to teach content area vocabulary. *The Reading Teacher, 45,* 36–43.

Stahl, S. A., & Nagy, W. E. (2006). *Teaching word meanings.* Mahwah, NJ: Erlbaum.

Stahl, S. A., Richek, M. G., & Vandevier, R. (1991). Learning word meanings through listening: A sixth grade replication. In J. Zutell & S. McCormick (Eds.), *Learning factors/teacher factors: Issues in literacy research. Fortieth yearbook of the National Reading Conference* (pp. 185–192). Chicago: National Reading Conference.

Stanovich, K. E. (1986). Matthew effects in reading: Some consequences of individual differences in the acquisition of literacy. *Reading Research Quarterly, 21,* 360–406.

Swanborn, M. S. W., & de Glopper, K. (1999). Incidental word learning while reading: A meta-analysis. *Review of Educational Research, 69,* 261–285.

Tanaka, S. (1996). *On board the Titanic: What it was like when the great liner sank.* New York: Hyperion Books.

Terban, M. (2006). *Scholastic dictionary of idioms.* New York: Scholastic.

Tompkins, G. E., & Yaden, D. B., Jr. (1986). *Answering students' questions about words.* Urbana, IL: ERIC Clearinghouse on Reading and Communication Skills and the National Council of Teachers of English.

Venezky, R. L. (1999). *The American way of spelling: The structure and origins of American English orthography.* New York: Guilford Press.

White, E. E. (1998). *Voyage on the great Titanic: The diary of Margaret Ann Brady.* New York: Scholastic.

White, T. G., Sowell, J., & Yanagihara, A. (1989). Teaching elementary students to use word-part clues. *The Reading Teacher, 42,* 302–308.

Williams, K. T. (2006). *Expressive vocabulary test-2.* Bloomington, MN: American Guidance Service/Pearson.

Wittels, H., & Greisman, J. (2001). *A first thesaurus.* Racine, WI: Golden Books.

Wood, A. (1982). *Quick as a cricket.* London: Child's Play.

Chapter 8

Promoting Comprehension: Reader Factors

PLAN: Preview the Learning Outcomes

After studying this chapter, you'll be prepared to respond to these points:

8.1 Define *comprehension*.

8.2 Name the comprehension strategies and explain their role in comprehension.

8.3 Discuss how teachers teach the reader factors.

8.4 Describe teachers' and students' roles in motivation.

Ms. Ali Teaches Comprehension Strategies. Posters about comprehension strategies, including connecting, questioning, repairing, and summarizing, hang on the wall in Ms. Ali's classroom. She introduced comprehension strategies by explaining that sixth graders think while they read, and they do different kinds of thinking, called *strategies*. Her students made the posters as they studied each strategy. Check the figure Sixth Graders' Strategy Poster to see Tanner, Vincente, and Ashante's poster for monitoring.

The first strategy that Ms. Ali taught was *predicting*, and even though her students were familiar with it, they didn't know why they were using it. She explained that predictions guide their thinking. Together they made a chart about the strategy and practiced making predictions as Ms. Ali read *The Garden of Abdul Gasazi* (Van Allsburg, 1993), the story of an evil magician who hates dogs. The students made predictions about *The Garden of Abdul Gasazi* based on the title and the cover illustration, but making predictions got harder in the middle of the surrealistic story because they didn't know whether the dog would escape the magician's garden after he was turned into a duck. Ms. Ali emphasized the importance of continuing to think about the story and to make predictions when it gets confusing. She stopped reading and talked first about why the dog was likely to be successful and then why he wouldn't be. Only about two thirds of the students predicted he would make it home safely, but he did.

The next day, they read *La Mariposa* (Jiménez, 1998), the autobiographical picture-book story about a migrant child with exceptional artistic ability. The title, which means "the butterfly," and the cover

illustration of a boy flying toward the sun didn't provide enough information on which to base a prediction, so the students learned that sometimes they have to read a few pages before they can make useful predictions. After reading about Spanish-speaking Francisco's difficult first day of school in an English-only classroom, Norma figured out that the caterpillar the boy is watching in the classroom will become a butterfly, and that the boy on the front cover is flying like a butterfly, but she didn't know why that connection was important. Several students pointed out that the butterfly might symbolize freedom. Moises predicted that the boy will be rescued from the migrant tent city where he and his family live, and Lizette suggested that he'll move to a bilingual classroom where his teacher will understand him and he'll make friends. Even though those predictions were wrong, the students became more engaged in the story and were eager for their teacher to continue reading. Ms. Ali wrote their predictions on small self-stick notes and attached them to the edge of the pages as she read. She modeled how to use these notes because she wanted to make their thinking more visible, and she explained that she wants them to use self-stick notes, too: "I want you to show me your thinking."

Next, she taught the connecting strategy using *So Far From the Sea* (Bunting, 1998), a story about life at a Japanese relocation camp during World War II. She explained that readers make three kinds of connections—text-to-self, text-to-world, and text-to-text. As she read each book aloud, she modeled making connections and encouraged the sixth graders to share their connections. Each time they made a connection, Ms. Ali wrote it on a self-stick note; after she finished reading the book, she collected the notes. The students sorted them according to the kind of connection, and posted them in columns on a chart. For an example, check the figure Connections Chart.

SIXTH GRADERS' STRATEGY POSTER

MONITORING

What is it?	It is checking that you are understanding what you are reading.
Why use it?	Monitoring helps you solve problems so you can be successful.
When?	You should use this strategy while you are reading.
What do you do?	1. Keep asking: Does this make sense? If you are understanding, keep reading, but if it doesn't make sense, take action to solve the problem. 2. Try these solutions: • Go back several pages or to the beginning of the chapter and reread. • Keep reading one or two more pages. • Reread the last prediction, connection, or summary you wrote. • Talk to a friend about the problem. • Write a quickwrite about the problem. • Talk to Ms. Ali.

CONNECTIONS CHART

Text-to-Self	Text-to-World	Text-to-Text
My grandmother takes flowers when she goes to the cemetery because one of her husbands died.	I know that in World War II, Americans were fighting the Japanese because of Pearl Harbor, and they were fighting Hitler and the Germans, too.	This story is like The Bracelet. That girl and her family were taken to a camp in the desert. It was miserable there and she didn't deserve to have to go.
My great-granddad had to go, and it wasn't fair because he was a loyal American, but his parents were from Japan.	In the book it's World War II, but I'm thinking about our war in Afghanistan.	Another book I know is Journey to Topaz. Topaz was a terrible war relocation center.
I know how to make origami birds. I learned last summer.		I've heard about a book called Anne Frank. She was Jewish and this sorta happened to her in Germany and she died, too.
We have an American flag on our car so everyone knows we love the U.S.A.		

Ms. Ali reviewed each comprehension strategy because she wanted the sixth graders to be familiar with all of them. Next, she introduced *Joey Pigza Loses Control*, a Newbery Honor book by Jack Gantos (2005), so that students could practice integrating their use of the comprehension strategies in an authentic reading experience. The teacher explained that readers rarely use only one strategy; instead, they use many of them at the same time.

Ms. Ali introduced the book: "This is a story about a boy named Joey who is about your age. His parents are divorced, and he's going to spend the summer with his dad. Joey is ADHD. His mother says he's 'wired,' and he uses medicine patches to control his behavior. He doesn't know his dad very well, so he doesn't know what to expect. His mom tells him not to expect too much." She asks the sixth graders to think about what they know about divorced parents, summer vacations, and ADHD kids. They talk about what they know about each topic, and then they brainstorm these questions to stimulate their thinking about the story:

What is Joey's dad like?
Will they have fun together?
Will Joey be in the way?
Does he hope his parents will get back together?
Does Joey's dad love him?

Will Joey's dad disappoint him?

Will Joey disappoint his dad?

Will Joey's medicine work or will he be "wired"?

Will Joey's mom be lonely without him?

Will Joey stay with his dad all summer or come back home sooner?

The teacher passes out copies of the book and stacks of small self-stick notes for students to use to record their thinking as they read. They read the first chapter together, and then students continue to read on their own or with a partner. The book is contemporary realism, and it's easy reading for most students. Ms. Ali chose it because it would be interesting but easy to read, so they'd have the cognitive resources available while reading to concentrate on their strategy use.

After reading the first chapter, the students come together to talk about it in a **grand conversation**. They begin by talking about what they remember from the chapter, and then Ms. Ali reads the sentence from page 10 where Joey says this to his mom about the dad he doesn't know very well: "I just want him to love me as much as I already love him." Ms. Ali asks, "How do parents show that they love their children?" She hangs up a sheet of chart paper, divides it into two columns, and writes the question at the top of the first column. The students suggest a number of ways, including giving them presents, taking care of them, spending time with them, taking them to church, keeping them safe, and having dinner with them. Ms. Ali writes their ideas under the question in the first column of the chart. Then she narrows the question and asks, "What do you think Joey is looking for from his dad?" Ashante says, "He wants his dad to pay attention to him." Leticia suggests, "He wants him to say, 'I love you, son,' tell him he's missed him, and play basketball with him." Students continue to offer ideas, which the teacher adds to the chart. Then she asks, "How do kids show love to their parents?" and she writes the question at the top of the second column. The students suggest that children show their love by behaving, making their parents proud, being responsible, and doing their chores; she writes these answers under the question in the second column. Finally, Ms. Ali asks, "What is Joey's dad expecting from his son?" It's much harder for the students to put themselves in this role. Henry offers, "I think he just wants to have him live with him every day." The sixth graders also reflect on their strategy use. Several students talk about predictions they made, and others share how they monitored their reading and made connections while they were reading.

After reading and discussing each chapter, the students collect the self-stick notes they've used to keep track of their thinking, and they write about the strategies they've used in a **double-entry journal**. Normally, double-entry journals have two columns, but Ms. Ali asks the students to include three columns—she's calling it a triple-entry journal: They write what was happening in the text or copy a quote from the text in the first column, explain their thinking in the second column, and identify the strategy they used in the third column. Check the figure A Triple-Entry Thinking Journal to read excerpts from Tanner's journal.

The students continue to read, discuss, and write about their strategy use as they read *Joey Pigza Loses Control*. After they've read half the book, Ms. Ali brings the class together for a **minilesson**. She explains that she's reviewed their thinking journals and has noticed that students weren't summarizing very much. They talk about the summarizing strategy and how, when, and why they should use it. Ms. Ali demonstrates how to summarize as she reads the beginning of the next chapter aloud, and then she encourages students to try to use the strategy as they read the next chapter.

After they finish reading the book, the students have another grand conversation. They talk about how Joey's mom rescues him and how disillusioned Joey is about his dad. Next, they return to the list of questions they brainstormed before they began reading and talk about the questions and answers. Jake answers the question "Does Joey's dad love him?" this way: "I think his dad does love him but it's a strange kind of love because his dad is selfish. He loves him as much as he can, but it's not very good love." Lizette answers these two questions: "Will Joey's dad disappoint him?" and "Will Joey disappoint his dad?" She says, "I'm positive that Joey's dad disappointed

A TRIPLE-ENTRY THINKING JOURNAL

Chapter	In the Book	My Thinking	Strategy
1	Joey's mom warns him that his dad is wired like he is.	I'm thinking that this book is about a kid who doesn't know his dad and he's going to be disappointed by him. His Mom doesn't think it's going to be a good vacation.	Identifying big ideas
4	Joey's dad doesn't act like a dad and his Grandma doesn't act like a grandma.	My stomach feels queasy. Joey doesn't belong with these people. His dad doesn't stop talking to listen to him and his grandma doesn't even like him. I predict bad things are going to happen.	Predicting
7	After the game they go to the mall to see Leezy.	My mind is asking questions. Why would Carter let Joey drive the car to the mall? Why would his dad tell him it's OK to steal money out of the wishing pond? Is the author trying to show us what a terrible dad he is? We already know that.	Questioning
8	His dad thinks Joey doesn't need the patches and he won't let him have them.	What is wrong with his dad? The patch is medicine that he needs. I am so mad at his dad. That's all I can think. I'm glad my parents take good care of me.	Connecting
14	Joey calls his mom to come get him at the mall.	I think Joey is really a smart kid. He knows how to save himself. He calls his mom and she comes to get him. Joey is right to call his dad a J-E-R-K because that's what he is. The visit was a fiasco just like I predicted. This is a really great book and I want to read it all over again.	Evaluating

him. His dad wasn't a good dad. The second question is harder to answer. I know Joey tried to be a good son, but it's impossible to satisfy his dad. His dad made him hyper and then got mad at him for being hyper."

Students then reread the chart they began after reading the first chapter about parents showing their love for their children and children showing their love for their parents. They talk about the things they learned that Joey wanted from his dad: for his dad to listen to him, to take care of him, to be responsible for him. They also talk about what Joey's dad wanted from him. Dillan explains, "I think Joey's dad wanted Joey to be his friend and to take care of him. I think Joey would be a better dad than his dad was." Then Ms. Ali asks about Joey's mom: "Does Joey's mom love him?" Everyone agrees that she does, and they name many ways that she shows her love, including giving him money so he can call her, listening to him, worrying about him, hugging him, and telling him she loves him. They complete the chart by adding the new suggestions and then circling the behaviors that his dad exemplified in blue, his mom's in green, and Joey's in red. Later, students will use the information on this chart as they write an essay about how parents and children show their love for one another.

As they reflect on their strategy use, the students are amazed that they remember so much from the story and how well they understand it. Jake says, "I was thinking all the time in this story. I guess that's why I know so much about it. This thinking is a good idea." Richard agrees, saying,

"I don't even have to remember to use strategies now. I just naturally think that way." Ms. Ali smiles at Richard's comment. Her goal is for her students to use comprehension strategies independently. She'll continue to emphasize strategies and remind the sixth graders to use self-stick notes to track their thinking for several more months, but she'll gradually remove this scaffold once she sees that they've become strategic readers.

STANDARDS CHECK!

Ms. Ali addressed the Common Core State Standards as she taught comprehension strategies in the vignette you've just read. Review the sixth grade literacy Standards document online at http://www.corestandards.org/ELA-Literacy, and identify the Standards that Ms. Ali addressed through her instruction. Create your list, and compare it with Ms. Ali's.

Comprehension is the goal of reading; it's the reason why people read. Students must understand what they're reading to learn from the experience; they must make sense of the words in the text to maintain interest; and they must enjoy reading to become lifelong readers. Ms. Ali taught her students to use comprehension strategies in the vignette because strategic readers are more likely to comprehend what they're reading. Struggling readers, in contrast, are frustrated; they don't understand what they're reading, don't like to read, and aren't likely to choose to read in the future.

Comprehension involves different levels of thinking, from literal to inferential, critical, and evaluative. The most basic level is **literal comprehension**: Readers pick out main ideas, sequence details, notice similarities and differences, and identify explicitly stated reasons. The higher levels differ from literal comprehension because readers use their own knowledge along with the information presented in the text. The second level is **inferential comprehension**. Readers use clues in the text, implied information, and their background knowledge to draw inferences. They make predictions, recognize cause and effect, and determine the author's purpose. **Critical comprehension** is next: Readers analyze symbolic meanings, distinguish fact from opinion, and draw conclusions. The most sophisticated level is **evaluative comprehension**: Readers judge the value of a text using generally accepted criteria and personal standards. They detect bias, identify faulty reasoning, determine the effectiveness of persuasive techniques, and assess the quality of a text. These levels point out the range of thinking readers do. Because it's important to involve students in higher level thinking, teachers ask questions and involve students in activities that require them to use inferential, critical, and evaluative comprehension.

What Is *Comprehension*?

Comprehension is a creative, multifaceted thinking process in which students engage with the text (Tierney, 1990). You've read about the word *process* before—both reading and writing have been described as processes. A process is more complicated than a single action: It involves a series of behaviors that occur over time. The comprehension process begins during prereading as students activate their background knowledge and preview the text, and it continues to develop as students read, respond, explore, and apply their reading. Readers construct a mental "picture" or representation of the text and its interpretation through the comprehension process (Van Den Broek & Kremer, 2000).

Judith Irwin (1991) defines comprehension as a reader's process of using prior experiences and the author's text to construct meaning that's useful to that reader for a specific purpose. This definition emphasizes that comprehension depends on both the reader and the text. Whether comprehension is successful, according to Sweet and Snow (2003), depends on the interaction of reader factors and text factors.

Reader and Text Factors

Readers are actively engaged with the text they're reading; they think about many things as they comprehend the text. For example, they do the following:

Activate prior knowledge
Examine the text to uncover its organization
Make predictions
Connect to their own experiences
Create mental images
Draw inferences
Notice symbols and other literary devices
Monitor their understanding

These activities can be categorized as reader and text factors (National Reading Panel, 2000). Reader factors include the background knowledge that readers bring to the reading process as well as the strategies they use while reading and their motivation and engagement during reading. Text factors include the author's ideas, the words the author uses to express those ideas, and how the ideas are organized and presented. Both reader factors and text factors affect comprehension. Figure 8–1 presents an overview of these factors; this chapter focuses on reader factors, and Chapter 9 addresses text factors.

Text Complexity

Text complexity is a new way of examining comprehension to determine the cognitive demands of books, or more specifically, how well readers can complete an assigned task with a particular text (Fisher, Frey, & Lapp, 2012). Traditionally, teachers have identified students' independent, instructional, and frustration levels and matched books to students using readability formulas, but the Common Core State Standards movement has drawn new attention to the topic because the 10th reading Standard specifies that students will read and comprehend challenging fiction and nonfiction texts independently and proficiently at each grade level. This Standard emphasizes two goals: First, students read books at their grade-level placements, and second, students learn to read and understand these books on their own, without teachers reading them aloud or leading them through comprehension activities. Booklist: Complex Texts shows examples of fiction and nonfiction texts from the Common Core State Standards document.

A number of factors affect text complexity; the Common Core State Standards identified these three components:

Qualitative Dimensions. Teachers make informed judgments about a book's grade appropriateness by examining its layout; its text structure, language features, and purpose and meaning; and the demands placed on readers' background knowledge. These dimensions are difficult to evaluate because they can't easily be quantified.

FIGURE 8–1	The Comprehension Factors

TYPE	FACTORS	ROLES IN COMPREHENSION
Reader	Background Knowledge	Students activate their world and literary knowledge to link what they know to what they're reading.
	Vocabulary	Students recognize the meaning of familiar words and apply word-learning strategies to understand what they're reading.
	Fluency	Students have adequate cognitive resources available to understand what they're reading when they read fluently.
	Strategies	Students actively direct their reading, monitor their understanding, and troubleshoot problems when they occur.
	Skills	Students automatically note details that support main ideas, sequence ideas, and use other skills.
	Motivation	Motivated students are more engaged in reading, more confident, and more likely to comprehend successfully.
Text	Genres	Genres have unique characteristics, and students' knowledge of them provides a scaffold for comprehension.
	Text Structures	Students recognize the important ideas more easily when they understand the patterns that authors use to organize text.
	Text Features	Students apply their knowledge of the conventions and literary devices used in texts to deepen their understanding.

Quantitative Measures. Teachers use readability formulas or other scores to determine a book's grade appropriateness by calculating word length, word frequency, word difficulty, sentence length, text length, and other quantitative features. They often rely on computer software to determine reading levels, such as Lexile scores.

Reader and Task Considerations. Teachers reflect on how they expect students to interact with the book, and on students' literary knowledge and strategy use as well as their motivation and interests. With instruction, students grow in their understanding of how to read complex texts, and they learn to think about ideas and information in different ways. For instance, young students are often asked to examine the theme in one story, but older students are asked to investigate how the point of view in two novels influences the theme.

Teachers analyze these components to determine a book's text complexity for their students. Unfortunately, there's no easy formula for figuring out the complexity level of a book.

Booklist — Complex Texts

GRADE	FICTION	NONFICTION
K	dePaola, T. (1978). *Pancakes for breakfast*. New York: Harcourt. Haley, G. E. (1988). *A story, a story*. New York: Aladdin Books.	Aliki. (1989). *My five senses*. New York: HarperCollins. Jenkins, S., & Page R. (2003). *What do you do with a tail like this?* Boston: Houghton Mifflin.
1	Arnold, T. (2006). *Hi! Fly guy*. New York: Cartwheel Books. Atwater, R. (2011). *Mr. Popper's penguins*. Boston: Little, Brown.	Hodgkins, F. (2007). *How people learned to fly*. New York: HarperCollins. Pfeffer, W. (2004). *From seed to pumpkin*. New York: HarperCollins.
2–3	MacLachlan, P. (2005). *Sarah, plain and tall*. New York: Scholastic. White, E. B. (2006). *Charlotte's web*. New York: HarperCollins.	Aliki. (1986). *A medieval feast*. New York: HarperCollins. Floca, B. (2009). *Moonshot: The flight of Apollo 11*. New York: Atheneum.
4–5	Lin, G. (2011). *Where the mountain meets the moon*. Boston: Little, Brown. Thayer, E. L. (2000). *Casey at the bat: A ballad of the republic sung in the year 1888*. San Francisco: Chronicle Books.	Lauber, P. (1996). *Hurricanes: Earth's mightiest storms*. New York: Scholastic. Montgomery, S. (2009). *Quest for the tree kangaroo*. New York: Sandpiper.
6–8	Frost, R. (1993). "The road not taken." In *The road not taken and other poems*. Mineola, NY: Dover Books. Yep, L. (2000). *Dragonwings* (25th anniversary ed.). New York: Harper Trophy.	Douglass, F. (2007). *Narrative of the life of Frederick Douglass, an American slave*. New York: Book Jungle. Steinbeck, J. (2002). *Travels with Charlie: In search of America*. New York: Penguin Books.

The Common Core State Standards challenge teachers to provide a balance of instruction and scaffolding so students learn to read and comprehend complex texts. Teachers ensure that students are actively engaged with books they're reading, and they provide more support when students are reading more complex texts. In the vignette, Ms. Ali demonstrated how teachers teach students about challenging texts and then gradually release responsibility to them to apply what they've learned about comprehension when they're reading independently.

Prerequisites for Comprehension

For students to comprehend a text, they must have adequate background knowledge, understand most words in a text, and be able to read fluently. When any of these prerequisites for comprehension are lacking, students aren't likely to understand what they're reading. Teachers can ameliorate readers' difficulties through differentiated instruction.

BACKGROUND KNOWLEDGE. Having both world knowledge and literary knowledge is a prerequisite because they provide a bridge to a new text (Braunger & Lewis, 2006). When students don't have adequate background knowledge, they're likely to find the text very challenging, and it's doubtful that they'll be successful. Teachers use prereading activities to build students' background knowledge—both their understanding of the topic and their familiarity with the genre; first they determine whether students need world or literary knowledge and then provide experiences and information to develop their schema. They use a combination of experiences, visual representations, and talk to build knowledge. Involving students in authentic experiences such as taking field trips, participating in dramatizations, and examining artifacts is the best way to build background knowledge, but photos and pictures, picture books, websites, videos, and other visual representations can also be used. Talk is often the least effective way, especially for English learners, but sometimes explaining a concept or listing the characteristics of a genre does provide enough information.

VOCABULARY. Students' knowledge of words plays a tremendous role in comprehension because it's difficult to comprehend a text that's loaded with unknown words. It's also possible that when students don't know many words related to a topic, they don't have adequate background knowledge either. Blachowicz and Fisher (2011) recommend creating a word-rich classroom environment to immerse students in words and teaching word-learning strategies so they can figure out the meaning of new words. In addition, teachers preteach key words when they're building background knowledge using **KWL charts**, **anticipation guides**, and other prereading activities.

READING FLUENCY. Fluent readers read quickly and efficiently. Because they recognize most words automatically, their cognitive resources aren't depleted by decoding unfamiliar words, and they can devote their attention to comprehension (Pressley, 2002a). In the primary grades, developing reading fluency is an important component of comprehension instruction because children need to learn to recognize words automatically so they can concentrate on comprehending what they're reading (Samuels, 2002). For many struggling readers, their lack of fluency severely affects their ability to understand what they read. Teachers help older, struggling readers who aren't fluent readers by teaching or reteaching word-identification strategies, having students do repeated readings, and providing students with books at their reading levels so that they can be successful. When teachers use grade-level texts that are too difficult for struggling students, they read them aloud so that everyone can comprehend and participate in related activities.

 Check the Compendium of Instructional Procedures, which follows Chapter 12.

 MONITOR: Check Your Understanding 8.1

Comprehension Strategies

Comprehension strategies are thoughtful behaviors that students use to facilitate their understanding as they read (Afflerbach, Pearson, & Paris, 2008). Some strategies are **cognitive**—they involve thinking; others are **metacognitive**—students reflect on their thinking. For example, readers make predictions about a story when they begin reading: They wonder what will happen to the characters and whether they'll enjoy the story. Predicting is a cognitive strategy because it involves thinking. Readers also monitor their reading, and monitoring is a metacognitive strategy. They notice whether they're understanding; and if they're confused, they take action to solve the problem. For example, they may go back and reread or talk to a classmate to clarify their confusion. Students are being metacognitive when they're alert to the possibility that they might get confused, and they know several ways to solve the problem (Pressley, 2002b).

Students learn to use a variety of cognitive and metacognitive strategies, including *predicting*, *drawing inferences*, and *monitoring*, to ensure that they comprehend what they're reading. Figure 8–2 lists the comprehension strategies and explains how readers use them. These 12 strategies emphasize how readers think during the reading process; they're reader factors. Students use these comprehension strategies to understand not only what they're reading, but also while they're listening to books read aloud and when they're writing. For example, students use the determining importance strategy when they're listening or reading to identify the big ideas, and when

FIGURE 8–2 The Comprehension Strategies

STRATEGY	WHAT READERS DO	HOW IT AIDS COMPREHENSION
Activating Background Knowledge	Readers think about what they already know about the topic.	Readers use their background knowledge to fill in gaps in the text and enhance their comprehension.
Connecting	Readers make text-to-self, text-to-world, and text-to-text links.	Readers personalize their reading by relating what they're reading to their background knowledge.
Determining Importance	Readers identify the big ideas in the text and notice the relationships among them.	Readers focus on the big ideas so they don't become overwhelmed with details.
Drawing Inferences	Readers use background knowledge and clues in the text to "read between the lines."	Readers move beyond literal thinking to grasp meaning that isn't explicitly stated in the text.
Evaluating	Readers evaluate both the text itself and their reading experience.	Readers assume responsibility for their own strategy use.
Monitoring	Readers supervise their reading experience, checking that they're understanding the text.	Readers expect the text to make sense, and they recognize when it doesn't so they can take action.
Predicting	Readers make thoughtful "guesses" about what will happen and then read to confirm their predictions.	Readers become more engaged in the reading experience and want to continue reading.
Questioning	Readers ask themselves literal and inferential questions about the text.	Readers use questions to direct their reading, clarify confusions, and make inferences.
Repairing	Readers identify a problem interfering with comprehension and then solve it.	Readers solve problems to regain comprehension and continue reading.
Setting a Purpose	Readers identify a broad focus to direct their reading through the text.	Readers focus their attention as they read according to the purpose they've set.
Summarizing	Readers paraphrase the big ideas to create a concise statement.	Readers have better recall of the big ideas when they summarize.
Visualizing	Readers create mental images of what they're reading.	Readers use the mental images to make the text more memorable.

they're writing, they organize their writing around the big ideas so that readers also will comprehend what they're reading.

Activating Background Knowledge

Readers bring their background knowledge to every reading experience; in fact, they read a text differently depending on their prior experiences. Zimmermann and Hutchins (2003) explain that "the meaning you get from a piece is intertwined with the meaning you bring to it" (p. 45). Before they begin reading, readers think about the topic and call up relevant information and related vocabulary to use while reading. The more background knowledge and prior experiences readers have about a topic, the more likely they are to comprehend what they're reading (Harvey & Goudvis, 2007).

Teachers use a variety of prereading activities to scaffold students as they learn to activate their background knowledge, such as **anticipation guides**, **exclusion brainstorming**, graphic organizers, **KWL charts**, and **prereading plans**. Through these activities, students think about the topic, use related vocabulary, and get interested in reading the text.

Connecting

Readers make three types of connections between the text and their background knowledge: text-to-self, text-to-world, and text-to-text connections (Harvey & Goudvis, 2007). In text-to-self connections, students link the ideas they're reading about to events in their own lives; these are personal connections. A story event or character may remind them of something or someone in their own lives, and information in a nonfiction book may remind them of a past experience. In text-to-world connections, students relate what they're reading to their "world" knowledge, learned both in and out of school. When students make text-to-text connections, they link the text or an element of it to another text they've read or to a familiar film or television program. Students often compare different versions of familiar folktales, novels and their sequels, and sets of books by the same author. Text-to-text connections require higher level thinking, and they're often the most difficult, especially for students who have done less reading or who know less about literature.

One way that teachers teach this strategy is by making connection charts with three columns labeled *text-to-self*, *text-to-world*, and *text-to-text*. Then students write connections that they've made on small self-stick notes and post them in the correct column of the chart, as Ms. Ali did in the vignette at the beginning of the chapter. Students can also make connection charts in their **reading logs** and write connections in each column. Later in the reading process, during the exploring and applying stages, students make connections as they assume the role of a character and are interviewed by classmates during **hot seat**, create **open-mind portraits** to share the character's thinking, or write simulated journals from the viewpoint of a character, for example.

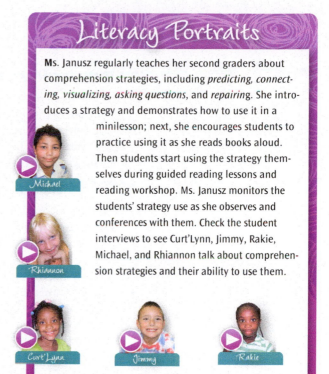

Literacy Portraits

Ms. Janusz regularly teaches her second graders about comprehension strategies, including *predicting, connecting, visualizing, asking questions,* and *repairing*. She introduces a strategy and demonstrates how to use it in a minilesson; next, she encourages students to practice using it as she reads books aloud. Then students start using the strategy themselves during guided reading lessons and reading workshop. Ms. Janusz monitors the students' strategy use as she observes and conferences with them. Check the student interviews to see Curt'Lynn, Jimmy, Rakie, Michael, and Rhiannon talk about comprehension strategies and their ability to use them.

Michael
Rhiannon
Curt'Lynn
Jimmy
Rakie

Determining Importance

Readers sift through the text to identify the important ideas as they read because it isn't possible to remember everything (Harvey & Goudvis, 2007; Keene & Zimmermann, 2007). Students learn to distinguish the big ideas and the details and to recognize what's important as they read and talk about the books they've read. This comprehension strategy is important because students need to be able to identify the big ideas in order to summarize.

Teachers often direct students toward the big ideas when they encourage them to make predictions. The way they introduce the text also influences students' thinking about what's important in the book they're about to read. Ms. Ali's introduction of *Joey Pigza Loses Control* (Gantos, 2005), for instance, directed her sixth graders' thinking about the story and its theme. When students read stories, they make diagrams about the plot, characters, and setting, and these graphic organizers emphasize the big ideas. Similarly, students make diagrams that reflect the structure of the text when they read informational articles and books and chapters in content area textbooks. Sometimes teachers provide the

Watch as two teachers demonstrate how they make connections. How does the teachers' modeling enhance their students' comprehension?

diagrams with the big ideas highlighted, but students often analyze the text to determine the big ideas and then create their own graphic organizers.

Drawing Inferences

Readers seem to "read between the lines" to draw inferences, but what they actually do is synthesize their background knowledge with the author's clues to ask questions that point toward inferences. Keene and Zimmermann (2007) explain that when readers draw inferences, they have "an opportunity to sense a meaning not explicit in the text, but which derives or flows from it" (p. 145). Readers make both conscious and unconscious inferences about characters in a story and its theme; the big ideas in a newspaper, magazine article, or nonfiction book; and the author's purpose in a poem (Pressley, 2002a). They may not be aware that they're drawing inferences, but when they wonder why the author included this or omitted that information, they probably are.

Students often have to read a picture-book story or an excerpt from a chapter of a novel two or three times in order to draw inferences because at first they focus on literal comprehension, which has to precede higher level thinking. Very capable students draw inferences on their own as they read, but other students don't notice opportunities to make them. Sometimes students do draw inferences when prompted by the teacher, but it's important to teach students how to draw inferences so that they can think more deeply when they read independently.

Teachers begin by explaining what inferences are, why they're important, and how inferential thinking differs from literal thinking. Then they teach these four steps in drawing inferences:

1. Activate background knowledge about topics related to the text.
2. Look for the author's clues as you read.
3. Ask questions, tying together background knowledge and the author's clues.
4. Draw inferences by answering the questions.

Teachers can create charts to make the steps more visible as students practice making inferences; Figure 8–3 shows an inference chart a seventh grade class developed as they read and analyzed *The Wretched Stone* (Van Allsburg, 1991). The story, told in diary format, is about a ship's crew that picks up a strange, glowing stone on a sea voyage; the stone captivates the sailors and has a terrible transforming effect on them. After reading the story and talking about what they understood and what confused them, students began making the chart. First, they completed the "background knowledge" column. The students thought about what they needed to know to understand the story: the meaning of the word *wretched*, sailors, the author/illustrator Chris Van Allsburg, and the fantasy genre because fantasies are different from other types of stories. Then they reread the story, searching for clues that might affect the meaning. They noticed that the ship captain's name was Hope, the island was uncharted, and the sailors who could read recovered faster, and they wrote these clues in the second column. Next, they thought about questions they had about the story and wrote them in the third column of the chart. Finally, the teacher reread the book one more time; this time, students listened more confidently, recognizing clues and drawing the

Teach Kids to BE STRATEGIC

Reader Factors

Teach students to apply comprehension strategies:

- Activate background knowledge
- Connect
- Determine importance
- Draw inferences
- Evaluate
- Monitor
- Predict
- Question
- Repair
- Set a purpose
- Summarize
- Visualize

Students learn to use each strategy and make posters to highlight their new knowledge. They apply strategies as they read and use self-stick notes to record their strategy use. Monitor students' growing use of strategies during independent reading activities, and if they struggle, reteach the strategies, making sure to name them and model their use.

FIGURE 8–3 Inference Chart

BACKGROUND KNOWLEDGE	CLUES IN THE STORY	QUESTIONS	INFERENCES
• The word <u>wretched</u> means "causing misery." • The people who work on a ship are sailors or the crew. Usually they're hard workers but not readers and musicians. • Chris Van Allsburg writes and illustrates fantasy picture books. He has brown hair and a beard. He wears glasses. • In fantasies, magic and other impossible things happen.	• The captain's last name is Hope. • The crew can read, play music, and tell stories. • It's odd that the island isn't on any maps. • The odor on the island seems sweet at first, but then it stinks. • The crew stare at the glowing stone. They lose interest in reading and stop working. • The crew change into monkeys because they watch the stone. • Capt. Hope looks just like Chris Van Allsburg. • Sailors who could read recovered faster.	• Why did Chris Van Allsburg make himself the captain? • Was it a real island or was it magic? • What is the wretched stone? • Why did the sailors turn into monkeys? • Why did the sailors who could read get well faster?	• Chris Van Allsburg wrote this book with hope for kids. • The wretched stone is television. • This book is a warning that watching too much TV is bad for you. • He wants kids to spend more time reading books because reading is good for you. • He wants kids to watch less TV. • Watching television is like the odor on the island. It's sweet at first, but too much of it stinks and isn't good for you.

inferences they had missed earlier. Finally, they completed the last column of the chart with their inferences.

Evaluating

Readers reflect on their reading experience and evaluate the text and what they're learning (Owocki, 2003). As with the other comprehension strategies, students use the evaluating strategy throughout the reading process. They monitor their interest from the moment they pick up the book and judge their success in solving reading problems when they arise. They evaluate their reading experience, including these aspects:

❧ Their ease in reading the text
❧ The adequacy of their background knowledge
❧ Their use of comprehension strategies
❧ How they solved reading problems
❧ Their interest and attention during reading

They also consider the text:

❧ Whether they like the text
❧ Their opinions about the author
❧ The world knowledge they gain
❧ How they'll use what they're learning

Students usually write about their reflections in **reading log** entries and talk about their evaluations in conferences with the teacher. Evaluating is important because it helps students assume more responsibility for their own learning.

New LITERACIES

Online Comprehension Strategies

Websites are dynamic learning contexts that create new challenges for readers because online texts differ from print texts in significant ways (Castek, Bevans-Mangelson, & Goldstone, 2006). Print texts are linear and unchanging, with a finite number of pages and with information arranged in predictable narrative, nonfiction, and poetic genres; online texts, in contrast, are multilayered, with unlimited multimodal information accessed through hypertext links.

Students use these traditional comprehension strategies to read Web-based texts, but they use them in new ways (Coiro & Dobler, 2007):

Activating Background Knowledge. Readers need to know about websites and how to navigate search engines to locate useful ones.

Predicting. Readers predict which links will be useful; otherwise, they get distracted or waste time finding their way back from unproductive links.

Evaluating. Students determine the accuracy, objectivity, relevance, and quality of information at websites, because some information is erroneous or biased.

Monitoring. Students monitor their navigational choices and decide whether the links they've reached are useful.

Repairing. Readers use the repairing strategy to correct poor navigational choices.

As researchers learn more about online reading, it's likely that they'll identify additional ways students adapt traditional comprehension strategies.

Readers also learn comprehension strategies that address the unique characteristics and complex applications of online texts (Coiro, 2003). *Coauthoring* is a comprehension strategy that readers use to impose an organization on online texts (Leu, Kinzer, Coiro, & Cammack, 2004). Coiro and Dobler (2007) examined the strategies that sixth graders used for Internet reading and found that these students use a self-directed process of text construction: They make a series of decisions as they move from one link to another, searching for information, and they plan, predict, monitor, and evaluate with each navigational choice. More than 30 years ago, Tierney and Pearson (1983) asserted that reading is a composing process, and these strategies emphasize the interrelatedness of reading and writing.

It's essential that teachers prepare students to use 21st-century technology. Students need to understand how print and Web-based texts differ so they can adjust how they apply traditional comprehension strategies and learn ones to use for Internet texts.

Monitoring

Readers monitor their understanding as they read, although they may be aware that they're using this strategy only when their comprehension breaks down and they have to take action to solve their problem. Harvey and Goudvis (2007) describe monitoring as the inner conversation that students carry on in their heads with the text as they read—for example, expressing wonder, making connections, asking questions, reacting to information, drawing conclusions, and noticing confusions.

Monitoring involves regulating reader and text factors at the same time. Readers often ask themselves these questions:

Ꮚ What's my purpose for reading?
Ꮚ Is this book too difficult for me to read on my own?
Ꮚ Do I need to read the entire book or only parts of it?
Ꮚ What's special about the genre of this book?
Ꮚ How does the author use text structure?
Ꮚ What is the author's viewpoint?
Ꮚ Do I understand the meaning of the words I'm reading? (Pressley, 2002b)

Once students detect a problem, they shift into problem-solving mode to repair their comprehension.

Teachers use **think-alouds** to demonstrate the monitoring strategy during **mini-lessons** and when they're reading aloud to students. They show that capable readers ask themselves if they understand what they're reading or if they realize that they don't remember what they've just read and what they do when they run into difficulty. Students also write about their thinking on small self-stick notes and place them in their books, next to text that stimulated their thinking. Later, students share their notes during a discussion about how they monitor their reading.

Predicting

Readers make thoughtful "guesses" or predictions about what will happen or what they'll learn in the book they're reading. These guesses are based on what students already know about the topic and genre or on what they've read thus far. Students often make a prediction before beginning to read and several others at pivotal points in a text—no matter whether they're reading stories, nonfiction books, or poems—and then as they read, they either confirm or revise their predictions. Predictions about nonfiction are different than for stories and poems; here students are generating questions about the topic that they would like to find answers to as they read.

When teachers share a big book with young children using **shared reading**, they prompt children to make predictions at the beginning of the book and again at key points during the reading. They model how to make reasonable predictions and use think-alouds to talk about their predictions.

Questioning

Readers ask themselves questions about the text as they read (Duke & Pearson, 2002). They ask self-questions out of curiosity, and as they use this strategy, they become more engaged with the text and want to keep reading to find answers (Harvey & Goudvis, 2007). These questions often lead to making predictions and drawing inferences. Students also ask themselves questions to clarify misunderstandings as they read. They use this strategy throughout the reading process—to activate background knowledge and make predictions before reading, to engage with the text and clarify confusions during reading, and to evaluate and reflect on the text after reading.

Traditionally, teachers have been the question-askers and students have been the question-answerers, but when students learn to generate questions about the text, their comprehension improves. In fact, students comprehend better when they generate their own questions than when teachers ask questions (Duke & Pearson, 2002). Many students don't know how to ask questions to guide their reading, so it's important to teach them how to do so. Teachers model generating questions and then encourage students to do the same. Tovani (2000) suggests having students brainstorm a list of "I wonder" questions on a topic because they need to learn how to generate questions; in the vignette at the beginning of the chapter, for example, Ms. Ali's sixth graders brainstormed questions before they began reading *Joey Pigza Loses Control* (Gantos, 2005).

The questions students ask shape their comprehension: If they ask literal questions, their comprehension will be literal, but if students generate inferential, critical, and evaluative questions, their comprehension will be higher level. **Question-Answer-Relationships** (QAR) (Raphael, Highfield, & Au, 2006) is an effective way to

Classroom INTERVENTIONS

Strategic Readers

Struggling students often complain that they don't understand what they're reading. Comprehension difficulties are due to a variety of problems, but one of the most common is that students don't read strategically (Cooper, Chard, & Kiger, 2006). They read passively, without using comprehension strategies to think about what they're reading. Unless they learn to thoughtfully engage in the reading process, it's unlikely that students who struggle with comprehension will improve very much.

The good news is that teachers can help struggling students become more thoughtful and strategic readers by teaching them to use comprehension strategies (Allington, 2012). The most important strategies for struggling readers are *activating background knowledge, determining importance, summarizing, questioning, visualizing,* and *monitoring.*

As teachers teach comprehension strategies, they explain each strategy, including how, when, and why to use it, and they make the strategy visible by demonstrating how to use it during minilessons, interactive read-alouds, and guided reading lessons. They use think-alouds to show that capable readers are active thinkers while they're reading. Students participate in small-group and partner activities as they practice using the strategy and verbalize their thinking. At first, teachers provide lots of support, and they withdraw it slowly as students become responsible for using the strategy independently. Once students have learned to apply two or three strategies, they begin to use them together. Integrating strategy use is important because capable readers don't depend on a single comprehension strategy; instead, they have a repertoire of strategies available that they use as needed while they're reading (Allington, 2012).

teach students about the different types of questions they can ask about a text. QAR was developed for analyzing the end-of-chapter questions in content area textbooks, but it's also useful for teaching students to categorize questions and ultimately to ask higher level questions.

Repairing

Readers use repairing to fix comprehension problems that arise while reading (Zimmermann & Hutchins, 2003). When students notice that they're confused or bored, can't remember what they just read, or aren't asking questions, they need to use this strategy (Tovani, 2000). Repairing involves identifying the problem and taking action to solve it: Sometimes students go back and reread or skip ahead and read, or they try questioning or another strategy that might help. At other times, they check the meaning of an unfamiliar word, examine the structure of a confusing sentence, learn more about an unfamiliar topic related to the text, or ask the teacher for assistance. These solutions are often referred to as *fix-up strategies*.

Setting a Purpose

Readers read for different reasons—for entertainment, to learn about a topic, for directions to accomplish a task, or to find the answer to a specific question, for instance—and the purposes they set direct their attention during reading (Tovani, 2000). Setting a purpose activates a mental blueprint, which aids in determining how readers focus their attention and how they sort relevant from irrelevant information as they read (Blanton, Wood, & Moorman, 1990). Before they begin to read, students identify a single, fairly broad purpose that they sustain while reading the entire text; it must fit both students' reason for reading and the text. To help them set a purpose, students can ask themselves "Why am I going to read this text?" or "What do I need to learn from this book?" It's important that students have a purpose when they read, because readers vary how they read and what they remember according to their purpose. When students don't have a purpose, they're likely to misdirect their attention and focus on unimportant ideas.

Summarizing

Readers pick out the most important ideas and the relationships among them and briefly restate them so they can be remembered (Harvey & Goudvis, 2007). It's crucial that students determine which ideas are the most important because if they focus on tangential ideas or details, their comprehension is compromised. To create effective summaries, students need to learn to paraphrase, or restate ideas in their own words.

Summarizing is a difficult task, but instruction and practice improve not only students' ability to summarize but their overall comprehension as well (Duke & Pearson, 2002). One way to teach students to summarize is to have them create graphic organizers after reading a chapter in a novel or a content area textbook: They emphasize the big ideas and relationships among them in their diagram, and then they use the information to write a brief summary statement.

Visualizing

Readers create mental images of what they're reading (Harvey & Goudvis, 2007; Keene & Zimmermann, 2007). They often place themselves in the images they

FIGURE 8–4	How the Comprehension Strategies Fit Into the Reading Process	
STAGE	**WHAT READERS DO**	**STRATEGIES READERS USE**
Prereading	Students prepare to read by setting purposes, thinking about the topic and genre of the text, and planning for the reading experience.	Activating background knowledge Predicting Questioning Setting a purpose
Reading	Students read the text silently or orally, thinking about it as they read, monitoring their understanding, and solving problems as they arise.	Monitoring Repairing All other strategies
Responding	Students share their reactions, making tentative and exploratory comments, asking questions, and clarifying confusions, by talking with classmates and the teacher and writing in reading logs.	Connecting Determining importance Drawing inferences Evaluating Questioning Visualizing
Exploring	Students reread parts of the text, examine it more analytically, and study the genre and writer's craft.	Determining importance Drawing inferences Evaluating Summarizing
Applying	Students create projects to deepen their understanding of the text they've read and reflect on their reading experience.	Connecting Evaluating Questioning

create, becoming a character in the story they're reading, traveling to that setting, or facing the conflict situations the characters face. Teachers sometimes ask students to close their eyes to help visualize the story or to draw pictures of the scenes and characters they visualize. How well students use visualization often becomes clear when they view film versions of books they've read: Students who are good visualizers are often disappointed with the film version and the actors portraying the characters, but those who don't visualize are often amazed by the film and prefer it to the book.

Students use comprehension strategies at every stage in the reading process, but their activities vary from stage to stage, depending on the strategy being used. Figure 8–4 explains what readers do to comprehend at each stage and the strategies they use. Sometimes strategies are grouped into before-reading, during-reading, and after-reading strategies, but that categorization doesn't work: Although setting a purpose is almost always a prereading strategy and monitoring and repairing are usually reading-stage strategies, students use connecting, drawing inferences, questioning, and other strategies in more than one stage.

Comprehension Skills

Even though there's controversy regarding the differences between comprehension strategies and skills, it's possible to identify some comprehension skills that students need to learn to become successful readers. These skills are related to strategies, but the big difference is that skills involve literal thinking; they're like questions to which there's one correct answer. One group of skills focuses on main ideas and details.

Students use the determining importance strategy to identify main ideas, and they use these related skills:

Recognizing details
Noticing similarities and differences
Identifying topic sentences
Comparing and contrasting main ideas and details
Matching causes with effects
Sequencing details
Paraphrasing ideas
Choosing a good title for a text

In contrast, when main ideas and relationships among them aren't explicitly stated in the text, students use the drawing inferences strategy to comprehend them because higher level thinking is required. Another group of comprehension skills is related to the evaluating strategy:

Recognizing the author's purpose
Detecting propaganda
Distinguishing between fact and opinion

Teachers teach these skills and students practice them until they become automatic procedures that don't require conscious thought or interpretation.

 MONITOR: Check Your Understanding 8.2

Teaching Students About Reader Factors

Comprehension instruction involves teaching students how to understand what they're reading. Teachers use explicit instruction, reading, and writing to develop students' understanding of fiction and nonfiction texts. Researchers emphasize the need to establish the expectation that the books students read and the compositions they write will make sense (Duke & Pearson, 2002). Teachers create an expectation of comprehension in these ways:

- Involving students in authentic reading activities every day
- Providing access to well-stocked classroom libraries
- Teaching students to use comprehension strategies
- Ensuring that students are fluent readers
- Providing opportunities for students to talk about the books they're reading
- Linking vocabulary instruction to underlying concepts

Teachers can't assume that students will learn to comprehend simply by doing lots of reading; instead, students develop an understanding of comprehension and what readers do to be successful through a combination of instruction and authentic reading activities (Block & Pressley, 2007). To examine the effectiveness of your comprehension instruction, use the Teacher Checklist: How do I teach reader factors?

The Common Core State Standards for English Language Arts emphasize the importance of reader factors: They focus on having students read increasingly complex texts through the grades and on teaching them how to comprehend the author's message. Students learn to understand precisely what authors say, but also to question authors' assumptions and assess the veracity of their claims. The document identifies these reader factors:

Key Ideas and Details. Students demonstrate their understanding of a text, ask and answer both literal and inferential questions, and explain relationships among ideas.

Integration of Knowledge and Ideas. Students analyze visual and multimedia elements, use reasons and evidence to support ideas, and make comparisons between two texts.

Range of Reading. Students read and understand grade-level fiction and nonfiction texts independently and proficiently.

Level of Text Complexity. Students learn how to read increasingly challenging texts.

The Standards place equal emphasis on teaching students how to use reader factors to comprehend fiction and nonfiction texts. For more information, check the feature Common Core State Standards: Reader Factors.

TEACHER Checklist

How do I teach reader factors?

○ Do I address Standards in my instruction?

○ Do I explain that strategies are problem-solving tactics?

○ Do I teach comprehension strategies using a combination of explanations, demonstrations, and practice activities?

○ Do I have students apply comprehension strategies in literacy activities as well as in thematic units?

○ Do I teach groups of strategies in routines so that students learn to orchestrate their use of multiple strategies?

○ Do I display student-made charts about the strategies in the classroom?

○ Do I have students read and analyze increasingly complex texts?

○ Do I have students read and comprehend grade-appropriate fiction and nonfiction texts?

Explicit Instruction

The fact that comprehension is an invisible mental process makes it difficult to teach; however, through explicit instruction, teachers can make comprehension more visible. They explain what comprehension is and why it's important, and they model how to use strategies by thinking aloud. Next, teachers encourage students to direct their thinking as they read, gradually releasing responsibility to students through guided and independent practice. Finally, they move students from focusing on a single comprehension strategy to integrating several strategies in routines. Ms. Ali demonstrated the concept of gradual release in the vignette at the beginning of the chapter as she reviewed each comprehension strategy and had the students practice it as they read picture books; then she had them apply all the strategies as they read *Joey Pigza Loses Control* (Gantos, 2005).

TEACHING STRATEGIES. Teachers teach individual comprehension strategies and then show students how to integrate several strategies simultaneously (Block & Pressley, 2007). They introduce each comprehension strategy in a series of **minilessons**. Teachers describe the strategy, model it for students as they read a text aloud, use it collaboratively with students, and provide opportunities for guided and then independent practice (Duke & Pearson, 2002); the independent practice is important because it's motivational. The Minilesson: Teaching Students to Ask Self-Questions shows how Mrs. Macadangdang teaches her third graders to use the questioning strategy.

Teachers also support students' learning about comprehension strategies in other ways; Figure 8–5 suggests several activities for each strategy. For example, second graders practice

COMMON CORE STATE STANDARDS

Reader Factors

The Common Core State Standards for English Language Arts emphasize that students are expected to read a broad range of high-quality and increasingly challenging texts. Students must be able to understand precisely what authors say and make interpretations based on textual evidence. The Standards specify these comprehension requirements:

● Students determine the central ideas of a text and analyze their development.

● Students make connections with background knowledge and other texts.

● Students draw inferences from the textual evidence.

● Students cite textual evidence that supports their answers to questions or supports their positions.

● Students comprehend grade-level stories, informational books, and other texts independently and proficiently.

The Standards emphasize that students use reader factors to comprehend increasingly complex fiction and nonfiction texts. To learn more about the Standards, go to http://www.corestandards.org/ELA-Literacy, or check your state's educational standards website.

Minilesson

TOPIC: Teaching Students to Ask Self-Questions
GRADE: Third Grade
TIME: Three 30-minute periods

Mrs. Macadangdang (the students call her Mrs. Mac) introduced questioning by talking about why people ask questions and by asking questions about stories they were reading. She encouraged the third graders to ask questions, too. They made a list of questions for each chapter of *Chang's Paper Pony* (Coerr, 1993), a story set in the California gold rush era, as she read it aloud, and then they evaluated their questions, choosing the ones that focus on the big ideas and that help them understand the story better. Now all of her students can generate questions, so she's ready to introduce the questioning strategy.

① Introduce the Topic

Mrs. Mac reads the list of comprehension strategies posted in the classroom that they've learned to use and explains, "Today, we're going to learn a new thinking strategy—questioning. Readers ask themselves questions while they're reading to help them think about the book." She adds "Questioning" to the list.

② Share Examples

The teacher introduces *The Josefina Story Quilt* (Coerr, 1989), the story of a pioneer family going to California in a covered wagon. She reads aloud the first chapter, thinking aloud and generating questions about the story. Each time she asks a question, she places in a pocket chart a sentence strip on which the question has already been written. Here are the questions: Why is Faith excited? Why are they going in a covered wagon? Who is Josefina? Can a chicken be a pet? Can Josefina do anything useful? Why is Faith crying?

③ Provide Information

Mrs. Mac explains, "Questions really turn your thinking on! I know it's important to think while I'm reading because it helps me understand. I like to ask questions about things I think are important and things that don't make sense to me." They reread the questions in the pocket chart and talk about the most helpful ones. Many students thought the question about the covered wagon was important, but as they continue reading, they'll learn that Josefina does indeed do something useful—she turns out to be a "humdinger of a watch dog" (p. 54)! Then Mrs. Mac reads aloud the second chapter, stopping often for students to generate questions. The students write their questions on sentence strips and add them to the pocket chart.

④ Guide Practice

The following day, Mrs. Mac reviews the questioning strategy, and students reread the questions for Chapters 1 and 2. Then the students form pairs, get copies of the book, and read the next two chapters of *The Josefina Story Quilt* together, generating questions as they read. They write their questions on small self-stick notes and place them in the book. Mrs. Mac monitors students, noticing which ones need additional practice. Then the class comes together to share their questions and talk about the chapters they've read. On the third day, they read the last two chapters and generate more questions.

⑤ Assess Learning

As she monitors the students, Mrs. Mac makes a list of those who need more practice generating questions, and she'll work with them as they read another book together.

FIGURE 8–5   Ways to Teach the Comprehension Strategies

STRATEGY	INSTRUCTIONAL PROCEDURES
Activating Background Knowledge	• Students complete an anticipation guide. • Students do an exclusion brainstorming activity. • Students develop a KWL chart.
Connecting	• Students add text-to-self, text-to-world, and text-to-text connections to a class chart. • Students write a double-entry journal with quotes and reflections about each one. • Students become a character and participate in a hot seat activity.
Determining Importance	• Students create graphic organizers. • Students make posters highlighting the big ideas.
Drawing Inferences	• Students use small self-stick notes to mark clues in the text. • Students create charts with author's clues, questions, and inferences. • Students quickwrite about an inference they've made.
Evaluating	• Students write reflections and evaluations in reading logs. • Students conference with the teacher about a book they've read.
Monitoring	• Students think aloud to demonstrate how they monitor their reading. • Students write about their strategy use on small self-stick notes and in reading logs.
Predicting	• Students make and share predictions during read-alouds. • Students write a double-entry journal with predictions in one column and summaries in the other. • Students make predictions during interactive read-alouds.
Questioning	• Students brainstorm a list of questions before reading. • Students ask questions during grand conversations and other discussions. • Students analyze the questions they pose using the QAR levels.
Repairing	• Students make personal charts of the ways they solve comprehension problems. • Students think aloud to demonstrate how they use the repairing strategy. • Students write about their repairs on small self-stick notes and place them in a book they're reading.
Setting a Purpose	• Students identify their purpose in a discussion before beginning to read. • Students write about their purpose in a reading log entry before beginning to read.
Summarizing	• Students write a summary using interactive writing. • Students create visual summaries on charts using words, diagrams, and pictures.
Visualizing	• Students create open-mind portraits of characters. • Students draw pictures of episodes from a book they're reading. • Students role-play episodes from a book they'e reading.

questioning by asking questions instead of giving answers during a grand conversation, and sixth graders practice connecting when they write favorite quotes in one column of a **double-entry journal** and then explain in the second column why each quote is meaningful. When teachers involve students in these activities, it's important to explain that they'll be practicing a particular strategy as they complete an activity so that they think about what they're doing and how it's helping them to comprehend better.

Once students know how to use individual strategies, they need to learn how to use routines, or combinations of strategies, because capable readers rarely use comprehension strategies one at a time (Duke & Pearson, 2002). In the vignette at the beginning of the chapter, for example, Ms. Ali was teaching her sixth graders to use multiple strategies as they read *Joey Pigza Loses Control* (Gantos, 2005) and reflect on their strategy use in their thinking logs.

CLOSE READING. Teachers use close reading to help students understand the deeper meaning of complex texts, those they haven't comprehended through the reading and responding stages of the reading process. Texts are complex when the ideas are sophisticated, the problems are complicated, and the story is told through multiple perspectives. For example, the concept of collective bargaining makes *Click, Clack, Moo: Cows That Type* (Cronin, 2011), a story about cows that go on strike for electric blankets, a complex text for first graders; and the intertwined story lines in *Holes* (Sachar, 2008), a novel about Stanley Yelnats, who suffers because of a family curse, make this text challenging for seventh graders.

Not all books are complex texts. For instance, *Number the Stars* (Lowry, 2011), a Holocaust story of a Christian girl and her Jewish friend, and *Bunnicula: A Rabbit-Tale of Mystery* (Howe & Howe, 2006), a dog's hilarious version of what happens when his family brings home a bunny from a theatre showing the movie *Dracula*, are both rated at the fourth–fifth grade level, but *Number the Stars* is far more complex than the other: Students must have background knowledge about the Holocaust when they read *Number the Stars* to understand the Jewish girl's predicament and the dangers the Christian family face for hiding her.

Teachers and students reread specific sections of the text in response to teachers' questions about words, phrases, sentences, and paragraphs in the book. For example, in *Number the Stars*, teachers ask text-dependent questions to direct students back into the text to grapple with complex ideas:

Chapter 1	On page 5, the girls tell each other how frightened they were when the Nazi soldiers stopped them. Why do you think they were scared?
Chapter 3	On page 21, the girls wonder what happened to Mrs. Hirsch. What clues does the author give about Mrs. Hirsch's fate?
Chapter 4	At the end of Chapter 3, Annemarie questions her bravery and says that she's glad she's an ordinary person who doesn't have to be courageous. Is she right?
	On page 36, the author says that only Ellen can stay with Annemarie's family. Why don't Ellen's parents stay, too?
	The chapter title is "It Will Be a Long Night." What night does the title refer to?
Chapter 5	The title of this chapter is "The Dark Haired One." Who does the title refer to?
	On page 48, how does Papa "prove" that Ellen is his daughter?
	On page 49, why does the German soldier tear up and stomp on Lise's baby picture?
Chapter 6	On page 53, Papa tells Uncle Henrik that Mama is bringing cigarettes, but Annemarie knows that cigarettes aren't available in Nazi-occupied Copenhagen. Why does he say that?
Chapter 7	On page 63, Mama asks if the girls talked to anyone, and reminds them to come inside if anyone approaches them. Why is Mama being so careful?
Chapter 8	On page 71, Annemarie recognizes the phrase "a day for fishing." What does it mean?

Chapter 9	On page 76, the author says that it's easier to be brave "if you do not know everything." What does Annemarie know, and what doesn't she know?
Chapter 11	On page 90, why does Peter give the baby some medicine?
	On page 91, Peter gives Ellen's father a packet to take to Uncle Henrik. Why doesn't he ask what's in it?
	The author talks about *pride*, meaning self-respect, on pages 93–94. Does the author think Ellen and her parents have lost their pride when they escape to Sweden wearing other people's old clothes?
Chapter 16	On page 123, Uncle Henrik tells Annemarie that she was very brave. What did she do that showed her bravery? Are there other examples of her bravery in the story?
Chapter 17	What would have happened to Ellen and her family if Annemarie hadn't gotten the handkerchief to Uncle Henrik before the soldiers searched the ship?

Teachers use text-dependent questions that direct students to reread short sections of the book and use the text as evidence in their responses. Through these discussions, students delve more deeply into the text to better understand the author's message. Sometimes teachers do close-reading activities with the whole class, or students work with partners or in small groups to answer questions and then report back to the class. Teachers also ask students to revisit the text and then respond to questions in reading log entries.

Stephanie Harvey (2015) describes close reading as strategic reading because these text-dependent questions require students to activate background knowledge, reread, visualize characters and episodes, think inferentially, ask questions, and use other comprehension strategies. Students use comprehension strategies during the first reading and subsequent readings and when they listen to teachers read aloud.

Developing Comprehension Through Reading

Students need to spend lots of time reading authentic texts independently and talking about their reading with classmates and teachers. Having students read interesting books written at their reading level is the best way for them to apply comprehension strategies. As they read and discuss their reading, students are practicing what they're learning about comprehension. Reading a selection in a basal reader each week is not enough; instead, students need to read many, many books representing a range of genres during reading workshop or **Sustained Silent Reading**.

In addition to providing opportunities for students to read independently, teachers read books aloud to young children who are not yet fluent readers and to struggling readers who can't read age-appropriate books themselves. When teachers do the reading, students have more cognitive resources available to focus on comprehension. Teachers often read books aloud when they introduce comprehension strategies so that they can model procedures and scaffold students' thinking.

Students also develop their comprehension abilities when they discuss the stories they're reading in **grand conversations** and nonfiction books and chapters in content-area textbooks in other discussions. As students talk about their reading, draw inferences, ask questions to clarify confusions, and reflect on their use of the comprehension strategies, they elaborate and refine their comprehension.

To read about three students' understanding of reader and text factors, check the feature Differentiated Instruction: Fifth Graders Vary in Knowledge About Comprehension.

Differentiated INSTRUCTION

Fifth Graders Vary in Knowledge About Comprehension

This Differentiated Instruction feature highlights three students from Ms. Reid's fifth grade class who vary in their knowledge about comprehension and how they use reader and text factors. Ms. Reid is currently teaching a literature focus unit on *Number the Stars* (Lowry, 2011), a story about bravery set during World War II, and the students are examining the novel's structure. As you read, think about what these students understand about reading comprehension and how you'd personalize instruction for them while addressing grade-level standards.

Meet *Crystal*, a Struggling Fifth Grader

Twelve-year-old Crystal, the tallest student in Ms. Reid's class, wishes she were shorter. Even though she yearns to fit in, she's a confident performer. She writes song lyrics that she calls "poems—but not the kind that rhyme," and then performs them at the school talent show. She also makes her own clothing using her mom's sewing machine. "The fun part," Crystal says, "is adding rhinestone decorations." She wears her own clothing almost every day to school and to family events.

This girl is an athlete! Crystal loves to play sports. "I'm the only girl on the Panther football team, and that's really cool, but basketball is my favorite," Crystal explains. Her mom and dad show their support by attending all of her games.

Crystal lives with her mom and dad and her little brother and sister, and she's attended the same school, beginning with a preschool program. She claims to read lots of books, but she can't name any books she's read recently "because I never look at the title of the book I'm reading." Even though school is challenging for her, Crystal plans to go to college and become a hairdresser. "I'm really good at doing hair, you know," she explains.

Crystal describes herself as a good reader, but she's very concerned about reading aloud in class. "I'm not good at reading aloud because I don't know how to pronounce all the words, and that's the most important part of reading," she explains. Crystal defines "comprehension" as getting all the words right, and she says that knowing every single word is what makes you a good reader.

Reader Factors

Crystal isn't comfortable talking about comprehension strategies. "I don't really like talking about my brain," she explains, but with prompting, Crystal says that she makes predictions "because you have to know the beginning to understand what's happening later in the book." She says she makes pictures in her mind, because description is the most important part of a story. She can't name any other strategies even though there's a list of comprehension strategies hanging in the classroom.

When Crystal has trouble reading, she skips over the "hard" word and tries to keep reading. Even if that strategy doesn't work, she keeps reading whether the words make sense or not. "The most important thing is to never give up," she says. She's not familiar with the term "context clues" and doesn't have other ideas for dealing with unfamiliar words. "Here's what I do: I just keep reading until I get to the end," she announces proudly.

Text Factors

Crystal's favorite books are from the Junie B. Jones series by Barbara Park, about a sassy 7-year-old. The reading level is first–second grade. She likes the books because they're easy to read and they're funny. Crystal's familiar with the terms "fiction" and "nonfiction," but she confuses them, calling the Junie B. Jones book she's reading a "nonfiction" book. She says that she reads both genres the same way—focusing on saying the words right.

She's heard the terms "characters," "plot," "setting," "theme," and "point of view," but she's not comfortable talking about the terms or citing examples from *Number the Stars*, the book her class is reading now. Crystal concedes that *Number the Stars* is a good book, and she likes it best when Ms. Reid reads aloud. "When the teacher is reading, I learn lots of details—you know, the important parts—like what's it like during a war. That's the theme."

Crystal loves science! She flips through her science textbook and points out the Vocabulary Preview at the beginning of each chapter and says, "This is what I like best. Teachers need to teach you the vocabulary so you can be better at learning." She doesn't notice other nonfiction features, such as headings and diagrams, or understand how they could help her comprehend the text. In addition, she's unfamiliar with the glossary.

This fifth grader's understanding of reader and text factors is summarized in the chart Crystal's Knowledge About Comprehension.

CRYSTAL'S KNOWLEDGE ABOUT COMPREHENSION

Reader Factors

☐ Activates background information
☐ Determines the meaning of academic vocabulary
☐ Reads fluently and expressively
☐ Applies comprehension strategies
☐ Monitors comprehension
☐ Is engaged in the reading experience

Text Factors

☐ Recognizes the characteristics of genres
☑ Has a favorite book or author
☐ Is interested in learning about authors
☐ Examines the text to uncover its organization
☐ Notices literary devices in stories and poems
☐ Understands the purpose of nonfiction text features

Instructional Implications

"Crystal, who's a native English speaker, scored in the lowest band level on the state achievement tests," Ms. Reid explains, "but she's developed strong survival skills. Her independent reading level is second grade, her instructional level is third grade, and the fifth grade instructional materials I'm required to use are at her frustration level. I read most texts aloud because she understands when she listens to me read aloud. Then she rereads it with a supportive classmate. Crystal likes to work with partners and frequently gets help from them." She fails to make important connections between Ms. Reid's lessons and her background knowledge, and her preoccupation with vocabulary limits her learning. "I've differentiated instruction for Crystal," Ms. Reid says. "I'm required to use grade-level textbooks, but I make sure she has books at her reading level, and I devise tiered activities so she can be successful."

Meet *Edgar*, a Capable Fifth Grader

Edgar's a friendly and outgoing 11-year-old who has a mischievous twinkle in his eyes. He lives with his parents, three brothers, and one sister. His parents speak Spanish at home, but Edgar's become a fluent English speaker. "I'm quite athletic," he says. "I play in a soccer league and on my school's softball team." Every summer his family goes to Mexico to visit relatives for 3 weeks, and he especially likes to stay with his Tia Rosa. Edgar definitely plans on going to college—he's visited the University of California, Santa Cruz and thinks he'd like to attend college there. He says that he'll probably read nonfiction manuals when he's an adult because he wants to be an engineer and build cars.

Edgar's favorite book is *Diary of a Wimpy Kid* (Kinney, 2007), the hilarious story of Greg Heffley's middle school experiences. He's read all seven books in the series, plus he's seen the movie twice. He likes the books because of Greg's irreverent attitude. Edgar reads every day during SSR, and his parents expect him to bring home a library book to read for 30 minutes every night after he finishes his homework.

Edgar considers himself a good reader; he explains, "Comprehension is important because you have to understand what you're reading." As he talks about what he does to comprehend, he focuses on thinking: "You always have to keep thinking about what's happening the book."

Reader Factors

Edgar knows about comprehension strategies: "We've been learning comprehension strategies all year because thinking has to go along with reading. See the list of comprehension strategies on that poster on the wall. Ms. Reid keeps reminding us to use them when we're reading in our anthology [basal reader] and during SSR. Sometimes I forget, but I usually remember to use them." He uses the predicting, visualizing, questioning, rereading, monitoring, and repairing strategies. "You want to know about repairing?" he asks. "Well, it's what you do when you're in trouble. You're reading something that's hard for you. Maybe the words are too hard or you get confused. You stop reading and do something to fix the problem. You think about the part you did understand, you go back and reread, and you figure out any really hard words. If that doesn't work and you can't keep reading, you go and ask Ms. Reid for help. You don't keep reading if nothing makes sense."

"I think you use mostly the same strategies for nonfiction books," Edgar says, "but I don't read many of them. I can think of one different strategy—taking notes. In fourth grade, I learned to take notes from my social studies textbook and some nonfiction books for a report I was writing on the California Gold Rush."

Text Factors

"Now we're reading *Number the Stars*, and we have grand conversations to talk about the characters, plot, and theme. Ms. Reid likes for us to ask questions because it makes us think. I learn a lot when I listen to what the other kids say and, of course, what Ms. Reid says. Most teachers ask lots of questions, but in Ms. Reid's classroom, we ask most of the questions."

Edgar points out the features of nonfiction books, including the glossary, index, headings, and diagrams in his science textbook. He explains that headings help you locate the main ideas, and diagrams "tell you information better than words could." When he examined a section of the textbook written using a sequence structure and another using comparison, he didn't notice any differences other than the topics. "Well, one was about volcanoes and one was about atoms, but I read them the same way. They're both nonfiction." He didn't recognize that the structure of nonfiction texts highlights the big ideas.

This fifth grader's understanding of reader and text factors is summarized in the chart Edgar's Knowledge About Comprehension.

Instructional Implications

Edgar reads and comprehends grade-level books. He scored at fifth grade level on the state achievement tests. His independent reading level is fourth grade, and his instructional level is fifth grade. Ms. Reid explains, "Edgar's a reader: He decodes most words easily, and his comprehension is good, but he uses only a handful of comprehension strategies independently. I'd like him to learn additional strategies to be able to understand more complex texts. I'd like to see him read more challenging books because he rereads the *Diary of a Wimpy Kid* books week after week. I think his biggest difficulty is limited background knowledge, so I've encouraged him to read a wide variety of fiction and nonfiction books.

"I'm required to use fifth grade textbooks and provide instruction to meet grade-level standards, so I feel like I'm meeting most of Edgar's academic needs," Ms. Reid explains, "but I differentiate instruction by building his background knowledge, focusing on unfamiliar academic vocabulary, and offering Edgar choices about the books he reads and the literacy activities he completes."

EDGAR'S KNOWLEDGE ABOUT COMPREHENSION

Reader Factors
- ☐ Activates background information
- ☐ Determines the meaning of academic vocabulary
- ☑ Reads fluently and expressively
- ☑ Applies comprehension strategies
- ☑ Monitors comprehension
- ☑ Is engaged in the reading experience

Text Factors
- ☐ Recognizes the characteristics of genres
- ☑ Has a favorite book or author
- ☐ Is interested in learning about authors
- ☑ Examines the text to uncover its organization
- ☐ Notices literary devices in stories and poems
- ☑ Understands the purpose of nonfiction text features

Eleven-year-old Elias comes from a Spanish-speaking home and was an English learner in the primary grades, but now he's a fluent English speaker. He lives with his parents, two older sisters, and younger brother. His parents speak Spanish, and Elias often translates for them. He's proud of his Lego collection, which his cousin started for him; his newest piece is a Ninjago motorcycle. His family has a computer, but after it crashed last winter, they haven't gotten it fixed. "I wish I had a Kindle," Elias says wistfully, "because it looks like a fun way to read."

Elias is a voracious reader. He loves graphic novels. "I've read every one in the school library so I just keep reading them again and again except when Ms. Reid tells me to choose something else. Graphic novels are so good because they show action and you don't have to imagine what's happening in your head." Right now he's rereading *Bone, Vol. 4: The Dragonslayer*, by Jeff Smith (2006), a book in the popular series about a character named Fone Bone who confronts the forces of evil.

When Elias isn't reading graphic novels, he reads science fiction and nonfiction books about topics that interest him, such as chemistry and tsunamis. He especially enjoyed Eoin Coifer's series of Artemis Fowl books, but one book he really didn't like was *The Original Adventures of Hank the Cowdog* (Erickson, 2011), a fantasy tale about Hank, the smart-alecky head of security on a Texas ranch. "My fourth grade teacher had us read it. Everybody loved it but me. They said it was so funny, but I thought it was boring. I didn't like the dialogue; it was hard to read."

Reader Factors

"Yes, I know about 'comprehension.' It's about understanding what you read," Elias explains. He's learned comprehension strategies and uses them: "I know about the easy strategies, like predicting, connecting, and asking questions, of course, but this year I've been learning about the 'deep thinking' ones, like drawing inferences, noticing propaganda, and making judgments." Elias continues, "These strategies go way beyond the words on the page. Take drawing inferences, for example. You really have to think while you're reading. You look for clues, and you have to know how to find them. Ms. Reid calls it 'reading between the lines.' I do that if I think the author has left some clues for me to figure out. Some authors are really good at giving you clues. I like reading books like that."

Elias is gaining a perspective about authors and their viewpoints: "I've learned that authors always have a viewpoint. It's not exactly propaganda, but they want you to think like they do. In *Number the Stars*, for example, they want you to think that the Nazis were bad people, and that Annemarie's and Ellen's families were brave. When I'm reading, I ask myself questions so I can figure out the author's viewpoint and decide whether or not I agree."

Text Factors

Elias is familiar with the fiction and nonfiction genres and knows that he likes to read graphic novels and science fiction books. He has favorite authors, and he can explain why he likes them. He's also internalized his knowledge about story structure. "I want to be an architect when I get older, and I think authors are a lot like architects. They build stories with characters, plot, setting, theme, and the rest. Stories, like houses, have to be unique."

Elias opens his science textbook to talk about nonfiction texts. He turns to a unit on natural disasters and points to "Volcano," a nonfiction text written by Seymour Simon. "I remember reading this selection and comparing it to a story about volcanoes in my anthology. They're both about volcanoes," he says, "but the author's purpose is different. This one provides information, and the other one tells a story." His project was a flip book: "It was a nonfiction book," he explains. "I printed the headings in red and the important science words in blue, and I made diagrams and labels for them."

This fifth grader's understanding of reader and text factors is summarized in the chart Elias's Knowledge About Comprehension.

Instructional Implications

Elias scored in the above-grade-level band on the state achievement test. His independent reading level is sixth grade, and his instructional level is seventh grade. "He doesn't have any difficulty reading our textbooks and trade books," Ms. Reid explains. "Sometimes, however, he's not familiar with academic vocabulary or science/social studies concepts.

Elias is quick to get on a computer to research an unfamiliar concept. He prefers to work alone, but he's willing to work with two other high achievers in my class. He must learn how to work as part of a team. Whenever Elias has free time, he picks up a book to read. I've encouraged him to read more challenging books, because that's how he'll expand his background knowledge and build academic vocabulary."

ELIAS'S KNOWLEDGE ABOUT COMPREHENSION

Reader Factors

☑ Activates background information
☐ Determines the meaning of academic vocabulary
☑ Reads fluently and expressively
☑ Applies comprehension strategies
☑ Monitors comprehension
☑ Is engaged in the reading experience

Text Factors

☑ Recognizes the characteristics of genres
☑ Has a favorite book or author
☑ Is interested in learning about authors
☑ Examines the text to uncover its organization
☐ Notices literary devices in stories and poems
☑ Understands the purpose of nonfiction text features

Nurturing English Learners

How do teachers teach comprehension? Comprehension is often difficult for English learners for a number of reasons (Bouchard, 2005). Many ELs lack the necessary background knowledge for understanding the book they're attempting to read. Sometimes they lack culturally based knowledge, and at other times, they're unfamiliar with a genre or can't understand the meaning of figurative vocabulary. There can be a mismatch between the students' level of English proficiency and the reading level of the book, too: Like all students, ELs won't understand what they're reading if the book is too difficult.

Teachers address these issues by carefully choosing books that are appropriate for English learners, building their world and literary knowledge, and introducing key vocabulary words in advance. Peregoy and Boyle (2013) also point out that many ELs read texts passively, as if they were waiting for the information they're reading to organize itself and highlight the big ideas. To help these students become more active readers, teachers explicitly teach the comprehension strategies. During the lessons, teachers explain each strategy, including why it will help students become better readers and how and when to use it. They spend more time modeling how to apply each strategy and thinking aloud to share their thoughts. Next, teachers provide guided practice with the students working together in small groups and with partners, and they assist students as they use the strategy. Finally, students use the strategy independently and apply it in new ways.

Assessing Reader Factors

Teachers use the integrated instruction–assessment cycle to ensure that students are growing in their ability to understand complex texts and to use increasingly more sophisticated strategies to deepen their understanding of grade-level texts. They also use diagnostic tests with struggling readers.

STEP 1: Planning. Teachers make decisions about how they'll teach comprehension strategies and other reader factors, and they decide how to monitor students' progress during instruction and evaluate it afterward.

STEP 2: Monitoring. Teachers assess students' comprehension informally every day; for example, they listen to the comments students make during grand conversations, conference with students about books they're reading, and examine their entries in reading logs. Students' interest in a book is sometimes an indicator, too: When students dismiss a book as "boring," they may mean that it's confusing or too difficult.

Teachers use these informal assessment procedures to monitor students' use of comprehension and their understanding of books they're reading:

Watch as a science teacher uses the cloze procedure to demonstrate how much students have learned in an ecology unit. How does this procedure illustrate students' comprehension?

Cloze Procedure. Teachers examine students' understanding of a text using the **cloze procedure**, in which students supply the deleted words in a passage taken from a text they've read. Although filling in the blanks may seem like a simple activity, it isn't because students need to consider the content of the passage, vocabulary words, and sentence structure to choose the exact word that was deleted.

Story Retellings. Teachers often have young children retell stories they've read or listened to read aloud to assess their literal comprehension (Morrow, 2002). Students' **story retellings** should be coherent and well organized and should include the big ideas and important details. When teachers prompt students with questions and encourage them to "tell me more," they're known as *aided retellings*; otherwise they're *unaided retellings*. Teachers often use checklists and **rubrics** to score students' story retellings.

Running Records. Teachers use **running records** (Clay, 2015) to examine children's oral reading behaviors, analyze their comprehension, and determine their reading levels. Although they're most commonly used with young children, running records can also be used with older students. Children read a book, and afterward they orally retell what they remember of it.

Think-Alouds. Teachers assess students' ability to apply comprehension strategies by having them **think aloud** and share their thinking as they read a passage (Wilhelm, 2001). Students usually think aloud orally, but they can also write their thoughts on small self-stick notes that they place beside sections of text, write entries in reading logs, and do **quickwrites**.

View a fourth grade teacher modeling the think-aloud procedure for her students. Why is it important for teachers to model strategic thinking?

STEP 3: Evaluating. Teachers assess students' knowledge about reading strategies and other reader factors using many of the same ways that they monitor students' progress during instruction. For instance, they ask students to think aloud about the strategies they applied as they read a book. Students also create projects, including **double-entry journals**, **hot seat**, **sketch-to-stretch**, and **open-mind portraits**.

STEP 4: Reflecting. Students reflect on what they've learned about reader factors through conferences with the teacher, and they also write entries in reading logs

ASSESSMENT TOOLS

Comprehension

Teachers use a combination of informal assessment procedures, including retelling and think-alouds, and commercially available tests to measure students' comprehension. Here are several tests that are commonly used in K–8 classrooms:

- **Comprehension Thinking Strategies Assessment**
  The Comprehension Thinking Strategies Assessment (Keene, 2006) examines first through eighth graders' ability to use these strategies to think about fiction and nonfiction texts they're reading: activating background knowledge, determining importance, drawing inferences, noticing text structure, questioning, setting a purpose, and visualizing. As students read a passage, they pause and reflect on their strategy use. Teachers score students' responses using a rubric. This 30-minute test can be administered to individuals or to the class, depending on whether students' responses are oral or written. This flexible assessment tool can be used to evaluate students' learning after teaching a strategy, to survey progress at the beginning of the school year, or to document achievement at the end of the year. It's available from Shell Education.

- **Developmental Reading Assessment, 2nd Edition PLUS (DRA2+)**
  Teachers use the K–3 or 4–8 DRA2+ kit to determine students' reading levels; assess their strengths and weaknesses in word identification, fluency, and comprehension; and make instructional decisions. To measure comprehension, teachers have students read a leveled book and then retell what they've read; their retellings are scored using a 4-point rubric. Both DRA2+ kits are available from Pearson.

- **Informal Reading Inventories (IRIs)**
  Teachers use individually administered IRIs to assess students' comprehension of narrative and informational texts. Comprehension is measured by students' ability to retell what they've read and to answer questions about the passage. The questions examine both how well students use literal and higher level thinking and their knowledge about word meanings. A number of commercially published IRIs are available, including the following:

  Analytical Reading Inventory (Woods & Moe, 2015)
  The Flynt/Cooter Comprehensive Reading Inventory-2 (Cooter, Flynt, & Cooter, 2014)
  Critical Reading Inventory (Applegate, Quinn, & Applegate, 2008)
  Qualitative Reading Inventory (Leslie & Caldwell, 2011)

  These IRIs can be purchased from Pearson. Other IRIs accompany basal reading series. IRIs typically are designed for grades 1–8, but first and second grade teachers often find that running records provide more useful information about beginning readers.

These tests provide valuable information about whether students meet grade-level comprehension standards.

about the strategies they've learned and can use independently. Teachers also reflect on the effectiveness of their instruction and how they might improve it.

DIAGNOSTIC ASSESSMENT. Teachers also use diagnostic assessment tools to screen the entire class for comprehension problems or to evaluate struggling students and plan for intervention. Check Assessment Tools: Comprehension for more information about informal reading inventories and other tests.

 MONITOR: Check Your Understanding 8.3

🌀 Motivation

Motivation is intrinsic, the innate curiosity that makes us want to figure things out. It involves feeling self-confident, believing you'll succeed, and viewing the activity as pleasurable (Guthrie & Wigfield, 2000). It's based on the engagement theory that you read about in Chapter 1. Motivation is social, too: People want to socialize, share ideas, and participate in group activities. Motivation is more than one characteristic, however; it's a network of interacting factors (Alderman, 1999). Often students' motivation to become better readers and writers diminishes as they reach the middle grades, and struggling students demonstrate significantly less enthusiasm for reading and writing than other students do.

Many factors contribute to students' engagement or involvement in reading and writing. Some focus on the teachers' role—what they believe and do—and others focus on students (Pressley, Dolezal, Raphael, Mohan, Roehrig, & Bogner, 2003; Unrau, 2008). Figure 8–6 summarizes the factors affecting students' engagement in literacy activities and what teachers can do to nurture students' interest.

Teachers' Role

Everything teachers do affects their students' interest and engagement with literacy, but four of the most important factors are teachers' attitude, the community teachers create, the instructional approaches they use, and their reward systems:

FIGURE 8–6 Factors Affecting Students' Motivation

ROLES	FACTORS	WHAT TEACHERS DO
Teachers	Attitude	• Show students that you care about them. • Display excitement and enthusiasm about what you're teaching. • Stimulate students' curiosity and desire to learn.
	Community	• Create a nurturing and inclusive classroom community. • Insist that students treat classmates with respect.
	Instruction	• Focus on students' long-term learning. • Teach students to be strategic readers and writers. • Engage students in authentic activities. • Offer students choices of activities and reading materials.
	Rewards	• Employ specific praise and positive feedback. • Use external rewards only when students' interest is very low.
Students	Expectations	• Expect students to be successful. • Teach students to set realistic goals.
	Collaboration	• Encourage students to work collaboratively. • Minimize competition. • Allow students to participate in making plans and choices.
	Reading and Writing Competence	• Teach students to use reading and writing strategies. • Provide guided reading lessons for struggling readers. • Use interactive writing to teach writing skills to struggling writers. • Provide daily reading and writing opportunities.
	Choices	• Have students complete interest inventories. • Teach students to choose books at their reading levels. • Encourage students to write about topics that interest them.

Attitude. It seems obvious that when teachers show that they care about their students and exhibit excitement and enthusiasm for learning, students are more likely to become engaged. Effective teachers also stimulate students' curiosity and encourage them to explore ideas. They emphasize intrinsic over extrinsic motivation because they understand that students' intrinsic desire to learn is more powerful than grades, rewards, and other extrinsic motivators.

Community. Students are more likely to engage in reading and writing when their classroom is a learning community that respects and nurtures everyone. Students and the teacher show respect for each other, and students learn how to work well with classmates in small groups. In a community of learners, students enjoy social interaction and feel connected to their classmates and their teacher.

Instruction. The types of literacy activities students are involved in affect their interest and motivation. Turner and Paris (1995) compared authentic literacy activities such as reading and writing workshop with skills-based reading programs and concluded that students' motivation was determined by the daily classroom activities. They found that the most successful were open-ended activities and projects in which students were in control of the processes they used and the products they created.

Rewards. Many teachers consider using rewards to encourage students to do more reading and writing, but Alfie Kohn (2001) and others believe that extrinsic incentives are harmful because they undermine students' intrinsic motivation. Incentives such as pizzas, free time, or "money" to spend in a classroom "store" are most effective when students' interest is very low and they're reluctant to participate in literacy activities. Once students become more interested, teachers withdraw these incentives and use less tangible ones, including positive feedback and praise (Stipek, 2002).

Students' Role

Motivation isn't something that teachers or parents can force on students; rather, it's an innate, intrinsic desire that students must develop themselves. They're more likely to become engaged with reading and writing when they expect to be successful, when they work collaboratively with classmates, when they're competent readers and writers, and when they have opportunities to make choices and develop ownership of their work. These factors influence students' motivation:

Expectations. Students who believe they have little hope of success are unlikely to become engaged in literacy activities. Teachers play a big role in shaping students' expectations, and teacher expectations are often self-fulfilling (Wentzel & Brophy, 2014): If teachers believe that their students can be successful, it's more likely that they will be. Stipek (2002) found that in classrooms where teachers take a personal interest in their students and expect that all of them can learn, the students are more successful.

Collaboration. When students work with classmates in pairs and in small groups, they're often more interested and engaged in activities than when they read and write alone. Collaborative groups support students because they have opportunities to share ideas, learn from each other, and enjoy the collegiality of their classmates. Competition, in contrast, doesn't develop intrinsic motivation; instead, it decreases many students' interest in learning.

Reading and Writing Competence. Not surprisingly, students' competence in reading and writing affects their motivation: Students who read well are more likely to be motivated to read than those who read less well, and the same is true for writers. Teaching students how to read and write is an essential factor in developing their motivation. Teachers find that once struggling students improve their reading and writing performance, they become more interested.

Choices.   Students want to have a say in which books they read and which topics they write about. By making choices, students develop more responsibility for their work and ownership of their accomplishments. Reading and writing workshop are instructional approaches that honor students' choices: In reading workshop, students choose books they're interested in reading and that are written at their reading level, and in writing workshop, students write about topics that interest them.

How to Engage Students

Oldfather (1995) conducted a 4-year study to examine the factors influencing students' motivation. She found that students were more highly motivated when they had opportunities for authentic self-expression as part of literacy activities. The students she interviewed reported that they were more highly motivated when they had ownership of the learning activities. Oldfather mentioned these specific activities:

- Students express their own ideas and opinions.
- Students choose topics for writing and books for reading.
- Students talk about books they're reading.
- Students share their writing with classmates.
- Students pursue authentic activities—not worksheets—using reading, writing, listening, and talking.

Ivey and Broaddus (2001) reported similar conclusions from their study of the factors that influence sixth graders' desire to read. Three of their conclusions are noteworthy. First, students are more interested in reading when their teachers make them feel confident and successful; a nurturing classroom community is an important factor. Second, students are more intrinsically motivated when they have ownership of their literacy learning; students place great value on being allowed to choose interesting books and other reading materials. Third, students become more engaged with books when they have time for independent reading and opportunities to listen to the teacher read aloud. Students reported that they enjoy listening to teachers read aloud because teachers make books more comprehensible and more interesting through the background knowledge they provide.

Some students aren't strongly motivated to learn to read and write, and they adopt defensive tactics for avoiding failure rather than strategies for being successful (Paris, Wasik, & Turner, 1996). Unmotivated readers give up or remain passive, uninvolved in reading. Some students feign interest or pretend to be involved even though they aren't. Others don't think reading is important, and they choose to focus on other curricular areas—math or sports, for instance. Some students complain about feeling ill or that classmates are bothering them. They place the blame anywhere but on themselves.

Other students avoid reading and writing entirely; they just don't do it. Still others read books that are too easy for them or write short pieces so that they don't have to exert much effort. Even though these strategies are self-serving, students use them because they lead to short-term success. The long-term result, however, is devastating because these students fail to learn to read and write well. Because it takes quite a bit of effort to read and write strategically, it's especially important that students experience personal ownership of the literacy activities going on in their classrooms and know how to manage their own reading and writing behaviors.

Assessing Motivation

Because students' motivation and engagement affect their success in reading as well as writing, it's important that teachers learn about their students and work to ensure that they're motivated and have positive attitudes about literacy. Teachers observe

ASSESSMENT TOOLS

Motivation

Teachers assess students' motivation in several ways. They observe students as they read and write, read entries in their reading logs, and conference with them about their interests and attitudes. At the beginning of the school year, teachers often have students create interest inventories with lists of things they're interested in, types of books they like to read, and favorite authors. Teachers also administer attitude surveys. These surveys assess students' motivation:

● **Elementary Reading Attitude Survey**
The Elementary Reading Attitude Survey (McKenna & Kear, 1990) assesses first through sixth grade students' attitudes toward reading at home and in school. The 20 items begin with the stem "How do you feel . . ." and students mark one of four pictures of Garfield, the cartoon cat; each picture depicts a different emotional state, ranging from positive to negative. This survey enables teachers to quickly estimate their students' attitudes.

● **Motivation to Read Profile**
The Motivation to Read Profile (Gambrell, Palmer, Codling, & Mazzoni, 1996) consists of two parts, a group test and an individual interview. The test is a survey with 20 items about self-concept as a reader and the value of reading that students respond to using a 4-point Likert scale. The interview is a series of open-ended questions about the types of books students like best and where they get reading materials. Each part takes about 15 minutes to administer.

● **Reader Self-Perception Scale**
The Reader Self-Perception Scale (Henk & Melnick, 1995) measures how students feel about reading and about themselves as readers. It's designed for third to sixth graders. Students respond to "I think I am a good reader" and other statements using a 5-point Likert scale where responses range from "strongly agree" to "strongly disagree." Teachers score students' responses and interpret the results to determine both overall and specific attitude levels.

● **Writing Attitude Survey**
The Writing Attitude Survey (Kear, Coffman, McKenna, & Ambrosio, 2000) examines students' feelings about the writing process and types of writing. It has 28 items, including "How would you feel if your classmates talked to you about making your writing better?" As in the Elementary Reading Attitude Survey, it features Garfield, the cartoon cat; students indicate their response by marking the picture of Garfield that best illustrates their feelings.

● **Writer Self-Perception Scale**
The Writer Self-Perception Scale (Bottomley, Henk, & Melnick, 1997/1998) assesses third through sixth graders' attitudes about writing and how they perceive themselves as writers. Students respond to statements such as "I write better than my classmates do," using the same 5-point Likert scale that the Reader Self-Perception Scale uses.

These attitude surveys were originally published in *The Reading Teacher* and are readily available at libraries, online, and in collections of assessment instruments, such as *Assessment for Reading Instruction* (McKenna & Dougherty Stahl, 2015).

students and conference with them and their parents to understand students' reading and writing habits at home, their interests and hobbies, and their view of themselves as readers and writers. There are also surveys that teachers can administer to quickly estimate students' motivation toward reading and writing; these surveys are described in Assessment Tools: Motivation.

Comparing Capable and Less Capable Students

Researchers have compared students who are capable readers and writers with other students who are less successful and have found some striking differences (Baker & Brown, 1984; Faigley, Cherry, Jolliffe, & Skinner, 1985; Paris, Wasik, & Turner, 1996). The researchers have found that more capable readers do the following:

- Read fluently
- View reading as a process of creating meaning
- Decode rapidly
- Have large vocabularies
- Understand the organization of stories, plays, nonfiction books, and poems
- Use comprehension strategies
- Monitor their understanding as they read

Similarly, capable writers do the following:

- Vary how they write depending on their purpose and audience
- Use the writing process flexibly
- Focus on developing ideas and communicating effectively
- Turn to classmates for feedback on how they're communicating
- Monitor how well they're communicating in the piece of writing
- Use formats and structures for stories, poems, letters, and other texts
- Postpone attention to mechanical correctness until the editing stage

All of these characteristics of capable readers and writers relate to comprehension, and because these students know and use them, they're better readers and writers than students who don't use them.

A comparison of the characteristics of capable and less capable readers and writers is presented in Figure 8–7. Young children who are learning to read and write often exemplify many of the characteristics of less capable readers and writers, but older students who are less successful readers and writers also exemplify them.

Less successful readers exemplify few of the characteristics of capable readers or behave differently when they're reading and writing. Perhaps the most remarkable difference is that more capable readers view reading as a process of comprehending or creating meaning, but less capable readers focus on decoding. In writing, less capable writers make cosmetic changes when they revise, rather than changes to communicate meaning more effectively. These important differences indicate that capable students focus on comprehension and the strategies readers and writers use to understand what they read and to make sure that what they write will be comprehensible to others.

Another important difference between capable and less capable readers and writers is that those who are less successful aren't strategic. They seem reluctant to use unfamiliar strategies or those that require much effort. They don't seem to be motivated or to expect that they'll be successful. Less capable readers and writers don't understand all stages of the reading and writing processes or use them effectively. They don't monitor their reading and writing (Keene & Zimmermann, 2007). Or, if they do use strategies, they remain dependent on primitive ones. For example, as they

FIGURE 8–7 Capable and Less Capable Readers and Writers

COMPONENT	READER CHARACTERISTICS	WRITER CHARACTERISTICS
Belief Systems	Capable readers view reading as a comprehending process, but less capable readers view reading as a decoding process.	Capable writers view writing as communicating ideas, but less capable writers see writing as putting words on paper.
Purpose	Capable readers adjust their reading according to purpose, but less capable readers approach all reading tasks the same way.	Capable writers adapt their writing to meet the demands of audience, purpose, and form, but less capable writers don't.
Fluency	Capable readers read fluently, but less capable readers read word by word, don't chunk words into phrases, and sometimes point at words as they read.	Capable writers sustain their writing for longer periods of time and pause as they draft to think and reread what they've written, but less capable writers write less and without pausing.
Background Knowledge	Capable readers relate what they're reading to their background knowledge, but less capable readers don't make this connection.	Capable writers gather and organize ideas before writing, but less capable writers don't plan before beginning to write.
Decoding/ Spelling	Capable readers identify unfamiliar words efficiently, but less capable readers make nonsensical guesses or skip over unfamiliar words and invent what they think is a reasonable text when they're reading.	Capable writers spell many words conventionally and use the dictionary to spell unfamiliar words, but less capable writers can't spell many high-frequency words, and they depend on phonics to spell unfamiliar words.
Vocabulary	Capable readers have larger vocabularies than less capable readers do.	Capable writers use more sophisticated words and figurative language than less capable writers do.
Strategies	Capable readers use a variety of strategies as they read, but less capable readers use fewer strategies or less effective ones.	Capable writers use many strategies effectively, but less capable writers use fewer strategies or less effective ones.
Monitoring	Capable readers monitor their comprehension, but less capable readers don't realize or take action when they don't understand.	Capable writers monitor that their writing makes sense, and they turn to classmates for revising suggestions, but less capable writers don't.

Based on Faigley, L., Cherry, R. D., Jolliffe, D. A., & Skinner, A. M. (1985). *Assessing writers' knowledge and processes of composing*; Paris, S. G., Wasik, B. A., & Turner, J. C. (1991). The development of strategic readers. In R. Barr, M. L. Kamil, P. B. Mosenthal, & P. D. Pearson (Eds.), *Handbook of reading research* (Vol. 2, pp. 609–640).

read, less successful readers seldom look ahead or back into the text to clarify misunderstandings or make plans. Or, when they come to an unfamiliar word, they often stop reading, unsure of what to do. They may try to sound out an unfamiliar word, but if that's unsuccessful, they give up. In contrast, capable readers know a variety of strategies, and if one strategy isn't successful, they try another.

Less capable writers move through the writing process in a lockstep, linear approach. They use a limited number of strategies, most often a "knowledge-telling" strategy in which they write everything they know about a topic with little thought to choosing information to meet the needs of their readers or to organizing the information to put related ideas together (Faigley et al., 1985). In contrast, capable writers understand the recursive nature of the writing process and turn to classmates for feedback about how well they're communicating. They're more responsive to the needs of the audience that will read their writing, and they work to organize their writing in a cohesive manner.

This research on capable and less capable readers and writers has focused on comprehension differences and students' use of strategies. It's noteworthy that all research comparing readers and writers focuses on how students use strategies, not on their use of reading and writing skills.

MONITOR: Check Your Understanding 8.4

Review

TEACHING ABOUT READER FACTORS

Effective teachers demonstrate their responsibility and commitment to facilitating their students' comprehension when they address reader factors according to the information in this chapter, these points in particular:

8.1 Teachers emphasize that comprehension is a process involving both reader factors and text factors.

8.2 Students use comprehension strategies to direct their reading, monitor their understanding, and troubleshoot problems when they occur.

8.3 Teachers teach students how to apply comprehension strategies to support their understanding of texts.

8.4 Teachers nurture students' motivation and engagement in literacy activities.

 **EVALUATE & REFLECT**

Apply your understanding of the reader factors that affect comprehension. The questions ask you to collect and analyze data, and report the results. Your response should meet academic standards and adhere to Standard English conventions.

1. Read an award-winning novel in the grades 4–8 range. Suggested books: *Joey Pigza Loses Control* (Gantos, 2005), *The Tale of Despereaux* (DiCamillo, 2003), *The Giver* (Lowry, 2006), *The Wednesday Wars* (Schmidt, 2009), and *The Higher Power of Lucky* (Patron, 2006). As you read, mark your thoughtful use of at least six comprehension strategies with small self-stick notes, as students might do. In your response, provide bibliographic information and a brief summary of the novel, list the strategies you employed, and describe the insights you've gained about teaching students about comprehension strategies.

2. Read aloud an appropriate picture book in a kindergarten or first grade classroom and teach the connecting strategy by creating a connections chart with children, as Ms. Ali did the vignette. In your response, provide bibliographic information and a brief summary about the book, describe the classroom and your lesson, and draw conclusions about these children's use of the connecting strategy. Include a copy of the chart you create.

3. Observe two struggling students in grades 4–6 to determine if they lack any of the prerequisites for comprehension. Watch as students participate in classroom literacy activities, and then interview them to gather more information. Talk with students about the book they're reading to judge their background and vocabulary knowledge, and listen to them read to determine their reading fluency. Also question them about comprehension strategies; that is, the kinds of thinking they do when they're reading. In your response, provide background information about the students, the results of your observation, and the conclusions you've drawn.

4. Reflect on how you use comprehension strategies. Ask yourself these questions:
   - Am I aware that I'm using cognitive strategies?
   - Which cognitive strategies do I use most often?
   - Am I aware that I'm using metacognitive strategies?
   - Am I a strategic reader?
   - How does my strategy use affect my comprehension?
   - How might I become a more strategic reader?

In your response, describe your strategy knowledge, how your use of strategies affects comprehension, and what you might do to become a more strategic reader.

5. Observe in a second to sixth grade classroom to learn more about motivation. Examine the classroom environment, and notice whether the teacher and the students exemplify the factors described in Figure 8–6. In your response, describe the teacher and the students, report the results of your observation, and make recommendations to enhance students' motivation based on your observations.

REFERENCES

Afflerbach, P., Pearson, P. D., & Paris, S. G. (2008). Clarifying differences between reading skills and strategies. *The Reading Teacher, 61,* 364–373.

Alderman, M. K. (1999). *Motivation for achievement: Possibilities for teaching and learning.* Mahwah, NJ: Erlbaum.

Allington, R. L. (2012). *What really matters for struggling readers: Designing research-based programs* (3rd ed.). Boston: Pearson.

Applegate, M. D., Quinn, K. B., & Applegate, A. J. (2008). *The critical reading inventory: Assessing students' reading and thinking* (2nd ed.). Upper Saddle River, NJ: Merrill/Prentice Hall.

Baker, L., & Brown, A. (1984). Metacognitive skills of reading. In P. D. Pearson, M. Kamil, P. Mosenthal, & R. Barr (Eds.), *Handbook of reading research* (pp. 353–394). New York: Longman.

Blachowicz, C. L. Z., & Fisher, P. J. (2011). Best practices in vocabulary instruction revisited. In L. M. Morrow & L. B. Gambrell (Eds.), *Best practices in literacy instruction* (4th ed., pp. 224–249). New York: Guilford Press.

Blanton, W. E., Wood, K. D., & Moorman, G. B. (1990). The role of purpose in reading instruction. *The Reading Teacher, 43,* 486–493.

Block, C. C., & Pressley, M. (2007). Best practices in teaching comprehension. In L. B. Gambrell, L. M. Morrow, & M. Pressley (Eds.), *Best practices in literacy instruction* (3rd ed., pp. 220–242). New York: Guilford Press.

Bottomley, D. M., Henk, W. A., & Melnick, S. A. (1997/1998). Assessing children's views about themselves as writers using the Writer Self-Perception Scale. *The Reading Teacher, 51,* 286–296.

Bouchard, M. (2005). *Comprehension strategies for English language learners.* New York: Scholastic.

Braunger, J., & Lewis, J. P. (2006). *Building a knowledge base in reading* (2nd ed.). Newark, DE: International Reading Association/National Council of Teachers of English.

Bunting, E. (1998). *So far from the sea.* Boston: Houghton Mifflin.

Castek, J., Bevans-Mangelson, J., & Goldstone, B. (2006). Reading adventures online: Five ways to introduce the new literacies of the Internet through children's literature. *The Reading Teacher, 59,* 714–728.

Clay, M. M. (2015). *An observation survey of early literacy achievement* (3rd ed.). Portsmouth. NH: Heinemann.

Coerr, E. (1989). *The Josefina story quilt.* New York: HarperCollins.

Coerr, E. (1993). *Chang's paper pony.* New York: HarperCollins.

Coiro, J. (2003). Reading comprehension on the Internet: Expanding our understanding of reading comprehension to encompass new literacies. *The Reading Teacher, 56,* 458–464.

Coiro, J., & Dobler, E. (2007). Exploring the online reading comprehension strategies used by sixth-grade skilled readers to search for and locate information on the Internet. *Reading Research Quarterly, 42,* 214–257.

Cooper, J. D., Chard, D. J., & Kiger, N. D. (2006). *The struggling reader: Interventions that work,* New York: Scholastic.

Cooter, R. B., Jr., Flynt, E. S., & Cooter, K. S. (2014). *The Flynt/Cooter comprehensive reading inventory-2.* Boston: Pearson.

Cronin, D. (2011). *Click, clack, moo: Cows that type.* New York: Simon & Schuster.

DiCamillo, K. (2003). *The tale of Despereaux.* New York: Candlewick Press.

Duke, N. K., & Pearson, P. D. (2002). Effective practices for developing reading comprehension. In A. E. Farstrup & S. J. Samuels (Eds.), *What research has to say about reading instruction* (3rd ed., pp. 205–242). Newark, DE: International Reading Association.

Erickson, J. R. (2011). *The original adventures of Hank the cowdog.* San Antonio, TX: Maverick Books.

Faigley, L., Cherry, R. D., Jolliffe, D. A., & Skinner, A. M. (1985). *Assessing writers' knowledge and processes of composing.* Norwood, NJ: Ablex.

Fisher, D., Frey, N., & Lapp, D. (2012). *Text complexity: Raising rigor in reading.* Newark, DE: International Reading Association.

Gambrell, L. B., Palmer, B. M., Codling, R. M., & Mazzoni, S. A. (1996). Assessing motivation to read. *The Reading Teacher, 49,* 518–533.

Gantos, J. (2005). *Joey Pigza loses control.* New York: HarperCollins.

Guthrie, J. T., & Wigfield, A. (2000). Engagement and motivation in reading. In M. L. Kamil, P. B. Mosenthal, P. D. Pearson, & R. Barr (Eds.), *Handbook of reading research* (Vol. 3, pp. 403–422). Mahwah, NJ: Erlbaum.

Harvey, S. (2015, March/April). Digging deeper: At its core, close reading is strategic reading. *Reading Today 32*(5), 30–31.

Harvey, S., & Goudvis, A. (2007). *Strategies that work: Teaching comprehension for understanding and engagement* (2nd ed.). Portland, ME: Stenhouse.

Henk, W. A., & Melnick, S. A. (1995). The Reader Self-Perception Scale (RSPS): A new tool for measuring how children feel about themselves as readers. *The Reading Teacher, 48,* 470–482.

Howe, D., & Howe, J. (2006). *Bunnicula: A rabbit-tale of mystery.* New York: Aladdin Books.

Irwin, J. W. (1991). *Teaching reading comprehension processes* (2nd ed.). Boston: Allyn & Bacon.

Ivey, G., & Broaddus, K. (2001). "Just plain reading": A survey of what makes students want to read in middle school classrooms. *Reading Research Quarterly, 36,* 350–377.

Jiménez, F. (1998). *La mariposa.* Boston: Houghton Mifflin.

Kear, D. J., Coffman, G. A., McKenna, M. C., & Ambrosio, A. L. (2000). Measuring attitude toward writing: A new tool for teachers. *The Reading Teacher, 54,* 10–23.

Keene, E. (2006). *Assessing comprehension thinking strategies.* Huntington Beach, CA: Shell Education.

Keene, E. O., & Zimmermann, S. (2007). *Mosaic of thought: The power of comprehension strategy instruction* (2nd ed.). Portsmouth, NH: Heinemann.

Kinney, J. (2007). *Diary of a wimpy kid*. New York: Amulet Books.

Kohn, A. (2001). *Punished by rewards: The trouble with gold stars, incentive plans, A's, praise, and other bribes*. Boston: Houghton Mifflin.

Leslie, L., & Caldwell, J. (2011). *Qualitative reading inventory* (5th ed.). Boston: Allyn & Bacon/Pearson.

Leu, D. J., Jr., Kinzer, C. K., Coiro, J., & Cammack, D. W. (2004). Toward a theory of new literacies emerging from the Internet and other communication technologies. In R. Ruddell & N. Unrau (Eds.), *Theoretical models and processes of reading* (5th ed., pp. 1570–1613). Newark, DE: International Reading Association.

Lowry, L. (2006). *The giver*. New York: Delacorte.

Lowry, L. (2011). *Number the stars*. New York: Sandpiper.

McKenna, M. C., & Dougherty Stahl, K. A. (2015). *Assessment for reading instruction* (3rd ed.). New York: Guilford Press.

McKenna, M. C., & Kear, D. J. (1990). Measuring attitude toward reading: A new tool for teachers. *The Reading Teacher, 43,* 626–639.

Morrow, L. M. (2002). *Organizing and managing the language arts block*. New York: Guilford Press.

National Reading Panel. (2000). *Teaching children to read: An evidence-based assessment of the scientific research literature on reading and its implications for reading instruction*. Washington, DC: National Institute of Child Health and Human Development.

Oldfather, P. (1995). Commentary: What's needed to maintain and extend motivation for literacy in the middle grades. *Journal of Reading, 38,* 420–422.

Owocki, G. (2003). *Comprehension: Strategic instruction for K–3 students*. Portsmouth, NH: Heinemann.

Palincsar, A. S., & Brown, A. L. (1986). Interactive teaching to promote independent learning from text. *The Reading Teacher, 39,* 771–777.

Paris, S. G., Wasik, B. A., & Turner, J. C. (1996). The development of strategic readers. In R. Barr, M. L. Kamil, P. B. Mosenthal, & P. D. Pearson (Eds.), *Handbook of reading research* (Vol. 2, pp. 609–640). Mahwah, NJ: Erlbaum.

Patron, S. (2006). *The higher power of Lucky*. New York: Atheneum.

Peregoy, S. F., & Boyle, W. F. (2013). *Reading, writing, and learning in ESL: A resource book for teaching K–12 English learners* (6th ed.). Boston: Pearson.

Pressley, M. (2002a). Comprehension strategies instruction: A turn-of-the-century status report. In C. C. Block & M. Pressley (Eds.), *Comprehension instruction: Research-based best practices* (pp. 11–27). New York: Guilford Press.

Pressley, M. (2002b). Metacognition and self-regulated comprehension. In A. E. Farstrup & S. J. Samuels (Eds.), *What research has to say about reading instruction* (3rd ed., pp. 291–309). Newark, DE: International Reading Association.

Pressley, M., Dolezal, S. E., Raphael, L. M., Mohan, L., Roehrig, A. D., & Bogner, K. (2003). *Motivating primary-grade students*. New York: Guilford Press.

Raphael, T. E., Highfield, K., & Au, K. H. (2006). *QAR now: A powerful and practical framework that develops comprehension and higher-level thinking in all students*. New York: Scholastic.

Sachar, L. (2008). *Holes*. New York; Farrar, Straus & Giroux.

Samuels, S. J. (2002). Reading fluency: Its development and assessment. In A. E. Farstrup & S. J. Samuels (Eds.), *What research has to say about reading instruction* (3rd ed., pp. 166–185). Newark, DE: International Reading Association.

Schmidt, G. D. (2009). *The Wednesday wars*. New York: Houghton Mifflin Harcourt.

Smith, J. (2006). *Bone, Vol. 4: The dragonslayer*. New York: Graphix.

Stipek, D. J. (2002). *Motivation to learn: Integrating theory and practice* (4th ed.). Boston: Allyn & Bacon.

Sweet, A. P., & Snow, C. E. (2003). Reading for comprehension. In A. P. Sweet & C. E. Snow (Eds.), *Rethinking reading comprehension* (pp. 1–11). New York: Guilford Press.

Tierney, R. J. (1990). Redefining reading comprehension. *Educational Leadership, 47,* 37–42.

Tierney, R., & Pearson, P. D. (1983). Toward a composing model of reading. *Language Arts, 60,* 568–580.

Tovani, C. (2000). *I read it, but I don't get it: Comprehension strategies for adolescent readers*. Portland, ME: Stenhouse.

Turner, J., & Paris, S. G. (1995). How literacy tasks influence children's motivation for literacy. *The Reading Teacher, 48,* 662–673.

Unrau, N. (2008). *Content area reading and writing: Fostering literacies in middle and high school cultures* (2nd ed.). Boston: Pearson.

Van Allsburg, C. (1991). *The wretched stone*. Boston: Houghton Mifflin.

Van Allsburg, C. (1993). *The garden of Abdul Gasazi*. Boston: Houghton Mifflin.

Van Den Broek, P., & Kremer, K. E. (2000). The mind in action: What it means to comprehend during reading. In B. M. Taylor, M. F. Graves, & P. van Den Broek (Eds.), *Reading for meaning: Fostering comprehension in the middle grades* (pp. 1–31). New York: Teachers College Press.

Wentzel, K. R., & Brophy, J. E. (2014). *Motivating students to learn* (4th ed.). New York: Routledge.

Wilhelm, J. D. (2001). *Improving comprehension with think-aloud strategies*. New York: Scholastic.

Woods, M. L., & Moe, A. J. (2015). *Analytical reading inventory* (10th ed.). Boston: Pearson.

Zimmermann, S., & Hutchins, C. (2003). *Seven keys to comprehension: How to help your kids read it and get it!* New York: Three Rivers Press.

Chapter 9

Promoting Comprehension: Text Factors

PLAN: Preview the Learning Outcomes

After studying this chapter, you'll be prepared to respond to these points:

9.1 Explain the text factors of stories.

9.2 Describe the text factors of nonfiction.

9.3 Discuss the text factors of poems.

9.4 Explain how to teach students about text factors.

Reading and Writing About Frogs. The fourth graders in Mr. Abrams's class are studying frogs. They began by making a class **KWL chart** (Ogle, 1986), listing what they already know about frogs in the "K: What We Know" column and things they want to learn in the "W: What We Wonder" column. At the end of the unit, students will finish the chart by listing what they've learned in the "L: What We Have Learned" column. The fourth graders want to know how frogs and toads are different and if it's true that you get warts from frogs. Mr. Abrams assures them that they'll learn the answers to many of their questions and makes a mental note to find the answer to their question about warts.

Aquariums with frogs and frog spawn are arranged in one area in the classroom; Mr. Abrams has brought in five aquariums and filled them with frogs he collected in his backyard and others he "rented" from a local pet store, and he has also brought in frog spawn from a nearby pond. The fourth graders are observing the frogs and the frog spawn daily and drawing diagrams and making notes in their **learning logs**.

Mr. Abrams places a text set with books about frogs representing the three genres—stories, nonfiction books, and poetry books—on a special shelf in the classroom library. He reads many of the books aloud to the class. When he begins, he reads the title and shows students several pages and asks them whether the book is a story, a nonfiction book, or a poem. After they determine the genre, they talk about their purpose for listening. For a nonfiction book, the teacher writes a question or two on the whiteboard to guide their listening, and then after reading, the students answer the questions as part of their discussion. They also read and reread many of these books during an independent reading time.

The teacher also has a class set of *Amazing Frogs and Toads* (Clarke, 1990), a nonfiction book with striking photographs and well-organized presentations of information. He reads it once with the whole class using **shared reading**, and they discuss the interesting information in the book. Next, he divides the class into small groups, and each group chooses a question about frogs to research in the book. Students reread the book, hunting for the answer to their question. Mr. Abrams has already taught the students to use the table of contents and the index to locate facts in a nonfiction book. After they locate and reread the information, they use the writing process to develop a poster to answer the question and share what they've learned. He meets with each group to help them design their posters and revise and edit their writing.

From the vast amount of information in *Amazing Frogs and Toads*, Mr. Abrams chooses nine questions, which address some of the questions on the "W: What We Wonder" section of the KWL chart, to highlight important information in the text and to focus on the five expository text structures, the organizational patterns used for nonfiction texts that students read and write. Mr. Abrams is teaching the fourth graders that nonfiction books, like stories, have special organizational elements. Here are his questions organized according to the expository structures:

What are amphibians? (Description)

What do frogs look like? (Description)

What is the life cycle of a frog? (Sequence)

How do frogs eat? (Sequence)

How are frogs and toads alike and different? (Comparison)

Why do frogs hibernate? (Cause and Effect)

How do frogs croak? (Cause and Effect)

How do frogs use their eyes and eyelids? (Problem and Solution)

How do frogs escape from their enemies? (Problem and Solution)

After the students complete their posters, they share them with the class through brief presentations, and the posters are displayed in the classroom. Check the figure Two Posters About Frogs: The life cycle poster emphasizes the sequence structure, and the "Frogs Have Big Eyes" poster explains that the frog's eyes help it solve problems—finding food, hiding from enemies, and seeing underwater.

Mr. Abrams's students use the information in the posters to write books about frogs. They choose three posters and write one- to three-paragraph chapters to report the information from them. They meet in **revising groups** to revise their rough drafts and then edit with a classmate and with Mr. Abrams. Finally, students word process their final copies and add illustrations, a title page, and a table of contents. Then they compile their books and "publish" them by sharing them with classmates from the author's chair.

Armin wrote this chapter on "Hibernation" in his book:

Hibernation means that an animal sleeps all winter long. Frogs hibernate because they are cold blooded and they might freeze to death if they didn't. They find a good place to sleep like a hole in the ground, or in a log, or under some leaves. They go to sleep and they do not eat, or drink, or go to the bathroom. They sleep

all winter and when they wake up it is spring. They are very, very hungry and they want to eat a lot of food. Their blood warms up when it is spring because the temperature warms up and when they are warm they want to be awake and eat. They are awake in the spring and in the summer, and then in the fall they start to think about hibernating again.

Jessica wrote this chapter on "The Differences Between Frogs and Toads" for her book:

You might think that frogs and toads are the same but you would be wrong. They are really different but they are both amphibians. I am going to tell you three ways they are different.

First of all, frogs really love water so they stay in the water or pretty close to it. Toads don't love water. They usually live where it is dry. This is a big difference between frogs and toads.

Second, you should look at frogs and toads. They look different. Frogs are slender and thin but toads are fat. Their skin is different, too. Frogs have smooth skin and toads have bumpy skin. I would say that toads are not pretty to look at.

Third, frogs have long legs but toads have short legs. That probably is the reason why frogs are wonderful jumpers and toads can't. They move slowly. They just hop. When you watch them move, you can tell that they are very different.

Frogs and toads are different kinds of amphibians. They live in different places, they look different, and they move in different ways. You can see these differences when you look at them and it is very interesting to study them.

Mr. Abrams helps his students develop a **rubric** to assess their books. The rubric addresses the following points about the chapters:

- The title describes the chapter.
- The information in each chapter is presented clearly.
- Vocabulary from the **word wall** is used in each chapter.
- The information in each chapter is written in one or more indented paragraphs.
- The information in each chapter has very few spelling, capitalization, and punctuation errors.
- There is a useful illustration in each chapter.

Other points on the rubric consider the book as a whole:

- The title page lists the title and the author's name.
- All pages in the book are numbered.
- The table of contents lists the chapters and the pages for each chapter.
- The title is written on the cover of the book.
- The illustrations on the cover of the book relate to frogs.

The students evaluate their books using a 4-point scale; Mr. Abrams also uses the rubric to assess their writing. He conferences with students and shares his scoring with them. Also, he helps the students set goals for their next writing project.

To end the unit, Mr. Abrams asks his students to finish the KWL chart. In the third column, "L: What We Have Learned," students list some of the information they've learned:

Tadpoles breathe through gills but frogs breathe through lungs.
Tadpoles are vegetarians but frogs eat worms and insects.
Snakes, rats, birds, and foxes are the frogs' enemies.
Some frogs in the rainforest are brightly colored and poisonous, too.
Some frogs are hard to see because they have camouflage coloring.
Male frogs puff up their air sacs to croak and make sounds.
Frogs have teeth but they swallow their food whole.
Frogs have two sets of eyelids and one set is clear so frogs can see when they are underwater.
Frogs can jump ten times their body length but toads can't—they're hoppers.

Mr. Abrams stands back to reread the fourth graders' comments. "I can tell how much you've learned when I read the detailed information you've added in the L column," he remarks with a smile. He knows that one reason why his students are successful is because he taught them to use text structure as a tool for learning.

 STANDARDS CHECK!

Mr. Abrams addressed the Common Core State Standards as he taught fourth graders about nonfiction text factors in the vignette you've just read. Review the fourth grade literacy Standards document online at http://www.corestandards.org/ELA-Literacy, and identify the Standards that Mr. Abrams addressed through his instruction. Create your list, and compare it with Mr. Abrams's.

*W*hat readers know and do during reading has a tremendous impact on how well they comprehend, but comprehension involves more than just reader factors: It also involves text factors. Stories, nonfiction books, and poems can be easier or more difficult to read depending on factors that are inherent in them (Harvey & Goudvis, 2007). These three types of text factors are the most important:

Genres. The three broad categories of literature are *stories, informational books* or *nonfiction,* and *poetry,* and there are subgenres within each category. For example, science fiction, folktales, and historical fiction are subgenres of stories.

Text Structures. Authors use text structures to organize texts and emphasize the most important ideas. Sequence, comparison, and cause and effect, for example, are three internal patterns used to organize nonfiction texts.

Text Features. Authors use text features to achieve a particular effect in their writing. Literary devices and conventions include symbolism and tone in stories, headings and indexes in nonfiction books, and page layout for poems.

When students understand how authors organize and present their ideas, this knowledge about text factors serves as a scaffold, making comprehension easier (Meyer & Poon, 2004; Sweet & Snow, 2003). Text factors make a similar contribution to students' writing: Students apply what they've learned about genres, text structures, and text features when they're writing (Mooney, 2001).

Text Factors of Stories

Stories are narratives about characters trying to overcome problems or deal with difficulties. They've been described as "waking dreams" that people use to find meaning in their lives. Children develop an understanding of what constitutes a story beginning in the preschool years when their parents read aloud to them, and they refine and expand their understanding of stories through literacy instruction at school (Applebee, 1978; Appleyard, 1994). Students learn about the subgenres of stories and read stories representing each one, examine the structural patterns that authors use to organize stories, and point out the narrative devices that authors use to breathe life into their stories.

Formats of Stories

Stories are available in picture-book and chapter-book formats. Picture books have brief texts, usually spread over 32 pages, in which text and illustrations combine to tell a story. The text is minimal, and the illustrations supplement the sparse text. The illustrations in picture books are often striking. Many picture books, such as *Rosie's Walk* (Hutchins, 2005), about a clever hen who outwits a fox, are for primary grade students, but others, such as *Show Way* (Woodson, 2005), a multimedia story about the generations of women in the author's family, from slavery to the Civil Rights movement to the present, were written with middle grade students in mind. Others are wordless picture books, such as *Flotsam* (Wiesner, 2006) and *Journey* (Becker, 2013), in which the story is told entirely through the illustrations.

Novels are longer stories written in a chapter format. Most are written for older students, but some, such as Dan Greenburg's collection of weird adventures called The Zack Files, Barbara Park's stories about the precocious girl Junie B. Jones, and Lenore Look's series about Alvin Ho, a kid who's afraid of almost everything, are for students reading at first through third grade levels. Chapter books for middle grade students include *Shiloh* (Naylor, 2012) and *Esperanza Rising* (Ryan, 2002). Complex stories such as *Holes* (Sachar, 2008) are more suitable for upper grade students. Chapter books have few illustrations, if any, because they don't usually play an integral role in the story.

Narrative Genres

Stories can be categorized in different ways, one of which is according to **genres** (Buss & Karnowski, 2000). Three general subcategories are *folklore*, *fantasies*, and *realistic fiction*. Figure 9–1 presents an overview of these narrative genres.

FOLKLORE. Stories that began hundreds of years ago and were passed down from generation to generation by storytellers before being written down are *folk literature*. These stories, including fables, folktales, and myths, are an important part of our

FIGURE 9–1 Narrative Genres

CATEGORY	GENRES	DESCRIPTIONS
Folklore	Fables	Brief tales told to point out a moral. For example: *Town Mouse, Country Mouse* (Brett, 2003) and *The Boy Who Cried Wolf* (Hennessy, 2006).
	Folktales	Stories in which heroes demonstrate virtues to triumph over adversity. For example: *Jouanah: A Hmong Cinderella* (Coburn, 1996) and *Rumpelstiltskin* (Zelinsky, 1996).
	Myths	Stories created by ancient peoples to explain natural phenomena. For example: *Why Mosquitoes Buzz in People's Ears* (Aardema, 2004) and *Raven* (McDermott, 2001).
	Legends	Stories, including hero tales and tall tales, that recount the courageous deeds of people who struggled against each other or against gods and monsters. For example: *John Henry* (J. Lester, 1999) and *The Adventures of Robin Hood* (Williams, 2007).
Fantasy	Modern Literary Tales	Stories written by modern authors that are similar to folktales. For example: *The Ugly Duckling* (Mitchell, 2007) and *Sylvester and the Magic Pebble* (Steig, 2010).
	Fantastic Stories	Imaginative stories that explore alternate realities and contain elements not found in the natural world. For example: *Jeremy Thatcher, Dragon Hatcher* (Coville, 2007b) and *Poppy* (Avi, 2005).
	Science Fiction	Stories that explore scientific possibilities. For example: *Aliens Ate My Homework* (Coville, 2007a) and *The Giver* (Lowry, 2006).
	High Fantasy	Stories that focus on the conflict between good and evil and often involve quests. For example: the Harry Potter series and *The Lion, the Witch and the Wardrobe* (Lewis, 2005).
Realistic Fiction	Contemporary Stories	Stories that portray today's society. For example: *Going Home* (Bunting, 1998) and *Seedfolks* (Fleischman, 2004).
	Historical Stories	Realistic stories set in the past. For example: *Sarah, Plain and Tall* (MacLachlan, 2005) and *Roll of Thunder, Hear My Cry* (Taylor, 2001).

cultural heritage. Fables are brief narratives designed to teach a moral. The story format makes the lesson easier to understand, and the moral is usually stated at the end. Fables exemplify these characteristics:

- They are short, often less than a page long.
- The characters are usually animals.
- The characters are one-dimensional: strong or weak, wise or foolish.
- The setting is barely sketched; the stories could take place anywhere.
- The theme is usually stated as a moral at the end of the story.

The best known fables, including "The Hare and the Tortoise" and "The Ant and the Grasshopper," are believed to have been written in the 6th century B.C. by a Greek slave named Aesop. Individual fables have been retold as picture-book stories, including *The Hare and the Tortoise* (Wildsmith, 2007) and *The Lion and the Mouse* (Pinkney, 2009).

Folktales began as oral stories, told and retold by medieval storytellers as they traveled from town to town. The problem in a folktale usually revolves around one of four situations: a journey from home to perform a task, a journey to confront a monster, the miraculous change from a harsh home to a secure home, or a confrontation between a wise beast and a foolish beast. Here are other characteristics:

- The story often begins with the phrase "Once upon a time . . ."
- The setting is generalized and could be located anywhere.
- The plot structure is simple and straightforward.
- Characters are one-dimensional: good or bad, stupid or clever, industrious or lazy.
- The end is happy, and everyone lives "happily ever after."

Some folktales are cumulative tales, such as *The Gingerbread Boy* (Galdone, 2008); these stories are built around the repetition of words and events. Others are talking animal stories; in these stories, such as *The Three Little Pigs* (Kellogg, 2002), animals act and talk like humans. The best known folktales are fairy tales. They have motifs or small recurring elements, including magical powers, transformations, enchantments, magical objects, trickery, and wishes that are granted, and they feature witches, giants, fairy godmothers, and other fantastic characters. Well-known examples are *Cinderella* (Ehrlich, 2004) and *Jack and the Beanstalk* (Kellogg, 1997).

People around the world have created myths to explain natural phenomena. Some explain the seasons, the sun, the moon, and the constellations, and others tell how the mountains and other physical features of the earth were created. Ancient peoples used myths to explain many things that have since been explained by scientific investigations. Myths exemplify these characteristics:

- Myths explain creations.
- Characters are often heroes with supernatural powers.
- The setting is barely sketched.
- Magical powers are required.

For example, the Greek myth *King Midas: The Golden Touch* (Demi, 2002) tells about the king's greed, and the Native American myth *The Legend of the Bluebonnet* (dePaola, 1996) recounts how these flowers came to beautify the countryside. Other myths tell how animals came to be or why they look the way they do. *Legends* are myths about heroes who have done something important enough to be remembered in a story; they may have some basis in history but aren't verifiable. Stories about Robin Hood and King Arthur, for example, are legends; American legends about Johnny Appleseed, Paul Bunyan, and Pecos Bill are known as *tall tales*.

FANTASIES. *Fantasies* are imaginative stories. Authors create new worlds for their characters, but these worlds must be based in reality so that readers will believe they exist. One of the most beloved fantasies is *Charlotte's Web* (White, 2012). Four types of fantasies are *modern literary tales*, *fantastic stories*, *science fiction*, and *high fantasy*.

Modern literary tales are related to folktales and fairy tales because they often incorporate many characteristics and conventions of traditional literature, but they've been written more recently and have identifiable authors. The best known author of modern literary tales is Hans Christian Andersen, a Danish writer of the 1800s who wrote *The Snow Queen* (Ehrlich, 2006) and *The Ugly Duckling* (Mitchell, 2007). Other examples of modern literary tales include *Alexander and the Wind-Up Mouse* (Lionni, 2006) and *The Wolf's Chicken Stew* (Kasza, 1996).

Fantastic stories are realistic in most details, but some events require readers to suspend disbelief. Fantasies exemplify these characteristics:

ℯ The events in the story are extraordinary, things that couldn't happen in today's world.
ℯ The setting is realistic.
ℯ Main characters are people or personified animals.
ℯ Themes often deal with the conflict between good and evil.

Some are animal fantasies, such as *Babe: The Gallant Pig* (King-Smith, 2005); the main characters in these stories are animals endowed with human traits. Students often realize that the animals symbolize human beings and that these stories explore human relationships. Some are toy fantasies, such as *The Miraculous Journey of Edward Tulane* (DiCamillo, 2006); they're similar to animal fantasies except that the main characters are talking toys, usually stuffed animals or dolls. Other fantasies involve enchanted journeys during which wondrous things happen. The journey must have a purpose, but it's usually overshadowed by the thrill and delight of the fantastic world, as in Roald Dahl's *Charlie and the Chocolate Factory* (2007).

In science fiction stories, authors create a world in which science interacts with society. Many stories involve traveling through space to distant galaxies or meeting alien societies. Authors hypothesize scientific advancements and imagine technology of the future to create the plot. Science fiction exemplifies these characteristics:

ℯ The story is set in the future.
ℯ Conflict is usually between the characters and natural or mechanical forces, such as robots.
ℯ The characters believe in the advanced technology.
ℯ A detailed description of scientific facts is provided.

Time-warp stories, in which the characters move forward and back in time, are also classified as science fiction. Jon Scieszka's Time Warp Trio stories, including *Knights of the Kitchen Table* (2004), are popular with middle grade students.

Heroes confront evil for the good of humanity in high fantasy. The primary characteristic is the focus on the conflict between good and evil, as in C. S. Lewis's *The Lion, the Witch and the Wardrobe* (2005) and J. K. Rowling's Harry Potter stories. High fantasy is related to folk literature in that it's characterized by motifs and themes. Most stories include magical kingdoms, quests, tests of courage, magical powers, and superhuman characters.

REALISTIC FICTION. These stories are lifelike and believable. The outcome is reasonable, and the story is a representation of action that seems truthful. Realistic fiction helps students discover that their problems aren't unique and that they aren't alone in experiencing certain feelings and situations. Realistic fiction also broadens students' horizons and allows them to experience new adventures. Two types are *contemporary stories* and *historical stories*.

In contemporary stories, readers identify with characters who are their own age and have similar interests and problems. In *The Higher Power of Lucky* (Patron, 2006),

A New Generation of Books

Many of the best new books for kids blur the lines between genres and incorporate innovative forms. Students read these texts differently, much like they approach online texts (Kiefer, Price-Dennis, & Ryan, 2006). In *The Invention of Hugo Cabret* (Selznick, 2007), the first novel to win the Caldecott Medal, the author combined storytelling, meticulous drawings, and cinematic techniques to create a touching story about a Parisian orphan. Half of the 500-page novel is told through illustrations that readers must "read" as carefully as they do the text.

Some authors combine genres. *Hate That Cat* (Creech, 2010), about a boy who learns the power of poetry, *Becoming Joe DiMaggio* (Testa, 2005), about a kid who escapes his difficult life by listening to baseball games with his grandfather, and *The Crossover* (Alexander, 2014), about twin 12-year-old basketball stars who deal differently with adolescence, are poetic narratives—stories told in verse. Students focus on the characters and the plot, but they're aware of the unique page layout and appreciate the figurative qualities of the language.

Other authors invent multiple voices to tell their stories. *Day of Tears: A Novel in Dialogue* (J. Lester, 2005) tells about an 1859 slave auction using different voices to emphasize the anguish of slave families and the greed of owners; *Good Masters! Sweet Ladies! Voices From a Medieval Village* (Schlitz, 2007) is an award-winning collection of 23 monologues, featuring people living at an English manor; and *Because of Mr. Terupt* (Buyea, 2011) features seven fifth graders who tell about their beloved teacher and how he helps them become better people. In these books, students read flexibly, adjusting to a new viewpoint in each chapter.

Book-length comics called *graphic novels* are a popular new genre. *Diary of a Wimpy Kid* (Kinney, 2007) and its sequels combine text and graphics to recount Greg Heffley's trials and tribulations in middle school, and *El Deafo* (Bell, 2014) is a memoir in which the author shares her struggles to lip read and make friends after an illness leaves her deaf. Students read the visual information in each frame and use their imagination to understand what's happening between frames.

Wordless picture books aren't just for young children; some present imaginative, multilayered adventures for older students. Middle graders like *Fossil* (Thomson, 2013), the story of a boy and his dog who find some fossils that spring to life and must be captured, and *Quest* (Becker, 2014), the story of two children who follow a map through enchanted lands to rescue the king. For upper grade students, *The Arrival* (Tan, 2007) is a compelling story of an immigrant's journey to build a better future. Readers develop a sense of the immigrant's isolation as they study the illustrations and recognize the visual metaphors.

Primary source materials are also being used to craft multigenre stories. *Middle School Is Worse Than Meatloaf: A Year Told Through Stuff* (Holm, 2011) incorporates diary entries, refrigerator notes, instant messages, and greeting cards to recount a girl's day-to-day experiences; and *The Wall: Growing Up Behind the Iron Curtain* (Sís, 2007) combines drawings, diary entries, and photos to create a powerful graphic memoir of the author's childhood in Soviet-ruled Prague. Students combine visual and textual information to comprehend across genres, text structures, and conventions.

---

for example, students read about an eccentric 10-year-old girl named Lucky who comes to terms with her mother's death and finds stability in her life. Here are the characteristics of contemporary fiction:

- Characters act like real people or like real animals.
- The setting is in the world as we know it today.
- Stories deal with everyday occurrences or "relevant subjects."

Other contemporary stories include *Granny Torrelli Makes Soup* (Creech, 2005) and *I Am Not Joey Pigza* (Gantos, 2007).

In contrast, historical stories are set in the past. Details about food, clothing, and culture must be typical of the era in which the story is set because the setting influences the plot. Historical stories illustrate these characteristics:

- The setting is historically accurate.
- Conflict is often between characters or between a character and society.
- The language is appropriate to the setting.
- Themes are universal, both for the historical period of the book and for today.

Examples of historical fiction include *Witness* (Hesse, 2005) and *Crispin: The Cross of Lead* (Avi, 2004). In these stories, students are immersed in historical events, they appreciate the contributions of people who lived before them, and they learn about human relationships.

Elements of Story Structure

Stories have unique structural elements that distinguish them from other genres. The most important story elements are *plot, characters, setting, point of view,* and *theme*; check the Booklist: Stories Illustrating the Elements of Story Structure. These elements work together to structure a story, and authors manipulate them to develop their stories.

PLOT. **Plot** is the sequence of events involving characters in conflict situations; it's based on the goals of one or more characters and the processes they go through to attain them (Lukens, Smith, & Miller Coffel, 2012). The main characters want to achieve the goal, and other characters are introduced to prevent them from being successful. Characters set the story events in motion as they attempt to overcome conflict and solve their problems. Stories with well-developed plots are included in Booklist: Stories Illustrating the Elements of Story Structure.

The most basic aspect of plot is the division of the main events into the beginning, middle, and end. In *The Tale of Peter Rabbit* (Potter, 2006), for instance, the

Watch a second grade teacher teach story structure by having students compare the structural elements in two stories. What helps children uncover the common elements for these stories?

Booklist — Stories Illustrating the Elements of Story Structure

ELEMENT	BOOKS
Plot	Brett, J. (2000). *Hedgie's surprise*. New York: Putnam. P
	Fleming, D. (2003). *Buster*. New York: Henry Holt. P
	Paulsen, G. (2007). *Hatchet*. New York: Simon & Schuster. U
	Sachar, L. (2008). *Holes*. New York: Farrar, Straus & Giroux. U
	Steig, W. (2010). *Sylvester and the magic pebble*. New York: Atheneum. PM
Characters	Cushman, K. (2012). *Catherine, called Birdy*. New York: Sandpiper. U
	Dahl, R. (2007). *James and the giant peach*. New York: Puffin Books. MU
	DiCamillo, K. (2015). *Flora & Ulysses: The illuminated adventures*. Somerville, MA: Candlewick Press. M
	Henkes, K. (2006). *Lilly's purple plastic purse*. New York: Greenwillow. P
	Lowry, L. (2006). *The giver*. New York: Delacorte. U
Setting	Bunting, E. (2006). *Pop's bridge*. San Diego: Harcourt. PM
	Choldenko, G. (2006). *Al Capone does my shirts*. New York: Puffin Books. MU
	Hale, S. (2005). *Princess Academy*. New York: Bloomsbury. MU
	Lowry, L. (2011). *Number the stars*. New York: Sandpiper. MU
	Patron, S. (2006). *The higher power of Lucky*. New York: Atheneum. U
Point of View	Bunting, E. (2006). *One green apple*. New York: Clarion Books. PM
	Hesse, K. (2005). *Witness*. New York: Scholastic. U
	Lewis, C. S. (2005). *The lion, the witch and the wardrobe*. New York: HarperCollins. U
	MacLachlan, P. (2005). *Sarah, plain and tall*. New York: Scholastic. M
	Pinkney, J. (2006). *The little red hen*. New York: Dial Books. P
Theme	Babbitt, N. (2007). *Tuck everlasting*. New York: Square Fish Books. U
	Bunting, E. (1999). *Smoky night*. San Diego: Harcourt Brace. M
	DiCamillo, K. (2006). *The miraculous journey of Edward Tulane*. Cambridge, MA: Candlewick Press. MU
	Naylor, P. R. (2012). *Shiloh*. New York: Atheneum. MU
	Woodson, J. (2001). *The other side*. New York: Putnam. PM

P = primary grades (K–2); M = middle grades (3–5); U = upper grades (6–8)

FIGURE 9–2 A Beginning-Middle-End Story Map

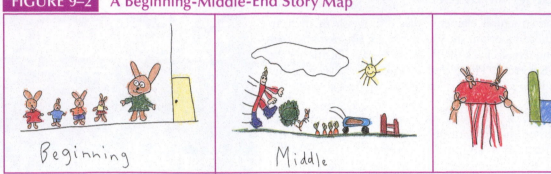

three story parts are easy to pick out. As the story begins, Mrs. Rabbit sends her children out to play after warning them not to go into Mr. McGregor's garden. In the middle, Peter goes to the garden and is almost caught. Then Peter finds his way out of the garden and gets home safely—the end of the story. Students can make a story map of the beginning-middle-end of a story using words and pictures, as the story map for *The Tale of Peter Rabbit* in Figure 9–2 shows.

Specific types of information are included in each part. In the beginning, the author introduces the characters, describes the setting, and presents a problem; together, the characters, setting, and events develop the plot and sustain the theme through the story. In the middle, the plot unfolds, with each event preparing readers for what follows. Conflict heightens as the characters face roadblocks that keep them from solving their problems; how the characters tackle these problems adds suspense to keep readers interested. In the end, all is reconciled, and readers learn whether the characters' struggles are successful.

Conflict is the tension or opposition between forces in the plot, and it's what interests readers enough to continue reading the story (Lukens et al., 2012). Conflict occurs in these four ways:

Between a Character and Nature. Conflict between a character and nature occurs in stories in which severe weather plays an important role and in stories set in isolated geographic locations, such as *Holes* (Sachar, 2008), in which Stanley struggles to survive at Camp Green Lake, a boys' juvenile detention center.

Between a Character and Society. Sometimes the main character's activities and beliefs differ from those of others, and conflict arises between that character and society. In *The Witch of Blackbird Pond* (Speare, 2001), for example, Kit Tyler is accused of being a witch because she continues activities in a New England Puritan community that were acceptable in the Caribbean community where she grew up but aren't in her new home.

Between Characters. Conflict between characters is very common. In *Tales of a Fourth Grade Nothing* (Blume, 2007), for instance, the never-ending conflict between Peter and his little brother, Fudge, is what makes the story entertaining.

Within a Character. The main character struggles to overcome challenges in his or her own life. In *Esperanza Rising* (Ryan, 2002), the title character must come to terms with her new life as a migrant worker after she leaves her family's ranch in Mexico.

Plot is developed through conflict that's introduced at the beginning, expanded in the middle, and finally resolved at the end. The development of the plot involves these components:

ℰ A problem that introduces conflict is presented at the beginning of the story.
ℰ Characters face roadblocks in attempting to solve the problem in the middle.

℮ The high point in the action occurs when the problem is about to be solved. This high point separates the middle and the end.

℮ The problem is solved and the roadblocks are overcome at the end of the story.

Figure 9–3 presents a plot diagram shaped like a mountain that incorporates these four components, which fifth graders completed after reading *Esperanza Rising* (Ryan, 2002). The problem in *Esperanza Rising* is that Esperanza and her mother must create a new life for themselves in California because they can't remain at their Mexican ranch home. Certainly, there's conflict between characters here and conflict with society, too, but the most important conflict is within Esperanza as she leaves her comfortable life in Mexico to become a migrant laborer in California. Esperanza and her mother face many roadblocks. They become farm laborers, and the work is very difficult. Esperanza wants to bring her grandmother to join them, but they don't have enough money for her travel expenses. Then Esperanza's mother becomes ill, and Esperanza takes over her mother's work. Finally, Esperanza saves enough money to bring her grandmother to California, but her money disappears. The high point of the action occurs when Esperanza's mother recovers enough to return to the farm labor camp, and it turns out that her money wasn't stolen after all: Esperanza's friend Miguel used it to bring her grandmother to California. As the story ends, the problem is solved: Esperanza adjusts to her new life in California with her mother and

FIGURE 9–3   **A Plot Diagram**

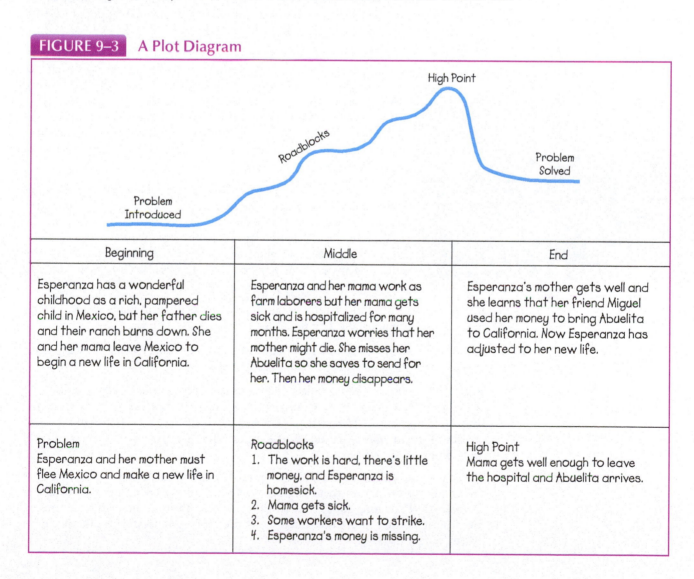

Beginning	Middle	End
Esperanza has a wonderful childhood as a rich, pampered child in Mexico, but her father dies and their ranch burns down. She and her mama leave Mexico to begin a new life in California.	Esperanza and her mama work as farm laborers but her mama gets sick and is hospitalized for many months. Esperanza worries that her mother might die. She misses her Abuelita so she saves to send for her. Then her money disappears.	Esperanza's mother gets well and she learns that her friend Miguel used her money to bring Abuelita to California. Now Esperanza has adjusted to her new life.
Problem Esperanza and her mother must flee Mexico and make a new life in California.	Roadblocks 1. The work is hard, there's little money, and Esperanza is homesick. 2. Mama gets sick. 3. Some workers want to strike. 4. Esperanza's money is missing.	High Point Mama gets well enough to leave the hospital and Abuelita arrives.

grandmother. *Esperanza* means "hope" in Spanish, and readers have reason to be optimistic that the girl and her family will create a good life for themselves.

CHARACTERS. *Characters* are the people or personified animals in the story. They're the most important structural element when stories are centered on a character or group of characters. Main characters have many character traits, both good and bad; that is to say, they have all the characteristics of real people. Inferring a character's traits is an important part of comprehension: Through character traits, readers get to know a character well, and the character seems to come to life. A list of stories with fully developed main characters is included in Booklist: Stories Illustrating the Elements of Story Structure. Characters are developed in four ways:

Appearance. Readers learn about characters through descriptions of their facial features, body shapes, habits of dress, mannerisms, and gestures. On the first page of *Tacky the Penguin* (H. Lester, 1990), the illustration of Tacky wearing a bright floral shirt and a purple-and-white tie suggests to readers that Tacky is an "odd bird"! Lester confirms this impression as she describes Tacky's behavior.

Action. The best way to learn about characters is through their actions. In Van Allsburg's *The Stranger* (1986), readers deduce that the stranger is Jack Frost because of what he does: He watches geese flying south for the winter, blows a cold wind, labors long hours without becoming tired, has an unusual rapport with wild animals, and is unfamiliar with modern conveniences.

Dialogue. Authors use dialogue to breathe life into their characters, develop the plot, provide information, move the story forward, and spark reader interest. For example, in *The Higher Power of Lucky* (Patron, 2007), the Newbery Award story set in the tiny, dusty town of Hard Pan, California, the author uses dialogue to reveal both Lucky's bravado and her fear of being abandoned by her guardian. *Said* is the most common dialogue tag, but authors often use more descriptive tags, including *nagged, roared, bragged, argued, whimpered,* and *giggled.*

Monologue. Authors provide insight into characters by revealing their thoughts. In *Sylvester and the Magic Pebble* (Steig, 2010), thoughts and wishes are central to the story. Sylvester, a foolish donkey, wishes to become a rock, and he spends a miserable winter that way. Steig shares the donkey's thinking with readers: He thinks about his parents, who are frantic with worry, and readers learn how Sylvester feels in the spring when his parents picnic on the rock he has become.

Watch fourth grade students delve deeper into the story of *The Three Little Pigs* to determine character motivation. Why does the teacher want students to find evidence in the text to identify the wolf's thoughts, actions, and feelings?

Sometimes authors use all four ways to develop characters, but in many stories, one or two ways are more important than the others.

SETTING. The setting is generally thought of as the location where the story takes place, but that's only one aspect. Setting has four dimensions:

Location. Many stories take place in predictable settings that don't contribute to a story's effectiveness, but sometimes the location is integral. For instance, the Boston Commons in *Make Way for Ducklings* (McCloskey, 2004) and the Alaskan North Slope in *Julie of the Wolves* (George, 2005) are artfully described and add uniqueness to the story.

Weather. Severe weather, such as a blizzard, a rainstorm, or a tornado, is crucial in some stories. A rainstorm is essential to the plot development in *Bridge to Terabithia* (Paterson, 2005), but in other books, the weather isn't mentioned because it doesn't affect the outcome of the story. Many stories take place on warm, sunny days.

Time Period. For stories set in the past or in the future, the time period is important. If *The Witch of Blackbird Pond* (Speare, 2001) and *Number the Stars* (Lowry, 2011), for example, were set in different eras, they would lose much of their impact: Today, few people would believe that Kit Tyler is a witch or that Jewish people are the focus of government persecution.

Time. This dimension involves both the time of day and the passage of time. Most stories take place during the day, except for scary stories that are set after dark. Many stories span a brief period of time. *Hatchet* (Paulsen, 2007) takes place in less than 2 months; other stories, such as *The Ugly Duckling* (Mitchell, 2007), span a year—long enough for the main character to grow to maturity.

In some stories, the setting is barely sketched; these are called *backdrop settings*. The setting in many folktales, for instance, is relatively unimportant, and the convention "Once upon a time . . ." is enough to set the stage. In other stories, the setting is elaborated and essential to the story's effectiveness; these settings are called *integral settings* (Lukens et al., 2012). Stories with integral settings also are presented in Booklist: Stories Illustrating the Elements of Story Structure.

POINT OF VIEW. Stories are written from a particular viewpoint, and this perspective determines to a great extent reader's understanding of the characters and events of the story (Lukens et al., 2012). Stories written from different viewpoints are presented in Booklist: Stories Illustrating the Elements of Story Structure. Here are the points of view:

First-Person Viewpoint. This point of view is used to tell a story through the eyes of one character using the first-person pronoun *I*. The narrator, usually the main character, speaks as an eyewitness and a participant in the events. For example, in *The True Story of the 3 Little Pigs!* (Scieszka, 1999), the wolf tries to explain away his bad image in his version of the familiar folktale.

Omniscient Viewpoint. The author is godlike, seeing and knowing all, telling readers about the thought processes of each character without worrying about how the information is obtained. *Doctor De Soto* (Steig, 1990), a story about a mouse dentist who outwits a fox with a toothache, is told from the omniscient viewpoint. Steig lets readers know that the fox wants to eat the dentist as soon as his toothache is cured and that the mouse dentist is aware of the fox's thoughts and plans a clever trick.

Limited Omniscient Viewpoint. This viewpoint is used so that readers know the thoughts of one character. It's told in third person, and the author concentrates on the thoughts, feelings, and experiences of the main character or another important character. Gary Paulsen used this viewpoint for *Hatchet* (2007) to be able to explore both Brian's thoughts as he struggled to survive in the wilderness and his coming to terms with his parents' divorce.

Objective Viewpoint. Readers are eyewitnesses to the story and are confined to the immediate scene. They learn only what's visible and audible and aren't aware of what any characters think. Most fairy tales, such as *Rumpelstiltskin* (Zelinski, 1996), are told from the objective viewpoint. The focus is on recounting events, not on developing the personalities of the characters.

Some stories are told from multiple viewpoints, such as *Seedfolks* (P. Fleischman, 2004b), the story of a community garden that brings hope to a blighted neighborhood. Each chapter is told from a first-person viewpoint by a different character.

THEME. **Theme** is the underlying meaning of a story; it embodies general truths about human nature (Lehr, 1991; Lukens et al., 2012). Themes usually deal with the characters' emotions and values, and can be either explicit or implicit: Explicit themes are stated clearly in the story, but implicit themes must be inferred. In a fable, the theme is often stated at the end, but in most stories, the theme emerges through the thoughts, speech, and actions of the characters as they try to overcome the obstacles that prevent them from reaching their goals. In *A Chair for My Mother* (V. B. Williams, 1993), for example, a young girl demonstrates the importance of sacrificing personal wants for her family's welfare as she and her mother collect money to buy a new chair after they lose all of their belongings in a fire.

Novels usually have more than one theme, and their themes generally can't be articulated with a single word. *Charlotte's Web* (White, 2012), for example, has several "friendship" themes, one explicitly stated and others that must be inferred. Friendship is a multidimensional theme—qualities of a good friend, unlikely friends, and sacrificing for a friend, for instance. Teachers probe students' thinking as they work to construct a theme and move beyond simplistic one-word labels. Minilesson: Analyzing the Theme demonstrates how Mrs. Miller, a seventh grade teacher, reviewed the concept of theme; afterward, her students analyzed the theme of books they were reading in literature circles.

Narrative Devices

Authors use narrative devices to make their writing more vivid and memorable (Lukens et al., 2012). Figure 9–4 describes the more common literary devices used in stories. Imagery is probably the most frequently used convention; many authors use it as they paint rich word pictures that bring their characters and settings to life. Flashbacks are commonly used in stories, such as the Time Warp Trio series, by Jon Scieszka, and the Magic Tree House series, by Mary Pope Osborne, where readers travel back in time for adventures. Authors also create symbols as they use one thing

FIGURE 9–4 Narrative Devices

DEVICE	DESCRIPTION
Dialogue	Written conversation where characters speak to each other. Authors use dialogue to move the story forward while bringing the characters to life.
Flashback	An interruption, often taking readers back to the beginning of the story. Authors use flashback in time-warp stories where characters travel back in time to a particular historical period.
Foreshadowing	Hinting at events to come later in the story to build readers' expectations. Authors often use foreshadowing in the beginning of the story.
Imagery	Descriptive words and phrases used to create a picture in the readers' minds. Authors also use metaphors and similes as they craft images.
Suspense	An excited uncertainty about the outcome of conflict in a story. Authors use suspense in the middle of the story as characters attempt to thwart one roadblock after another.
Symbolism	A person, place, or thing used to represent something else. For example, a lion often symbolizes courage and a dove symbolizes peace. Authors use symbols to enhance the theme of a story.
Tone	The overall feeling or mood in a story, ranging from humorous to serious and sad. Authors create the tone through their choice of words and use of other narrative devices.

Minilesson

TOPIC: Analyzing the Theme
GRADE: Seventh Grade
TIME: 20 minutes

Mrs. Miller's seventh graders are studying the Middle Ages and are reading novels set in that period, such as *Catherine, Called Birdy* (Cushman, 2012), in literature circles. Mrs. Miller brings the class together to teach a minilesson on theme before asking the students in each literature circle to analyze the theme of the book they're reading.

1 Introduce the Topic

"It's time to talk about theme because most of you are reaching the end of the book you're reading," Mrs. Miller begins. "Before, I asked you to focus on the setting to learn more about medieval life as you were reading and discussing the book. Now, I want you to think about your book in a different way: I want you to think about the theme. Let's review: Theme is the universal message in the book. It might be about friendship, courage, acceptance, determination, or some other important quality."

2 Share Examples

Mrs. Miller uses *Hatchet* (Paulsen, 2007), a survival story that students read in September, as an example. "Did Brian save himself?" the teacher asks. Everyone agrees that he did. "So what is the theme of the story?" Mrs. Miller asks. Students identify survival as the theme, and Mrs. Miller asks them to explain it in a sentence. Jared suggests, "Sometimes you have to do a lot of disgusting things if you want to survive." Mrs. Miller agrees. Carole offers, "I think the theme is that you may not think that you have the guts and the brains to survive, but if you get trapped in the wilderness, you will find that you do." Again she agrees. Jo-Jo expresses the theme another way: "It's like in the movie *Castaway*. Brian has to get mad—really mad and a little crazy, too, but he gets mad enough to survive. You have to stand up and prove to yourself that you can survive." Again she agrees. Mrs. Miller draws a cluster on the whiteboard and writes *survival* in the center circle. Then she draws out rays and writes on them the sentences that the students offered.

3 Provide Information

"Theme isn't obvious the way plot, characters, and setting are," Mrs. Miller explains. She tells the class that in order to uncover the theme, they need to think about the conflicts facing the character and how the character goes about solving the problem. "Then you have to answer the question: 'What is the author trying to tell me about life?'"

4 Guide Practice

The minilesson ends as the students return to their literature circles to talk about the theme of their book. Mrs. Miller asks them to think of one or more one-word qualities and then to draw out at least three possible sentence-long themes. As they analyze the theme, they draw clusters on chart paper.

5 Assess Learning

Mrs. Miller moves from group to group, talking with students about theme. She checks their clusters and helps them draw out additional themes to add to them.

to represent something else. In Chris Van Allsburg's *The Wretched Stone* (1991), for example, the glowing stone that distracts the crew from reading, from spending time with their friends, and from doing their jobs symbolizes television or computers. To understand the theme of many stories, students must recognize symbols and understand what they represent. The author's style conveys the tone or overall feeling: Some stories are humorous, some are uplifting celebrations of life, and others are sobering commentaries on society.

Looking at the Text Factors in a Story

Project Mulberry (Park, 2007) is a contemporary realistic novel about Julie Song, a seventh grade Korean American girl, and her friend Patrick, who team up to create a project to win a blue ribbon at the state fair. This multicultural novel is appropriate for fourth through eighth graders, and the reading level is fifth grade. Newbery Medal–winning author Linda Sue Park has written a lively, engaging first-person narrative. Julie is a compelling character, and her thoughts and actions drive the story forward. Her mother suggests that she and Patrick raise silkworms for their state fair project, but at first Julie isn't interested because she thinks it's too Korean; instead, she wants to do something "American."

Self-acceptance is the most important theme in this story. The conflict is within Julie as she struggles to fit in while honoring her Korean heritage. Another theme is prejudice: Julie fears that her mother may be racist because she doesn't want her to spend time with Mr. Dixon, the African American man who gives her mulberry leaves to feed to the silkworms. The story emphasizes the importance of doing small things to increase tolerance.

The most interesting feature in the book is a series of conversations between Julie and the author that are inserted between chapters. In these exchanges, Julie complains about her character and asks questions about how Ms. Park thinks of ideas and writes books. These witty conversations provide useful insights about the writing process. Most students will enjoy reading them, but those who don't can easily skip over them because they're set off from the rest of the story.

 MONITOR: Check Your Understanding 9.1

 # Text Factors of Nonfiction

Stories have been the principal genre for reading and writing instruction in the primary grades because it's been assumed that constructing stories in the mind is a fundamental way of learning; however, many students prefer to read nonfiction books, and they're able to understand them as well as they do stories (Stead & Duke, 2005). The shift to nonfiction traditionally happens in fourth grade. Certainly, students are interested in learning about their world—about the difference between dolphins and whales, how a road is built, threats to the environment of Antarctica, or Amelia Earhart's ill-fated flight around the world—and nonfiction books provide this knowledge.

Nonfiction Genres

Nonfiction books provide facts on just about any topic you can think of. Consider, for example: *Flick a Switch: How Electricity Gets to Your Home* (Seuling, 2003), *Taj Mahal* (Arnold & Comora, 2007), *Saguaro Moon: A Desert Journal* (Pratt-Serafini, 2002), *The Brain* (Simon, 2006), *Groundhog Day!* (Gibbons, 2007), *Ancient Inca* (Gruber, 2006), and *The Right Dog for the Job: Ira's Path From Service Dog to Guide Dog* (Patent, 2004). Some of these books are picture books that use a combination of text and illustrations to present information, and others are chapter books that depend primarily on the text to provide information.

Other books present information within a story context; the Magic School Bus series is perhaps the best known. In *The Magic School Bus and the Science Fair Expedition* (Cole, 2006), for example, Ms. Frizzle and her class travel through time to learn how scientific thinking developed. The page layout is innovative, with charts and reports containing factual information presented at the outside edges of most pages.

ALPHABET BOOKS. Many alphabet books are designed for young children who are learning to identify the letters of the alphabet. Some are predictable, featuring a letter and an illustration of a familiar object on each page, but others, such as *Alphabet Adventure* (Wood, 2001) and *The Alphabet Room* (Pinto, 2003), are more imaginative presentations. Other alphabet books are intended for older students. *The Alphabet From A to Y With Bonus Letter Z!* (Martin & Chast, 2007) is a clever wordplay book, and others, such as *SuperHero ABC* (McLeod, 2006) and *Q Is for Quark: A Science Alphabet Book* (Schwartz, 2001), provide a wealth of information about various topics. In these books, words representing each letter are explained in paragraph-long entries.

BIOGRAPHIES. Students read biographies to learn about a person's life. A wide range of biographies are available for kids today, from those featuring well-known personalities, such as *Eleanor Roosevelt: A Life of Discovery* (Freedman, 1997), *Muhammad* (Demi, 2003), *Escape! The Story of the Great Houdini* (S. Fleischman, 2006), and *Isaac Newton* (Krull, 2006), to those about unsung heroes, such as *Delivering Justice: W. W. Law and the Fight for Civil Rights* (Haskins, 2006). These books are individual biographies because they focus on a single person; others are collective biographies with short vignettes about a group of people who are related in some way, such as *Rad American Women A–Z: Rebels, Trailblazers, and Visionaries Who Shaped Our History . . . and Our Future!* (Schatz, 2015) and *Honky-Tonk Heroes and Hillbilly Angels: The Pioneers of Country and Western Music* (George-Warren, 2006).

Autobiographies are life stories written by the people themselves. One of the most noteworthy is *I Am Malala: How One Girl Stood Up for Education and Changed the World* (Yousafzai, 2014), the story of the Pakistani girl who became a children's rights activist and the youngest person ever to receive the Nobel Peace Prize. Unfortunately, only a few other autobiographies are available for K–8 students, but the Meet the Author series for kindergarten through fifth grade students and the Author at Work series for older students, from Richard C. Owen Publisher, are interesting to students who have read these authors' books. These autobiographies of contemporary authors, including Jane Yolen's *On the Slant* (2009) and Ralph Fletcher's *Reflections* (2007), present information about their lives and insights about writing.

REFERENCE BOOKS. Students use reference books, such as almanacs, dictionaries, and atlases, to track down information and research topics. *The World Almanac for Kids* (Janssen, 2015) is an eye-catching book, filled with kid-friendly information about fashion, disasters, movies, prizes and contests, mythology, and census data, for example. This almanac is completely updated each year, so the topics vary. Dorling Kindersley Publishers is well known for their wide variety of visually stunning reference books,

Literacy Portraits

Ms. Janusz's classroom is filled with stories and informational books. She uses these books for instructional purposes, and plenty of books are available for students to read independently. These second graders know about genres. They can identify books representing each genre and talk about the differences between them. Ms. Janusz teaches minilessons on genres and points out the genre of books she's reading aloud. She doesn't call all books "stories."

Click on the play button for Rhiannon to watch her compare fiction and nonfiction. As you listen to Rhiannon, think about the information provided in this chapter. What conclusions can you draw about what Ms. Janusz has taught about text factors? Also, look at other video clips of Rhiannon to see how she applies her knowledge about genres in both reading and writing.

Rhiannon

including *Mesopotamia* (Steele, 2007) and *Science: A visual encyclopedia* (Woodland & Parker, 2014). Other noteworthy reference books, such as *National Geographic Beginner's World Atlas* (2011), are published by the National Geographic Society.

Expository Text Structures

Nonfiction books are organized in particular ways called **expository text structures** (McGee & Richgels, 1985). Figure 9–5 describes these patterns, presents sample passages and cue words that signal use of each pattern, and suggests a graphic organizer for each structure. When readers are aware of these patterns, it's easier to understand what they're reading, and when writers use these structures to organize their writing, it's easier for readers to understand. Sometimes the pattern is signaled through the title, a topic sentence, or cue words, but sometimes it isn't. These are the most common expository text structures:

Description. The author describes a topic by listing characteristics, features, and examples. Phrases such as *for example* and *characteristics are* cue this structure. When students delineate any topic, such as the Mississippi River, eagles, or Alaska, they use description.

Sequence. The author lists or explains items or events in numerical, chronological, or alphabetical order. Cue words for sequence include *first, second, third, next, then,* and *finally.* Students use this pattern to write directions for completing a math problem or the stages in an animal's life cycle. The events in a biography are often written in the sequence pattern, too.

Comparison. The author compares two or more things. *Different, in contrast, alike,* and *on the other hand* are cue words and phrases that signal this structure. When students compare and contrast book and movie versions of a story, reptiles and amphibians, or life in ancient Greece with life in ancient Egypt, they use this organizational pattern.

Cause and Effect. The author explains one or more causes and the resulting effect or effects. *Reasons why, if . . . then, as a result, therefore,* and *because* are words and phrases that cue this structure. Explanations of why dinosaurs became extinct, the effects of pollution, or the causes of the Civil War use this pattern.

Problem and Solution. The author states a problem and offers one or more solutions. A variation is the question-and-answer format, in which the writer poses a question and then answers it. Cue words and phrases include *the problem is, the puzzle is, solve,* and *question . . . answer.* Students use this structure when they write about why money was invented, why endangered animals should be saved, or why dams are needed to ensure a permanent water supply.

Booklist: Expository Text Structures presents books for all grade levels exemplifying these text structures.

Nonfiction Features

Nonfiction books have unique text features that stories and poems normally don't have, such as margin notes and glossaries. The purpose of these features is to make text easier to read and to facilitate students' comprehension. Nonfiction texts often include these features:

೮ Headings and subheadings to direct reader's attention to the big ideas
೮ Photos and drawings to illustrate the big ideas

FIGURE 9–5   The Five Expository Text Structures

PATTERN	GRAPHIC ORGANIZER	SAMPLE PASSAGE
Description The author describes a topic by listing characteristics and examples. Cue words include *for example* and *characteristics are.*		The Olympic symbol consists of five interlocking rings that represent the continents that athletes come from to compete in the games. The rings are colored black, blue, green, red, and yellow. At least one of these colors is found in the flag of every country sending athletes to the Olympics.
Sequence The author lists items or events in numerical or chronological order. Cue words include *first, second, third, next, then,* and *finally.*	1. _____ 2. _____ 3. _____ 4. _____ 5. _____	The Olympics began as athletic festivals to honor the Greek gods. The most important festival honored Zeus, and it became the Olympics in 776 B.C. The games ended in A.D. 394, and weren't held for 1,500 years. The modern Olympics began in 1896. Nearly 300 male athletes competed in these games. In 1900, female athletes also competed. The games have continued every four years since 1896 except during World War II.
Comparison The author explains how two or more things are alike and/or how they're different. Cue words include *different, in contrast, alike, same as,* and *on the other hand.*	Alike / Different	The modern Olympics are different than the ancient games. There weren't swimming races, but there were chariot races. No female contestants participated, and all athletes competed in the nude. Of course, the ancient and modern Olympics are alike in many ways. The javelin and discus throws are the same, for example. Some people say that cheating, professionalism, and nationalism in the modern games are a disgrace, but according to ancient Greek writers, they existed in their Olympics, too.
Cause and Effect The author lists one or more causes and the resulting effect or effects. Cue words include *reasons why, if . . . then, as a result, therefore,* and *because.*	Cause → Effect #1, Effect #2, Effect #3	There are several reasons why so many people attend the Olympics or watch the games on television. One reason is tradition. The word *Olympics* reminds people of the ancient games. People escape the ordinariness of daily life by attending or watching the Olympics. They like to identify with someone else's accomplishment. National pride is another reason, and an athlete's hard-earned victory becomes a nation's victory.
Problem and Solution The author states a problem and lists one or more solutions. A variation is the question-and-answer format. Cue words include *problem is, dilemma is, puzzle is, solved,* and *question . . . answer.*	Problem → Solution	One problem with the modern games is that they're very expensive. A stadium, pools, and playing fields must be built for the athletic events, and housing is needed for the athletes. And these facilities are used for only 2 weeks! In 1984, Los Angeles solved these problems by charging a fee for official sponsors and using many existing buildings in the area. The Coliseum where the 1932 games were held was used again, and local colleges became playing and living sites.

Booklist Expository Text Structures

STRUCTURE	BOOKS
Description	Cooper, M. L. (2007). *Jamestown, 1607*. New York: Holiday House. MU
	Davies, N. (2014). *Tiny creatures: The world of microbes*. Somerville, MA: Candlewick Press. PM
	Floca, B. (2007). *Lightship*. New York: Atheneum. PM
	Gibbons, G. (2007). *Groundhog day!* New York: Holiday House. P
	Patent, D. H. (2014). *Super sniffers*. New York: Bloomsbury. M
	Simon, S. (2007). *Snakes*. New York: HarperCollins. M
Sequence	Cole, J. (2006). *The magic school bus and the science fair expedition*. New York: Scholastic. M
	Jenkins, M. (2014). *The history of money: From bartering to banking*. Somerville, MA: Candlewick Press. MU
	Kelly, I. (2007). *It's a butterfly's life*. New York: Holiday House. P
	Minor, W. (2006). *Yankee Doodle America: The spirit of 1776 from A to Z*. New York: Putnam. M
	Morgan, E. (2014). *Next time you see a maple seed*. Arlington, VA: National Science Teachers Association. M
	Royston, A. (2006). *The life and times of a drop of water: The water cycle*. Chicago: Raintree. M
Comparison	Bidner, J. (2007). *Is my cat a tiger? How your cat compares to its wild cousins*. New York: Lark Books. M
	Hall, K. (2014). *Polar bears and penguins*. Mt. Pleasant, SC: Arbordale. PM
	Jenkins, S. (2007). *Dogs and cats*. Boston: Houghton Mifflin. MU
	Munro, R. (2001). *The inside-outside book of Washington, DC*. San Francisco: Chronicle Books. MU
	Spier, P. (2014). *We the People: The Constitution of the United States*. New York: Doubleday. M
	Thomas, I. (2006). *Scorpion vs. tarantula*. Chicago: Raintree. M
Cause-Effect	Bang, M., & Chisholm, P. (2014). *Buried sunlight: How fossil fuels have changed the earth*. New York: Scholastic. PM
	Barretta, G. (2008). *Now and Ben: The modern inventions of Benjamin Franklin*. New York: Square Fish Books. PM
	Brown, C. L. (2006). *The day the dinosaurs died*. New York: HarperCollins. P
	Burns, L. G. (2007). *Tracking trash: Flotsam, jetsam, and the science of ocean movement*. Boston: Houghton Mifflin. MU
	Collins, A. (2006). *Violent weather: Thunderstorms, tornadoes, and hurricanes*. Washington, DC: National Geographic. M
	Rockwell, A. (2006). *Why are the ice caps melting? The dangers of global warming*. New York: HarperCollins. PM
Problem-Solution	Bledsoe, L. J. (2006). *How to survive in Antarctica*. New York: Holiday House. MU
	Calmenson, S. (2007). *May I pet your dog? The how-to guide for kids meeting dogs (and dogs meeting kids)*. New York: Clarion Books. PM
	Kudlinski, K. V. (2005). *Boy, were we wrong about dinosaurs*. Boston: Houghton Mifflin. PM
	Montalvan, L. C. (2014). *Tuesday tucks me in: The loyal bond between a soldier and his service dog*. New York: Roaring Brook Press. PM
	Morrison, M. (2006). *Mysteries of the sea: How divers explore the ocean depths*. Washington, DC: National Geographic. M
	Thimmesh, C. (2006). *Team moon: How 400,000 people landed Apollo 11 on the moon*. Boston: Houghton Mifflin. MU

- Figures, maps, and tables to provide diagrams and detailed information visually
- Margin notes that provide supplemental information or direct readers to additional facts about a topic
- Highlighted vocabulary words to identify key terms
- A glossary to assist readers in pronouncing and defining key terms
- Review sections or charts at the end of chapters or the entire book
- An index to assist readers in locating specific information

It's important that students understand these nonfiction text features so they can use them to make their reading more effective and improve their comprehension (Harvey & Goudvis, 2007).

Looking at the Text Factors in a Nonfiction Book

The Down-to-Earth Guide to Global Warming (David & Gordon, 2007) is a 112-page paperback nonfiction book that explains climate change and its disastrous consequences using examples that students can relate to. It's organized into four sections: The first section explains global warming, the second examines weather changes, the next addresses extinction of plants and animals, and the fourth is a call to action. The authors present serious information in an entertaining way using concrete examples, and they provide practical suggestions to show students how they can help combat global warming in their homes and communities.

This nonfiction book is reader-friendly; it incorporates most of the conventions of the nonfiction genre. Readers will find a table of contents and a "dear reader" letter at the beginning. Margin notes are used again and again to highlight important information and add interesting facts. Key terms and important facts are printed in color and in a font that's larger than the surrounding text. Photos and cartoon illustrations add interest, and diagrams, pie charts, and maps make the information being presented easier to understand. In the back of the book are a glossary, an index, a bibliography, and suggestions for further reading, including websites for students to check out.

The authors use a problem-and-solution organizational structure: The problem is climate change, and the authors suggest ways that children can help to solve the problem, including recycling, conserving power, replacing conventional light bulbs with compact fluorescent bulbs, using canvas bags instead of paper or plastic bags, and pursuing a career in the environmental field. Other text structures are also used within chapters. For example, the authors describe global warming, explain the water cycle, and identify effects of global warming that children can appreciate, such as worse allergies and less maple syrup for pancakes.

This brightly colored, inviting paperback book is appropriate for third through sixth graders, both for students who are interested in learning more about climate change and for those who are collecting information for a report or other project.

Watch this teacher's explanation of text factors in a nonfiction book, and notice the chart she uses in her explanation. What might she have the students do next?

 MONITOR: Check Your Understanding 9.2

🌀 Text Factors of Poetry

It's easy to recognize a poem because the text looks different than a page from a story or a nonfiction book. Layout, or the arrangement of words on a page, is an important text factor. Poems are written in a variety of forms, ranging from free verse to haiku, and poets use poetic devices to make their writing more effective. Janeczko (2003) explains that its important to point out poetic forms and devices to establish a common vocabulary for talking about poems, and because poems are shorter than other types of text, it's often easier for students to examine the text, notice differences in poetic forms, and find examples of poetic devices that authors have used.

Formats of Poetry Books

Three types of poetry books are published for children. Picture-book versions of *The Midnight Ride of Paul Revere* (Longfellow, 2001) and other classic poems are the first type; in these books, each line or stanza is presented and illustrated on a page. Others

Booklist | Collections of Poetry

FORMAT	BOOKS
Picture-Book Versions of Single Poems	Carroll, L. (2007). *Jabberwocky* (C. Myers, illus.). New York: Jump at the Sun. U
	Frost, R. (2001). *Stopping by woods on a snowy evening* (S. Jeffers, illus.). New York: Dutton. MU
	Thayer, E. L. (2006). *Casey at the bat.* Tonawanda, NY: Kids Can Press. MU
	Westcott, N. B. (2003). *The lady with the alligator purse.* New York: Little, Brown. P
Specialized Collections	Florian, D. (2007). *Comets, stars, the moon, and Mars: Space poems and paintings.* Orlando, FL: Harcourt. MU
	Havill, J. (2006). *I heard it from Alice Zucchini: Poems about the garden.* San Francisco: Chronicle Books. PM
	Issa, K. (2007). *Today and today.* New York: Scholastic. MU
	Kuskin, K. (2003). *Moon, have you met my mother? The collected poems of Karla Kuskin.* New York: HarperCollins. PMU
	Larios, J. (2006). *Yellow elephant: A bright bestiary.* Orlando, FL: Harcourt. PM
	Prelutsky, J. (2006). *Behold the bold umbrellaphant and other poems.* New York: Greenwillow. PM
	Sidman, J. (2006). *Butterfly eyes and other secrets of the meadow.* Boston: Houghton Mifflin. MU
	Soto, G. (2006). *A fire in my hands.* Orlando, FL: Harcourt. U
Comprehensive Anthologies	Driscoll, M., & Hamilton, M. (Sels.). (2003). *A child's introduction to poetry.* New York: Black Dog & Leventhal. PM
	Paschem, E., & Raccah, D. (Sels.). (2005). *Poetry speaks to children.* Naperville, IL: Sourcebooks MediaFusion. M
	Prelutsky, J. (Sel.). (1983). *The Random House book of poetry for children.* New York: Random House. PMU
	Sword, E. H. (Sel.). (2007). *A child's anthology of poetry.* New York: HarperCollins/Ecco. MU

are specialized collections of poems, either written by a single poet or related to a single theme, such as *Tour America: A Journey Through Poems and Art* (Siebert, 2006). Comprehensive anthologies are the third type, and these books feature 50 to 500 or more poems arranged by category; one of the best is Jack Prelutsky's *The Random House Book of Poetry for Children* (1983). Booklist: Collections of Poetry includes poetry books representing each format.

VERSE NOVELS. *Verse novels* are stories that are told through poems rather than prose. Some are one long poem, and others are a collection of shorter poems. Novels in verse are unique in that they're musical and create powerful visual images. Karen Hesse's Newbery-winning *Out of the Dust* (1999) describes the grim realities of living in the Oklahoma Dust Bowl, and in *Locomotion* (2004), Jacqueline Woodson uses a collection of 60 poems to tell the sad but hopeful story of a New York City fifth grader who grieves, and then slowly recovers after his parents are killed in a house fire. Poets use a variety of poetic forms in their stories: Sharon Creech wrote *Love That Dog* (2001) in free verse, Lois Lowry used rhyming couplets in *Stay! Keeper's Story* (1999), and Jen Bryant used free verse in a journal format in *Pieces of Georgia* (2007). Check the Booklist: Verse Novels for additional books.

Cadden (2011) explains that verse novels combine elements of stories, poetry, and drama. Voice is the most powerful story element: Readers "hear" the voices of the characters as they narrate the story, and when authors use multiple storytellers, each character offers a unique but incomplete perspective. The structure is different, too. Prose stories are constructed with a beginning, middle, and end, but Campbell (2004) compares the structure of a verse novel to a wheel: The event is the hub, and the narrators are the spokes. Authors commonly use free verse in verse novels, and this poetic form allows them to develop characters through their careful choice of words and how the words are arranged on the page. These books also exemplify oral characteristics of drama. Verse novels, like plays, are rich in dialogue; narrators recount events without adding description or summaries.

Booklist — Verse Novels

LEVEL	BOOKS
Middle Grades	Creech, S. (2001). *Love that dog*. New York: HarperCollins.
	Creech, S. (2010). *Hate that cat*. New York: HarperCollins.
	Creech, S. (2005). *Heartbeat*. New York: HarperCollins.
	Grimes, N. (2013). *Words with wings*. Honesdale, PA: WordSong.
	Wardlaw, L. (2011). *Won Ton: A cat tale told in haiku*. New York: Holt.
	Weston, R. P. (2008). *Zorgama Zoo*. New York: Razorbill Books.
	Wissinger, T. W. (2013). *Gone fishing: A novel*. Boston: Houghton Mifflin Harcourt.
	Wong, J. S. (2008). *Minn and Jake*. New York: Sunburst.
Middle and Upper Grades	Applegate, K. (2012). *The one and only Ivan*. New York: HarperCollins.
	Havill, J. (2011). *Grow: A novel in verse*. Atlanta, GA: Peachtree.
	Hesse, K. (2009). *Out of the dust*. New York: Scholastic.
	Lowry, L. (1999). *Stay! Keeper's story*. New York: Yearling.
	Woodson, J. (2005). *Locomotion*. New York: Putnam.
Upper Grades	Alexander, K. (2014). *The crossover*. Boston: Houghton Mifflin Holt.
	Bryant, J. (2005). *The trial*. New York: Yearling.
	Bryant, J. (2007). *Pieces of Georgia*. New York: Yearling.
	Burg, A. E. (2013). *Serafina's promise*. New York: Scholastic.
	Hesse, K. (2005). *Witness*. New York: Scholastic.
	Montgomery, H. (2003). *Voyage of the Arctic tern*. London: Walker Books.
	Woodson, J. (2014). *brown girl dreaming*. New York: Nancy Paulsen Books.

Poetic Forms

Poets who write for K–8 students employ a variety of poetic forms. Rhymed verse is the most common type, as in *My Parents Think I'm Sleeping* (Prelutsky, 2007). Another common form is narrative poems, such as Clement Moore's classic, "The Night Before Christmas," and Longfellow's *The Midnight Ride of Paul Revere* (2001), illustrated by Christopher Bing. These poems tell a story. A contemporary form is free verse: It's unique because writers aren't required to use traditional poetic techniques, including structure, rhyme, and rhythm. Instead, writers choose words to express ideas precisely and create powerful images, and they divide the lines so they flow like speech. Conventional capitalization and punctuation are optional. Carl Sandburg's classic poem "Fog" (Prelutsky, 1983), *Desert Voices* (Baylor, 1993), and *Canto Familiar* (Soto, 2007) are examples.

Students write funny verses, vivid word pictures, powerful comparisons, and expressions of deep sentiment. The key to successful poetry is poetic formulas, which serve as scaffolds, or temporary frameworks, so that students focus on ideas rather than on the rhyme scheme. Most of these formulas incorporate free verse, but others use rhyme or spatial arrangement on the page:

Acrostics. Students use a key word to structure acrostic poems. They choose a word and write it vertically on a sheet of paper, and then they create lines of poetry, each line beginning with a letter in their key word.

Apology Poems. Using William Carlos Williams's poem "This Is Just to Say" as the model, students write apology poems in which they apologize for something they're secretly glad they did (Koch, 1990). Middle and upper graders are familiar with offering apologies and enjoy writing humorous ones, as shown in *This Is Just to Say: Poems of Apology and Forgiveness* (Sidman, 2007).

Bilingual Poems. Students write free verse poems and insert words from another language into their poems (Cahnmann, 2006). Gary Soto's *Neighborhood Odes* (2005) and Jan Felipe Herrera's *Laughing Out Loud, I Fly* (1998) are examples of Spanish-English bilingual poems. The words that are written in a second language are key words, chosen to elicit strong images and cultural memories.

Color Poems. Students write color poems by beginning each line or stanza with a color word (Koch, 2000). Instead of writing "The spooky night sky was black," students write the color word first: "Black is the spooky night sky." For example, sixth graders wrote these free-verse couplets about the color red:

> Red is eye-catching,
> noticing a shiny, red sports car speeding by.
>
> Red is anticipation,
> waiting for Santa Claus on Christmas Eve.
>
> Red is patriotic,
> Saluting Betsy Ross's red, white, and blue flag.
>
> Red is tasty,
> eating spicy salsa and sweet strawberries.
>
> Red is loving,
> giving red roses to your sweetie.
>
> Red is life,
> feeling the blood pulsing through my body.

Concrete Poems. The words and lines in concrete poems are arranged on the page to help convey the meaning. When the words and lines form a picture or outline the objects they describe, they're called *shape poems*. Sometimes the layout of words, lines, and stanzas is spread across a page or two to emphasize the meaning. *A Poke in the I: A Collection of Concrete Poems* (Janeczko, 2005) and *Doodle Dandies: Poems That Take Shape* (J. P. Lewis, 2002) are two collections of concrete poems.

Found Poems. Students create found poems by clipping key words and phrases from stories, newspaper, Internet, and magazine articles, and nonfiction books and arranging the clippings to make a poem. A sixth grader crafted this found poem, "The Man in the Garage," after reading *Skellig* (Almond, 1998), a haunting story about redemption:

> His face, pale as dry plaster
> With hundreds of tiny creases and cracks
> And a few colorless hairs growing on his chin.
> His hair, black with a tangle of knots.
> Wearing a filthy black suit, hanging like a sack on his thin bones,
> Great bulges on his back, beneath his jacket.
> Feather-covered wings folded on his shoulders.
> His name, Skellig.

When students write found poems, they experiment with more sophisticated words and language structures than they might write themselves, and they also document their understanding of the stories and other texts they've read.

Haiku. Haiku is a Japanese poetic form that contains just 17 syllables, arranged in three lines of 5, 7, and 5 syllables. It's a concise form, much like a telegram, and the poems normally deal with nature, presenting a single clear image. Books of haiku to share with students include *Dogku* (Clements, 2007) and *Cool Melons— Turn to Frogs! The Life and Poems of Issa* (Gollub, 2004). The artwork in these picture books may give students ideas for illustrating their own haiku poems.

List Poems. Students create list poems using words and phrases from a list they've brainstormed about a topic, following models in Georgia Heard's (2009) book of list poems. Each line in the poem follows the same structure, and the last line is a twist or sums up the topic. Third grade Jeremy wrote this list poem, titled "Jeremy's Favorite Pizza":

Crispy crust
Tomato sauce
Italian seasoning
Pepperoni slices
Sausage meatballs
Mushrooms—O.K.
NO olives
Mozzarella cheese
PIPING HOT!

Jeremy proudly pointed out that each of his lines has two words, and he used uppercase letters to indicate which words should be emphasized when reading the poem aloud.

Odes. Odes celebrate everyday objects, especially those things that aren't usually appreciated. The unrhymed poem, written directly to that object, tells what's good about the thing and why it's valued. The ode is a venerable poetic form, going back to ancient Greece. Traditionally, odes were sophisticated lyrical verses, such as Keats's "Ode to a Nightingale," but Chilean poet Pablo Neruda (2000) introduced this contemporary variation that's more informal. The best collection of odes for students is Gary Soto's *Neighborhood Odes* (2005), which celebrates everyday things, such as water sprinklers and tennis shoes, in the Mexican American community in Fresno, California, where he grew up.

Poems for Two Voices. In this unique format, students write poems in two side-by-side columns that two readers read simultaneously; one reads the left column, and the other reads the right column. When both readers have words—either the same words or different ones—written on the same line, they read them together so that the poem sounds like a duet. Two books of poems for two voices are Paul Fleischman's *I Am Phoenix: Poems for Two Voices* (1989), about birds, and the Newbery Medal–winning *Joyful Noise: Poems for Two Voices* (2004a), about insects. And if two voices aren't enough, check *Big Talk: Poems for Four Voices* (Fleischman, 2008).

The Booklist: Poetic Forms presents a variety of books illustrating these forms. To learn about other poetic forms, check *The Teachers & Writers Handbook of Poetic Forms* (Padgett, 2000). Students use some of these forms when they write their own poems, including odes and concrete poems.

Booklist — Poetic Forms

FORM	BOOKS
Acrostics	Harley, A. (2009). *African acrostics: A word in edgeways.* Cambridge, MA: Candlewick Press. PM
	Paolilli, P., & Brewer, D. (2003). *Silver seeds.* New York: Puffin Books. PM
Apology Poems	Levine, G. C. (2012). *Forgive me, I meant to do it: False apology poems.* New York: HarperCollins. MU
	Sidman, J. (2007). *This is just to say: Poems of apology and forgiveness.* Boston: Houghton Mifflin. M
Bilingual Poems	Mora, P. (1999). *Confetti: Poems for children.* New York: Lee & Low. PM
	Soto, G. (2005). *Neighborhood odes.* Orlando: Harcourt. M
	Herrera, J. F. (1998). *Laughing out loud, I fly.* New York: HarperCollins. MU
Color Poems	O'Neill, M. (1990). *Hailstones and halibut bones.* New York: Doubleday. M
Concrete Poems	Cleary, B. P. (2014). *Ode to a commode: Concrete poems.* Minneapolis: Millbrook Press. PM
	Franco, B. (2011). *A dazzling display of dogs: Concrete poems.* Berkeley, CA: Tricycle Press. M
	Grandits, J. (2004). *Technically, it's not my fault: Concrete poems.* New York: Sandpiper. MU
	Janeczko P. B. (2005). *A poke in the I.* Cambridge, MA: Candlewick Press. M
Found Poems	Heard, G. (2012). *The arrow finds its mark: A book of found poetry.* New York: Roaring Brook Press. MU
Haiku	Cleary, B. P. (2014). *If it rains pancakes: Haiku and lantern poems.* Minneapolis: Millbrook Press. PM
	Clements, A. (2007). *Dogku.* New York: Atheneum. PM
	Gollub, M. (2004). *Cool melons—Turn to frogs!* New York: Lee & Low. MU
	Muth, J. J. (2014). *Hi Koo! A year of seasons.* New York: Scholastic. PM
	Prelutsky, J. (2004). *If not for the cat.* New York: Greenwillow. PM
	Raczka, B. (2010). *Guyku: A year of haiku for boys.* Boston: Houghton Mifflin. PM
Limericks	Brooks, L. (2009). *Timericks: The book of tongue-twisting limericks.* New York: Workman. M
	Marshall, J. (2003). *Pocketful of nonsense.* Boston: Houghton Mifflin. M
List Poems	Heard, G. (Ed.). (2009). *Falling down the page: A book of list poems.* New York: Roaring Brook Press. MU
Odes	Bennett, K. (2010). *Dad and pop: An ode to fathers & stepfathers.* Cambridge, MA: Candlewick Press. PM
	Soto, G. (2005). *Neighborhood odes.* Orlando: Harcourt. M
Poems for Two Voices	Fleischman, P. (1989). *I am phoenix: Poems for two voices.* New York: HarperCollins. MU
	Fleischman, P. (2004). *Joyful noise: Poems for two voices.* New York: HarperCollins. MU
	Fleischman, P. (2008). *Big talk: Poems for four voices.* Cambridge, MA: Candlewick Press. PM
	Franco, B. (2009). *Messing around on the monkey bars: And other school poems for two voices.* Cambridge, MA: Candlewick Press. PM
	Gerber, C. (2013). *Seeds, bees, butterflies, and more! Poems for two voices.* New York: Holt. M

Poetic Devices

Poetic devices are especially important tools because poets express their ideas very concisely. Every word counts! They use these poetic devices:

- Assonance: the type of alliteration where vowel sounds are repeated in nearby words.
- Consonance: the type of alliteration where consonant sounds are repeated in nearby words.
- Imagery: words and phrases that appeal to the senses and evoke mental pictures.
- Metaphor: a comparison between two unlikely things, without using *like* or *as*.
- Onomatopoeia: words that imitate sounds.
- Repetition: words, phrases, or lines that are repeated for special effect.
- Rhyme: words that end with similar sounds used at the end of the lines.
- Rhythm: the internal beat in a poem that's felt when poetry is read aloud.
- Simile: a comparison incorporating the word *like* or *as*.

Narrative and poetic devices are similar, and many of them, such as imagery and metaphor, are important in both genres.

Poets use other conventions, too. Capitalization and punctuation are used differently; poets choose whether to use capital letters or punctuation marks. They think about the meaning they're conveying and the rhythm of their writing as they decide how to break poems into lines and whether to divide the lines into stanzas. Layout is another consideration: Although the arrangement of lines on the page matters for all poems, it's especially important in concrete poems.

Looking at the Text Factors in a Book of Poetry

This Is Just to Say: Poems of Apology and Forgiveness (Sidman, 2007) is a collection of poems purportedly written and compiled by Mrs. Merz's sixth graders at the Florence Scribner School as part of a poetry unit. In the introduction, student-editor Anthony K. explains that he and his classmates wrote the apology poems using William Carlos Williams's poem "This Is Just to Say" as a model, and then the recipients wrote poems of forgiveness back to the students.

The book is arranged in two parts. The first part, Apologies, contains the sixth graders' apology poems, with each student's poem featured on a separate page with a drawing of the student-author and other illustrations related to the content of the poem. Readers are told that the line drawings and mixed-media illustrations were created by Bao Vang, an artistic student in the class. The second part, Responses, contains the forgiveness poems that the sixth graders received. These poems are arranged in the same order as the apology poems, with each one on a separate page and accompanied by Bao's whimsical illustrations.

Short poems written on a wide variety of topics are included in this captivating anthology; some are humorous, and others heartfelt or sad. José, for example, wrote an apology to his dad for throwing a rock and breaking the garage window. Other topics include stealing brownies, the death of a pet, insensitive comments, and rough play during a dodge ball game. José's dad responds, telling him to forget about the broken window and expressing his pride in his son's accomplishments. Other recipient's poems convey feelings of love, grief, and acceptance.

Most of the poems follow the pattern of William Carlos Williams's model poem, but many of the students modified it to fit their ideas and words; a handful use different forms, including haiku, poems for two voices, odes, found poems, and free verse. The poems are typed in different fonts, and their arrangement on the page varies, too. The most striking feature of the poems is the range of voices: Some sound as if they were written by sixth grade girls, some by boys, and others by siblings, parents, and grandparents.

In the author biography, Joyce Sidman confesses that she assumed the personas of the students and the recipients and wrote the poems in this book. Years before, she'd written an apology poem with a class of fourth graders and sent it to her mother, who responded with a letter of forgiveness, and the idea for this book was born! This collection of poems is appropriate for third through sixth graders. Many of the poems can be used as models for students' writing, and teachers may want to have their students write their own collections of apology and forgiveness poems.

 MONITOR: Check Your Understanding 9.3

Teaching About Text Factors

Researchers have documented that when teachers teach students about text factors, their comprehension increases (Fisher, Frey, & Lapp, 2008; Sweet & Snow, 2003). In addition, when students are familiar with the genres, organizational patterns, and literary devices in books they're reading, they're better able to create those text factors in their own writing (Buss & Karnowski, 2000). It's not enough to focus on stories, however; students need to learn about a variety of genres. In the vignette at the beginning of the chapter, Mr. Abrams used text factors to scaffold his students' learning about frogs. He taught them about the unique characteristics of nonfiction books, emphasized text structures through the questions he asked, and used graphic organizers to help students visualize big ideas. To evaluate your effectiveness in teaching students about the unique text factors of stories, nonfiction, and poetry, use the Teacher Checklist: How do I teach text factors?

The Common Core State Standards for English Language Arts emphasize that at each grade level, kindergarten through eighth grade, students grow in their ability to use text factors to comprehend stories and nonfiction texts, particularly complex texts, more effectively. Teachers teach about genres, structural patterns, and literary devices so students can accomplish these tasks:

- Noticing how point of view and other elements of story structure shape the content and style of stories
- Making connections among big ideas and details
- Integrating information presented visually and through media
- Examining sentences and paragraphs to see how they relate to each other and the whole text
- Analyzing texts to draw conclusions
- Citing textual evidence to support conclusions
- Becoming more sensitive to poor reasoning in texts

After instruction and guided practice, students learn to apply their knowledge about text factors when they read grade-level texts independently. To learn more about the Standards, check the feature Common Core State Standards: Text Factors.

Minilessons

Check the Compendium of Instructional Procedures, which follows Chapter 12.

Teachers teach students about text factors directly—often through **minilessons** (L. Simon, 2005). They highlight a genre, explain its characteristics, and then read aloud books representing that genre, modeling their thinking about text factors. Later, students make charts of the information they're learning and hang them in the classroom. Similarly, teachers introduce structural patterns and have students examine how authors use them to organize a book or an excerpt from a book they're reading. Students often create graphic organizers to visualize the structure of nonfiction books they're reading and appreciate how the organization emphasizes the big ideas (Opitz, Ford, & Zbaracki, 2006). Teachers also focus on the literary devices that authors use to make their writing more vivid and the conventions that make a text more reader-friendly. Students often collect sentences with narrative devices from stories they're reading and lines of poetry with poetic devices from poems to share with classmates, and they create charts with nonfiction features they've found in books to incorporate in reports they're writing.

Comprehension Strategies

It's not enough that students can name the characteristics of a myth, identify cue words that signal expository text structures, or define *metaphor* or *assonance*: The goal is for them to actually use what they've learned about text factors when they're reading and writing. The comprehension strategy they use when they're applying what they've learned is called *noticing text factors*; it involves considering genre, recognizing text structure, and attending to literary devices. Lattimer (2003) explains the strategy this way: Students need to think about "what to expect from a text, how to approach it, and what to take away from it" (p. 12). Teachers teach students about text factors through minilessons and other activities, but the last step is to help students internalize the information and apply it when they're reading and writing. One way teachers do this is by demonstrating how they apply the strategy as they read books aloud using **think-alouds** (Harvey & Goudvis, 2007). Teachers also use think-alouds to demonstrate this strategy as they do modeled and shared writing.

Reading and Writing Activities

Students need opportunities to read books and listen to teachers read books aloud while they're learning about text factors. Lattimer (2003) recommends teaching genre studies where students learn about a genre while they're reading and exploring books representing that genre and then apply what they're learning through writing. For example, a small group of fifth graders wrote this poem for two voices as a project after reading *Number the Stars* (Lowry, 2011), the story of the friendship between two Danish girls, a Christian and a Jew, during World War II:

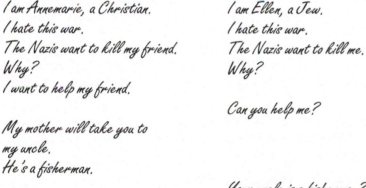

I am Annemarie, a Christian.
I hate this war.
The Nazis want to kill my friend.
Why?
I want to help my friend.

My mother will take you to
my uncle.
He's a fisherman.

He will hide you on his ship.

He will take you to Sweden.
To freedom.
I am Annemarie, a Christian.

I want to help my friend.

I hate this war.

I am Ellen, a Jew.
I hate this war.
The Nazis want to kill me.
Why?

Can you help me?

Your uncle is a fisherman?

He will hide me on his ship?

To freedom.

I am Ellen, a Jew.

I need the help of my friends
or I will die.
I hate this war.

The fifth graders used Paul Fleischman's Newbery Award book, *Joyful Noise* (2004a), as the model for their poem. They knew how to write poems for two voices because they participated in a genre study about poetry several months earlier. Their choice of this poetic form is especially appropriate because it highlights one of the story's themes: These characters are very much alike even though one is Christian and the other is Jewish.

Teach Kids to BE STRATEGIC

Text Factors

Teach students how to recognize and analyze text factors using these strategies so they can increase their comprehension of complex texts:

- Consider genre
- Recognize text structure
- Attend to literary devices

Introduce these strategies in minilessons and have students practice using them as they read books and listen to books read aloud. If students struggle, reteach the strategies, model their use, and think aloud about their application.

TEACHER Checklist

How do I teach text factors?

- O Do I address Standards through my instruction?
- O Do I ask students to categorize books by genre?
- O Do I teach students to identify plot, theme, and other structural elements of stories?
- O Do I teach students to recognize imagery, flashbacks, symbolism, and other narrative devices?
- O Do I have students explain how authors use expository text structures to organize nonfiction texts?
- O Do I teach students to use headings and other nonfiction features to improve their comprehension of textbooks and nonfiction books?
- O Do I ask students to recognize poetic forms of the poems they read?
- O Do I have students apply poetic formulas and devices in the poems they write?
- O Do I ask students to apply what they've learned about text factors in reading and writing?

Assessing Text Factors

Although there aren't formal tests to assess students' knowledge of text factors, students demonstrate what they're learning as they participate in reading and writing activities and develop oral and written projects. Teachers use this instruction–assessment cycle:

Step 1: Planning. As they plan for instruction, teachers determine which text factors they'll teach and how they'll monitor students' progress and assess students' learning.

Step 2: Monitoring. Teachers monitor students' progress as they observe and conference with them about their reading and writing activities. For example, they notice whether students choose sentences containing literary devices when asked to share favorite sentences with the class from a book they're reading or whether they mention text factors during grand conversations. They also take note of students' understanding of text structures as they make graphic organizers and their awareness of structural elements and literary devices in their **reading log** entries.

Step 3: Evaluating. Teachers encourage students to apply their knowledge of genres, structural elements, and literary devices as they respond to literature, develop projects, and write stories and other compositions. One way to do this is to include items on **rubrics** and checklists that pertain to text factors.

Step 4: Reflecting. Teachers ask students during conferences to reflect on how they're growing in their ability to use text factors to comprehend complex texts, and students also write reading log entries, letters, and essays to reflect on their learning. Teachers also consider the effectiveness of their instruction and think about ways they can adapt instruction to emphasize text factors to enhance students' comprehension abilities.

It's up to teachers to notice how students are applying their knowledge about text factors, and to find new ways for them to share their understanding.

 **MONITOR: Check Your Understanding 9.4**

Review

FACILITATING STUDENTS' COMPREHENSION OF TEXT FACTORS

Effective teachers teach students to use their knowledge of genres, structural elements, and literary devices to increase their comprehension of complex texts using the information presented in this chapter, these points in particular:

9.1 Teachers teach students that stories have unique text factors: narrative genres, story elements, and narrative devices.

9.2 Teachers teach students that nonfiction books have unique text factors: nonfiction genres, expository text structures, and nonfiction features.

9.3 Teachers teach students that poems have unique text factors: book formats, poetic forms, and poetic devices.

9.4 Teachers teach students about text factors and the role they play in comprehension.

EVALUATE & REFLECT

Evaluate your understanding of text factors. The questions ask you to collect and analyze data, and report the results. Your response should meet academic standards and adhere to Standard English conventions.

1. Read a novel written for students in grades 4–8, and analyze the book's text factors, the genre, elements of story structure, and narrative devices. Check the Booklist: Stories Illustrating the Elements of Story Structure for recommended novels. In your response, provide bibliographic information and a brief summary of the novel and your analysis of the book's text factors. Use the section "Looking at the Text Factors in a Story" as your model.

2. Read a nonfiction book for K–3 students, and analyze the book's text factors, the genre, expository text structures, and nonfiction features. In your response, provide bibliographic information, a brief summary of the book, and its text factors. Use the section "Looking at the Text Factors in a Nonfiction Book" as your model.

3. Read a novel in verse and analyze the narrative and poetic text factors the author used. In your response, provide bibliographic information, a brief summary of the book, and its narrative and poetic text factors

4. Teach a minilesson on one of the poetic forms to a small group of students, and work with them to apply what they've learned to write their own poems. In your response, describe the students, explain your instructional procedure, supply students' poems, and finish with a reflection about teaching poetry

5. Reread the vignette at the beginning of the chapter and analyze Mr. Abrams's instruction about nonfiction text factors using the questions in the Teacher Checklist: How do I teach text factors? In your response, briefly describe and analyze Mr. Abrams's instruction, and offer recommendations on how the teacher might improve his instruction.

REFERENCES

Aardema, V. (2004). *Why mosquitoes buzz in people's ears*. New York: Puffin Books.

Alexander, K. (2014). *The crossover*. Boston: Houghton Mifflin Harcourt.

Almond, D. (1998). *Skellig*. New York: Random House.

Applebee, A. N. (1978). *The child's concept of story: Ages two to seventeen*. Chicago: University of Chicago Press.

Appleyard, J. A. (1994) *Becoming a reader: The experience of fiction from childhood to adulthood*. New York: Cambridge University Press.

Arnold, C., & Comora, M. (2007). *Taj Mahal*. Minneapolis, MN: Carolrhoda.

Avi. (2004). *Crispin: The cross of lead*. New York: Hyperion Books.

Avi. (2005). *Poppy*. New York: Harper Trophy.

Baylor, B. (1993). *Desert voices*. New York: Aladdin Books.

Becker, A. (2013). *Journey*. Somerville, MA: Candlewick Press.

Becker, A. (2014). *Quest*. Somerville, MA: Candlewick Press.

Bell, C. (2014). *El deafo*. New York: Abrams.

Blume, J. (2007). *Tales of a fourth grade nothing*. New York: Puffin Books.

Brett, J. (2003). *Town mouse, country mouse*. New York: Putnam.

Bryant, J. (2007). *Pieces of Georgia*. New York: Yearling.

Bunting, E. (1998). *Going home*. New York: Harper Trophy.

Buss, K., & Karnowski, L. (2000). *Reading and writing literary genres*. Newark, DE: International Reading Association.

Buyea, R. (2011). *Because of Mr. Terupt*. New York: Yearling.

Cadden, M. (2011, Fall). The verse novel and the question of genre. *The ALAN Review, 39*(1), 21–27.

Cahnmann, M. (2006). Reading, living, and writing bilingual poetry as scholARTisry in the language arts classroom. *Language Arts, 83*, 341–351.

Campbell, P. (2004). The sand in the oyster: Vetting the verse novel. *Horn Book Magazine, 80*, 611–616.

Clarke, B. (1990). *Amazing frogs and toads*. New York: Knopf.

Clements, A. (2007). *Dogku*. New York: Atheneum.

Coburn, J. R. (1996). *Jouanah: A Hmong Cinderella*. San Francisco: Shen's Books.

Cole, J. (2006). *The magic school bus and the science fair expedition*. New York: Scholastic.

Coville, B. (2007a). *Aliens ate my homework*. New York: Aladdin Books.

Coville, B. (2007b). *Jeremy Thatcher, dragon hatcher*. San Diego: Harcourt/Magic Carpet Books.

Creech, S. (2001). *Love that dog*. New York: HarperCollins.

Creech, S. (2005). *Granny Torrelli makes soup*. New York: Harper Trophy.

Creech, S. (2010). *Hate that cat*. New York: HarperCollins.

Cushman, K. (2012). *Catherine, called Birdy*. New York: Sandpiper.

Dahl, R. (2007). *Charlie and the chocolate factory*. New York: Puffin Books.

David, L., & Gordon, C. (2007). *The down-to-earth guide to global warming*. New York: Orchard/Scholastic.

Demi. (2002). *King Midas: The golden touch*. New York: McElderry.

Demi. (2003). *Muhammad*. New York: McElderry.

dePaola, T. (1996). *The legend of the bluebonnet*. New York: Putnam.

DiCamillo, K. (2006). *The miraculous journey of Edward Tulane*. Cambridge, MA: Candlewick Press.

Ehrlich, A. (2004). *Cinderella*. New York: Dutton.

Ehrlich, A. (2006). *The snow queen*. New York: Dutton.

Fisher, D., Frey, N., & Lapp, D. (2008). Shared readings: Modeling comprehension, vocabulary, text structures, and text features for older readers. *The Reading Teacher, 61*, 548–556.

Fleischman, P. (1989). *I am phoenix: Poems for two voices*. New York: HarperCollins.

Fleischman, P. (2004a). *Joyful noise: Poems for two voices*. New York: HarperCollins.

Fleischman, P. (2004b). *Seedfolks*. New York: Harper Trophy.

Fleischman, P. (2008). *Big talk: Poems for four voices*. Cambridge, MA: Candlewick Press.

Fleischman, S. (2006). *Escape! The story of the Great Houdini*. New York: Greenwillow.

Fletcher, R. (2007). *Reflections*. Katonah, NY: Richard C. Owen.

Freedman, R. (1997). *Eleanor Roosevelt: A life of discovery*. New York: Clarion Books.

Galdone, P. (2008). *The gingerbread boy*. New York: Clarion Books.

Gantos, J. (2007). *I am not Joey Pigza*. New York: Farrar, Straus & Giroux.

George, J. C. (2005). *Julie of the wolves*. New York: Harper Trophy.

George-Warren, H. (2006). *Honky-tonk heroes and hillbilly angels: The pioneers of country and western music*. Boston: Houghton Mifflin.

Gibbons, G. (2007). *Groundhog Day!* New York: Holiday House.

Gollub, M. (2004). *Cool melons—turn to frogs! The life and poems of Issa*. New York: Lee & Low.

Gruber, B. (2006). *Ancient Inca*. Washington, DC: National Geographic Children's Books.

Harvey, S., & Goudvis, A. (2007). *Strategies that work: Teaching comprehension for understanding and engagement* (2nd ed.). York, ME: Stenhouse.

Haskins, J. (2006). *Delivering justice: W. W. Law and the fight for civil rights*. Cambridge, MA: Candlewick Press.

Heard, G. (Ed.). (2009). *Falling down the page*. New York: Roaring Brook Press.

Hennessy, B. G. (2006). *The boy who cried wolf*. New York: Simon & Schuster.

Herrera, J. P. (1998). *Laughing out loud, I fly*. New York: HarperCollins.

Hesse, K. (1999). *Out of the dust*. New York: Scholastic.

Hesse, K. (2005). *Witness*. New York: Scholastic.

Holm, J. L. (2011). *Middle school is worse than meatloaf: A year told through stuff*. New York: Atheneum.

Hutchins, P. (2005). *Rosie's walk*. New York: Aladdin Books.

Janeczko, P. B. (2003). *Opening a door: Reading poetry in the middle school classroom*. New York: Scholastic.

Janeczko, P. B. (2005). *A poke in the I: A collection of concrete poems*. Cambridge, MA: Candlewick Press.

Janssen, S. (2015). *The world almanac for kids*. New York: World Almanac Books.

Kasza, K. (1996). *The wolf's chicken stew*. New York: Putnam.

Kellogg, S. (1997). *Jack and the beanstalk*. New York: Harper Trophy.

Kellogg, S. (2002). *The three little pigs*. New York: Harper Trophy.

Kiefer, B. Z., Price-Dennis, D., & Ryan, C. L. (2006). Children's books in a multimodal age. *Language Arts, 84*, 92–98.

King-Smith, D. (2005). *Babe: The gallant pig*. New York: Knopf.

Kinney, J. (2007). *Diary of a wimpy kid*. New York: Abrams.

Koch, K. (1990). *Rose, where did you get that red?* New York: Vintage.

Koch, K. (2000). *Wishes, lies, and dreams*. New York: HarperPerennial.

Krull, K. (2006). *Isaac Newton*. New York: Viking.

Lattimer, H. (2003). *Thinking through genre*. Portland, ME: Stenhouse.

Lehr, S. S. (1991). *The child's developing sense of theme: Responses to literature*. New York: Teachers College Press.

Lester, H. (1990). *Tacky the penguin*. Boston: Houghton Mifflin.

Lester, J. (1999). *John Henry*. New York: Puffin Books.

Lester, J. (2005). *Day of tears: A novel in dialogue*. New York: Hyperion Books.

Lewis, C. S. (2005). *The lion, the witch and the wardrobe*. New York: HarperCollins.

Lewis, J. P. (2002). *Doodle dandies! Poems that take shape*. New York: Aladdin Books.

Lionni, L. (2006). *Alexander and the wind-up mouse*. New York: Knopf.

Longfellow, H. W. (2001). *The midnight ride of Paul Revere* (C. Bing, Illus.). Brooklyn, NY: Handprint Books.

Lowry, L. (1999). *Stay! Keeper's story*. New York: Yearling.

Lowry, L. (2006). *The giver*. New York: Delacorte.

Lowry, L. (2011). *Number the stars*. New York: Sandpiper.

Lukens, R. J., Smith, J. J., & Miller Coffel, C. (2012). *A critical handbook of children's literature* (9th ed.). Boston: Allyn & Bacon.

MacLachlan, P. (2005). *Sarah, plain and tall*. New York: Scholastic.

Martin, S., & Chast, R. (2007). *The alphabet from A to Y with bonus letter Z!* New York: Flying Dolphin Press.

McCloskey, R. (2004). *Make way for ducklings*. New York: Square Fish Books.

McDermott, G. (2001). *Raven*. San Diego: Voyager.

McGee, L. M., & Richgels, D. J. (1985). Teaching expository text structures to elementary students. *The Reading Teacher, 38*, 739–745.

McLeod, B. (2006). *Superhero ABC*. New York: HarperCollins.

Meyer, B. J. F., & Poon, L. W. (2004). Effects of structure strategy training and signaling on recall of text. In R. B. Ruddell & N. J. Unrau (Eds.), *Theoretical models and processes of reading* (5th ed., pp. 810–850). Newark, DE: International Reading Association.

Mitchell, S. (2007). *The ugly duckling*. Cambridge, MA: Candlewick Press.

Mooney, M. E. (2001). *Text forms and features: A resource for intentional teaching*. Katonah, NY: Richard C. Owen.

National Geographic Beginner's World Atlas. (2011). Washington, DC: National Geographic.

Naylor, P. R. (2012). *Shiloh*. New York: Atheneum.

Neruda, P. (2000). *Selected odes of Pablo Neruda*. Berkeley: University of California Press.

Ogle, D. M. (1986). K-W-L: A teaching model that develops active reading of expository text. *The Reading Teacher, 39*, 564–570.

Opitz, M. F., Ford, M. P., & Zbaracki, M. D. (2006). *Books and beyond: New ways to reach readers*. Portsmouth, NH: Heinemann.

Padgett, R. (2000). *The teachers & writers handbook of poetic forms* (2nd ed.). New York: Teachers & Writers Collaborative.

Park, L. S. (2007). *Project mulberry*. New York: Yearling.

Patent, D. H. (2004). *The right dog for the job: Ira's path from service dog to guide dog*. New York: Walker.

Paterson, K. (2005). *Bridge to Terabithia*. New York: Harper Trophy.

Patron, S. (2006). *The higher power of Lucky*. New York: Atheneum.

Paulsen, G. (2007). *Hatchet*. New York: Simon & Schuster.

Pinkney, J. (2009). *The lion and the mouse*. Boston: Little, Brown.

Pinto, S. (2003). *The alphabet room*. New York: Bloomsbury.

Potter, B. (2006). *The tale of Peter Rabbit*. New York: Warne.

Pratt-Serafini, K. J. (2002). *Saguaro moon: A desert journal*. Nevada City, CA: Dawn.

Prelutsky, J. (Sel.). (1983). *The Random House book of poetry for children*. New York: Random House.

Prelutsky, J. (2007). *My parents think I'm sleeping*. New York: Greenwillow.

Ryan, P. M. (2002). *Esperanza rising*. New York: Scholastic.

Sachar, L. (2008). *Holes*. New York: Farrar, Straus & Giroux.

Schatz, K. (2015). *Rad American women A–Z: Rebels, trailblazers, and visionaries who shaped our history…and our future!* San Francisco: City Lights.

Schlitz, L. A. (2007). *Good masters! Sweet ladies! Voices from a medieval village*. Cambridge, MA: Candlewick Press.

Schwartz, D. M. (2001). *Q is for quark: A science alphabet book*. Berkeley, CA: Tricycle Press.

Scieszka, J. (1999). *The true story of the 3 little pigs!* New York: Viking.

Scieszka, J. (2004). *Knights of the kitchen table*. New York: Puffin Books.

Selznick, B. (2007). *The invention of Hugo Cabret*. New York: Scholastic.

Seuling, B. (2003). *Flick a switch: How electricity gets to your home*. New York: Holiday House.

Sidman, J. (2007). *This is just to say: Poems of apology and forgiveness*. Boston: Houghton Mifflin.

Siebert, D. (2006). *Tour America: A journey through poems and art*. San Francisco: Chronicle Books.

Simon, L. (2005). *Write as an expert: Explicit teaching of genres*. Portsmouth, NH: Heinemann.

Simon, S. (2006). *The brain: Our nervous system*. New York: HarperCollins.

Sís, P. (2007). *The wall: Growing up behind the iron curtain*. New York: Farrar, Straus & Giroux.

Soto, G. (2005). *Neighborhood odes*. San Diego: Harcourt.

Soto, G. (2007). *Canto familiar*. Orlando: Harcourt.

Speare, E. G. (2001). *The witch of Blackbird Pond*. Boston: Houghton Mifflin.

Stead, T., & Duke, N. K. (2005). *Reality checks: Teaching reading comprehension with nonfiction, K–5*. York, ME: Stenhouse.

Steele, P. (2007). *Mesopotamia*. New York: DK Publishing.

Steig, W. (1990). *Doctor De Soto*. New York: Farrar, Straus & Giroux.

Steig, W. (2010). *Sylvester and the magic pebble*. New York: Atheneum.

Sweet, A. P., & Snow, C. E. (2003). Reading for comprehension. In C. E. Snow & A. P. Sweet (Eds.), *Rethinking reading comprehension* (pp. 1–11). New York: Guilford Press.

Tan, S. (2007). *The arrival*. New York: Arthur A. Levine/Scholastic.

Taylor, M. D. (2001). *Roll of thunder, hear my cry*. New York: Dial Books.

Testa, M. (2005). *Becoming Joe DiMaggio*. Cambridge, MA: Candlewick Press.

Thomson, B. (2013). *Fossil*. New York: Two Lions.

Van Allsburg, C. (1986). *The stranger*. Boston: Houghton Mifflin.

Van Allsburg, C. (1991). *The wretched stone*. Boston: Houghton Mifflin.

White, E. B. (2012). *Charlotte's web*. New York: HarperCollins.

Wiesner, D. (2006). *Flotsam*. New York: Clarion Books.

Wildsmith, B. (2007). *The hare and the tortoise*. New York: Oxford University Press.

Williams, M. (2007). *The adventures of Robin Hood*. New York: Walker.

Williams, V. B. (1993). *A chair for my mother*. New York: Harper Trophy.

Wood, A. (2001). *Alphabet adventure*. New York: Blue Sky Press.

Woodland, C., Parker, S. (2014). *Science: A visual encyclopedia*. New York: DK Publishing.

Woodson, J. (2004). *Locomotion*. New York: Puffin Books.

Woodson, J. (2005). *Show way*. New York: Putnam.

Yolen, J. (2009). *On the slant*. Katonah, NY: Richard C. Owen.

Yousafzai, M. (2014). *I am Malala: How one girl stood up for education and changed the world*. Boston: Little, Brown.

Zelinsky, P. O. (1996). *Rumpelstiltskin*. New York: Puffin Books.

three

Organizing for Instruction

Teachers generally use two or more of these instructional approaches to teach reading and writing:

- ℮ **Guided reading**
- ℮ **Basal reading programs**
- ℮ **Literature focus units**
- ℮ **Literature circles**
- ℮ **Reading and writing workshop**

No single approach is a complete literacy program, so teachers combine approaches or components from several approaches to ensure that students receive explicit instruction and opportunities for authentic reading and writing. Many teachers add guided reading or another instructional program to differentiate instruction and address their students' needs. In addition, they teach students how to use reading and writing as tools for learning and as ways to demonstrate new knowledge through thematic units that focus on social studies and science topics.

These instructional approaches differ in significant ways. Probably the most important difference is theoretical orientation: Basal reading programs reflect behaviorism; literature circles, in contrast, reflect sociolinguistics. The instructional materials differ, too: Students read leveled books in guided reading groups and textbooks in basal reading programs, but they read trade books in the other approaches. Teachers organize for literacy instruction according to their beliefs about how children learn, district requirements, and the available materials.

In this part opener, I introduce you to five teachers who talk about basal readers, differentiation, thematic units, and other topics related to organizing for literacy instruction.

Basal Readers

My name is Tashelle King, and I'm required to use basal readers in third grade. I understand the district's decision, but I'd prefer using a balanced approach because that's what I believe is best. So, what I do is a combination: We read selections in the anthology, and I teach the related skills; then my students apply them using real books. Right now we're comparing fiction and nonfiction books. After reading and comparing stories and articles in our anthology, my students have formed literature circles to read one of Mary Pope Osborne's stories and the accompanying nonfiction fact tracker. One group is reading *Twister on Tuesday* [Osborne, 2001] and its companion, *Twisters and Other Terrible Storms* [Osborne, 2003], and another group is reading *Monday With a Mad Genius* [Osborne, 2009] and its companion, *Leonardo da Vinci* [Osborne & Boyce, 2009]. Afterward, the groups create projects to share what they've learned with the class. Lots of kids are doing slide shows, movies, and other digital projects. They're amazing!

Differentiation

My name is Dawna Crawford, and this year I'm teaching a fourth/fifth grade combination class. "Differentiation" means modifying your instruction to make sure that every student can learn what you're teaching. Don't get me wrong; differentiating instruction isn't easy to do, but it's what every good teacher does. You just can't let students keep struggling until they give up; you have to step in. What do I do? First of all, I get to know my students. It's not just their academic strengths and weaknesses; I get to know them as people—who's in their families, what they do after school, and what their dreams are. Second, I treat my students with love and respect and I insist they do the same. We're a family in room 19. One more thing: I match my students to my instructional plans. I use leveled books for guided reading lessons, have them work in small groups, preteach difficult topics to my students with less background knowledge—all those things experts tell us to do.

Interventions

My name is Becky Boyd-Vega. I love sixth graders, but I'm dealing with kids reading at the third through eighth grade levels. Our school takes the first 25 minutes of the school day for an intervention period. I work with 14 kids reading at levels N and O; that's third grade level, mind you. It's such a big group that I divided them into two groups, and I do guided reading using leveled books. Each day I begin with a quickie 5-minute minilesson for the whole class, and then I work with one group while the other group reads independently. Today's minilesson topic was homonyms; that's a topic I keep revisiting. At the end of the 25-minute intervention session, each of the kids reading independently turns in a

"ticket" to leave the classroom. I vary their assignments; sometimes I ask them to tell me how many pages they've read that day, recall a pair of homonyms, or write a connection they made while reading.

Diverse Learners

My name is Tami Christensen, and we have students from 34 countries, speaking 18 languages, at our school. I teach second grade, and it can be a real challenge teaching children who are learning English and adapting to a new cultural environment at the same time, but, oh my, the rewards are huge! My classroom is a community where we know, respect, and support each other. I reward my students for asking questions and taking risks. I really believe that the quality of classroom life fosters students' academic achievement. What do I do? I integrate my students' language and culture into the classroom, and I find out about their interests and build on them. Students share their knowledge, sometimes with their parents' and grandparents' assistance. My students often work with partners and in small groups so they can support and learn from each other. One more thing: I always try to make learning fun, and we celebrate each other's successes.

Thematic Units

My name is Arturo "Artie" Romero, and I'm an eighth grade Core teacher. I teach integrated English and history 90-minute classes, focusing on American literature and history from precolonial days to the 20th century. I organize my instruction into thematic units, and I utilize three components—textbooks, novels, and writing workshop. I'm expected to use both the literature anthology and the history textbooks, which I do. I like having the skills laid out for me to teach. In addition, we read great novels together as a class, including *My Brother Sam Is Dead* (Collier & Collier, 2005), *Breaking Through* (Jiménez, 2002), *Chinese Cinderella* (Mah, 2010), and *Roll of Thunder, Hear My Cry* (Taylor, 2004). I do close reading and emphasize using comprehension strategies to deepen our understanding of the books. And, I teach language mechanics and grammar through writing workshop. The students develop and refine essays to investigate the recurring themes in American literature and history.

REFERENCES

Collier, J. L., & Collier, C. (2005). *My brother Sam is dead*. New York: Scholastic.

Jiménez, F. (2002). *Breaking through*. New York: Sandpiper.

Mah, A. Y. (2010). *Chinese Cinderella*. New York: Ember.

Osborne, M. P. (2001). *Twister on Tuesday*. New York: Random House.

Osborne, M. P. (2003). *Twister and other terrible storms*. New York: Random House.

Osborne, M. P. (2009). *Monday with a mad genius*. New York: Random House.

Osborne, M. P., & Boyce, N. P. (2009). *Leonardo da Vinci*. New York: Random House.

Taylor, M. D. (2004). *Roll of thunder, hear my cry*. New York: Puffin Books.

Chapter 10

Organizing for Instruction

PLAN: Preview the Learning Outcomes

After studying this chapter, you'll be prepared to respond to these points:

10.1 Explain how to teach reading using guided reading.

10.2 Discuss the strengths and weaknesses of basal reading programs.

10.3 Describe how to use literature focus units in a balanced literacy approach.

10.4 Explain how teachers use literature circles to teach reading.

10.5 Describe the reading and writing workshop program.

A Yearlong Author Study. There's a busy hum in Mr. Singh's fourth grade classroom. The students are involved in a 40-minute writing workshop; it's the time when they develop and refine pieces of writing on topics they've chosen themselves. They word process their rough drafts on laptops and work with classmates to revise and edit them. Then they print out clean copies of their drafts for a final editing conference with Mr. Singh, and afterward, they format the text and print the finished copy.

The class has been involved in an ambitious yearlong project on Chris Van Allsburg, the popular author and illustrator of award-winning fantasy picture books, including *Probuditi* (2006) and *The Polar Express* (2005). The students have read some of these stories in their basal readers and during literature circles, and Mr. Singh has read others aloud. The stories they've been writing accompany the illustrations in *The Mysteries of Harris Burdick* (Van Allsburg, 1996).

The unit began in September when Mr. Singh read aloud *Jumanji* (Van Allsburg, 1982), the story of two children who play a jungle adventure board game that comes to life. He also read aloud the sequel, *Zathura* (2002), about a space adventure board game, and students watched the movie version. They also made board games and wrote directions for playing them. The teacher used the story to emphasize the importance of listening to directions in the classroom, following parents' directions at home, and reading directions on state achievement tests.

Mr. Singh regularly teaches **minilessons** on writing strategies that students then apply in their own writing. He began with a series of lessons on revising and proof-reading that students use during writing workshop. Next, he taught lessons about the elements of story structure. Posters about each story element hang in the classroom, testimony to the learning taking place there. Students apply what they've

In this chapter, you'll read about five ways to organize literacy instruction: Teachers use a combination of guided reading, basal readers, literature focus units, literature circles, reading and writing workshop, and other approaches to create a balanced literacy program. As you read this vignette, notice how Mr. Singh integrates these approaches in a yearlong study of award-winning author/illustrator Chris Van Allsburg. He combines explicit instruction with authentic reading and writing to expand students' learning.

learned as they craft their own stories, using the writing process to draft and refine their stories; check the figure Writing Process Activities. Last year, these students took an after-school touch-typing course, so they know the fundamentals of finger placement on the keyboard and are developing typing fluency as they use laptops.

Today during writing workshop, Mr. Singh is meeting with Alfonso, Martha, and Yimleej to proofread their stories and correct errors. Other students are word processing their last stories or printing out final copies and gluing them into their books. Miguel and Lindsey have finished their books, so they're helping classmates word process, transfer to the computer, and print out their stories. Mr. Singh's optimistic that everyone will be finished by lunchtime tomorrow. He plans to start author's chair during writing workshop tomorrow: Students will take turns reading their favorite stories aloud to classmates. Author's chair is a popular classroom activity; most students are eager to share their stories, and their classmates enjoy listening to them because they've learned how to read with expression and hold their classmates' interest.

WRITING PROCESS ACTIVITIES

STAGE	ACTIVITIES	DESCRIPTIONS
Prewriting	Story Cards	Students create story cards to develop their ideas, characters, setting, problem, climax, and solution.
	One-on-One	Students meet with a classmate to share their story cards and talk out their ideas.
Drafting	Rough Drafts	Students write rough drafts on laptops, working from their story cards.
Revising	Revising Groups	Students share clean copies of their drafts with two classmates, getting feedback about their stories. Then they make revisions based on the feedback they received.
	Conference With Mr. Singh	Mr. Singh reads and responds to their stories. Students conference with him to discuss their drafts and later make additional revisions based on his feedback.
Editing	Proofreading	Students print out clean copies of their drafts, proofread them, and correct the errors they notice. Then two classmates proofread their drafts to identify and correct remaining spelling, capitalization, punctuation, and grammar errors.
	Conference With Mr. Singh	Students print out clean copies and meet with Mr. Singh to proofread and correct any remaining errors.
Publishing	Final Copy	Students print out final copies, glue the pages into books, and add illustrations.

Last week, the class created this introductory page for their story collections:

> *Thirty-five years ago Harris Burdick came by Peter Wenders's publishing office. He claimed he had written and illustrated 15 stories but all he brought with him were the illustrations. The next day Harris Burdick planned on bringing the stories to Mr. Wenders, but he never returned.*
>
> *Chris Van Allsburg met with Mr. Wenders and that's how he learned about the illustrations. Mr. Wenders gave Mr. Van Allsburg a dusty box of drawings, and Chris Van Allsburg decided to make them into a book for children.*
>
> *The fourth graders in room 18 have worked hard to create stories for each of the illustrations. Even though we have written our stories, we are here to tell you that the mystery of Harris Burdick still remains.*

It's a class collaboration: Mr. Singh and the students developed the introduction together, and copies were made for each student. By collaborating, the teacher ensured that they had a useful introduction for their books.

Mr. Singh continued to read stories each month. In October, he and his students read *The Stranger* (Van Allsburg, 1986), a story included in their basal readers. In the story, the Baileys take in an injured stranger, a man who doesn't speak or seem to know who he is, but he appears to be attuned with the seasons and has an amazing connection with wild animals. Although it's never explicitly stated in the story, the stranger is Jack Frost. The class takes several days to read the story. On the first day, the teacher introduced the key vocabulary words, including *autumn*, *etched*, and *peculiar*, and the class previewed the story, examining the illustrations and making predictions. Mr. Singh used **shared reading**: The students listened to the story read aloud on the professional CD that accompanies the textbook and followed along in their textbooks. Some inferred that the stranger was Jack Frost, but others didn't. That's when Mr. Singh introduced the drawing inferences strategy, which he called "reading between the lines."

They read the story a second time, searching for clues about the stranger's identity, and then they made a cluster, a spider web–like diagram, with the clues. They wrote the words *The Stranger* in the center circle, drew out rays from this circle, and wrote these clues at the end of each one: he wears odd clothing, is confused by buttons, and works hard but doesn't get tired. Afterward, they completed page 156 in the Practice Book that accompanies the textbook as well as other pages that emphasize comprehension. Then Mr. Singh asked students to closely examine the illustrations in the story. They noticed how the perspective in the illustrations varies to draw readers into the scenes and create the mood. The students read the story a third time with partners, talking about how Chris Van Allsburg used viewpoint in the illustrations.

In November, students read other books by Chris Van Allsburg in literature circles. First, Mr. Singh presented **book talks** about these four books: *Two Bad Ants* (Van Allsburg, 1988), *Just a Dream* (Van Allsburg, 1990), *The Sweetest Fig* (Van Allsburg, 1993b), and *The Wreck of the* Zephyr (Van Allsburg, 1983). Students formed small groups to read one of them, assuming roles and taking on responsibilities in the small groups as they read and discussed the book. Then they read another book during a second literature circle in January.

Mr. Singh read aloud the award-winning holiday story *The Polar Express* (Van Allsburg, 2005) in December. In the story, being able to hear Santa's bells jiggle represents belief in the magic of Christmas, so Mr. Singh gave each student a small bell to jiggle each time it was mentioned in the story. The students discussed the story in a **grand conversation**; much of their discussion focused on the theme and how the author states it explicitly at the end of the story. "What an awesome story!" Hunter concluded, and his classmates agreed. They also talked about their own holiday traditions and wrote about them during writing workshop.

They continued to read other books by Chris Van Allsburg: In February, Mr. Singh read *The Garden of Abdul Gasazi* (Van Allsburg, 1993a), and in March, he read *The Wretched Stone* (Van Allsburg, 1991). These books are difficult for students to comprehend because they have to draw inferences: In *The Garden of Abdul Gasazi*, readers have to decide whether the magician really changes the dog into a duck, and in *The Wretched Stone*, they need to understand that the stone is a symbol, representing television, computers, or video games. Mr. Singh taught a series of mini-lessons on drawing inferences, and he modeled the strategy as he reread the stories, showing the

fourth graders how to use their background knowledge, the clues in the story, and self-questions to read between the lines. Then students reread the stories with partners, talked about clues in the stories, and drew inferences as their teacher had.

In March, Mr. Singh also taught a series of minilessons on the fantasy genre. Then students divided into small groups to reread the Chris Van Allsburg books and examine them for fantasy characteristics. They developed a chart with the titles of the books written across the top and the characteristics of fantasies written down the left side. Then they completed the chart by indicating how the characteristics were represented in each book.

This month, students are reading Chris Van Allsburg's books independently; some are reading books they haven't already read, and others are rereading favorites. As they read, they search for the white dog that Van Allsburg includes in each book. In some books, such as *The Garden of Abdul Gasazi*, the dog is alive, but in others, he's a puppet, a hood ornament, or a picture. In several books, only a small part of him shows; in *The Wretched Stone*, for example, you see only his tail. In addition, they continue to notice the fantasy elements of the stories, draw inferences when needed, and reflect on Van Allsburg's use of perspective in his illustrations. As a culminating activity, Mr. Singh plans to read aloud *The Chronicles of Harris Burdick: Fourteen Amazing Authors Tell the Tales* (Van Allsburg, 2011), a collection of stories for the pictures in *The Mysteries of Harris Burdick* written by Sherman Alexie, Kate DiCamillo, Linda Sue Park, Lemony Snicket, and other best-selling authors.

 STANDARDS CHECK!

Mr. Singh addressed the Common Core State Standards as he taught fourth graders about writing workshop in the vignette you've just read. Review the fourth grade literacy Standards document online at http://www.corestandards.org/ELA-Literacy, and identify the Standards that Mr. Singh addressed through his instructional activities. Create your list, and compare it with Mr. Singh's.

There's no one best way to teach reading and writing; instead, teachers create a balanced literacy program using two or more approaches. Five of the most commonly used literacy programs for kindergarten through eighth grade are *guided reading*, *basal reading programs*, *literature focus units*, *literature circles*, and *reading and writing workshop*. Mr. Singh's author study in the vignette was successful because his literacy program was balanced with a combination of explicit instruction, small-group and whole-class literacy activities, and independent reading and writing opportunities. By combining several instructional approaches, he juggled the district's adopted basal reading program with other approaches that enriched and extended his students' literacy learning. To evaluate your instructional program, use the Teacher Checklist: How effective is my instructional program?

The purpose of the Common Core State Standards for English Language Arts (2010) is to delineate what students are expected to know and be able to do to be prepared for

TEACHER *Checklist*

How effective is my instructional program?

- ○ Do I combine several instructional programs to meet students' needs?
- ○ Do I use texts at students' instructional level for reading instruction?
- ○ Do students read and respond to award-winning grade-appropriate books?
- ○ Do I provide explicit instruction on strategies and skills?
- ○ Do I incorporate whole-class, small-group, and independent activities?
- ○ Do students have daily opportunities to read books independently?
- ○ Do students participate in authentic reading and writing activities?
- ○ Do I monitor and assess students' progress?
- ○ Do I intervene and modify instruction when students struggle?

college and career literacy demands, but they don't prescribe how teachers are to teach reading or which instructional programs to use. However, the Standards document does make several important points about instruction. First, teachers should differentiate instruction to increase opportunities for all students to be successful. Next, the Standards aren't taught separately; instead, teachers should integrate reading and writing so that most literacy activities address several Standards. Third, across the curriculum connections to reading instruction are crucial; teachers should incorporate reading instruction into thematic units using a text set of stories, informational books, media, and digital texts. Mr. Singh demonstrated some of these guidelines in the vignette. The feature Common Core State Standards: Reading reviews the recommendations.

Conducting Guided Reading Lessons

Teachers use guided reading to teach reading to small groups of four to six students who read at the same level. They use books written at students' instructional level, and support their application of reading strategies (Fountas & Pinnell, 1996). Students do the actual reading themselves, although the teacher often reads the first page aloud to get the group off to a successful start. Beginning readers mumble-read the words, which helps the teacher keep track of students' knowledge of high-frequency words and use of decoding and other reading strategies, but more fluent readers read silently. This instructional program is typically used in kindergarten through third grade, but it can also be used with older students, especially struggling readers. Check the Overview of the Instructional Approach: Guided Reading.

Components

Guided reading lessons last approximately 20 minutes. To begin, students reread, either individually or with a partner, familiar books they've already read during previous lessons. Then teachers introduce a new book and guide students as they read it. Beginning readers generally read picture books in one sitting, but more fluent readers take several days to a week to read chapter books.

To introduce a new book, teachers activate and build students' background knowledge, build their interest, and take the students on a "walk" through the book, talking about the illustrations and the text. Teachers also set a purpose for reading. Next, students read the entire book, with the teacher providing assistance when needed. They read softly to themselves while the teacher monitors each student's progress by listening in as the student reads, stops to decode unfamiliar words, and rereads confusing passages.

Once everyone in the group has finished reading, the students talk about the book as in a **grand conversation**, sharing ideas, making connections, asking clarifying questions, and reading from the text to make a point. Teachers also use words from the book to teach and practice phonics, new vocabulary words, and reading strategies.

Sometimes students extend the reading experience through writing. Teachers design projects based on the book: Sometimes students write about a personal experience

Check the Compendium of Instructional Procedures, which follows Chapter 12.

OVERVIEW OF THE INSTRUCTIONAL APPROACH

Guided Reading

TOPIC	DESCRIPTION
Purpose	To develop independent readers who use strategies flexibly to decode unfamiliar words, read fluently, and comprehend what they're reading.
Components	Guided reading lessons begin with students rereading a familiar leveled book, and then the teacher introduces a new leveled book for that day's lesson and students read it independently. Afterward, they discuss the selection and the teacher uses the book for phonics, vocabulary, and strategy lessons. Sometimes students extend their reading by doing a writing project.
Theory Base	Teacher-centered. Guided reading reflects the constructivist and information processing theories, because teachers use reading groups to differentiate instruction, and they teach reading strategies.
Applications	Teachers often use guided reading in conjunction with literature focus units or reading and writing workshop so students have opportunities to apply the reading strategies they're learning and integrate reading and writing.
Strengths	• Students read books at their instructional reading levels. • Teachers teach reading strategies. • Teachers differentiate instruction to address students' needs. • Teachers supervise students as they read to provide assistance when needed.
Limitations	• Teachers often feel a loss of control because while they work with a small group, classmates work at centers. • Teachers have to locate multiple copies of appropriate leveled books for each group.

that's related to the book's events, or they write their own pattern book using a sentence stem from the book. Students also use interactive writing to create a group project.

Reading Strategies

The goal of this instructional program is to develop independent readers, and students who read independently are strategic: They can read fluently, monitor their progress, and solve problems as they arise. Students learn to use these reading strategies through guided reading lessons:

- Self-monitoring
- Checking predictions
- Decoding unfamiliar words
- Determining if a word makes sense
- Checking that the word is appropriate in the syntax of the sentence
- Using all sources of information
- Chunking phrases to read more fluently

Teachers observe students as they read. They spend a minute or two with each reader, sitting either in front of or beside the student and watching for evidence that the student is using strategies to identify words and solve reading problems. Teachers take notes about their observations and use the information when choosing the next book for that student to read.

Watch as students prepare to read a story on their laptops. Why does the teacher introduce the story, activate background knowledge, and introduce vocabulary?

Instructional Materials

Teachers choose leveled books for guided reading that match students' instructional reading levels. Many schools purchase grade-level kits of leveled books, such as Scholastic Guided Reading Book Collections; these kits typically include six copies of a fiction and a nonfiction book at each level. Or, teachers put together their own kits using books they've leveled themselves.

Applying the Reading Process

As they teach reading, teachers apply the reading process, which provides the structure or skeleton for instruction. They use this structure for guided reading lessons:

Prereading. Teachers build students' background knowledge, introduce vocabulary, and preview the book.

Reading. Students read the entire book independently while the teacher listens to them read to monitor their progress.

Responding. Students talk about the book in discussions that are similar to grand conversations, sharing ideas, asking questions, and making connections.

Exploring. Teachers use words and sentences from the book to teach phonics, vocabulary, and reading strategies.

Applying. Students practice rereading the book, gaining confidence and knowledge with each rereading experience. Sometimes they create writing projects related to the book they've read.

Teachers apply the reading process as they teach guided reading lessons. There's an emphasis on the reading and exploring stages in this instructional program; the emphasis varies in each of the programs.

Managing Guided Reading

Teachers organize the small-group lessons so that they work with each group three to five times a week; students who are struggling meet with the teacher more often than those reading at grade level do. The groupings are flexible because whenever teachers observe a student who's struggling or one who's moving ahead of other group members, they change that student to a more appropriate group.

While teachers teach guided reading lessons, the rest of the class is involved in other literacy activities. Most teachers have students work at literacy centers that they've set up around the classroom. These centers are inviting, and students know how to work independently or cooperatively in small groups at the centers using all sorts of literacy materials, including books, online games, and digital media. Teachers place sign-in sheets at the centers or use another accounting system to monitor students' work. Whenever possible, they enlist parents, teacher aides, and older students to supervise the centers so they can focus on the guided reading lessons they're teaching.

Other teachers have students participate in other instructional programs: literature focus units, literature circles, and reading and writing workshop. Students create projects about books they've read, read books independently, participate in small-group discussions, and participate in writing projects.

 **MONITOR: Check Your Understanding 10.1**

⟲ Teaching With Basal Reading Programs

Commercial reading programs, commonly called *basal readers*, have been a staple in reading instruction for more than 150 years. Before 1850, William Holmes McGuffey wrote the McGuffey Readers, the first textbooks published with increasingly challenging books designed for each grade level. The lessons featured literature selections that emphasized religious and patriotic values. As they read aloud to classmates, students used phonics to sound out words, studied vocabulary words in the context of stories, and practiced proper enunciation. These books were widely used until the beginning of the 20th century. Probably the most famous basal reading program is the Scott Foresman program, introduced in 1930 and used through the 1960s. The first grade textbooks featured stories about two children named Dick and Jane; their little sister, Sally; their pets, Puff and Spot; and their parents. To teach words, the books relied on repetition through contrived sentences such as "See Jane. See Sally. See Jane and Sally." Students were expected to memorize words rather than use phonics to decode them; this whole-word method was known as "look and say." The Scott Foresman program has been criticized for its lack of phonics instruction as well as for centering stories on an "ideal" middle-class white family.

Today's basal readers include more authentic literature selections that celebrate diverse cultures, and they emphasize an organized presentation of strategies and skills, especially phonics in the primary grades. Walsh (2003) reviewed five widely used series and found that they all provide visually stimulating artwork to engage students, similar methods of teaching decoding and comprehension, and teacher's guides with detailed lesson plans. She also uncovered a common problem: None of the programs provided for the sustained development of students' background knowledge, but when students don't develop a strong foundation of world and word knowledge, they have difficulty reading and understanding more conceptually demanding books, beginning at fourth grade level. This drop in achievement is known as the "fourth grade slump," and children from economically disadvantaged families are more likely to fall behind than their classmates are (Chall, Jacobs, & Baldwin, 1991).

Publishers of basal reading textbooks tout their programs as complete literacy programs containing all the materials, including digital components, needed for students to become successful readers. The accessibility of reading materials is one advantage: Teachers have copies of grade-level textbooks for every student. Another advantage is the instructional program is planned for them: Teachers follow step-by-step directions to teach strategies and skills, and workbooks provide practice materials. It's unrealistic, however, to assume that any commercial reading program could be a complete literacy program. Students who read above or below grade level need reading materials at their levels, and all students need many more opportunities than a basal reading program provides to listen to books read aloud and to read and reread books. In addition, a complete literacy program involves more than reading; students also need opportunities to learn the writing process, draft and refine compositions, and learn writing strategies and skills. For more information, check the Overview of the Instructional Approach: Basal Reading Programs.

Components

A number of commercial programs are available today, and most include these components:

- ⟲ Selections in grade-level textbooks
- ⟲ Instruction about decoding and comprehension strategies and skills
- ⟲ Workbook assignments
- ⟲ Independent reading opportunities

OVERVIEW OF THE INSTRUCTIONAL APPROACH

Basal Reading Programs

TOPIC	DESCRIPTION
Purpose	To teach the strategies and skills that successful readers need using an organized program that includes grade-level reading selections, workbook practice assignments, and frequent testing.
Components	Basal reading programs involve five components: reading selections in the grade-level textbook, instruction on strategies and skills, workbook assignments, independent reading opportunities, and a management plan that includes flexible grouping and regular assessment.
Theory Base	Teacher-centered. Basal reading programs are based on behaviorism because teachers provide explicit instruction and students are passive rather than active learners.
Applications	Basal reading programs organize instruction into units with weeklong lessons that include reading, strategy and skill instruction, and workbook activities. They should be used with other instructional approaches to ensure that students also read books at their instructional levels and have opportunities to participate in writing projects.
Strengths	• Textbooks are aligned with grade-level standards. • Students read selections at their grade level. • Teachers teach strategies and skills in a sequential program, and students practice them through reading and workbook assignments. • The teacher's guide provides detailed instructions for teaching reading. • Assessment materials are included in the program.
Limitations	• Selections may be too difficult for some students and too easy for others. • Selections may lack the authenticity of good literature or not include a variety of genres. • Programs include many workbook assignments. • Most instruction is presented to the whole class.

Basal readers are recognized for their strong skills component: Teachers teach skills in a predetermined sequence, and students apply what they're learning in the textbook selections they read and the workbook assignments they complete.

SELECTIONS IN GRADE-LEVEL TEXTBOOKS. Basal reading programs are organized into units on topics such as challenges, folktales, and friends. Units include four to six weeklong lessons, each with a featured selection. The selections in the kindergarten and first grade textbooks contain decodable text so that children can apply the phonics skills they're learning, but as students develop stronger word-identification skills and a bank of familiar high-frequency words, textbooks transition to literature selections that were originally published as trade books.

Everyone reads the same selections in the grade-level textbook each week, no matter their reading level. These commercial programs argue that it's important to expose all students to grade-level instruction because some students, especially minority students, have been denied equal access to instruction. The teacher's guide offers suggestions for supporting struggling readers and English learners. Many programs also provide video, audio, and Internet resources. Audiotapes of the selections, which teachers often play as students follow along in their copies of the textbook, are an especially useful resource. After this shared reading experience, some less successful readers can then read the selection, but many teachers complain that a few students can't read the selections no matter how much support they provide.

INSTRUCTION IN STRATEGIES AND SKILLS. Teachers use basal reading programs to deliver explicit and systematic instruction that is aligned with the Common Core State Standards. Most textbooks include instruction in phonemic awareness, phonics, high-frequency words, word-identification skills, spelling, grammar, and writing mechanics (capitalization and punctuation). The programs also emphasize comprehension strategies, including evaluating, monitoring, predicting, questioning, summarizing, and visualizing.

The teacher's guide—usually available as a book or an eBook—provides detailed lesson plans for teaching strategies and skills with each selection. Teachers explain the strategies and skills and model their use as they read with students, then students apply them as they read selections and complete workbook pages. Scope-and-sequence charts for each grade level that are included in the teacher's guide show the recommended sequence for teaching strategies and skills and explain how they're introduced at one grade level and reinforced and expanded at the next level. These programs claim that their explicit, systematic instruction ensures success.

WORKBOOK ASSIGNMENTS. For each reading selection, students complete workbook pages before, during, and after reading to reinforce instruction; 10 to 12 workbook pages that focus on phonics, vocabulary, comprehension, grammar, spelling, and writing accompany each selection. On these pages, students write words, letters, or sentences; match words and sentences; or complete graphic organizers.

Teachers vary how they use the workbook pages. Once students know how to complete a page, such as those that focus on practicing spelling words, they work independently or with partners. However, for more challenging assignments, such as those dealing with comprehension strategies or newly introduced skills, teachers have the whole class do the assignment together at their direction. They also devise various approaches for monitoring completion of workbook assignments: They may have students check their own work, or they may grade the assignments themselves.

INDEPENDENT READING OPPORTUNITIES. Most basal reading programs include a collection of easy, on-grade-level, and challenging paperback books for students to read independently. Multiple copies of each book are available, and teachers set them out for students to read after finishing each selection. Some of these books, especially in the primary grades, have been written to reinforce phonics skills and vocabulary words, but others are authentic trade books. The goal is for the collection to meet the needs of all students, but sometimes teachers still need to supplement with much easier books for English learners or struggling readers.

Instructional Materials

At the center of a basal reading program is the student textbook, sometimes called an *anthology*. In the primary grades, two or more books are provided at each grade level, and in fourth through sixth grades, there's usually one book. Most basal reading programs end in sixth grade. The books are colorful and inviting, often featuring pictures of children and animals on the covers of primary-level books and exciting adventures and fanciful locations on the covers of fourth through sixth grade books. The selections are grouped into units, and each unit includes stories, poems, and informational articles. Many multicultural selections have been added, and illustrations usually feature ethnically diverse people. Information about authors and illustrators is provided for many selections. Textbooks contain a table of contents and a glossary.

Commercial reading programs provide a wide variety of print and digital materials to support student learning. Consumable workbooks are probably the best known support material; students write letters, words, and sentences in these books to practice phonics, comprehension, and vocabulary strategies and skills. Big books and kits with letter and word cards, wall charts, and manipulatives are included in the kindergarten and first grade programs.

Some multimedia materials, such as audiocassettes, CDs, and videos, are available, which teachers can use at listening and computer centers. Collections of trade books are available for each grade level to provide opportunities for supplemental reading. In the primary grades, many books have decodable text to provide practice on phonics skills and high-frequency words; in the upper grades, the books are related to unit topics.

Basal reading programs also offer a variety of assessment tools, often available online. Teachers use placement evaluations or informal reading inventories to determine students' reading levels and for placement in reading groups, and they use **running records** to informally monitor students' reading. There are also selection and unit tests to determine students' phonics, vocabulary, and comprehension knowledge. Information is provided on how to administer the assessments, analyze the results, and manage the assessment program.

A teacher's instructional guide is provided for each grade level. This oversize handbook gives comprehensive information about how to plan lessons, teach the selections, and assess students' progress. The selections are shown in reduced size in the guide, and each page includes background information about the selection, instructions for reading the selections, and ideas for coordinating skill and strategy instruction. In addition, information is presented about which supplemental books to use with each selection and how to assess students' learning. These guides are typically available in both print and eBook editions. Figure 10–1 summarizes the materials provided in most basal reading programs.

Applying the Reading Process

When teachers implement basal reading programs, they use the reading process, even though many activities are different than in other approaches:

Prereading. Teachers follow directions in the teacher's guide to activate and build students' background knowledge, introduce vocabulary, teach word-identification and comprehension strategies, and preview the selection.

Reading. Students read the selection independently, but if it's too difficult, teachers read it aloud or play an audiotape before students read it themselves.

Responding. Teachers follow directions in the teacher's guide to enhance students' comprehension by asking questions about the author's purpose, modeling **think-alouds**, encouraging students to draw inferences, and summarizing the selection. Students also complete workbook assignments that focus on comprehension.

Exploring. Teachers teach phonics, word analysis, spelling, and grammar skills, and students practice the skills by completing workbook assignments. They also teach students about authors, genres, and text structures.

Watch as third graders identify character traits from a story they've read and support their ideas with text evidence. How does the teacher differentiate this lesson to accommodate both students who understood the task and a student who needed assistance?

Applying. Students read related selections in the basal reader or in supplemental books that accompany the program and participate in writing activities related to the selection or genre they're studying.

One of the most striking differences is that students complete practice activities in workbooks during several of the stages rather than applying what they're learning in more authentic ways.

FIGURE 10–1	Materials in Basal Reading Programs

MATERIALS	DESCRIPTION
Textbook	The student's grade-level book of thematically arranged reading selections. Textbooks are available in a series of softcover books in the primary grades and a single hardcover book in the middle and upper grades. Some programs also have online student textbooks.
Big Books	Enlarged copies of books for shared reading. These books are used in kindergarten and first grade.
Supplemental Books	Collections of paperback trade books for each grade level. Kindergarten-level books often feature familiar songs and wordless stories. First and second grade books often include decodable words for practicing phonics skills and high-frequency words. In grades 3 to 6, books are often related to unit themes.
Workbooks	Consumable practice books of phonics, comprehension, vocabulary, spelling, and grammar worksheets that are coordinated with reading selections and the strategies and skills being taught. Some programs also have online practice drills and games.
Kits	Alphabet cards, word cards, and other instructional materials for emergent and beginning readers. These kits are used in kindergarten through second grade.
Teacher's Guide	An oversize book with comprehensive information about how to teach reading using the basal reading program. Reading selections are shown in reduced size, and background information about the selection, instructions for teaching the selections, and ideas on coordinating skill and strategy instruction are given on each page. Suggestions for differentiating instruction, correlations with grade-level standards, and assessment options are provided. In addition, information is presented about which supplemental books to use with each selection. Some programs have online teacher's guides.
Home–School Connections	Resources to strengthen home–school partnerships, including information about the reading program and lists of ways parents can work with their children. These materials are available in English, Spanish, and several other languages.
Assessment System	An online testing and reporting system with a library of standards-based tests to monitor student achievement, diagnose problems, and report to parents and administrators.
Multimedia Resources	Audio, visual, and digital materials for students and teachers, including CDs of selections, information and updates on the textbook's website, Internet links, and online assessments.
Lesson Planner	An online management tool that teachers download to use in planning for instruction and aligning lessons with state literacy standards.

Managing a Basal Reading Program

The teacher's guide provides a management plan for the basal reading program. Daily and weekly lesson plans are included with suggestions for pacing for each unit, ideas for flexible grouping, and regular assessment activities. There are letters to send home to parents at the beginning of each unit, usually available in several languages, as well as a variety of assessment materials, including phonics tests, end-of-selection and end-of-unit tests, writing rubrics, and observation guidelines. Teachers are encouraged to assess students' learning regularly to monitor their progress and to evaluate the effectiveness of the instructional program.

 MONITOR: Check Your Understanding 10.2

Teaching With Literature Focus Units

Teachers plan literature focus units featuring popular and award-winning stories, nonfiction books, or books of poetry. Some literature focus units feature a single book, either a picture book or a chapter book, and others feature several books for a genre unit or an author study. Teachers direct students as they read and respond to a book, but the emphasis in this instructional approach is on teaching students about literature and developing lifelong readers. For more information, check the Overview of the Instructional Approach: Literature Focus Units.

OVERVIEW OF THE INSTRUCTIONAL APPROACH

Literature Focus Units

TOPIC	DESCRIPTION
Purpose	To teach reading through literature, using high-quality, grade-appropriate picture books and novels.
Components	Teachers involve students in three activities: Students read and respond to a trade book together as a class; the teacher teaches minilessons on phonics, vocabulary, and comprehension using the book they're reading; and students create projects to extend their understanding of the book.
Theory Base	Teacher/student-centered. Literature focus units represent a transition between teacher-centered and student-centered learning because teachers support students as they read a book. This approach reflects information processing theory because teachers develop students' background knowledge, read aloud when students can't read fluently, and teach vocabulary words and comprehension strategies. It also reflects Rosenblatt's transactional theory because students participate in grand conversations and write in reading logs to deepen their comprehension, and critical literacy theory because issues of social justice often arise in the trade books.
Applications	Teachers teach units featuring a picture book or a novel, generally using books on a district-approved list, or units featuring a genre or author. Literature focus units are often alternated with another approach where students read books at their own reading levels.
Strengths	• Teachers select award-winning literature for these units. • Teachers scaffold students' comprehension as they read with the class or small groups. • Teachers teach minilessons on reading strategies and skills. • Students learn vocabulary through word walls and other activities. • Students learn about text factors—genres, story structure, and literary devices.
Limitations	• All students read the same book whether or not they like it and whether or not it's written at their reading level. • Many activities are teacher directed.

Literature focus units include activities incorporating the five stages of the reading process:

Prereading. Teachers involve students in activities to build background knowledge and interest them in reading the book, including sharing book boxes, reading related books, showing DVDs, and talking about related topics.

Reading. Students read the featured selection independently, or the teacher reads it aloud or uses **shared reading** if it's too difficult for students to read themselves.

Responding. Students participate in **grand conversations** to talk about the book and write entries in **reading logs** to deepen their understanding.

Exploring. Students post vocabulary on **word walls**, participate in word-study activities, learn comprehension strategies, examine text factors, and research the book's author or related topics.

Applying. Students apply their learning as they create oral, written, visual, and digital projects and share them with their classmates.

Through these activities, teachers guide students as they read and respond to high-quality literature.

Steps in Developing a Unit

Teachers develop a literature focus unit through a series of steps, beginning with choosing the literature and setting goals, then identifying and scheduling activities, and finally deciding how to assess students' learning. Effective teachers don't simply follow directions in literature focus unit planning guides that are available for purchase in school supply stores; rather, they do the planning themselves because they're the ones who are most knowledgeable about their students, the time available for the unit, the strategies and skills they need to teach, and the activities they want students to pursue.

Usually literature focus units featuring a picture book are completed in a week, and units featuring a novel or other longer book are completed in 3 or 4 weeks. Genre and author units often last 3 or 4 weeks. Rarely, if ever, do literature focus units continue for more than a month; when teachers drag out a unit, they risk killing students' interest in that particular book or, worse yet, their interest in literature and reading.

STEP 1: Select the Literature. Teachers select the book for the literature focus unit—a picture-book story, a novel, a nonfiction book, or a book of poetry. They collect multiple copies so students will each have their own copy to read. Many school districts have class sets of selected books available; however, sometimes teachers have to ask administrators to purchase multiple copies or buy books themselves through book clubs.

Teachers select related books for the text set, too, including other versions of the same story, sequels, other books written by the same author, or other books in the same genre. They collect one or two copies of 10, 20, 30, or more books for the text set and add them to the classroom library for the unit; these books are placed on a special shelf or in a crate in the library center. At the beginning of the unit, teachers introduce the books and provide opportunities for students to read them during independent reading time.

Teachers also identify and collect supplemental materials related to the featured selection, including puppets, stuffed animals, and toys; charts and diagrams; book boxes of materials to use in introducing the book; and information about the author and the illustrator. For many picture books, big-book versions are also available that can be used for shared reading. Teachers also locate multimedia resources, including videotapes of the featured selection, DVDs to provide background knowledge on the topic, and websites about the author and the illustrator.

STEP 2: Set Goals. Teachers decide what they want their students to learn during the unit, and they connect the goals they set with the standards that their students are expected to learn.

STEP 3: Develop a Unit Plan. Teachers read or reread the selected book and then think about the focus they'll use for the unit. Sometimes they focus on an element of story structure, the historical setting, wordplay, the author or genre, or a topic related to the book, such as weather or desert life. After determining the focus, they choose activities to use at each of the five stages of the reading process and think about how they'll differentiate instruction so all students can be successful. Teachers often jot notes on a chart divided into sections for each stage; then they use the ideas they've brainstormed as they plan the unit. Generally, not all of the brainstormed activities will be used, but teachers select the most important ones according to their focus and the time available.

STEP 4: Coordinate Grouping Patterns With Activities. Teachers think about how to incorporate whole-class, small-group, partner, and individual activities into their unit plans. It's important that students have opportunities to read and write independently as well as to work with small groups and to come together as a class. If the class will read the book together, then students need opportunities to reread it with a partner or to read related books independently. These grouping patterns should be alternated during various activities in the unit. Teachers often go back to their planning sheet and highlight activities with colored markers according to grouping patterns.

STEP 5: Create a Time Schedule. Teachers create a schedule that provides sufficient time for students to move through the five stages of the reading process and to complete the activities planned for the unit. They also plan minilessons to teach reading and writing strategies and skills identified in their goals and those needed for students to complete the unit activities. Teachers usually have a set time for minilessons in their weekly schedule, but sometimes they arrange their schedules to teach minilessons just before they introduce specific activities or assignments.

STEP 6: Assess Students. Teachers link assessment with instruction using the four-step cycle of *planning, monitoring, evaluating,* and *reflecting.* They begin thinking about assessment as they choose the featured book and plan the unit. Next, they use informal assessment tools to monitor students' progress during the literature focus unit so they can reteach lessons or adapt their instruction so that all students are successful. At the end of the literature focus unit, they evaluate the projects that students create. In the final step, *reflecting,* teachers think about the effectiveness of their teaching, and students self-assess their learning and work habits.

Teachers often distribute unit folders in which students save their work. Keeping all the materials together makes the unit easier for both students and teachers to manage. Teachers also plan ways to document students' learning and assign grades. One type of record keeping is an assignment checklist, which teachers develop with students and distribute at the beginning of the literature focus unit. Students track their progress during the unit and sometimes negotiate to change the checklist as the unit evolves. They put the lists in their unit folders and mark off each item as it's completed. At the end of the unit, students turn in their assignment checklist and other completed work. Although this list doesn't include every activity students were involved in, it identifies those that will be graded.

Units Featuring a Picture Book

In literature focus units featuring picture books, younger children read predictable picture books or books with very little text, such as *Rosie's Walk* (Hutchins, 2005), a humorous story about a hen that walks leisurely around the barnyard, unwittingly leading the silly fox that is following her into one mishap after another; older students read more sophisticated picture books with more elaborate story lines, such as *Train to Somewhere* (Bunting, 2000), a story about an orphan train taking children to adoptive families in the West set in the late 1800s. Teachers use the same six-step approach for developing units featuring a picture book for younger and older students.

Watch as a teacher educator talks about using historical and realistic fiction to build students' background knowledge. How do teachers broaden students' world knowledge during literature focus units?

Units Featuring a Novel

Teachers develop literature focus units using novels, such as *Bunnicula: A Rabbit-Tale of Mystery* (Howe & Howe, 2006), *Sarah, Plain and Tall* (MacLachlan, 2005), and *Number the Stars* (Lowry, 2011). The biggest difference between picture-book stories and novels is their length, and when teachers plan literature focus units featuring a novel, they need to decide how to schedule the reading of the book. Will students read one or two chapters each day? How often will they respond in reading logs or grand conversations? It's important that teachers reread the book to note the length of chapters and identify key points in the book where students will want time to explore and respond to the ideas presented there.

Figure 10–2 presents a 4-week lesson plan for Lois Lowry's *Number the Stars*, a story of friendship and courage set in Nazi-occupied Denmark during World War II. The daily routine during the first 2 weeks is as follows:

Reading. Students and the teacher read two chapters using shared reading.

Responding After Reading. Students participate in a grand conversation about the chapters they've read, write in reading logs, and add important words to the class word wall.

Minilesson. The teacher teaches a minilesson on a reading strategy or presents information about World War II or about the author.

More Reading. Students read related books from the text set independently.

The schedule for the last 2 weeks is different. During the third week, students choose a class project (interviewing people who were alive during World War II) and individual projects. They work in teams on activities related to the book and continue to read other books about the war. During the final week, students finish the class interview project and share their completed individual projects.

Units Featuring a Genre

During a genre unit, students learn about the characteristics of a particular genre, such as folktales, science fiction, or biographies. Students read several books illustrating the genre, participate in a variety of activities to deepen their knowledge about the genre's text factors, and sometimes apply what they've learned through a project. For example, after reading and comparing Cinderella tales from around the world, third graders often create picture books to retell their favorite version, and seventh graders who are studying the Middle Ages often write stories incorporating details that they've learned about the historical period. During a genre unit on biographies, fifth graders choose a person to research, read a biography, do more online research, and then create a

FIGURE 10–2 A Unit Lesson Plan

	Monday	Tuesday	Wednesday	Thursday	Friday
Week 1	Build background on World War II The Resistance movement ML: Reading maps of Nazi-occupied Europe Read aloud <u>The Lily Cupboard</u>	Introduce NTS Begin word wall Read Ch. 1 & 2 Grand conversation Reading log Add to word wall Book talk on text set	Read Ch. 3 & 4 Grand conversation Reading log Word wall ML: Connecting with a character Read text set books	Read Ch. 5 Grand conversation Reading log Word wall ML: Visualizing Nazis in apartment (use drama)	Read Ch. 6 & 7 Grand conversation Reading log Word wall ML: Information about the author and why she wrote the book
Week 2	Read Ch. 8 & 9 Grand conversation Reading log Word wall ML: Compare home front and war front Read text set books	Read Ch. 10 & 11 Grand conversation Reading log Word wall ML: Visualizing the wake (use drama) Read text set books	Read Ch. 12 & 13 Grand conversation Reading log Word wall ML: Compare characters—make Venn diagram Read text set books	Read Ch. 14 & 15 Grand conversation Reading log Word wall ML: Make word maps of key words Read text set books	Finish book Grand conversation Reading log Word wall ML: Theme of book Read text set books
Week 3	Plan class interview project Choose individual projects Work on projects	Activities at Centers: 1. Story map 2. Word sort 3. Plot profile 4. Quilt Work on projects	Activities at Centers Work on projects	Activities at Centers Work on projects	Activities at Centers Work on projects
Week 4	Revise interviews Work on projects	Revise interviews Work on projects	Edit interviews Share projects	Make final copies Share projects	Compile interview book Share projects

multigenre project to share what they've learned; or during a genre unit on poetry, students write poems applying the forms of the poetry they've learned about.

Units Featuring an Author

During an author study, students learn about an author's life and read one or more books he or she has written. Most authors post websites where they share information about themselves, their books, and how they write, and Richard C. Owen Publisher developed two series of fascinating picture-book author autobiographies. As students learn about authors, they develop a concept of author; this awareness is important so that students will think of them as real people who eat breakfast, ride bikes, and take out the garbage, just as they do. When students think of authors as real people, they view reading in a more personal way. This awareness also carries over to their writing: Students gain a new perspective as they realize that they, too, can write books. They learn about the writing process and the writer's craft that authors use, too.

In first grade, for example, many children read Eric Carle's books and experiment with his illustration techniques, and in the vignette at the beginning of the chapter, Mr. Singh's students participated in a yearlong author study on Chris Van Allsburg. They read his fantasy picture books, hunted for the picture of the white dog in every book, and wrote their own fantasy stories based on *The Mysteries of Harris Burdick* (Van Allsburg, 1996). Figure 10–3 presents a list of recommended writers for author studies; the list is divided into primary, middle, and upper grade levels, but many authors are appropriate for students at more than one level. Jerry Spinelli, for instance, writes books that appeal to both middle and upper grade students.

FIGURE 10–3 Recommended Writers for Author Studies

PRIMARY GRADES	MIDDLE GRADES	UPPER GRADES
Caroline Arnold	Eve Bunting	Avi
Jan Brett	Joanna Cole	Sharon Creech
Ashley Bryan	Gail Gibbons	Christopher Paul Curtis
Eric Carle	Nikki Giovanni	Paul Fleischman
Doreen Cronin	Eric Kimmel	Karen Hesse
Tomie dePaola	Patricia MacLachlan	Lois Lowry
Arthur Dorros	Phyllis Reynolds Naylor	Walter Dean Myers
Lois Ehlert	Patricia Polacco	Linda Sue Park
Denise Fleming	Pam Muñoz Ryan	Gary Paulsen
Kevin Henkes	Jon Scieszka	J. K. Rowling
Steven Kellogg	Jerry Spinelli	Louis Sachar
Patricia McKissack	Janet Stevens	Gary Soto
Rosemary Wells	Chris Van Allsburg	Suzanne Fisher Staples
Mo Willems	Carole Boston Weatherford	Jacqueline Woodson
Audrey Wood	David Wiesner	Laurence Yep

Managing Literature Focus Units

Literature focus units are somewhat teacher directed, and teachers play several important roles. They share their love of literature and direct students' attention to comprehension strategies and text factors. They model the strategies that capable readers use and guide students to read more strategically. Teachers also scaffold students, providing support and guidance so that they can be successful. Through this instruction and support, students learn about reading and literature, and they apply what they've learned as they participate in literature circles and reading workshop, two other student-centered approaches.

 MONITOR: Check Your Understanding 10.3

Orchestrating Literature Circles

One of the best ways to nurture students' love of reading and ensure that they become lifelong readers is through literature circles—small, student-led book discussion groups that meet regularly in the classroom (Daniels, 2001). Sometimes literature circles are called *book clubs*. The reading materials are quality books of children's literature, including stories, poems, biographies, and other nonfiction books, and what matters most is that students are reading something that interests them and is manageable. Students choose the books to read and form temporary groups. Next, they set a reading and discussion schedule. Then they read independently or with partners and come together to talk about their reading in discussions that are like grand conversations. Sometimes the teacher meets with the group, but at other times, the group meets independently. Depending on the length of the book and the age of the students, a literature circle on one book may last from several days to a week or two.

Key Features of Literature Circles

The key features of literature circles are *choice*, *literature*, and *response*. As teachers organize for literature circles, they make decisions about these features: They structure the program so that students can make choices about what to read, and they develop a plan for response so that students can think deeply about books they're reading and respond to them.

CHOICE. Students make many choices in literature circles. They choose the books they'll read and the groups they participate in. They share in setting the schedule for reading and discussing the book, and the roles they assume in the discussions. They also decide how they'll share the book with classmates. Teachers structure literature circles so that students have these opportunities, but even more importantly, they prepare students for making choices by creating a community of learners in their classrooms in which students assume responsibility for their learning and can work collaboratively with classmates.

LITERATURE. The books chosen for literature circles should be interesting and at students' reading level. They must seem manageable to the students, especially during their first literature circles. Samway and Whang (1996) recommend choosing shorter books or picture books at first so that students don't become bogged down. It's also important that teachers have read and liked the books because otherwise they won't be able to do convincing **book talks** when they introduce them. In addition, they won't be able to contribute to the book discussions.

Students typically read stories during literature circles, but they can also read nonfiction books or nonfiction books paired with stories (Heller, 2006; Stien & Beed, 2004).

Students read nonfiction books related to thematic units or biographies during a genre unit. Second graders often choose books from the Magic Tree House series of easy-to-read chapter books that features pairs of fiction and nonfiction books, including *Hour of the Olympics* (Osborne, 1998) and *Olympics of Ancient Greece* (Osborne & Boyce, 2004), or the popular Magic School Bus picture-book series, including *The Magic School Bus Explores the Senses* (Cole, 1999).

RESPONSE. Students meet several times during a literature circle to discuss the book. Through these discussions, students summarize their reading, make connections, learn vocabulary, and explore the author's use of text factors. They learn that comprehension develops in layers. From an initial comprehension gained through reading, students deepen their understanding through the discussions. They learn to return to the text to reread sentences and paragraphs in order to clarify a point or state an opinion. Gilles (1998) examined students' talk during literature circle discussions and identified four types of talk, which are presented in Figure 10–4.

Karen Smith (1998) describes the discussions her upper grade students have as "intensive study," often involving several group meetings. At the first session, students share personal responses, talking about the characters and events of the story, sharing favorite parts, and asking questions to clarify confusions. At the end of the first session, students and the teacher decide what they want to study at the next session, such as an element of story structure. Students prepare for the second discussion by rereading excerpts from the book related to the chosen focus. Then, during the second session, they talk about how the author used that element of story structure, and they often make charts and diagrams, such as **open-mind portraits**, to organize their thoughts.

Students need many opportunities to respond to literature before they'll be successful in literature circles. One of the best ways to prepare students is by reading aloud to them and involving them in grand conversations. Teachers demonstrate ways to respond that are reflective and thoughtful, encourage students to respond to the books, and reinforce

FIGURE 10–4 Types of Talk During Literature Circle Discussions

Talk About the Book

Students summarize their reading and talk about the book by applying what they've learned about text factors as they do the following:

- Retell events or big ideas
- Examine the theme or genre
- Explore the organizational elements or patterns the author used
- Find examples of literary devices

Talk About Connections

Students make connections between the book and their own lives, the world, and other literature they've read in these ways:

- Explain connections to their lives
- Compare this book to another book
- Make connections to a film or television show they've viewed

Talk About the Reading Process

Students think metacognitively and reflect on the strategies they used to read the book as they do the following:

- Reflect on how they used strategies
- Explain their reading problems and how they solved them
- Identify sections that they reread and why they reread them
- Talk about their thinking as they were reading
- Identify parts they understood or misunderstood

Talk About Group Process and Social Issues

Students use talk to organize the literature circle and maintain the discussion. They also examine social issues and current events related to the book, such as homelessness and divorce, as they do the following:

- Decide who will be group leader
- Determine the schedule, roles, and responsibilities
- Draw in nonparticipating students
- Bring the conversation back to the topic
- Extend the discussion to social issues and current events

FIGURE 10–5   Roles Students Play in Literature Circles

ROLE	RESPONSIBILITIES
Discussion Director	The discussion director guides the group's discussion and keeps the group on task. To get the discussion started or to redirect it, the student may ask: • What did the reading make you think of? • What questions do you have about the reading? • What do you predict will happen next?
Passage Master	The passage master focuses on the literary merits of the book. This student chooses several memorable passages to share with the group and tells why each one was chosen.
Word Wizard	The word wizard is responsible for vocabulary. This student identifies four to six important, unfamiliar words from the reading and looks them up in the dictionary. He or she selects the most appropriate meaning and other interesting information about the word to share with the group.
Connector	The connector points out links between the book and students' lives. These connections might include happenings at school or in the community, current events or historical events from around the world, or something from the connector's own life. Or the connector can make comparisons with other books by the same author or on the same topic.
Summarizer	The summarizer prepares a brief summary of the reading to convey the big ideas to share with the group. This student often begins the discussion by reading the summary aloud to the group.
Illustrator	The illustrator draws a picture or diagram related to the reading. The illustration might relate to a character, an exciting event, or a prediction. The student shares the illustration with the group, and the group talks about it before the illustrator explains it.
Investigator	The investigator locates some information about the book, the author, or a related topic to share with the group. This student may search the Internet, check an encyclopedia or library book, or interview a person with special expertise on the topic.

Based on Daniels, H. (2001). Literature circles: Voice and choice in book clubs and reading groups; Daniels, H., & Bizar, M. (1998). *Methods that matter: Six structures for best practice classrooms.*

students' comments when they share their thoughts and feelings and talk about their use of comprehension strategies as they listened to the teacher reading aloud.

Many teachers have students assume roles and complete assignments in preparation for discussion group meetings (Daniels, 2001). One student is the discussion director, and he or she assumes the leadership role and directs the discussion. This student chooses topics and formulates questions to guide the discussion. Other students prepare by selecting a passage to read aloud, drawing a picture or making a graphic related to the book, or investigating a topic connected to the book. The roles are detailed in Figure 10–5. Although having students assume specific roles may seem artificial, it teaches them about the ways they can respond in literature circles.

Teachers often prepare assignment sheets for each of the roles their students assume during a literature circle and then pass out copies before students begin reading;

FIGURE 10–6 A Literature Circle Role Sheet

Word Wizard

Name *Ray*   Date *Dec. 7*   Book *Holes*

You are the Word Wizard in this literature circle. Your job is to look for important words in the book and learn about them. Complete this chart before your literature circle meets.

Word and Page Number	Meanings	Etymology
callused p. 80 "his callused hands"	✓ to toughen ✓ to make hard ? unsympathetic	Latin 1565
penetrating p. 82 "a penetrating stare"	? to enter ✓ sharp or piercing	Latin 1520
condemned p. 88 "a condemned man"	✓ found guilty	Latin 1300
writhed p. 91 "his body writhed with pain"	✓ to twist the body in pain	English 900

students complete one of the assignment sheets before each discussion. Figure 10–6 shows a "word wizard" assignment sheet that an eighth grader completed as he read *Holes* (Sachar, 2008), the story of a boy named Stanley Yelnats, who is sent to a hellish correctional camp where he finds a real friend, a treasure, and a new sense of himself. As word wizard, this student chose important words from the story to study. In the first column on the assignment sheet, he wrote the words and the pages on which they were found. Next, he checked the dictionary for each word's meaning, and in the second column listed several meanings when possible and placed checkmarks next to the appropriate ones for how a word was used in the book. The student also checked the etymology of the word in the dictionary, and in the third column, he listed the language the word came from and when it entered English.

During the discussion about the second section of *Holes*, the word *callused* became important. The "word wizard" explained that *callused* means "toughened" and "hardened," and that in the story, Stanley's and the other boys' hands became callused from digging holes. He continued to say that the third meaning, "unsympathetic," didn't make sense. This comment provided an opportunity for the teacher to explain how *callused* could mean "unsympathetic," and students decided to make a chart to categorize characters in the story who had callused hands and those who were unsympathetic. The group concluded that the boys with callused hands were sympathetic to each other, but the adults at the correctional camp who didn't have callused hands were often unsympathetic and had callused hearts. Talking about the meaning of a single word—*callused*—led to a new way of looking at the characters in the story.

Literature circles are an effective instructional approach because of the three key features—*choice*, *literature*, and *response*. As students read and discuss books with classmates, they often become more engaged and motivated than in more teacher-directed

Watch as fifth grade English learners listen to their teacher explain the roles they'll engage in as they read *Winn Dixie* together. What does the teacher do to ensure that students will be successful?

approaches. For more information, check the Overview of the Instructional Approach: Literature Circles.

Implementing Literature Circles

For literature circles to be successful, classrooms need to become communities of learners. Before teachers begin to implement literature circles, they need to ensure that students can work collaboratively with classmates, in particular that they've learned to be responsible for their own learning and are supportive to group members. Then teachers organize literature circles using a seven-step series of activities.

STEP 1: Select Books. Teachers prepare text sets with five to seven related titles and collect six or seven copies of each book. They give a brief book talk to introduce the books, and then students sign up for the one they want to read. Students need time to preview the books, and then they decide what to read after considering the topic and the difficulty level. Once in a while, students don't get to read their first choice, but they can always read it another time, perhaps during another literature circle or during reading workshop.

STEP 2: Form Literature Circles. Students get together to read each book; usually no more than six students participate in a group. They begin by setting a schedule for reading and discussing the book within the time limits set by the teacher. Students also choose discussion roles so that they can prepare for the discussion after reading.

OVERVIEW OF THE INSTRUCTIONAL APPROACH

Literature Circles

TOPIC	DESCRIPTION
Purpose	To provide students with opportunities for authentic reading and literary analysis.
Components	Students form literature circles to read and discuss books that they choose themselves. They often assume roles for the book discussion.
Theory Base	Student-centered. Literature circles reflect sociolinguistic, transactional, and critical literacy theories because students work in small, supportive groups to read and discuss books, and the books they read often involve cultural and social issues that require students to think critically.
Applications	Teachers often use literature circles in conjunction with a basal reading program or with literature focus units so students have opportunities to do independent reading and literary analysis.
Strengths	• Books are available at a variety of reading levels. • Students are more strongly motivated because they choose the books they read. • Students have opportunities to work with their classmates. • Students participate in authentic literacy experiences. • Students learn how to respond to literature. • Teachers may participate in discussions to help students clarify misunderstandings and think more critically about the book.
Limitations	• Teachers often feel a loss of control because students are reading different books. • Students must learn to be task oriented and to use time wisely to be successful. • Sometimes students choose books that are too difficult or too easy for them.

STEP 3: Read the Book. Students read all or part of the book independently or with a partner, depending on the book's difficulty level. Afterward, they prepare for the discussion by doing the assignment for the role they assumed.

STEP 4: Participate in a Discussion. Students meet to talk about the book; these grand conversations usually last about 30 minutes. The discussion director or another student who has been chosen as the leader begins the discussion, and then classmates continue as in any other grand conversation, taking turns sharing their responses according to the roles they assumed. The talk is meaningful because students talk about what interests them or confuses them in the book.

STEP 5: Teach Minilessons. Teachers teach **minilessons** before or after group meetings on a variety of topics, including asking insightful questions, completing role sheets, using comprehension strategies, and examining text factors (Daniels & Steineke, 2004). They address the procedures that students use in small-group discussions as well as literary concepts and strategies and skills.

STEP 6: Share With the Class. Students in each literature circle share the book they've read with their classmates through a book talk or another presentation.

STEP 7: Assess Learning. Teachers monitor students' progress in the literature circle, checking that they're responsible group members, engaged in the book they're reading, actively participating in the group, and developing their comprehension. At the end of the literature circle, students write self-reflections to assess their participation in the group and their learning.

Using Literature Circles With Young Children

First and second graders can meet in small groups to read and discuss books, just as older, more experienced readers do (Frank, Dixon, & Brandts, 2001; Marriott, 2002; Martinez-Roldan & Lopez-Robertson, 1999/2000). These young children choose books at their reading levels, listen to the teacher read a book aloud, or participate in a **shared reading** activity. Children probably benefit from listening to a book read aloud two times or reading it several times before participating in the discussion. In preparation for the literature circle, children often draw and write **reading log** entries to share with the group. Or, they can write a letter to their group telling about the book. The literature circle often begins with one child sharing a reading log entry or letter with the small group.

Groups meet with the teacher to talk about a book. The teacher guides the discussion at first and models how to share ideas and to participate in a discussion. The talk is meaningful because children share what interests them in the book, make text-to-self, text-to-world, and text-to-text connections, point out illustrations and other book features, ask questions, and discuss themes. Young children don't usually assume roles as older students do, but teachers often notice a few of the first and second graders beginning to take on leadership roles. During a literature circle, the other children in the classroom are usually reading books or writing in reading logs in preparation for their upcoming literature circle meeting with the teacher.

Applying the Reading Process

As students participate in literature circles, they're involved in activities representing all five stages of the reading process:

> **Prereading.** Teachers give book talks, and then students choose books to read, form groups, and get ready to read by making schedules and choosing roles.

Reading. Students read the book independently or with a partner, and prepare for the group meeting.

Responding. Students talk about the book and take responsibility to come to the discussion prepared to participate actively.

Exploring. Teachers teach minilessons during which students rehearse literature circle procedures, learn comprehension strategies, and examine text factors.

Applying. Students give brief presentations to the class about the books they've read.

As students make choices and move through the reading process, they assume increasingly more responsibility for their own learning.

Managing Literature Circles

When teachers introduce literature circles, they teach students how to participate in small-group discussions and respond to literature. At first, many teachers participate in discussions, but they quickly step back as students become comfortable with the procedures and get engaged in the discussions.

Unfortunately, groups don't always work well. Sometimes conversations get off track because of disruptive behavior, or students monopolize the discussion, hurl insults at classmates, or exclude certain students. Clarke and Holwadel (2007) describe an inner-city sixth grade classroom where literature circles deteriorated because of race, gender, and class tensions. They identified students' negative feelings toward classmates and their limited conversation skills as two problems they could address, and they improved the quality of literature circles in this classroom through these activities:

Minilessons. The teachers taught minilessons to develop more positive relationships among group members and build more effective discussion skills, including learning how to listen to each other and take turns when talking (Daniels & Steineke, 2004).

Videotapes. The teachers videotaped students participating in a literature circle and viewed it with group members to make them more aware of how their behavior affected their discussions. They talked about how the discussions went, identified problems, and brainstormed ways to solve them.

Books. The teachers reconsidered the books they'd chosen and looked for books that might relate better to students' lives and inspire more powerful discussions. These books were especially effective in this classroom: *Sang Spell* (Naylor, 1998), *Hush* (Woodson, 2002), *Slave Dancer* (Fox, 2001), and *Stargirl* (Spinelli, 2004).

Coaching. The teachers became coaches to guide students in becoming more effective participants. They modeled positive group behavior and appropriate discussion skills and demonstrated how to use their responses to deepen their understanding of a book. At times, they assumed the teacher role to ensure that everyone participated and to keep the discussion on track.

Even though some problems persisted, Clarke and Holwadel improved the quality of their students' literature circles. The classroom environment became more respectful, and students' improved conversation skills transferred to other discussions. And, once students became more successful, their interest in reading increased, too.

MONITOR: Check Your Understanding 10.4

Implementing Reading and Writing Workshop

Students are involved in authentic reading and writing projects during reading and writing workshop. This approach involves three key characteristics: *time, choice,* and *response*. First, students have large chunks of time and the opportunity to read and write. Instead of being add-ons for after students finish assignments, reading and writing become the core of the literacy curriculum.

Second, students assume ownership of their learning through self-selection of books they read and their topics for writing. Instead of reading books that the teacher has selected or reading the same book together as a group or class, students choose the books they want to read, books that are suitable to their interests and reading levels. Usually students choose whatever book they want to read—a story, a collection of poems, or a nonfiction book—but sometimes teachers set parameters. For example, during a genre unit on science fiction, teachers ask students to select a science fiction story to read. During writing workshop, students plan their writing projects: They choose topics related to hobbies, content area units, and other interests, and they also select the genre for their writing. Often they choose to publish their writing as books.

The third characteristic is *response*. Students respond to books they're reading in reading logs that they share during conferences with the teacher. They also do book talks to share books they've finished reading with classmates. Similarly, in writing workshop, students share with classmates rough drafts of books and other compositions they're writing, and they share their completed and published compositions with genuine audiences.

Reading workshop and writing workshop are different types of workshops. Reading workshop fosters real reading of self-selected books. Students read hundreds of books during reading workshop. At the first grade level, students might read or reread three or four books each day, totaling close to a thousand books during the school year, and older students read fewer, longer books. Even so, upper grade teachers report that their students read between 25 and 100 books during the school year.

Similarly, writing workshop fosters real writing (and the use of the writing process) for genuine purposes and for authentic audiences. Each student writes and publishes as many as 50 to 100 short books in the primary grades and 20 to 25 longer books in the middle and upper grades. As they write, students come to see themselves as authors and become interested in learning about the authors of the books they read.

Teachers often use both workshops, or if their schedule doesn't allow, they may alternate the two. Schedules for reading and writing workshop at the first, third, sixth, and eighth grade levels are presented in Figure 10–7. Kindergarten teachers can implement reading and writing workshop in their classrooms, too (Cunningham & Shagoury, 2005); even though they do more of the reading and writing themselves, teachers involve 5-year-olds in authentic literacy experiences and teach them about comprehension strategies and text factors.

Reading and writing workshop can be used as the primary instructional approach in a classroom, or it can be used along with guided reading or another instructional approach to provide authentic opportunities for students to read and write. This approach is student centered because students make many choices and work independently as they read and write. Providing authentic activities and independent work opportunities reflects the constructivist theory, which emphasizes that learners create their own knowledge through exploration and experimentation.

FIGURE 10–7   Schedules for Reading and Writing Workshop

First Grade	
9:00–9:10	The teacher rereads several familiar big books. Then the teacher introduces a new big book and reads it aloud.
9:10–9:30	Children read matching small books independently and reread other familiar books.
9:30–9:40	Children choose one of the books they've read or reread during independent reading and draw and write a quickwrite.
9:40–9:50	Children share the favorite book and the quickwrite.
9:50–10:05	The teacher teaches a reading/writing minilesson.
10:05–10:30	Children write independently on self-selected topics and conference with the teacher.
10:30–10:40	Children share their published books with classmates.
10:40–10:45	The class uses choral reading to enjoy poems and charts hanging in the classroom.
Third Grade	
10:30–11:00	Students read self-selected books and respond to them in reading logs.
11:00–11:15	Students share with classmates books they've finished reading and do informal book talks about them. Students often pass books to classmates who want to read them next.
11:15–11:30	The teacher teaches a reading/writing minilesson.
11:30–11:55	The teacher reads aloud, and then students participate in a grand conversation. —Continued after lunch—
12:45–1:15	Students write books independently.
1:15–1:30	Students share their published books with classmates.
Sixth Grade	
8:20–8:45	The teacher reads aloud a chapter book, and students talk about it in a grand conversation.
8:45–9:30	Students write independently and conference with the teacher.
9:30–9:40	The teacher teaches a reading/writing minilesson.
9:40–10:25	Students read self-selected books independently.
10:25–10:40	Students share published writings and give book talks about books they've read.
Eighth Grade	
During alternating months, students participate in reading or writing workshop.	
1:00–1:45	Students read or write independently.
1:45–2:05	The teacher presents a minilesson on a reading or writing procedure, concept, strategy, or skill.
2:05–2:15	Students share the books they've read or compositions they've published.

Reading Workshop

Nancie Atwell introduced reading workshop in 1987 as an alternative to traditional reading instruction. In reading workshop, students read books that they choose themselves and respond to books through writing in reading logs and conferencing with teachers and classmates (Atwell, 1998). This approach represented a dramatic change in what teachers believe about how children learn and how literature should be used in the classroom. Traditional reading programs emphasized dependence on a teacher's guide to determine how and when particular strategies and skills should be taught; in contrast, reading workshop is an individualized reading program. Atwell developed reading workshop with her middle school students, but it's been adapted and used successfully at every grade level, first through eighth. There are several versions of reading workshop, but they usually contain five components: *reading, responding, sharing, teaching minilessons,* and *reading aloud to students.*

READING. Students spend 30 to 60 minutes independently reading books. They choose the books they read, often using recommendations from classmates. They also choose books on favorite topics—horses, science fiction, and dinosaurs, for example— or written by favorite authors, such as Audrey Wood, Chris Van Allsburg, and Louis Sachar. It's crucial that students be able to read the books they choose. Ohlhausen and Jepsen (1992) developed a strategy for choosing books called the "Goldilocks Strategy." Using "The Three Bears" folktale as their model, these teachers created three categories of books—"Too Easy" books, "Too Hard" books, and "Just Right" books. The books in the "Too Easy" category were those students had read before or could read fluently; "Too Hard" books were unfamiliar and confusing; and books in the "Just Right" category were interesting, with just a few unfamiliar words. The books in each category vary according to students' reading levels. This approach works at any grade level. Figure 10–8 presents a chart about choosing books using the Goldilocks Strategy.

FIGURE 10–8 **The Goldilocks Strategy**

How to Choose the Best Books for YOU

"Too Easy" Books
1. The book is short.
2. The print is big.
3. You have read the book before.
4. You know all the words in the book.
5. The book has a lot of pictures.
6. You are an expert on this topic.

"Just Right" Books
1. The book looks interesting.
2. You can decode most of the words.
3. Your teacher has read this book aloud to you.
4. You have read other books by this author.
5. There's someone to give you help if you need it.
6. You know something about this topic.

"Too Hard" Books
1. The book is long.
2. The print is small.
3. There aren't many pictures in the book.
4. There are a lot of words that you can't decode.
5. There's no one to help you read this book.
6. You don't know much about this topic.

Classroom libraries need to contain hundreds of books, including books written at a range of reading levels, so that every student can find books to read. Primary teachers often worry about finding books that their students can handle independently. Predictable books, leveled books, easy-to-read books, and books that have been read aloud several times are often the most accessible for young children. Teachers introduce students—especially reluctant readers—to the books in the classroom library so that they can more effectively choose books to read. The best way to preview books is using a very brief book talk to interest students in the book: Teachers tell a little about the book, show the cover, and perhaps read the first paragraph or two.

Teachers often read their own books or a book of children's literature during reading workshop; through their example, they model the importance of reading. Teachers also conference with students about the books they're reading while the rest of the class reads. As they conference, they talk briefly and quietly with students about their reading. Students may also read aloud favorite quotes or an interesting passage to the teacher.

RESPONDING. Students usually keep reading logs in which they write their initial responses. Sometimes students dialogue with the teacher about the books they're reading; a journal allows for ongoing written conversation between the teacher and individual students (Atwell, 1998). Responses often demonstrate students' use of reading strategies and offer insights into their thinking about literature; seeing how students think about their use of reading helps teachers guide and monitor their learning.

Teachers play an important role in helping students expand and enrich their responses to literature. They collect students' reading logs periodically to monitor their responses. They write back and forth with students, with the idea that students write more if the teacher responds. However, because responding to students' journals is very time-consuming, teachers should keep their responses brief and not respond to every entry.

Hancock (2007) classified students' written responses to stories they're reading into these three categories: immersion responses, involvement responses, and literary connections. The categories and the various patterns that exemplify each one are summarized in Figure 10–9. In most reading log entries, students write responses that address several patterns as they reflect on the story and explore their understanding.

In the first category, *immersion responses*, students indicate whether the book is making sense to them. They draw inferences about characters, offer predictions, ask questions, or discuss confusions. Here are some responses excerpted from sixth graders' reading logs about *Bunnicula: A Rabbit-Tale of Mystery* (Howe & Howe, 2006):

I predict the Monroes will find out what Chester and Harold are up to.

I don't think a bunny can be a vampire. A bunny couldn't suck the blood out of vegetables.

Now I'm thinking that Bunnicula really is a vampire.

I knew Harold and Chester would take care of Bunnicula. What I didn't know was that the Monroes would come home early.

I wonder why the vegetables are turning white. It can't be Bunnicula but I don't know what's happening.

In the second category, *involvement responses*, students show that they're personally involved with a character, often giving advice or judging a character's actions.

FIGURE 10–9 Response Patterns

CATEGORY	PATTERNS	DESCRIPTIONS
Immersion Responses	**Understanding**	Students write about their understanding of characters and plot. Their responses include personal interpretation as well as summarizing.
	Character Introspection	Students share their insights into the feelings and motives of a character. They often begin their comments with "I think . . ."
	Predicting	Students speculate about what will happen later in the story and confirm predictions they made previously.
	Questioning	Students ask "I wonder why" questions and write about confusions.
Involvement Responses	**Character Identification**	Students show personal identification with a character, sometimes writing "If I were _____, I would . . ." They express empathy, share related experiences from their own lives, and sometimes give advice to the character.
	Character Assessment	Students judge a character's actions and often use evaluative terms, such as *nice* or *dumb*.
	Story Involvement	Students reveal their involvement as they express satisfaction with how the story's developing. They may comment on their desire to continue reading or use terms such as *disgusting, weird,* or *awesome* to react to sensory aspects of the story.
Literary Connections	**Connections**	Students make text-to-self, text-to-world, text-to-text, and text-to-media (TV shows and movies) connections.
	Literary Evaluation	Students evaluate part or all of the book. They may offer "I liked/I didn't like" opinions and praise or condemn an author's style.

Based on Hancock, M. R. (2007). *Language arts: Extending the possibilities.*

They reveal their own involvement in the story as they express satisfaction with how the story is developing. Here are some examples:

I know how Chester and Harold feel. It's like when I got a new baby sister and everyone paid attention to her. I got ignored a lot.

Bunnicula isn't safe in that house! He better run away—NOW.

Awesome!!! The vegetables are white and there are little fang holes in them.

This book is wicked cool. I can't stop reading.

In the third category, *literary connections*, students make connections and evaluate the book. They offer opinions, sometimes saying "I liked . . ." or "I didn't like . . ." and compare the book to others they've read. Here are some examples:

My dog Diesel is a lot like Harold. He gets on my bed with me and he loves to eat snacks, but my mother says you should never feed a dog chocolate.

I love this book! I know it's fantasy and stuff like this couldn't happen but it would be awesome if it could.

This book reminds me of Charlotte's Web because the animals can talk. They have a whole life that the people in the story don't know about. But the books are different because Bunnicula is much funner than Charlotte's Web. It made me laugh and Charlotte's Web made me cry.

When students use only a few types of responses, teachers teach minilessons to model the types they aren't using and ask questions to prompt them to think and respond in new ways.

Some students write minimal responses. It's important that they choose books to read that they find personally interesting and that they feel free to share their thoughts, feelings, and questions with a trusted audience—usually the teacher. Sometimes writing entries on a computer and using email to share them with students in another class or with other interested readers increase students' interest in writing more elaborated responses.

During reading and responding, there's little or no talking because students are engaged in reading and writing independently. Rarely do students interrupt classmates, go to the rest room, or get drinks of water, except in case of emergency, nor do they use reading workshop time to do homework or other schoolwork.

SHARING. For the last 15 minutes of reading workshop, the class gathers together to discuss books they've finished reading. Students talk about a book and why they liked it. Sometimes they read a brief excerpt aloud or formally pass the book to a classmate who wants to read it. Sharing is important because it helps students become a classroom community to value and celebrate each other's accomplishments.

TEACHING MINILESSONS. The teacher also spends 5 to 15 minutes teaching **minilessons** on reading workshop procedures, comprehension strategies, and text factors. Sometimes minilessons are taught to the whole class, and at other times, they're taught to small groups. At the beginning of the school year, teachers teach minilessons to the whole class on choosing books to read and other reading workshop procedures; later in the year, they teach minilessons on drawing inferences and other comprehension strategies and text factors. Teachers teach minilessons on particular authors when they introduce their books to the whole class and on literary genres when they set out collections of books representing a genre in the classroom library.

READING ALOUD TO STUDENTS. Teachers use the **interactive read-aloud** procedure to read picture books and chapter books to the class as part of reading workshop. They choose high-quality literature that students might not be able to read themselves, award-winning books that they believe every student should be exposed to, or books that relate to a thematic unit. After reading, students talk about the book and share the reading experience. This activity is important because students listen to a book read aloud and respond to it together as a community of learners, not as individuals.

Applying the Reading Process

Even though reading workshop is different from other instructional approaches, students work through the same five stages of the reading process:

Prereading. Students choose books at their reading level to read and activate background knowledge as they look at the cover and think about the title.

Reading. Students read the books they've selected independently, at their own pace.

Responding. Students talk about the books they're reading when they conference with the teacher, and they often write responses in reading logs.

Exploring. Teachers teach students about text factors, authors, and comprehension strategies through minilessons.

Applying. Students often give book talks to their classmates about the books they've finished reading.

IS SUSTAINED SILENT READING THE SAME AS READING WORKSHOP? **Sustained Silent Reading** (SSR) is an independent reading time set aside during the school day for students in one class or the entire school to silently read self-selected books. It's used to increase the amount of reading students do and to encourage them to develop the habit of daily reading (Pilgreen, 2000). Reading workshop and SSR are similar. The goal is to provide opportunities for students to read self-selected books independently. Both programs work best in classrooms that are communities of learners. It seems obvious that students need to feel relaxed and comfortable to engage with books and read for pleasure, and a community of learners is a place where students do feel comfortable because they're respected and valued by classmates and the teacher.

There are important differences, however. Reading workshop has five components—reading, responding, sharing, teaching minilessons, and reading aloud to students—but SSR has only one—reading. Reading workshop is recognized as an instructional approach because it includes both independent reading and explicit instruction. In contrast, SSR is a supplemental program without an instructional component.

Literacy Portraits

The second graders in Ms. Janusz's classroom participate in writing workshop every morning. They use the writing process as they craft stories, poems, and informational books, usually on topics they've chosen themselves. Click on the play button for Rakie to watch her participate in writing workshop. Recently, Ms. Janusz taught a minilesson about how to write about a memory, and now Rakie's writing about a memory—a trip she took to Africa with her mom and sister. As you view the clip, try to identify some of the writing workshop activities that are described in this chapter. Since it's not possible to see every activity in one video clip, think about what might be going on during the other activities. Also, watch the video clip again to identify the stages of the writing process that Rakie's using.

Rakie

Writing Workshop

Writing workshop is the best way to implement the writing process (Atwell, 1998; Fletcher & Portalupi, 2001). Students write on topics that they choose themselves and assume ownership of their writing and learning. At the same time, the teacher's role changes from being a provider of knowledge to serving as a facilitator and guide. The classroom becomes a community of writers who write and share their writing, and there's a spirit of pride and acceptance.

Students have writing folders in which they keep all papers related to the writing project they're working on. They also keep writing notebooks in which they jot down images, impressions, dialogue, and experiences that they can build on for writing projects (Calkins, 1994). Students have access to different kinds of paper, some lined and some unlined, as well as writing instruments, including pencils and red and blue pens. They also have access to the classroom library because many times, students' writing grows out of books they've read; for example, they may write a sequel to a book or retell a story from a different viewpoint. Primary grade students often use patterns from books they've read to structure books they're writing.

Writing workshop is a 60- to 90-minute period scheduled each day. During this time, students are involved in three components: *writing*, *sharing*, and *minilessons*. Sometimes teachers add a fourth activity, *reading aloud to students*, when it's not used in conjunction with reading workshop. For more information, check the Overview of the Instructional Approach: Reading and Writing Workshop.

WRITING. Students spend 30 to 45 minutes or longer working independently on writing projects. Just as students in reading workshop choose books and read at their own pace, in writing workshop, they work at their own pace on writing projects they've chosen themselves. Most students move at their own pace through all five stages of the writing process, but young children often use an abbreviated process consisting of prewriting, drafting, and publishing.

OVERVIEW OF THE INSTRUCTIONAL APPROACH

Reading and Writing Workshop

TOPIC	DESCRIPTION
Purpose	To provide students with opportunities for authentic reading and writing activities.
Components	Reading workshop involves reading, responding, sharing, teaching minilessons, and reading aloud to students. Writing workshop consists of writing, sharing, and teaching minilessons.
Theory Base	Student-centered. The workshop approach reflects sociolinguistic and information processing theories because students participate in authentic activities that encourage them to become lifelong readers and writers.
Applications	Teachers often use reading workshop in conjunction with a basal reading program or with literature focus units so students have opportunities to do independent reading. They often add writing workshop to any of the other instructional approaches so students have more sustained opportunities to use the writing process to develop and refine compositions.
Strengths	• Students read books that are appropriate for their reading levels. • Students are more motivated because they choose the books to read that interest them. • Students work through the stages of the writing process. • Activities are student directed, and students work at their own pace. • Teachers have opportunities to work individually with students during conferences.
Limitations	• Teachers often feel a loss of control because students are reading different books and working at different stages of the writing process. • Teachers have the responsibility to teach minilessons on strategies and skills, in both whole-class groups and small groups. • Students must learn to be task oriented and to use time wisely to be successful.

Teachers conference with students as they write. Many teachers prefer moving around the classroom to meet with students rather than having students come to a table to meet with them: Too often, a line forms as students wait, and they lose precious writing time. Some teachers move around the classroom in a regular pattern, meeting with one fifth of the students each day. In this way, they're sure to conference with everyone during the week.

Other teachers spend the first 15 to 20 minutes of writing workshop stopping briefly to check on 10 or more students each day. Many use a zigzag pattern to get to all parts of the classroom each day. These teachers often kneel down beside each student, sit on the edge of the student's seat, or carry their own stool around to each student's desk. During the 1- or 2-minute conferences, teachers ask students what they're writing, listen to them read a paragraph or two, and then ask what they plan to do next. Then these teachers use the remaining time during writing workshop to conference more formally with students who are revising and editing their compositions; during revising conferences, they identify strengths in students' writing, ask questions, and discover possibilities. Some teachers like to read the pieces themselves, and others like to listen to students read their papers aloud. As they interact with students, teachers model the kinds of responses that students are learning to give to each other.

As students meet to share their writing during revising, they continue to develop as a community of writers. They share their rough drafts in **revising groups** composed of four or five students. Sometimes teachers join in, but students normally run the groups themselves. They take turns reading their rough drafts to each other and listen as their classmates offer compliments and suggestions for revision. Students also participate in revising and editing centers that are set up in the classroom. They know how to work at each center and the importance of working with classmates to make their writing better.

After proofreading their drafts with a classmate and then meeting with the teacher for a final editing, students make the final copy of their writings. They often want to print their writing out on the computer so that it looks professional. Many times, students compile their final copies to make books, but sometimes they attach their writing to artwork, make posters, write letters that will be mailed, or perform scripts as skits or puppet shows. Not every piece is necessarily published; sometimes students decide not to continue with a piece of writing, and they file that piece in their writing folders and start something new.

A first grade teacher begins writing workshop by reading aloud a nonfiction book about turkeys and then having her students describe and identify parts of a turkey. What does this teacher then model for students to make the workshop successful?

SHARING. For the last 10 to 15 minutes of writing workshop, the class gathers together to share their new publications. Younger students often sit in a circle or on a rug for sharing time. Students take turns sitting in the special author's chair to read their compositions aloud. After each sharing, classmates clap and offer compliments. They may also make other comments and suggestions, but the focus is on celebrating completed writing projects, not on revising the composition to make it better.

TEACHING MINILESSONS. During this 5- to 30-minute period, teachers provide minilessons on writing workshop procedures, the writer's craft, and writing strategies and skills, such as organizing ideas, proofreading, and using quotation marks with dialogue (Fletcher & Portalupi, 2007). In the middle and upper grades, teachers often display an anonymous piece of writing (perhaps from a student in another class or from a previous year). Students read the writing, and the teacher uses it to teach the lesson, which may focus on giving suggestions for revision, combining sentences, proofreading, or writing a stronger lead sentence. Teachers also select excerpts from books students are reading for minilessons to show how published authors use writing strategies and skills.

Applying the Writing Process

Writing workshop is the best way for students to apply the writing process: Teachers teach students how to complete the activities during each stage, and then students practice what they've learned during writing workshop. Students move through the five stages of the writing process as they plan, draft, revise, edit, and, finally, publish their writing:

Prewriting. Students choose topics and set their own purposes for writing. Then they gather and organize ideas, often drawing pictures, making graphic organizers, or talking out their ideas with classmates.

Drafting. Students work independently to write their rough drafts.

Revising. Students participate in **revising groups** to share their rough drafts and get feedback to help them revise their writing.

Editing. Students work with classmates to proofread and correct mechanical errors in their writing, and they also meet with the teacher for a final editing.

Publishing. Students prepare a final "published" copy of their writing, and sit in the author's chair to read it to classmates.

As students participate in writing workshop, they gain valuable experience using the writing process.

Managing a Workshop Classroom

It takes time to establish a workshop approach because students need to develop new ways of working and learning, and they have to form a community of readers and writers in the classroom (Gillet & Beverly, 2001). For reading workshop, students need to learn how to select books and use other reading workshop procedures. For writing workshop, they need to learn how to use the writing process to develop and refine a piece of writing, how to make books for their compositions, and other writing workshop procedures. Sometimes students complain that they don't know what to write about, but in time, they learn how to brainstorm possible topics and to keep a list of topics in their author's notebooks.

Beginning on the first day of the school year, teachers establish the workshop environment in their classroom. They provide time for students to read and write and teach them how to respond to books and to their classmates' writing. Through their interactions with students, the respect they show to students, and the way they model reading and writing, teachers establish the classroom as a community of learners.

Teachers develop a schedule for reading and writing workshop with time allocated for each component, as was shown in Figure 10–7. In their schedules, teachers allot as much time as possible for students to read and write. After developing the schedule, teachers post it in the classroom and talk with students about the activities and their expectations. They teach the workshop procedures and continue to model them until students become comfortable with the routines. As students gain experience with the workshop approach, their enthusiasm grows and the workshop approach is successful.

Many teachers use a classroom chart, which Nancie Atwell (1998) calls "status of the class," to monitor students' work. At the beginning of reading workshop, students

TEACHER'S NOTE

Most students are making good progress, but several are struggling. Charlie gets stuck during revising and then abandons his drafts. Dina is working very slowly, and Eddie rushes through the process; his writing reflects this. Elsa works quickly, too, but her writing is well developed and polished.

ASSESSMENT *Snapshot*

Writing Workshop Chart

Name	Dates						
	3/16	3/17	3/18	3/19	3/20	3/23	3/24
Antonio	4	5	5	5	5	1	1
Bella	2	2	2 3	2	2	4	5
Charlie	3	3 1	1	2	2 3	3	3
Dina	4 5	5	5	1	1	1	1
Dustin	3	3	4	4	4	5	5 1
Eddie	2 3	2	2 4	5	5	1	1 2
Elizabeth	2	3	3	4	4	4 5	5
Elsa	1 2	3 4	4 5	5	5	1	2

Code: 1 = Prewriting 2 = Drafting 3 = Revising 4 = Editing 5 = Publishing (or the teacher) record the book they're reading or if they're writing in a reading log, waiting to conference with the teacher, or browsing in the classroom library. For writing workshop, students identify the stage of the writing process they're involved in. Check the Assessment Snapshot: Writing Workshop Chart. Teachers can also use the chart to award weekly "effort" grades, to have students indicate their need to conference with the teacher, or to have students announce that they're ready to share the book they've read or publish their writing. Teachers can review students' progress and note which students they need to meet with. When students fill in the chart themselves, they develop responsibility and a stronger desire to accomplish tasks they set for themselves.

Teachers take time during reading and writing workshop to observe students as they work together in small groups. Researchers who have observed in reading and writing workshop classrooms report that some students, even as young as first graders, are excluded from group activities because of gender, ethnicity, or socioeconomic status (Henkin, 1995); the socialization patterns in classrooms seem to reflect society's. Henkin recommends that teachers be alert to the possibility that boys might share books only with other boys or that some students won't find anyone willing to be their editing partner. If teachers see instances of discrimination, they should confront the situation directly and work to foster a classroom environment where students treat each other equitably.

Many teachers fear that when they implement the workshop approach in their classrooms, students' scores on standardized achievement tests will decline, even though teachers have reported either an increase in test scores or no change at all. Swift (1993) reported the results of a yearlong study comparing two groups of her students; one group read basal reader selections, and the other participated in reading workshop. The reading workshop group showed significantly greater improvement, and Swift also reported that students participating in reading workshop showed more positive attitudes toward reading.

 MONITOR: Check Your Understanding 10.5

Review

ORGANIZING FOR INSTRUCTION

Effective teachers organize for instruction using a combination of instructional approaches to ensure that students can read grade-level texts and meet reading and writing standards. They follow the guidelines presented in this chapter, these points in particular:

10.1 Teachers use leveled books to teach reading in guided reading lessons.

10.2 Teachers supplement basal reading programs with authentic reading and writing activities.

10.3 Teachers present literature focus units to teach students about award-winning books.

10.4 Teachers incorporate choice, literature, and response into literature circles.

10.5 Teachers provide opportunities for students to read self-selected books during reading workshop and write on self-selected topics during writing workshop.

✔ EVALUATE & REFLECT

Apply your understanding about the five instructional approaches. The questions ask you to collect and analyze data, and report the results. Your response should meet academic standards and adhere to Standard English conventions.

1. Reread and analyze the Overview features that examine each of the five instructional programs, and then compare one topic, such as purpose or strengths, across the five programs. In your response, explain what you've learned about the instructional programs through your analysis.

2. Observe in a classroom using one or more of the instructional programs described in the chapter. In your response, describe the classroom and the instruction you observed, and draw conclusions about the programs.

3. Participate in a literature circle for a fiction or nonfiction book in your college classroom. Follow the format described in this chapter, and assume roles before beginning to read. Keep a journal of your experiences as you participate in the literature circle. In your response, provide bibliographic information and a summary of the featured book, describe your experiences, and draw conclusions about using literature circles in a K–8 classroom. Include the journal of your experiences.

4. Create a lesson plan for a one-week unit featuring a picture book, similar to the lesson plan shown in Figure 10–2. Choose a book from a district, state, or other list of recommended books, determine the appropriate grade level, and design a literature focus unit that applies all five stages of the reading process. In the response, provide bibliographic information and a summary of the book, identify the grade level for the unit, present a diagram of the unit, and explain how the unit applies the five stages of the reading process.

5. Choose an author from the list in Figure 10–3 to study. Research the author, and examine at least five of his or her books. Then draw conclusions about why this author is recommended for an author unit. In your response, present information about the author and summaries of the books, and explain how the author makes contributions to children's literature.

REFERENCES

Atwell, N. (1998). *In the middle: New understandings about reading and writing with adolescents* (2nd ed.). Upper Montclair, NJ: Boynton/Cook.

Bunting, E. (2000). *Train to somewhere*. New York: Clarion Books.

Calkins, L. M. (1994). *Teaching writing* (Rev. ed.). Portsmouth, NH: Heinemann.

Chall, J. S., Jacobs, V. A., & Baldwin, L. E. (1991). *The reading crisis: Why poor children fall behind*. Cambridge, MA: Harvard University Press.

Clarke, L. W., & Holwadel, J. (2007). "Help! What is wrong with these literature circles and how can we fix them?" *The Reading Teacher, 61*, 20–29.

Cole, J. (1999). *The magic school bus explores the senses*. New York: Scholastic.

Common core state standards for English language arts. (2010). Retrieved from http://www.corestandards.org

Cunningham, A., & Shagoury, R. (2005). *Starting with comprehension: Reading strategies for the youngest learners*. Portland, ME: Stenhouse.

Daniels, H. (2001). *Literature circles: Voice and choice in book clubs and reading groups*. York, ME: Stenhouse.

Daniels, H., & Bizar, M. (1998). *Methods that matter: Six structures for best practice classrooms*. York, ME: Stenhouse.

Daniels, H., & Steineke, N. (2004). *Mini-lessons for literature circles*. Portsmouth, NH: Heinemann.

Fletcher, R., & Portalupi, J. (2001). *Writing workshop: The essential guide*. Portsmouth, NH: Heinemann.

Fletcher, R., & Portalupi, J. (2007). *Craft lessons: Teaching writing K–8* (2nd ed.). York, ME: Stenhouse.

Fountas, I. C., & Pinnell, G. S. (1996). *Guided reading: Good first teaching for all children*. Portsmouth, NH: Heinemann.

Fox, P. (2001). *Slave dancer*. New York: Atheneum.

Frank, C. R., Dixon, C. N., & Brandts, L. R. (2001). Bears, trolls, and pagemasters: Learning about learners in book clubs. *The Reading Teacher, 54*, 448–462.

Gilles, C. (1998). Collaborative literacy strategies: "We don't need a circle to have a group." In K. G. Short & K. M. Pierce (Eds.), *Talking about books: Literature discussion groups in K–8 classrooms* (pp. 55–68). Portsmouth, NH: Heinemann.

Gillet, J. W., & Beverly, L. (2001). *Directing the writing workshop: An elementary teacher's handbook*. New York: Guilford Press.

Hancock, M. R. (2007). *Language arts: Extending the possibilities.* Upper Saddle River, NJ: Merrill/Prentice Hall.

Heller, M. F. (2006). Telling stories and talking facts: First graders' engagement in a nonfiction book club. *The Reading Teacher, 60,* 358–369.

Henkin, R. (1995). Insiders and outsiders in first-grade writing workshops: Gender and equity issues. *Language Arts, 72,* 429–434.

Howe, D., & Howe, J. (2006). *Bunnicula: A rabbit-tale of mystery.* New York: Aladdin Books.

Hutchins, P. (2005). *Rosie's walk.* New York: Aladdin Books.

Lowry, L. (2011). *Number the stars.* New York: Sandpiper.

MacLachlan, P. (2005). *Sarah, plain and tall.* New York: Scholastic.

Marriott, D. (2002). *Comprehension right from the start: How to organize and manage book clubs for young readers.* Portsmouth, NH: Heinemann.

Martinez-Roldan, C. M., & Lopez-Robertson, J. M. (1999/ 2000). Initiating literature circles in a first grade bilingual classroom. *The Reading Teacher, 53,* 270–281.

Naylor, P. R. (1998). *Sang spell.* New York: Atheneum.

Ohlhausen, M. M., & Jepsen, M. (1992). Lessons from Goldilocks: "Somebody's been choosing my books but I can make my own choices now!" *The New Advocate, 5,* 31–46.

Osborne, M. P. (1998). *Hour of the Olympics.* New York: Random House.

Osborne, M. P., & Boyce, N. P. (2004). *Olympics of Ancient Greece.* New York: Random House.

Pilgreen, J. L. (2000). *The SSR handbook: How to organize and manage a sustained silent reading program.* Portsmouth, NH: Boynton/ Cook/Heinemann.

Sachar, L. (2008). *Holes.* New York: Farrar, Straus & Giroux.

Samway, K. D., & Whang, G. (1996). *Literature study circles in a multicultural classroom.* York, ME: Stenhouse.

Smith, K. (1998). Entertaining a text: A reciprocal process. In K. G. Short & K. M. Pierce (Eds.), *Talking about books: Literature discussion groups in K–8 classrooms* (pp. 17–31). Portsmouth, NH: Heinemann.

Spinelli, J. (2004). *Stargirl.* New York: Laurel Leaf.

Stien, D., & Reed, P. L. (2004). Bridging the gap between fiction and nonfiction in the literature circle setting. *The Reading Teacher, 57,* 510–518.

Swift, K. (1993). Try reading workshop in your classroom. *The Reading Teacher, 46,* 366–371.

Van Allsburg, C. (1982). *Jumanji.* Boston: Houghton Mifflin.

Van Allsburg, C. (1983). *The wreck of the Zephyr.* Boston: Houghton Mifflin.

Van Allsburg, C. (1986). *The stranger.* Boston: Houghton Mifflin.

Van Allsburg, C. (1988). *Two bad ants.* Boston: Houghton Mifflin.

Van Allsburg, C. (1990). *Just a dream.* Boston: Houghton Mifflin.

Van Allsburg, C. (1991). *The wretched stone.* Boston: Houghton Mifflin.

Van Allsburg, C. (1993a). *The garden of Abdul Gasazi.* Boston: Houghton Mifflin.

Van Allsburg, C. (1993b). *The sweetest fig.* Boston: Houghton Mifflin.

Van Allsburg, C. (1996). *The mysteries of Harris Burdick.* Boston: Houghton Mifflin.

Van Allsburg, C. (2002). *Zathura.* Boston: Houghton Mifflin.

Van Allsburg, C. (2005). *The polar express.* Boston: Houghton Mifflin.

Van Allsburg, C. (2006). *Probuditi.* Boston: Houghton Mifflin.

Van Allsburg, C. (2011). *The chronicles of Harris Burdick: Fourteen amazing authors tell the tales.* Boston: Houghton Mifflin.

Walsh, K. (2003, Spring). Basal readers: The lost opportunity to build the knowledge that propels comprehension. *American Educator, 27,* 24–27.

Woodson, J. (2002). *Hush.* New York: Scholastic.

Chapter 11

Differentiating for Success

PLAN: Preview the Learning Outcomes

After studying this chapter, you'll be prepared to respond to these points:

11.1 Explain the three ways to differentiate instruction.

11.2 Describe how to work with struggling readers and writers.

Classroom Interventions. The 31 students in Mrs. Lee's sixth grade class are reading *The Bread-winner* (Ellis, 2001), the story of a girl who seeks work disguised as a boy to support her family during the Taliban era in Afghanistan. Before beginning to read, the students participated in a WebQuest activity to learn about Afghan culture and listened to an interview with the author, Deborah Ellis.

Today, some students are lounging on floor pillows in the reading center as they read independently. Others are clustered around Mrs. Lee, listening as she reads aloud; she reads softly to avoid distracting the students reading in the reading center. Some of the students sitting close to Mrs. Lee follow along in their copies, but others look at the teacher, listening intently. She provides two ways to read the novel because her students' reading levels range from third through seventh grade. Students reading at the fifth, sixth, and seventh grade levels can read the book independently, but her 10 students reading at the third and fourth grade levels need extra support; that's why she reads aloud to them.

After she finishes reading each chapter, the class comes together for a **grand conversation**. Because the students have many questions about life under Taliban rule, Mrs. Lee often takes more of the discussion time than she'd like to answer their questions, but gradually the students are developing the background knowledge they need to understand the story. This is the time when Mrs. Lee teaches comprehension, so she asks inferential questions that require students to go beyond literal thinking. For example, she asks, "Why did the Taliban arrest Parvana's father?" Hector quickly answers with what he remembers reading in the novel: "Because he went to college in another country, and they don't want teachers to do that." Mrs. Lee persists, "Why doesn't the Taliban want teachers to study in another country?" No one has an idea, so Mrs. Lee asks the question another way: "Lots of teachers in America go to other countries to study. You know that I went to visit schools in China last summer. Why is that a good idea?" The students offer several reasons—to learn about other people, to learn new things, and to learn new ways of teaching. So Mrs. Lee asks, "Wouldn't the Taliban want teachers to do these things, too?" Marisela replies, "No, the Taliban

In this chapter, you'll learn more about differentiating instruction. Teachers modify the content, the topics they teach; the process, their instructional procedures; and the product, the projects that students create. As you read this vignette, notice how Mrs. Lee adapts instruction to meet the needs of all students in her class. She accomplishes this during both her literacy block and her after-school intervention program that she calls "The Reading Club."

closed the schools because they want to control everyone. They don't like teachers who have new ideas because they could make trouble." "How could they make trouble?" Mrs. Lee continues. Jared suggests, "Parvana's father and the other teachers could tell people that there is a better way to live, and then everyone could get together and fight the Taliban and have a free country like ours."

Literature study is only one part of Mrs. Lee's literacy block; check the figure Mrs. Lee's Schedule. She differentiates instruction during the literacy block to ensure that her students are successful. Mrs. Lee begins the literacy block each morning with Accelerated Reader. All students read independently in leveled books for 30 minutes and complete online comprehension checks after each book. Mrs. Lee supervises as students read, moving from desk to desk and listening to individual students read softly, and she monitors their progress on the comprehension checks. A chart is posted in the classroom so students can track their reading growth.

Next, students participate in a literature study of a novel. Mrs. Lee usually chooses books from the district's sixth grade recommended reading list, and she supplements with timely books such as *The Breadwinner* that she thinks would appeal to her students. The novel becomes a vehicle for teaching reading strategies and literary analysis.

Mrs. Lee teaches **minilessons** on comprehension strategies, literary analysis, and other grade-level standards; sometimes the whole class participates, and at other times, she teaches lessons to specific groups of students. She ties lessons to the novel, and her focus for this book is on how

MRS. LEE'S SCHEDULE

ACTIVITY	GRADE-LEVEL STUDENTS	STRUGGLING STUDENTS
8:30–9:00 Accelerated Reader	Students read books at their reading level and check their comprehension online.	Students read books at their reading level and check their comprehension online.
9:00–10:00 Literature Study	Students read the featured novel independently and participate in grand conversations.	Students listen to the teacher read the featured novel aloud and participate in grand conversations.
10:00–10:15 Minilessons	Mrs. Lee presents whole-class minilessons on grade-level literacy topics.	Mrs. Lee presents whole-class minilessons on grade-level literacy topics and other minilessons for small groups according to need.
10:15–11:15 Activities/ Guided Reading	Students participate in activities related to the featured novel.	Students participate in guided reading groups and work in small groups to do activities related to the featured novel.
11:15–11:45 Word Study	Students participate in whole-class and small-group word-study activities and lessons. They use an individualized approach to spelling.	Students participate in whole-class and small-group word-study activities and lessons. They use an individualized approach to spelling.

authors use elements of story structure to develop theme. Today, she reviews character development with the whole class and explains that authors develop characters in four ways: through appearance, actions, talking, and thinking. She asks students to think about Parvana, the main character, and how Deborah Ellis developed her. As the students share ideas, Mrs. Lee draws a weblike diagram on chart paper and writes Parvana's name in the center circle. She divides the diagram into four sections, writes *appearance*, *actions*, *talking*, and *thinking* in the sections, and adds a sentence or two that students suggest in each section. Mrs. Lee steps back and asks, "Which of the four ways of character development is most important?" The students are torn between "appearance" and "actions." Nita says, "It's her clothes. She has to dress like a boy," but Javier disagrees, "No, it's what she's doing. She's pretending to be a boy to help her family." After more discussion, most students agree with Javier. Check the figure A Character Diagram.

Next week, Mrs. Lee will introduce human rights with this scenario: Imagine that when you wake up tomorrow morning, life is totally different—it's like Parvana's life. What will you do? What won't you be able to do? How will you feel? Students will talk, draw, and write about the ways their lives would change. Mrs. Lee will explain what human rights are and describe the rights guaranteed in the Constitution's Bill of Rights. Afterward, students will play an interactive online game about human rights, and they'll participate in differentiated activities to think more deeply about the human rights they enjoy and those denied to Parvana.

While students are working on activities, Mrs. Lee meets with small groups of struggling readers for guided reading lessons. One group is reading at early third grade level (Level M), the second group is reading at late third grade/early fourth grade level (Level P), and the third group is reading at fourth grade level (Level R). She usually meets with two groups each day for 25 to 30 minutes each, and they read short chapter books at their reading levels; they read and discuss one or two chapters, and then they reread the chapters independently or with a partner before they meet again.

The group at the early third grade level is reading Greenburg's wacky series, The Zack Files, about an amazing fifth grader named Zack. In the book they've just finished reading, *How I Went From Bad to Verse* (Greenburg, 2000), Zack is bitten by an insect and catches Rhyme Disease. He

A CHARACTER DIAGRAM

When she was a girl she kept her face covered and tried to be invisible.
She cut her hair and pretended to be a boy.

Appearance

She dressed as a boy to go to the market and buy food.
She was a reader and writer.
She dug up graves.

Actions

(Parvana)

Talking

"I can do this".

"I am working to get my family back".

Thinking

She dident like the hard work but she did it to help her family.
She was very lonely.

speaks only in rhyme, and worse yet, he floats above the ground and turns blue. Finally, his science teacher, Mrs. Coleman-Levin, cures him and his life returns to normal—at least until the next book. The students silently reread the last two chapters, and they talk again about Zack's weird symptoms and his teacher's unusual cures.

Mrs. Lee draws a chart about symptoms and cures on a whiteboard beside her, and the students list Zack's symptoms (rhyming, floating, and blue skin) on the chart; then they explain how Mrs. Coleman-Levin cured each one. The students check Chapter 8 to be sure that they remember the cures (wearing a reversible jacket, reciting a poem backward, and thinking happy thoughts) and complete the chart.

After conducting another guided reading lesson, Mrs. Lee moves the class to the last segment of the literacy block: word study. Students do a combination of vocabulary and individualized spelling activities. On Monday, Mrs. Lee takes the entire 30 minutes for spelling. She administers the pretest, and students check it themselves. Then they choose the words they'll study during the week and make two copies of their word list, one for themselves and one for Mrs. Lee to keep. Because she's implemented an individualized spelling program, students study different words, depending on their developmental levels. They practice their spelling words each day, and on Friday, they take the final test.

On Tuesday, Wednesday, and Thursday, students participate in vocabulary lessons to study the meanings of specific words, examine root words and affixes, and learn to use a dictionary and a thesaurus. Over the past month, Mrs. Lee has taught lessons on these root words:

ann/enn (year): *annual, anniversary, millennium*
graph (write): *paragraph, autobiography, photograph*
tele (far): *telecast, telephone, telethon*
volv (roll): *revolution, evolution, revolver*

The students have made posters about these root words, and they're displayed around the classroom.

Because Mrs. Lee wants to do more to help her struggling readers, she developed a twice-a-week after-school intervention program that she calls "The Reading Club." She invited the 10 students reading at third and fourth grade levels to stay after school each Tuesday and Thursday to participate in the club. She began the club after parent conferences in early October; she explained to parents the importance of providing students with personalized instruction and additional time for reading. All parents agreed to pick up their children after club meetings and to provide 30 minutes of independent reading time at home 4 days a week.

During the 45-minute reading club meeting, students read self-selected books independently and participate in guided reading groups. Mrs. Lee is pleased to see these students' growth over the past 4 months. She's noticed that her struggling students behave during the reading club the way her grade-level readers do during the school day: Instead of being reticent and unsure of themselves, they participate willingly in discussions and confidently assume leadership roles.

As the club meeting begins, the students pick up the books they've been reading and settle on floor pillows in the reading center. Mrs. Lee checks that everyone has an appropriate book to read and calls a group of four students reading at Level P who are reading Jon Scieszka's The Time Warp Trio series of easy-reading chapter books. Currently, they're reading *Knights of the Kitchen Table* (2004), in which the boys travel back to the days of King Arthur. A giant and a dragon threaten Camelot, and the boys arrive to help the king and his knights. The first few chapters were difficult because the students weren't familiar with the King Arthur tales, but Mrs. Lee told the stories to build their background knowledge. The vocabulary was new, too—*vile knaves, methinks,* and *foul-mouthed enchanters,* for example—but now the group is into the story. They read about the boys reaching Camelot and meeting King Arthur, Queen Guenevere, and Merlin when they read Chapter 5 today in class. They begin by rereading the chapter and doing a read-around, where they take turns randomly reading aloud their favorite sentences from the chapter. Then Mrs. Lee takes them on a text walk of Chapter 6, and they examine a full-page illustration of the giant. Hector predicts, "I think Sir Joe the Magnificent will kill the giant." "You should say he will *slay* him. *Slay* means to kill," Jesus explains. Mrs. Lee asks how the students might slay the giant, and the boys quickly suggest using swords or guns, but the illustrations don't provide any clues.

Mrs. Lee explains that this riddle is going to be important in the chapter: *Why did the giant wear red suspenders?* The students aren't familiar with suspenders, so Mrs. Lee shows them a pair of her husband's. She explains that sometimes her husband wears suspenders instead of a belt to hold his pants up. Marisela, who's been listening quietly while the boys eagerly talked about slaying giants, asks, "So, why did the giant wear suspenders?" The teacher explains that they'll learn the answer as they read the chapter, and then Marisela predicts, "You have to be smart to know the answer to a riddle, so I think those boys will use their brains to save Camelot." Mrs. Lee smiles in agreement and says, "Let's read Chapter 6 to see if Marisela's prediction is right."

The students read the five-page chapter quickly, and Mrs. Lee helps students decode several unfamiliar words and explains a confusing section when two boys ask about it. Now the group knows the answer to the riddle: The giant wore red suspenders to hold his pants up. The students are hooked: They want to read more riddles. Mrs. Lee promises to get some riddle books tomorrow. They continue talking about the chapter, and Jesus sums up the group's feelings by saying, "Bleob [the giant] should be dead and gone by now. I just want to keep reading and find out what happens." Because the giant destroys himself in the next chapter, Mrs. Lee lets them take their books back to the reading center and read the next chapter to find out what happens.

Then Mrs. Lee calls a second group for a guided reading lesson while the other two groups continue reading on their own. The second group finishes reading with Mrs. Lee with only several minutes remaining before the club meeting ends, so she joins the students in the reading center and asks them to briefly tell what they've been reading.

 STANDARDS CHECK!

Mrs. Lee addressed the Common Core State Standards as she taught sixth graders about reading comprehension in the vignette you've just read. Even though differentiation *and* struggling readers and writers *aren't specifically mentioned, review the sixth grade literacy Standards document online at http://www.corestandards.org/ELA-Literacy, and identify the Standards that Mrs. Lee addressed through her instructional activities. Create your list, and compare it with Mrs. Lee's.*

Teachers know that their students vary—in their interests and motivation, their background knowledge and prior experiences, and their culture and language proficiency as well as their reading and writing achievement—so it's important to take these individual differences into account as they plan for instruction. **Differentiated instruction** is based on this understanding that students differ in important ways. According to Tomlinson (2014), differentiated instruction "means 'shaking up' what goes on in the classroom so that students have multiple options for taking in information, making sense of ideas, and expressing what they learn" (p. 1). Differentiating instruction is especially important for struggling readers and writers who haven't been successful and who can't read grade-level textbooks.

In the vignette, for example, Mrs. Lee personalized her instruction to meet her students' needs and provided support for her struggling readers and writers so that they could be successful. First, she provided additional support for struggling students during regular classroom reading and writing activities: During the literature focus unit, Mrs. Lee read aloud to students who couldn't read the featured novel independently. Second, she provided additional instruction for her struggling students: During the activities period, Mrs. Lee taught guided reading lessons for those students. Third, she provided an after-school intervention program: She met with her struggling readers twice a week for The Reading Club and got these students' parents to commit to providing time for independent reading at home.

Ways to Differentiate Instruction

The expectation that all students are to meet the same literacy standards at each grade level implies that all students should receive the same instructional program, but teachers know that some of their students are working at grade level but others are struggling or advanced. Because students' achievement levels differ and their interests and preferred ways of learning vary, teachers modify their instructional programs so that all students can be successful. Tomlinson (2014) explains that in differentiated classrooms, "teachers provide specific ways for students to learn as deeply as possible and as quickly as possible without assuming one student's road map for learning is identical to anyone else's" (p. 4). Heacox (2002) characterizes differentiated instruction as rigorous, relevant, flexible, and complex:

Rigorous means that teachers provide challenging instruction that encourages students' active engagement in learning.

Relevant means that teachers address literacy standards to assure that students learn essential knowledge, strategies, and skills.

Flexible means that teachers use a variety of instructional procedures and grouping techniques to support students.

Complex means that teachers engage students in thinking deeply about books they're reading, compositions they're writing, and concepts they're learning.

It's crucial that teachers recognize the diversity of learners in 21st-century classrooms and understand that students don't need to participate in the same learning activities or read and write in whole-class groups all day long. To assess your effectiveness in modifying instruction to meet the needs of all students, use the Teacher Checklist: How do I differentiate instruction?

Teachers modify instruction in three ways: They modify the *content* that students need to learn, the instructional *process* used to teach students, and the *products* students create to demonstrate their learning (Heacox, 2002; Tomlinson, 2014):

Differentiating the Content. The content is the "what" of teaching, the literacy knowledge, strategies, and skills that students are expected to learn at each grade level. The content reflects Common Core grade-level Standards. Teachers concentrate on teaching the essential content, and to meet students' needs, they provide more instruction and practice for some students and less for others. For those who are already familiar with the content, they increase the complexity of instructional activities. Teachers decide how they'll differentiate the content by assessing students' knowledge before they begin teaching, and then they match students with appropriate activities.

Differentiating the Process. The process is the "how" of teaching, the instruction that teachers provide, the materials they use, and the activities students are involved in to ensure that they're successful. Teachers group

TEACHER *Checklist*

How do I differentiate instruction?

○ Do I maintain a commitment to meeting grade-level standards for all students?

○ Do I use assessment procedures to diagnose students' needs and plan instruction to address those needs?

○ Do I use flexible grouping and have students work individually, in small groups, and as a class?

○ Do I change grouping arrangements to reflect students' achievement levels and interests?

○ Do I teach with collections of books and other reading materials, written at varying difficulty levels?

○ Do I design activities with multiple options to match students' instructional levels?

○ Do I modify instruction to respond to students' specific learning needs and continue to make adjustments during instruction?

○ Do I respect all students and value their work?

○ Do I focus on individual students' academic achievement and success?

students for instruction and choose reading materials at appropriate levels of difficulty. They also make decisions about involving students in activities that allow them to apply what they're learning through oral, written, or visual means.

Differentiating the Product. The product is the result of learning; it demonstrates what students understand and how well they can apply what they've learned. Students usually create projects, such as posters, multimodal reports, board games, puppet shows, and new versions of stories. Teachers often vary the complexity of the projects they ask students to create by changing the level of thinking that's required to complete the project.

Teachers create a classroom culture that promotes acceptance of individual differences and is conducive to matching instruction to individual students. Having a classroom community where students respect their classmates and can work collaboratively is vital. They learn that students don't always do the same activity or read the same book, and they focus on their own work rather than on what their classmates are doing. Students become more responsible for their own learning and develop more confidence in their ability to learn.

Grouping for Instruction

Teachers use three grouping patterns: Sometimes students work together as a whole class, and at other times, they work in small groups or individually. Decisions about

Computer-Based Programs

Scholastic's Reading Counts!, Renaissance Learning's Accelerated Reader, and Learning A-Z's Raz-Kids.com are popular computer-based programs that manage students' daily independent reading practice. They're consistent with differentiated instruction because students choose books to read from a leveled collection and read at their own pace. Afterward, students take computer-generated quizzes to check their comprehension, and the teacher retrieves computer-generated reports to track their progress. More than half of American schools use these programs.

Reading volume is related to achievement, and these programs provide daily opportunities for reading practice (Snow, Burns, & Griffin, 1998; Topping & Paul, 1999). Students who do more reading are better readers than those who do less. The programs are predicated on these principles:

- Students read authentic books at their reading levels.
- The quizzes provide frequent comprehension monitoring.
- Teachers use the test results to intervene with struggling students.
- Students' motivation grows as they read and score well on quizzes.

These principles reflect the balanced approach to reading instruction.

Students take computer-generated quizzes after reading each book. Each quiz has 5 to 20 multiple-choice items, depending on the reading level; the questions focus on literal comprehension. The minimum passing score is 60%, and the optimal score is 85%. Students get the results immediately, so they can learn from their errors and alert the teacher if they're having difficulty. Software provides information about students' comprehension, reading rates, and reading volume to assist teachers in monitoring their progress. The software also generates classroom, school, and district reports.

Researchers have found that students participating in computer-based reading programs score higher on standardized tests than students who don't use the programs; nonetheless, the programs are controversial for several reasons (Holmes & Brown, 2003; Schmidt, 2008). First, quizzes focus on literal comprehension, not higher level thinking, but proponents counter that the purpose is to determine whether students have read a book, not to assess higher level comprehension. Next, detractors argue that students are limited in which books they can read because they can read only books at their reading level, but proponents say that students can read other books at different times. Third, detractors contend that students read books with the goal of passing the quiz, rather than for enjoyment or to learn about interesting topics, but proponents point out that students need to learn to read for varied purposes. Many teachers like the programs because they can effectively manage students' reading and monitor their progress.

which type of grouping to use depend on the teacher's purpose, the complexity of the activity, and students' specific learning needs. Small groups are used flexibly to provide a better instructional match between students and their needs. In differentiated classrooms, students are grouped and regrouped often; they aren't always grouped according to achievement levels or with the same classmates.

Teachers use a combination of the three grouping patterns in each instructional program: Basal reading programs and literature focus units use primarily whole-class groups, literature circles and guided reading are predominantly small-group programs, and reading and writing workshop feature mostly individual literacy activities. Nonetheless, each instructional program incorporates all three grouping patterns. The activities are categorized by program in Figure 11–1.

Teachers use the three types of groups for a variety of activities. Whole-class activities typically include **interactive read-alouds** and **word walls**. Revising groups and **shared reading** are small-group activities. Other activities, including the **Language Experience Approach** and **reading logs**, are often done individually. Some activities, such as **minilessons** and **interactive writing**, are used with more than one type of group. In addition, when teachers introduce an activity, students work together as a class to learn the steps involved; then, once they understand the procedure, they work in small groups or individually.

GUIDED READING. Guided reading was developed to use with beginning readers, but teachers also use it with older students, especially English learners and struggling

Watch as a third grade teacher differentiates instruction for a lesson on inferencing. How does she modify her instruction for this small group of English learners?

Check the Compendium of Instructional Procedures, which follows Chapter 12.

FIGURE 11–1   Grouping Patterns

PROGRAM	WHOLE CLASS	SMALL GROUPS	INDIVIDUALS
Basal Readers	Introduce the book. Teach vocabulary. Teach strategies and skills. Read the featured selection.	Reread the selection. Practice vocabulary and skills. Work at centers.	Complete workbook assignments. Read related books.
Literature Focus Units	Read a featured book. Participate in grand conversations. Teach minilessons. Do word-study activities. Learn about author and genre. Create projects.	Read a featured book. Participate in grand conversations. Teach minilessons. Do word-study activities. Learn about author and genre. Create projects.	Read a featured book. Respond in reading logs. Read related books. Create projects.
Literature Circles	Introduce books.	Read and discuss a book together.	Choose a book to read. Assume roles to examine the book. Contribute to group discussions.
Reading Workshop	Read aloud to students. Teach minilessons. Share books.	Teach minilessons.	Read self-selected books. Conference with the teacher.
Writing Workshop	Read aloud to students. Teach minilessons. Share writing from the author's chair.	Teach minilessons. Participate in revising groups. Edit with a partner.	Write on self-selected topics. Conference with the teacher.

readers who need more teacher support to decode and comprehend books they're reading, learn reading strategies, and become independent readers. Sometimes guided reading is confused with round-robin reading and literature circles, but these three small-group instructional activities are different. In round-robin reading, an approach that's no longer recommended, students take turns reading aloud to the group rather than doing their own reading. In literature circles, students read books on their own with very limited teacher guidance.

TEXT SETS. Teachers create **text sets** of books and digital reading materials for students to read during literature focus units and thematic units. These collections include reading materials representing several genres, bookmarked digital resources, and books that vary in difficulty level. If teachers can't locate a wide enough range of reading materials, they can create them with students to add to the text set. Booklist: Text Set for *The Breadwinner* presents Mrs. Lee's text set of books and digital articles and WebQuests related to *The Breadwinner* (Ellis, 2001), Afghanistan, Muslim religious holidays, and Arab immigrants. The list includes all three books in Deborah Ellis's trilogy of stories about Parvana, and it features two books of poetry by Naomi Shihab Nye (2002a, 2002b), an esteemed Arab American poet and anthologist. Teachers use **book talks** to introduce books at the beginning of the unit and then display the books on a special shelf in the classroom library. They often read some of the books aloud to the class, have students read others in literature circles, and encourage students to read additional books during reading workshop.

Text sets are only a small part of well-stocked classroom libraries. Teachers set out collections of stories, nonfiction books, magazines, and books of poetry, written at a range of levels for students to read independently. They also make available lots of other books that are interesting, familiar, and easy enough for reluctant and struggling students to read and reread on their own, including books they read the previous year.

Tiered Activities

To match students' needs, teachers create several tiered or related activities that focus on the same essential knowledge but vary in complexity (Robb, 2008). These activities are alternative ways of reaching the same goal because "one-size-fits-all" activities can't benefit on-grade-level students, support struggling readers, and challenge advanced students. Creating tiered lessons, according to Tomlinson (2014), increases the likelihood that all students will be successful. Even though the activities are different, they should be interesting and engaging and require the same amount of effort from students.

Teachers vary activities in several ways. First, they vary them by complexity of thinking. In recall-level activities, students identify, retell, or summarize; in analysis-level activities, they compare and categorize; and in synthesis-level activities, students evaluate, draw conclusions, and invent. Second, teachers vary activities according to the level of reading materials. They use books and other print and online materials written at students' reading level, or they vary the way they share the materials with students. Third, teachers vary activities by the form of expression. Students are involved in visual, oral, and written expression as they complete an activity: Examples of visual expression are charts, posters, and dioramas; examples of oral expression are dramatizations, oral reports, and choral readings; and examples of written expression are stories, poems, and reports. Some activities require a combination of forms of expression; for example, students might write a poem from the viewpoint of a book character (written) and dress up as the character (visual) to read the poem aloud to the

Booklist

Text Set For *The Breadwinner*

GENRE	TEXTS
Stories	Bunting, E. (2006). *One green apple*. New York: Clarion Books.
	Ellis, D. (2001). *The breadwinner*. Toronto, ON: Groundwood Books.
	Ellis, D. (2003). *Parvana's journey*. Toronto, ON: Groundwood Books.
	Ellis, D. (2004). *Mud city*. Toronto, ON: Groundwood Books.
	Khan, R. (2004). *The roses in my carpets*. Markham, ON: Fitzhenry & Whiteside.
	Oppenheim, S. L. (1997). *The hundredth name*. Honesdale, PA: Boyds Mills Press.
	Williams, K. L., & Mohammed, K. (2007). *Four feet, two sandals*. New York: Eerdmans.
Autobiographies	Yousafzai, M. (2014). *I am Malala: How one girl stood up for education and changed the world*. Boston: Little, Brown.
Nonfiction Books	Banting, E. (2003). *Afghanistan: The culture*. Minneapolis, MN: Crabtree.
	Banting, E. (2003). *Afghanistan: The land*. Minneapolis, MN: Crabtree.
	Banting, E. (2003). *Afghanistan: The people*. Minneapolis, MN: Crabtree.
	Ellis, D. (2012). *Kids of Kabul: Living bravely through a never-ending war*. Toronto, ON: Groundwood Books.
	Ellis, D. (2012). *Parvana*. Toronto, ON: Groundwood Books.
	Haskins, J., & Benson, K. (2006). *Count your way through Afghanistan*. Minneapolis, MN: Millbrook Press.
	Mobin-Uddin, A. (2007). *The best Eid ever*. Honesdale, PA: Boyds Mills Press.
	Whitfield, S. (2008). *National Geographic countries of the world: Afghanistan*. Washington, DC: National Geographic Children's Books.
	Winter, J. (2009). *Nasreen's secret school: A true story from Afghanistan*. New York: Beach Lane Books.
	Wolf, B. (2003). *Coming to America: A Muslim family's story*. New York: Lee & Low.
	Zucker, J. (2004). *Fasting and dates: A Ramadan and Eid-ul-Fitr story*. New York: Barron's.
Poetry	Nye, N. S. (Compiler). (2002). *The flag of childhood: Poems from the Middle East*. New York: Aladdin Books.
	Nye, N. S. (2002). *19 varieties of gazelle: Poems of the Middle East*. New York: Greenwillow.
Websites and WebQuests	Time for Kids Around the World report "Afghanistan"
	Scholastic Special Report "Kids in Afghanistan"
	National Geographic Kids article "Afghanistan"
	Create WebQuest on *The Breadwinner*
	Create WebQuest on Afghanistan
	Literacy Net's Webquest on Afghanistan
	Literacy Net's WebQuest on *The Breadwinner*
	Quest Garden's WebQuest on *The Breadwinner*

class (oral). Creating tiered activities doesn't mean that some students do more work and others do less; each activity must be equally interesting and challenging to the students.

Tomlinson (2014) recommends that teachers begin by designing an interesting activity that focuses on elemental knowledge and requires high-level thinking. Next, they visualize a ladder where the top rung represents advanced students, the middle rung on-grade-level students, and the bottom rung struggling students, and then they decide where the activity they've created fits on the ladder. The third step is to create other versions of the activity. Teachers create one, two, or three versions of the activity at different levels of difficulty to meet the needs of their students. Versions can vary according to the difficulty level of reading materials they use, thinking levels, or forms of expression. Finally, teachers decide which students will do each version of the activity. It's important to make tiering invisible. Heacox (2002) recommends that teachers alternate the order in which they introduce activities to students, show similar enthusiasm for each one, and use neutral ways of identifying groups of students who will pursue each activity.

One of the Common Core State Standards that Mrs. Lee addressed as her sixth graders read and responded to *The Breadwinner* (Ellis, 2001) was to analyze the theme conveyed through the characters and the plot. She decided to explore the theme of human rights and, in particular, what happens when they're denied. She began by talking about human rights during a close-reading activity as the class discussed the book, and students looked for examples of human rights that the Taliban denied to Parvana and her family. Later, students worked in small groups to create lists of human rights, including religious freedom, the right to safe food and drinking water, the right to speak your mind, the right to education, freedom to work and earn a living, civil rights, and equal rights for all people. They played the interactive game "Save the Bill of Rights" at the National Constitution Center's website to learn more about the rights that Americans are guaranteed.

Once students understood what human rights are and could find examples of these rights and freedoms being denied in *The Breadwinner*, Mrs. Lee designed this activity:

> Information, please! Create a Venn diagram on chart paper to compare the human rights we have in America to those Parvana and her family had in Taliban-controlled Afghanistan. Then create a statement to summarize the information presented in the Venn diagram and write it underneath the diagram.

Mrs. Lee decided that this graphic activity was appropriate for her on-grade-level students. She developed this version for her struggling students:

> A celebration of human rights! Choose the human right that you value most and create a quilt square using color, images, and words to describe it. Then we'll connect the squares and create a human rights quilt.

Finally, Mrs. Lee designed this activity for her advanced students:

> Let's get involved! Students in our class are passionate about human rights and want to help people like Parvana and her family. Find a way for us to get involved, and create a brochure about your idea to share with everyone.

The advanced students researched organizations that aid refugees and promote human rights, including UNICEF, Habitat for Humanity, Heifer International, and Doctors Without Borders, before they heard about REACH: Relief and Education for Afghan Children, a nonprofit charitable organization dedicated to building schools in rural Afghanistan. The students explained the project, showed their classmates the project's website, told them about the six schools REACH had already built, and proposed that their class collect money for this worthy endeavor. Before long, the class had gotten the entire school involved, and they raised $4,037 to contribute to the organization.

LITERACY CENTERS. Literacy centers contain meaningful, purposeful literacy activities that students can work at in small groups. Students practice phonics skills at the phonics center, sort word cards at the vocabulary center, or listen to books related to a book they're reading at the listening center. Figure 11–2 describes 20 literacy

FIGURE 11–2   Literacy Centers

CENTER	DESCRIPTION
Alphabet	Young children sing the ABC song, sort upper- and lowercase letters, read alphabet books, and practice other activities the teacher has introduced.
Author	Students examine information about authors they're studying, and interested students write letters to them.
Collaborative Books	Students write pages for a class book following the format indicated at the center, and afterward the teacher compiles and binds the pages into a book.
Computer	Students do word processing, read interactive books, complete WebQuests, search the Internet, and play online games.
Dramatic Play	Students work with puppets, small manipulative materials related to books they're reading, and book boxes as they retell stories and create sequels.
Grammar	Students examine grammar concepts, such as identifying parts of speech and marking capitalization and punctuation on sample compositions.
Library	Students look at books and magazines, choose books to read from text sets, and read books classmates have written.
Listening	Students use a tape player and headphones to listen to stories and other books read aloud. Often copies of the books are available so students can read along.
Making Words	Students arrange letter cards to spell words using the procedure their teacher has taught them.
Message	Kindergartners write notes to classmates and post them on a message board. They also check for messages their classmates and the teacher have written to them.
Nonfiction Books	Students read nonfiction books on a special topic, complete graphic organizers emphasizing the big ideas, and examine genres and nonfiction features.
Phonics	Children practice phonics concepts the teacher has introduced using a variety of small objects, picture cards, and games.
Pocket Charts	Children arrange sentence strips for a familiar poem or song in the pocket chart, and then they read or sing it.
Poetry	Students read poems and locate examples of poetic devices. They also write poems, referring to charts describing various poetic formulas posted in the center.
Proofreading	Students proofread with partners and then use spell checkers, high-frequency word lists, and dictionaries to correct mechanical errors in their rough drafts.
Sequencing	Students retell stories by sequencing story boards (made by cutting apart two copies of a picture book) or illustrations students have drawn.
Spelling	Students practice spelling words, do word sorts to review spelling concepts, and play spelling games at the center.
Stories	Students collect objects for story boxes, and use them in telling and writing stories.
Vocabulary	Students learn about idioms; match synonyms, homophones, or antonyms; make word posters or maps; and sort words according to meaning or structural form.
Writing	Students locate needed writing materials, work on writing projects, get feedback about their writing, and make books.

centers. These centers are usually organized in special places in the classroom or at groups of tables (Fountas & Pinnell, 1996).

Although literacy centers are generally associated with primary classrooms, they can be used effectively to differentiate instruction at all grade levels, even in seventh and eighth grades. In most classrooms, the teacher works with a small group of students while the others work at centers, but sometimes all students work at centers at the same time.

The activities in these literacy centers relate to concepts, strategies, and skills that the teacher recently taught in minilessons, and they vary from simple to complex. Other center activities relate to books students are reading and to thematic units. Students manipulate objects, sort word cards, reread books, complete graphic organizers related to books, and practice skills in centers. Some literacy centers, such as reading and writing centers, are permanent, but others change according to the books students are reading and the activities planned. Teachers provide clear directions at the center so students know what to do and what they should do after they finish an activity.

In some classrooms, students flow freely from one center to another according to their interests; in other classrooms, students are assigned to centers or are required to work at some "assigned" centers and choose among other "choice" centers. Students can sign attendance sheets when they work at each center or mark off their names on a class list posted there. Rarely do students move from center to center in a lockstep approach every 15 to 30 minutes; instead, they move from one center to the next when they finish what they're doing.

Assessment Snapshot: U.S. Constitution Centers Checklist shows a form that eighth graders used as they worked at centers during a unit on the Constitution. Some centers were required; they're marked with an asterisk. Students were expected to complete the "required" centers and two others of their choice; when they finished work at a center, they put a checkmark in the "Student's Check" column. Students keep their checklists in their unit folders, and they add any worksheets or papers they do at the center. Having a checklist or another approach to monitor students' progress helps them develop responsibility for completing their assignments.

DIFFERENTIATED PROJECTS. Students often create projects at the end of a unit to apply what they've learned and to bring closure to the unit. Possible projects include charts, murals, and other visual representations; poems, essays, and other compositions; PowerPoint reports, readers theatre productions, and other oral presentations; websites and other Internet products; and community-based projects that reflect students' synthesis of the big ideas and high-quality workmanship. Projects are an important part of differentiated instruction because students follow their interests, demonstrate what they've learned in authentic ways, and feel successful (Yatvin, 2004).

At the end of some units, students work together on a class project. When fifth graders are studying idioms, for example, they often create a collection of posters or write and compile a collaborative book about idioms, showing their literal and figurative meanings. Most of the time, however, students choose their own projects. Some students work independently or with a partner, and others work in small groups.

Projects are especially valuable for both advanced and struggling students (Yatvin, 2004). When advanced students create projects, they have opportunities to pursue special interests and extend their learning beyond the classroom. For example, they often choose to get involved in community and social issues that they're passionate about,

ASSESSMENT *Snapshot*

U.S. Constitution Centers Checklist

Center	Activity	Student's Check	Teacher's Check
Word Wall	Choose three words from the word wall and make word-study cards for each word.		
Puzzle Center	Complete the "Branches of Government" puzzle.	✓	✓
Library Center	Use the informational books at the center to complete the Constitution time line.		
Internet Center	Research the Constitution on the Internet and complete the study guide.		
Writing Center	Study Howard Christy's painting "The Signing of the Constitution" and write a poem or descriptive essay about it.		
* Legislative Branch Center	Complete activities at this student-developed center.	✓	✓
* Executive Branch Center	Complete activities at this student-developed center.	✓	✓
* Judicial Branch Center	Complete activities at this student-developed center.	✓	✓
* The Bill of Rights Center	Complete activities at this student-developed center.	✓	✓
* Alphabet Book Center	Choose a letter and create a page for the Class Constitution Alphabet Book.	✓	✓

* = required

TEACHER'S NOTE

Raven completed all 5 "required" centers successfully, but she finished only 1 of the 2 "choice" centers. Her folder includes the work she did at each center but no explanation about the undone center.

such as homelessness, climate change, and disaster relief, through the projects they do. Similarly, struggling students are often more successful in demonstrating their learning when they work with classmates in small, collaborative groups and use their special talents and expertise, such as drawing, making oral presentations, and using computers, to create a high-quality project.

To learn more about how students at one grade level vary in achievement, check the feature Differentiated Instruction. It profiles three eighth graders: Ales, a capable student, Graciela, a struggling student, and Kolei, an advanced student.

Differentiated INSTRUCTION

Eighth Graders Differ in Achievement

This Differentiated Instruction feature highlights three eighth graders in Mr. Garcia's English classroom who vary in their literacy development and their views about how teachers can help them to be more successful. One student works at the eighth grade level, the second is struggling, and the third is advanced in his academic achievement. As you read, think about what these students know about reading and writing and how you'd personalize instruction for them in developmentally appropriate ways.

Meet Ales, a Capable Eighth Grader

Fourteen-year-old Ales is an on-grade-level student. Her favorite color is pink, and she loves Hip Hop music. She's very knowledgeable about caring for animals because she helps her mother take care of their tropical fish. Ales is on the girls' basketball team at her school; she plays wing because she's strong and an excellent shooter.

Ales is part of a large blended family. She lives with her mother, her stepdad, two sisters, two stepsisters, and a stepbrother. Her dad lives in Nevada, and she visits him every summer. Everyone in her family speaks English, but Ales wants to learn Spanish because so many people in her community speak Spanish, and she wants to be able to talk to them and know what they're saying.

There's a computer with Internet access set up in a quiet part of her living room. Ales uses it for homework, and on weekends, she plays games and downloads the lyrics to new Hip Hop songs. She reads a lot because her mom insists that she read for 30 minutes every night after finishing her homework. She checks out books from the public library and also brings home books from the school library to read.

Ales hopes to attend college in New York. She wants to become either a vet, because she loves animals, or a crime scene investigator, because it's an interesting career that she's learned about by watching *CSI* on TV.

explains. "I visualize, make connections, summarize, and monitor so I'll understand." She applies fix-up strategies—especially slowing down and rereading—when she gets confused.

"I want to become a better reader so I can go to college," Ales says. "I think the most important thing my teachers can do to help me become a better reader is to give me more time for reading. My mom makes me read 30 minutes every night and that's why I get good grades."

Ales likes to read realistic fiction, especially inspirational stories about girls. Now she's reading *Reach for Tomorrow* (McDaniel, 1999), a book in the One Last Wish series about the residents and counselors of Jenny House, a group home for critically ill girls. Ales explains that she likes reading about miracles, and the stories teach her how to cope in a crisis. She also reads *Essence* magazine. Her favorite author is Sharon Flake, author of *The Skin I'm In* (2007) and other novels about hope and perseverance set in inner-city neighborhoods. Ales reads Sharon Flake's blog, and she likes to visit the author's website.

Reading

Ales is a grade-level reader who likes to read and who knows about comprehension. "I think about what I'm reading," she

Writing

"Of course, I like to write!" Ales declares. "It's fun, and it helps me become a better reader." Her favorite genre is essays because that's what she's learning now. She's written descriptive, comparison-contrast, and persuasive essays, and she's proudest of her persuasive essay about conserving water in her drought-stricken community. Her mom reads everything she writes and saves her papers in a special box.

Ales uses the computer at home to word process her writing assignments. "I'm just learning to type, so you could say I just hunt and peck when I'm word processing on the computer," she explains. "I'm getting better, but I need to take a word processing course next summer."

Ales has learned to use the writing process. She explains, "I make notes with all my ideas before I start writing. Then I keep thinking about what I'm writing. I ask myself if my writing is good, and I know I can revise to make it better. I think a lot faster than I write, so I skip words. When I'm revising, I go back and add them. I like sharing and getting feedback. Proofreading is the easiest part; I'm a good speller."

Ales writes at home, too: "I have a diary that I write in almost every day. I keep it hidden so no one reads it. And I write letters to my dad, and he always writes back to me."

Instructional Implications

Most instruction reflects grade-level standards, so it's appropriate for Ales and other capable, grade-level students.

"Because Ales is responsible about completing reading assignments and projects, it's easy to just assume I'm meeting her needs," Mr. Garcia explains. "But sometimes I worry about Ales and my other grade-level students because I don't want to ignore them. I need to personalize their instruction, taking into account their interests, too." For more information, check the chart How to Differentiate Instruction for Ales.

Ales asked Mr. Garcia for opportunities to make choices, especially about the projects she creates. "I really like school," Ales reflects, "but me and my friends wish we could work together on stuff we're really interested in. I wish we could be doing more important things at school—stuff like saving the world."

Meet Graciela, a Struggling Eighth Grader

Graciela is an angry teenager who struggles with reading and writing. She's a native Spanish speaker who's lived in the United States all her life. This 13-year-old is an athlete; last week, she ran an 8:32 mile in PE. She loves to play flag football with her girlfriends.

"Troublemaker!" That's what Graciela calls herself. Her mother had to accompany her to school every day in first and second grades. She remembers being angry, pulling girls' hair, and hitting classmates. She doesn't know why she did it, but her behavior improved in third grade as she learned English. She still gets in trouble when a teacher is grouchy or a classmate bothers her, and she overreacts.

Graciela lives with her mom and her younger brother. They speak Spanish at home and watch the Telemundo and Univision channels on TV. She says she doesn't do much homework, but her mom buys Hispanic magazines for her.

Graciela likes to go to the movies with her friends; scary movies are her favorite. She dreams of becoming a model, but her mother wants her to be a doctor.

Reading

Graciela's instructional reading level is fourth grade, 4 years below her grade-level placement; even so, she describes herself as "a pretty good reader." The most important thing when you're reading is "to say all the words right," according to Graciela. She thinks she's better at comprehension than at getting the words right. Sometimes her teacher talks about the comprehension strategies, but Graciela doesn't listen because she doesn't plan to use them. "They're for thinking," she says, "not for reading."

She claims to have read the Harry Potter books but doesn't remember anything about them. She does know about the 6-year-old main character in the Junie B. Jones chapter-book series, and she has *Junie B. Jones Is a Party Animal* (Park, 1997) tucked into her backpack; the book's reading level is second grade.

In Graciela's language arts class, students read independently for 20 minutes each day, and she's been reading the books in the Junie B. Jones series for several months now. "They're pretty good stories, and they're easy for me," she says. "I don't really like to read very much," Graciela admits.

Writing

Graciela says she doesn't do much writing at school, and she can't remember any compositions she's written. When asked specifically about the writing project that's going on in her classroom this week, she admits that she's supposed to be writing a response to *Freak the Mighty* (Philbrick, 2001), the compelling story of an extraordinary friendship between two eighth grade misfits, which her teacher has read aloud. Graciela has participated in a series of grand conversations about the book but laments that she probably wouldn't complete the assignment.

In response to questions about the writing process, this struggling writer explains, "I just pick up my pen and start writing. It's hard to think of things to write about, so I just try to get done." She doesn't like to share her writing and tries to get everything right the first time so she doesn't have to revise. Her friend Angela is a good proofreader, so Graciela asks her to check her writing.

HOW TO DIFFERENTIATE INSTRUCTION FOR GRACIELA

Content
- Prioritize instructional goals for Graciela.
- Build Graciela's background knowledge about the topic and introduce vocabulary.
- Stimulate Graciela's interest in the topic by making it personal.

Process
- Provide a text set of reading materials, including texts at Graciela's reading level.
- Use tiered activities so Graciela can be successful.
- Have Graciela work with a nurturing classmate.

Product
- Allow Graciela to choose the projects she creates.
- Encourage Graciela to develop oral or artistic projects to share her new knowledge.
- Provide adequate time at school or enlist her mother's help so that Graciela can complete projects.

"Writing is good when it's neat and there aren't any mistakes," according to Graciela. "I erase my mistakes, and if my paper is messy, I throw it away." Graciela claims to write at home, but later she admits that she never does.

Instructional Implications

School is difficult for Graciela. Her teachers send her to the principal's office for talking back to them, and "just because my teachers don't like me, they give me bad grades," she explains. Her grades the first quarter were Bs, but by the second quarter, they'd dropped to Ds and Fs. Graciela doesn't take responsibility; she blames her teachers: "The reason I get bad grades is because my teachers are mean, and they make me so mad." It's not surprising that Graciela's frustrated: Her instructional level is 4 years below her grade placement. Instruction doesn't make sense, and the academic language her teachers use is unfamiliar.

"I want my teachers to have interesting stuff for me to learn, and I want it to make sense," Graciela explains. "I don't like when they give me Fs. It's not my fault!" In many ways, it isn't Graciela's fault. She reads four grades below most of her classmates, and she needs intensive intervention to build background knowledge, increase her reading level, and learn study skills. Mr. Garcia does his best: He tries to modify the content, process, and product dimensions of his instruction to address Graciela's needs, but it's hard to find suitable books at her reading level, and Graciela complains that his instruction doesn't make sense even though he uses lots of visuals. In addition, even her most nurturing classmates frustrate her, and her anger interferes with completing activities. For more information, check the chart How to Differentiate Instruction for Graciela.

Meet Kolei, an Advanced Eighth Grader

Fourteen-year-old Kolei is a self-assured, high-achieving student. His family came to the United States from the South Pacific island country of Tonga when his father was a child. Kolei has visited Tonga twice and wants to live there someday. This high achiever is poised and articulate, describing himself as "a deep thinker." Kolei is a native English speaker; he and his family speak English at home, and his grandmother taught him to speak and read Tongan and a bit of Tahitian. He's interested in fashion design and thinks it would be cool to be a supermodel. He watches *Project Runway* and *America's Next Top Model*, two fashion-themed reality-TV shows.

There are six other people in Kolei's family: his mother, father, grandmother, and three siblings, an older brother and two younger sisters. He's an integral part of his family's Polynesian catering and dancing business. He plays traditional Tahitian drums, has received awards for his dancing, and often helps out by lugging heavy trays of food at events.

Kolei studies for 3 hours each night. He has a computer but rarely uses it because he's so busy doing homework. His family expects him to go to college, and he wants to earn a doctorate and become a psychologist.

Reading

Kolei reads at 10th grade level, two grade levels above his current grade placement. He says, "I love to read because that's how I learn." Mr. Garcia and his other teachers often call on him to read aloud in class because he's such an expressive reader. "I always use strategies to understand what I'm reading." Kolei explains, "I think about the topic and the purpose before I start reading, and I'm good at drawing inferences and summarizing. I monitor my reading so I'll know when I don't understand."

"I don't do much reading at school except in textbooks," Kolei says. "Usually we're assigned to read for homework so I read for an hour or more most days at home. We did reading workshop in sixth grade, and I loved reading all the books that I'd chosen. Our teacher had a huge classroom library and I read at least one book every week. It was awesome!"

In addition to textbook assignments, he's read the popular Harry Potter and Lemony Snicket series, but he doesn't really like fantasy. He prefers historical fiction because "history is interesting." He really enjoyed Avi's *The Fighting Ground* (1994), a novel set during the American Revolution. The book he prizes most is a biography set in his homeland, *Queen Salote of Tonga* (Wood-Ellem, 2001).

His parents often buy books for him, and on weekends he can often be found browsing in the psychology section at the local Barnes & Noble bookstore.

Writing

Kolei prefers writing to reading, and he's interested in a variety of genres. He recently completed a lengthy science report on the accuracy of eyewitness testimony; in it, he concluded that girls and boys provide similar eyewitness testimony. He also likes to write poetry: "Have you noticed that words have color? I use words to create pictures in my poems. Rhyme isn't important; word choice is what matters."

Like most writers, Kolei says that revising is the toughest part for him. He rereads his drafts, thinking about the audience's needs more than his own, checks to make sure his writing is well organized, and deletes or "tosses" lots of sentences because that's what authors do when they revise. He also gets feedback from classmates and uses their suggestions when he revises.

When asked about what makes writing effective, Kolei identified these traits: introductions that grab readers' attention, well-developed ideas, clear organization, precise words, interesting sentences, and a powerful voice. This dedicated writer keeps three notebooks at home. In one journal, Kolei

HOW TO DIFFERENTIATE INSTRUCTION FOR KOLEI

Content
- Determine Kolei's background knowledge about the topic before beginning instruction.
- Increase the complexity of instruction.
- Use tiered activities to challenge Kolei.

Process
- Provide a text set of reading materials, including books at Kolei's reading level.
- Incorporate online materials and activities.
- Encourage Kolei to work with other advanced students.

Product
- Encourage Kolei's creativity through multimodal projects.
- Require Kolei to use higher level thinking skills.
- Have Kolei pursue both individual and small-group projects.

writes song lyrics; in the second, he invents stories; and in the third, he sketches fashion designs.

Instructional Implications

Kolei is successful in school, and differentiating instruction might not seem very important for advanced students, but it is. He needs to expand his knowledge, investigate challenging topics, and get involved in community projects. For more information, check the chart How to Differentiate Instruction for Kolei.

According to Kolei, he usually either works alone or spends instructional time assisting classmates who need help. "I don't mind helping kids, but I'm not the teacher," he explains. "Sometimes they don't want help, and I tell them how important it is to get an education, but they just laugh. And, I worry about getting my own work done. I think I'd like to work with Colin, Ivan, and some of the other smarter kids." Kolei reflects: "I like to have choices, and I like projects that make me think, you know, to do research to find answers. I like projects that my dad and I do together. He'll take me anywhere to interview people or visit exhibits at museums. I'd like to do more of projects like that."

 MONITOR: Check Your Understanding 11.1

Struggling Readers and Writers

Why are some students more successful than others in learning to read and write? Researchers report that young children with strong oral language skills and in families where parents read aloud to them and provide other early literacy experiences are more likely to be successful in school. They've also found that children who aren't fluent English speakers, children whose parents had difficulty learning to read and write, and children from low-SES communities are more likely to have difficulty reaching grade-level proficiency in reading and writing (Strickland, 2002).

Struggling Readers

It's crucial to identify students at risk for reading problems early so these problems can be addressed quickly, before they're compounded. Fink (2006) identified these factors that predict early reading difficulty in kindergarten or first grade:

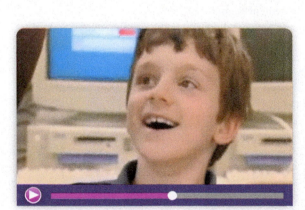

Watch as an educator explains how the achievement gap between high and low achievers widens year after year. Why do teachers need to address the needs of students who struggle?

- Difficulty developing concepts about written language, phonemic awareness, letter names, and phoneme–grapheme correspondences
- Slower to respond than classmates when asked to identify words
- Behavior that deviates from school norms

In addition, children with a family history of reading problems are more likely to experience difficulty in learning to read.

Although many struggling readers are identified in the primary grades, other students who have been successful begin to exhibit reading problems in fourth or fifth grade; this phenomenon is known as the "fourth grade slump" (Chall & Jacobs, 2003). Many teachers attribute this problem to the increased use of nonfiction books and content area textbooks that may be poorly written, that lack reader-friendly features, or that present unfamiliar topics using new vocabulary words.

Struggling readers exhibit a variety of difficulties. Some have ineffective decoding skills or don't read fluently, and others have insufficient vocabulary knowledge or difficulty understanding and remembering the author's message. Still others struggle because they're unfamiliar with English language structures. Figure 11–3 identifies some of the problems that struggling readers face and suggests ways to solve each one. When teachers suspect that a student is struggling, they take action and assess him or her to diagnose any problems, and they intervene if problems are present because expert instruction helps overcome reading difficulties (Snow, Burns, & Griffin, 1998).

Struggling Writers

Many students struggle with writing. It's easy to notice some of their problems when you examine their compositions: Some students have difficulty developing and organizing ideas, some struggle with word choice and writing complete sentences and effective transitions, and others have problems with spelling, capitalization, punctuation, and grammar skills. Other students struggle with the writing process and using writing strategies effectively; they may be unsure about what writers do as they develop and refine their compositions or the thinking that goes on during writing (Christenson, 2002). There are some students, too, who complain that their hands and arms hurt when they write, some who show little interest and do the bare minimum, and others who are so frustrated with writing that they refuse to write at all. Figure 11–4 lists some problems that struggling writers face and suggests ways to address them.

To build their confidence and become more successful, struggling students need to learn more about writing and have more opportunities to practice writing. Teachers address students' specific problem areas through a combination of instruction and authentic practice activities.

High-Quality Instruction

Struggling students have significant difficulty learning to read and write. Some students are at risk for reading and writing problems in kindergarten and first grade, but others develop difficulties in fourth or fifth grade or even later. The best way to help these students is to prevent their difficulties in the first place by providing high-quality classroom instruction and adding an intervention, if it's needed (Cooper, Chard, & Kiger, 2006). Unfortunately, there's no quick fix for low-achieving students. Helping struggling students requires both high-quality classroom instruction and sustained, personalized intervention (Allington, 2012).

Teachers use a balanced approach that combines explicit instruction in decoding, fluency, vocabulary, comprehension, and writing along with daily opportunities for students to apply what they're learning in authentic literacy activities (Allington, 2012). It's standards driven and incorporates research-based procedures and activities. Teachers address these four components to enhance the literacy development of struggling readers and writers:

Watch as this eighth grade teacher explains how students are to collect and revise important writing assignments over the school year. Why might this portfolio process improve students' writing, including those with special needs?

Personalizing Instruction. Teachers adjust their instructional programs to match students' needs using flexible grouping, tiered activities, and respectful tasks (Opitz & Ford, 2008). Results of ongoing assessment are used to vary instructional content, process, and assignments according to students' developmental levels, interests, and learning styles.

FIGURE 11–3   How to Address Struggling Readers' Problems

PROBLEMS	SOLUTIONS
Written Language Concepts Student doesn't understand print concepts.	• Use the Language Experience Approach to record the student's language and demonstrate print concepts. • Use shared reading and have the student point out examples of print concepts in big books. • Have the student dictate and write messages.
Alphabet Knowledge Student can't name letters or match upper- and lowercase letters.	• Identify letters in the student's name and in environmental print. • Teach the student to use the ABC song to identify specific letters. • Teach the student to use an alphabet chart to identify matching letters. • Play matching games with the student. • Have the student sort upper- and lowercase letters.
Phonemic Awareness Student can't manipulate speech sounds.	• Sing songs, read poems, and have the student identify rhyming words. • Ask the student to match rhyming picture cards. • Pronounce individual sounds in a word and have the student orally blend them into words. • Have the student orally segment words into individual sounds using Elkonin boxes. • Have the student substitute beginning, medial, and ending sounds in words.
Decoding Student can't identify high-frequency words.	• Make a personal word wall with words the student recognizes. • Use a routine to teach and practice high-frequency words. • Ask the student to look for high-frequency words in familiar books. • Have the student write words on a whiteboard or using magnetic letters.
Student can't identify consonant and vowel sounds.	• Have the student sort objects or picture cards according to sounds. • Play phonics games, including those online, with the student. • Have the student substitute initial consonants to create a list of words using a phonogram. • Do interactive writing.
Student can't decode one-syllable words.	• Involve the student in making words activities. • Have the student spell words using magnetic letters. • Teach the student about vowel patterns. • Have the student sort word cards according to vowel patterns. • Teach the student to decode by analogy. • Have the student read and write lists of words created from one phonogram.
Student can't identify multisyllabic words.	• Teach the procedure for decoding multisyllabic words. • Have the student remove prefixes and suffixes to identify the root word. • Brainstorm lists of words from a single root word. • Have the student write words with affixes on a whiteboard.
Fluency Student omits, substitutes, or repeats words when reading.	• Teach high-frequency words that the student doesn't know. • Ensure that the level of reading materials is appropriate for the student. • Have the student read the text quietly before reading it aloud. • Have the student reread familiar texts, including big books and classroom charts. • Use choral reading in small groups.
Student reads word by word, without expression.	• Have the student practice rereading easier texts to develop fluency. • Ask the student to echo read, imitating the teacher's expression. • Have the student do repeated readings. • Break the text into phrases for the student to read aloud. • Do choral reading in small groups.

FIGURE 11–3 *(Continued)*

Vocabulary Student doesn't understand the meanings of words.	• Create a KWL chart or do an anticipation guide before reading. • Teach key vocabulary before reading. • Have the student sort words from a featured book or a thematic unit. • Have the student make diagrams and posters about key words. • Read books aloud every day to build the student's vocabulary. • Teach idioms, synonyms and antonyms, and word-learning strategies.
Comprehension Student can't retell or answer questions after reading.	• Build the student's background knowledge before reading. • Ensure that the book is appropriate for the student. • Read the book aloud instead of having the student read it. • Have the student sequence story boards and use them to retell the story. • Set a purpose for reading by having the student read a brief text to find the answer to one literal-level question.
Student can't draw inferences or do higher level thinking.	• Read the book aloud instead of having the student read it. • Do think-alouds to model drawing inferences and higher level thinking. • Teach comprehension strategies. • Teach the student about text structure. • Use QARs to teach the student about types of questions. • Involve the student in small-group grand conversations and literature circles.
Student is a passive reader.	• Use the interactive read-aloud procedure. • Teach the student to self-select books using the Goldilocks Strategy. • Have the student read a book with a partner or in a literature circle. • To stimulate interest, have the student view the movie version before reading a novel. • Involve the student in hot seat, grand conversations, and other participatory activities.
Study Skills Student can't locate information in reference materials.	• Teach the student to use an index to locate information. • Have the student practice locating information in almanacs and print and online reference materials. • Teach the student to skim and scan to find information in a text. • Teach the student to navigate the Web to locate information online.
Student can't take notes.	• Demonstrate how to take notes using a graphic organizer or small self-stick notes. • Make a copy of a text and have the student mark the big ideas with a highlighter pen. • Have the student identify big ideas and create a graphic organizer to represent them. • Have the student work with a partner to take notes on small self-stick notes.

Based on McKenna, 2002; Cockrum & Shanker, 2013.

Using Appropriate Instructional Materials. Most of the time, students read interesting books written at their reading levels in small groups or individually. Teachers usually have plenty of books available for on-grade-level readers, but finding appropriate books for struggling readers can be difficult. Booklist: Easy-to-Read Chapter Book Series presents a list of suitable paperback series for older struggling students. Teachers also choose award-winning books for literature focus units, but even though these "teaching-texts" are important, Allington (2012) recommends using a single text with the whole class only 25% of the time because students need more opportunities to read books at their reading levels.

Expanding Teachers' Expertise. Teachers continue to grow professionally during their careers (Allington, 2012): They join professional organizations,

FIGURE 11–4 How to Address Struggling Writers' Problems

PROBLEMS	SOLUTIONS
Ideas Student complains, "I don't know what to write."	• Have the student brainstorm a list of ideas and pick the most promising one. • Invite the student to talk with classmates to get ideas.
Composition lacks focus.	• After writing a draft, have the student highlight sentences that pertain to the focus, cut the other parts, and elaborate the highlighted ideas. • Give the student a very focused assignment. • Share samples of unfocused writing for the student to revise.
Composition lacks interesting details and vocabulary.	• Have the student brainstorm words related to each of the five senses and then add some of the words to the composition. • Have the student refer to word walls posted in the classroom for vocabulary. • Teach vivid verbs and adjectives. • Demonstrate the visualization strategy.
Organization Composition is poorly organized.	• Help the student decide on paragraph organization before beginning to write. • Teach the concept of "big idea" using many types of texts, and then help the student identify the big idea for each paragraph before beginning to write. • Teach sequence words, such as *first, next, last,* and *finally.* • Have the student create a graphic organizer before beginning to write.
Composition is divided into paragraphs, but some sentences don't belong.	• Have the student reread each paragraph, checking that each sentence belongs. • Encourage the student to work with a partner to check sentences in each paragraph. • Have the student examine paragraphs and locate sentences that don't belong.
Composition lacks a strong lead.	• Have the student try several leads with an experience, a question, a quotation, or a comparison. • Encourage the student to get feedback about the effectiveness of the lead in a revising group. • Have the student examine the leads in stories and informational books.
Writing Process Student doesn't reread or revise composition, or doesn't make constructive revisions.	• Compare the quality of sample unrevised and revised compositions. • Include revision as a requirement in the assessment rubric. • Use revising groups. • Conference with the student to examine the revisions during the revising stage.
Student plagiarizes.	• Make the student accountable for clusters, graphic organizers, or note cards. • Have the student use the writing process and do the research and writing in class, not at home. • Teach the student how to take notes and develop a composition.
Conventions Composition is difficult to read because of misspellings and mechanical and grammar errors.	• Have the student refer to high-frequency and content area word walls when writing. • Arrange for the student to edit with a partner. • Conference with the student to correct remaining errors in the editing stage. • Teach the student to proofread. • Have the student examine and correct errors in sample compositions.
Composition has weak sentence structure.	• Have editing partners address sentence structure during the editing stage. • Teach sentence combining and then have the student practice it.
Composition is difficult to read because of poor handwriting or messiness.	• Have the student use word processing. • Encourage the student to use manuscript rather than cursive handwriting. • Take the student's dictation if necessary.

FIGURE 11-4   *(Continued)*

Motivation Student does the bare minimum, or even refuses to write.	• Conference with the student to determine why he/she is hesitant. • Brainstorm with the student during prewriting. • Model how to expand a sentence into a paragraph, or a brief composition into a better developed one. • Try the Language Experience Approach and interactive writing. • Have the student write a collaborative composition with a small group or a partner. • Keep first writing assignments very short to ensure success.
Student is too dependent on teacher approval.	• Have the student check with a classmate before coming to the teacher. • Ask the student to sign up for conferences with the teacher. • Make sure the student understands expectations and procedures.

participate in professional book clubs, attend workshops and conferences, and find answers to questions that puzzle them through teacher-inquiry projects. Figure 11–5 outlines some ways that teachers stretch their knowledge and teaching expertise.

Collaborating With Literacy Coaches. Literacy coaches are experienced teachers with special expertise in working with struggling readers and writers (Casey, 2006). They support teachers by working alongside them in their classrooms, demonstrating instructional procedures and evaluation techniques, and they collaborate with teachers to design instruction to address students' needs. Toll (2005) explains that "literacy coaching is not about telling others what to do, but rather bringing out the best in others" (p. 6). Through their efforts, teachers are becoming more expert, and schools are becoming better learning environments.

The quality of classroom instruction has a tremendous impact on how well students learn to read and write, and studies of exemplary teachers indicate that teaching expertise is the critical factor (Block, Oakar, & Hurt, 2002).

Interventions

Schools use **intervention** programs to address low-achieving students' reading and writing difficulties and accelerate their literacy learning (Cooper, Chard, & Kiger, 2006). They're used to build on effective classroom instruction, not as a replacement for it. The classroom teacher or a specially trained reading teacher meets daily with struggling students. Using paraprofessionals is a widespread practice but not recommended because they aren't as effective as certified teachers (Allington, 2012). During interventions, teachers diagnose, provide intensive, expert instruction, and scaffold individuals or very small groups of students. Interventions take various forms: They can be provided by adding a second lesson during the regular school day, offering extra instruction in an after-school program, or holding extended-school-year programs during the summer. Figure 11–6 summarizes the recommendations for effective intervention programs.

EARLY INTERVENTIONS. Until recently, most interventions were designed for students in fourth through eighth grades who were already failing; now the focus has changed to early intervention for at-risk children to eliminate the pattern of school failure that begins early and persists throughout some students' lives (MacDonald &

Booklist   Easy-to-Read Chapter-Book Series

READING LEVEL	SERIES	GENRE
Grade 1	*Bones*, by David Adler	Fantasy
	Elephant and Piggie, by Mo Willems	Adventure
	Fly Guy, by Tedd Arnold	Humor
	Fox, by Edward Marshall	Adventure
Grade 2	*A to Z Mysteries*, by Ron Roy	Mystery
	Amber Brown, by Paula Danziger	Realism
	Andrew Lost, by J. C. Greenburg	Fantasy
	Bones, by David Adler	Mystery
	Commander Toad, by Jane Yolen	Science Fiction
	Fitch and Chip, by Lisa Wheeler	Adventure
	Jigsaw Jones Mysteries, by James Preller	Mystery
	Junie B. Jones, by Barbara Park	Adventure
	Magic Tree House, by Mary Pope Osborne	Adventure
	Marvin Redpost, by Louis Sachar	Adventure
	Minnie and Moo, by Denys Cazet	Adventure
	Ricky Ricotta's Mighty Robots, by Dav Pilkey	Science Fiction
	The Zack Files, by Dan Greenburg	Fantasy
Grade 3	*Abracadabra!* by Peter Lerangis	Mystery
	Adventures of the Bailey School Kids, by Debbie Dadey and Marcia Jones	Adventure
	Amber Brown, by Paula Danziger	Realism
	Boxcar Children, by Gertrude Chandler Warner	Mystery
	Captain Underpants, by Dav Pilkey	Humor
	Hank the Cowdog, by John R. Erickson	Fantasy
	Magic School Bus Chapter Books, by Joanna Cole	Nonfiction
	Secrets of Droon, by Tony Abbott	Fantasy
	Sports, by Matt Christopher	Sports
	The Unicorn's Secret, by Kathleen Duey	Fantasy
	The Zack Files, by Dan Greenburg	Fantasy
Grade 4	*Animal Ark*, by Ben M. Baglio	Animals
	The Babysitters Club, by Ann M. Martin	Adventure
	Deltora Quest, by Emily Rodda	Fantasy
	Dolphin Diaries, by Ben M. Baglio	Animals
	Encyclopedia Brown, by Donald J. Sobol	Mystery
	Goosebumps, by R. L. Stine	Horror
	Guardians of Ga'hoole, by Kathryn Lasky	Fantasy
	Pyrates, by Chris Archer	Adventure
	The Time Warp Trio, by Jon Scieszka	Fantasy
Grade 5	*The Amazing Days of Abby Hayes*, by Anne Mazer	Realism
	Animorphs, by K. A. Applegate	Science Fiction
	The Black Stallion, by Walter Farley	Animals
	Dinotopia, by Peter David	Science Fiction
	From the Files of Madison Finn, by Laura Dower	Contemporary
	Heartland, by Lauren Brooke	Animals
	The Saddle Club, by Bonnie Bryant	Animals
	Thoroughbred, by Joanna Campbell	Animals

Figueredo, 2010; Strickland, 2002). Teachers have developed three types of interventions for preschoolers, kindergartners, and first graders:

ᴥ Preventive programs to create more effective early-childhood programs
ᴥ Family-focused programs to develop young children's awareness of literacy, parents' literacy, and parenting skills
ᴥ Early interventions to resolve reading and writing problems and accelerate literacy development for low-achieving K–3 students

Intervention programs still exist, of course, for older low-achieving students, but teachers believe that earlier and more intensive intervention will solve many of the difficulties that older students exhibit today.

To prevent literacy problems and break the cycle of poverty in the United States, the federal government directs two early-intervention programs for economically disadvantaged children and their parents. The best known program is Head Start, which began in the mid-1960s as part of President Lyndon Johnson's War on Poverty. It currently serves more than one million children and their families each year. Young children grow rapidly in their knowledge of concepts about written language and understanding of literacy behaviors, but these remarkable gains aren't usually sustained after children start school. A newer program that began as part of the No Child Left Behind legislation is the Even Start Family Literacy Program, which integrates early-childhood education and literacy instruction for parents into one program.

FIGURE 11–5 Ways to Develop Professional Knowledge and Expertise

Professional Organizations	International Literacy Association (ILA) National Council of Teachers of English (NCTE) Teachers of English to Speakers of Other Languages (TESOL)
Journals	*Journal of Adolescent and Adult Literacy* (ILA) *Reading Online* (ILA) *The Reading Teacher* (ILA) *Language Arts* (NCTE) *Voices From the Middle* (NCTE) *Essential Teacher* (TESOL) *The Internet TESL Journal*
Literacy Workshops and Conferences	Teachers attend local, state, and national conferences sponsored by ILA, NCTE, and TESOL to learn more about teaching reading and writing, and they also attend workshops sponsored by local sites affiliated with the National Writing Project (NWP).
Collaboration	Teachers at one grade level or at one school can participate in teacher book clubs, view videos about classroom practices, and discuss ways to improve teaching and meet the needs of their students.
Teacher-Inquiry Projects	To learn how to conduct teacher research, consult one of these books: *The Art of Classroom Inquiry: A Handbook for Teacher-Researchers* (Hubbard & Power, 2003), *The Power of Questions: A Guide to Teacher and Student Research* (Falk & Blumenreich, 2005), and *What Works? A Practical Guide for Teacher Research* (Chiseri-Strater & Sunstein, 2006).
National Writing Project	Teachers attend programs at local National Writing Project sites and apply to participate at invitational summer institutes. To locate the nearest NWP site, check their website.
Professional Books	Teachers read books about research-based instructional strategies, current issues, and innovative practices published by ILA, NCTE, TESOL, Heinemann, Scholastic, Stenhouse, and other publishers.

READING RECOVERY. Reading Recovery is the most widely known intervention program for the lowest-achieving first graders (Clay, 1993, 2005a, 2005b). It involves 30-minute daily one-on-one tutoring by specifically trained and supervised teachers for 12 to 30 weeks. Reading Recovery lessons involve these components:

- Rereading familiar books
- Independently reading the book introduced in the previous lesson
- Learning decoding and comprehension strategies
- Writing sentences
- Reading a new book with teacher support

Once students reach grade-level standards and demonstrate that they can work independently in their classroom, they leave the program. The results of the intervention are impressive: 75% of students who complete the Reading Recovery program meet grade-level literacy standards and continue to be successful.

RESPONSE TO INTERVENTION. Response to Intervention (RTI) is a schoolwide initiative to identify struggling students quickly, promote high-quality classroom instruction, provide effective interventions, and increase the likelihood that students

---

FIGURE 11–6 High-Quality Interventions

Scheduling
Interventions take place daily for 20–45 minutes, depending on students' age and instructional needs. Classroom teachers often provide the interventions as second reading lessons in the classroom or during after-school programs, but at other times, specially trained reading teachers provide the interventions.

Grouping
Teachers work with students individually or in small groups of no more than three students; larger groups of students, even when they exhibit the same reading or writing problems, aren't as effective.

Reading Materials
Teachers match students to books at their instructional level for lessons and at their independent level for voluntary reading. The reading materials should engage students and provide some challenge without frustrating them.

Instruction
Teachers provide lessons that generally include rereading familiar books, reading new books, word study (phonics, word identification, and vocabulary), and writing activities. The content of the lessons varies according to students' identified areas of difficulty.

Reading and Writing Practice
Teachers provide additional opportunities for students to spend time reading and writing to practice and apply what they're learning.

Assessment
Teachers monitor progress on an ongoing basis by observing students and collecting work samples. They also use diagnostic tests to document students' learning according to grade-level standards.

Professional Development
Teachers continue their professional development to improve their teaching expertise, and they ensure that the aides and volunteers who work in their classroom are well trained.

Home–School Partnerships
Teachers keep parents informed about students' progress and involve them in supporting independent reading and writing at home.

will be successful (Lipson & Wixson, 2010; Mellard & Johnson, 2008). It involves three tiers:

Tier 1: Screening and Prevention. Teachers provide high-quality instruction that's supported by scientifically based research, screen students to identify those at risk for academic failure, and monitor their progress. If students don't make adequate progress toward meeting grade-level standards, they move to Tier 2.

Tier 2: Early Intervention. Trained reading teachers provide enhanced, individualized instruction targeting students' specific areas of difficulty. If the intervention is successful and students' reading problems are resolved, they return to Tier 1; if they make some progress but need additional instruction, they remain in Tier 2; and if they don't show improvement, they move to Tier 3, where the intensity of intervention increases.

Tier 3: Intensive Intervention. Special education teachers provide more intensive intervention to individual students and small groups and more frequent progress monitoring. They focus on remedying students' problem areas and teaching compensatory strategies.

This schoolwide instruction and assessment program incorporates data-driven decision making, and special education teachers are optimistic that it will be a better way to diagnose learning-disabled students.

INTERVENTIONS FOR OLDER STUDENTS. Despite teachers' best efforts, approximately one quarter of students in the upper grades are struggling readers, and they need effective classroom interventions in addition to high-quality reading instruction (Allington, 2011). In most middle school classrooms today, teachers don't teach reading; instead, they teach literature, grammar, and writing, but struggling students require expert reading instruction, particularly on comprehension and vocabulary strategies, to reach grade-level proficiency (Schmitt, 2011).

Richard Allington (2011) recommends that teachers design intervention programs that include these components:

High-Quality Instruction. Teachers provide high-quality, appropriate literacy instruction that's tailored to students' needs. Even though many intervention programs emphasize phonics, researchers have found that decoding is a strength for most struggling readers, and instructional time is better spent on vocabulary and comprehension (Ivey & Baker, 2004).

Instructional-Level Reading Materials. Teachers teach reading using books at students' instructional level that are also appropriate for their age. Selecting appropriate reading materials is especially important for students who read three or four levels below their grade placement.

More Time for Reading. Teachers increase the amount of time students spend reading independent level books each day, and they ensure that students choose interesting books to read.

In some schools, teachers design their own programs using these components, as Mrs. Lee did in the vignette at the beginning of the chapter, but in others, administrators purchase intervention programs. Figure 11–7 lists a variety of comprehensive intervention programs for struggling readers and writers.

FIGURE 11–7   Comprehensive Intervention Programs

PROGRAM	PUBLISHER	DESCRIPTION
Accelerated Literacy Learning	Accelerated Literacy Learning	A balanced literacy intervention program for K–8 struggling readers. It uses assessment results to differentiate and personalize reading and writing instruction.
AMP Reading System	Pearson	An intervention system for struggling sixth to eighth graders who read at the third to sixth grade levels. It focuses on reading comprehension, fluency, and vocabulary.
Destination Reading	Houghton Mifflin Harcourt	A flexible reading intervention program for K–3 at-risk students. Teachers provide explicit instruction with ample practice opportunities. The instruction is individualized.
Earobics	Houghton Mifflin Harcourt	An intensive intervention program for K–3 students that delivers instruction through interactive software, teacher-directed activities, manipulative activities, and books.
Merit Software	Merit Software	A software program for struggling elementary and middle school students that addresses reading comprehension, vocabulary, grammar, and writing. Students receive personal feedback, and there's a built-in tracking system for teachers.
Read 180	Scholastic	An intensive, individualized intervention program for elementary and middle school students. It uses a combination of Read 180 software and teachers' instruction on reading comprehension, vocabulary, word study, and writing.
Reading Recovery	Reading Recovery Council of North America	A short-term, one-on-one tutoring program for the lowest achieving first graders. Specially trained teachers provide intensive instruction on reading and writing in 30-minute lessons.

 **MONITOR: Check Your Understanding 11.2**

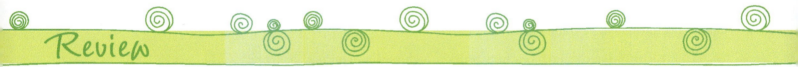

DIFFERENTIATING LITERACY INSTRUCTION

Effective teachers demonstrate their responsibility and commitment to teaching all students effectively by personalizing instruction using the guidelines presented in this chapter, these points in particular:

11.1 Teachers differentiate instruction by modifying the content, the process, and the product to meet the needs of all students, including those who struggle.

11.2 Teachers use a balanced approach to teach struggling students that incorporates effective instruction, materials at students' reading levels, and extra time for reading and writing.

✔ EVALUATE & REFLECT

Evaluate your knowledge about differentiated instruction. The questions ask you to collect and analyze data, and report the results. Your response should meet academic standards and adhere to Standard English conventions.

1. Study the vignette at the beginning of the chapter to locate examples of differentiation according to content, process, and product. In your response, report the results of your examination, and suggest ways that Mrs. Lee might further differentiate her instruction.

2. Create a text set for a literature focus unit for a specific grade level that includes at least eight fiction, nonfiction, and digital texts ranging across three appropriate grade levels. In your response, describe the literature focus unit, list the texts by grade level in one chart and in another chart according to genre, and reflect on what you've learned about creating text sets.

3. Develop a list of four tiered projects for a literature focus unit at a specific grade level, K–8, that takes into account individual interests and academic achievement. In your response, summarize the literature focus unit and grade level, explain each project, and classify the projects according to how they differ; they might differ according to content, process, and product, or according to oral, visual, digital, and written language.

4. Interview two students at the same grade level in the grades 3–6 band who differ in academic achievement, following the Differentiated Instruction special feature in this chapter. In your response, describe each student, his/her reading and writing achievement, and instructional implications. Include a chart about how to differentiate instruction for each student.

5. Research Reading Recovery or Response to Intervention to learn about the topic and its effectiveness, and prepare a digital presentation to share what you've learned. In your response, write an essay about the intervention program, present your reading list, and include a flash drive of your digital presentation.

REFERENCES

Allington, R. L. (2011). Reading intervention in the middle grades. *Voices From the Middle, 19*(2), 10–16.

Allington, R. L. (2012). *What really matters for struggling readers: Designing research-based programs* (3rd ed.). Boston: Pearson.

Avi. (1994). *The fighting ground*. New York: Harper Trophy.

Block, C., Oakar, M., & Hurt, N. (2002). The expertise of literacy teachers: A continuum from preschool–grade 5. *Reading Research Quarterly, 37*, 178–206.

Casey, K. (2006). *Literacy coaching: The essentials*. Portsmouth, NH: Heinemann.

Chall, J. S., & Jacobs, V. A. (2003). Poor children's fourth-grade slump. *American Educator, 27*(1), 14–15, 44.

Chiseri-Strater, E., & Sunstein, B. S. (2006). *What works? A practical guide for teacher research*. Portsmouth, NH: Heinemann.

Christenson, T. A. (2002). *Supporting struggling writers in the elementary classroom*. Newark, DE: International Reading Association.

Clay, M. M. (1993). *Reading Recovery: A guidebook for teachers in training*. Portsmouth, NH: Heinemann.

Clay, M. M. (2005a). *Literacy lessons: Designed for individuals*, part one: *Why? When? and How?* Portsmouth, NH: Heinemann.

Clay, M. M. (2005b). *Literacy lessons: Designed for individuals*, part two: *Teaching procedures*. Portsmouth, NH: Heinemann.

Cockrum, W.. & Shanker, J. L., (2013). *Locating and correcting reading difficulties* (10th ed.). Boston: Pearson.

Cooper, J. D., Chard, D. J., & Kiger, N. D. (2006). *The struggling reader: Interventions that work*. New York: Scholastic.

Ellis, D. (2001). *The breadwinner*. Toronto, ON: Groundwood Books.

Falk, B., & Blumenreich, M. (2005). *The power of questions: A guide to teacher and student research*. Portsmouth, NH: Heinemann.

Fink, R. (2006). *Why Jane and John couldn't read—and how they learned: A new look at striving readers*. Newark, DE: International Reading Association.

Flake, S. (2007). *The skin I'm in*. New York: Hyperion Books.

Fountas, I. C., & Pinnell, G. S. (1996). *Guided reading: Good first teaching for all children*. Portsmouth, NH: Heinemann.

Greenburg, D. (2000). *How I went from bad to verse*. New York: Grosset & Dunlap.

Heacox, D. (2002). *Differentiating instruction in the regular classroom: How to reach and teach all learners, grades 3–12*. Minneapolis: Free Spirit Publishing.

Holmes, C. T., & Brown, C. L. (2003). *A controlled evaluation of a total school improvement process, School Renaissance* (Technical report). Athens: University of Georgia.

Hubbard, R. S., & Power, B. M. (2003). *The art of classroom inquiry: A handbook for teacher-researchers* (Rev. ed.). Portsmouth, NH: Heinemann.

Ivey, G., & Baker, M. I. (2004). Phonics instruction for older students? Just say no. *Educational Leadership, 61*(6), 35–39.

Lipson, M. Y, & Wixson, K. K. (Eds.). (2010). *Successful approaches to RTI: Collaborative practices for improving K–12 literacy*. Newark, DE: International Reading Association.

MacDonald, C., & Figueredo, L. (2010). Closing the gap early: Implementing a literacy intervention for at-risk kindergartners in urban schools. *The Reading Teacher, 63*, 404–419.

McDaniel, L. (1999). *Reach for tomorrow*. New York: Laurel Leaf.

McKenna, M. C. (2002). *Help for struggling readers: Strategies for grades 3–8*. New York: Guilford Press.

Mellard, D. F., & Johnson, E. (2008). *RTI: A practitioner's guide to implementing Response to Intervention*. Thousand Oaks, CA: Corwin and the National Association of Elementary School Principals.

Nye, N. S. (Compiler). (2002a). *The flag of childhood: Poems from the Middle East*. New York: Aladdin Books.

Nye, N. S. (2002b). *19 varieties of gazelle: Poems of the Middle East.* New York: Greenwillow.

Opitz, M. F., & Ford, M. P. (2008). *Do-able differentiation: Varying groups, texts, and supports to reach readers.* Portsmouth, NH: Heinemann.

Park, B. (1997). *Junie B. Jones is a party animal.* New York: Random House.

Philbrick, R. (2001). *Freak the mighty.* New York: Scholastic.

Robb, L. (2008). *Differentiating reading instruction: How to teach reading to meet the needs of each student.* New York: Scholastic.

Schmidt, R. (2008). Really reading: What does Accelerated Reader teach adults and children? *Language Arts, 85,* 202–211.

Schmitt, M. C. (2011). Using a network of strategies rubric to become a self-regulated learner. *Voices From the Middle, 19*(2), 33–38.

Scieszka, J. (2004). *Knights of the kitchen table.* New York: Puffin Books.

Snow, C. E., Burns, S., & Griffin, P. (Eds.). (1998). *Preventing reading difficulties in young children.* Washington, DC: National Academy Press.

Strickland, D. S. (2002). The importance of effective early intervention. In A. E. Farstrup & S. J. Samuels (Eds.), *What research has to say about reading instruction* (3rd ed., pp. 69–86). Newark, DE: International Reading Association.

Toll, C. A. (2005). *The literacy coach's survival guide: Essential questions and practical answers.* Newark, DE: International Reading Association.

Tomlinson, C. A. (2014). *The differentiated classroom: Responding to the needs of all learners* (2nd ed.). Alexandria, VA: Association for Supervision and Curriculum Development.

Topping, K. J., & Paul, T. D. (1999). Computer-assisted assessment of practice at reading: A large scale survey using Accelerated Reader data. *Reading & Writing Quarterly, 15,* 213–231.

Wood-Ellem, E. (2001). *Queen Salote of Tonga.* Honolulu: University of Hawai'i Press.

Yatvin, J. (2004). *A room with a differentiated view: How to serve ALL children as individual learners.* Portsmouth, NH: Heinemann.

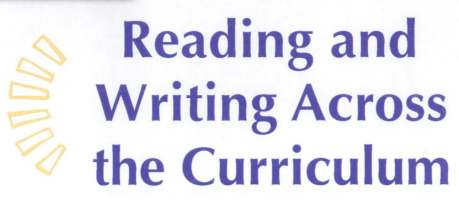

Chapter 12

Reading and Writing Across the Curriculum

PLAN: Preview the Learning Outcomes

After studying this chapter, you'll be prepared to respond to these points:

12.1 Describe how students use reading and writing as learning tools.

12.2 Explain how students use writing to demonstrate learning.

12.3 Discuss how to use content area textbooks.

12.4 Explain how to develop a thematic unit.

Third Graders' Multigenre Projects. Mrs. Zumwalt's third graders are studying ocean animals, and her focus is adaptation: How do animals adapt to survive in the ocean? As her students learn about ocean life, they take special notice of how individual animals adapt: Alyssa learns that whelks have hard shells to protect them, Aidan knows that small fish travel together in schools, Cody reports that clams burrow into the sand to be safe, and Christopher read that sea otters have thick fur to keep them warm in the cold ocean water. Students add what they're learning about adaptation to a chart hanging in the classroom.

A month ago, Mrs. Zumwalt began the thematic unit by passing out a collection of nonfiction picture books for students to examine. After they looked at the books and read excerpts for 30 minutes or so, she brought them together to begin a **KWL chart**. This huge chart covers half of the back wall of the classroom; three sheets of poster paper hang vertically, side by side. The sheet on the left is labeled "K—What We Know About Ocean Animals," the middle sheet is labeled "W—What We Wonder About Ocean Animals," and the one on the right is labeled "L—What We Learned About Ocean Animals." Mrs. Zumwalt asked what students already knew about ocean animals, and they offered many facts, including "sea stars can grow a lot of arms," "sharks have three rows of teeth," and "jellyfish and puffer fish are poisonous," which the teacher recorded in the K column. Students also asked questions, including "Can an animal live inside a jellyfish?" "Is it true that father seahorses give birth?" and "How do some fish light up?" which she wrote in the W column. They continued to think of questions for several days, and Mrs. Zumwalt added them to the W column. At the end of the unit, students will add facts they've learned to the L column.

In this chapter, you'll learn how to integrate literacy instruction with content area study. Teachers develop thematic units in which students read nonfiction and content area textbooks and participate in a combination of "writing to learn" and "writing to demonstrate learning" activities. As you read this vignette, notice how Mrs. Zumwalt uses reading and writing as learning tools and how her students create multigenre reports to share what they've learned about ocean animals.

Mrs. Zumwalt talked about the six ocean habitats—seashore, open ocean, deep ocean, seabed, coral reefs, and polar seas—and the animals living in each one. She began with the seashore, and the class took a field trip to the Monterey Bay Aquarium to learn about the animals that live at the seashore. She focused on several animals in each habitat, reading aloud books and emphasizing how animals have adapted. For each habitat, they made a class chart, and students recorded information in their learning logs. They hung the charts in the classroom, and after all six habitats were introduced, Mrs. Zumwalt set out a pack of cards with names of animals and pictures of them for students to sort according to habitat. Check the animals listed in the figure Ocean Habitat Sort.

Students have **learning logs** with 20 sheets of lined paper for writing, 10 sheets of unlined paper for drawing and charting, and 15 information sheets about ocean animals. There's also a page for a personal word wall that's divided into boxes and labeled with letters of the alphabet; students record words from the class **word wall** on their personal word walls. Mrs. Zumwalt introduces new words during her presentations and as she reads aloud books from the text set on ocean animals; then she adds them to the word wall.

Eight of her 20 third graders come from homes where Spanish is spoken, and these students struggle with spoken and written English. Mrs. Zumwalt brings them together most days for an

OCEAN HABITAT SORT

Seashore	Open Ocean	Deep Ocean	Seabed	Coral Reefs	Polar Seas
shrimp	puffer fish	nautilus	sting ray	sea fan	penguin
sea gull	swordfish	sperm whale	nurse shark	coral	narwhal
sea otter	sea turtles		clam	barracuda	elephant seal
crab	manta ray		scallop		walrus
lobster	porpoise		sponge		leopard seal
octopus	dolphin		whelk		krill
pelican	squid				

extra lesson while their classmates work on other activities. She either previews the next lesson she'll teach or the next book she'll read, or she reviews her last lesson or the last book she read. In this small-group setting, students talk about what they're learning, ask questions, examine artifacts and pictures, and practice vocabulary. They often create **interactive writing** charts to share what they've discussed with their classmates. Here's their chart about schools of fish:

There are two kinds of schools. Kids go to school to be smart and little fish travel in groups that are called "schools." Fish are safer when they stick together in schools.

Once the class became familiar with a variety of ocean animals, each student picked a favorite animal to study; they chose sting rays, dolphins, squids, sea anemones, sand dollars, great white sharks, seals, penguins, sea turtles, jellyfish, octopuses, seahorses, pelicans, killer whales, barracudas, tunas, electric eels, lobsters, manatees, and squid. They researched their animals using the Internet and books in the text set; one of their best resources was the 11-volume encyclopedia *Aquatic Life of the World* (2001). Once they became experts, Mrs. Zumwalt introduced the idea of developing multigenre projects about the animals they'd studied. In multigenre projects, students create a variety of items representing different genres and package them in a box, on a display board, or in a notebook. Earlier in the year, the students worked collaboratively to develop a class multigenre project, so they were familiar with the procedure and the format.

The students decided to create four items for their multigenre projects: a chapter book with information about their animal's physical traits, diet, habitat, and enemies together with three other items. Other possible items include an adaptation poster, a life-cycle chart, a poem, an alliterative sentence, a diagram of the animal, and a pack of true/false cards about the animal. They plan to package their projects in cereal boxes brought from home and decorated with pictures, interesting information, and a big-idea statement about how that animal has adapted to ocean life.

The third graders use the writing process to prepare their books. These students know how writers develop, draft, and refine their writing, and earlier in the year, they created charts describing each stage of the writing process that now hang in the classroom. For prewriting, they used large, multicolored index cards to jot notes; the green one is for "Physical Traits," the yellow one is for "Diet," the blue one is for "Habitat," the purple one is for "Enemies," and the pink one is for "Other Interesting Information."

After students took notes using book resources from the text set and Internet resources, they shared the information they'd gathered one-on-one with classmates, who asked questions about things that confused them and encouraged the students to add more information about incomplete topics. Next, students wrote rough drafts and shared them with the partners they worked with earlier. Then they met in **revising groups** with Mrs. Zumwalt and several classmates and refined their drafts using the feedback they received from their group.

Now students are proofreading and correcting their revised drafts and creating published books. Once they correct the mechanical errors and meet with Mrs. Zumwalt for an editing conference, they word process their chapters, add illustrations, and compile the pages into a hardbound book. They're also preparing their boxes and the other items for their multigenre projects.

Christian researched pelicans; to see his nonfiction book, check the figure Christian's Book About Pelicans. For his other three items, he drew a life-cycle chart showing a pelican egg, a newly hatched bird in the nest, a young adult bird flapping its wings, and an older adult diving into the ocean for food; he made a Venn diagram comparing white and brown pelicans; and he wrote an alliterative sentence about pelicans using only words beginning with P. He decorated his multigenre project box with pictures of pelicans and interesting facts, including "Their wings are nine feet long." and "Pelicans can live to be 25 years old." The adaptation statement on his multigenre box reads, "Pelicans have web feet and they can dive underwater to catch their food. That's how they survive at the seashore."

Today, the third graders complete the KWL chart by adding comments about what they've learned. Cody offers that "octopuses can change shape and color to camouflage themselves," Hernan reports that "dolphins' tails go up and down but fishes' tails go side to side," and Carlos adds that "jellyfish are related to sea anemones because neither one has teeth."

CHRISTIAN'S BOOK ABOUT PELICANS

Chapter 1
Introduction

Pelicans are birds that live on the seashore. They have web feet for walking on sand and swimming. They can dive underwater to catch their food. That's how they live near the ocean.

Chapter 2
Physical Traits

Pelicans have some interesting physical traits. The pelican is easy to identify. They have big pouches and you can tell them by their big necks and plump bodies. The pelican has big legs and colors brown and white.

Chapter 3
Diet

Diet is what an animal eats. The pelican swallows a lot of fish. Pelicans gobble up meat. Pelicans attack sea stars and they chomp on seahorses.

Chapter 4
Habitat

A habitat is where an animal lives. The pelican lives in many countries. Pelicans are found where there's air and where it's warm. Some pelicans are now living in Monterey. Pelicans live by water, too.

Chapter 5
Enemies

Most animals are both prey and predator. That means animals are usually both the hunted and the hunter. The pelican eats seahorses and sea stars. Pelicans are hunted by sharks and people. Why do people hurt these birds? People dump waste into the water and it kills the fishes that the pelicans eat!

Chapter 6
Conclusion

I hope pelicans will always live in Monterey Bay but they could die if people dump pollution into the ocean and that would be very sad.

Next week, the third graders will share their completed multigenre boxes one-on-one with second graders, and they'll share them with their parents at back-to-school night. In preparation for this sharing, the students have been taking turns presenting their projects to small groups of classmates.

 STANDARDS CHECK!

Mrs. Zumwalt addressed the Common Core State Standards as she taught a third grade unit on ocean animals in the vignette you've just read. Review the third grade literacy Standards document online at http://www.corestandards.org/ELA-Literacy, and identify the Standards that Mrs. Zumwalt addressed through her instructional activities. Create your list, and compare it with Mrs. Zumwalt's.

Just as Mrs. Zumwalt's third graders learned about ocean animals through reading and writing, students at all grade levels—even kindergartners and first graders—use reading and writing as tools to learn and share their new knowledge about insects, the water cycle, Australia, pioneers, astronomy, World War II, and other content area topics. Teachers organize content area study into thematic units and identify big ideas for students to investigate. Units are time-consuming because student-constructed learning takes time. Teachers can't briefly touch on every topic; if they do, their students will learn very little. Instead, teachers make smart choices as they plan units, because only a relatively few topics can be presented in depth during a school year. During thematic units, students need opportunities to question, discuss, explore, and apply what they're learning (Harvey, 1998).

Content area textbooks are resources that many students use to learn about social studies, science, and other content areas, but they aren't a complete instructional program. Students need to know how to read content area textbooks because these books differ from other reading materials: They have unique conventions and structures that students use as aids in reading and remembering the big ideas. Because many students find textbooks more challenging to read than other books, teachers need to know how to support their students' reading so that they'll be successful.

The Common Core State Standards for English Language Arts stress the importance of teaching students to read nonfiction texts and to write reports and essays to be ready for college and careers. The document places a growing emphasis on nonfiction, both in language arts and in content area classes. By fourth grade, students are expected to balance their reading between fiction and nonfiction texts, and by eighth grade, to focus more on nonfiction texts. Students who master the Standards build strong content knowledge by reading nonfiction texts purposefully to gain knowledge, by using research and study strategies, and by sharing their knowledge through speaking and writing. Specific Standards address reading nonfiction texts and writing reports and essays to develop these abilities:

- Students integrate and evaluate information presented in diverse media and formats.
- Students delineate and evaluate the arguments and specific claims in a text.
- Students analyze how two or more texts address a topic.
- Students conduct research to build and present knowledge.
- Students write arguments to support claims and evidence.
- Students write informative texts to examine and convey complex ideas.

These competencies come from the Reading: Informational Text and the Writing Standards. Check the feature Common Core State Standards: Content Area Learning to read more about how the Standards uphold reading and writing in the content areas.

Learning Tools

Reading and writing are learning tools because reading has a powerful impact on writing, and vice versa (Tierney & Shanahan, 1996): When students read about a topic first, their writing is enhanced because of what they learn, and when they write about an idea from a book they're reading, their comprehension is deepened because they're exploring big ideas and relationships among them. Making these connections is especially important when students are learning content area information because of the added challenges that unfamiliar topics, text complexity, and technical vocabulary present.

Reading to Learn

A wide variety of high-quality picture books and chapter books are available today for teachers to use in teaching thematic units. Two outstanding science-related trade books, for example, are *Team Moon: How 400,000 People Landed Apollo 11 on the Moon* (Thimmesh, 2006), a stunning book that highlights the contributions of the people working behind the scenes on that space mission, and *Oh, Rats! The Story of Rats and People* (Marrin, 2006), a riveting book of facts about a survival champion. Two notable trade books on social studies topics are *Freedom Riders: John Lewis and Jim Zwerg on the Front Lines of the Civil Rights Movement* (Bausum, 2006), a powerful book that contrasts black America and white America in the 1960s by describing the journeys of two young men, and *One Thousand Tracings: Healing the Wounds of World War II* (Judge, 2007), a moving picture-book story of an American family who started a relief effort that reached 3,000 people in war-ravaged Europe. These books are both entertaining and informative, and the authors' engaging writing styles and formats keep readers interested. They're relevant, too, because many students make connections to their own lives and background knowledge as they read these books, and teachers use them to build students' background knowledge at the beginning of a thematic unit.

Watch as fifth graders use nonfiction books to support their content area learning. How do nonfiction books assist struggling students to read content area textbooks?

TEXT SETS. Teachers collect text sets of books and other reading materials on topics to use in teaching thematic units, as Mrs. Zumwalt did in the vignette. Materials for text sets are carefully chosen to include different genres, a range of reading levels to meet the needs of students, and multimedia resources that present a variety of perspectives. It's especially important to include plenty of books and other materials that English learners and struggling readers can read (Robb, 2002).

Teachers collect as many types of materials as possible, for example:

atlases and maps	nonfiction books
brochures and pamphlets	photographs
digital articles	poems and songs
films and videos	primary source materials
magazines	reference books
models and diagrams	stories
newspaper articles	websites and WebQuests

They collect single copies of some books and multiple copies of others to use for literature focus units and literature circles. Too often, teachers don't think about using magazines to teach social studies and science, but many excellent magazines are available, including *Click* and *National Geographic Little Kids* for young children and *Cobblestone* and *Time for Kids* for older students. Some magazines are also available in digital editions, including *Time for Kids*. Figure 12–1 presents a list of print and digital magazines for K–8 students.

MENTOR TEXTS. Teachers use stories, nonfiction books, and poems that students are familiar with to model the writer's craft (Dorfman & Cappelli, 2007). Picture books are especially useful mentor texts because they're short enough to be reread quickly. Teachers begin by rereading a mentor text and pointing out a specific feature such as adding punch with strong verbs, writing from a different perspective, or changing the tone by placing adjectives after nouns. Then students imitate the feature in brief collaborative compositions and in their own writing. They have opportunities to experiment with literary devices, imitate sentence and book structures, try out new genres, or explore different page arrangements.

FIGURE12–1	Magazines for K–8 Students		
MAGAZINE		**PRINT**	**DIGITAL**
Appleseeds (social studies) MU		●	
Ask (science/history) P		●	●
Big Backyard (nature) P		●	●
ChickaDEE (science) PM		●	
Click (science) P		●	
Cobblestone (history) MU		●	
Dig Into History (history/archeology) MU		●	●
FACES: People, Places, and Cultures (multicultural) M		●	
Ladybug (stories, poems, and songs) P		●	
Muse (science and the arts) MU		●	●
National Geographic Kids (geography and culture) MU		●	
National Geographic Little Kids (science) P		●	
OWL (science) MU		●	●
Ranger Rick (nature) M		●	●
Sports Illustrated for Kids (sports) MU		●	●
Time for Kids (current events) U		●	●

P = primary grades (K–2); M = middle grades (3–5); U = upper grades (6–8)

Nonfiction books are often used as mentor texts to teach students about new genres, organizational structures, and page formats. For example, *Gone Wild: An Endangered Animal Alphabet* (McLimans, 2006) is a graphic masterpiece where letters of the alphabet are transformed into vulnerable animals, and text boxes accompanying each letter provide facts about the animal. Students can use the format of *Gone Wild* to write a class alphabet book during a science or social studies unit. Another excellent mentor text is *Good Masters! Sweet Ladies! Voices From a Medieval Village* (Schlitz, 2007), a collection of 23 first-person character sketches of young people living in an English village in 1255. This book was designed as a play or a **readers theatre** presentation. Each character has a distinct personality and societal role, and historical notes are included in the margins. During a unit on ancient Rome or World War II, for example, students can use this

Check the Compendium of Instructional Procedures, which follows this chapter.

mentor text as a model for their own collection of character sketches and present them for students in other classrooms or their parents.

Teachers also use mentor texts in **minilessons** to teach students how to make their writing more powerful, and students use these books as springboards for writing as part of thematic units. Dorfman and Cappelli (2007) explain that "mentor texts serve as snapshots into the future. They help students envision the kind of writers they can become" (p. 3).

Writing to Learn

Students use writing as a tool for learning during thematic units to take notes, categorize ideas, draw graphic organizers, and write summaries. The focus is on using writing to help students think and learn, not on spelling every word correctly. Nevertheless, students should use classroom resources, such as **word walls**, to spell most words correctly and write as neatly as possible so that they can reread their own writing. Armbruster, McCarthey, and Cummins (2005) also point out that writing to learn serves two other purposes as well: When students write about what they're learning, it helps them become better writers, and teachers can use students' writing to assess their learning.

LEARNING LOGS. Students use **learning logs** to record and react to what they're learning in social studies, science, or other content areas. Laura Robb (2003) explains that learning logs are "a place to think on paper" (p. 60). Students write in these journals to discover gaps in their knowledge and to explore relationships between what they're learning and their past experiences. Through these activities, students practice taking notes, writing descriptions and directions, and making graphic organizers. Figure 12–2 presents

FIGURE 12–2   A Page From a Learning Log

FIGURE 12–3   A Note-Taking/Note-Making Sheet

Where Electricity Comes From	
Note-Taking (My Notes After Reading)	Note-Making (My Questions and Ideas)
1. <u>Coal, Oil, and Gas Energy</u> Power plants burn these fuels to make electricity. This is the most common kind but we need more because these are NOT renewable.	Our house has electricity for TV, refrigerator, lights and lots of other stuff. I don't know where it comes from. Maybe it comes from gas because we have gas heat, but I will ask my mom.
2. <u>Water Energy</u> Hydroelectric power plants turn falling water into electricity. They are located at dams like the Grand Coulee Dam. It's renewable.	I've never heard of this before but there's a dam near where my Nana lives. Does it make electric power?
3. <u>Sun Energy</u> Solar generators use the sun's energy to make electricity. They are most common in places where there's lots of sunshine.	My dad said we might get solar panels on our roof because our bills are too high. I need to find out how solar panels work and how much they cost.
4. <u>Wind Energy</u> Huge windmills collect wind energy and then turbines make electricity. There are windmills in places where there is lots of wind.	I saw some of these windmills on the side of Interstate 5. They use renewable energy—that is good, but they also kill lots of birds—that is bad.
5. <u>Nuclear Energy</u> Uranium atoms are split in nuclear reactors to release energy. This is kind of dangerous because of radiation and it's hard to get rid of radioactive waste.	There was a tsunami in Japan that ruined a nuclear power plant and people had to escape because of deadly radiation. Some people died. They could never turn the reactor back on.

a page from a second grader's learning log about penguins; the chart shows that penguins have three enemies—leopard seals, skua gulls, and people.

DOUBLE-ENTRY JOURNALS. Double-entry journals are just what the name suggests: Students divide their journal pages into two parts and write different types of information in each one (Daniels & Zemelman, 2004). For example, they write important facts in one column and their reactions to the information in the other column, or questions about the topic in the left column and answers in the right column. Figure 12–3 shows a fifth grader's double-entry journal about electricity. In the left column, the student wrote information he was learning, and in the right column, he asked questions and made personal connections to the information.

SIMULATED JOURNALS. In some stories, such as *Catherine, Called Birdy* (Cushman, 2012), the author assumes the role of a character and writes a series of diary entries from his or her point of view; these books are *simulated journals*. They're rich with historical details, and the book's language typifies the vocabulary and the sentence structure of the period. At the end of the book, authors often include information about how they researched the period and explanations about the liberties they took with the characters or events that are recorded. Younger students read *Diary of a Spider* (Cronin, 2011) and other books in the series about a worm and a fly to learn scientific information written in an entertaining journal format.

Scholastic has created two series of historical journals; one is for girls, and the other for boys. *I Walk in Dread: The Diary of Deliverance Trembly, Witness to the Salem Witch Trials* (Fraustino, 2004), *A Picture of Freedom: The Diary of Clotee, a Slave Girl* (McKissack, 1997), and *Survival in the Storm: The Dust Bowl Diary of Grace Edwards* (Janke, 2002) are from the Dear America series; each book provides a glimpse into American history from a young girl's perspective. The My Name Is America series features books written from a boy's point of view; they include *The Journal of Patrick Seamus Flaherty: United States Marine Corps* (White, 2002), *The Journal of Ben Uchida: Citizen 13559, Mirror Lake Internment Camp* (Denenberg, 1999), and *The Journal of Jesse Smoke: A Cherokee Boy, Trail of Tears, 1838* (Bruchac, 2001). Both sets of books are handsomely bound to look like old journals with heavy paper, rough-cut around the edges.

Students, too, write simulated journals by assuming the role of another person and writing from that person's viewpoint. They assume the role of a historical figure when they read biographies or as part of social studies units, and as they read stories, students assume the role of a character in the story. When students write from the viewpoint of a famous person, they begin by making a "life line," a time line of the person's life. Then they pick key dates in the person's life and write entries about what happened on those dates. A fifth grader wrote these diary entries as Benjamin Franklin:

December 10, 1719

Dear Diary,

My brother James is so mad at me. He just figured out that I'm the one who wrote the articles for his newspaper and signed them Mistress Silence Dogood. He says I can't do any more of them. I don't understand why. My articles are funny. Everyone reads them. I bet he won't sell as many newspapers anymore. Now I have to just do the printing.

February 15, 1735

Dear Diary,

I have printed my third "Poor Richard's Almanack." It is the most popular book in America and now I am famous. Everyone reads it. I pretend that somebody named Richard Saunders writes it, but it's really me. I also put my wise sayings in it. My favorite wise saying is "Early to bed, early to rise, makes a man healthy, wealthy, and wise."

June 22, 1763

Dear Diary,

I've been an inventor for many years now. There are a lot of things I have invented like the Franklin stove (named after me) and bifocal glasses, and the lightning rod, and a long arm to get books off of the high shelves. That's how I work. I see something that we don't have and if it is needed, I figure out how to do it. I guess I just have the knack for inventing.

May 25, 1776

Dear Diary,

Tom Jefferson and I are working on the Declaration of Independence. The patriots at the Continental Congress chose us to do it but it is dangerous business. The Red Coats will call us traitors and kill us if they can. I like young Tom from Virginia. He'll make a good king of America some day.

April 16, 1790

Dear Diary,

I am dying. I only have a day or two to live. But it's OK because I am 84 years old. Not very many people live as long as I have or do so many things in a life. I was a printer by trade but I have also been a scientist, an inventor, a writer, and a statesman. I have lived to see the Philadelphia that I love so very much become part of a new country. Good-bye to my family and everyone who loves me.

These entries show how the fifth grader chose the important dates for each entry and wove in factual information.

Students can use simulated journals in two ways: as a journal or as a refined and polished composition—a demonstration-of-learning project. When students use simulated journals as a tool for learning, they write entries as they're reading a book to get to know the character better, or during a thematic unit as they're learning about the historical period. In these entries, students explore concepts and make connections between what they're learning and what they already know. These journal entries are less polished than when students write a simulated journal as a culminating project. When they're developing a project, students plan out their journals carefully, identify important dates, and use the writing process to draft, revise, and edit their entries. They often add covers typical of the historical period. For example, a simulated journal written during a unit on ancient Greece might be written on a long sheet of butcher paper and rolled like a scroll, or a pioneer journal might be backed with brown paper cut to resemble an animal hide.

QUICKWRITING. When students do **quickwriting**, they write on a topic for 5 to 10 minutes, letting thoughts flow from their minds to their pens without focusing on mechanics or revisions. Young children often draw pictures or use a combination of drawing and writing to explore ideas. Teachers use quickwriting to activate students' background knowledge at the beginning of a thematic unit, monitor their progress and clarify misconceptions during the unit, and review big ideas at the end (Readence, Moore, & Rickelman, 2000).

Toward the end of a thematic unit on the solar system, for example, fourth graders each chose a word from the word wall for a quickwrite, and then they shared their writing with classmates. This is one student's quickwrite on Mars:

Mars is known as the red planet. Mars is Earth's neighbor. Mars is a lot like Earth. On Mars one day lasts 24 hours. It is the fourth planet in the solar system. Mars may have life forms. Two rovers have been exploring Mars. One named Curiosity found something exciting. There is water on Mars! It is under the dusty and rocky surface. Mars has no rings.

After writing, students usually share their writing in small groups, and then one student in each group shares with the class. Sharing takes about 10 minutes, so the entire quickwriting activity can be completed in 20 minutes or less.

 MONITOR: Check Your Understanding 12.1

Demonstrating Learning

Students research topics and then use writing to demonstrate their learning. This writing is more formal, and students apply their knowledge of the writing process to revise and edit their writing before making the final copy. Four ways that students demonstrate learning are by writing reports, developing essays, crafting poems, and constructing multigenre projects.

Reports

Reports are the best known type of writing to demonstrate learning; students write many types of reports, ranging from posters to collaborative books and individual reports. Too often, students aren't exposed to report writing until they're faced with writing a term paper in high school, and then they're overwhelmed with learning how to take notes on note cards, organize information, write the paper, and compile a bibliography. There's absolutely no reason to postpone report writing! Early, successful experiences with nonfiction writing teach students about content area topics as well as how to share information and demonstrate learning (Harvey, 1998; Tompkins, 2012).

POSTERS. Students combine visual and verbal elements when they make posters (Moline, 1995); English learners are often better able to demonstrate their new knowledge through a combination of words and pictures than by words alone (Guccione, 2011). They draw pictures and diagrams and write labels and commentary. For example, students draw diagrams of the inner and outer planets in the solar system, label the clothing a Revolutionary War soldier wore and the supplies he carried, identify important events of a person's life on a life line, or chart the explorers' voyages to America and around the world on a map. Students plan the information they want to include in the poster and devise an attention-getting display using headings, illustrations, captions, boxes, and rules. They prepare a rough draft of their posters, section by section, and then revise and edit each section. Then they make a final copy of each section, glue the sections onto a sheet of posterboard, and share their posters with classmates as they would share finished pieces of writing. As part of a reading and writing workshop focusing on nonfiction books, a fifth grader read *The Magic School Bus Inside a Beehive* (Cole, 1996) and created the poster shown in Figure 12–4 to share what he had learned.

FIGURE 12–4   A Report Poster

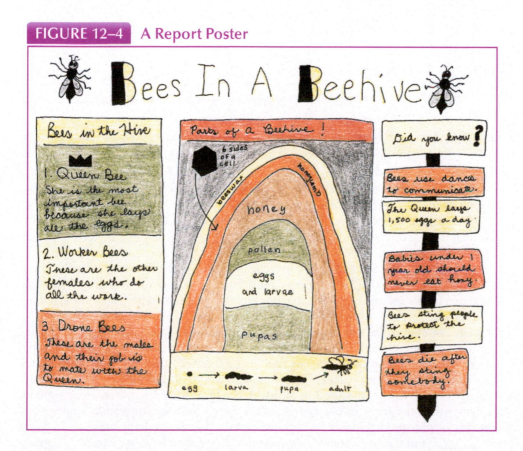

FIGURE 12–5   **A Page From an "All About Penguins" Book**

Penguins lay eggs
and keep them
worm with ther
feets and ther
stomechs.

"ALL ABOUT . . ." BOOKS. The first reports that young children write are "All About . . ." books, in which they provide information about familiar topics, such as "Firefighters," "Planting Seeds," and "Penguins." Young children write an entire booklet on a single topic; usually one piece of information and an illustration appear on each page. A page from a first grader's "All About Penguins" book is shown in Figure 12–5. In the figure, Rosa drew a picture at the top of the page and wrote a sentence explaining the picture underneath.

ALPHABET BOOKS. Students work together as a class to write alphabet books, using the letters of the alphabet to organize the information they want to share. These collaborative books incorporate the sequence structure, because the pages are arranged in alphabetical order. Alphabet books such as *Z Is for Zamboni: A Hockey Alphabet* (Napier, 2002) and *The Queen's Progress: An Elizabethan Alphabet* (Mannis, 2003) are useful mentor texts. Students begin by brainstorming information related to the topic being studied and identify a word or fact for each letter of the alphabet. Then they work individually or with partners to compose pages for the book. The format for the pages is similar to the one used in alphabet books written by professional authors: Students write the letter in one corner of the page, draw an illustration, and write a sentence or paragraph to describe the word or fact. The text usually begins "_____ is for _____," and then a sentence or paragraph description follows. In a fourth grade class's alphabet book on the California missions, for instance, Ramon wrote the "*U* is for *Unbearable*" page:

> *Life was UNBEARABLE at the missions for many Indians because they couldn't hunt or do the things they used to. They had to stay at the mission and obey the padres. Sometimes the padres even beat them if they tried to go home to see their families.*

CLASS COLLABORATIONS. Students work together to write **collaborative books**. Sometimes students each write one page for the report, or they can work together in small groups to write chapters. Students create collaborative reports on almost any science or social studies topic. They write collaborative biographies: Each student or small group writes about one event or accomplishment in the subject's life, and then the pages are assembled in chronological order. Or, students work in small groups to write chapters for a collaborative report on the planets in the solar system, ancient Egypt, or the Oregon Trail.

INDIVIDUAL REPORTS. Students also write individual reports after doing authentic research, in which they explore topics that interest them or hunt for answers to questions they've posed (Harvey, 1998; Stead, 2002). They read books and interview people with special knowledge, and increasingly they're turning to the Internet for information. After learning about their topics, students write reports, using the writing process, to share their new knowledge. Students often word process the text, add photos from the Internet, and publish their reports in book format.

Essays

Students write essays to explain, analyze, and persuade; sometimes their topics are personal, such as the death of a parent or adjusting to a new school, and at other times, they address national and international issues such as gun safety, famine, and immigration. These compositions are short, usually no longer than two pages. They're classified as nonfiction but often include some story elements, especially in personal essays. Students write essays from their own viewpoints, and their voices should come clearly through the writing (Pryle, 2007). They learn to write personal essays, in which they recount an experience, shaping it to illustrate a theme or generalization; comparison essays, in which they compare two or more things to emphasize important differences and sometimes offer an opinion; and persuasive essays, in which they try to persuade readers to accept an idea, agree with an opinion, or take a course of action.

Another type is the five-paragraph essay; it's tightly structured with the introduction, body, and conclusion divided into five paragraphs, as the name suggests. In the first paragraph, the writer introduces the topic, often using a thesis statement. In the next three paragraphs, the writer presents three ideas with supporting evidence and examples, one in each paragraph. In the last paragraph, the writer summarizes the ideas and restates the thesis. The five-paragraph essay is very controversial: Proponents argue that it teaches students how to organize their thoughts, but opponents counter that its rigid structure limits thinking. In addition, essays can't always be organized into a predetermined number of paragraphs; instead, the topic and the writer's ideas drive the organization and determine the number of paragraphs (Robb, 2004). Because of its limitations, use of this type of essay isn't recommended.

Poems

Students often write poems as projects after reading books and to demonstrate content area learning as part of thematic units. They write formula poems by beginning each line or stanza with a word or line, they create free-form poems, and they follow the structure of model poems as they create their own poems.

"I AM . . ." POEMS. Students assume the role of a person and write a poem from that person's viewpoint. They begin and end the poem (or each stanza) with "I am _____" and begin all the other lines with "I." For example, an eighth grader wrote an "I Am . . ." poem from the viewpoint of John F. Kennedy after reading a biography about the 35th president:

> I am John Fitzgerald Kennedy.
> I commanded a PT boat in World War II.
> I saved my crew after a Japanese ship hit us.
> I became a politician because that's
> what my dad wanted me to do.
> I was elected the 35th president of the United States.
> I said, "Ask not what your country can do for you—
> ask what you can do for your country."
> I believed in equal rights for blacks and whites.
> I began the Peace Corps to help the world live free.
> I cried the tears of assassination because
> Lee Harvey Oswald shot me dead.
> I left my young family in America's love.
> I am John Fitzgerald Kennedy.

POEMS FOR TWO VOICES. Students take on two, often contrasting, roles to write poems for two voices. This poetic form is arranged in two columns, with lines written side by side. It's read simultaneously by two readers or two groups of readers: One reads the left column, and the other reads the right column. When both readers have words—either the same words or different words—written on the same line, they read them simultaneously so that the poem sounds like a musical duet. Two eighth graders wrote the following poem during a unit on slavery, after learning about Harriet Tubman and her work with the Underground Railroad. The left column is written from the slave's perspective, and the right column from the conductor's.

FREEDOM!	FREEDOM!
	I hide slaves in my house;
	It's my moral duty.
I dodge the law wherever I go;	
I follow the north star.	
	I feed them until they get
	to the next stop.
I hide in closets and cellars	
and sleep whenever I can.	
	It is a big risk.
I am in grave danger.	
BUT IT'S WORTH IT!	BUT IT'S WORTH IT!
Harriet Tubman is the Moses	
of our people.	
	I am a conductor,
	helping my passengers
	along the way.
Once I reach Canada,	
I'll be free.	
Will freedom be sweet?	
	Oh, yes it will.
FREE AT LAST!	FREE AT LAST!

FOUND POEMS. Students create poems by culling words and phrases from a book they're reading and arranging the words and phrases into a free-form poem. Fourth graders created this poem about a saguaro cactus after reading *Cactus Hotel* (Guiberson, 2007):

> A young cactus sprouts up.
> After 10 years only four inches high,
> after 25 years two feet tall,
> after 50 years 10 feet tall.
> A welcoming signal across the desert.
> A Gila woodpecker,
> a white-winged dove,
> an elf owl
> decide to stay.
> After 60 years an arm grows,
> the cactus hotel is 18 feet tall.
> After 150 years 7 long branches
> and holes of every size
> in the cactus hotel.

Multigenre Projects

Students explore a science or social studies topic through several genres in a **multigenre project** (Allen, 2001). They combine content area study with writing in significant

Booklist Multigenre Books

GRADE LEVEL	BOOKS
Primary Grades (K–2)	Andrews-Goebel, N. (2002). *The pot that Juan built.* New York: Lee & Low.
	Martin, J. B. (2009). *Snowflake Bentley.* New York: Sandpiper.
	Teague, M. (2002). *Dear Mrs. La Rue: Letters from obedience school.* New York: Scholastic. (And other books in the series.)
Middle Grades (3–5)	Bang, M. (2001). *Nobody particular: One woman's fight to save the bay.* New York: Henry Holt.
	Cole, J. (2001). *The magic school bus explores the senses.* New York: Scholastic. (And other books in the series.)
	Geronimo Stilton, secret agent. (2008). New York: Scholastic. (And other books in the series.)
	Hoyt-Goldsmith, D. (2002). *Celebrating Ramadan.* New York: Holiday House.
	Kinney, J. (2007). *Diary of a wimpy kid.* New York: Scholastic. (And other books in the series.)
	Kurlansky, M. (2001). *The cod's tale.* New York: Putnam.
	Matthews, J. (2006). *Pirates.* New York: Atheneum.
Upper Grades (6–8)	Avi. (2010). *Nothing but the truth: A documentary novel.* New York: Scholastic.
	Conrad, P. (2005). *Our house: Stories of Levittown.* New York: Scholastic.
	Holm, J. L. (2011). *Middle school is worse than meatloaf: A year told through stuff.* New York: Atheneum.
	Klise, K. (1999). *Regarding the fountain: A tale, in letters, of liars and leaks.* New York: Avon. (And other books in the series.)
	Lester, J. (2005). *To be a slave.* New York: Puffin Books.
	Ryan, P. M. (2012). *The dreamer.* New York: Scholastic.
	Snicket, L. (2003). *Lemony Snicket: The unauthorized autobiography.* New York: HarperCollins.
	Thayer, E. L. (2000). *Ernest L. Thayer's Casey at the bat: A ballad of the republic sung in the year 1888.* New York: Chronicle Books.

and meaningful ways. Romano (2000) explains that the benefit of this approach is that each genre offers ways of learning and understanding that the others don't; students gain different understandings, for example, by writing a simulated journal entry, an alphabet book, and a time line. Teachers or students identify a **repetend**, a common thread or unifying theme for the project, which helps students move beyond the level of remembering facts to a higher, more analytical level of understanding. In the vignette at the beginning of the chapter, Mrs. Zumwalt's repetend was adaptation; in their multigenre projects, her students highlighted how the animal they studied adapted to life in the ocean.

Depending on the information they want to present and their repetend, students use a variety of genres such as these for their projects:

acrostics	feature articles	questions and answers
"All About . . ." books	found poems	quotes
alphabet books	"I Am . . ." poems	reports
artifacts	letters	riddles
biographical sketches	life lines	simulated journals
blogs	maps	slide shows
book boxes	newspaper articles	songs
cartoons	open-mind portraits	time lines
clusters	photo galleries	Venn diagrams
cubes	poems	video clips
data charts	postcards	websites and wikis
double-entry journals	posters	word clouds
essays	PowerPoint presentations	word sorts

New LITERACIES

WebQuests

WebQuests are inquiry-oriented digital projects that enhance students' learning by scaffolding their thinking and involving them in meaningful tasks. These projects foster students' ability to use the Internet to search and retrieve information from websites and understand multimodal presentations (Ikpeze & Boyd, 2007). Students often waste time searching for online resources, but in WebQuests, the resources are bookmarked for easier use. WebQuests have these components:

- **Introduction.** An engaging scenario with background information and the roles that students will assume, such as time traveler, botanist, or superhero
- **Task.** The creative activity that students will complete, such as making a map, writing a song, or creating a board game
- **Process.** Steps that students follow to complete the task
- **Resources.** Bookmarked websites and any other resources that students will need
- **Evaluation.** A rubric for students to self-assess their work
- **Conclusion.** Opportunities for students to share the experience and reflect on their learning

These online learning projects were created by Bernie Dodge of San Diego State University. His website provides useful information about locating teacher-made WebQuests and creating your own.

Teachers have created hundreds of WebQuests on a wide range of literature, social studies, and science topics that are available online. A few are designed for younger children, but most are for older students. For example, in one WebQuest, students who have read *Hatchet* (Paulsen, 2007) embark on a wilderness journey and answer scavenger-hunt questions as they learn survival skills, and in another, students who are studying ancient Egypt travel back to 1250 B.C. to find King Tut's burial mask and decode the message hidden inside it. Other WebQuest topics include chocolate, biomes, voting, World War II, and hurricanes, as well as popular books, such as *The Outsiders* (Hinton, 2007) and *Whirligig* (Fleischman, 2010).

Most digital resources are informational websites that include multimodal features such as graphics, photos, maps, video clips, sound, and interactive activities. It's harder to locate good resources for literature WebQuests, but effective websites about authors and on topics related to a story's setting and social issues, such as gangs and drunk driving, are available.

When teachers choose WebQuests, they examine them to be sure they include the components described here, and that resource links are active, or teachers need to replace them. Also, they consider whether completing a digital inquiry project will enhance students' understanding and promote higher level thinking.

Students generally use three or more genres in a multigenre project and include both textual and visual genres. What matters most is that the genres extend and amplify the repetend.

Not only can students create multigenre projects, but some authors use the technique in trade books; *The Magic School Bus Inside a Hurricane* (Cole, 1996) and others in the Magic School Bus series are examples of multigenre books. Each book features a story about Ms. Frizzle and her students on a fantastic science adventure, and on the side panels of pages, a variety of explanations, charts, diagrams, and essays are presented. Together the story and informational side panels present a more complete, multigenre presentation or project. Other multigenre books for older students are *To Be a Slave* (Lester, 2005), *Nothing But the Truth* (Avi, 2010), *Lemony Snicket: The Unauthorized Autobiography* (Snicket, 2003), *Middle School Is Worse Than Meatloaf* (Holm, 2011), and *Ernest L. Thayer's Casey at the Bat: A Ballad of the Republic Sung in the Year 1888* (Thayer, 2000). Booklist: Multigenre Books presents a collection of books for all grade levels.

 MONITOR: Check Your Understanding 12.2

Content Area Textbooks

Textbooks have traditionally been the centerpiece of social studies and science classes, but these books have shortcomings that limit their effectiveness. Too often, content area textbooks are unappealing and too difficult for students to read and understand, and they cover too many topics superficially. It's up to teachers to plan instruction to make content area textbooks more comprehensible and to supplement students' learning with other reading and writing activities during thematic units. To assess your effectiveness using content area textbooks, see the Teacher Checklist: How do I use content area textbooks?

Textbook Features

Content area textbooks look different than other types of books and have unique conventions, such as the following:

Headings and subheadings to direct readers' attention to the big ideas

Photographs and drawings to illustrate the big ideas

Charts and maps to provide detailed information visually

Margin notes to provide supplemental information or to direct readers to additional information on a topic

Highlighted words to identify key vocabulary

An index for locating specific information

A glossary to assist readers in pronouncing and defining technical words

Study questions at the end of the chapter to check readers' comprehension

Because these features make the textbook easier to read, it's essential that students learn to use them to make reading

---

TEACHER *Checklist*

How do I use content area textbooks?

○ Do I teach students about the unique conventions of textbooks, and show how to use them as comprehension aids?

○ Do I have students create questions before reading each section of a chapter and then read to find the answers?

○ Do I introduce key terms before students read the textbook assignment?

○ Do students focus on the big ideas instead of trying to remember lots of facts?

○ Do students complete graphic organizers as they read because these visual representations emphasize the big ideas and the connections among them?

○ Do I include small-group activities to make textbooks more comprehensible?

○ Do I teach students to take notes about the big ideas as they read?

○ Do I encourage students to be active readers, to ask themselves questions and to monitor their reading?

○ Do I use the listen-read-discuss format when textbook assignments are too difficult for students to read on their own?

○ Do I create text sets to supplement content area textbooks?

Watch this video to see how quickwrites become an important part of a social studies lesson. How does the teacher integrate quickwriting with other strategies to create a meaningful lesson?

content area textbooks more effective and improve their comprehension (Harvey & Goudvis, 2007). Teachers teach **minilessons** about these features and demonstrate how to use them to read more effectively.

Making Textbooks More Comprehensible

Teachers use a variety of activities during each stage of the reading process to make content area textbooks more reader friendly and to improve students' comprehension of what they've read. Figure 12–6 lists ways teachers can make content area textbooks more comprehensible at each stage of the reading process. Teachers choose one or more activities at each stage to support their students' reading but never try to do all of the activities listed in the figure during a single reading assignment.

STAGE 1: Prereading. Teachers prepare students to read the chapter and nurture their interest in the topic in these ways:

- Activate and build students' background knowledge about the topic
- Introduce big ideas and technical words
- Set purposes for reading
- Preview the text

Teachers use a variety of activities to activate and build students' background knowledge about the topic, including developing **KWL charts**, reading aloud stories and nonfiction books, reading digital articles, and viewing videos and DVDs. They also use the gamelike formats of anticipation guides and exclusion brainstorming to heighten students' interest. In **anticipation guides**, teachers introduce a set of statements on the topic of the chapter, students agree or disagree with each statement, and then they read the assignment to see if they were right. In **exclusion brainstorming**, students examine a list of words and decide which ones they think are related to the

FIGURE 12–6 Activities to Make Textbooks More Comprehensible

STAGE	ACTIVITIES	
Prereading	KWL charts	Possible sentences
	Text set of books	Prereading plan
	Websites, videos, and DVDs	Question-Answer-Relationships
	Anticipation guides	Text walk
	Exclusion brainstorming	Word walls
Reading	Interactive read-aloud	Graphic organizers
	Partner reading	Note taking
	Small-group read and share	
Responding	Discussions	Learning logs
	Think-pair-square-share	Double-entry journals
	Graphic organizers	Quickwriting
Exploring	Word walls	Semantic feature analysis
	Word sorts	Hot seat
	Data charts	Tea party
Applying	WebQuests	Multigenre projects
	PowerPoint presentations	Oral reports
	Essays	

textbook chapter, and then they read the chapter to check their predictions.

Teachers introduce the big ideas in a chapter when they create a **prereading plan** in which they present an idea discussed in the chapter and then have students brainstorm words and ideas related to it. They begin a **word wall** with some key words. Another activity is **possible sentences**, in which students compose sentences that might be in the textbook chapter using two or more vocabulary words from the chapter. Later, as they read the chapter, students check to see if their sentences are included or are accurate enough so that they could be used in the chapter.

Students are more successful when they have a purpose for reading. Teachers set the purpose through prereading activities, and they also can have students read the questions at the end of the chapter, assume responsibility for finding the answer to a specific question, and then read to find the answer. After reading, students share their answers with the class. To preview the chapter, teachers take students on a "text walk" page by page through the chapter, noting main headings, looking at illustrations, and reading diagrams and charts. Sometimes students turn the main headings into questions and prepare to read to find the answers to the questions or check the questions at the end of the chapter to determine the **Question-Answer-Relationships**.

STAGE 2: Reading. Teachers support students as they read the textbook chapter in these ways:

- Ensure that students can read the assignment
- Assist students in identifying the big ideas
- Help students organize ideas and details

It's essential that students can read the chapter. Sometimes the prereading activities provide enough scaffolding so that students can read the assignment successfully, but sometimes they need more support. When students can't read the chapter, teachers have several options. They can read the chapter aloud before students read it independently, or students can read with a partner. Teachers also can divide the chapter into sections and assign groups of students to read each section and report back to the class; in this way, the reading assignment is shorter, and students can read along with their group members. Students learn the material from the entire chapter as they listen to classmates share their sections. After this sharing experience, students may then be able to go back and read the chapter.

Teachers help students identify and organize the big ideas in a variety of ways. Two of the best ways are taking notes about the big ideas and completing graphic organizers that focus on the big ideas as they read.

STAGE 3: Responding. Teachers help students develop and refine their comprehension in this stage as they think, talk, and write about the information they've read in these ways:

- Clarify students' misunderstandings
- Help students summarize the big ideas

Classroom INTERVENTIONS

Content Area Textbooks

Struggling readers need to know how to read content area textbooks. Typically they approach all reading assignments the same way—they open to the first page and read straight through—and afterward complain that they don't remember anything. This approach doesn't work because students aren't actively involved in the reading experience, and they're not taking advantage of the special features used in content area textbooks, including headings, highlighted words, illustrations, end-of-chapter questions, and a glossary, that make the books easier to read.

Successful readers think about the text while they're reading, and the textbook features encourage students' active engagement. Before beginning to read, students activate their background knowledge by previewing the chapter. They read the introduction, the headings, the conclusion, and the end-of-chapter questions and examine photos and illustrations. They locate highlighted vocabulary words, use context clues to figure out the meaning of some words, and check the meaning of others in the glossary. Now they're thinking about the topic. As they read, students try to identify the big ideas and the relationships among them. They stop after reading each section to add information to a graphic organizer, take notes using small self-stick notes, or talk about the section with a classmate. After students finish reading the entire chapter, they make sure they can answer the end-of-chapter questions.

Teachers need to teach students how to read a content area textbook, pointing out the special features and demonstrating how to use them. Next, students work in small groups or with partners as they practice using the features to engage their thinking and improve their comprehension. With guided practice and opportunities to work collaboratively with classmates, students can become more successful readers.

ⓒ Make connections to students' lives

Students talk about the big ideas, ask questions to clarify confusions, and make connections as they participate in class discussions. They also talk about the chapter in small groups. One popular technique is *think-pair-square-share*, in which students think about a topic individually for several minutes; then they pair up with classmates to share their thoughts and hear other points of view. Next, each pair of students gets together with another pair, forming a square, to share their thinking. Finally, students come back together as a class to discuss the topic.

Writing is another way for students to respond: They do **quickwrites**, write in learning logs, or use **double-entry journals** to record quotes or important information from the chapter and make connections to their own lives. Students also write summaries in which they synthesize the big ideas and describe the relationships among them. Summary writing requires students to think strategically as they analyze what they've read to determine which ideas are important. Minilesson: Writing Summaries of Informational Articles shows how Mr. Surabian teaches his fourth graders about a new writing genre.

STAGE 4: Exploring. Teachers ask students to dig into the text during the exploring stage to focus on vocabulary, examine the text, and analyze the big ideas in these ways:

ⓒ Have students study vocabulary words
ⓒ Review the big ideas in the chapter
ⓒ Help students to connect the big ideas and details

As they study the technical words in the chapter, students post them on word walls, make posters to study their meaning, and do **word sorts** to emphasize the relationships among the big ideas. To focus on the big ideas, students make data charts to record information according to the big ideas or create a **semantic feature analysis** chart to classify important information. Figure 12–7 shows an excerpt from a data chart that fourth graders made as they studied the regions of their state. Students often keep these charts and refer to them to write reports or create other projects. They also participate in **hot seat** and **tea party** to talk about what they're learning.

STAGE 5: Applying. Teachers support students as they apply what they've learned by creating projects in these ways:

ⓒ Expand students' knowledge about the topic
ⓒ Have students personalize their learning
ⓒ Expect students to share their knowledge

Students participate in WebQuests, read additional books from the text set, conduct research online, and interview people to expand their knowledge, and then they share what they've learned by writing reports and essays, creating PowerPoint presentations and multigenre projects, presenting oral reports, and doing other projects.

Learning How to Study

Students are often asked to remember content area material that they've read for a discussion, to take a test, or for an oral or written project. The traditional way to study is to memorize a list of facts, but it's more effective to use strategies that require students to think critically and to elaborate ideas. As they study, students do the following:

ⓒ Restate the big ideas in their own words

Minilesson

TOPIC: Writing Summaries of Informational Articles
GRADE: Fourth Grade
TIME: Five 30-minute sessions

Mr. Surabian plans to teach his students how to write a summary; only a few seem familiar with the term *summary writing*, and no one knows how to write one. Writing a summary is one of the fourth grade standards, and the prompt for the district's writing assessment often requires summary writing.

① Introduce the Topic

Mr. Surabian explains that a summary is a brief statement of the main points of an article. He presents a poster with these characteristics of a summary:

- A summary tells the big ideas.
- A summary shows the connections between the big ideas.
- A summary has a generalization or a conclusion.
- A summary is written in your own words.
- A summary is brief.

② Share Examples

Mr. Surabian shares a one-page article about Wilbur and Orville Wright and the summary he's written about it. The students check that the summary meets all of the characteristics on the poster. Then he shares a second article about mummification, and the students pick out the big ideas and highlight them. Next, Mr. Surabian draws a diagram to show the relationships among the ideas, and they develop a generalization or conclusion statement. Then he shares his summary, and the fourth graders check that he included the big ideas and that the summary meets all of the characteristics on the poster.

③ Provide Information

The next day, Mr. Surabian reviews the characteristics of a summary and shares an article about motorcycles. The students read it, identify and highlight the big ideas, draw a diagram to illustrate the relationships among the ideas, and create a generalization. After this preparation, they write a summary of the article, checking that it meets the characteristics listed on the classroom poster. On the third day, Mr. Surabian's students repeat the process with an article about rain forests.

④ Guide Practice

On the fourth day, Mr. Surabian shares an article about the Mississippi River. The students read and discuss it, identifying the big ideas, relationships among them, and possible conclusions. Then the teacher divides the students into small groups, and each group writes a summary. Afterward, they share their summaries and check them against the poster. The class repeats this activity the next day; this time, they read about porpoises. Mr. Surabian shortens the time spent discussing the article and identifying the big ideas and conclusions so that students must assume more responsibility for developing and writing the summary.

⑤ Assess Learning

Mr. Surabian assesses students' learning by monitoring them as they work in small groups. He identifies several students who need practice, and he plans additional minilessons with them.

FIGURE 12–7   An Excerpt From a Data Chart

REGION	VEGETATION	ANIMALS	PLACES	HISTORY	ECONOMY
North	Redwood tres	Grizzly Bears Salmon	Eureka Napa Valley	Sutter's Fort GOLD!	Logging Wine
North Coast	Redwood trees Giant sequoia tres	seals Sea Otters Monarch Butterflies	San Francisco	Chinatown Cable Cars Earthquake	Computers Ghirardelli chocolate Levis
South Coast	Palm tres Orange tres	Gray whales Condors	Los Angeles Hollywood	El Camino Real missions O.J. Simpson Earthquake	Disneyland TV + movies airplanes
Central Valley	Poppies	Quail	Fresno Sacramento	capital Pony Express Railroad	grapes Peaches Cotton Almond
Sierra Nevada	Giant Sequoia Lupine	Mule Deer Golden eagles Black Baers	Yosemite	John Muir	skiing

☍ Make connections among the big ideas
☍ Add details to each of the big ideas
☍ Ask questions about the importance of the ideas
☍ Monitor whether they understand the ideas

Students use these procedures as they study class notes, complete graphic organizers to highlight the big ideas, and orally rehearse by explaining the big ideas to themselves.

TAKING NOTES. When students take notes, they identify what's most important and then restate it in their own words. They select and organize the big ideas, identify organizational patterns, paraphrase and summarize information, and use abbreviations and symbols to take notes more quickly. Copying information verbatim is less effective than restating information because students are less actively involved in understanding what they're reading.

Students take notes in different ways: They can make outlines or bulleted lists; draw flow charts, webs, and other graphic organizers; or make **double-entry journals** with notes in one column and interpretations in the other column. Or, if students can mark on the text they're reading, they underline or highlight the big ideas and write notes in the margin.

Too often, teachers ask students to take notes without teaching them how to do it. It's important that teachers share copies of notes they've taken so students see different styles of note taking, and that they demonstrate note taking—identifying the big ideas, organizing them, and restating information in their own words—as students read an article or an excerpt from a content area textbook. Once students understand how to identify the big ideas and to state them in their own words, they need opportunities to practice note taking. First, they work in small groups to take notes collaboratively, and then they work with a partner.

Teachers often use study guides to direct students toward the big ideas when they read content area textbooks. They create the study guides with diagrams, charts, lists, and sentences, and students complete them as they read using information and vocabulary from the chapter. Afterward, they review their completed study guides with partners, small groups, or the whole class and check that their work is correct.

It's also important that teachers teach students how to review notes to study for quizzes and tests. Too often, students think they're done with notes once they've written them because they don't understand that the notes are a study tool.

QUESTION-ANSWER-RELATIONSHIPS. Students use Taffy Raphael's **Question-Answer-Relationships** (QAR) technique (1986) to understand how to answer questions written at the end of content area textbook chapters. The technique teaches students to become aware of whether they're likely to find the answer to a question "right there" on the page, between the lines, or beyond the information provided in the text. By being aware of a question's requirements, students are in a better position to answer it correctly and to use the activity as a study strategy.

THE SQ4R STUDY STRATEGY. Students in the seventh and eighth grades also learn how to use the SQ4R study strategy, a six-step technique in which students survey, question, read, recite, relate, and review as they study a content area reading assignment. This study strategy, which incorporates before-, during-, and after-reading components, was devised in the 1930s and recently revised to include the "relate" step. It's been researched and thoroughly documented as a very effective technique; however, when students are in a hurry and skip some of the steps, the strategy won't be as successful (Topping & McManus, 2002).

Why Aren't Content Area Textbooks Enough?

Sometimes content area textbooks are used as the entire instructional program in social studies or science, but that's not a good idea. Textbooks typically only survey topics; other instructional materials are needed to provide depth and understanding. Students need to read, write, and discuss topics. It's most effective to use the reading process and then extend students' learning with projects. Developing thematic units with content area textbooks as one resource is a much better idea than using content area textbooks as the only reading material.

 MONITOR: Check Your Understanding 12.3

Thematic Units

Thematic units are interdisciplinary units that integrate reading and writing with social studies, science, and other curricular areas. Students are often involved in planning the thematic units and identifying some of the questions they want to explore and the activities that interest them. Textbooks are used as a resource, but only one of many.

Students explore topics that interest them and research answers to questions they've posed and are genuinely interested in answering. They share their learning at the end of the unit, as Mrs. Zumwalt's students did in the vignette, and are assessed on what they've learned as well as on the processes they used in learning and working in the classroom.

How to Develop a Unit

To begin planning a thematic unit, teachers choose the general topic and determine the instructional focus using literacy and content area standards. Next, they identify the resources they have available for the unit and develop their teaching plan, integrating content area study with reading and writing activities. They move through these steps in developing a thematic unit:

1. **Determine the focus.** Teachers identify three or four big ideas to emphasize in the unit because the goal isn't to teach a collection of facts but to help students grapple with several big understandings. Teachers also choose the grade-level standards to address during the unit.

2. **Collect a text set.** Teachers collect stories, nonfiction books, and poems on topics related to the unit for the text set and place them in a special area in the classroom library. They'll read some books aloud, and students will read others independently or in small groups. Other books are used for minilessons or as models or patterns for writing projects.

3. **Coordinate textbook readings.** Teachers review the content area textbook chapters related to the unit and decide how to use them most effectively. For example, they might use one as an introduction, have students read others during the unit, or read the chapters to review the big ideas. They also think about how to make the textbook more comprehensible, especially for English learners and struggling readers.

4. **Locate digital and multimedia materials.** Teachers locate websites, DVDs, maps, models, artifacts, and other materials for the unit. Some materials are used to build students' background knowledge and others to teach the big ideas. Also, students create multimedia materials to display in the classroom.

Watch a fourth grade teacher create and use a KWL chart with her students at the beginning of a thematic unit. What steps do students take to complete each column of the chart?

5. **Plan instructional activities.** Teachers think about ways to teach the unit using reading and writing as learning tools, brainstorm possible activities, and then develop a planning map with possible activities. They also make decisions about coordinating the thematic unit with a literature focus unit using a related book, literature circles featuring books from the text set, or reading and writing workshop.

6. **Identify minilesson topics.** Teachers plan **minilessons** to teach strategies and skills related to reading and writing nonfiction as well as content area topics connected to the unit, based on state standards and needs they've identified from students' work.

7. **Plan ways to differentiate instruction.** Teachers devise ways to use flexible grouping to adjust instruction to meet students' developmental levels and language proficiency levels, provide appropriate books and other instructional materials for all students, and scaffold struggling students and challenge high achievers with tiered activities and projects.

8. Brainstorm possible projects. Teachers think about projects students can develop to apply and personalize their learning at the end of the unit. They often use the **RAFT** procedure to design tiered projects so students have alternative ways to demonstrate their learning. This planning makes it possible for teachers to collect needed supplies and have suggestions ready for students who need assistance in choosing a project. Students usually work independently or in small groups, but sometimes the whole class works together on a project.

9. Plan for assessment. Teachers consider how they'll monitor students' progress and evaluate learning at the end of the unit. In this way, they can explain to students at the beginning of the unit how they'll be evaluated and check to see that their assessment emphasizes students' learning of the big ideas.

After considering unit goals, standards to teach, the available resources, and possible activities, teachers are prepared to develop a time schedule, write lesson plans, and create rubrics and other assessment tools.

Nurturing English Learners

How do teachers adjust content area instruction? Teachers have two goals in mind as they consider how to accommodate English learners' instructional needs when they develop thematic units: They want to maximize students' opportunities to learn English and develop content area knowledge, and they have to consider the instructional challenges facing their students and how to adjust instruction and assessment to meet their needs (Peregoy & Boyle, 2013).

CHALLENGES IN LEARNING CONTENT AREA INFORMATION. English learners often have more difficulty learning during thematic units than during literacy instruction because of the additional language demands of unfamiliar topics, vocabulary words, and nonfiction books (Rothenberg & Fisher, 2007). These are the most important challenges facing many of these students:

English Language Proficiency. Students' ability to understand and communicate in English has an obvious effect on their learning. Teachers address this challenge by teaching English and content area information together. They use realia and visual materials to support students' understanding of the topics they're teaching and simplify the language, when necessary, in their explanations of the big ideas. They consider the reading levels of the nonfiction books and content area textbooks they're using, and when students can't read these books themselves, they read them aloud. But if the books are still too difficult, they find others to use instead. Teachers also provide frequent opportunities for ELs to use the new vocabulary as they talk informally about the topics they're learning.

Background Knowledge. English learners often lack the necessary background knowledge about content area topics, especially about American history, so teachers need to take time to expand students' knowledge base using artifacts, photos, models, picture books, videos, and field trips, and they need to make clear links between the topics and students' past experiences and previous thematic units; otherwise, the instruction won't be meaningful. Finding time to preteach this information isn't easy, but without it, English learners aren't likely to learn much during the unit. Teachers also involve all students, including ELs, in making **KWL**

Listen to a teacher talk about why writing is difficult for English learners. Which instructional procedures are effective with English learners?

charts, doing **exclusion brainstorming**, and marking **anticipation guides** to activate their background knowledge.

Vocabulary. English learners are often unfamiliar with content area vocabulary because these words aren't used in everyday conversation; they're technical terms, such as *prairie schooner*, *democracy*, *scavenger*, and *photosynthesis*. Because some words, such as *democracy*, are cognates, students who speak Spanish or another Latin-based language at home may be familiar with them, but not other technical terms that have entered English from other languages. Teachers address this challenge by preteaching key vocabulary words, posting words (with picture clues, if needed) on **word walls**, and using realia, photos, and picture books to introduce the words. They also involve students in a variety of vocabulary activities, including doing **word sorts**, making a **semantic feature analysis**, and drawing diagrams and posters about the words.

Reading. Nonfiction books and content area textbooks aren't the same as stories: Authors organize information differently, incorporate special features, and use more sophisticated sentence structures. In addition, nonfiction text is dense, packed with facts and technical vocabulary. Teachers address the challenge of an unfamiliar genre in three ways. First, they teach students about nonfiction books, including the expository text structures and the distinctive text features of this genre. Next, they teach the strategies that readers use to comprehend nonfiction books, including determining the big ideas and summarizing. Third, they teach ELs to make graphic organizers and take notes to highlight the big ideas and the relationships among them. Through this instruction, English learners are equipped with the necessary tools to read nonfiction books and textbooks more effectively.

Writing. Writing is difficult for English learners because it reflects their English proficiency, but it also supports their learning of content knowledge and English. All students should use writing as a tool for learning during thematic units: As they **quickwrite**, draw graphic organizers, make charts and diagrams, take notes, and write in learning logs, they're grappling with the big ideas and the vocabulary they're learning. Students also use writing to demonstrate learning. This more formal type of writing is much more difficult for English learners because of increased language demands. Teachers address this challenge by choosing a project that requires less writing or by having students work with partners or in small groups.

These challenges are primarily the result of the students' limited knowledge of English, and when teachers address them, ELs are more likely to be successful in learning content area information and developing English-language proficiency.

ADJUSTING INSTRUCTION. Teachers address the challenges facing English learners as they adjust instruction to maximize students' learning. They also find ways to maximize students' participation in instructional activities because many ELs avoid interacting with mainstream classmates or fear asking questions in class (Peregoy & Boyle, 2013; Rothenberg & Fisher, 2007). Teachers adjust their instruction in these ways:

- Use visuals and manipulatives, including artifacts, videos, photographs, and models
- Preteach big ideas and key vocabulary
- Teach students about expository text structures
- Practice taking notes with students
- Use graphic organizers and other diagrams to highlight relationships among big ideas
- Organize students to work in small, collaborative groups and with partners
- Include frequent opportunities for students to talk informally about big ideas
- Provide opportunities for students to use oral language, reading, and writing
- Collect text sets, including picture books and online resources
- Use a textbook as only one resource
- Review big ideas and key vocabulary

These suggestions take into account students' level of English development, their limited background knowledge and vocabulary related to many unit topics, and their reading and writing levels.

CHOOSING ALTERNATIVE ASSESSMENTS. Teachers monitor English learners' progress using a combination of observing them and asking questions. Too often, teachers ask ELs if they understand, but that usually isn't effective because they tend respond positively, even when they're confused. It's more productive to interact with students, talking with them about the activity they're involved in or asking questions about the book they're reading.

Teachers also devise alternative assessments to learn more about English learners' achievement when they have difficulty on regular evaluations (Rothenberg & Fisher, 2007). For example, instead of writing an essay, students can draw pictures or graphic organizers about the big ideas and add words from the word wall to label them to demonstrate their learning, or they can talk about what they've learned in a conference with the teacher. Instead of giving written tests, teachers can simplify the wording of the test questions and have ELs answer them orally. When it's important to have English learners create written projects, they'll be more successful if they work collaboratively in small groups. Portfolios are especially useful in documenting ELs' achievement. Students also place work samples in their portfolios to show what they've learned about content area topics and how their English proficiency has developed. 🐚

A First Grade Unit on Trees

During this 4-week unit, first graders learn about trees and their importance to people and animals. Children observe trees in their community and learn to identify the parts of a tree and types of trees. Teachers use the **interactive read-aloud** procedure to share books from the text set and list important words on the **word wall**. A collection of leaves, photos of trees, pictures of animals that live in trees, and products that come from trees is displayed in the classroom, and children learn about categorizing as they sort types of leaves, shapes of trees, foods that grow on trees and those that don't, and animals that live in trees and those that don't. Children learn how to use writing as a tool for learning as they make entries in **learning logs**, and teachers use **interactive writing** to make charts about the big ideas. They also view information on bookmarked websites to learn more about trees. As a culminating activity, children plant a tree at their school or participate in a community tree-planting campaign. Check the Planning Guide: A First Grade Unit on Trees.

A Fourth Grade Unit on Desert Ecosystems

During this 3-week unit, students investigate the plants, animals, and people that live in the desert and learn how they support each other. They keep learning logs in which they take notes and write reactions to books they're reading. Students divide into book clubs during the first week to read books about the desert. During the second week of the unit, students participate in an author study of Byrd Baylor, a woman who lives in the desert and writes about desert life, and they read many of her books. During the third week, students participate in reading workshop to read other desert books and reread favorites. To extend their learning, they create projects, including writing desert riddles, making a chart of a desert ecosystem, and drawing a desert mural. Together as a class, students write a desert alphabet book. Check the Planning Guide: A Fourth Grade Unit on Desert Ecosystems.

A Sixth Grade Unit on Ancient Egypt

Students learn about this great ancient civilization during a monthlong unit. Key concepts include the influence of the Nile River on Egyptian life, the contributions of this civilization to contemporary America, a comparison of ancient to modern Egypt, and the techniques Egyptologists use to locate tombs of the ancient rulers and decipher Egyptian hieroglyphics. Students read books in literature circles and read other books from the text set independently. They also consult online resources and complete a WebQuest about ancient Egypt. Teachers teach minilessons on map-reading skills, taking notes from content area textbooks, Egyptian gods, and writing poems. At the end of the unit, students create projects and share them on Egypt day, when they assume the roles of ancient Egyptians, dressing as ancient people did and eating foods of the period. Check the Planning Guide: A Sixth Grade Unit on Ancient Egypt.

 MONITOR: Check Your Understanding 12.4

Planning Guide
A First Grade Unit on Trees

GRAPHIC ORGANIZERS

- Venn diagram comparing ways people and animals use trees.
- Circle diagram with the life cycle of a tree.
- Data chart about the shapes of trees or features of leaves.

How do people and animals use trees?

People — wood, enjoy flowers, decorate
(shared) shade, play, food
Animals — home, safety

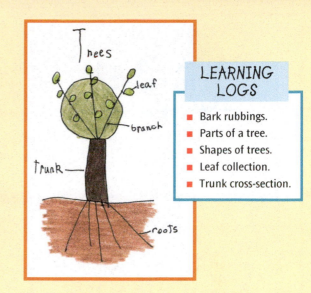

LEARNING LOGS

- Bark rubbings.
- Parts of a tree.
- Shapes of trees.
- Leaf collection.
- Trunk cross-section.

FIELD TRIPS

- Walking field trip of neighborhood.
- Visit to a forest.
- Visit to a plant nursery.

PROJECTS

- Plant a tree.
- Write "All About Trees" books.
- Create books of tree riddles.
- Develop multigenre projects.

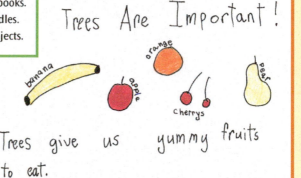

TEXT SET

Brown, R. (2007). *The old tree.* Cambridge, MA: Candlewick.

Cherry, L. (2000). *The great kapok tree.* San Diego: Harcourt Brace.

Ehlert, L. (1999). *Red leaf, yellow leaf.* San Diego: Harcourt Brace.

Ganeri, A. (2006). *From seed to apple.* Portsmouth, NH: Heinemann.

Gibbons, G. (2002). *Tell me, tree: All about trees for kids.* Boston: Little, Brown.

Hiscock, B. (1999). *The big tree.* Honesdale, PA: Boyds Mills Press.

Iverson, D. (1999). *My favorite tree: Terrific trees of North America.* Nevada City, CA: Dawn.

Miller, D. S. (2002). *Are trees alive?* New York: Walker.

Pfeffer, E. W. (2007). *A log's life.* New York: Simon & Schuster.

What Trees Need
Trees need 3 things to live. They need sunlight to shine on them. They need water because they get thirsty. They need good soil to grow strong. With these 3 things trees will be healthy.

INTERACTIVE WRITING

- Parts of a tree.
- Shapes of trees.
- How we use trees.
- What trees need to live.
- How to take care of trees.
- Trees in our community.

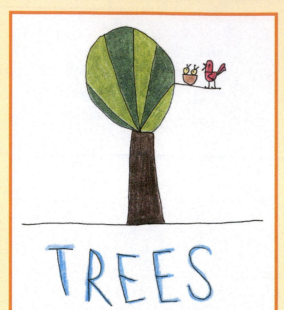

TREES

LANGUAGE EXPERIENCE APPROACH

- Make a scrapbook of tree photos and dictate a sentence to describe each photo.
- Compile a class collaboration book with each student drawing a picture and dictating a sentence on one page.
- Paint pictures of trees in each season, display them on a poster, and dictate a sentence to describe each painting.

vein

vein

Food gos in the vein to the leaf.

OBJECT AND WORD SORTS

- Types of leaves.
- Shapes of trees.
- Foods from trees.
- Animals that live in trees.
- Ways people and animals use trees.

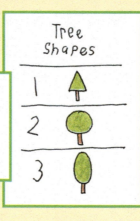

Tree Shapes

1

2

3

VOCABULARY

- Make word posters.
- Collect pictures and objects to represent words.
- Do word and object sorts.

WEBSITE

- Exploring the Secret Life of Trees

LITERACY STRATEGIES

- Summarize information.
- Locate words on word wall.
- Sort objects and word cards.
- Make word posters.
- Write learning log entries.
- Write "All About . . . " books.

WORD WALL

ABCD	EFGHI	JKLM	NO
bark	fruit	leaf	needle
branch	flower	leaves	nuts
birds	evergreen	jagged	nest
acorn		maple syrup	owl
chocolate			oak
beaver			oxygen
PQR	ST	UVW	XYZ
root	trunk	wood	
paper	shade	wide	
rough	smooth	vein	
palm tree	seed		
pine	squirrel		

Planning Guide
A Fourth Grade Unit on Desert Ecosystems

LITERACY STRATEGIES

- Read nonfiction books to locate information.
- Identify big ideas.
- Write information on a data chart.
- Use an index.
- Draw a life cycle chart.
- Create riddles.
- Recognize problem-and-solution structure.
- Compare ecosystems.

CONTENT AREA TEXTBOOK

- Teach students about unique features of content area textbooks.
- Have students listen to teacher read the chapter aloud before reading it independently or with partners.
- Use modeling to teach students how to take notes.

VOCABULARY ACTIVITIES

- Make word posters and word maps.
- Do a word sort.
- Create a semantic feature analysis about how plants and animals survive in a desert habitat.

PROJECTS

- Create a multigenre project.
- Write desert riddles.
- Draw a chart of the desert ecosystem.
- Make a tabletop desert scene.
- Write an "I Am . . ." poem patterned on *Desert Voices*.
- Research a question about the desert.
- Paint a desert mural.

CENTERS

- Add information about desert plants and animals to a data chart.
- Listen to a book at the listening center.
- Draw the life cycle of a desert animal.
- Write a class alphabet book about deserts.
- Read Byrd Baylor's books and others from the text set.
- Write letters to author Byrd Baylor.
- Sort words from the word wall.
- Compare hot and cold deserts.
- Participate in making a tabletop desert diorama.

MAPS AND DIAGRAMS

- Read landform maps.
- Draw a map of the desert.
- Draw the life cycle of a desert animal.
- Make a problem-solution chart on desert adaptations.
- Identify deserts on a world map.
- Compare deserts and forests.

TEXT SET

Bash, B. (2002). *Desert giant.* Boston: Little, Brown.

Baylor, B. (1993). *Desert voices.* New York: Scribner.

Fowler, A. (1997). *It could still be a desert.* Chicago: Children's Press.

George, J. C. (1996). *One day in the desert.* New York: Harper Trophy.

Gibbons, G. (1999). *Deserts.* New York: Holiday House.

Guiberson, B. Z. (2007). *Cactus hotel.* New York: Holt.

Johnson, R. L. (2000). *A walk in the desert.* Minneapolis: Carolrhoda.

Mora, P. (2008). *The desert is my mother.* Houston: Piñata Books.

Siebert, D. (1992). *Mojave.* New York: Harper Trophy.

Simon, S. (1990). *Deserts.* New York: Morrow.

Taylor, B. (1998). *Desert life.* New York: Dorling Kindersley.

Wallace, M. D. (1996). *America's deserts.* Golden, CO: Fulcrum Kids.

WORD WALL

ABC	DEFGH	IJKL
cactus	desert	kangaroo rat
coral snake	Death Valley	king snake
camouflage	dunes	jackrabbit
camels	Gobi Desert	Joshua tree
coyote	exoskeleton	lizard
cacti	hawk	javelina

MNOP	QRST	UVWXYZ
Mojave Desert	Sahara Desert	yucca
oasis	scorpion	
owl	spines	
	saguaro	
	tortoise	
	sidewinder	

AUTHOR STUDY

- Share information about Byrd Baylor.
- Read her books set in the desert.
- Write letters to the author.

Byrd Baylor

I ♥ Deserts

TECHNOLOGY

- View websites about the desert and the plants, animals, and people living there.
- Complete a WebQuest about desert life.
- Develop a multimodal presentation about the desert.
- Create a website about the desert.

KWL CHART

- Use to introduce the theme.
- Identify research questions.
- Use to conclude the unit.

LEARNING LOGS

- Take notes.
- Write quickwrites.
- Draw a food chain.
- List vocabulary words.

Planning Guide

A Sixth Grade Unit on Ancient Egypt

KWL CHART

- Introduce KWL chart at the beginning of the unit.
- Identify research questions for collaborative or individual reports.
- Use to conclude the unit.

PROJECTS

- Keep a simulated journal as an ancient Egyptian.
- Make a time line of the ancient civilization.
- Make a poster about a god or goddess.
- Present an oral report about how to mummify someone.
- Create a website about ancient Egypt.
- Write a collection of poems about ancient Egypt using *Voices of Ancient Egypt* as a model.
- Complete a WebQuest.
- Present an "interview" of several ancient Egyptians.
- Write a book about the ways the Egyptian civilization has influenced ours.
- Research the Rosetta stone.
- Make a chart comparing ancient and modern Egypt.
- Create a multigenre project.

MAPS AND DIAGRAMS

- Make a time line of ancient Egypt.
- Create a Venn diagram comparing ancient and modern Egypt.
- Read maps of ancient and modern Egypt.
- Draw maps of Egypt.

LITERACY STRATEGIES

- Use anticipation guides.
- Learn to take notes.
- Analyze expository text structures.
- Make a time line.
- Analyze Greek root words.
- Examine QAR in content area textbooks.

TEXT SET

Aliki. (1985). *Mummies made in Egypt.* New York: HarperCollins.

Der Manuelian, P. (1996). *Hieroglyphs from A to Z.* New York: Scholastic.

Giblin, J. C. (1993). *The riddle of the Rosetta stone.* New York: HarperCollins.

Gregory, K. (1999). *Cleopatra VII, daughter of the Nile.* New York: Scholastic.

Harris, G. (1993). *Gods and pharaohs from Egyptian mythology.* New York: Peter Bedrick.

Hart, G. (2004). *Ancient Egypt.* New York: DK Publishing.

Hinshaw, K. C. (2007). *Ancient Egypt.* San Francisco: Chronicle Books.

Honan, L. (1999). *Spend the day in ancient Egypt.* New York: Wiley.

Lattimore, D. N. (1995). *The winged cat: A tale of ancient Egypt.* New York: HarperCollins.

Macaulay, D. (1982). *Pyramid.* Boston: Houghton Mifflin.

Milton, J. (2000). *Hieroglyphs.* New York: Grosset & Dunlap.

Perl, L. (1990). *Mummies, tombs, and treasure: Secrets of ancient Egypt.* New York: Clarion Books.

Rubalcaba, J. (2007). *Ancient Egypt: Archaeology unlocks the secrets of Egypt's past.* Washington, DC: National Geographic Children's Books.

Stanley, D., & Vennema, P. (1997). *Cleopatra.* New York: Harper Trophy.

Winters, K. (2003). *Voices of ancient Egypt.* Washington, DC: National Geographic Children's Books.

WORD-STUDY ACTIVITIES

- Make word maps.
- Do a word sort.
- Create a semantic feature analysis.
- Make a word chain.
- Write an alphabet book on Egypt.

WORD WALL

ABCD	EFGH	IJKLM
canopic jars	Egypt	irrigation
Africa	Hatshepsut	lotus
Champollion	embalming	Imhotep
Amun-Ra	hieroglyphs	Luxor
dynasty	Egyptologist	Memphis
Cleopatra		mummification
		Middle Kingdom

NOPQ	RST	UVWXYZ
pharaohs	Ramses the Great	Valley of the Kings
Nile River	Tutankhamun	vizier
Nefertiti	senet	
natron	scribes	
pyramid	Rosetta stone	
Old Kingdom		
New Kingdom		
obelisk		
papyrus		

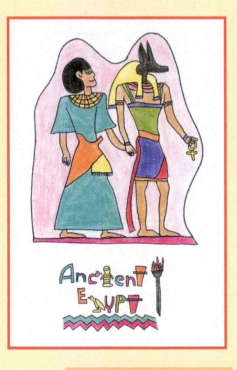

LITERATURE CIRCLES

Have students read and discuss a book about ancient Egypt in small groups.

CONTENT AREA TEXTBOOK

- Preview chapter with students before reading.
- Divide chapter into sections and have a small group read each section and report to the class.
- Have students complete study guides.
- Use QAR procedure to answer end-of-chapter questions.

CENTERS

- Draw a map of Egypt.
- Make a mummy.
- Write hieroglyphics.
- Make a god or goddess poster.
- Sort words from the word wall.
- Write in learning logs.
- Read text set books.
- Research ancient Egypt online.

TECHNOLOGY

- View websites about ancient Egypt, including the British Museum's website.
- Complete a WebQuest. Many teacher-made WebQuests about ancient Egypt are available online.
- Create a multigenre project on life in ancient Egypt that includes a digital component.

Review

READING AND WRITING ACROSS THE CURRICULUM

Effective teachers integrate reading and writing instruction with content area study. They develop thematic units and teach minilessons to ensure that students learn how to comprehend nonfiction books and content area textbooks and how to use reading and writing as tools for learning and to demonstrate new knowledge. Teachers follow the guidelines presented in this chapter, these points in particular:

12.1 Teachers teach students to use reading and writing as learning tools.

12.2 Teachers have students use writing to demonstrate what they've learned.

12.3 Teachers teach students to use content area textbooks effectively.

12.4 Teachers focus on the big ideas in thematic units.

✔ EVALUATE & REFLECT

Evaluate your knowledge about teaching reading and writing across the curriculum. The questions ask you to collect and analyze data, and report the results. Your response should meet academic standards and adhere to Standard English conventions.

1. Choose a level in the grades 3–8 range, and compile a text set of books and digital resources representing a variety of genres for a thematic unit on a social studies or science topic. The texts should range from two grade levels below to two grades above the identified level; for example, a text set for fifth grade should include materials ranging from third to seventh grade. In your response, present the text set, explain how you compiled it, and reflect on what you've learned about text sets.

2. Reread the sections "Mentor Texts" in this chapter and "The Writer's Craft" in Chapter 2, and then develop a text set of books for teaching each of the six traits. Include at least 12 books in your set. In your response, present the text set, organized by trait, and then explain how you'll use each book to teach the writer's craft.

3. Work with a small group of students in the grades 3–6 range who are involved in a thematic unit, and help them develop a multigenre project. In your response, describe the students and the thematic unit, explain the items in the multigenre project and its repetend, and include a photo or video clip of the project.

4. Analyze a social studies or science textbook and support materials at one level in the grades 4–8 range. Note the unique features of the book, and identify ways that the publisher worked to make the textbook more comprehensible. In your response, describe the textbook, noting its unique features and the publisher's attempts to make the book more comprehensible. Evaluate the textbook's effectiveness and conclude how you'd use it as part of a thematic unit in your classroom.

5. Plan a thematic unit for any level in the K–8 range using the steps in this chapter, and create a planning guide similar to the ones in the chapter. In your response, provide background information about the grade level and the unit, include your planning guide, and reflect on the experience of planning a unit.

REFERENCES

Allen, C. A. (2001). *The multigenre research paper: Voice, passion, and discovery in grades 4–6*. Portsmouth, NH: Heinemann.

Aquatic life of the world. (2001). New York: Marshall Cavendish.

Armbruster, B. B., McCarthey, S. J., & Cummins, S. (2005). Writing to learn in elementary classrooms. In R. Indrisano & J. R. Paratore (Eds.), *Learning to write, writing to learn: Theory and research in practice* (pp. 71–96). Newark, DE: International Reading Association.

Avi. (2010). *Nothing but the truth*. New York: Scholastic.

Bausum, A. (2006). *Freedom riders: John Lewis and Jim Zwerg on the front lines of the civil rights movement*. Washington, DC: National Geographic Children's Books.

Bruchac, J. (2001). *The journal of Jesse Smoke: A Cherokee boy, Trail of Tears, 1838*. New York: Scholastic.

Cole, J. (1996). *The magic school bus inside a hurricane*. New York: Scholastic.

Cole, J. (1998). *The magic school bus inside a beehive*. New York: Scholastic.

Cronin, D. (2011). *Diary of a spider*. New York: Scholastic.

Cushman, K. (2012). *Catherine, called Birdy*. New York: Sandpiper.

Daniels, H., & Zemelman, S. (2004). *Subjects matter: Every teacher's guide to content-area reading*. Portsmouth, NH: Heinemann.

Denenberg, B. (1999). *The journal of Ben Uchida: Citizen 13559, Mirror Lake Internment Camp*. New York: Scholastic.

Dorfman, L. R., & Cappelli, R. (2007). *Mentor texts: Teaching writing through children's literature, K–6*. Portland, ME: Stenhouse.

Fleischman, P. (2010). *Whirligig*. New York: Square Fish Books.

Fraustino, L. R. (2004). *I walk in dread: The diary of Deliverance Trembly, witness to the Salem witch trials*. New York: Scholastic.

Guccione, L. M. (2011). Integrating literacy and inquiry for English learners. *The Reading Teacher, 64*, 567–577.

Guiberson, B. Z. (2007). *Cactus hotel*. New York: Henry Holt.

Harvey, S. (1998). *Nonfiction matters: Reading, writing, and research in grades 3–8*. York, ME: Stenhouse.

Harvey, S., & Goudvis, A. (2007). *Strategies that work: Teaching comprehension for understanding and engagement* (2nd ed.). York, ME: Stenhouse.

Hinton, S. E. (2007). *The outsiders*. New York: Viking.

Holm, J. L. (2011). *Middle school is worse than meatloaf: A year told through stuff*. New York: Atheneum.

Ikpeze, C. H., & Boyd, F. B. (2007). Web-based inquiry learning: Facilitating thoughtful literacy with WebQuests. *The Reading Teacher, 60*, 644–654.

Janke, K. (2002). *Survival in the storm: The dust bowl diary of Grace Edwards*. New York: Scholastic.

Judge, L. (2007). *One thousand tracings: Healing the wounds of World War II*. New York: Hyperion Books.

Lester, J. (2005). *To be a slave*. New York: Puffin Books.

Mannis, C. D. (2003). *The queen's progress: An Elizabethan alphabet*. New York: Viking.

Marrin, A. (2006). *Oh, rats! The story of rats and people*. New York: Dutton.

McKissack, P. C. (1997). *A picture of freedom: The diary of Clotee, a slave girl*. New York: Scholastic.

McLimans, D. (2006). *Gone wild: An endangered animal alphabet*. New York: Walker.

Moline, S. (1995). *I see what you mean: Children at work with visual information*. York, ME: Stenhouse.

Napier, M. (2002). *Z is for Zamboni: A hockey alphabet*. Chelsea, MI: Sleeping Bear Press.

Paulsen, G. (2007). *Hatchet*. New York: Simon & Schuster.

Peregoy, S. F., & Boyle, O. F. (2013). *Reading, writing, and learning in ESL: A resource book for teaching K–12 English learners* (6th ed.). Boston: Pearson.

Pryle, M. (2007). *Teaching students to write effective essays*. New York: Scholastic.

Raphael, T. E. (1986). Teaching question-answer-relationships, revisited. *The Reading Teacher, 39*, 516–523.

Readence, J. E., Moore, D. W., & Rickelman, R. J. (2000). *Prereading activities for content area reading and learning* (3rd ed.). Newark, DE: International Reading Association.

Robb, L. (2002). Multiple texts: Multiple opportunities for teaching and learning. *Voices From the Middle, 9*(4), 28–32.

Robb, L. (2003). *Teaching reading in social studies, science, and math*. New York: Scholastic.

Robb, L. (2004). *Nonfiction writing: From the inside out*. New York: Scholastic.

Romano, T. (2000). *Blending genre, alternating style: Writing multiple genre papers*. Portsmouth, NH: Heinemann/Boynton/Cook.

Rothenberg, C., & Fisher, D. (2007). *Teaching English language learners: A differentiated approach*. Upper Saddle River, NJ: Merrill/Prentice Hall.

Schlitz, L. A. (2007). *Good masters! Sweet ladies! Voices from a medieval village*. Cambridge, MA: Candlewick Press.

Snicket, L. (2003). *Lemony Snicket: The unauthorized autobiography*. New York: HarperCollins.

Stead, T. (2002). *Is that a fact? Teaching nonfiction writing K–3*. Portland, ME: Stenhouse.

Thayer, E. L. (2000). *Ernest L. Thayer's Casey at the bat: A ballad of the republic sung in the year 1888* (C. Bing, Illus.). Brooklyn, NY: Handprint Books.

Thimmesh, C. (2006). *Team moon: How 400,000 people landed* Apollo 11 *on the moon*. Boston: Houghton Mifflin.

Tierney, R. J., & Shanahan, T. (1996). Research on the reading-writing relationship: Interactions, transactions, and outcomes. In R. Barr, M. L. Kamil, P. Mosenthal, & P. D. Pearson (Eds.), *Handbook of reading research* (Vol. 2, pp. 246–280). Mahwah, NJ: Erlbaum.

Tompkins, G. E. (2012). *Teaching writing: Balancing process and product* (6th ed.). Boston: Allyn & Bacon/Pearson.

Topping, D., & McManus, R. (2002). *Real reading, real writing: Content-area strategies*. Portsmouth, NH: Heinemann.

White, E. E. (2002). *The journal of Patrick Seamus Flaherty: United States Marine Corps*. New York: Scholastic.

four

Compendium of Instructional Procedures

- Anticipation Guides
- Book Talks
- Choral Reading
- Cloze Procedure
- Collaborative Books
- Double-Entry Journals
- Exclusion Brainstorming
- Grand Conversations
- Hot Seat
- Interactive Read-Alouds
- Interactive Writing
- KWL Charts
- Language Experience Approach
- Learning Logs
- Making Words
- Minilessons
- Open-Mind Portraits
- Possible Sentences
- Prereading Plan

- Question-Answer-Relationships
- Quickwriting
- RAFT
- Readers Theatre
- Reading Logs
- Revising Groups
- Rubrics
- Running Records
- Semantic Feature Analysis
- Shared Reading
- Sketch-to-Stretch
- Story Boards
- Story Retelling
- Sustained Silent Reading
- Tea Party
- Think-Alouds
- Word Sorts
- Word Walls

Note: Look for hyperlinked *Standards in the Classroom* features to read how teachers implement various instructional procedures to address Common Core English Language Arts Standards. The orange Compendium terms don't hyperlink to the instructional procedures they name because full descriptions of the procedures are also located in Part 4.

Anticipation Guides   Teachers use anticipation guides (Head & Readence, 1986) to activate students' background knowledge before they read nonfiction books, and content area textbooks in particular. Teachers prepare a list of statements about the topic for students to discuss; some statements are true and others are incorrect, often based on common misconceptions. Students discuss each statement and decide whether they agree with it. Then after reading the selection, students discuss the statements again and decide whether they agree with them. Usually they change some of their opinions, and they realize that they've refined their understanding of the topic through the activity.

An anticipation guide about immigration that eighth graders considered before reading a chapter in their history textbook included these statements:

> There are more people immigrating to the United States today than ever before in history.
>
> The government sets a quota for the number of people allowed to enter the United States each year.
>
> Most people immigrate to the United States because they want to find better jobs and earn more money.
>
> Aliens are people who are in the United States illegally.
>
> Refugees are people who are forced to flee from their homeland because of war or other disasters.
>
> Many immigrants have difficulty adjusting to the new ways of life in America.

You probably agree with some of these statements and disagree with others; perhaps you're unsure about a couple of them. Having these questions in mind when you begin reading gives you a purpose for reading and directs your attention to the big ideas. And, as you read, you might find that your initial assessment of one or two statements wasn't accurate, and when you repeat the assessment afterward, you'll make some changes.

THE STEPS.   Teachers follow these steps to develop and use anticipation guides:

1. *Identify several major concepts in the reading assignment.* Teachers keep in mind students' knowledge about the topic and any misconceptions they might have about it.

2. *Develop a list of statements.* Teachers compose four to six statements that are general enough to stimulate discussion and are useful in clarifying misconceptions, and they make copies for students. The guide has space for students to mark whether they agree with each statement before and again after reading.

3. *Discuss the anticipation guide.* Teachers introduce the anticipation guide and have students respond to the statements. Working in small groups, in pairs, or individually, students decide whether they agree with each one. Then, as a class, students discuss their responses to each statement and defend their positions.

4. *Read the text.* Students read the text and compare their responses to what's stated in the reading material.

5. *Discuss each statement again.* Students talk about the statements again, citing information in the text that supports or refutes each one. Or, students can again respond to each of the statements and compare their answers before and after reading. When students use the anticipation guide, teachers have them fold back their first set of responses on the left side of the paper and then respond to each item again on the right side.

ANTICIPATION GUIDE FOR *THE OUTSIDERS*

Before Reading		Gangs	After Reading	
Agree	Disagree		Agree	Disagree
✓		1. Gangs are bad.	✓	
✓		2. Gangs are exciting.	✓	
✓		3. It is safe to be a gang member.		✓
	✓	4. Gangs make a difference in a gang member's life.	✓	
	✓	5. Gangs fill a need.	✓	
	✓	6. Once you join a gang, it is very difficult to get out.	✓	

Although anticipation guides are more commonly used before reading content area textbooks, they can also be used to explore complex issues in novels, including homelessness, crime and punishment, and immigration. An eighth grade class, for example, studied gangs in preparation for reading S. E. Hinton's *The Outsiders* (2006), and they completed an anticipation guide before and again after reading the novel. To see how Lanie's thinking changed after reading the novel, check the figure Anticipation Guide for *The Outsiders*. The statements about gangs in the anticipation guide probed important points and led to lively discussion and thoughtful responses.

STANDARDS IN THE CLASSROOM. Click here to read how Mr. Vin addresses eighth grade Standards when his students use an anticipation guide. 🌀

Book Talks *Book talks* are brief teasers that teachers give to introduce students to particular books and interest them in reading the books. To hook students' interest, teachers show the book, summarize it without giving away the ending, and read a short excerpt aloud. Then they pass the book off to an interested reader or place it in the classroom library for students to read.

Students use the same steps when they give book talks to share the books they've read during reading workshop. Here's a transcript of a third grader's book talk about Paula Danziger's *Amber Brown Is Not a Crayon* (2006a):

> This is my book: <u>Amber Brown Is Not a Crayon</u>. It's about these two kids—Amber Brown, who is a girl, and Justin Daniels, who is a boy. See? Here's their picture. They are in third grade, too, and their teacher—his name is Mr. Cohen—pretends to take them on airplane trips to the places they study. They move their chairs so that it's like they are on an airplane and Amber and Justin always put their chairs side by side. I'm going to read you the very beginning of the book. [She reads the first three pages aloud to the class.] This story is really funny and when you're reading you think the author is telling you the story instead of you

*reading it. And there are more stories about Amber Brown. This is the one I'm reading now—*You Can't Eat Your Chicken Pox, Amber Brown *[2006b].*

There are several reasons why this student and others in her class are so successful in giving book talks. The teacher has modeled the procedure, and students are reading books that they've chosen—books they really like. In addition, these students are experienced in talking with their classmates about books.

THE STEPS. Teachers follow these steps to conduct a book talk:

1. *Select a book to share.* Teachers choose a new book to introduce to students or a book that students haven't shown much interest in. They familiarize themselves with the book by reading or rereading it.

2. *Plan a brief presentation.* Teachers plan how they'll present the book to interest students in reading it. They usually begin with the title and author of the book, and they mention the genre or topic and briefly summarize the plot without giving away the ending. Teachers also decide why they liked the book and think about why students might be interested in it. Sometimes they choose a short excerpt to read and an illustration to show.

3. *Present the book talk.* Teachers present the book talk and show the book. Their comments are usually enough so that at least one student will ask to borrow the book to read.

Teachers use book talks to introduce books in the classroom library. At the beginning of the school year, they take time to present many of the books, and during the year, they introduce new books that they add to the library. They also talk about the books for a literature circle, or a text set of books for a thematic unit (Gambrell & Almasi, 1996). During a seventh grade unit on the Underground Railroad, for example, teachers might introduce five books about Harriet Tubman and the Underground Railroad and then have students form literature circles to read one of them. 🍂

Choral Reading   Students use choral reading to orally share poems and other brief texts. This group reading activity provides students, especially struggling readers, with valuable oral reading practice; they learn to read more expressively and increase their reading fluency (Rasinski, Padak, & Fawcett, 2010). In addition, it's a great activity for English learners because they practice reading aloud with classmates in a nonthreatening group setting (McCauley & McCauley, 1992). As they read with English-speaking classmates, they hear and practice English pronunciation of words, phrasing of words in a sentence, and intonation patterns.

Many arrangements for choral reading are possible. Students may read the text together as a class or divide it and read sections in small groups, or individual students may read particular lines or stanzas while the class reads the rest of the text using these arrangements:

Echo Reading. A leader reads each line and the group repeats it.

Leader and Chorus Reading. A leader reads the main part, and the group reads the refrain in unison.

Small-Group Reading. The class divides into two or more groups, and each group reads part of the poem.

Cumulative Reading. One student reads the first line or stanza, and another student joins in as each line or stanza is read to create a cumulative effect.

Students read the text aloud several times, experimenting with different arrangements until they decide which one conveys meaning most effectively.

THE STEPS. Teachers follow this procedure:

1. *Select a poem.* Teachers choose a poem or other text and copy it onto a chart or make multiple copies for students to read.

2. *Arrange the text.* Teachers work with students to decide how to arrange the text. They add marks to the chart, or they have students mark individual copies so that they can follow the arrangement.

3. *Rehearse the poem.* Teachers read the poem with students several times at a natural speed, pronouncing words carefully.

4. *Read the poem aloud.* Teachers emphasize that students pronounce words clearly and read with expression. They can record students' reading so that they can hear themselves; sometimes students want to rearrange the choral reading after hearing their presentation.

Choral reading makes students active participants in the poetry experience, and it helps them learn to appreciate the sounds, feelings, and magic of poetry. Many poems can be used for choral reading, and poems with repetitions, echoes, refrains, or questions and answers work well. Try these poems, for example:

"My Parents Think I'm Sleeping," by Jack Prelutsky (2007)
"I Woke Up This Morning," by Karla Kuskin (2003)
"Every Time I Climb a Tree," by David McCord (Paschen, 2005)
"Ode to La Tortilla," by Gary Soto (2005)
"The New Kid on the Block," by Jack Prelutsky (1983)
"Mother to Son," by Langston Hughes (2007)
"A Circle of Sun," by Rebecca Kai Dotlich (Yolen & Peters, 2007)

Poems written specifically for two readers are very effective, including Donald Hall's book-length poem *I Am the Dog/I Am the Cat* (1994) and Paul Fleischman's collection of insect poems, *Joyful Noise: Poems for Two Voices* (2004). Teachers can also use speeches, songs, and longer poems for choral reading. Try, for example, *Brother Eagle, Sister Sky: A Message From Chief Seattle* (Jeffers, 1993) and Woody Guthrie's *This Land Is Your Land* (2002).

STANDARDS IN THE CLASSROOM. Click here to read how Mr. Abbott addresses Standards using choral reading with his struggling fourth graders.

Cloze Procedure The cloze procedure is an informal diagnostic assessment that teachers use to gather information about readers' ability to deal with the complexity of texts they're reading (Taylor, 1953). Teachers construct a cloze passage by selecting an excerpt from a story, a nonfiction book, or a content area textbook that students have read and deleting every fifth word in the passage; the deleted words are replaced with blanks. Then students read the passage and fill in the missing words, using their knowledge of syntax and semantics to successfully predict the missing words in the text passage. Only the exact word is considered a correct answer.

This cloze passage is about wolves:

The leaders of a wolf pack are called the alpha wolves. There is an _____ male and an alpha _____ . They are usually the _____ and the strongest wolves _____ the pack. An alpha _____ fight any wolf that _____ to take over the _____. When the alpha looks _____ other wolf in the _____, the other wolf crouches _____ and tucks its tail _____ its hind legs. Sometimes _____ rolls over and licks _____ alpha wolf's face as _____ to say, "You are _____ boss."

The missing words are *alpha, female, largest, in, will, tries, pack, the, eye, down, between, it, the, if,* and *the.*

The cloze procedure assesses sentence-level comprehension (Tierney & Readence, 2005). It's a useful classroom tool for determining which texts are at students' instructional level and for monitoring students' understanding of novels they're reading. A caution, however: Cloze doesn't measure comprehension globally; it only assesses students' ability to use syntax and semantics within individual sentences and paragraphs.

THE STEPS. Teachers follow these steps to use the cloze procedure:

1. *Select a passage.* Teachers select a passage from a textbook or trade book and retype it. The first sentence is typed exactly as it appears in the original text, but beginning with the second sentence, one of the first five words is deleted and replaced with a blank. Then every fifth word in the remainder of the passage is deleted and replaced with a blank.

2. *Complete the cloze activity.* Students silently read the passage all the way through once and then reread it and predict or "guess" the word that goes in each blank. They write the deleted words in the blanks.

3. *Score students' work.* Teachers award one point each time the missing word is identified. A percentage of correct answers is determined by dividing the number of points by the number of blanks. If students score more than 60% correct replacements, the text is likely at their independent reading level; if they score 40–60% correct replacements, the text is probably at their instructional level; and if they score less than 40% correct replacements, the text is likely at their frustration level.

The cloze procedure can be used to judge students' reading level in unfamiliar books, or to assess their comprehension after reading a book. When teachers use the cloze procedure to check students' comprehension, specific words, such as character names, facts related to the setting, or key events, are deleted, rather than every fifth word. This assessment procedure can also be used to judge whether a particular book is appropriate for classroom instruction. Teachers prepare a cloze passage and have students follow the steps described here to predict the missing words (Jacobson, 1990). Then they score students' predictions and use a one-third to one-half formula to determine the text's appropriateness: If students correctly predict more than 50% of the deleted words, the text is easy reading, but if they predict less than 30%, it's too difficult for classroom instruction. The instructional range is 30–50% correct predictions (Reutzel & Cooter, 2008). 🌀

Collaborative Books   Students work together in small groups to make collaborative books. They each contribute one page or work with a classmate to write a page or a section of the book, using the writing process as they draft, revise, and edit their pages. Teachers often make class collaborations with students as a first bookmaking project and to introduce the stages of the writing process. Students write collaborative books to retell a favorite story, illustrate a poem with one line or a stanza on each page, or write a nonfiction book or biography. The benefit of collaborative books is that students share the work so the books are completed much more quickly and easily than individual books. Because students write only one page or section, it takes less time for teachers to conference with them and assist them with time-consuming revising and editing.

THE STEPS. Teachers follow these steps in making collaborative books with their students:

1. *Choose a topic.* Teachers choose a topic related to a literature focus unit or thematic unit. Then students choose specific topics or pages to prepare.

2. *Introduce the page or section design.* If students are each contributing one page for a class book on penguins, for example, they choose a fact or other piece of information about penguins to write. They might draw a picture related to the fact at the top of the page and write the fact underneath the picture. Teachers often model the procedure and write one page of the book together as a class before students begin working on their pages.

3. *Make rough drafts.* Students share their pages in **revising groups**, and they revise their pictures and text after getting feedback from classmates. Then they correct mechanical errors and make the final copy of their pages.

4. *Compile the pages.* Students add a title page and covers. Older students might also prepare a table of contents, an introduction, and a conclusion, and add a bibliography at the end. To make the book sturdier, teachers often laminate the covers (or all pages in the book) and have the book bound.

5. *Make copies of the book.* Teachers often make copies of the book for each student. The specially bound copy is then placed in the class or school library.

As part of literature focus units, students often retell a story or create an innovation or new version of a story in a collaborative book. They retell a novel by having each student summarize one chapter. Students also illustrate a poem or song by writing one line or stanza on a page and then drawing or painting an illustration. *The Lady With the Alligator Purse* (Hoberman, 2003), *There Was an Old Lady Who Swallowed a Fly* (Taback, 1997), and *America the Beautiful* (Bates, 2003) are picture-book examples of song and poem retellings that students can examine before they write their own collaborative retellings. ☜

Double-Entry Journals   A *double-entry journal* is a special type of **reading log** in which the pages are divided into two columns; students write different types of information in each column (Berthoff, 1981). In the left column, students write quotes from the story or nonfiction book they're reading, and in the right column, they reflect on each quote. They may relate a quote to their own lives, react to it, write a question, or make some other connection. Check the figure Excerpts From a Fifth Grader's Double-Entry Journal about *The Lion, the Witch and the Wardrobe*. Teachers use double-entry journals to help students structure their thinking about a text (Tovani, 2000). The quotes that students select indicate what they think is important, and the responses they make in the right column reveal their understanding of what they've read.

THE STEPS. Students usually write double-entry journals independently after reading each chapter or two of a novel, or more often with a nonfiction book or content area textbook, and they follow these steps:

1. *Design journal pages.* Students divide the pages in their reading logs into two columns. They may label the left column "Quotes" or "Facts" and the right column "Reflections" or "Connections."

EXCERPTS FROM A FIFTH GRADER'S DOUBLE-ENTRY JOURNAL

Quotes	Reflections
Chapter 1 I will tell you this is the sort of house where no one is going to mind what we do.	I remember the time that I went to Beaumont, Texas, to stay with my aunt. My aunt's house was very large. She had a piano and she let us play it. She told us that we could do whatever we wanted to.
Chapter 5 "How do you know?" he asked, "that your sister's story is not true?"	It reminds me of when I was little and I had an imaginary place. I would go there in my mind. I made up all kinds of make-believe stories about myself in this imaginary place. One time I told my big brother about my imaginary place. He laughed at me and told me I was silly. But it didn't bother me because nobody can stop me from thinking what I want.
Chapter 15 They're nibbling at the cords.	This reminds me of the story where the lion lets the mouse go and the mouse helps the lion.

2. ***Write quotes or facts in the left column.*** As students read, or immediately after reading, they copy one or more important or interesting quotes or facts in the left column.

3. ***Complete the right column.*** Students reread the quotes or facts and make notes in the right column about their reasons for choosing each one or what it means to them. Sometimes it's easier if students share the quotes or facts with a partner or in a **grand conversation** before they complete the right column.

Sometimes teachers change the headings for the two columns. Young children, who use the double-entry format in their journals, label the left column "Predictions" and the right one "What Happened" (Macon, Bewell, & Vogt, 1991). In the left column, they write or draw what they think will happen before they begin to read, and afterward, they draw or write what actually happened in the right column. 🌀

Exclusion Brainstorming

Teachers use exclusion brainstorming to activate students' background knowledge and expand their understanding about a social studies or science topic before reading (Blachowicz, 1986). They present a list of words, and students identify the ones that they believe don't relate to the topic. Then after reading, students review the list and decide whether they chose correctly. Exclusion brainstorming is a useful prereading activity because as students talk about the words on the list to decide which ones aren't related, they refine their knowledge, think about some key vocabulary words, and develop a purpose for reading.

THE STEPS. Teachers follow this procedure for exclusion brainstorming:

1. ***Prepare a word list.*** Teachers identify words related to a nonfiction book or content area textbook chapter that students will read and include a few words that don't fit with the topic. They project the list on an interactive whiteboard or make copies for students.

2. ***Read the list of words.*** Teachers read the list, and then, in small groups or together as a class, students decide which words they think aren't related to the text and draw circles around them.

AN EXCLUSION BRAINSTORMING		
✔ smallest ocean	✔ North Pole	✔ Atlantic Ocean
✔ ice-covered	✔ (ancient Greeks)	✔ (military importance)
(fresh water)	✔ Pacific Ocean	✔ sea water
✔ icebergs	✔ aurora borealis	✔ (United States)
✔ bitterly cold	✔ Vikings	~~precipitation~~
✔ Eskimos	✔ whales	✔ cod
✔ polar bears	~~penguins~~	✔ research stations
✔ Robert E. Peary	✔ Siberia	✔ USS Nautilus
✔ (commercial importance)	✔ Northwest passage	~~South Pole~~

3. ***Learn about the topic.*** Students read the text, noticing whether the words in the exclusion brainstorming exercise are mentioned in it.

4. ***Review the list.*** Students check their exclusion brainstorming list and make corrections based on their reading. They put checkmarks by related words and cross out unrelated words, whether they circled them earlier or not.

Teachers use exclusion brainstorming as a prereading activity to familiarize students with key concepts and vocabulary before reading nonfiction books and magazine and online articles. An eighth grade teacher prepared the list of words shown in the figure An Exclusion Brainstorming before his students read an article on the Arctic Ocean; all of the words except *penguins*, *South Pole*, and *precipitation* are related to the Arctic Ocean. Students circled seven words as possibly unrelated, and after reading, they crossed out the three words that their teacher expected them to eliminate. 🌀

Grand Conversations

Grand conversations are discussions about stories in which students explore the big ideas and reflect on their understanding (Peterson & Eeds, 2007). They're different from traditional discussions because they're student centered. Students do most of the talking as they voice their opinions and support their views with examples from the story. They talk about what puzzles them, what they find interesting, their personal connections to the story, connections to the world, and connections they see between this story and others they've read. Students don't raise their hands to be called on by the teacher; instead, they take turns and speak when no one else is speaking, much as adults do when they talk with friends. Students also encourage their classmates to contribute to the conversation. Even though teachers participate, the talk is primarily among the students.

Grand conversations have two parts. The first part is open-ended: Students talk about their reactions to the book, and their comments determine the direction of the conversation; teachers share their responses, ask questions, and provide information. Later, teachers do close reading to focus students' attention on one or two topics that they didn't talk about in the first part of the conversation. For English learners to participate successfully in grand conversations, they need to feel comfortable and safe in the group (Graves & Fitzgerald, 2003).

THE STEPS. Teachers follow these steps in using this instructional procedure:

1. ***Read the book.*** Students read a story or part of a story, or they listen to the teacher read it aloud.

2. *Prepare for the grand conversation.* Students think about the story by drawing pictures or writing in **reading logs**. This step is especially important when students don't talk much because with this preparation, they're more likely to have ideas to share with classmates.

3. *Hold small-group conversations.* Students form small groups to talk about the story before getting together as a class. This step is optional and is generally used when students are uncomfortable about sharing with the whole class or when they need more time to talk about the story.

4. *Begin the grand conversation.* Students form a circle for the class conversation so that everyone can see each other. Teachers begin by asking, "Who would like to begin?" or "What are you thinking about?" One student makes a comment, and classmates take turns talking about the idea the first student introduced.

5. *Continue the conversation.* A student introduces a new idea, and classmates talk about it, sharing ideas, asking questions, and reading excerpts to make a point. Students limit their comments to the idea being discussed, and after students finish discussing this idea, a new one is introduced. To ensure that everyone participates, teachers often ask students to make no more than three comments until everyone has spoken at least once.

6. *Ask questions.* Teachers ask questions to direct students to aspects of the story that they've missed; for example, they might focus on an element of story structure or the writer's craft. Or they may ask students to compare the book to the film version of the story or to other books by the same author.

7. *Conclude the conversation.* After all of the big ideas have been explored, teachers end the conversation by summarizing and drawing conclusions about the story or the chapter of the novel.

8. *Reflect on the conversation.* Students write (or write again) in reading logs to reflect on the ideas discussed in the grand conversation.

When students get together for a whole-class conversation during literature focus units, a feeling of community is established. Young children usually meet as a class; older students get together as a class when they're participating in a literature focus unit or listening to the teacher read a book aloud, but during literature circles, students meet in small groups because they're reading different books. When the entire class meets, students have fewer opportunities to talk, but they hear a wide variety of comments; however, when they meet in small groups, they have many more opportunities to share their ideas, but they hear fewer interesting responses from classmates.

STANDARDS IN THE CLASSROOM. **Click here** to read how Mrs. Mendes addresses Standards using a grand conversation in her second grade classroom. ☙

Hot Seat Hot seat is a role-playing activity that builds students' comprehension. Students assume the persona of a character from a story, the featured person in a biography they're reading, or an author whose books they've read, and they sit in a chair designated as the "hot seat" to be interviewed by classmates. It's called hot seat because students have to think quickly and respond to their classmates' questions and comments. Wilhelm (2002) explains that through the hot seat activity, students explore the characters, analyze story events, draw inferences, and try out different interpretations. Students aren't intimidated by performing for classmates; in fact, in most classrooms, the activity is very popular. Students are usually eager for their turn to sit on the hot seat. They often wear a costume they've created when they assume the character's persona and share objects they've collected and artifacts they've made.

THE STEPS. Students follow these steps for a hot seat interview:

1. *Learn about the character.* Students prepare for the hot seat activity by reading a story or a biography to learn about the character they'll impersonate.

2. *Create a costume.* Students design a costume appropriate for their character. In addition, they often collect objects or create artifacts to use in their presentations.

3. *Prepare opening remarks.* Students think about the most important things they'd like to share about the character and plan what they'll say at the beginning of the activity.

4. *Introduce the character.* One student sits in front of classmates in a chair designated as the "hot seat," tells a little about the character he or she is role-playing using a first-person viewpoint (e.g., "I said, 'One small step for man, one giant leap for mankind'"), and shares artifacts.

5. *Ask questions and make comments.* Classmates ask thoughtful questions to learn more about the character and offer advice, and the student remains in the role to respond to them.

6. *Summarize the ideas.* The student on the hot seat selects a classmate to summarize the important ideas that were presented about the character. He or she clarifies any misunderstandings and adds any big ideas that classmates don't mention.

During literature focus units, students take turns role-playing characters and being interviewed. Students representing different characters can also come together for a conversation—a group hot seat activity. For example, during a literature focus unit on *The View From Saturday* (Konigsburg, 1998), the story of a championship sixth grade Academic Bowl team that's told from the perspectives of the team members, students representing Noah, Nadia, Ethan, Julian, and their teacher, Mrs. Olinski, take turns sitting on the hot seat, or they come together to talk about the story. Similarly, when students are participating in literature circles, they can take turns role-playing characters from the story they're reading, or each student in the group can assume the persona of a different character at the same time for a group hot seat activity.

STANDARDS IN THE CLASSROOM. Click here to read how Mr. Jones addresses Standards using hot seat interviews with his fifth graders. 🌀

Interactive Read-Alouds   Teachers use interactive read-alouds to share books with students. The focus is on enhancing students' comprehension by engaging them in the reading process before, during, and after reading. Teachers introduce the book and activate students' background knowledge before beginning to read. Next, they engage students during reading through conversation and other activities. Afterward, they involve students in responding to the book. What's most important is how teachers engage students while they're reading aloud (Fisher, Flood, Lapp, & Frey, 2004).

Teachers often engage students by pausing periodically to talk about what's just been read. The timing is crucial: When reading stories, it's more effective to stop where students can make predictions and connections, after episodes that students might find confusing, and just before the ending becomes clear. When reading nonfiction, teachers stop to talk about big ideas as they're presented, briefly explain technical terms, and emphasize connections among the ideas. Teachers often read a poem from beginning to end once, and then stop as they're rereading it for students to play

INTERACTIVE TECHNIQUES

Stories	• Make and revise predictions at pivotal points. • Share personal, world, and literary connections. • Draw a picture of a character or an event. • Assume the persona of a character and share the character's thoughts. • Reenact a scene from the story.
Nonfiction	• Ask questions or share information. • Raise hands when specific information is read. • Restate the headings as questions. • Take notes. • Complete graphic organizers.
Poetry	• Add sound effects. • Mumble-read along with the teacher. • Repeat lines after the teacher. • Clap when rhyming words, alliteration, or other poetic devices are heard.

with words, notice poetic devices, and repeat favorite words and lines. Deciding how often to pause for an activity and knowing when to continue reading develop through practice and vary from one group of students to another. For additional ideas, check the figure Interactive Techniques.

THE STEPS. Teachers follow these steps to conduct interactive read-alouds:

1. *Pick a book.* Teachers choose award-winning and other high-quality books that are appropriate for students and that fit into their instructional programs.

2. *Prepare to share the book.* Teachers practice reading the book to ensure that they can read it fluently and to decide where to pause and engage students with the text; they write prompts on self-stick notes to mark these pages. Teachers also think about how they'll introduce the book and highlight difficult vocabulary words.

3. *Introduce the book.* Teachers activate students' background knowledge, set a clear purpose for listening, and preview the text.

4. *Read the book interactively.* Teachers read the book aloud, modeling fluent reading. They stop periodically to ask questions to focus students on specific points in the text and involve them in other activities.

5. *Involve students in after-reading activities.* Students participate in discussions and other response activities.

Teachers use this instructional procedure whenever they're reading aloud, no matter whether it's an after-lunch read-aloud period or during a literature focus unit, reading workshop, or a thematic unit. Reading aloud has always been an important activity in kindergarten and first grade classrooms. Sometimes teachers think they should read to children only until they learn to read, but reading aloud to share the excitement of books, especially those that students can't read themselves, should remain an important part of the literacy program at all grade levels. Older students report that when they listen to the teacher read aloud, they get more interested in the book and understand it better, and the experience often makes them want to read it themselves (Ivey, 2003).

STANDARDS IN THE CLASSROOM. Click here to read how Ms. Perez addresses Standards using interactive read-alouds in her first grade classroom. ✿

Interactive Writing

Teachers use interactive writing to create a message with students and write it on chart paper (Button, Johnson, & Furgerson, 1996). The text is composed by the group, and the teacher guides students as they write it word by word. Students take turns writing known letters and familiar words, adding punctuation marks, and marking spaces between words. As students participate in creating and writing the text on chart paper, they also write it on small whiteboards. Afterward, students read and reread the text using **shared reading** at first, and then read it independently.

Interactive writing is used to demonstrate how writing works and show students how to construct words using their knowledge of phoneme–grapheme correspondences and spelling patterns, and it's a powerful instructional procedure to use with English learners, no matter whether they're first graders or eighth graders (Tompkins & Collom, 2004). It was developed by the well-known English educator Moira McKenzie, who based it on Don Holdaway's work in shared reading (Fountas & Pinnell, 1996).

THE STEPS. Teachers follow these steps to do interactive writing with small groups of students or the entire class:

1. **Collect materials.** Teachers collect chart paper, colored marking pens, white correction tape, an alphabet chart, magnetic letters or letter cards, and a pointer. They also collect these materials for individual students' writing: small whiteboards, pens, and erasers.

2. **Pass out writing supplies.** Teachers distribute individual whiteboards, pens, and erasers for students to use to write the text individually as it's written together as a class on chart paper. They periodically ask students to hold their boards up so they can see what the students are writing.

3. **Set a purpose.** Teachers present a stimulus activity or set a purpose for interactive writing. Often they read or reread a trade book as a stimulus, but students also share daily news summaries or information they're learning in social studies or science.

4. **Choose a sentence to write.** Teachers negotiate the text—often a sentence or two—with students. Students repeat the sentence several times and segment it into words. The teacher also helps the students remember the sentence as it's written.

5. **Write the first sentence.** The teacher and students slowly pronounce the first word, "stretching" it out, and students identify the sounds and the letters that represent them and write the letters on chart paper. The teacher chooses students to write letters and words, depending on their knowledge of phonics and spelling. They use one color pen, and the teacher uses another color to write words students can't spell to keep track of how much writing students are able to do. Teachers have an alphabet poster with upper- and lowercase letters available for students to refer to when they're unsure how to form a letter, and white correction tape (sometimes called "boo-boo" tape) to correct poorly formed letters and misspellings. After writing each word, one student serves as the "spacer" and uses his or her hand to mark the space between words. This procedure is repeated to write each word in the sentence, and students reread the sentence from the beginning after each new word is completed. When appropriate, teachers point out capital letters, punctuation marks, and other conventions of print.

6. **Write additional sentences.** Teachers follow the procedure described in step 5 to write the remaining sentences to finish the text.

7. **Display the completed text.** After completing the message, teachers post the chart in the classroom and have students reread it using **shared reading** or independent reading. Students often reread interactive charts when they "read the

room," and teachers use the charts in teaching high-frequency words and phonics concepts.

Interactive writing can be used as part of literature focus units, in social studies and science thematic units, and for many other purposes, too:

Write predictions before reading	Write responses after reading
Write letters and other messages	Write information or facts
Make KWL charts	Create new versions of a familiar text
Write class poems	Make posters

When students begin interactive writing in kindergarten, they use letters to represent the beginning sounds in words and write familiar words such as *the*, *a*, and *is*. As they learn more about phoneme–grapheme correspondences and spelling patterns, they do more of the writing. Once they're writing words fluently, students do interactive writing in small groups. Each group member uses a different color pen and takes turns writing words. They also sign their names in color on the page so that the teacher can track which words each student wrote.

STANDARDS IN THE CLASSROOM. **Click here** to read how Mrs. Perry addresses Standards during an interactive writing activity. 🌀

KWL Charts Teachers use KWL charts during thematic units to activate students' background knowledge about a topic and to scaffold them as they ask questions and organize the information they're learning (Ogle, 1986). Teachers create a KWL chart by hanging up three sheets of butcher paper on a classroom wall and labeling them *K*, *W*, and *L*; the letters stand for "What We Know," "What We Wonder," and "What We Learned." To see a KWL chart a kindergarten class developed as they were hatching chicks, check the figure A Kindergarten Class's KWL Chart. The teacher did the actual writing on the chart, but the children generated the ideas and questions. It often takes several weeks to complete this activity because teachers introduce the KWL chart at the beginning of a unit and use it to identify what students already know and what they wonder about the topic. Toward the end of the unit, students complete the last section of the chart, listing what they've learned.

This procedure helps students activate background knowledge, combine new information with prior knowledge, and learn technical vocabulary related to a thematic unit. Students become curious and more engaged in the learning process, and teachers can introduce complex ideas and academic vocabulary in a nonthreatening way. Teachers direct, scribe, and monitor the development of the KWL chart, but it's the students' talk that makes this instructional procedure so powerful. Students use talk to explore ideas as they create the K and W columns and to share new knowledge as they complete the L column.

THE STEPS. Teachers follow this procedure:

1. *Post a KWL chart.* Teachers hang three charts side by side on the classroom wall and label them *K* (What We Know), *W* (What We Wonder), and *L* (What We Learned).

2. *Complete the K column.* At the beginning of a thematic unit, teachers ask students to brainstorm what they know about the topic and write this information in

A KINDERGARTEN CLASS'S KWL CHART

Baby Chicks

K What We Know	W What We Wonder	L What We Learned
They hatch from eggs. They sleep. They can be yellow or other colors. They have 2 legs. They have 2 wings. They eat food. They have a tail. They live on a farm. They are little. They have beaks. They are covered with fluff.	Are their feet called wabbly? Do they live in the woods? What are their bodies covered with? How many toes do they have? Do they have a stomach? What noises do they make? Do they like the sun?	Chickens' bodies are covered with feathers. Chickens have 4 claws. Yes, they do have stomachs. Chickens like to play in the sun. They like to stay warm. They live on farms.

the K column. Sometimes students suggest information that isn't correct; these statements should be turned into questions and added to the W column.

3. **Complete the W column.** Teachers write the questions that students suggest in the W column. They continue to add questions to the W column during the unit.

4. **Complete the L column.** At the end of the unit, students reflect on what they've learned, and teachers record this information in the L column of the chart.

Sometimes teachers organize the information on the KWL chart into categories to highlight the big ideas and to help students remember more of what they're learning; this procedure is called KWL Plus (Carr & Ogle, 1987). Teachers either provide three to six big-idea categories when they introduce the chart, or ask students to decide on categories after they brainstorm information about the topic for the K column. Students then focus on these categories as they complete the L column, classifying each piece of information according to one of the categories. When categories are used, it's easier to make sure students learn about each of the big ideas being presented.

Students also make individual KWL charts. As with class charts, they brainstorm what they know about a topic, identify questions, and list what they've learned. They can make their charts in **learning logs** or construct flip books with K, W, and L columns. Students make individual flip charts by folding a legal-size

A FOURTH GRADER'S FLIP CHART

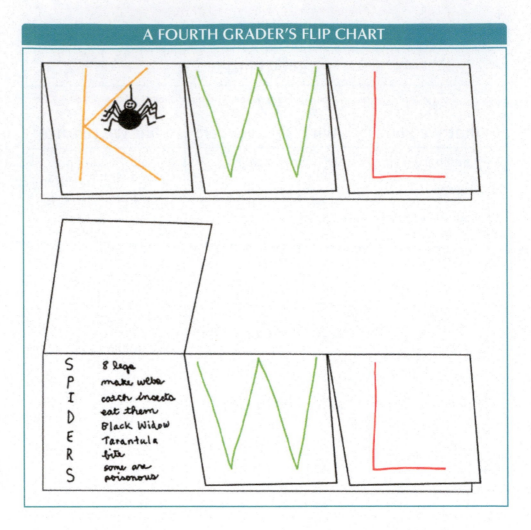

sheet of paper in half, lengthwise, cutting the top flap into thirds, and labeling the flaps *K*, *W*, and *L*. Then students lift the flaps to write in each column, as shown in the figure A Fourth Grader's Flip Chart. Checking students' completed L columns is a good way to evaluate their learning.

Language Experience Approach The Language Experience Approach (LEA) is a reading and writing procedure that's based on students' language and experiences (Ashton-Warner, 1965). A student dictates words and sentences about an experience, and the teacher writes the dictation. As the words and sentences are written, the teacher models how written language works, and then the text becomes the student's reading material. Because the language comes from the student and because the content is based on his or her experiences, the student is usually able to read the text. It's an effective way to help children begin reading; even those who haven't been successful with other types of reading activities can read what they've dictated.

Teachers use LEA to create reading materials that English learners can read. The student cuts pictures out of magazines and glues them in a book. Then the teacher and the student label several important words in a picture and create a related sentence that the teacher writes underneath the picture for the student to read. LEA is effective because students' texts are meaningful to them (Crawford, 2003).

THE STEPS. Depending on the teacher's purpose, this flexible procedure can be used with the entire class, with small groups, and with individual students. Teachers follow these steps when working with individual students:

1. ***Provide a stimulus for writing.*** Teachers identify a stimulus for writing; it can be an experience shared in school, a book read aloud, a field trip, or an outside-of-school experience that the student is familiar with, such as having a pet or playing in the snow.

2. ***Talk about the experience.*** The teacher and the student talk about the experience to generate words and review the experience so that the student's dictation will be more interesting and complete. Teachers often begin with an open-ended question, such as "What are we going to write about?" The student talks about the experience to clarify and organize ideas and use more specific vocabulary.

3. ***Record the student's dictation.*** The teacher takes the student's dictation. If the student hesitates, the teacher rereads what has been written and encourages him or her to continue. Teachers print neatly and spell words correctly, but they preserve students' language as much as possible. It's a great temptation to change the student's language to their own, in either word choice or grammar, but editing should be kept to a minimum so that students don't get the impression that their language is inferior or inadequate.

4. ***Read the text aloud.*** The teacher reads the text aloud, pointing at each word as it's read; this reading reminds the student of the content of the text and demonstrates how to read it aloud with appropriate intonation. Then the student reads along with the teacher, and after several joint readings, he or she reads the text alone.

5. ***Make sentence strips.*** The teacher rewrites the text on sentence strips that the student keeps in an envelope attached to the back of the paper. The student reads and sequences the sentence strips, and once he or she can read them smoothly, the student cuts the strips into individual words. He or she arranges the words into the familiar sentence and then creates new sentences with the word cards.

6. ***Add word cards to a word bank.*** The student adds the word cards to his or her word bank (a small box that holds the word cards) after working with this text. The word cards are used for a variety of activities, including **word sorts**.

LEA is often used to create texts students can read and use as a resource for writing. For example, during a thematic unit on insects, first graders learned about ladybugs and created a big book with this dictated text:

Part 1: What Ladybugs Do

Ladybugs are helper insects. They help people because they eat aphids. They make the earth pretty. They are red and they have 7 black spots. Ladybugs keep their wings under the red wing cases. Their wings are transparent and they fly with these wings. Ladybugs love to eat aphids. They love them so much that they can eat 50 aphids in one day!

Part 2: How Ladybugs Grow

Ladybugs live on leaves in bushes and in tree trunks. They lay eggs that are sticky and yellow on a leaf. The eggs hatch and out come tiny and black larvae. They like to eat aphids, too. Next the larva becomes a pupa and then it changes into a ladybug. When the ladybugs first come out of the pupa, they are yellow but they change into red and their spots appear. Then they can fly.

Part 3: Ladybugs Are Smart

Ladybugs have a good trick so that the birds won't eat them. If a bird starts to attack, the ladybug turns over on her back and squeezes a stinky liquid from her legs. It smells terrible and makes the bird fly away.

Each part was written on a large sheet of paper, and the pages were bound into a book. After reading and rereading the book, the children each chose a sentence to be written on a sentence strip; some wrote their own sentences, and the teacher wrote them for others. They practiced reading their sentences, then they cut the sentences apart and rearranged them, and finally they used the sentences in writing their own "All About Ladybugs" books.

STANDARDS IN THE CLASSROOM. <u>Click here</u> to read how Ms. Salam addresses Standards when she uses the Language Experience Approach in her kindergarten classroom.

| Learning Logs | Students write in learning logs as part of thematic units. Like other journals, *learning logs* are booklets of paper in which students record information they're learning, write questions, summarize big ideas, draw diagrams, and reflect on their learning. Their writing is impromptu, and the emphasis is on using writing as a learning tool rather than creating polished products. Even so, students should be encouraged to work carefully and to spell content-related words posted on the **word wall** correctly. Teachers monitor students' logs, and they can quickly see how well students understand the big ideas they're learning.

THE STEPS. Students construct learning logs at the beginning of a thematic unit and then make entries in them during the unit. Here are the steps in this instructional procedure:

1. *Prepare learning logs.* At the beginning of a thematic unit, students construct learning logs using a combination of lined and unlined paper that's stapled into booklets with tagboard or laminated construction paper covers.

2. *Make entries in learning logs.* Students take notes, draw diagrams, list vocabulary words, do **quickwrites**, and write summaries.

3. *Monitor students' entries.* Teachers read students' learning logs and answer their questions and clarify confusions.

4. *Write reflections.* Teachers often have students review their entries at the end of the thematic unit and write reflections about what they've learned.

Students use learning logs during social studies units to make notes and respond to information they're learning as they read nonfiction books and content area textbooks. During a thematic unit on pioneers, for example, fourth graders do these activities in learning logs:

- Write questions to investigate during the unit
- Draw and label pictures of covered wagons
- List items the pioneers carried west
- Mark the Oregon Trail on a map of the United States
- Write responses to videos about pioneers
- Write a rough draft of a poem about life on the Oregon Trail
- Write a letter to the teacher at the end of the unit listing five things they learned

Learning logs are used for similar purposes in science units. During a unit on rocks and minerals, for example, seventh graders drew graphic organizers that they completed as they read a chapter in the science textbook, compiled lab reports as they did

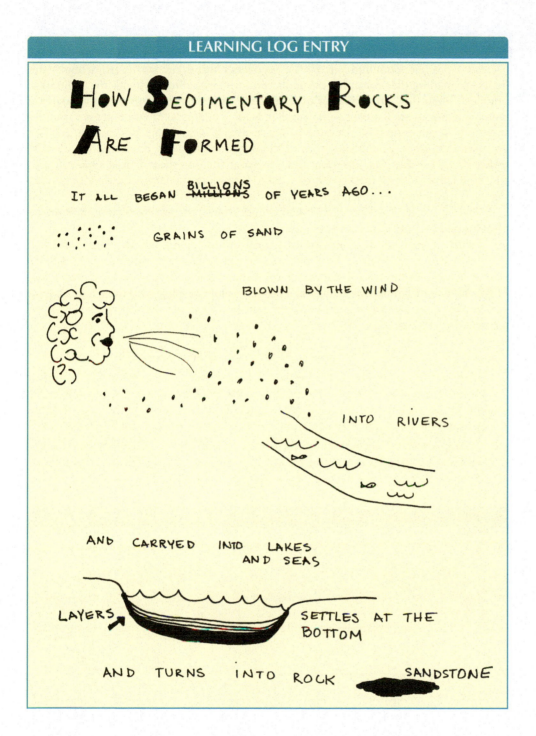

LEARNING LOG ENTRY

How Sedimentary Rocks Are Formed

IT ALL BEGAN ~~MILLIONS~~ BILLIONS OF YEARS AGO...

GRAINS OF SAND

BLOWN BY THE WIND

INTO RIVERS

AND CARRYED INTO LAKES AND SEAS

LAYERS

SETTLES AT THE BOTTOM

AND TURNS INTO ROCK

SANDSTONE

experiments, did quickwrites after watching videos, and drew diagrams and charts about scientific information. One student drew a series of illustrations to explain how sedimentary rocks form; check the figure Learning Log Entry.

STANDARDS IN THE CLASSROOM. **Click here** to read how Mr. Willson addresses Standards as his third graders write in learning logs. 🌀

Making Words   *Making words* is a teacher-directed spelling activity in which students arrange letter cards to spell words (Cunningham & Cunningham, 1992). Teachers choose key words from books students are reading that exemplify particular phonics or spelling patterns for students to practice. Then they prepare a set of letter cards that small groups or individual students can use to spell words. The teacher leads students as they create a variety of words using the letters. For example, after reading *Diary of a Spider* (Cronin, 2011), a group of first graders built these short-*i* and long-*i* words using the letters in the word *spider*: *is, sip, rip, dip, drip, side, ride,* and *ripe*. After spelling these words, children used all of the letters to spell the key word—*spider*. As students make words, they're practicing what they know about phoneme–grapheme correspondences and spelling patterns, and teachers get feedback on what students understand, correct confusions, and review phonics and spelling concepts when necessary.

Teachers often use this activity with small groups of English learners to practice spelling strategies and skills. It's effective because ELs collaborate with classmates, and the activity is both nonthreatening and hands-on. Sometimes teachers bring together a group of ELs to do a making words activity as a preview before doing it with the whole class (or afterward as a review), and sometimes a different word is used to reinforce a spelling pattern that they're learning.

THE STEPS. Teachers follow these steps for the making words activity:

1. *Make letter cards.* Teachers prepare a set of small letter cards with multiple copies of each letter, especially common letters such as *a, e, i, r, s,* and *t,* printing the lowercase letterform on one side and the uppercase form on the reverse. They package the cards letter by letter in small plastic bags or partitioned plastic boxes.

2. *Choose a word.* Teachers choose a word to use in the word-making activity, and without disclosing it, have a student distribute the needed letter cards to classmates.

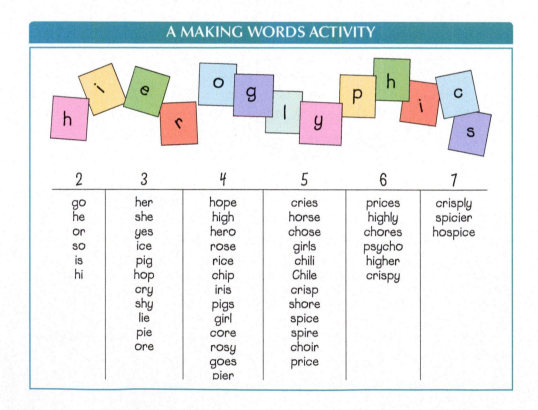

A MAKING WORDS ACTIVITY

h i e o g l y p h i c s
        r   s

2	3	4	5	6	7
go	her	hope	cries	prices	crisply
he	she	high	horse	highly	spicier
or	yes	hero	chose	chores	hospice
so	ice	rose	girls	psycho	
is	pig	rice	chili	higher	
hi	hop	chip	Chile	crispy	
	cry	iris	crisp		
	shy	pigs	shore		
	lie	girl	spice		
	pie	core	spire		
	ore	rosy	choir		
		goes	price		
		pier			

3. *Name the letter cards.* Teachers ask students to name the letter cards and arrange them on their desks with consonants in one group and vowels in another.

4. *Make words.* Students use the letter cards to spell words containing two, three, four, five, six, or more letters, and they list the words they can spell on a chart. Teachers monitor students' work and encourage them to fix any misspelled words.

5. *Share words.* Teachers have students identify two-letter words they made with the letter cards and continue to report longer and longer words until they identify the chosen word made using every letter card. After students share all of the words, teachers suggest any words they missed and point out recently taught spelling patterns.

Teachers choose words for word-making lessons from books they're reading with students. For example, for Eric Carle's *A House for Hermit Crab* (2005), *hermit crabs* offers many word-making possibilities; and for *Number the Stars* (Lowry, 2011), *resistance fighters* can be used. Teachers also choose words for making words activities from thematic units. While a sixth grade class was studying ancient Egypt, they completed the activity shown in the figure A Making Words Activity using the word *hieroglyphics*. Teachers can get additional ideas for word-making activities using books that Patricia Cunningham and Dorothy Hall have compiled (1994a, 1994b).

STANDARDS IN THE CLASSROOM. **Click here** to read how Mrs. Ford addresses Standards through a making words activity with second graders.

Minilessons Teachers teach short, focused lessons called *minilessons* on literacy strategies and skills (Atwell, 1998; Hoyt, 2000). Topics include how to write an entry in a reading log, use commas in a series, draw inferences, and use sentence combining. In these lessons, teachers introduce a topic and connect it to the reading or writing students are involved in, provide information, and supervise as students practice the topic. Minilessons usually last 15 to 30 minutes, and sometimes teachers extend the lesson over several days as students apply the topic in reading and writing activities. The best time to teach a minilesson is when students will have immediate opportunities to apply what they're learning.

It's not enough to simply explain strategies and skills and remind students to use them; minilessons are an effective way to teach strategies and skills so that students actually learn to apply them. Teachers must actively engage students, encourage and scaffold them while they're learning, and then gradually withdraw their support (Dorn & Soffos, 2001).

THE STEPS. Teachers follow these steps as they teach minilessons to small groups and to the whole class:

1. *Introduce the topic.* Teachers introduce the strategy or skill by naming it and making a connection between the topic and activities going on in the classroom.

2. *Share examples.* Teachers show how to use the topic with examples from students' own writing or from books they're reading.

3. *Provide information.* Teachers provide information, explaining and demonstrating the strategy or skill.

4. *Supervise practice.* Students practice using the strategy or skill with teacher supervision.

5. *Assess learning.* Teachers monitor students' progress and evaluate their use of newly learned strategies or skills.

Teachers teach minilessons during literature focus units, reading and writing workshop, and other instructional approaches. Some address strategies and skills, and others focus on instructional procedures, such as how to use a dictionary or share writing from the author's chair, and concepts, such as homophones or adjectives.

STANDARDS IN THE CLASSROOM. <u>Click here</u> to read how Mrs. Waters addresses Standards when she teaches a minilesson during writing workshop in her fifth grade classroom. ⟲

Open-Mind Portraits Students draw open-mind portraits to help them think more deeply about a character, reflect on story events from the character's viewpoint, and analyze the theme (McLaughlin & Allen, 2001). The portraits have two parts: the character's face on the top, the "portrait" page, and several "thinking" pages revealing the character's thoughts at pivotal points in the story. The two pages of a fourth grader's open-mind portrait on Sarah, the mail-order bride in *Sarah, Plain and Tall* (MacLachlan, 2005), are shown in the figure Open-Mind Portrait. The words and pictures on the "thinking" page represent her thoughts at the end of the story.

THE STEPS. Students follow these steps to make open-mind portraits either as they're reading a story or immediately afterward:

1. *Make a portrait of a character.* Students draw and color a large portrait of the head and neck of a character in a story they're reading.

OPEN-MIND PORTRAIT

2. *Cut out the "portrait" and "thinking" pages.* Students cut out the portrait and attach it with a brad or staple on top of several more sheets of drawing paper. It's important that students place the fastener at the top of the portrait so that there's room to draw and write on the "thinking" pages.

3. *Design the "thinking" pages.* Students lift the portrait page and draw and write about the character's thoughts at key points in the story.

4. *Share the completed open-mind portraits.* Students share their portraits with classmates and talk about the words and pictures they chose to include on the "thinking" pages.

Students create open-mind portraits to think more deeply about a character in a story they're reading in literature focus units and literature circles. They often reread parts of the story to recall specific details about the character's appearance before they draw the portrait, and they write several entries in a simulated journal to start thinking from that character's viewpoint before making the "thinking" pages. In addition to making open-mind portraits of characters in stories they're reading, students can make open-mind portraits of historical figures as part of social studies units, and of well-known personalities after reading biographies.

Possible Sentences

Possible sentences is a prereading activity that activates students' background knowledge about content area topics and related academic vocabulary (Blachowicz & Fisher, 2015; Lenski, Wham, & Johns, 1999). Students use what they know about a topic and their familiarity with English sentence structure to make predictions about word meanings and craft possible sentences; then after learning more, they review their sentences and make changes if they aren't accurate. This instructional procedure is typically used before reading nonfiction texts, especially content area textbook chapters, but teachers also use it before giving oral presentations on social studies and science topics or viewing DVDs.

A third grade teacher introduced a unit on honeybees by listing these key words on a whiteboard:

drones	hive	nectar
eggs	honey	queen
flowers	honeycomb	workers

The students eagerly began a conversation to share what they knew about honeybees, and soon they were asking lots of questions. Next, the teacher distributed *The Life and Times of the Honeybee* (Micucci, 1997), *The Honey Makers* (Gibbons, 2000), *Bees!* (Time for Kids, 2005), and other nonfiction books about honeybees for students to examine. Afterward, the students shared what they learned and created possible sentences that they called "rough draft sentences" using the key words. These sentences are shown in the figure A Possible Sentences Chart; the key words are underlined. Some of the sentences were accurate, but others would be revised after students learned more. The next day, the students read and discussed *The Magic School Bus Inside a Beehive* (Cole, 1998). Then they evaluated their possible sentences and revised them to correct factual errors and to add more information; these sentences are also shown in the figure, and their revisions are in red. The third graders expanded their background knowledge and academic vocabulary, and were now prepared to read and learn more about honeybees.

THE STEPS. Teachers follow these steps in this prereading procedure:

1. *Choose words.* Teachers choose 8–10 key words related to a content area topic; some words will probably be somewhat familiar to students, but others are likely to be unfamiliar or used in a new way.

A POSSIBLE SENTENCES CHART

Rough Draft Sentences	Evaluation	Revised Sentences
Bees live in <u>hives</u>.	+	Bees live in <u>hives</u>.
Bees get <u>nectar</u> from <u>flowers</u>.	−	Worker bees get <u>nectar</u> from <u>flowers</u>.
The <u>queen</u> bees use the <u>nectar</u> to make honey.	−	The worker bees use the <u>nectar</u> to make honey.
Bees store the <u>honey</u> in the <u>honeycomb</u>.	+	Bees store the <u>honey</u> in the <u>honeycomb</u>.
The <u>drones</u> don't eat the honey.	?	The <u>drones</u> are the male bees, and they don't do much work at all.
The <u>queen</u> is the most important bee.	+	The <u>queen</u> is the ruler bee and she's the biggest.
The <u>queen</u> bee lays all the <u>eggs</u>.	+	The <u>queen</u> bee lays thousands of <u>eggs</u>.
The <u>workers</u> are the male bees.	−	The <u>workers</u> are small female bees who do most of the work in the hive.

2. *Introduce the topic.* Teachers introduce the topic, making connections to topics previously studied and asking students to share their ideas. If students have limited knowledge about the topic and the vocabulary, teachers often read aloud a picture book about the topic.

3. *Define the words.* Teachers have students define or explain the words. Upper grade students often group the words into related pairs.

4. *Write sentences.* Students compose sentences using each word or each related pair of words. Even though they're not sure about the meanings or how to use the words in sentences, they give it a try. They make a prediction, understanding that this possible sentence is like a rough draft, and it can be revised later.

5. *Share the sentences.* Students share their possible sentences with classmates and talk about the plausibility of each one.

6. *Teach the lesson.* Students read the selection or listen to the presentation to test the accuracy of their predictions.

7. *Evaluate the sentences.* Students evaluate the accuracy of their sentences and mark them as accurate (+), inaccurate (−), or don't know (?).

8. *Revise the inaccurate sentences.* Students revise the sentences that aren't accurate and share them with classmates.

Possible sentences is a demanding activity because students must have a little background knowledge about the topic and be willing to make educated guesses about the meaning of academic vocabulary; nonetheless, it's effective because students learn to apply their background knowledge and word knowledge to predict the meanings of words. In addition, students become more engaged and eager to learn because they want to determine whether their predictions are accurate. ❧

Prereading Plan Teachers use the prereading plan (PReP) to diagnose and build necessary background knowledge before students read nonfiction books and content area textbooks (Langer, 1981; Vacca, Vacca, & Mraz, 2014). Teachers introduce a key concept discussed in the reading assignment and ask students to brainstorm related words and ideas. Teachers and students talk about the concept, and afterward students **quickwrite** to reflect on it. This activity is especially important for English learners who have limited background knowledge about a topic and technical vocabulary because it prepares them to read nonfiction books or content area textbooks. An added benefit is that students' interest in the topic often increases as they participate in this activity.

THE STEPS. Teachers follow these steps when they use this instructional procedure:

1. *Discuss a key concept.* Teachers introduce a key concept using a word, phrase, object, or picture to initiate a discussion.

2. *Brainstorm.* Teachers ask students to brainstorm words about the topic and record their ideas on a chart. They also help students make connections among the brainstormed ideas.

3. *Introduce vocabulary.* Teachers present additional vocabulary words that students need to read the assignment and clarify any misconceptions.

4. *Quickwrite about the topic.* Teachers have students quickwrite about the topic using words from the brainstormed list.

5. *Share the quickwrites.* Students share their quickwrites with the class, and teachers ask questions to help classmates clarify and elaborate their thinking.

6. *Read the assignment.* Students read the assignment and relate what they're reading to what they learned before reading.

Teachers use this instructional procedure during thematic units. Before reading a social studies textbook chapter about the Bill of Rights, for example, an eighth grade teacher used PReP to introduce the concept that citizens have freedoms and responsibilities. Students brainstormed this list during a discussion about the Bill of Rights:

guaranteed in the Constitution	James Madison
1791	10 amendments
citizens	freedom of speech
freedom of religion	owning guns and pistols
no searches without a search warrant	act responsibly
limits on these freedoms for everyone's good	serve on juries
"life, liberty, and the pursuit of happiness"	right to a jury trial
no cruel or unusual punishments	vote intelligently

Then before reading the chapter, students wrote quickwrites to make personal connections to the ideas they'd brainstormed. Here's one student's quickwrite:

> I always knew America was a free country but I thought it was because of the Declaration of Independence. Now I know that the Bill of Rights is a list of our freedoms. There are 10 freedoms in the Bill of Rights. I have the freedom to go to any church I want, to own guns, to speak my mind, and to read newspapers. I never thought of serving on a jury as a freedom and my Mom didn't either. She was on a jury about a year ago and she didn't want to do it. It took a whole week. Her boss didn't like her missing work. The trial was about someone who robbed a store and shot a man but he didn't die. I'm going to tell her that it is important to do jury duty. When I am an adult, I hope I get to be on a jury of a murder trial. I want to protect my freedoms and I know it is a citizen's responsibility, too.

When the teacher read this student's quickwrite, she noticed that the student confused the number of amendments with the number of freedoms listed in the amendments, so she clarified the misunderstandings individually with her. 🐚

Question-Answer-Relationships

Taffy Raphael's Question-Answer-Relationships (QAR) procedure teaches students to be aware of whether they're likely to find the answer to a comprehension question "right there" on the page, between the lines, or beyond the information provided in the text so that they're better able to answer it (Raphael, Highfield, & Au, 2006). Students use the QAR procedure when they're reading both stories and nonfiction and answering comprehension questions independently.

This procedure differentiates among the types of questions and the kinds of thinking required to answer them: Some questions require only literal thinking, but others demand higher levels of thinking. Raphael identified these four types of questions:

Right There Questions. Readers find the answer "right there" in the text, usually in the same sentence as words from the question. These are literal-level questions.

Think and Search Questions. The answer is in the text, but readers must search for it in different parts of the text and put the ideas together. These are inferential-level questions.

Author and Me Questions. Readers use a combination of the author's ideas and their own to answer the question. These questions combine inferential and evaluation levels.

On My Own Questions. Readers use their own ideas to answer the question; sometimes they don't need to read the text to answer it. These are evaluation-level questions.

The first two types of questions are known as "in the book" questions because the answers can be found in the book, and the last two types are "in the head" questions because they require information and ideas not presented in the book. An eighth grader's chart describing these types of questions is shown in the figure QAR Chart.

THE STEPS. Students follow these steps when they use the QAR procedure:

1. *Read the questions first.* Students preview the questions before reading the text to give them an idea of what to think about as they read.
2. *Predict how to answer the questions.* Students consider which of the four types each question represents and the level of thinking required to answer it.
3. *Read the text.* Students read the text while thinking about the questions they'll answer afterward.
4. *Answer the questions.* Students reread the questions, determine where to find the answers, locate the answers, and write them.
5. *Share answers.* Students read their answers aloud and explain how they answered the questions. They should again refer to the type of question and whether the answer was "in the book" or "in the head."

Students use the QAR procedure whenever they answer questions after reading a story, nonfiction book, or content area textbook. They can also write their own "in the book" and "in the head" questions. A seventh grade teacher, for instance, asked his students to write questions representing the four levels in their **reading logs** as they read *The Giver* (Lowry, 2006). Here are some of their questions:

Right There Questions
What was the first color Jonas could see?
What does a Receiver do?

QAR CHART

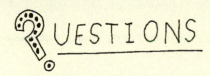

ℚUESTIONS

RIGHT THERE — The answer is easy to find in the book. It is near the Question.

THINK AND SEARCH — The answer is in the book but it isn't all in one place. I have to search for it and put the parts together.

AUTHOR AND ME — The answer is a combination of ideas in the book and my own ideas.

ON MY OWN — The answer is NOT in the book. I have to do my own thinking.

<u>Think and Search Questions</u>

How is Jonas different than the other people?

Why did Rosemary ask to be released?

<u>Author and Me Questions</u>

What happened to Jonas and Gabe at the end of the book?

Was the Giver an honorable person?

<u>On My Own Questions</u>

What would you have done if you were Jonas?

Could this happen in the United States?

Students also write questions when reading nonfiction books and content area textbooks. 🌀

Quickwriting

Quickwriting is an impromptu writing activity in which students explore a topic or respond to a question (Brozo & Simpson, 2007). They write for 5 to 10 minutes, letting their thoughts flow without stopping to make revisions or correct misspelled words; the focus is on generating ideas and developing writing fluency. Students think about ideas, reflect on what they know about a topic, ramble on paper, and make connections among ideas. Here's a series of quickwrites that a fifth grader wrote as she listened to her teacher read aloud *The Higher Power of Lucky* (Patron, 2006), an award-winning story of a plucky 10-year-old girl named Lucky who tries to surmount her problems and bring stability to her life:

Prompt: Why do you think the main character is named Lucky?

> I don't know. At this point I don't think Lucky is lucky at all. Her mom died and her dad doesn't want her. She seems pretty unlucky. All that I can think is that Lucky is going to get more lucky at the end of the book. I hope something really good happens to her because she deserves it.

Prompt: Do you think Brigitte will abandon Lucky?

> Lucky is really afraid that Brigitte will go back home to Paris. I don't think Brigitte is going to leave. It would be a really mean thing to do and Brigitte is sort of a mom and moms don't do that. I also think it's bad for a girl to have to worry about being abandoned. That's really sad. I predict that Lucky will have a real family at the end of the book.

Prompt: What happened when Lucky hit bottom?

> It happened when she ran away from home. There was a bad dust storm and Miles was lost and it was her fault that Miles was lost. She was wearing Brigitte's beautiful red dress and she probably ruined it. I thought she'd get in big trouble and maybe she'd even die and so would Miles and her dog but it didn't happen that way. Everybody in town drove their cars out to the caves to find her and they were so happy to see her and Miles that they didn't even get mad. Lots of good things happened. Best of all, she found out that Brigitte was going to adopt her and would always be her mom. I love this book.

Students wrote their quickwrites after the teacher finished reading each chapter or two, and the quickwrites helped them reflect on what was happening in the story and prepare for the **grand conversations**.

THE STEPS. Teachers follow these steps in the quickwriting procedure:

1. *Choose a topic.* Students choose a topic or question (or the teacher assigns one) for the quickwrite, and they write it at the top of their papers.

2. *Write about the topic.* Students write sentences and paragraphs to explore the topic for 5 to 10 minutes. They focus on interesting ideas, make connections between the topic and their own lives, and reflect on their reading or learning. They rarely, if ever, stop writing to reread or correct errors in what they've written.

3. *Read quickwrites.* Students meet in small groups to read their quickwrites, and then one student in each group is selected to share with the class. That student rereads his or her quickwrite in preparation for sharing with the whole class and adds any missing words and completes any unfinished thoughts.

4. *Share selected quickwrites.* Students who have been chosen to share their quickwrites with the whole class take turns reading them aloud.

5. *Write a second time.* Sometimes students write a second time on the same topic or on a new topic that emerged through writing and sharing; this second quickwrite is usually more focused than the first. Or students can expand their first quickwrite after listening to classmates share theirs or after learning more about the topic.

Teachers use quickwriting to promote thinking during literature focus units and thematic units. It's used as a warm-up at the beginning of a lesson or to promote reflection at the end. Sometimes students identify the topics or questions for the quickwrite, and at other times, the teacher provides them. Quickwrites are also an effective prewriting procedure (Routman, 2004). Students often do several quickwrites to explore what they know about a topic before beginning to write; they brainstorm ideas and vocabulary, play with language, and identify ideas they need to learn more about before moving on to the drafting stage.

RAFT Teachers use RAFT to create project topics and other assignments to enhance students' comprehension of novels they're reading and information they're learning in thematic units (Buehl, 2001; Holston & Santa, 1985). RAFT stands for *role*, *audience*, *format*, and *topic*, and teachers consider these four dimensions as they design projects:

Role. Students assume the role of a person or the voice of a group of people for this project. Sometimes they take on the role of a book character, historical figure, or contemporary personality, such as Oprah, but at other times, they remain themselves.

Audience. The audience is the person or people who will read or view the project; they may include students, teachers, parents, or community members, as well as simulated audiences, such as book characters and historical personalities.

Format. The format is the genre or activity that students create; it might be a letter, brochure, cartoon, journal, poster, essay, newspaper article, speech, or digital scrapbook.

Topic. The topic is the subject of the project; it may be an issue related to the text, an essential question, or something of personal interest.

When students develop projects, they process ideas and information in different ways as they assume varied viewpoints and complete projects directed to specific audiences. Their thinking is imaginative and interpretive; in contrast, students' comprehension tends to be more literal when they do more traditional assignments, such as writing answers to questions.

RAFT IDEAS FOR *THE WEDNESDAY WARS*

Role	Audience	Format	Topic
Holling and William Shakespeare	Our class	Interview	Explain "To thine own self be true" and other life lessons.
Mrs. Baker	Her son, a U.S. soldier in Vietnam	Letter	Tell why you took such an interest in Holling.
You	Our class	Poster	Describe the cultural and political uproar of the 1960s.
You	Newbery Award Committee	Persuasive essay	Present reasons why this book should win the Newbery Award.
Bullies	Students at Camillo Jr. High	Speech	Research bullying, and explain how to deal with bullies.
Mai Thi (Holling's classmate)	Our class	Digital scrapbook	Share information about Vietnam and the war's effect on you and your home country.
Holling	Mrs. Baker	Letter, written when Holling is 30 years old	Explain how you've followed Mrs. Baker's advice: "Learn everything you can—everything. And then use all that you have learned to be a wise and good man."

THE STEPS. Teachers follow these steps to create projects:

1. *Establish the purpose.* Teachers reflect on what they want students to learn through this activity and consider how it can enhance students' comprehension of a book they're reading or a social studies or science topic they're learning.

2. *Prepare a RAFT chart.* Teachers prepare a RAFT chart of possible projects by brainstorming roles, choosing audiences, identifying genres and other formats for projects, and listing topics.

3. *Read the book or study the topic.* Students read and discuss a novel or learn about a topic before they develop RAFT projects.

4. *Choose projects.* Sometimes teachers assign the same project for groups of students, but at other times, they let students choose a project from the RAFT chart.

5. *Create projects.* Students prepare their oral, written, or multimedia projects and get feedback from the teacher as they work.

6. *Share completed projects.* Students share their projects with small groups or the whole class and other appropriate audiences.

RAFT is an effective way to differentiate instruction by providing tiered activities; projects on the same text or topic can be adjusted according to students' achievement levels, English proficiency, and interests. For example, check the figure RAFT Ideas for *The Wednesday Wars* to see a seventh grade teacher's project ideas for Gary Schmidt's (2007) Newbery Honor book; this coming-of-age novel chronicles the everyday trials of Holling Hoodhood, who's at odds with his seventh grade English teacher, Mrs. Baker. ꙮ

Readers Theatre Readers theatre is a dramatic performance of a script by a group of readers (Black & Stave, 2007). Students each assume a part, rehearse by reading and rereading their characters' lines in the script, and then do a performance for their classmates. Students can read scripts in trade books and textbooks, or they can create their own scripts. The Booklist: Readers Theatre Scripts includes books of both narrative and nonfiction scripts.

What's valuable about readers theatre is that students interpret the story with their voices, without using much action. They may stand or sit, but they must carry the whole communication of the plot, characterization, mood, and theme by using their voices, gestures, and facial expressions. In addition, readers theatre avoids many of the problems inherent in theatrical productions: Students don't memorize their parts; elaborate props, costumes, and backdrops aren't needed; and long, tedious hours aren't spent rehearsing. They have opportunities to read good literature, and through this procedure they engage with text, interpret characters, and bring the text to life (Keehn, Martinez, & Roser, 2005; Worthy & Prater, 2002). Moreover, English learners and other students who aren't yet fluent readers gain valuable oral reading practice in a relaxed, small-group setting. They practice reading high-frequency words, increase their reading speed, learn how to phrase and chunk words in sentences, and read with more expression.

THE STEPS. Teachers follow these steps for readers theatre as they work with a small group or the whole class:

1. *Select a script.* Students select a script and then read and discuss it as they would any story. Afterward, they volunteer to read each part.

2. *Rehearse the reading.* Students decide how to use their voice, gestures, and facial expressions to interpret the characters they're reading. They read the script several times, striving for accurate pronunciation, voice projection, and appropriate

Booklist — Readers Theatre Scripts

Barchers, S. I. (1997). *50 fabulous fables: Beginning readers theatre.* Portsmouth, NH: Teacher Ideas Press.

Barchers, S. I., & Pfeffinger, C. R. (2006). *More readers theatre for beginning readers.* Portsmouth, NH: Teacher Ideas Press.

Fredericks, A. D. (2007). *Nonfiction readers theatre for beginning readers.* Portsmouth, NH: Teacher Ideas Press.

Laughlin, M. K., Black, P. T., & Loberg, M. K. (1991). *Social studies readers theatre for children: Scripts and script development.* Portsmouth, NH: Teacher Ideas Press.

Martin, J. M. (2002). *12 fabulously funny fairy tale plays.* New York: Scholastic.

Pugliano-Martin, C. (1999). *25 just-right plays for emergent readers.* New York: Scholastic.

Pugliano-Martin, C. (2008). *Greek myth plays.* New York: Scholastic.

Shepard, A. (2005). *Stories on stage: Children's plays for reader's theater with 15 play scripts from 15 authors.* Olympia, WA: Shepard.

Wolf, J. M. (2002). *Cinderella outgrows the glass slipper and other zany fractured fairy tale plays.* New York: Scholastic.

Wolfman, J. (2004). *How and why stories for readers theatre.* Portsmouth, NH: Teacher Ideas Press.

Worthy, J. (2005). *Readers theatre for building fluency: Strategies and scripts for making the most of this highly effective, motivating, and research-based approach to oral reading.* New York: Scholastic.

inflections. Less rehearsal is needed for an informal, in-class presentation than for a more formal production; nevertheless, interpretations should always be developed as fully as possible.

3. **Stage the reading.** Readers theatre can be presented on a stage or in a corner of the classroom. Students stand or sit in a row and read their lines. They stay in position through the production or enter and leave according to the characters' appearances "onstage." If readers are sitting, they stand to read their lines; if they're standing, they step forward to read. The emphasis isn't on production quality; rather, it's on the interpretive quality of readers' voices and expressions. Costumes and props aren't necessary; however, adding a few small props enhances interest as long as they don't interfere with the interpretive quality of the reading.

Students create their own readers theatre scripts from stories they've read and about topics related to thematic units (Flynn, 2007). When students are creating a script, it's important to choose a story with lots of conversation; any parts that don't include dialogue can become narrator parts. Depending on the number of narrator parts, one to four students can take the narrator duties. Teachers often make photocopies of the story for students to mark up or highlight as they develop the script. Sometimes students simply use their marked-up copies as the finished script, and at other times, they retype the finished script, omitting the unnecessary parts.

Reading Logs *Reading logs* are journals in which students write their reactions and opinions about books they're reading or listening to the teacher read aloud. Through their reading log entries, students clarify misunderstandings, explore ideas, and deepen their comprehension (Barone, 1990; Hancock, 2008). They also add lists of words from the word wall, diagrams about story elements, and information about authors and genres. For a chapter book, students write after reading every chapter or two, and they often write single entries after reading picture books or short stories. Often students write a series of entries about a collection of books written by the same author, such as books by Eric Carle or Chris Van Allsburg, or about versions of the same folktale or fairy tale.

Sometimes students choose what they'll write about in reading log entries, and at other times, they respond to questions or prompts that teachers have prepared. Both student-choice and teacher-directed entries are useful: When students choose their own topics, they delve into their own ideas and questions, sharing what's important to them, and when teachers prepare prompts, they direct students' thinking to topics and questions that students might otherwise miss. When teachers know their students well and are familiar with the books students are reading, they choose the best mix of student-choice and teacher-directed entries.

THE STEPS. Students follow these steps as they write independently in reading logs:

1. *Prepare reading logs.* Students make reading logs by stapling paper into booklets, and they write the title of the book on the cover.

2. *Write entries.* Students write their reactions and reflections about the book or chapter. Sometimes they choose their own topics, and at other times, teachers pose topics and questions. Students often summarize events and make connections to the book. They also list interesting or unfamiliar words, jot down memorable quotes, and take notes about characters, plot, or other story elements.

3. *Share entries.* Students share their reading logs with teachers so they can monitor students' work. Teachers also write comments back to students about their interpretations and reflections.

Students at all grade levels can write and draw reading log entries to help them understand stories they're reading and listening to read aloud during literature focus units and literature circles (Daniels, 2001). As a sixth grade class read *The Giver* (Lowry, 2006), a Newbery Award–winning story of a not-so-perfect society, students discussed each chapter and brainstormed several possible chapter titles. Then they wrote entries in their reading logs and labeled each chapter with the number and the title they thought was most appropriate. The following three reading log entries show how a sixth grader grappled with the idea of "release":

> Chapter 18: "Release"
> I think release is a very rude thing to do. People have a right to live where they want to. Just because they're different they should NOT have to go somewhere else. I think release means that you have to go and live elsewhere. And you can't come back to the community.

> Chapter 19: "Release—The Truth"
> It is wrong to kill people that didn't do anything bad. They kill perfectly innocent people! If I were Jonas I would probably go insane. The people who kill the people that are to be released don't know what they're doing. I think they've been brain-washed.

> Chapter 20: "Mortified"
> Jonas really can't go home and face his father. What can he do? Now that he knows what release is, he will probably decide to stay with The Giver for the rest of his life.

After reading and discussing Chapter 18, this student doesn't understand that "release" means "killing," but he grasps the awful meaning of the word as he reads Chapter 19. 🌀

Revising Groups   During the revising stage of the writing process, students meet in revising groups to share their rough drafts and get feedback on how well they're communicating (Tompkins, 2012). Revising group members offer compliments about things writers have done well and make suggestions for improvement. Their comments reflect these topics and other aspects of the writer's craft:

leads	word choice	voice
dialogue	sentences	rhyme
endings	character development	sequence
description	point of view	flashbacks
ideas	organization	alliterations

These topics are used for both compliments and suggestions. When students are offering a compliment, they might say, "I liked your lead. It grabbed me and made me keep listening," and when they're making a suggestion, they say, "I wonder if you could start with a question to make your lead more interesting. Maybe you could say, 'Have you ever ridden in a police car? Well, that's what happened to me!'"

Teaching students how to share their rough drafts and offer constructive feedback isn't easy. When teachers introduce revision, they model appropriate responses because students may not know how to offer specific and meaningful comments tactfully. Teachers and students can brainstorm a list of appropriate compliments and suggestions and post it in the classroom to refer to. Comments should usually begin with "I," not "you." Notice the difference in tone in these two sentence stems: "I wonder if . . ." versus "You need to . . ." Here are some ways to begin compliments:

I like the part where . . .
I learned how . . .
I like the way you described . . .
I like how you organized the information because . . .

Students also offer suggestions about how classmates can revise their writing, and it's important that they phrase what they say in helpful ways. Writers often begin suggestions this way:

I got confused in the part about . . .
I wonder if you need a closing . . .
I'd like you to add more about . . .
I wonder if these paragraphs are in the right order . . .
I think you might want to combine these sentences . . .

Student-writers also ask classmates for help with specific problems they've identified; looking to classmates for feedback is a big step in learning to revise. Writers ask questions such as these:

What do you want to know more about?
Is there a part that I should throw away?
What details can I add?
What do you think is the best part of my writing?
Are there some words I need to change?

Revising groups work effectively once students understand how to support and help their classmates by offering compliments, making suggestions, and asking questions.

Revising is the most difficult part of the writing process because it's hard for students to stand back and evaluate their writing objectively in order to make changes to communicate more effectively. As students participate in revising groups, they learn how to accept compliments and suggestions and to provide useful feedback to classmates.

THE STEPS. Teachers teach students how to use this instructional procedure so that they can then work in small groups to get ideas for revising their writing. Here are the steps:

1. **Read drafts aloud.** Students take turns reading their rough drafts aloud to the group. Everyone listens politely, thinking about compliments and suggestions they'll make after the writer finishes reading. Only the writer looks at the composition because when classmates look at it, they quickly notice and comment on mechanical errors, even though the emphasis during revising is on content. Listening to the writing read aloud keeps the focus on content.

2. **Offer compliments.** After listening to the rough draft read aloud, classmates in the revising group tell the writer what they liked about the composition. These positive comments should be specific, focusing on strengths, rather than the often-heard "I liked it" or "It was good"; even though these are positive comments, they don't provide effective feedback.

3. **Ask clarifying questions.** Writers ask for assistance with trouble spots they identified earlier when rereading their writing, or they may ask questions that reflect more general concerns about how well they're communicating.

4. **Offer other revision suggestions.** Group members ask questions about things that were unclear to them and make suggestions about how to revise the rough draft.

5. **Repeat the process.** Members of the revising group repeat the first four steps so that all students can share their rough drafts.

6. **Make plans for revision.** Students each make a commitment to revise their writing based on the comments and suggestions of the group members. The final decision on what to revise always rests with the writers themselves, but with the understanding that their rough drafts aren't perfect comes the realization that some revision will be necessary. When students verbalize their planned revisions, they're more likely to complete the revision stage.

Students meet in revising groups whenever they're using the writing process. Once they've written a rough draft, students are ready to share their writing and get some feedback from classmates. They often meet with the same revising group throughout the school year, or students can form groups when they're ready to get feedback about their rough drafts. Many teachers have students sign up on the whiteboard; this way, whenever four students are ready, they form a group. Both established and spontaneously formed groups can be effective. What matters most is that students get feedback about their writing when they need it.

STANDARDS IN THE CLASSROOM. Click here to read how Ms. Feingold addresses Standards using revising groups in her third grade classroom.

Rubrics *Rubrics* are scoring guides that teachers use to assess students' achievement (Spandel, 2005). These guides usually have 4, 5, or 6 levels, ranging from high to low, and assessment criteria are described at each level. Students receive a copy of the rubric as they begin a project so that they understand what's expected and how they'll be assessed. Depending on the rubric's intricacy, teachers mark the assessment criteria either while they're reading or examining the project or immediately afterward and then determine the overall score.

The assessment criteria on rubrics vary. The requirements in rubrics for oral presentations often focus on eye contact, composure, and the quality of the content; and the criteria in rubrics for museum projects describe the quality of artifacts and curator's notes, accuracy and completeness of information, Standard English conventions used in written text, and bibliographic resources. Criteria in general writing rubrics address the writer's craft, such as ideas, organization, word choice, and mechanics. Other rubrics are genre specific, and deal with genre characteristics; teachers often use these rubrics to assess stories, reports, and autobiographies. No matter which assessment criteria are used, the same ones are addressed at each achievement level. If a criterion addresses sentence fluency, for example, descriptors about sentence fluency are included at each level; the statement "contains short, choppy sentences" might be used at the lowest level and "uses sentences that vary in length and style" at the highest level. Each level represents a one-step improvement in students' application of that criterion.

Rubrics can be constructed with any number of levels, but it's easier to show growth when a rubric has more levels: Much more improvement is needed for students to move from one level to another if the rubric has 4 levels than if it has 6 levels. A rubric with 10 levels would be even more sensitive, but rubrics with many levels are harder to construct and more time-consuming to use. Researchers usually recommend that teachers use rubrics with either 4 or 6 levels so that there's no middle score—each level is either above or below the middle—because teachers are inclined to score students at the middle level, when there is one.

Rubrics are often used for determining proficiency levels and assigning grades. The level that's above the midpoint is usually designated as "proficient," "competent," or "passing"—that's a 3 on a 4-point rubric and a 4 on a 5- or 6-point rubric. The levels on a 6-point rubric can be described this way:

1 = minimal level	4 = proficient level
2 = beginning or limited level	5 = excellent level
3 = developing level	6 = superior level

Teachers also equate levels to letter grades.

These scoring guides help students achieve higher grades because they lay out the qualities that constitute excellence and clarify teachers' expectations so students understand how the project will be assessed. Students, too, can use rubrics to improve the quality of their projects: Based on the rubric's criteria, they can examine their work-in-progress and decide how to strengthen it. In addition, Vicki Spandel (2005) claims that rubrics are time savers: She says that rubrics drastically reduce the time it takes to read and respond to students' work because the criteria on the rubric guide the assessment and reduce the need to write lengthy comments back to students.

THE STEPS. Teachers follow these steps when they use rubrics to assess students' achievement:

1. *Choose a rubric.* Teachers choose or create a rubric that's appropriate to the project.
2. *Introduce the rubric.* Teachers distribute copies of the rubric to students and talk about the criteria used at each level, focusing on the requirements at the proficient level.
3. *Self-assess progress.* Students use the rubric to self-assess their work-in-progress. They highlight phrases in the rubric or check off items that best describe their achievement. Then they determine which level has the most highlighted words or checkmarks; that level is the overall score, and students circle it.
4. *Assess students' projects.* Teachers assess students' projects by highlighting phrases in the rubric or checking off items that best describe the work. Then they assign the overall score by determining which level has the most highlighted words or checkmarks and circle it.
5. *Conference with students.* Teachers talk with students about the assessment, identifying strengths and weaknesses. Then students set goals for the next project.

Many commercially prepared rubrics are currently available: State departments of education post rubrics for mandated writing tests on their websites, and school districts hire teams of teachers or consultants to develop reading and writing rubrics for each grade level. Spandel (2005) provides rubrics that assess the six traits of writing. Other rubrics are provided with basal reading programs, in professional books for teachers, and on the Internet.

Even though commercially prepared rubrics are convenient, they may not be appropriate for some groups of students or for certain types of projects. The rubrics may have only 4 levels when 6 would be better, or they may have been designed for a different grade level. They also may not address a specific genre, or they may have been written for teachers, not in kid-friendly language. Because of these limitations, teachers often decide to develop their own rubrics or adapt commercial rubrics to meet their own needs.

STANDARDS IN THE CLASSROOM. Click here to read how Mr. Alvarez addresses Standards in the rubrics he uses in his fourth grade classroom. ⟡

Running Records In this reading-stage activity, teachers observe individual students as they read aloud and record information to analyze their reading fluency (Clay, 2000). They calculate the percentage of words the student reads correctly and then analyze the miscues or errors. Teachers make a checkmark on a copy of the text as the student reads each word correctly and use other marks to indicate words that the student mispronounces or doesn't know.

THE STEPS. Teachers conduct running records with individual students using these steps:

1. *Choose a book.* Teachers have the student choose an excerpt for the assessment at least 100 words in length from a book he or she is reading. For beginning readers, the text can be shorter.

2. *Take the running record.* As the student reads the excerpt aloud, the teacher records information about the words read correctly as well as those misread. The

HOW TO MARK MISCUES

MISCUE	EXPLANATION	MARKING
Incorrect word	If the student reads a word incorrectly, the teacher writes the incorrect word above the correct word.	take / taken
Self-correction	If the student self-corrects an error, the teacher writes SC (for "self-correction") following the incorrect word.	for SC / from
Unsuccessful attempt	If the student attempts to pronounce a word, the teacher records each attempt above the correct word.	be-bēf-before / before
Skipped word	If the student skips a word, the teacher marks the error with a dash.	— / the
Inserted word	If the student says words that aren't in the text, the teacher writes an insertion symbol called a *caret* where the student made the error and records the inserted words.	out / go ⌃ for a walk
Supplied word	If the student can't identify a word, the teacher supplies it and writes T above the word.	T / which
Repetition	If the student repeats a word or phrase, it isn't scored as a miscue, but the teacher notes it by making a checkmark for each repetition.	✓✓✓ / so

teacher makes checkmarks on a copy of the text for each word read correctly and uses other marks for miscues. Check the figure How to Mark Miscues.

3. **Calculate the percentage of miscues.** Teachers calculate the percentage of miscues by dividing the number of miscues by the total number of words read. When the student makes 5% or fewer errors, the book is considered to be at his or her independent level. When there are 6–10% errors, the book is at the student's instructional level, and when there are more than 10% errors, the book is too difficult—the student's frustration level.

4. **Analyze the miscues.** Teachers look for patterns in the miscues in order to determine how the student is growing as a reader and what strategies and skills should be taught next.

Many teachers conduct running records on all their students at the beginning of the school year and at the end of grading periods. In addition, they do running records more often during guided reading groups and with students who aren't making expected progress in reading to diagnose their reading problems and make instructional decisions.

Semantic Feature Analysis Teachers create a semantic feature analysis to help students examine the characteristics of vocabulary words or content area concepts (Pittelman, Heimlich, Berglund, & French, 1991). They draw a grid for the analysis with words or concepts listed on one axis and the characteristics or components listed on the other. Students reading a novel, for example, can do a semantic feature analysis with vocabulary words listed on one axis and the characters' names on the other; they decide which words relate to which characters and use pluses and minuses to mark the relationships on the grid. Teachers often do a semantic feature analysis with the whole class, but students can work in small groups or individually to complete the grid. The examination should be done as a whole-class activity, however, so that students can share their insights.

THE STEPS. Teachers follow these steps to do a semantic feature analysis:

1. **Create a grid.** Teachers create a grid with vocabulary or concepts listed on the vertical axis and characteristics or categories on the horizontal axis.

SEMANTIC FEATURE ANALYSIS

Immigration

	Arrived in the 1600s	Arrived in the 1700s	Arrived in the 1800s	Arrived in the 1900s	Came to Ellis Island	Came for religious freedom	Came for safety	Came for opportunity	Were refugees	Experienced prejudice
English	+	+	−	−	−	+	−	+	−	−
Africans	+	+	+	−	−	−	−	−	−	+
Irish	−	−	+	−	−	−	+	+	+	+
Other Europeans	−	+	+	+	+	−	+	+	+	+
Jews	−	−	+	+	+	+	+	−	+	+
Chinese	−	−	+	−	−	−	−	−	−	+
Latinos	−	−	−	+	−	−	−	+	−	+
Southeast Asians	−	−	−	+	−	−	+	+	+	+
Code: + = yes; − = no; ? = don't know										

2. **Complete the grid.** Students complete the grid, cell by cell, by considering the relationship between each item on the vertical axis and the items on the horizontal axis. Then they mark the cell with a plus to indicate a relationship, a minus to indicate no relationship, and a question mark when they're unsure.

3. **Examine the grid.** Students and the teacher examine the grid for patterns and then draw conclusions based on the patterns.

Teachers have students do a semantic feature analysis as part of a literature focus unit or a thematic unit. For example, check the figure Semantic Feature Analysis to see how a fifth grade class reviewed what they were learning about America as a culturally pluralistic society during a thematic unit on immigration. They listed the groups of people who immigrated to the United States on one axis and historical features on the other. Next, they completed the grid by marking each cell. Afterward, the students examined it for patterns and identified these big ideas:

> Different peoples immigrated to America at different times.
> The Africans who came as slaves were the only people who were brought to America against their will.
> The English were the only immigrants who didn't suffer prejudice.

Shared Reading   Teachers use shared reading to read authentic literature—stories, nonfiction books, and poems—with students who couldn't read those books independently (Holdaway, 1979). Teachers use big books with young children and read the book aloud, modeling fluent reading. Then they read the book again and again for several days. The focus for the first reading is students' enjoyment; during the next couple of readings, teachers draw students' attention to concepts about print, comprehension, and interesting words and sentences. Finally, students focus on decoding particular words during the last reading or two.

Students are actively involved in shared reading. Teachers encourage them to make predictions and to chime in on reading repeated words and phrases. Individual students or small groups take turns reading brief parts once they begin to recognize words and phrases. Students examine interesting features that they notice in the book—punctuation marks, illustrations, tables of contents, for example—and teachers point out others. They also talk about the book, both while they're reading and afterward. Shared reading builds on students' experience listening to their parents read bedtime stories (Fisher & Medvic, 2000).

THE STEPS. Teachers follow these steps to use shared reading with the whole class or small groups of young children:

1. **Introduce the text.** Teachers talk about the book or other text by activating or building background knowledge on topics related to the book and by reading the title and the author's name aloud.

2. **Read the text aloud.** Teachers read the story aloud, using a pointer (a dowel rod with a pencil eraser on the end) to track as they read. They invite children to be actively involved by making predictions and by joining in the reading, if the story is repetitive.

3. **Have a grand conversation.** Children talk about the story in a **grand conversation**, ask questions, and share their responses.

4. **Reread the story.** Children take turns using the pointer to track the reading and turning pages. Teachers invite students to join in reading familiar and predictable

words. Also, they take opportunities to teach and use graphophonic cues and reading strategies while reading. Teachers vary the support that they provide, depending on children's reading expertise.

5. ***Continue the process.*** Teachers continue to reread the story with children over a period of several days, again having them turn pages and take turns using the pointer to track the text while reading. They encourage children who can read the text to read along with them.

6. ***Read independently.*** After children become familiar with the text, teachers distribute individual copies of the book or other text for them to read independently and use for a variety of activities.

Teachers use shared reading during literature focus units, literature circles, and thematic units. When doing shared reading with young children, teachers use enlarged texts, including big books, poems written on charts, **Language Experience** stories, and **interactive writing** charts, so that children can see the text and read along. Teachers also use shared reading techniques to read books that older students can't read themselves (Allen, 2002). Students each have a copy of the novel, content area textbook, or other book, and the teacher and students read together. The teacher or another fluent reader reads aloud while students follow along in the text, reading to themselves.

STANDARDS IN THE CLASSROOM. **Click here** to read how Ms. Clark addresses Standards during a shared reading lesson in her first grade classroom. ᎧᎧ

Sketch-to-Stretch	Sketch-to-stretch is a tool for helping students deepen their comprehension of stories they've read (Short & Harste, 1996). Students draw pictures or diagrams that represent what the story means

to them, not pictures of their favorite character or episode. In particular, they focus on theme and on symbols to represent the theme as they make sketch-to-stretch drawings (Dooley & Maloch, 2005). An added benefit is that students learn that stories rarely have only one interpretation and that by reflecting on the characters and events, they usually discover one or more themes.

Students need many opportunities to experiment with this activity before they move beyond drawing pictures of the story events or characters to be able to think symbolically. It's helpful to introduce this instructional procedure through a **minilesson** and to draw several sketches together as a class before students do their own. With practice, students learn that there isn't a single correct interpretation, and teachers help students focus on the interpretation rather than on their artistic talents. Check the figure A Fourth Grader's Sketch-to-Stretch, made after reading *The Ballad of Lucy Whipple* (Cushman, 1996), a story set during the California gold rush. The sketch-to-stretch emphasizes two themes of the book—you make your own happiness, and home is where you are.

THE STEPS. Teachers follow these steps as they implement this instructional procedure:

1. ***Read and respond to a story.*** Students read a story or several chapters of a longer book, and they respond to the story in a **grand conversation** or in **reading logs**.

2. ***Discuss the themes.*** Students and the teacher talk about the themes in the story and ways to symbolize meanings. Teachers remind students that there are many ways to represent the meaning of an experience, and they explain that students can use lines, colors, shapes, symbols, and words to visually represent what a story means to them. They talk about possible meanings and ways they might visually represent them.

A FOURTH GRADER'S SKETCH-TO-STRETCH

3. *Draw the sketches.* Students draw sketches that reflect what the story means to them. Teachers emphasize that students should focus on their thinking about the meaning of the story, not on their favorite part, and that there's no single correct interpretation of the story. They also remind students that the artistic quality of their drawings is less important than their interpretation.

4. *Share the sketches.* Students meet in small groups to share their sketches and talk about the symbols they used. Teachers encourage classmates to study each student's sketch and tell what they think the student is trying to convey.

5. *Share some sketches with the class.* Each group chooses one sketch from their group to share with the class.

6. *Revise sketches and make final copies.* Students add to their sketches based on feedback they received and ideas from classmates, and then they make a final copy of their sketches.

Students can use sketch-to-stretch whenever they're reading stories. In literature circles, for example, students create sketch-to-stretch drawings about themes and symbols that they share during group meetings (Whitin, 2002). Through this sharing, students gain insights about their classmates' thinking and clarify their own understanding. The same is true when students create and share sketch-to-stretch drawings during literature focus units.

STANDARDS IN THE CLASSROOM. Click here to read how Mr. Maldonado addresses Standards when his fifth graders use sketch-to-stretch.

Story Boards *Story boards* are cards on which the illustrations and text from a picture book have been attached. Teachers make story boards by cutting apart two copies of a picture book and gluing the pages on pieces of tagboard. The most important use of story boards is to sequence the events of a story by lining the cards up on a whiteboard marker tray or hanging them on a clothesline. Once the pages of the picture book have been laid out, students visualize

AN EIGHTH GRADE STORY BOARD FROM *DRAGONWINGS*

Moon Shadow meets his Uncle Bright Star. He had worked in the California Gold Rush and building the railroad. Then Windrider, Moon Shadow's dad, shows Moon Shadow around, to make him feel safe at home. They go past the Barbary Coast where the white demons live to his new home in Chinatown, the town of the Tang People. It looks like his old home in China. Moon Shadow's dad gave him a kite to fly. It was like a blue and green butterfly. Moon Shadow loved his new kite. Moon Shadow hasn't flown his kite yet, but I bet that he can't wait! They all go into a big house called the Company of the Peach Order Vow and then Uncle Bright Star's son named Black Dog comes. He is in a gang and he takes drugs. He tells everyone that the demons hate them and want to kill them. Then they heard the sound of a window shattering. So they went downstairs and they saw that a window was broken and the white demons were yelling and shouting at them. Moon Shadow is scared but Windrider protects him.

the story and its structure in new ways and examine the illustrations more closely. For example, students arrange story boards from *How I Became a Pirate* (Long, 2003) to retell the story and pick out the beginning, middle, and end. They use story boards to identify the dream sequences in the middle of *Abuela* (Dorros, 1997) and compare versions of folktales, such as *The Mitten* (Brett, 2009; Tresselt, 1989) and *The Woodcutter's Mitten* (Koopmans, 1995).

Teachers use this instructional procedure because it allows students to manipulate and sequence stories and examine illustrations more carefully. Story boards are especially useful tools for English learners who use them to preview a story before reading or to review the events in a story after reading. ELs also draw story boards because they can often share their understanding better through art than through language. In addition, story boards present many opportunities for teaching comprehension when only one copy of a picture book is available.

THE STEPS. Teachers generally use story boards with a small group of students or with the whole class, but individual students can reexamine them as part of center activities. Here are the steps:

1. *Collect two copies of a book.* Teachers use two copies of a picture book for the story boards; paperback copies are preferable because they're less expensive. In a few picture books, all the illustrations are on right-hand or left-hand pages, so only one copy is needed.

2. *Cut the books apart.* Teachers remove the covers and separate the pages, evening out the cut edges.

3. *Attach the pages to pieces of cardboard.* Teachers glue each page or double-page spread to a piece of cardboard, making sure that pages from each book are alternated so that each illustration is included.

4. *Laminate the cards.* Teachers laminate the cards so that they can withstand use by students.

5. *Use the cards in activities.* Teachers use the story board cards for a number of activities, including sequencing, story structure, rereading, and word study.

Students use story boards during literature focus units. For a sequencing activity, teachers pass out the cards in a random order, and students line up around the classroom to sequence the story events. Story boards can also be used when only a few copies of a picture book are available so that students can identify words for the **word wall**, notice literary language, examine an element of story structure, or study the illustrations. When students read novels, they create their own story boards. Partners work together to create a story board for one chapter: They make a poster with a detailed drawing illustrating events in the chapter and write a paragraph-length summary of it. Check the figure An Eighth Grade Story Board From *Dragonwings*, which two students created to summarize Chapter 2 from the Laurence Yep (2000) story.

STANDARDS IN THE CLASSROOM. Click here to read how Ms. O'Brien addresses Standards as she uses story boards with first graders. 🍂

Story Retelling

Teachers use story retelling to monitor students' comprehension (Morrow, 1985). Teachers sit one-on-one with individual students in a quiet area of the classroom and ask them to retell a story they've just read or listened to read aloud. While the student is retelling, teachers use a teacher-made scoring sheet to mark the information that he or she includes. If the student hesitates or doesn't finish retelling the story, teachers ask questions, such as "What happened next?" Students organize the information they remember to provide a personalized summary, which reveals their level of comprehension (Hoyt, 1999).

Teachers can't assume that students already know how to retell stories, even though many do. Through explanations and demonstrations of the retelling procedure, students learn what's expected of them. Students also need to practice retelling stories before they'll be good at it. They can retell stories with a classmate and to their parents at home.

Once teachers begin listening to students retell stories, they notice that students who understand a story retell it differently than those who don't. Good comprehenders' retellings make sense: They reflect the organization of the story and include all of the important story events. In contrast, weak comprehenders often recall events haphazardly or omit important events, especially those in the middle of the story.

Retelling is an instructional tool as well as an assessment tool. McKenna and Dougherty Stahl (2015) explain that through story retelling, students expand their oral language, enhance their use of comprehension strategies, and deepen their knowledge of story structure. When students participate regularly in retelling activities, their comprehension improves as they learn to focus on the big ideas in the story, and their oral language abilities are enhanced as they incorporate sentence patterns, vocabulary, and phrases from stories into their own talk.

THE STEPS. Teachers usually share a story with the class and then follow these steps as individual students retell it:

1. *Introduce the story.* Teachers introduce the story by reading the title, examining the cover of the book, or talking about a topic related to the story. They also explain that students will retell the story afterward.

2. *Read and discuss the story.* Students read the story or listen to it read aloud. When students are reading the story themselves, it's essential that the story is at their reading level. Afterward, they talk about the story, sharing ideas and clarifying confusions.

3. *Create a graphic organizer.* Students create a graphic organizer or a series of drawings to guide their retelling. (This step is optional, but it's especially helpful for students who have difficulty retelling stories.)

4. *Retell the story.* Teachers ask students to individually retell the story in their own words, asking questions, if necessary, to elicit more information:

   Who was the story about?
   What happened next?
   Where did the story take place?
   What did the character do next?
   How did the story end?

5. *Mark the scoring guide.* Teachers assess the retelling by marking a scoring guide as the student retells the story. The scoring guide lists important information about characters and events in the story, usually organized into beginning, middle, and end sections. As they listen to the retelling, teachers place checkmarks by each piece of information that the student recalls. If a student omits important information, teachers ask questions to prompt the student's recall, and they write P beside information that was recalled with prompting.

Teachers often use this instructional procedure during literature focus units and guided reading to monitor students' comprehension of stories they've read and listened to read aloud. Students can also retell nonfiction books; in these retellings, the focus is on summarizing the big ideas and their relationships rather than on story events (Flynt & Cooter, 2005). Their retellings should address these questions:

   What are the big ideas?
   How are the big ideas structured?
   What is the author's purpose?
   What did students learn that they didn't already know?

For students to remember the big ideas they're learning, it's essential that they make personal, world, and textual connections to them. They need adequate background knowledge about a topic to make connections—and if they can't make any connections, it's unlikely they'll understand or remember the big ideas.

STANDARDS IN THE CLASSROOM. **Click here** to read how Ms. Guzman addresses Standards when her first graders retell stories. 🐚

Sustained Silent Reading *Sustained Silent Reading* (SSR) is an independent reading time set aside during the school day for students in one class or the entire school to silently read self-selected books (Gardiner, 2005). In some schools, everyone—students, teachers, principals, secretaries, and custodians—stops to read, usually for a 15- to 30-minute period. SSR is a popular reading activity that's known by a variety of names, including "drop everything and read" (DEAR), "sustained quiet reading time" (SQUIRT), and "our time to enjoy reading" (OTTER).

Teachers use SSR to increase the amount of reading students do every day and to develop their ability to read silently and without interruption (Hunt, 1967). SSR follows these guidelines:

🌀 Students choose the books they read.

🌀 Students read silently.

🌀 The teacher serves as a model by reading.

🌀 Students choose one book or other reading material for the entire reading time.

🌀 The teacher sets a timer for a predetermined, uninterrupted time period, usually 15–30 minutes.

🌀 Everyone participates.

🌀 The teacher doesn't keep records or evaluate students on their performance. (Pilgreen, 2000)

Even though SSR was specifically developed without follow-up activities, many teachers use a few carefully selected and brief follow-up activities to sustain students' interest in reading books. For example, students often discuss their reading with a partner, or volunteers give **book talks** to tell the whole class about their books. As students listen to one another, they get ideas about books that they might like to read. In some classrooms, students develop a ritual of passing on the books they've finished reading to interested classmates.

Through numerous studies, SSR has proven to be beneficial in developing students' reading ability—fluency, vocabulary, and comprehension (Krashen, 1993; Marshall, 2002; Pilgreen, 2000). In addition, it promotes a positive attitude toward reading and encourages students to develop the habit of daily reading. Because students choose the books they'll read, they have the opportunity to develop their own tastes and preferences as readers.

THE STEPS. Teachers follow these steps in implementing this instructional procedure:

1. *Set aside a time for SSR.* Teachers allow time every day for uninterrupted, independent reading; it may last for only 10 minutes in first grade classrooms or 20 to 30 minutes or more in the upper grades. Teachers often begin with a 10-minute period and then extend the time as students build endurance and want to continue reading.

2. *Ensure that students have books to read.* Students read independently in books they keep at their desks. Beginning readers often reread three or four leveled readers that they've already read during SSR.

3. *Set a timer for a predetermined time.* Teachers set the timer for the SSR reading period. To ensure that students aren't disturbed during SSR, some teachers place a "do not disturb" sign on the door.

4. *Read along with students.* Teachers read a book, magazine, or newspaper for pleasure while students read to model what capable readers do and to show that reading is a pleasurable activity.

When all teachers in a school are working together to set up SSR, they meet to set a daily time for this special reading activity and lay the ground rules for the program. Many schools have SSR first thing in the morning or at some other convenient time during the day. What's most important is that SSR is held every day at the same time, and that all students and adults in the school stop what they're doing to read. If teachers use the time to grade papers or work with individual students, the program won't be effective. The principal and other staff members should also make a habit of visiting a different classroom each day to join in the reading activity.

Tea Party   Students participate in a tea party to read or reread excerpts from a story, nonfiction book, or content area textbook. It's an active, participatory activity with students moving around the classroom and socializing with classmates as they read short excerpts aloud to each other and talk about them (Beers, 2003). Teachers choose and make copies of excerpts, back them with tagboard, and laminate them. Then they distribute the excerpts to students, provide some rehearsal time, and have students participate in the tea party activity.

Teachers often use tea party as a prereading activity to introduce a new chapter in a content area textbook. They usually select the excerpts in order to introduce big ideas and related vocabulary, familiarize students with a new text, and build background knowledge. At other times, teachers invite students to reread favorite excerpts to celebrate a book they've finished reading. When tea party is used as a postreading activity, students review big ideas, summarize the events in a story, or focus on an element of story structure. Students can also create vocabulary cards, each featuring a word from the **word wall**, its definition, and an illustration. After making the cards, students participate in a tea party, sharing their word cards and explaining the words to their classmates.

This instructional procedure is especially valuable for English learners because students have opportunities to build background knowledge before reading and review texts after reading in a supportive, social classroom environment (Rea & Mercuri, 2006). It's important that teachers choose excerpts that are written at English learners' reading levels or adapt them so that these students will be able to read them fluently.

THE STEPS. Teachers follow these steps as they implement tea party:

1. *Make the cards.* Teachers make cards with excerpts from a story, nonfiction book, or content area textbook that students are reading. They laminate the cards, or they use sentence strips with younger students.

2. *Practice reading.* Students practice reading the excerpts to themselves several times until they can read them fluently.

3. *Share excerpts.* Students move around the classroom, stopping to read and discuss their excerpts with classmates. When students pair up, they take turns sharing their excerpts. After the first student reads, both students discuss the text; then the other student reads and both students comment on the second student's text. Then students move apart and find other classmates to share their cards with.

4. *Share excerpts with the class.* Students return to their desks after 10 to 15 minutes, and teachers invite several students to read their excerpts to the class or talk about what they learned through the tea party activity.

Tea party is a good way to celebrate the conclusion of a literature focus unit or a thematic unit, and the activity reinforces the main ideas taught during the unit. Teachers also use tea party to introduce a thematic unit by choosing excerpts from nonfiction books or content area textbooks that present the main ideas and key vocabulary students will learn during the unit. The figure Tea Party Cards shows cards from a class set that a seventh grade teacher used to introduce a unit on ecology. The teacher collected some of the sentences and paragraphs from nonfiction books and a textbook chapter that students would read, and she wrote other selections herself.

TEA PARTY CARDS

Recycling means using materials over and over or making them into new things instead of throwing them away.	Acid rain happens when poisonous gases from factories and cars get into rain clouds. Then the gases mix with rain and fall back to earth. It is harmful to our environment and to the people and animals on earth.
Plastic bottles, plastic forks, and plastic bags last forever! A big problem with plastic is that it doesn't biodegrade. Instead of filling landfills with plastic, it should be recycled.	Many cities have air filled with pollution called smog. This pollution is so bad that the sky looks brown, not blue.
The ozone layer around the earth protects us from the harmful rays of the sun. This layer is being damaged by gases called chloro-fluorocarbons or CFCs. These gases are used in air conditioners, fire extinguishers, and styrofoam.	Americans cut down 850 million trees last year to make paper products. Sound like a lot of trees? One tree can be made into approximately 700 grocery bags, and a large grocery store uses about that many bags in an hour!

Students read and discussed the excerpts and began a word wall with the key words. These two activities activated students' background knowledge about ecology and began to build new concepts. ✺

Think-Alouds Teachers use the think-aloud procedure to teach students how to direct and monitor their thinking during reading (Wilhelm, 2001). By making their thinking explicit, they're demonstrating what capable readers do implicitly (Keene & Zimmerman, 2007). After they watch teachers think aloud, students practice the procedure by thinking aloud about the literacy strategies they're learning. As they think aloud, students respond to the text, identify big ideas, ask self-questions, make connections, figure out how to solve problems that arise, and reflect on their use of strategies. This procedure is valuable because students learn to be more active readers. They learn how to think metacognitively and to regulate their own cognitive processes (Baker, 2002).

THE STEPS. Teachers use these steps to teach students to think aloud:

1. *Choose a book.* Teachers who work with younger children usually choose a big book, and those who teach older students often make copies of an excerpt from a book they're reading aloud to the class to demonstrate how to think aloud.

2. *Plan the think-aloud.* Teachers decide which strategies they want to demonstrate, where they'll pause, and the kinds of thinking they want to share.

3. *Demonstrate a think-aloud.* Teachers read the text, pausing to think aloud, explaining what they're thinking and how they're using a strategy or solving a

reading problem. They often use these "I" sentence starters to talk about their thinking:

> I wondered if . . .
> I don't know this word, so . . .
> I was confused by . . .
> I didn't understand why . . .
> I think the big idea is . . .
> I reread this part because . . .

4. ***Annotate the text.*** Teachers write a small self-stick note about their thinking and attach it beside the text that prompted the think-aloud. They often use a word or phrase, such as *picture in my mind, context clues,* or *reread,* to quickly document their thinking.

5. ***Continue thinking aloud.*** Teachers continue reading the book, pausing to think aloud again and annotate the text with additional notes about their thinking.

6. ***Reflect on the procedure.*** Teachers review their annotations, talk about their strategy use, and reflect on the usefulness of think-alouds as a tool for comprehending what they're reading.

7. ***Repeat the procedure.*** Teachers read another book and have students take turns thinking aloud and annotating the text. Once students are familiar with the procedure, they practice doing think-alouds in small groups and with partners.

Once students know how to think aloud, teachers can use this procedure as an assessment tool. During student–teacher conferences, students reflect on their reading and evaluate how well they use particular strategies, and they think about what they could do differently to comprehend more effectively. Students can also refer to their annotations and write reflections about their use of particular strategies.

STANDARDS IN THE CLASSROOM. Click here to read how Ms. Carle addresses Standards when she teaches her struggling second graders to use think-alouds. 🐚

Word Sorts Students use word sorts to examine and categorize words according to their meanings, phoneme–grapheme correspondences, or spelling patterns (Bear, Invernizzi, Templeton, & Johnston, 2016). The purpose of word sorts is to help students focus on conceptual and phonological features of words and identify recurring patterns. For example, as students sort cards with words such as *stopping, eating, hugging, running,* and *raining,* they discover the rule for doubling the final consonant in short-vowel words before adding an inflectional ending.

Teachers choose categories for word sorts, depending on instructional goals or students' developmental levels:

- Rhyming words, such as words that rhyme with *ball, fat, car,* and *rake*
- Consonant sounds, such as pictures of words beginning with *r* or *l*
- Phoneme–grapheme relationships, such as words in which the final *y* sounds like long *i* (*cry*) and others in which the final *y* sounds like long *e* (*baby*)
- Spelling patterns, such as long-*e* words with various spelling patterns (*sea, greet, be, Pete*)
- Number of syllables, such as *pig, happy, afternoon,* and *television*
- Root words and affixes
- Conceptual relationships, such as words related to different characters in a story or to big ideas in a thematic unit

A CONCEPT SORT

Stanley	Zero	Camp Green Lake	Mr. Sir	The Warden	The Escape
unlucky	nobody	wasteland	grotesque	Ms. Walker	miracle
sneakers	Hector Zeroni	guards	cowboy hat	holes	sploosh
Caveman	confession	investigation	swollen	venom	thumbs-up sign
overweight	homeless	yellow-spotted lizard	tattoo	miserable	impossible
callused	Clyde Livingston's shoes	scorpions	sunflower seeds	fingernail polish	ledges
million dollars	digger	girl scout camp	guard	make-up kit	Big Thumb
suitcase	frail	temperature	tougher	freckles	happiness

Many of the words chosen for word sorts come from books students are reading or from thematic units. The figures A Concept Sort and A Grammar Sort show two word sorts using words from *Holes* (Sachar, 2008).

Word sorts are effective for English learners because students build skills to understand how English differs from their native language, and they develop knowledge to help them predict meaning through spelling (Helman, Bear, Templeton, Invernizzi, & Johnston, 2012). Because word sorts can be done in small groups, teachers can choose words for the sorts that are appropriate for students' developmental levels.

THE STEPS. Teachers follow these steps for conducting a word sort:

1. *Choose a topic.* Teachers choose a language skill or content area topic for the word sort and decide whether it will be an open or closed sort: In an open sort, students determine the categories themselves based on the words they're sorting, and in a closed sort, teachers present the categories as they introduce the sorting activity.

2. *Compile a list of words.* Teachers compile a list of 6 to 20 words, depending on grade level, that exemplify particular categories, and they write the words on small cards. Or, small picture cards can be used.

3. *Introduce the sorting activity.* If it's a closed sort, teachers present the categories and have students sort word cards into these categories. If it's an open sort, students identify the words and look for possible categories. They arrange and rearrange the cards until they're satisfied with the sorting. Then they add category labels.

4. *Make a permanent record.* Students make a permanent record of their sort by gluing the word cards onto a large sheet of construction paper or poster board or by writing the words on a sheet of paper.

5. *Share word sorts.* Students share their word sorts with classmates, explaining the categories they used (for open sorts).

Teachers use word sorts to teach phonics, spelling, and vocabulary. During literature focus units, students sort vocabulary words according to the beginning, middle,

A GRAMMAR SORT

Adjectives	Nouns	Verbs	Adverbs
half-opened	wasteland	chewing	surely
scratchy	curiosity	waits	previously
tougher	fossil	howled	quickly
desolate	allergies	startled	well
throbbing	pitchfork	watches	intently
metallic	warden	gazes	supposedly
shriveled	sneakers	wiggled	always
callused	Caveman	scooped	angrily

or end of the story or according to character. During thematic units, students sort vocabulary words according to big ideas. 🌀

Word Walls *Word walls* are collections of words posted in the classroom that students use for word-study activities and refer to when they're writing (Wagstaff, 1999). Teachers make word walls using construction paper squares or sheets of butcher paper that have been divided into alphabetized sections. Students and the teacher write on the word wall interesting, confusing, or other important words from books they're reading and related to big ideas they're learning during thematic units. Usually students choose the words to write on the word wall, and they may even do the writing themselves, but teachers add any important Tier 2 words that students haven't chosen.

A second type of word wall for high-frequency words is used in primary grade classrooms: Teachers hang large sheets of construction paper, one for each letter of the alphabet, on a wall of the classroom, and then post high-frequency words such as *the, is, are, you, what,* and *to* as they're introduced (Cunningham, 2013; Lynch, 2005). This word wall remains on display, and additional words are added throughout the year. In kindergarten classrooms, teachers begin the school year by placing word cards with students' names on the wall chart and adding common environmental print, such as *K-Mart* and *McDonald's.* Later in the year, they add words such as *I, love, the, you, Mom, Dad, good,* and other words that students want to be able to read and write.

THE STEPS. Teachers usually create word walls with the whole class, and they follow these steps:

1. *Prepare the word wall.* Teachers prepare a blank word wall from sheets of construction paper or butcher paper, dividing it into 12 to 24 boxes and labeling the boxes with letters of the alphabet.

2. *Introduce the word wall.* Teachers introduce the word wall and write several key words on it before beginning to read.

3. *Add words to the word wall.* Students suggest "important" words for the word wall as they're reading a book or participating in thematic-unit activities. Students and the teacher write the words in the alphabetized blocks, making sure to write large enough so that most students can see the words. If a word is misspelled, it's corrected because students will be using the words in various activities. Sometimes the teacher adds a small picture or writes a synonym for a difficult word, puts a box around the root word, or writes the plural form or other related words nearby.

4. *Use the word wall.* Teachers use the word wall for a variety of vocabulary activities, and students refer to the word wall when they're writing.

Teachers use word walls during literature focus units and thematic units, and primary grade teachers also teach high-frequency words using word walls. They involve students in a variety of word-study activities. For example, students do **quickwrites** using words from the word wall and refer to the word wall when they're writing journal entries and books. Teachers also use words from the word wall for **word sorts** and **tea party** activities. In addition, primary grade teachers use words from high-frequency word walls for phonics and other word-study activities. One example is a popular word-hunt game: Teachers distribute small whiteboards and have students identify and write words from the word wall on them according to the clues they provide. For example, teachers say, "Find the word that begins like _____," "Look for the word that rhymes with _____," "Find the word that alphabetically follows _____," or "Think of the word that means the opposite of _____," depending on what students are learning. As they play this game, students read and reread the words, apply phonics and word-study concepts, and practice spelling high-frequency words.

STANDARDS IN THE CLASSROOM. Click here to read how Mrs. Greene addresses Standards as fifth graders create sentences using words from the word wall. ᘒᓫᕙ

REFERENCES

Allen, J. (2002). *On the same page: Shared reading beyond the primary grades.* York, ME: Stenhouse.

Ashton-Warner, S. (1965). *Teacher.* New York: Simon & Schuster.

Atwell, N. (1998). *In the middle: New understandings about writing, reading, and learning.* Portsmouth, NH: Heinemann/Boynton/Cook.

Baker, L. (2002). Metacognition in comprehension instruction. In C. C. Block & M. Pressley (Eds.), *Comprehension instruction: Research-based best practices* (pp. 77–95). New York: Guilford Press.

Barone, D. (1990). The written responses of young children: Beyond comprehension to story understanding. *The New Advocate, 3,* 49–56.

Bates, K. L. (2003). *America the beautiful.* New York: Putnam.

Bear, D. R., Invernizzi, M., Templeton, S., & Johnston, F. (2016). *Words their way: Word study for phonics, vocabulary, and spelling instruction* (6th ed.). Boston: Pearson.

Beers, K. (2003). *When kids can't read, what teachers can do.* Portsmouth, NH: Heinemann.

Berthoff, A. E. (1981). *The making of meaning.* Montclair, NJ: Boynton/Cook.

Blachowicz, C. L. Z. (1986). Making connections: Alternatives to the vocabulary notebook. *Journal of Reading, 29,* 643–649.

Blachowicz, C., & Fisher, P. J. (2015). *Teaching vocabulary in all classrooms* (5th ed.). Boston: Pearson.

Black, A., & Stave, A. M. (2007). *A comprehensive guide to readers theatre: Enhancing fluency and comprehension in middle school and beyond.* Newark, DE: International Reading Association.

Brett, J. (2009). *The mitten.* New York: Putnam.

Brozo, W. G., & Simpson, M. L. (2007). *Content literacy for today's adolescents: Honoring diversity and building competence* (5th ed.). Upper Saddle River, NJ: Prentice Hall.

Buehl, D. (2001). *Classroom strategies for interactive learning* (2nd ed.). Newark, DE: International Reading Association.

Button, K., Johnson, M. J., & Furgerson, P. (1996). Interactive writing in a primary classroom. *The Reading Teacher, 49,* 446–454.

Carle, E. (2005). *A house for hermit crab.* New York: Aladdin Books.

Carr, E., & Ogle, D. (1987). K-W-L Plus: A strategy for comprehension and summarization. *Journal of Reading, 31,* 626–631.

Ciardello, A. V. (1998). Did you ask a good question today? *Journal of Adolescent & Adult Literacy, 42,* 210–220.

Clay, M. M. (2000). *Running records for classroom teachers.* Portsmouth, NH: Heinemann.

Cole, J. (1998). *The magic school bus inside a beehive.* New York: Scholastic.

Crawford, A. N. (2003). Communicative approaches to second-language acquisition: The bridge to second-language literacy. In G. G. Garcia (Ed.), *English learners: Reaching the highest level of*

English literacy (pp. 152–181). Newark, DE: International Reading Association.

Cronin, D. (2011). *Diary of a spider*. New York: Scholastic.

Cunningham, P. M. (2013). *Phonics they use: Words for reading and writing* (6th ed.). Boston: Pearson.

Cunningham, P. M., & Cunningham, J. W. (1992). Making words: Enhancing the invented spelling-decoding connection. *The Reading Teacher, 46*, 106–115.

Cunningham, P. M., & Hall, D. P. (1994a). *Making big words*. Parsippany, NJ: Good Apple.

Cunningham, P. M., & Hall, D. P. (1994b). *Making words*. Parsippany, NJ: Good Apple.

Cushman, K. (1996). *The ballad of Lucy Whipple*. New York: Clarion Books.

Daniels, H. (2001). *Literature circles: Voice and choice in book clubs and reading groups*. York, ME: Stenhouse.

Danziger, P. (2006a). *Amber Brown is not a crayon*. New York: Puffin Books.

Danziger, P. (2006b). *You can't eat your chicken pox, Amber Brown*. New York: Puffin Books.

Dooley. C. M., & Maloch, B. (2005). Exploring characters through visual representations. In N. L. Roser & M. G. Martinez (Eds.), *What a character! Character study as a guide to literary meaning making in grades K–8* (pp. 111–123). Newark, DE: International Reading Association.

Dorn, L. J., & Soffos, C. (2001). *Shaping literate minds: Developing self-regulated learners*. York, ME: Stenhouse.

Dorros, A. (1997). *Abuela*. New York: Puffin Books.

Editors of Time for Kids. (2005). *Bees!* New York: HarperCollins.

Fisher, B., & Medvic, E. F. (2000). *Perspectives on shared reading: Planning and practice*. Portsmouth, NH: Heinemann.

Fisher, D., Flood, K., Lapp, D., & Frey, N. (2004). Interactive read-alouds: Is there a common set of implementation practices? *The Reading Teacher, 58*, 8–17.

Fleischman, P. (2004). *Joyful noise: Poems for two voices*. New York: Harper Trophy.

Flynn, R. M. (2007). *Dramatizing the content with curriculum-based readers theatre, grades 6–12*. Newark, DE: International Reading Association.

Flynt, E. S., & Cooter, R. B., Jr. (2005). Improving middle-grades reading in urban schools: The Memphis Comprehension Framework. *The Reading Teacher, 58*, 774–780.

Fountas, I. C., & Pinnell, G. S. (1996). *Guided reading: Good first teaching for all children*. Portsmouth, NH: Heinemann.

Gambrell, L. B., & Almasi, J. F. (Eds.). (1996). *Lively discussions! Fostering engaged reading*. Newark, DE: International Reading Association.

Gardiner, S. (2005). *Building students' literacy through SSR*. Alexandria, VA: Association for Supervision and Curriculum Development.

Gibbons, G. (2000). *The honey makers*. New York: HarperCollins.

Graves, M. F., & Fitzgerald, J. (2003). Scaffolding reading experiences for multilingual classrooms. In G. G. Garcia (Ed.), *English learners: Reaching the highest level of English literacy* (pp. 96–124). Newark, DE: International Reading Association.

Guthrie, W. (2002). *This land is your land*. Boston: Little, Brown.

Hall, D. (1994). *I am the dog/I am the cat*. New York: Dial Books.

Hancock, M. R. (2008). *A celebration of literature and response: Children, books, and teachers in K–8 classrooms* (3rd ed.). Upper Saddle River, NJ: Merrill/Prentice Hall.

Head, M. H., & Readence, J. E. (1986). Anticipation guides: Meaning through prediction. In E. K. Dishner, T. W. Bean, J. E. Readence, & D. W. Moore (Eds.), *Reading in the content areas* (2nd ed., pp. 229–234). Dubuque, IA: Kendall Hunt.

Helman, L., Bear, D., Templeton, S., Invernizzi, M., & Johnston, F. (2012). *Words their way with English learners: Word study for phonics, vocabulary, and spelling* (2nd ed.). Upper Saddle River, NJ: Merrill/Prentice Hall.

Hinton, S. E. (2006). *The outsiders*. New York: Penguin.

Hoberman, M. A. (2003). *The lady with the alligator purse*. Boston: Little, Brown.

Holdaway, D. (1979). *Foundations of literacy*. Auckland, NZ: Ashton Scholastic.

Holston, V., & Santa, C. (1985). RAFT: A method of writing across the curriculum that works. *Journal of Reading, 28*, 456–457.

Hoyt, L. (1999). *Revisit, reflect, retell: Strategies for improving reading comprehension*. Portsmouth, NH: Heinemann.

Hoyt, L. (2000). *Snapshots*. Portsmouth, NH: Heinemann.

Hughes, L. (2007). *The dream keeper and other poems*. New York: Knopf.

Hunt, L. (1967). Evaluation through teacher-pupil conferences. In T. C. Barrett (Ed.), *The evaluation of children's reading achievement* (pp. 111–126). Newark, DE: International Reading Association.

Ivey, G. (2003). "The teacher makes it more explainable" and other reasons to read aloud in the intermediate grades. *The Reading Teacher, 56*, 812–814.

Jacobson, J. M. (1990). Group vs. individual completion of a cloze passage. *Journal of Reading, 33*, 244–250.

Jeffers, S. (1993). *Brother eagle, sister sky: A message from Chief Seattle*. New York: Puffin Books.

Keehn, S., Martinez, M. G., & Roser, N. L. (2005). Exploring character through readers theatre. In N. L. Roser & M. G. Martinez (Eds.), *What a character! Character study as a guide to literary meaning making in grades K–8* (pp. 96–110). Newark, DE: International Reading Association.

Keene, E. O., & Zimmerman, S. (2007). *Mosaic of thought: The power of comprehension strategy instruction* (2nd ed.). Portsmouth, NH: Heinemann.

Konigsburg, E. L. (1998). *The view from Saturday*. New York: Aladdin Books.

Koopmans, L. (1995). *The woodcutter's mitten*. New York: Crocodile Books.

Krashen, S. (1993). *The power of reading*. Englewood, CO: Libraries Unlimited.

Kuskin, K. (2003). *Moon, have you met my mother? The collected poems of Karla Kuskin*. New York: HarperCollins.

Langer, J. A. (1981). From theory to practice: A prereading plan. *Journal of Reading, 25*, 152–157.

Lenski, S. D., Wham, M. A., & Johns, J. L. (1999). *Reading and learning strategies for middle and high school students*. Dubuque, IA: Kendall Hunt.

Lewis, C. S. (2005). *The lion, the witch and the wardrobe*. New York: HarperCollins.

Long, M. (2003). *How I became a pirate*. San Diego: Harcourt.

Lowry, L. (2006). *The giver*. New York: Delacorte.

Lowry, L. (2011). *Number the stars*. New York: Sandpiper.

Lynch, J. (2005). *High frequency word walls*. New York: Scholastic.

MacLachlan, P. (2005). *Sarah, plain and tall*. New York: Scholastic.

Macon, J. M., Bewell, D., & Vogt, M. E. (1991). *Responses to literature: Grades K–8*. Newark, DE: International Reading Association.

Marshall, J. C. (2002). *Are they really reading? Expanding SSR in the middle grades*. Portland, ME: Stenhouse.

McCauley, J. K., & McCauley, D. S. (1992). Using choral reading to promote language learning for ESL students. *The Reading Teacher, 45*, 526–533.

McKenna, M. C., & Dougherty Stahl, K. A. (2015). *Assessment for reading instruction* (3rd ed.). New York: Guilford Press.

McLaughlin, M., & Allen, M. B. (2001). *Guided comprehension: A teaching model for grades 3–8*. Newark, DE: International Reading Association.

Micucci, C. (1997). *The life and times of the honeybee*. New York: Sandpiper.

Morrow, L. M. (1985). Retelling stories: A strategy for improving children's comprehension, concept of story structure, and oral language complexity. *Elementary School Journal, 85,* 647–661.

Ogle, D. M. (1986). K-W-L: A teaching model that develops active reading of expository text. *The Reading Teacher, 39,* 564–570.

Paschen, E. (Ed.). (2005). *Poetry speaks to children*. Naperville, IL: Sourcebooks/MediaFusion.

Patron, S. (2006). *The higher power of Lucky*. New York: Atheneum.

Peterson, R., & Eeds, M. (2007). *Grand conversations: Literature groups in action* (Updated ed.). New York: Scholastic.

Pilgreen, J. L. (2000). *The SSR handbook: How to organize and manage a sustained silent reading program*. Portsmouth, NH: Heinemann/Boynton/Cook.

Pittelman, S. D., Heimlich, J. E., Berglund, R. L., & French, M. P. (1991). *Semantic feature analysis: Classroom applications*. Newark, DE: International Reading Association.

Prelutsky, J. (1983). *The Random House book of poetry for children*. New York: Random House.

Prelutsky, J. (2007). *My parents think I'm sleeping*. New York: Greenwillow.

Raphael, T. E., Highfield, K., & Au, K. H. (2006). *QAR now: A powerful and practical framework that develops comprehension and higher-level thinking in all students*. New York: Scholastic.

Rasinski, T., & Padak, N. (2010). *Teaching children who find reading difficult* (4th ed.). Boston: Pearson.

Rea, D. M., & Mercuri, S. P. (2006). *Research-based strategies for English language learners: How to teach goals and meet standards, K–8*. Portsmouth, NH: Heinemann.

Reutzel, D. R., & Cooter, R. B., Jr. (2008). *Teaching children to read: From basals to books* (5th ed.). Upper Saddle River, NJ: Merrill/Prentice Hall.

Routman, R. (2004). *Writing essentials: Raising expectations and results while simplifying teaching*. Portsmouth, NH: Heinemann.

Sachar, L. (2008). *Holes*. New York: Farrar, Straus & Giroux.

Schmidt, G. D. (2007). *The Wednesday wars*. New York: Clarion Books.

Short, K. G., & Harste, J. (1996). *Creating classrooms for authors and inquirers*. Portsmouth, NH: Heinemann.

Soto, G. (2005). *Neighborhood odes*. San Diego: Harcourt.

Spandel, V. (2005). *Creating writers through 6-trait writing assessment and instruction* (4th ed.). Boston: Allyn & Bacon.

Taback, S. (1997). *There was an old lady who swallowed a fly*. New York: Viking.

Taylor, W. L. (1953). "Cloze procedure": A new tool for measuring readability. *Journalism Quarterly, 30,* 415–433.

Tierney, R. J., & Readence, J. E. (2005). *Reading strategies and practices: A compendium* (6th ed.). Boston: Allyn & Bacon.

Tompkins, G. E. (2012). *Teaching writing: Balancing process and product* (6th ed.). Boston: Allyn & Bacon.

Tompkins, G. E., & Collom, S. (Eds.). (2004). *Sharing the pen: Interactive writing with young children*. Upper Saddle River, NJ: Merrill/Prentice Hall.

Tovani, C. (2000). *I read it, but I don't get it: Comprehension strategies for adolescent readers*. York, ME: Stenhouse.

Tresselt, A. (1989). *The mitten*. New York: Harper Trophy.

Vacca, R. T., Vacca, J. L., & Mraz, M. (2014). *Content area reading: Literacy and learning across the curriculum* (11th ed.). Boston: Pearson.

Wagstaff, J. (1999). *Teaching reading and writing with word walls*. New York: Scholastic.

Whitin, P. E. (2002). Leading into literature circles through the sketch-to-stretch strategy. *The Reading Teacher, 55,* 444–450.

Wilhelm, J. D. (2001). *Improving comprehension with think-aloud strategies*. New York: Scholastic.

Wilhelm, J. D. (2002). *Action strategies for deepening comprehension*. New York: Scholastic.

Worthy, J., & Prater, K. (2002). "I thought about it all night": Readers theatre for reading fluency and motivation. *The Reading Teacher, 56,* 294–297.

Yep, L. (2000). *Dragonwings* (25th anniversary ed.). New York: Harper Trophy.

Yolen, J., & Peters, A. F. (Eds.). (2007). *Here's a little poem*. Cambridge, MA: Candlewick Press.

Glossary

academic language The language used in the classroom, in books, and on tests. It's more difficult to understand than everyday, spoken English.

accommodation A Piagetian process in which learners create schemas because of new information or experiences.

aesthetic reading Reading for pleasure; the term was introduced by Louise Rosenblatt.

affix A syllable added to the beginning (prefix) or end (suffix) of a word to change its meaning (e.g., *il-* in *illiterate* and *-al* in *national*).

alliteration A sound device in which authors repeat a consonant sound in several words in a sentence or line of poetry.

alphabetic principle The assumption underlying alphabetical language systems that each sound has a corresponding graphic representation (or letter).

antonyms Words with opposite meanings (e.g., *good–bad*).

applying The fifth stage of the reading process, in which readers go beyond the text to use what they've learned in another literacy experience, often by making a project or reading another book.

assessment An ongoing process to monitor growth, diagnose problems, and improve learning; in contrast, *evaluation* is used at the end of instruction to make judgments and determine quality against a set of standards.

assimilation A Piagetian process in which learners modify or incorporate new information and experiences into existing schemas.

authentic Activities and materials related to real-world reading and writing.

automaticity Identifying words accurately and quickly when reading.

background knowledge A student's knowledge or previous experiences about a topic.

balanced approach An approach to literacy instruction in which teachers integrate instruction with authentic reading and writing experiences.

basal readers Reading textbooks that are leveled according to grade.

Basic Interpersonal Communicative Skills (BICS) The language skills used in everyday social situations; they're not cognitively demanding.

big books Enlarged versions of picture books that teachers read with children, usually in the primary grades.

blend To combine the sounds represented by letters to pronounce a word.

bound morpheme A morpheme that isn't a word and can't stand alone (e.g., *-s*, *tri-*).

breve A mark shaped like a smile that's placed over a vowel to indicate that it represents a short sound (e.g., *băth*, *ĕnd*, and *cŭt*).

close reading A procedure to deepen students' comprehension of challenging texts through repeated readings of a brief text passage and analysis of individual words and sentences.

cloze An activity in which students replace words that have been deleted from a text.

cluster A spider web–like diagram used to collect and organize ideas after reading or before writing; also called a *map* or a *web*.

cognition Thinking.

Cognitive Academic Language Proficiency (CALP) The formal academic language that's needed for school success. It's the language use in classrooms, in books, and on tests. In contrast to BICS, it's cognitively demanding.

cognitive strategy A learning process that requires thinking, such as predicting, inferring, and revising.

Common Core State Standards An initiative that describes what American K–12 students should learn in language arts and math at each grade level. The goal is to ensure that students graduating from high school are prepared for college or the workforce.

compound word A new word formed with two or more words that has its own meaning; it can be spelled as one word, joined together with a hyphen, or spelled as separate words (e.g., *makeup*, *newspaper*, *upside-down*, *mother-in-law*, *high school*, *police officer*).

comprehension The process of constructing meaning using both the author's text and the reader's background knowledge for a specific purpose.

concepts about written language Basic understandings about the way print works, including the direction of print, spacing, punctuation, letters, and words.

conditional knowledge Metacognitive knowledge about when to use a reading or writing strategy or perform the steps in a process, such as the writing process.

consonant A speech sound characterized by friction or stoppage of the airflow as it passes through the vocal tract; usually any letter except *a, e, i, o,* and *u.*

consonant blend Combinations of two or three consonants; each one is pronounced, in contrast to consonant digraphs. Examples include *swing, bump, clean,* and *bent.*

consonant digraph Two adjacent consonants that represent a sound not represented by either consonant alone (e.g., *th–this, ch–chin, sh–wash, ph–telephone*).

context clue Information from the words or sentences surrounding a word that helps to clarify the word's meaning.

conventions Mechanics of writing, including spelling, capitalization, punctuation, and grammar.

critical comprehension The third level of comprehension; readers analyze symbolic meanings, distinguish between facts and opinions, and draw conclusions.

critical literacy An instructional approach in which students read texts to understand issues of power, inequality, and injustice, and they're empowered through social action projects.

cueing systems The phonological, semantic, syntactic, and pragmatic information that students rely on as they read.

declarative knowledge Metacognitive knowledge or factual information about a reading or writing strategy or process, such as the writing process.

decoding Using word-identification strategies to pronounce and attach meaning to an unfamiliar word.

diagnosis Determining specific problems readers are having, generally using a test.

dialect A variety of language.

differentiated instruction Procedures for assisting students in learning, providing options, challenging students, and matching books to students to maximize their learning.

diphthong A sound produced when the tongue glides from one sound to another; it's represented by two vowels (e.g., *oy–boy, ou–house, ow–how*).

drafting The second stage of the writing process, in which writers pour out ideas in a rough draft.

echo reading The teacher or another reader reads a sentence and a group of students reread or "echo" what was read.

editing The fourth stage of the writing process, in which writers proofread to identify and correct spelling, capitalization, punctuation, and grammar errors.

efferent reading Reading for information.

Elkonin boxes A strategy for segmenting sounds in a word that involves drawing a box to represent each sound.

emergent literacy Children's early reading and writing development before conventional reading and writing instruction.

environmental print Signs, labels, and other print found in the community.

eponym Words created from people's names, such as *maverick, silhouette, diesel, Levi's,* and *sandwich.*

etymology The origin and history of words; the etymological information is enclosed in brackets in dictionary entries.

evaluation Summative assessment conducted after learning.

evaluative comprehension The fourth and most sophisticated level of comprehension; readers judge the value of the text they're reading.

explicit instruction Systematic instruction of concepts, strategies, and skills that builds from simple to complex.

exploring The fourth stage of the reading process, in which readers reread the text, study vocabulary words, and learn strategies and skills.

expository text Nonfiction.

expository text structures The organizational patterns of nonfiction texts—*description, comparison, sequence, cause-effect,* and *problem-solution.*

eZines Online literary magazines.

family literacy Home–school partnerships to enhance students' literacy development.

figurative meaning The symbolic meaning of a word or phrase; figures of speech, such as metaphors and symbols, are used to make the text more metaphorical.

fluency Reading smoothly, quickly, and with expression.

formative evaluation Informal assessment procedures that teachers use during the learning process.

free morpheme A morpheme that can stand alone as a word (e.g., *book, cycle*).

frustration reading level The level of reading material that's too difficult for students to read successfully; accuracy level is less than 90%.

genre A category of literature such as folklore, science fiction, biography, or historical fiction, or a writing form.

Goldilocks Strategy A strategy for choosing "just right" books.

grammar The structure of a language; that is, how words combine to form sentences.

grapheme A written representation of a sound using one or more letters.

graphic novels Book-length comics.

graphic organizers Diagrams that provide organized visual representations of information from texts.

graphophonemic Sound–symbol relationships.

high-frequency word A common English word, usually a word among the 100 or 300 most common words (e.g., *the, is, what*).

high-stakes tests Standardized achievement tests that are administered with the knowledge that important funding, placement, graduation, or tenure decisions are riding on the result.

homographs Words that are spelled alike but are pronounced differently (e.g., a *present* and to *present*).

homonyms Words that sound alike but are spelled differently (e.g., *sea–see, there–their–they're*); also called *homophones*.

homophones Words that sound alike but are spelled differently (e.g., *there–their–they're*); also called *homonyms*.

hyperbole A stylistic device involving obvious exaggerations.

idioms Expressions that mean something different than the literal meanings of the individual words (e.g., "kick the bucket," "a piece of cake," "hold your horses").

imagery The use of words and figurative language to create an impression.

independent reading level The level of reading material that students can read independently with high comprehension and an accuracy level of 95–100%.

inferential comprehension The second level of comprehension; readers draw inferences using clues in the text, implied information, and their own knowledge.

inflectional endings Suffixes that express plurality or possession when added to a noun (e.g., *girls, girl's*), tense when added to a verb (e.g., *walked, walking*), or comparison when added to an adjective (e.g., *happier, happiest*).

informal reading inventory (IRI) An individually administered reading test composed of word lists and graded passages that are used to determine students' independent, instructional, and frustration levels and listening capacity levels.

informational text Nonfiction books and articles.

instructional reading level The level of reading material that students can read with teacher support and instruction with 90–94% accuracy.

interpretation Comprehension.

intervention Intense, individualized instruction for struggling readers to solve reading problems and accelerate their growth.

invented spelling Students' attempts to spell words that reflect their developing knowledge about the spelling system.

leveled books Books that have been evaluated and ranked according to difficulty level.

Lexile scores A method of estimating the difficulty level of a text.

listening capacity level The highest level of graded passage that students can understand when it's read aloud to them.

literacy The ability to read and write.

literacy coach A reading specialist who provides professional development for teachers and supports their implementation of the instructional programs.

literal comprehension The most basic level of comprehension; readers pick out main ideas, sequence details, and notice similarities and differences to understand what's explicitly stated in a text.

literature circle An instructional approach in which students meet in small groups to read and respond to a book.

literature focus unit An approach to reading instruction in which the whole class reads and responds to a piece of literature.

literal meaning The direct meaning of a text; the words in the text have common, everyday meanings, and no figures of speech are used.

long vowels The vowel sounds that are also names of the alphabet letters: /ā/ as in *make*, /ē/ as in *feet*, /ī/ as in *ice*, /ō/ as in *coat*, and /ū/ as in *rule*.

lowercase letters The letters that are smaller and usually different from uppercase letters.

macron A horizontal mark that's placed over a vowel to indicate that it represents a long sound (e.g., *rūle, gō, bīke*, and *pāle*).

mechanics Conventions of writing, including spelling, capitalization, punctuation, and grammar.

metacognition Students' awareness of their own thinking and learning processes.

metacognitive strategy A learning process that requires reflection, such as monitoring or evaluating.

metaphor A comparison expressed directly, without using *like* or *as*.

miscue analysis A procedure for categorizing and analyzing a student's oral reading errors.

mood The tone of a story or poem.

morpheme The smallest meaningful part of a word; sometimes it's a word (e.g., *cup, hope*), and sometimes it isn't a whole word (e.g., *-ly, bi-*).

multigenre project A collection of student products and texts representing different genres that are related to a repetend or theme.

narrative A story.

new literacies The ability to use digital and multimodal technologies to communicate and learn effectively.

nonstandard English A dialect of English other than Standard English.

onomatopoeia Words that imitate sounds, such as *ker-plunk, zaaaap, wroom,* and *splat.*

onset The part of a syllable or one-syllable word that comes before the vowel (e.g., *c* in *cat, sh* in *shell,* and *str* in *string*).

orthography The spelling system.

oxymoron A figure of speech in which opposite ideas are joined to create an effect (e.g., *cruel kindness, jumbo shrimp,* and *walking dead*).

palindrome A word or phrase that reads the same forward and backward (e.g., *mom, eye, toot, racecar*).

personification Figurative language in which objects and animals have human qualities.

phoneme A sound; it's represented in print with slashes (e.g., /s/ and /th/).

phoneme–grapheme correspondence The relationship between a sound and the letter(s) representing it.

phonemic awareness The ability to manipulate the sounds in words orally.

phonics Predictable relationships between phonemes and graphemes.

phonogram A rime or word family (e.g., *-ill* is the phonogram used to create this word family: *bill, gill, hill, chill, will, quill, thrill*).

phonological awareness The ability to identify and manipulate phonemes, onsets and rimes, and syllables; it includes phonemic awareness.

phonology The sound system of language.

plot The events that make up a story.

polysyllabic Containing more than one syllable.

portfolio assessment An alternative form of assessment using students' collections of their work samples, including writings, multimedia projects, and other artifacts, to demonstrate growth and achievement over time.

portmanteau word A blended word made by combining two words (e.g., *motor + hotel = motel,* and *breakfast + lunch = brunch*).

pragmatics The social use system of language.

prefix A syllable added to the beginning of a word to change its meaning (e.g., *re-* in *reread*).

prereading The first stage of the reading process, in which readers activate background knowledge, set purposes, and make plans for reading.

prewriting The first stage of the writing process, in which writers gather and organize ideas for writing.

procedural knowledge Metacognitive knowledge about when to use a reading or writing strategy or do a process, such as stages in the writing process.

proofreading Reading a composition to identify spelling and other mechanical errors.

prosody The ability to orally read sentences expressively, with appropriate phrasing and intonation.

publishing The fifth stage of the writing process, in which writers make the final copy of their writing and share it with an audience.

***r*-controlled vowels** When vowels are followed by an *r*, it affects how the vowels are pronounced (e.g., *are, where,* and *scare*).

readability formula A method of estimating the difficulty level of a text.

reader factors The factors that enable students to comprehend what they read, including background knowledge, vocabulary, reading fluency, and comprehension strategies and skills.

reading The second stage of the reading process, in which readers read the text for the first time using independent reading, shared reading, or guided reading, or by listening to it read aloud. Also, the complex process of understanding written text.

reading process The process in which students use prereading, reading, responding, exploring, and applying to negotiate meaning and create an interpretation of a text.

reading rate Reading speed, usually reported as the average number of words read correctly in 1 minute.

repetend The theme of a multigenre project.

responding The third stage of the reading process, in which readers respond to the text, often through grand conversations and by writing in reading logs.

revising The third stage of the writing process, in which writers clarify meaning in their rough drafts.

rhyming words Words with the same rime sound (e.g., *white*, *bright*).

rime The part of a syllable or one-syllable word that begins with the vowel (e.g., *-at* in *cat*, *-ell* in *shell*, *-ing* and in *string*).

rubric A guide listing specific criteria for grading student work; it includes levels of achievement and is scored numerically.

scaffolding The support a teacher provides to students as they read and write.

schema A cognitive structure or mental file.

schwa The neutral vowel sound in an unaccented syllable of words with two or more syllables; the sound is marked with ə, an upside-down lowercase *e* (e.g., *əgain*, *sofə*, *pencəl*, and *vitəmin*).

segment To pronounce a word slowly, saying each sound distinctly.

self-efficacy Students' belief in their capability to succeed and reach their goals; students who have self-efficacy are more likely to be higher achieving readers and writers.

semantics The meaning system of language.

short vowels The vowel sounds represented by /ă/ as in *cat*, /ĕ/ as in *bed*, /ĭ/ as in *big*, /ŏ/ as in *hop*, and /ŭ/ as in *cut*.

simile A comparison expressed using *like* or *as*.

six traits An analytical model for teaching and assessing writing using these qualities of good writing: *ideas*, *organization*, *voice*, *word choice*, *sentence fluency*, *conventions*, and *presentation*.

skill An automatic processing behavior that students use in reading and writing, such as sounding out words, recognizing antonyms, and capitalizing proper nouns.

Standard English The variety of English that's the model for educated users.

standardized achievement tests Tests, usually created by commercial publishers, that measure academic achievement against grade-level standards; they employ uniform procedures for administering and scoring so that results across schools, districts, and states are comparable.

strategy A problem-solving behavior that students use in reading and writing, such as predicting, monitoring, visualizing, and summarizing.

struggling reader or writer A student who isn't meeting grade-level expectations in reading or writing.

suffix A syllable added to the end of a word to change its meaning (e.g., *-y* in *hairy*, *-ful* in *careful*).

summative evaluation Formal assessment procedures used after learning to judge the students' achievement and the effectiveness of instruction.

syllable An uninterrupted segment of speech that includes a vowel sound (e.g., *get*, *a-bout*, *but-ter-fly*, *con-sti-tu-tion*).

symbol An object used to represent something else.

synonyms Words that mean nearly the same thing (e.g., *road–street*).

syntax The structural system of language or grammar.

text complexity A way to determine the comprehension demands of a book or other text using reader and text factors.

text factors The genres, text structures, and text features that make books easier or more difficult to comprehend.

text features Literary devices and display conventions that authors use to achieve particular effects in their writing, such as point of view, metaphors, rhyme, and headings.

text set A collection of fiction and nonfiction books and digital resources at varied reading levels on a topic.

text structures Organizational patterns or genres.

theme The underlying meaning of a story.

think-aloud A procedure in which teachers or students verbalize their thoughts while reading or writing to describe their strategy use.

trade book A published book that isn't a textbook; the type of books in bookstores and libraries.

uppercase letters The letters that are larger and are used as first letters in a name or at the beginning of a sentence; also called "capital letters."

voice The author's writing style.

vowel A voiced speech sound made without friction or stoppage of the airflow as it passes through the vocal tract; the letters *a, e, i, o, u,* and sometimes *w* and *y.*

vowel digraph Two or more adjacent vowels in a syllable that represent a single sound (e.g., *bread, eight, pain, saw*).

word consciousness Students' interest in and awareness of words and their meanings.

word family A group of words with the same rime (e.g., *ball, call, fall, hall, mall, tall,* and *wall*).

word identification Strategies that students use to decode words, such as phonic analysis, analogies, syllabic analysis, and morphemic analysis.

writer's craft The language tools that writers use to convey meaning effectively, including imagery, humor, alliteration, sentence structure, and viewpoint.

writing genres Forms of writing, such as stories, friendly letters, essays, and poems.

writing process The process in which students use prewriting, drafting, revising, editing, and publishing to develop and refine a composition.

zone of proximal development The distance between students' actual developmental level and their potential developmental level that can be reached with scaffolding by the teacher or classmates.

Index